A History of Modern Indonesia since *c.* 1300

A History of Modern Indonesia since *c.* 1300

M. C. RICKLEFS

Second Edition

Stanford University Press
Stanford, California

Stanford University Press
Stanford, California
© 1981, 1993 M.C. Ricklefs
First edition published 1981
Second edition published 1993
Reprinted 1994
Originating publisher: Macmillan Press Ltd
  Hampshire, England
First published in the U.S.A. by
  Stanford University Press, 1993
Printed in Hong Kong
Cloth ISBN 0–8047–2194–7
Paper ISBN 0–8047–2195–5
This book is printed on acid-free paper
Original printing 1994
Last figure below indicates year of this printing
06 05 04 03 02 01 00 99 98 97

For Norman, Charles and Deborah

Contents

List of Maps   ix

Preface to the First Edition   x

Preface to the Second Edition   xii

A Note on Orthography   xiii

Abbreviations   xiv

I   The Emergence of the Modern Era

    1   The Coming of Islam   3

    2   General Aspects of Pre-Colonial States and Major Empires,

        c. 1300–1500   15

    3   The Arrival of the Europeans in Indonesia, *c.* 1509–1620   22

    4   The Rise of New States, *c.* 1500–1650   32

    5   Literary, Religious and Cultural Legacies   50

II   Struggles for Hegemony, *c.* 1630–1800

    6   Eastern Indonesia, *c.* 1630–1800   61

    7   Java, *c.* 1640–82   69

    8   Java, Madura and the VOC, *c.* 1680–1745   81

    9   Java and the VOC, *c.* 1745–92   94

III   The Creation of a Colonial State, *c.* 1800–1910

    10   Java, 1792–1830   109

    11   Java, 1830–1900   119

    12   The Outer Islands, *c.* 1800–1910   131

IV   **The Emergence of the Idea of Indonesia, *c.* 1900–42**

   13 A New Colonial Age   151

   14 The First Steps towards National Revival, *c.* 1900–27   163

   15 Repression and Economic Crisis, 1927–42   181

V   **The Destruction of the Colonial State, 1942–50**

   16 World War II and the Japanese Occupation, 1942–5   199

   17 The Revolution, 1945–50   212

VI   **Independent Indonesia**

   18 The Democratic Experiment, 1950–7   237

   19 Guided Democracy, 1957–65   257

   20 Creating the New Order, 1965–75   284

   21 The New Order since 1975   304

Notes and References   310

Bibliography   326

Maps   351

Index   361

List of Maps

The Indonesian Archipelago   352

Sumatra and the Malay Peninsula   353

Java and Madura   354

Bali and Lombok   356

Kalimantan   357

Eastern Indonesia   358

Archipelago Topography   359

World War II in the Pacific, with dates of major Allied
     battle victories, 1942–5   360

Preface to the First Edition, 1981

This is a textbook designed for the serious student who wishes to investigate the history of Indonesia since the coming of Islam. It is intended to meet a need found by those whose study has been hampered by the large number and specialised nature of the major works on the subject, the high proportion of these which are written in foreign languages and the difficulty of gaining access to some of them. Students have also found that the existing literature sometimes over-emphasises either colonial aspects or the exoticism of Indonesia, and fails to provide a clear chronology within which to orient their study. This book therefore aims to provide a basic but detailed narrative of Indonesian history since *c.* 1300, an introduction to the major issues of the period and a guide to the most important published secondary sources (or primary sources where no adequate secondary sources exist). My aim is, thus, to facilitate students' progress to more advanced levels of study. The need for such a book has been evident for some time, but it is only recently that the study of Indonesian history has reached a sufficient level of coverage and sophistication over the whole period for such a textbook to be possible. Significant gaps remain in our knowledge, but the major lacunae have now been investigated.

Indonesia's recorded history does not begin where this book begins, but about a thousand years before. The earliest inscriptions of the Indonesian archipelago are on seven stone pillars from Kutai in East Kalimantan, which on palaeographic grounds are dated to *c.* AD 400. Chinese references are also available from a very early time. Indigenous sources and Chinese records have enabled scholars to reconstruct much of the history of the pre-Islamic states of Indonesia, which included some of the major empires of the ancient world. One of the greatest of these, Majapahit, is discussed briefly in Chapter 2 simply because it falls within the chronological limits of this book.

These pre-Islamic states were Hindu-Buddist, and they left major literary and artistic legacies which, as will be seen in Chapter 5, continued to be influential long after the coming of Islam. The social, administrative and political traditions of these states also had an abiding influence. This early period has many problems of evidence and interpretation and is in much need of further study. For this reason, I decided not to attempt to cover it in this book. Some important works on Majapahit are listed in the notes and references for Chapter 2. On the other pre-Islamic states see Krom, *Hindoe-Javaansche geschiedenis;* Coedès, *Les états hindouisés* (in English as *Indianized states of Southeast Asia*); Wolters, *Early Indonesian commerce,* and van Naerssen's essay in van Naerssen and de Iongh, *Economic and administrative history of early Indonesia.*

The period since *c.* 1300 appears to me to make a coherent historical unit, which this book calls Modern Indonesian History. There are of course significant sub-periods within modern Indonesian history, as is reflected by the division of the book into parts and chapters. Three fundamental elements give the period historical unity. The first is cultural and religious: the Islamisation of Indonesia which began *c.* 1300 and continues today. The second is topical: the interplay between Indonesians and Westerners which began *c.* 1500 and still continues. The third is historiographical: primary sources throughout this period are written almost exclusively in the modern forms of Indonesian languages (Javanese, Malay, etc. rather than Old Javanese or Old Malay) and in European languages. Between *c.* 1300 and *c.* 1500 these elements emerged, and have remained ever since.

The writer of any history textbook must decide whether to give preference to broad interpretative themes or to the detailed, and sometimes confusing, progress of events. My experience suggests that students find interpretative treatments more readable but less useful than detailed narratives. I also prefer a detailed narrative in principle, for if the basic evidence is presented, readers are more able to arrive at their own generalisations or to question others'. I therefore decided that this book should give first place to the detailed historical evidence. There is no attempt here to impose any new synthesis upon Indonesian history, although of course my views are implicit throughout the volume.

This book gives the history of Java greater precedence than it may seem to deserve. There are four reasons for this. First, Java has received more historical study than the other islands and is therefore better known. Second, its people represent over half the population of Indonesia. Third, it has been the centre of much of the political history of both colonial and independent periods and exerted an influence over other areas greater than their influence outside their own regions, and thus carries greater significance for the history of Indonesia as a whole. And fourth, it is the area upon which all of my own research has concentrated and this personal element has naturally coloured the book. Further research will undoubtedly make it possible to study outer island areas more adequately in the future than is now the case.

No scholar masters more than a small portion of the primary sources for the topics covered in this book, nearly seven centuries of history over the world's largest archipelago. Much of this volume is thus a paraphrase or summary of the work of others, whose publications are listed in the Bibliography. Like any textbook, this one may at times simply repeat, and even add to, the mistakes of others. To minimise this problem I have called upon several colleagues and friends for comments upon draft chapters. Very substantial parts of the book have been read by Prof. C. D. Cowan, Prof. C. Fasseur, Dr H. J. de Graaf and Dr A. J. S. Reid. Dr J. S. Bastin, Dr P. B. R. Carey, Prof. James J. Fox, Dr E. U. Kratz, Prof. J. D. Legge, Dr Ruth T. McVey, Dr P. Voorhoeve and Prof. P. J. Zoetmulder, S. J., have also given me valuable suggestions on sections of this book. To all of them I am deeply indebted. The errors which remain are, of course, entirely my responsibility. I owe special gratitude to my students who read most of the book in draft, helped me to decide what was needed and encouraged me to believe that the book was worth writing. Many Indonesians gave me information which was invaluable for the last chapters of the book, but mostly on the understanding that it was not attributable to them.

M. C. Ricklefs

Preface to the Second Edition

In the decade after the first edition of this text book appeared, the study of Indonesian history advanced substantially. It was clearly necessary, therefore, to prepare a new edition if this work were to remain useful to students.

Research has gone forward in all fields with impressive results. Economic history generally, the history of the outer islands (notably Bali), nineteenth-century Java, nineteenth-century Sumatra, the history of the twentieth century generally and particularly of the Revolution and years since 1965, have all been served by substantial new publications. Major works of synthesis and interpretation have also appeared, notably Lombard's *Carrefour javanais*, a work so broad in its scope that it could not be cited in any particular chapter below. These publications have both opened up new topics and shed new light on previously studied subjects.

In revising this book, I have added new passages and corrected errors which came to light in the first edition. I am grateful to colleagues and students who brought such errors to my attention and thereby made it possible for this version to be better. Additions and alterations have been made throughout the text. More substantial sections have been added on nineteenth-century Java and the 1930s Depression. Two new chapters on the period since 1965 have been written. The changes to the bibliography are, not surprisingly, extensive.

I am grateful to those colleagues who have read and commented on drafts of this revised edition: Prof. Anne Booth, Dr. Ian Brown, Prof. C. Fasseur, Prof. R. William Liddle, Prof. A. J. S. Reid, Dr. Henk Shulte Nordholt, Dr. Helius Sjamsuddin and Dr. Adrian Vickers. None of them, of course, bears any responsibility for the final text of the book.

M. C. Ricklefs

A Note on Orthography

The various Indonoesian languages which appear in this book sometimes have differing transcription systems or orthography. For all words and proper names in modern Indonesian languages, I have used a standardised spelling based upon the reformed Indonesian system of 1972. Old Javanese appears in the standard Sanskrit transcription. For words which exist in both Indonesian and regional languages, I have ignored regional spellings (thus, Indonesian *dalang* rather than Javanese *dhalang*). For the twentieth century, however, there are exceptions which are explained below. Since the 1972 system does not distinguish among the different pronunciations of the letter *e*, I have added ĕ to represent /ə/ (like the *e* in 'fallen'). The character *e* is pronounced either /e/ or /ɛ/ (like either the *a* in 'fate' or the *e* in 'sct'). In some names which are commonly used in English, I have used a conventional spelling (thus, Malacca rather than Mĕlaka and Java rather than Jawa).

Consonants have generally the same value as in English except for *c* which is pronounced like the *ch* in 'chair' and *sy* which is pronounced like the *sh* in 'share'. Vowels arc also pronounced as in English, except for the *a* in Javanese words which is pronounced rather like English *o* when it appears in penultimate and final syllables without final consonants. Thus Mangkunĕgara is pronounced 'Mangkunĕgoro' but Mangkunĕgaran is pronounced as it is spelled. As an aid to pronunciation, it is generally true that the stress in Indonesian languages falls upon the penultimate syllable.

As local scripts gave way to romanisation in the twentieth century, a variety of spellings was used. In this book I have followed the principle of spelling personal names and publication titles as they were spelled at the time. Organisations, however, have been spelled according to the standard 1972 system unless there is a clearly established convention in modern scholarly works (thus, Budi Utomo rather than the correct form Budi Utama).

In the twentieth century individuals used Dutch orthography and either pre-1972 or (now) post-1972 Indonesian orthography. Javanese commonly use *o* rather than *a* where the latter is pronounced 'o'. The pre-1972 orthographies differ from the 1972 system primarily in using Dutch rather than English consonants: *tj* rather *c*, *dj* rather than *j*, and *j* rather than *y*. Dutch orthography additionally differs in using *oe* for *u*. Thus, in the twentieth century the Javanese name Sujana (pronounced 'Sujono') might be spelled Soedjana, Soedjono, Sudjono, Sudjana, Sujana or Sujono. In the last two cases, there is no way of knowing whether this is a person named Sujana using the 1972 system or one named Suyana using the pre-1972 system.

For Arabic words, names and titles, a conventional transcription system is used. Chinese names are given in Pinyin, but the first time a name is mentioned it is also given in the Wade-Giles transcription if this differs from Pinyin. Wherever I have been able to establish them, life- or reign-dates are given when an individual is first mentioned.

Abbreviations

AD   *Anno Domini*, the Christian era
AH   *Anno Hijrae*, the Islamic era
AJ   *Anno Javano*, the Javanese era
ASEAN   Association of South East Asian Nations
b.   born
CSI   Centraal Sarekat Islam, Sarekat Islam Central (headquarters)
d.   died
DPR(-GR)   Dewan Pĕrwakilan Rakyat (- Gotong Royong), (Mutual-
              Cooperation) People's Representative Council
f.   Dutch florins/guilders
HIS   Hollandsch-Inlandsche School, Dutch-Native School
IGGI   Inter-Governmental Group on Indonesia
IMF   International Monetary Fund
ISDV   Indische Sociaal-Democratische Vereniging, Indies Social-
              Democratic Association
KAMI   Kĕsatuan Aksi Mahasiswa Indonesia, Indonesian Students' Action
              Front
KNIP   Komite Nasional Indonesia Pusat, Central Indonesian National
              Committee
MIAI   Majlis Islam A'laa Indonesia, Supreme Islamic Council of Indonesia
MPR(S)   Majĕlis Pĕrmusyawaratan Rakyat (Sĕmĕntara), (Provisional) People's
              Consultative Assembly
MULO   Meer Uitgebreid Lager Onderwijs, More Extended Lower
              Education (school)
NU   Nahdatul Ulama/Nahdlatul 'Ulama, Rise of the Religious Scholars
              (organisation)
OPEC   Organisation of Petroleum Exporting Countries
OSVIA   Opleidingschool voor Inlandsche Ambtenaren, Training School for
              Native Officials
PDI   Partai Demokrasi Indonesia, Indonesian Democratic party
PKI   Partai Komunis Indonesia, Indonesian Communist Party
PNI   Partai Nasional Indonesia, Indonesian Nationalist Party
PNI-Baru   Pĕndidikan Nasional Indonesia, Indonesian Nationalist Education
              (party)
PPP   Partai Pĕrsatuan Pĕmbangunan, United Development Party
PRRI   Pĕmĕrintah Revolusioner Republik Indonesia, Revolutionary
              Government of the Indonesian Republic
PSI   Partai Sosialis Indonesia, Indonesian Socialist Party
PSII   Partai Sarekat Islam Indonesia, Indonesian Islamic Union Party
r.   reigned
Rp.   Rupiah
Ś   Śaka era
SI   Sarekat Islam, Islamic Union
SOBSI   Sentral Organisasi Buruh Sĕluruh Indonesia, Central All-Indonesia
              Workers' Organisation
STOVIA   School tot Opleiding van Inlandsche Artsen, School for Training
              Native Doctors
UN   United Nations
VOC   Vereenigde Oost-Indische Compagnie, (Dutch) United East India
              Company

I
The Emergence of the Modern Era

1 The Coming of Islam

The spread of Islam is one of the most significant processes of Indonesian history, but also one of the most obscure. Muslim traders had apparently been present in some parts of Indonesia for several centuries before Islam became established within the local communities. When, why and how the conversion of Indonesians began has been debated by several scholars, but no definite conclusions have been possible because the records of Islamisation which survive are so few, and often so uninformative. In general, two processes probably occurred. On the one hand, indigenous Indonesians came into contact with Islam and made an act of conversion. On the other, foreign Asians (Arabs, Indians, Chinese, etc.) who were already Muslims settled permanently in an Indonesian area, intermarried and adopted local lifestyles to such a degree that in effect they became Javanese or Malay or whatever. These two processes may often have occurred in conjunction with each other, and when a piece of evidence survives indicating, for instance, that a Muslim dynasty had been established in some area, it is often impossible to know which of these two processes was the more important.

There must have been an Islamic presence in maritime Southeast Asia from early in the Islamic era. From the time of the third caliph of Islam, 'Uthman (644–56), Muslim emissaries from Arabia began to arrive at the Chinese court. By at least the ninth century there were several thousand Muslim merchants in Canton. Such contacts between China and the Islamic world would have been maintained primarily via the sea routes through Indonesian waters. It is therefore not surprising that Muslims seem to have played an important role in the affairs of the great Sumatran Buddhist trading state of Śrīvijaya, which was founded in the later seventh century. Between 904 and the mid-twelfth century, envoys with Arabic names came from there to the Chinese court. In 1282 the king of Samudra in north Sumatra sent two emissaries with Arabic names to China. Unfortunately, the presence of foreign Muslims in the Indonesian area does not demonstrate either that local Islamic states had been established or that a significant level of local conversions had occurred.

The most reliable evidence for the spread of Islam within a local Indonesian society consists of Islamic inscriptions (mostly tombstones) and a few travellers' accounts. The earliest surviving Muslim gravestone on which the date is clear is found at Leran in East Java and is dated AH 475 (AD 1082). This was the gravestone of a woman, a daughter of someone named Maimun. It has, however, been doubted whether the grave to which the stone belongs was actually in Java, or whether the stone was for some reason transported to Java (for instance, as ballast on a ship) sometime after the lady's death. In any case, since the deceased appears to have been a non-Indonesian Muslim, this stone sheds no light on the establishment of Islam among Indonesians.

The first evidence of Indonesian Muslims concerns the northern part of Sumatra. When the Venetian traveller Marco Polo touched at Sumatra on his way home from China in 1292, he found that Pĕrlak was a Muslim town, while two nearby places which he called 'Basma(n)' and 'Samara' were not. 'Basma(n)' and 'Samara' have often been identified with Pasai and Samudra, but this identification is open to question. It is possible either that 'Samara' is not Samudra, or if it is that Polo was wrong in saying that it was non-Muslim. For the gravestone of the first Muslim ruler of Samudra, Sultan Malik as-Salih, has been found, and is dated AH 696 (AD 1297). This is the first clear evidence of the existence of a Muslim dynasty in the Indonesian-Malay area, and further gravestones demonstrate that from the late thirteenth century this part of North Sumatra remained under Islamic rule. The Moroccan traveller Ibn Battuta passed through Samudra on his way to and from China in 1345 and 1346, and found that the ruler was a follower of the Shafi'i school of law. This confirms the presence from an early date of the school which was later to dominate Indonesia, although it is possible that the other three Orthodox schools (Hanafi, Maliki and Hanbali) were also present at an early time.

Two late-fourteenth-century gravestones from Minye Tujoh in North Sumatra appear to document the continuing cultural transition there. The two stones are in the same form, but one has an Arabic inscription and the other an Old Malay inscription in paleo-Sumatran (Indian-type) characters, both inscriptions being Islamic. They both date the death of a daughter of a deceased Sultan Malik az-Zahir, but although they have the same month, date and day of the week, they differ by ten years (AH 781 and 791 / AD 1380, 1389). It seems likely that there is an error in one of the years, that both inscriptions refer to the same woman and that she was therefore commemorated with inscriptions in two languages and two scripts. After this time, the documents from North Sumatra are wholly in the Arabic script.

From the fourteenth century survives evidence of the spread of Islam to Brunei, Trĕngganu (in what is now northeast Malaysia) and East Java. An Arabic inscription on a tombstone from Brunei praises a dead ruler called both Sultan (Arabic) and Maharaja (Sanskrit) of Brunei; although the stone is undated, Chen argues that it must have been made in Quanzhou (Kwangchow), South China, and imported from there early in the fourteenth century, in any case before 1366. Another gravestone records in Chinese the death in Brunei in 1264 of a Chinese who was apparently a Muslim. The Trĕngganu stone is a fragment of a legal edict. The date at the end appears to be incomplete, however, and the possible range of dates for this inscription is between AD 1302 and 1387. The stone appears to represent the introduction of Islamic law into a previously non-Islamic area, as is suggested by the predominance of Sanskrit over Arabic words, even for such an important word as God, which is given in one case as *dewata mulia raya* rather than *Allah*.

A particularly significant series of gravestones is found in the East Javanese graveyards of Trawulan and Tralaya, near the site of the Hindu-Buddhist court of Majapahit (see Chapter 2). These stones mark the burial of Muslims, but with one exception they are dated in the Indian Śaka era rather than the Islamic *Anno*

Hijrae and use Old Javanese rather than Arabic numerals. The Śaka era was used by the Javanese courts from Old Javanese times down to AD 1633, and its presence on these tombstones and the use of Old Javanese numerals mean that these are almost certainly the tombs of Javanese, as opposed to foreign, Muslims. The earliest is found at Trawulan, bearing the date Ś 1290 (AD 1368–9). At Tralaya is a series of gravestones extending from Ś 1298 to 1533 (AD 1376–1611). These stones carry Qur'anic quotations and pious formulae. From the elaborate decoration on some of them and their proximity to the site of the Majapahit capital, Damais concluded that these were probably the graves of very distinguished Javanese, perhaps even members of the royal family.

These East Javanese stones therefore suggest that some members of the Javanese elite adopted Islam at a time when the Hindu-Buddhist state of Majapahit was at the very height of its glory. These were, moreover, the first Javanese Muslims of whom evidence survives. Since evidence is so scanty, of course it cannot be said with certainty that these were the first Javanese adherents to Islam. But the Trawulan and Tralaya gravestones certainly contradict, and therefore cast grave doubts upon, the view once held by scholars that Islam originated on the coast of Java and initially represented a religious and political force which opposed Majapahit.

The likelihood or otherwise of Javanese courtiers embracing Islam before Javanese coastal communities did so is influenced by one's view of the relative importance of traders and Sufis as the bringers of Islam; this issue is discussed below. There can be little doubt that Majapahit, with its far-flung political and trading contacts outside Java (see Chapter 2), would have seen foreign Muslim traders. The problem is whether its sophisticated courtiers would have been attracted to a religion of merchants. Mystical Islamic teachers, perhaps claiming supernatural powers, seem a more plausible agent of conversion in Javanese court circles, which had long been familiar with the mystical speculations of Hinduism and Buddhism.

When Islam began to be adopted among the communities of the north coast of Java is unclear. In 1416, the Chinese Muslim Ma Huan visited the coast of Java and left a report in his book *Ying-yai Sheng-lan* ('The overall survey of the ocean's shores', published in 1451) that there were only three kinds of people in Java: Muslims from the west, Chinese (some of them Muslims) and the heathen Java-nese. Since the Trawulan and Tralaya gravestones show that there were Javanese Muslims at the court some fifty years before this time, Ma Huan's report suggests that Islam was indeed adopted by Javanese courtiers before coastal Javanese began to convert. An early Muslim gravestone dated AH 822 (AD 1419) has been found at Grĕsik, one of the most important East Javanese ports. It marks the burial of one Malik Ibrahim, but since this gentleman was apparently not Javanese it merely confirms the presence of foreign Muslims in Java, and sheds no further light on the question of coastal Javanese conversion. Local traditions, however, say that Malik Ibrahim was one of the first nine apostles of Islam in Java (the *wali sanga)*, a tradition for which there is no documentary evidence.

Around the beginning of the fifteenth century, the great Malay trading state of Malacca was founded. Its history will be considered briefly in Chapter 2. Malacca was the most important trading centre of the western archipelago, and therefore became a centre for foreign Muslims and apparently a supporter of the spread of Islam. From Malacca and elsewhere survive gravestones showing this spread in the Malay Peninsula. The gravestone of Malacca's sixth Sultan, Mansur Syah (d. AH 822/AD 1477), has been found, as has the gravestone of the first Sultan of Pahang, Muhammad Syah (d. AH 880/AD 1475). From Pĕngkalan Kĕmpas in Nĕgĕri Sĕmbilan survives an inscription which appears to show that this region was in transition to an Islamic culture in the 1460s. The stone is in two parts, one written in Malay with Arabic script, and the other in Malay with Indian-type characters like those found on the Minye Tujoh inscription. The stone uses the Indian Śaka era, and apparently records the death of a local hero named Ahmat Majanu in Ś 1385 (AD 1463–4).

Returning to North Sumatra, late fifteenth- and sixteenth-century graves document the establishment of further Islamic states there. The first Sultan of Pĕdir, Muzaffar Syah, was buried in AH 902 (AD 1497), and the second, Ma'ruf Syah, in AH 917 (AD 1511). At the very tip of North Sumatra, the state of Aceh was founded in the early sixteenth century; it was soon to become the most powerful North Sumatran state and one of the most powerful states of the Malay-Indonesian area. The first Sultan of the Acehnese 'empire' was Ali Mughayat Syah, whose tombstone is dated AH 936 (AD 1530).

Outside of Java, Sumatra, Brunei and the Malay Peninsula, there is no evidence of the adoption of Islam by Indonesians before the sixteenth century. It is quite clear, however, that Islam had spread to some points farther east, for near Jolo (in the Sulu archipelago, southern Philippines) there was a tombstone dated AH 710 (AD 1310) marking the grave of a Muslim who was apparently of foreign origin but who had become some sort of local ruler. Much later legendary sources from Mindanao and Sulu, the Islamic areas of the Philippines, describe the bringing of Islam by Arabs and Malays from the western archipelago. It seems probable that Chinese Muslims also played a role in the spread of Islam in this area.

Before the sixteenth century, the fragmentary evidence shows that the spread of Islam began in the western archipelago. There does not, however, seem to have been a continuous rolling wave of Islam, with one contiguous area after another adopting the new faith. The evidence provides only a few brief hints of the process which was under way, but it was apparently complicated and rather slow. By the end of the thirteenth century, Islam was established in North Sumatra; in the fourteenth century in northeast Malaya, Brunei, the southern Philippines and among some courtiers in East Java; and in the fifteenth century in Malacca and other areas of the Malay Peninsula. A few gravestones or travellers' accounts can only provide evidence about the presence of indigenous Muslims in a certain place at a certain time. The fact that no evidence of Islamisation happens to have survived from other places does not necessarily mean that there were no Muslims there. And the surviving evidence cannot answer more complex questions – such as, for instance, how many of the people of Samudra other than the ruler were Muslims in 1297, or how deeply the lifestyles or religious ideas of the first Indonesian converts were affected by Islam. As will be seen in subsequent chapters, Islamisation is a process which has continued down to the present day. It must not be assumed that once an area is known to have had a Muslim ruler, the process of Islamisation was complete. Indeed, this probably symbolises more the beginning than the end of Islamisation among the populace.

In the early sixteenth century, an extraordinary European source makes possible a general survey of Islam in the Indonesian Archipelago. Tomé Pires was an apothecary from Lisbon who spent the years from 1512 to 1515 in Malacca, immediately after its conquest by the Portuguese in 1511. During this time he visited Java and Sumatra personally, and avidly collected information from others concerning the entire Malay-Indonesian area. His book *Suma Oriental* reveals a discriminating observer, whose descriptions are far superior to those of other Portuguese writers. It is full of invaluable material of many varieties, but in this chapter attention must be focused upon what Pires observed regarding Islam. His evidence cannot be presumed to be accurate in all details, of course. But so much of what he wrote seems consistent with the other fragments of evidence described above, and his description is so free of obviously erroneous statements about the area, that it seems to stand as one of the most important documents on the spread of Islam in Indonesia.

According to Pires, most of the kings of Sumatra were Muslims by his time, but there were still non-Islamic states. From Aceh in the north down the east coast as far as Palembang, the rulers were Muslims. South of Palembang and around the tip of Sumatra up the west coast, most of them were not. At Pasai there was a thriving international trading community and Pires attributed the original establishment of Islam in Pasai to the 'cunning' of these Muslim merchants. The ruler of Pasai had not, however, been able to convert the people of the interior. Similarly, the Minangkabau king and a hundred of his men were reportedly Muslims, although the remaining Minangkabau people were not. But Pires said that Islam was winning new adherents daily in Sumatra.

The Sundanese-speaking region of West Java was not yet Muslim in Pires's day, and indeed was hostile to Islam. Although Pires did not mention the name, this was the area ruled by the Hindu-Buddhist state of Pajajaran, concerning which there are hardly any reliable records. The Islamisation of this area by conquest in the sixteenth century is discussed in Chapter 4.

Central and East Java, the areas where the ethnic Javanese lived, was still claimed by the Hindu-Buddhist king living in the interior of East Java at Daha (Kědiri). The coastal areas as far east as Surabaya were, however, Islamised, and were often at war with the interior, except for Tuban, which remained loyal to the Hindu-Buddhist king. Some of the coastal Muslim lords were Javanese who had adhered to Islam. Some were not originally Javanese, but rather Muslim Chinese, Indians, Arabs and Malays who had settled on the coast and established trading states. Pires described a process of Javanisation under way among these latter groups, who so admired the culture of the Hindu-Buddhist court that they attempted to emulate its style and were becoming Javanese thereby. The fourteenth-century gravestones of Trawulan and Tralaya discussed above suggest that for its part the Hindu-Buddhist court was able, at least at times, to tolerate Muslims within its own circle. The warfare which Pires describes between coast and interior should not, therefore, be seen as necessarily a product of irreconcilable religious and cultural differences, for there was a process of cultural assimilation at work as Islam encountered the powerful high culture of Old Java. This process of assimilation and accommodation continued long after the vast majority of Javanese were at least nominally Muslim, and has made the Islam of Java rather different in style from that of Malaya or Sumatra. The warfare between coast and interior also continued long after both regions had adopted Islam, and its origins are probably to be sought more in the political and economic differences between the two areas which are discussed in following chapters. East of Surabaya, the Javanese coast was still pre-Islamic, and apparently Hindu, for widow-burning was practised. 'Thus,'said Pires, 'they lose their bodies in this life and their souls burn in the next' *(Suma Oriental,* 198).

In Kalimantan (Borneo), Pires reported that Brunei had a king who had recently become a Muslim. The rest of Kalimantan was non-Muslim, as were also the islands of Madura, Bali, Lombok, Sumbawa, Flores, Solor and Timor to the east of Java. The Bugis and Makasarese of South Sulawesi (Celebes) were also not yet Islamised.

Islam was, however, spreading in the 'Spice Islands' of Maluku in East Indonesia. Muslim Javanese and Malay merchants were established on the coast of Banda, but there was no king there and the interior still contained non-Muslims. Tĕrnate, Tidore and Bacan had Muslim kings. The rulers of Tidore and Bacan used the Indian title Raja, but that of Tĕrnate had adopted the title of Sultan and the Raja of Tidore had taken the Arabic name al-Mansur.

All the evidence taken together gives a general picture of the progress of Islam from the late thirteenth to the early sixteenth centuries. From a starting point in the north of Sumatra, it had spread as far as the spice-producing areas of East Indonesia. The areas where it was most firmly established were those which were most important in international trade: the Sumatran shores of the Straits of Malacca, the Malay Peninsula, the north coast of Java, Brunei, Sulu and Maluku. Yet not all important trade areas had, on Tomé Pires' evidence, been Islamised. For example, Timor and Sumba, which produced sandalwood, were still non-Islamic. And the presence of international trade does little to explain why there should have been Muslim aristocrats at the court of Majapahit in the fourteenth century, or why Trĕngganu is the earliest area of Malaya where Islamisation is documented. Some kind of link between trade and Islam is nonetheless apparent.

The general timing of the beginnings of Islamisation can thus be established to some degree, but there remain important questions which have provoked considerable controversy. After several centuries during which foreign Muslims had been passing through or residing in Indonesia, why was it that significant Indonesian conversions began only in the thirteenth, and especially in the fourteenth and fifteenth centuries? Where did the Islam of Indonesia come from? And how did Islam succeed in becoming the majority religion of Indonesia?

To attempt an answer to such questions, some scholars have thought it appropriate to turn from the primary historical records discussed above to the Indonesian legends which record how Indonesians themselves told the story of their conversion. All these legends are much later than the coming of Islam; although they may contain old stories, most of the texts are known only in eighteenth- and nineteenth-century versions. These are not reliable historical accounts, but in their shared emphasis upon the roles played by esoteric learning and magical powers, upon the foreign origins and trade connections of the first teachers, and upon a process of conversion which began with the elite and worked downwards, they may reveal something of the original events.

Hikayat Raja-raja Pasai ('Story of the kings of Pasai') is one such legendary source. The text is in Malay, but was copied at Dĕmak (north Java) in 1814. It tells how Islam came to Samudra, the first area where an Islamic state was founded; the gravestone of the first Sultan, Malik as-Salih, of 1297 was discussed above. In this story, the Caliph of Mecca hears of the existence of Samudra and decides to send a ship there in fulfilment of a prophecy of the Prophet Muhammad that there would one day be a great city in the East called Samudra, which would produce many saints. The ship's captain, Shaikh Ismail, stops en route in India to pick up a Sultan who has stepped down from his throne to become a holy man. The ruler of Samudra, Merah Silau (or Silu), has a dream in which the Prophet appears to him, magically transfers knowledge of Islam to him by spitting in his mouth, and gives him the title Sultan Malik as-Salih. Upon awakening, the new Sultan discovers that he can read the *Qur'an* although he has never been instructed and that he has been magically circumcised. His followers are understandably mystified by the Sultan's recitations in Arabic. But then the ship arrives from Mecca. When Shaikh Ismail hears Malik as-Salih's Confession of Faith, he installs him as ruler with regalia and state robes from Mecca. Ismail goes on to teach the populace how to recite the Confession – that there is no God but God and Muhammad is His messenger. He then departs, but the Indian holy man stays behind to establish Islam more firmly in Samudra.

Sĕjarah Mĕlayu ('Malay History') is another Malay text known in several versions. One text carries the date AH 1021 (AD 1612), but this exists only in an early-nineteenth-century copy. As well as a story about the conversion of Samudra which is like that of *Hikayat Raja-raja Pasai,* this text contains a tale about the conversion of the king of Malacca. He, too, has a dream in which the Prophet appears, teaches him the Confession of Faith, gives him the new name Muhammad, and tells him that on the following day a ship will arrive from Arabia carrying a teacher whom he is to obey. On waking, the king discovers that he has been magically circumcised, and as he goes about continually repeating the Confession of Faith the rest of the court (who cannot understand the Arabic phrases) become convinced that he has gone mad. But then the ship arrives, and from it Sayyid Abdul Aziz steps down to pray upon the shore, much to the wonderment of the population who ask the meaning of his ritual movements. The king announces that this is all as it was in his dream, and the court officials thereupon join him in embracing Islam. The king now takes the title Sultan Muhammad Syah and commands all the populace to embrace Islam. Sayyid Abdul Aziz becomes the teacher of the king.

These two Malay texts are different from the Islamisation legends concerning Java which have so far been studied. Whereas the Malay texts see Islamisation as a great turning point, marked by the formal signs of conversion such as circumcision, the Confession of Faith and the adoption of an Arabic name, the Javanese legends do not present Islamisation as such a great watershed. This seems consistent with the evidence discussed above, suggesting that a process of assimilation was at work in Java. But in Javanese stories, magical events still play a prominent role.

Babad Tanah Jawi ('History of the land of Java') is a generic title covering a large number of manuscripts in Javanese, which vary in their arrangement and details, and none of which exists in copies older than the eighteenth century. These texts ascribe the first Javanese conversions to the work of the nine saints *(wali sanga),* but the names and relationships among these nine differ in various texts. It is impossible to reduce these variations to a list of nine persons upon which all texts would agree; indeed some manuscripts accept the convention that there were nine, but nonetheless proceed to list ten. The following names would, however, be fairly widely found in the manuscripts: Sunan Ngampel-Dĕnta, Sunan Kudus, Sunan Murya, Sunan Bonang, Sunan Giri, Sunan Kalijaga, Sunan Sitijĕnar, Sunan Gunungjati and Sunan Walilanang. A tenth *wali*, Sunan Bayat, is also often found.

The term *wali* which is applied to all these figures is Arabic (meaning 'saint'), but the title *sunan* which they all carry is Javanese. The origin of the latter is somewhat unclear, but it may derive from *suhun*, meaning 'to do honour to', here in a passive form meaning 'honoured'. Several, but not all, of the *walis* are said to have been of non-Javanese descent, and several are said to have studied in Malacca (notably Sunans Giri, Bonang and Walilanang). Several are also said to have had commercial connections, Giri as the foster child of a female trader, Bayat as the employee of a woman rice merchant, and Kalijaga as a grass salesman.

The Babad Tanah Jawi story of how Sunan Kalijaga was brought to the rightful path is instructive. It is notable that the formal signs of conversion (circumcision, Confession of Faith, etc.) are so entirely absent that it is not in fact clear whether Kalijaga is already nominally Muslim at the time of his 'conversion'. In this story, Kalijaga is said to be the son of a Tumĕnggung Wilatikta in the service of Majapahit, whose religious affiliation is unspecified. The young man, however, has the name Said, which is Arabic. Having lost at gambling, Said becomes a highway robber on the north coast. One day Sunan Bonang passes and is accosted by Said, but Bonang tells him that it would be much better to rob a person who will later pass by, dressed entirely in blue with a red hibiscus flower behind his ear. Said takes this advice, and three days later this other person appears. It is, of course, Bonang himself in disguise. When Said attacks him, however, Bonang turns himself into four persons. Said is so shaken by the experience that he gives up his bad ways and adopts the life of an ascetic. He takes the name Kalijaga, becomes a *wali* and marries a sister of Sunan Gunungjati.

Sĕjarah Bantĕn ('History of Bantĕn') is another Javanese text containing conversion stories. Most manuscripts of this chronicle are late-nineteenth-century, but two are copies of originals written in the 1730s and 1740s. As is the case with the *Babad Tanah Jawi* legends, there are many magical events here, but conversions are not very explicitly described and there is no emphasis on the Confession of Faith, circumcision, etc. The story of the origins of Sunan Giri is of interest. According to *Sĕjarah Bantĕn*, a foreign holy man named Molana Usalam comes to Balambangan in the Eastern Salient *(Oosthoek)* of Java, an area where Islam was not in fact established until the late eighteenth century. The ruler of Balambangan has a daughter who is incurably ill, but she recovers when Molana Usalam gives her betel-nut to chew. She is then given in marriage to Molana Usalam, but when he also asks the ruler to adopt Islam the latter refuses. Molana Usalam therefore departs from Balambangan, leaving behind the princess who is already pregnant. When she bears a son, he is thrown into the sea in a chest, as in the story of Moses (which is found in *sura* XX of the *Qur'an* as well as in the Bible). The chest is fished out of the sea at Grĕsik, where the boy is raised as a Muslim and later becomes the first Sunan of Giri. It is worth noting that, so far as is known at present, Malay legends are devoid of stories such as that of Balambangan, where the supernatural powers of a foreign holy man are insufficient to cause conversion.

These kinds of legends cannot tell much about the actual events surrounding the coming of Islam, but they do at least reflect how later generations of Indonesian Muslims looked back upon Islamisation. There is a clear and significant difference between the Malay and Javanese legends, with Islamisation being a major turning point defined by clear outward signs of conversion in the former, but a much less clearly marked transition in the latter. There are also important consistencies between the two sets of traditions. Both reflect memories of the foreign origins of some of the early teachers, of magical events which attended Islamisation, and of the conversion process as something which began with the ruling elite of the area.

From the north coast of Java came two further documents which help to add substance to the story of Islamisation. These two manuscripts in Javanese contain Islamic teachings as they were being given in Java in the sixteenth century. Although neither manuscript is dated, both were brought back to the Netherlands by the first Dutch expedition to Java (1595–7) and are therefore prior to that time in date. Neither is a connected work of theology. One is a *primbon* (handbook) containing notes made by one or more students of some teacher. The other is attributed by G. W. J. Drewes to a teacher named Seh Bari, and contains considerations upon a series of disputed points. Both texts are orthodox, and both are mystical. That is to say, they do not reflect the austere legal interests associated with the four Orthodox schools of Islam, but rather the metaphysical considerations and ascetic ethos associated with the mystics of Islam, the Sufis, who by this time were accepted as part of the orthodox Islamic world.

The orthodoxy of these two manuscripts is significant. The Islam of Indonesia has been full of heterodoxy and heresy, a fact which later encouraged major reformist movements in the nineteenth and twentieth centuries. These texts are therefore important for showing that entirely orthodox Islam was being taught, at least in some areas, from an early time. These texts do reveal some adaptation to Javanese surroundings. For instance, God is referred to with the Javanese term *pangeran* and asceticism is described with the Javanese word *tapa*. Both texts use the Javanese script, which had originally developed from an Indian script, although in later centuries religious works in Javanese sometimes employed the Arabic script. These adjustments to the Javanese environment are, however, of little significance; the teachings of these texts could have been found in any orthodox mystical community in the Islamic world. The book ascribed to Seh Bari suggests that this orthodox viewpoint may not have been dominant throughout Java, for it has long passages attacking heretical doctrines. In particular, it denounces any identification of God and Man, which is one of the worst heresies in Islam, although it is excellent Hinduism and a doctrine that has persisted in some Javanese Muslim circles into the twentieth century.

G. W. J. Drewes proposes that a third Javanese manuscript, a 'code of Muslim ethics', is also to be dated to the early stages of Islamisation in Java. The antiquity of this text is, however, less certain than is true of the sixteenth-century *primbon* and Seh Bari works. The 'code' could be as late as the final wave of conversions in East Java in the eighteenth century. It is nonetheless valuable for depicting the strains in a society in the midst of Islamisation. Its author repeatedly denounces the practices of those who still clung to the traditional religion (called *agama Jawa*, 'Javanese religion'). This text, too, belongs within

a generally mystical understanding of Islam, but there also survives an anonymous Malay-language manuscript dating from before 1620 which demonstrates
that non-mystical Qur'anic exegesis was practised as well in the Indonesian
region.

The evidence concerning the coming of Islam to Indonesia which has been
discussed above does not easily lead to firm conclusions. It is for this reason that
scholars have differed sharply in their views of Islamisation. One rather lengthy
debate has concerned the area from which Islam came. Gujerat in northwest
India has been one favoured candidate; Gujerati influence is suggested by the
fact that the tombstone of Malik Ibrahim (d. 1419) at Grĕsik and several stones at
Pasai are believed to have been imported from Cambay in Gujerat. The Malabar
coast of southwest India, Coromandel in southeast India, Bengal, South China
and of course Arabia, Egypt and Persia have all been suggested as the source
of Indonesian Islam. Too often this debate seems to presuppose an unjustifiably
simplistic view of events. This was, after all, a process of religious change which
occupied several centuries. In this chapter, only evidence for the initial stages has
been examined, yet between the time of Malik as-Salih's gravestone and Tomé
Pires's account over two centuries elapsed. The area concerned is the largest
archipelago on the earth's surface, and at the time in question it was already
involved in international trade. It seems highly improbable that the Islamisation of
Indonesia can be explained with reference to only one source. Nor is it acceptable
to consider only external sources, for it seems clear that Islam was introduced in
many areas by Indonesians themselves, especially by Malay and Javanese Muslims
travelling in East Indonesia and by Muslim rulers who conquered non-Islamised
areas. There is sufficient evidence to suggest that foreign Muslims from many areas
and Indonesian Muslims themselves all played important roles in various areas at
various times.

But the major question remains; why was Islam adopted by a significant number
of Indonesians only in the thirteenth, fourteenth and fifteenth centuries? There
was at one time a widely accepted stereotype which described Islamisation solely
in terms of foreign traders who intermarried locally and formed Islamic communities in this way; these grew as Indonesians were attracted to the new faith, whose
egalitarian ethos supposedly provided relief from the Hindu caste system. This
idea is now, quite rightly, almost entirely rejected. There is no evidence whatsoever
that there was anything egalitarian about Islam in practice; all the evidence in
this chapter points to Islamisation from above, and none of the Islamic societies
which will be discussed in subsequent chapters was in any sense egalitarian. Nor
can the presence of traders alone explain Islamisation, for it seems certain that
Muslim traders had been present in Indonesia long before significant Indonesian
conversions began. On the other hand, conversion is inconceivable without trade,
for it was the international network of commerce that brought Indonesians into
contact with Islam.

The clear evidence of a mystical bias in much of Indonesian Islam has led to
the suggestion that the Sufis were the primary agents of conversion. A. H. Johns
is the main supporter of this argument, and he points out that the Islamisation of
Indonesia coincided with the period when Sufism came to dominate the Islamic
world, after the fall of Baghdad to the Mongols in 1258. He sees the Sufis, of all
nationalities, as travelling to Indonesia aboard trading ships and there successfully

propagating their more eclectic and less austere version of the faith. Although this view has much logical force, it does lack evidence, for no organised Sufi brother-hood is documented in Indonesia from this early period. On the other hand, there is of course little documentation to support any theory. Moreover, in India, where Islamisation also occurred within previously Hindu communities, some scholars have argued that Sufis were not normally the initial agents of conversion, but rather a second wave of Islam which deepened the orthodox commitment of already Islamised areas. This is similar to the role ascribed to the Indian holy man in the *Hikayat Raja-raja Pasai* story described above. And the Sufi theory seems irrelevant to those cases such as Tomé Pires described, where foreign Muslims settled and became Javanese, so that the question is more one of Javanisation than Islamisation. Nonetheless, the strong mystical strain in Indonesian Islam is perfectly clear in the two sixteenth-century Javanese religious texts and in later, better known, centuries. Mysticism is therefore clearly a part of Islamisation, but its precise role remains unclear.

Given the unsatisfactory nature of the evidence, great caution is essential in drawing conclusions. It seems perfectly clear that trade was an essential element in bringing Islam to Indonesia. It may also have been an incentive to conversion, for Indonesian rulers involved in trade may have thought it expedient to adopt the same religion as the majority of the traders. But traders are unlikely to have been intimates of the nobility of the Majapahit court, who would probably have regarded themselves as being far above merchants in social standing; they are more likely to have been influenced by learned Muslim mystics and holy men with claims to supernatural powers. And the problem remains of explaining why conversions only began several centuries after Muslim traders had been known in the region.

Distinctions must probably be drawn between different areas of Indonesia. There were parts of Sumatra and the Javanese coast of which nothing is known before Islamisation; in some cases towns emerged here as a result of foreign Muslims settling, in other cases Indonesians living there may have been little influenced by Hindu-Buddhist ideas and were therefore attracted to Islam for the cultural paraphernalia it brought, such as literacy. But in the ancient centres of high culture this was not true: in Majapahit and Bali Islam met profound cultural barriers. Majapahit's cultural influence was such that even non-Javanese Muslims on the coast emulated its style. It is symptomatic of this difference that in North Sumatra there were Sultans since the end of the thirteenth century, whereas no Javanese monarch is known definitely to have adopted that title until the seven-teenth century. It would be wrong, however, to overemphasise the superficiality of Islamisation in Java. Although Islam had a very limited impact on Javanese philosophy, it altered some fundamental social customs: eventually all Javanese converts accepted circumcision and burial, for instance, in place of Hindu-Buddhist rituals such as cremation. Entrance into this new religious community was, thus, clearly marked. In Bali, for reasons which are not clear, the cultural barriers were insurmountable and Bali has remained Hindu until the present day. In all areas of Indonesia, Islamisation was the beginning, not the end, of a major process of change. Seven centuries later, this process is still continuing.

One final point needs to be made. The debates about the relative importance of traders and Sufis, and about the foreign sources of Indonesian Islam, have obscured an important aspect of Islamisation. It is often thought of as a peaceful process, since there is no evidence of foreign military expeditions imposing Islam by conquest. But once an Indonesian Islamic state was founded, Islam was sometimes spread from there to other areas by warfare. Examples of this in sixteenth-century Sumatra and Java and in seventeenth-century Sulawesi will be seen in Chapter 4. This does not necessarily mean that such wars were fought primarily in order to spread Islam; the roots of these struggles were perhaps more commonly dynastic, strategic and economic. But Islamisation often followed upon conquest. Islam was spread in Indonesia not only by persuasion and commercial pressures, but by the sword as well.

2 General Aspects of Pre-Colonial States and Major Empires, c. 1300–1500

The political history of Indonesia in the fourteenth and fifteenth centuries is not well known, for the same reason that the process of Islamisation is so unclear – that is, the scarcity of evidence. But two major states clearly dominated this period: Majapahit in East Java and Malacca in Malaya. The former was the greatest of the pre-Islamic states of Indonesia; the latter was probably the greatest of the Muslim trading empires. Together they symbolise the transitional state of Indonesia in these centuries. Other states, such as the new Sultanate of Pasai, have left too little evidence to support historical reconstruction.

Before looking at Majapahit and Malacca, some of the general characteristics of pre-colonial Indonesian states must be considered. The evidence here derives from later centuries, but it is clear that certain general features of Indonesian states were constant for several centuries. In particular, the land forms and climate of the region had important implications not only for agriculture and trade, but for state formation as well.

Java has a chain of volcanic mountains forming an east–west spine along the island. Further mountains and highlands help to split the interior into a series of relatively isolated regions suitable for wet-rice cultivation. These rice lands of Java are among the richest in the world. The main avenues of communication in Java were the rivers, of which there are many relatively short ones. The only rivers suitable for long-distance communication were the Brantas and Sala, and it is not surprising that the valleys of these two were the centres of major kingdoms. By the mid-seventeenth century, and probably before, there was also a system of roads in Java, with toll gates and permanent bridges. In the dry season (approximately March-September) the major roads were usable for heavy wheeled traffic. Roads, however, were more vulnerable to disruption than rivers. Brigands or local over-lords could hamper the passage of traffic, during the wet season the roads could be impassable, and at all times considerable upkeep was needed.

Java thus consisted of pockets of population which were relatively isolated from one another. The population of Java in these early centuries is unknown. Reid has estimated that it might have been as high as 4 million in 1600, reaching 5 million by 1800, but there is much room for argument on this matter. Even if there was a population as high as this before the nineteenth century, Java was still extremely underpopulated by twentieth-century standards, and vast areas must have been uninhabited, thereby enhancing the isolation of the populated districts. Any major empire in the interior of Java required some form of central authority over several such isolated regions, a difficult task given the state of communications. Nonetheless, with the exceptions of Majapahit (see below) and Děmak (see Chapter 4), the great empires of Java were primarily inland states. Difficulties of communication meant that overseas trade was not a major activity for such inland empires.

In the outer islands, states were formed in somewhat different physical circumstances. There, too, much of the land surface consisted of mountains, highlands and forest, and many coastal areas were swamps. The vast bulk of Sumatra as seen on a map does not reveal how little of its surface was populated. There exist no estimates of outer island population before the colonial period. Reid suggests that the population of the outer islands may have been as high as 5.8 million in 1600 and 7.9 million in 1800. Thus by present-day standards this area, too, was underpopulated.

In most of the outer islands, states were formed in coastal areas suitable for rice agriculture. The attention of such states was directed to their hinterlands insofar as there was food or important trade products to be had, such as pepper, gold and so on. But the natural lines of communication for such states were outward, to the sea. The outer islands had few long-distance roads like those in Java to assist internal communication. Some rivers led into the hinterlands of these states, but navigation upstream was of course less attractive than sailing outwards to the sea. It will be seen in Chapter 4, for instance, that as Aceh expanded its power down the east coast of Sumatra, its main competitor was not another Sumatran state but Johor, across the Straits of Malacca. Similarly, South Kalimantan states had less to do with the vast interior of that island than with the ports of North Java. And when the Bugis of South Sulawesi began their great emigrations in the seventeenth and eighteenth centuries, they did not march northward in Sulawesi but instead took to their ships. For the outer islands, the seas were their highways.

The states of the archipelago which are described in this and the following chapters were all involved in both international and domestic commerce, which produced much of their wealth. Throughout the archipelago traders dealt in bulk items such as rice, pepper and textiles. Java was Southeast Asia's largest producer of rice until the nineteenth century. Sumatra was the archipelago's main exporter of pepper, the great boom product from the fifteenth to the seventeenth centuries. Many high-quality textiles were imported into Indonesia from India and China, but there was also a substantial trade in textiles produced in the archipelago, particularly in South Sulawesi and Java (which was, again, the largest producer). Traders from outside Indonesia came particularly to acquire Indonesia's high-value forest products such as camphor and sandalwood and the gold of Sumatra and West Kalimantan. Above all, they sought the pepper of western Indonesia and the clove, nutmeg and mace of Maluku in easter Indonesia – the crops which, as will be seen in the next chapter, did so much to attract the first Europeans to Indonesia.

Some observers have attempted to describe the clear distinction between the land-based states of Java and the seaborne states of the outer islands in terms of a differing economic base. Java is seen as a 'hydraulic' society, where the base was wet-rice agriculture, and the outer island states as areas which depended primarily on external trade. This stereotype is not entirely satisfactory. The outer island states normally depended on wet-rice agriculture to feed their populations, although it is true that some of the largest trading states such as Malacca, Aceh, Bantĕn and Gowa mainly fed their populations with rice imported from the north coast of Java. Indeed, the trading ports of north Java were more a part of this seaborne trade system than of the interior Javanese empires, and they had vast rice-producing hinterlands and were major rice exporters. The major difference between these two types of state was the way in which physical circumstances directed their activities: outward in the outer islands, inward in Java.

Many similar conditions existed throughout Indonesia, and affected the economic and political life of pre-colonial states. In all areas there was limited population, and therefore a limited base for taxation and manpower for rice cultivation and armies. It was sometimes one of the aims of warfare, therefore, to deport the population of conquered territories to the area of the victor. The physical isolation of populated territories and poor communications meant that it was difficult to maintain centralised authority over several populated areas. In Java, the solution to this was a system of limited kingship, with considerable autonomy granted to regional overlords. Similarly, outer island empires often were obliged to give considerable autonomy to vassal lords. There was, therefore, constant tension within large states between regional and central interests, and all such states were fragile entities. There was also a limit upon the degree of oppression that was possible, for the existence of large uninhabited tracts made it possible for the population to move to a new area beyond their lord's control if oppression reached intolerable limits. This is not to say that there was no oppression, for there was much, but certain limits were imposed upon it.

A central ruler had three major techniques available to maintain his authority. First, he could accord regional overlords and other potential opponents such as princes and regional leaders enough autonomy and direct benefits in the form of wealth, prestige and protection to make it worth their while to support him. Second, he could maintain a cult of glory about his person and court which appeared to reflect supernatural sanctions supporting him. Third, and most crucial of all, he must have the military strength to crush any opposition. All pre-colonial Indonesian states were founded ultimately on superior military power. Here the outer islands may have had some advantages. Although the pattern of monsoon winds made the open seas unusable in certain areas at certain times of the year, it was nonetheless probably easier to move a seaborne expeditionary force to a single target than to march a large Javanese army through difficult terrain over which other, potentially hostile, lords governed, and in which the troops could, if they wished, simply melt away. A successful ruler stayed on top of this precarious system by balancing and manipulating the interests of those below him, by demonstrating superior martial skills, and by appearing to have the support of the supernatural. He created thereby a consensus of lesser notables in support of his authority. He also of course needed a network of spies to keep him informed, and political marriages to tie the interests of others to his own future.

The two major states of the fourteenth and fifteenth centuries, Majapahit and Malacca, will be considered rather briefly, for although both were extremely important neither belongs within the main themes of this book. Majapahit was a Hindu–Buddhist state, whereas the main concern of this book is the Islamic period of Indonesian history. And Malacca, although the most important state of the western archipelago, was located in what is now Malaysia.

The detailed history of Majapahit is not very clear. The main sources are inscriptions in Old Javanese, the Old Javanese text *Nāgarakĕrtāgama* written in 1365 (known only in later manuscripts), the Middle Javanese text *Pararaton* (known from later copies found in Bali) and some Chinese records. The reliability of all the Javanese sources was questioned by C.C. Berg, who argued that they were to be seen not as historical but rather as supernatural documents, to be understood within the context of politico-religious myths which the authors of these records were concerned to support. It was his view that these texts were not intended to record the past, but rather by supernatural means to determine future events. Professor Berg's ideas have, however, found little support from other scholars.

Berg's general scepticism towards all Javanese sources seems exaggerated, and some certainty is possible about the history of Majapahit. What is reasonably clear is who were its rulers down to the later fifteenth century, and what sort of state it was in general. The rulers were as follows:

King Kĕrtarājasa Jayawardhana	AD 1294–1309
King Jayanagara	1309–28
Queen Tribhuwanā Wijayottunga Dewī	1328–50
King Rājasanagara (Hayam Wuruk)	1350–89
King Wikramawardhana	1389–1429
Queen Suhitā	1429–47
King Wijayaparākramawardhana	1447–51
King Rājasawardhana	1451–53

There was an interval of three kingless years, which may have resulted from a succession crisis. The Majapahit royal house now apparently split into two contending branches, and the tensions and conflicts between them may have lasted into the 1480s. The reign dates of two further kings are known:

King Girīśawardhana	1456–66
King Singhawikramawardhana	1466–78

Hayam Wuruk's reign was the golden age of Majapahit, and it was during his time that the *Nāgarakĕrtāgama* was written. Thereafter, events become less clear. There was apparently a civil war in 1405–6, a disputed succession in the 1450s and a major princely rebellion in 1468. But the Majapahit royal line (or a branch of it) remained in power throughout. Later Javanese chronicles say that Majapahit fell to the Islamic state of Dĕmak in 1478. The rise of Dĕmak and the final collapse of the Hindu–Buddhist state in the interior of Java *c.* 1527 will be discussed in Chapter 4. Here it need only be said that if Majapahit was conquered *c.* 1478, it was not by an Islamic enemy.

The *Nāgarakĕrtāgama* and the inscriptions make it possible to reconstruct something of the style and influence of Majapahit in the fourteenth century. It claimed a form of authority over far-flung vassal states throughout Sumatra, the Malay Peninsula, Kalimantan and eastern Indonesia. Although this may have constituted something of an 'empire' in Indonesian terms, it is clear from the general physical constraints described earlier in this chapter that there was unlikely to have been any regular centralised exercise of authority by Majapahit over such areas. It appears to have been trade connections which mainly linked these regions, and at the Majapahit end this trade was probably a royal monopoly. Thus, Majapahit was both a land-based and a trading empire at once. It exercised significant naval power, and in 1377 sent a punitive expedition against Palembang in Sumatra. Majapahit also claimed relationships with Champa, Cambodia, Siam, southern Burma and Vietnam, and sent missions to China. The memory of Majapahit's greatness has lived on in Indonesia, and it is sometimes seen as establishing a precedent for the present political boundaries of the Republic.

The capital was a grand affair, with great annual festivities. Both Buddhism and the worship of the Hindu gods Siwa (Śiva) and Wisnu (Viṣṇu) were practised, and there was a union of these faiths in the person of the king, who was regarded as 'Siwa-Buddha' and 'Nirguṇa' to the Wisnuite. The *Nāgarakĕrtāgama* makes no mention of Islam, although as was seen in Chapter 1 there were apparently Muslim courtiers by this time. Although the detailed history of Majapahit requires further research, it was clearly one of the greatest of Indonesian states. Its Islamised successors looked back upon it with pride and attempted to depict themselves as its dynastic successors.

In the late fourteenth and early fifteenth centuries, the influence of Majapahit throughout the archipelago began to decline. At the same time, a new Malay trading state arose in the western archipelago. The precise origins of Malacca are disputed. It appears that a prince of Palembang named Parameswara fled after the Majapahit attack in 1377 and eventually found his way to Malacca c. 1400. There he found a good port, accessible in all seasons and on the narrowest part of the Straits. With allies from the sea-people *(orang laut)*, the wandering proto-Malay privateers of the Straits, he proceeded to establish Malacca as a major international port by compelling passing ships to call there, and establishing fair and reliable facilities for warehousing and trade. Malacca was probably the purest example of an Indonesian entrepôt state, for it had no significant products of its own; indeed, it had to import food to feed its populace. It quickly became an enormously successful port, for it had a stranglehold on the Straits, one of the most crucial stages of the international trade system which reached from China and Maluku in the east to East Africa and the Mediterranean in the west.

The main threat to Malacca from the beginning was Siam, but Malacca sought and received Chinese protection as early as 1405. Thereafter repeated Malacca missions to China, in which the first three kings themselves all joined, and visits to Malacca by enormous Chinese fleets commanded by the Ming dynasty's admiral Zheng He (Cheng Ho), continued until 1434. This obvious Chinese protection helped Malacca to become firmly established. In the mid-fifteenth century, Malacca moved to conquer areas on both sides of the Straits which produced food, tin, gold and pepper, thereby increasing both its wealth and its strategic position. By the 1470s and 1480s the empire controlled the main populated centres throughout the southern Malay Peninsula and the central east coast of Sumatra.

At the beginning, Parameswara was a Hindu–Buddhist king, but he naturally compelled and encouraged Muslim traders to use his port. There has been some debate about his conversion to Islam. It appears that very late in his reign (? 1390–1413/14) he adopted Islam and the name Iskandar Syah. His two successors

Mĕgat Iskandar Syah (r. 1414–23/4) and Muhammad Syah (r. 1424–44?) were Muslims. But there may have been a Hindu–Buddhist reaction under the fourth king Parameswara Dewa Syah (r. 1445–6), who was apparently killed in a Muslim coup and replaced by his half-brother Sultan Muzaffar Syah (r. 1446–59). Thereafter the position of Islam was unchallenged.

The most interesting aspect of Malacca for this history of Indonesia is the vast trading network which reached out to the Indonesian islands. The Portugese writer Tomé Pires described the wealth of this system with an enthusiasm which may be exaggerated, but his general description is clearly reliable. The main stages and the most important products involved were as follows:

Malacca – east coast of Sumatra: gold, camphor, pepper, silk, benzoin and other wood resins, honey, wax, pitch, sulphur, iron, cotton, rattan, rice and other foodstuffs, slaves; exchanged primarily for Indian textiles; trading junks were also purchased in Malacca by the traders from some areas.

Malacca – Sunda (West Java): pepper, tamarind, slaves, gold, rice and other foodstuffs; exchanged for Indian textiles, areca, rosewater, etc.

Malacca – Central and East Java: rice and other foodstuffs, pepper, tamarind, semi-precious stones, gold, slaves and textiles to be used as trade-goods further east; exchanged for good quality Indian textiles and Chinese goods.

West Java – west coast of Sumatra: products like those from the east coast of Sumatra, and horses, were shipped to West Java; there was also direct trade with Gujerati shippers, who brought textiles.

Central and East Java – South Sumatra: cotton, honey, wax, pitch, rattan, pepper, gold, were shipped to Java.

Java – Bali, Lombok, Sumbawa: foodstuffs, coarse textiles, slaves, horses; exchanged for Javanese textiles.

Bali, Lombok, Sumbawa – Timor, Sumba: sandalwood from the latter areas; exchanged for coarse Indian and Javanese textiles.

Timor, Sumba – Maluku: nutmeg, clove and mace from Maluku (the 'Spice Islands'); exchanged for coarse Sumbawan textiles, Javanese cash and Indian trinkets.

Java and Malacca – South Kalimantan: foodstuffs, diamonds, gold, camphor; exchanged for Indian textiles.

South Sulawesi – Malacca, Java, Brunei, Siam, Malay Peninsula: slaves, rice and gold from Makasar were traded directly by the Bugis for Indian textiles, benzoin, etc.

At Malacca, this Indonesian trading system was linked to routes reaching westward to India, Persia, Arabia, Syria, East Africa and the Mediterranean, northward to

Siam and Pegu, and eastward to China and perhaps Japan. This was the greatest trading system in the world at this time, and the two crucial exchange points were Gujerat in northwest India and Malacca. The spices of Indonesia were one of the prize products of this system, but it needs to be remembered that the products which kept the system going were bulk items of a more mundane nature, especially Indian textiles and Javanese rice. Although there were undoubtedly more rats than rubies in Malacca, the wealth displayed there must have been impressive. The key to Malacca's success was less that it was a good port (for there were others) than that the ruler's policies had succeeded in creating an international community of traders who found its facilities advantageous. The Portugese were soon to discover that conquering the port was easier than creating such a community.

3 The Arrival of the Europeans in Indonesia, *c.* 1509–1620

The arrival of the first Europeans in Southeast Asia at the beginning of the sixteenth century has sometimes been regarded as the most important watershed in its history. This view is untenable. Although Europeans – above all the Dutch – were to have a great impact upon Indonesia, this was largely a phenomenon of later times. As the colonial period recedes into the past, questions are being asked about how lasting even this later impact was. Whatever the case, in the early years of the Europeans' presence, their influence was sharply limited in both area and depth.

Europe was not the most advanced area of the world at the start of the fifteenth century. Nor was it the most dynamic. The major expanding force in the world was Islam; in 1453 the Ottoman Turks conquered Constantinople, and at the eastern end of the Islamic world the faith was spreading in Indonesia and the Philippines. But the Europeans, and especially the Portuguese, were making certain technological advances which would launch the Portuguese nation on one of the most daring overseas adventures of all time. Through improved geographical and astronomical knowledge – much of which derived from Arab learning, often transmitted to European Christians *via* Jewish scholarship – the Portuguese became better navigators. By combining lateen and square rigging and improving construction, they produced ships that were faster, more manoeuvrable and more seaworthy. They began to use artillery aboard ship: the man-of-war was becoming a seaborne gunnery platform rather than primarily a floating castle for bowmen or a ramming device.

The Portuguese had not only the technological advances that would enable them to expand overseas; they had also the will and the need to do so. With the encouragement of Prince Henry 'the Navigator' (d. 1460) and other patrons, Portuguese seamen and adventurers began the long search down the west coast of Africa for gold, for the glory of battle and for a way to outflank the Muslim enemy. They also sought spices, which meant somehow finding the way to Asia to cut out the Muslim merchants who, with their Venetian outlet in the Mediterranean, monopolised spice imports to Europe. Spices were as much a matter of necessity as taste. During the European winter there was no way to keep large livestock herds alive; many animals were therefore slaughtered and the meat must then be preserved. For this, salt and spices were used, and among the imported spices the most valuable was the clove from East Indonesia. Indonesia also produced pepper, nutmeg and mace (the latter two deriving from the same plant); it was therefore a major goal for the Portuguese, although they had as yet little idea where the 'Spice Islands' of Indonesia might be, or how to get there.

In 1487 Bartolomeu Dias rounded the Cape of Good Hope and entered the Indian Ocean. In 1497 Vasco da Gama reached India. The Portuguese soon discovered, however, that the trade products they had hoped to sell could not compete in the sophisticated Indian market with those which flowed through the Asian trade network. They realised that they must therefore employ naval warfare to establish themselves. The man who was primarily responsible for this daring attempt was Afonso de Albuquerque (? 1459–1515), probably the greatest naval commander of the age. In 1503 Albuquerque went to India, and in 1510 he conquered Goa on the west coast as a permanent base for the Portuguese. By this time bases had already been established farther west, at Ormuz and Socotra. The plan was to dominate the seaborne trade of Asia by establishing permanent bases at crucial points, whence the superior military technology of the Portuguese could be directed. In 1510, after much fighting and hardship, as well as internal dissension and confusion, the Portuguese seemed near to achieving their aim. The most necessary task for them now was to assault the eastern terminus of Asian trade at Malacca.

Upon hearing the first reports of Malacca's great wealth which came from Asian traders, the Portuguese king sent Diogo Lopes de Sequeira to find Malacca, to make a friendly compact with its ruler and to stay on there as Portugal's representative east of India. All did not go well for Sequeira when he arrived in Malacca in 1509. At first he was well received by Sultan Mahmud Syah (r. 1488–1528), but then the international Muslim trading community of the city convinced Mahmud that the Portuguese posed a grave threat to him. He turned against Sequeira, captured several of his men and killed others, and attempted to assault the four Portuguese ships which, however, managed to sail away. As had been the case farther west, conquest was clearly the only means open to the Portuguese to establish themselves.

In April 1511, Albuquerque set sail from Portuguese Goa for Malacca with a force of some 1200 men and seventeen or eighteen ships. Hostilities commenced soon after his arrival and carried on sporadically throughout July and early August. The Malaccan side was hampered by a bitter dispute between Sultan Mahmud and his son Sultan Ahmad, who had just been given authority over the state and who was later killed upon his father's orders. Although Malacca seems to have been well supplied with artillery, the Portuguese combination of firepower, determination and fanatical courage carried them to victory. Malacca was conquered. Albuquerque stayed in Malacca until November 1511, by which time he had prepared Malacca's defences to resist any Malay counterattack and had ordered the first ships to set out in search of the 'Spice Islands'. He then set sail for India aboard a capacious but rotting vessel from which he escaped when it sank off Sumatra, taking with it to the bottom all the booty plundered at Malacca.

The Portuguese now controlled Malacca, but it very soon became evident that they did not control the Asian trade which had been centred on it. The Portuguese had many problems. They were never self-supporting, and were as dependent upon Asian suppliers for food as had been their Malay predecessors in Malacca. They were short of both money and manpower. Their organisation was typified by confused and overlapping commands, inefficiency and corruption. Even their own governors of Malacca traded for personal gain at the Malay port of Johor, where duties and prices were lower, in violation of the monopoly they were supposed to maintain. The Asian traders transferred much of their trade to other ports, and simply bypassed the Portuguese monopoly.

In the west of the archipelago the Portuguese fairly soon ceased to be such a revolutionary force. Their technological superiority consisted of navigational and military techniques which were quickly learned by their Indonesian competitors; Portuguese cannon were soon captured by Indonesian opponents. Portuguese Malacca became a part of a web of conflict in the Straits of Malacca, as Johor and Aceh competed to defeat each other and the Portuguese and to become the true successor of Malacca (see Chapter 4). By the second half of the sixteenth century, ships were seen in the Indonesian Archipelago which had part Portuguese and part Indonesian crews, or which were owned by Indonesians and chartered by Portuguese.

The importance of the conquest of Malacca must not, however, be under-estimated. The city began to die as a trading port under the Portuguese, they never monopolised Asian trade, they had little influence on the culture of Indonesians in the western archipelago, and they soon settled down as a rather odd part of their Indonesian surroundings. Nonetheless, the Portuguese had done one thing which had a lasting impact: they had fundamentally disrupted the organisation of the Asian trade system. There was no longer a central port where the wealth of Asia could be exchanged; there was no longer a Malay state to police the Straits of Malacca and make them safe for commercial traffic. Instead, there was a dispersal of the trading community to several ports, and bitter warfare in the Straits. After a century of success, Malacca was turned almost overnight into a name with a proud past but little future.

The most lasting cultural impact of the Portuguese was in Maluku (a name ultimately derived from the Arab traders' term for the region, *Jazirat al-Muluk*, the land of many kings). Here were located the 'Spice Islands' of East Indonesia. Immediately after the conquest of Malacca the first exploratory mission was sent eastward under Francisco Serrão. In 1512 he was shipwrecked, but he struggled to Hitu (northern Ambon), where he demonstrated martial skills against an attacking force which endeared him to the local ruler. This also led the rulers of the two competing islands Tĕrnate and Tidore both to inquire after the possibility of Portuguese assistance. There was a temporary decline in Javanese and Malay sailings to the eastern islands at this time, caused especially by the destruction of the Javanese fleet at Malacca in 1511. Thus, the Portuguese were also welcomed in the area because they could bring food and buy spices. The Asian trade soon revived, however, and the Portuguese never exercised an effective monopoly over the spices.

The Portuguese allied themselves with Tĕrnate and in 1522 began to build a fortress there. Their relations with the Muslim ruler were strained by rather feeble attempts at Christianisation, and by the generally poor behaviour of the Portuguese. This outpost at the other end of the earth rarely attracted any but the most desperate and avaricious. In 1535 the Portuguese in Tĕrnate deposed King Tabariji (or Tabarija) and sent him to Portuguese Goa. There he converted to Christianity, took the name Dom Manuel, and upon being declared innocent of the charges which had been brought against him he was sent back to reoccupy his throne. He died en route at Malacca in 1545, but not before he had given his Portuguese godfather Jordão de Freitas the island of Ambon. Finally the Portuguese, who murdered Sultan Hairun of Tĕrnate in 1570, were expelled by the Tĕrnatens after a five-year siege in 1575, after which they moved to Tidore and established a new fortress in 1578. The main centre of Portuguese activities in Maluku, however, now came to be Ambon. Tĕrnate meanwhile became an expanding, fiercely Islamic and anti-Portuguese state under the rule of Sultan Baab Ullah (r. 1570–83) and his son Sultan Said.

The Portuguese were also involved and beleaguered in Solor. In 1562 Dominican priests built a palm-trunk fortress there which Javanese Muslim attackers burned down the following year. The Dominicans persisted, however, rebuilding the fortress in more durable materials and commencing the Christianisation of the local population. There were further Javanese attacks in later years. Nor was the populace of Solor uniformly in favour of the Portuguese or their religion, for there were repeated displays of resistance. In 1598–9 a major Solorese uprising required the Portuguese to send an armada of 90 ships to put down the insurgents. Nevertheless the Portuguese remained in occupation of their Solor fortress until expelled by the Dutch in 1613 and again, after a Portuguese reoccupation, in 1636.

Amongst the Portuguese adventurers and desperadoes, there was one European whose work initiated a permanent change in East Indonesia. This was the Spaniard Saint Francis Xavier (1506–52), a co-founder of the Jesuit Order with Saint Ignatius Loyola. In 1546–7 Xavier worked among the peoples of Ambon, Tĕrnate and Morotai (Moro), and laid the foundations for a permanent mission there. He went on to carry his mission enterprise to Japan, but died before being able to enter China. After Xavier's departure from Maluku others continued his work. By the 1560s there were perhaps as many as 10 000 Catholics in the area, mostly on Ambon, and by the 1590s there were 50 000 to 60 000. The Dominicans, too, had some success in Christianising Solor; by the 1590s the Portuguese and local Christian population there probably numbered about 25 000 people. There continued to be Christian communities in eastern Indonesia through succeeding centuries, and this contributed to a sense of shared interests with Europeans, particularly among the Ambonese, which no other Indonesian people experienced to the same degree.

Banda, the source of nutmeg, was, however, rather an exception to the pattern of developments described here. There an oligarchic form of government led by *orang kaya* (powerful men) displayed no enthusiasm for Christianity or the Europeans who brought it. The Bandanese steadfastly refused the Portuguese permission to build a fortress and, probably because of the lack of such a base, the priests made no serious attempt to Christianise the Bandanese. Bandanese continued to play an active and independent role in archipelago trade until the early seventeenth century.

It is worth pointing out that this serious missionary endeavour took place in the latter half of the sixteenth century, after the pace of Portuguese conquest had stopped. The cross came seriously to East Indonesia rather a long time after the sword. By this time, the main Portuguese interest in the East was already shifting away from Maluku. Trade with Japan began in 1543 and the formal cession of Macao in 1557 made more regular trade possible with China. And the worldwide activities of the Portuguese were coming to be centred more on the sugar of Brazil and the slaves of Africa than on the eastern periphery of empire.

In Maluku the Portuguese left some other signs of their cultural influence. The romantic *kĕroncong* ballads sung to the guitar are of hybrid Portuguese origin. A considerable number of Indonesian words are from Portuguese, such as *pesta* (party), *sabun* (soap), *sĕpatu* (shoe), *bĕndera* (flag), *meja* (table), *Minggu* (Sunday), and so on. This reflects the role which the Portuguese language played, alongside Malay, as a *lingua franca* throughout the archipelago into the early nineteenth century. Many family names still found in Ambon are Portuguese: da Costa, Dias, de Fretas, Gonsalves, Mendosa, Rodrigues, da Silva, etc.

Given the grandeur of their original design to dominate the trade of Asia, the legacy left by the Portuguese in Indonesia was small; vocabulary items, family names, *kĕroncong*. And all of these are things which Indonesians themselves decided to make their own; it was not Portuguese military power which made a party a *pesta*. The greatest and most lasting effects of the arrival of the Portuguese were two: the disruption and disorganisation of the trade network caused by their conquest of Malacca, and the planting of Christianity in some parts of eastern Indonesia. The second, however, was less the work of the Portuguese empire than of a few devoted priests.

After the Portuguese came the Dutch, who inherited the aspirations and strategy of the Portuguese. The Dutch brought better organisation, better guns, better ships, better financial backing, and the same combination of courage and brutality. They very nearly achieved what the Portuguese had hoped but failed to achieve, control of the spices of Indonesia. But the Dutch did one thing the Portuguese had not done: they established a permanent foothold in Java. This was to make their involvement fundamentally different from the Portuguese, and was to lead ultimately to the Dutch becoming a land-based colonial power in Java.

In the late sixteenth century the United Provinces of the Netherlands (the most important being Holland and Zeeland) were under considerable pressure to expand overseas. The Dutch war of independence against Spain, which broke out in the 1560s and was not finally settled until 1648, had already brought important changes. The Dutch had acted as middlemen in retailing spices from Portugal in northern Europe, but the war and the union of the Spanish and Portuguese crowns in 1580 disrupted their access to spices brought from Asia by the Portuguese. This naturally only increased their desire to ship spices directly from Asia themselves. Moreover, the movements of population which occurred during the Dutch-Spanish war left the Netherlands a more homogeneous Calvinist society, while the southern Spanish provinces (in present-day Belgium) and, of course, Spain and Portugal themselves, were Catholic. Commercial competition was now to be associated with the animosities of the Reformation.

The Portuguese tried to keep secret the navigational details of the route to Asia, but there were Dutchmen in their service, the most famous of whom was Jan Huygen van Linschoten. In 1595–6 he published his *Itinerario naer Oost ofte Portugaels Indien* ('Itinerary to the East, or Portuguese, Indies'), containing maps and detailed descriptions of the Portuguese discoveries. The Dutch were now aware not only of the vast wealth of Asia, but also of Portuguese problems there. As the Dutch had improved their ship construction and seaborne armament, they believed that the Portuguese in Asia would be no match for them.

In 1595 the first Dutch expedition set sail for the East Indies. Four ships with two hundred and forty-nine men and sixty-four cannon set out under Cornelis de Houtman, who had spent many years in Lisbon and claimed vast knowledge of what the Portuguese were doing. His incompetent leadership caused much dissension on the expedition, however, and after undergoing great hardship and sickness, only three ships and eighty-nine men were to return to the Netherlands over two years later. In June 1596, de Houtman's ships reached Bantĕn, the main pepper port of West Java. There the Dutch soon became involved in conflict both with the Portuguese and with Indonesians. De Houtman left Bantĕn and sailed eastward along Java, causing insult and injury at each port of call. At Sidayu he lost twelve dead in a Javanese attack. Off Madura the Dutch killed a local ruler as he was rowed out to talk to them. Finally, in 1597 the remnants of the expedition returned to the Netherlands, with enough spices on board to show a profit. It had been demonstrated that even an incompetent voyage could make money.

Now began a period known as the 'wild' or 'unregulated' voyages (wilde vaart), as competing Dutch shippers scrambled for a share of the Indonesian spices. In 1598, twenty-two ships of five different companies set sail; fourteen eventually returned. The fleet under Jacob van Neck was the first to reach the 'Spice Islands' of Maluku in March 1599, where it was well received; his ships returned in 1599–1600 with enough spices to show a 400 per cent profit. Most of the 1598 fleets were profitable, and in 1601 fourteen separate expeditions sailed from the Netherlands.

By now it was becoming clear that this competition among Dutch shippers was undesirable. There were now four competing Dutch trading agents in Bantĕn; the competition throughout the spice-supplying areas of Indonesia was driving prices up and the increasing supply into Europe was driving profits down. In 1598 the States-General had proposed that the competing companies should merge in their own mutual interest. It was four years, however, before they could be brought to achieve such a merger.

In March 1602 the competing companies merged to form the United East India Company, the VOC (Vereenigde Oost-Indische Compagnie). The competing interests were represented by a system of Chambers (kamer) for each of six regions of the Netherlands. Each Chamber had an agreed number of Directors, who totalled seventeen and were referred to as the Heeren XVII (Seventeen Gentlemen). Amsterdam's preponderant role gave it eight of the seventeen Directors, and the VOC's headquarters was located there. The VOC was granted a charter by the States-General which gave it quasi-sovereign powers to enlist personnel on an oath of allegiance, wage war, build fortresses and conclude treaties throughout Asia.

The personnel of the VOC in Asia were, as one would expect, not always of the highest calibre, especially in its later years. Honourable men of vision who wished to undertake hazardous careers in Asia were hard to find. Although the VOC as an organisation was Dutch, many of its personnel were not. Adventurers, vagabonds, criminals, and the unfortunate from throughout Europe took its oath of allegiance. Inefficiency, dishonesty, nepotism and alcoholism were widespread in the VOC. There was much brutality which modern minds find repellent, but it must be remembered that this was a brutal age, and Indonesians showed no greater gentleness.

In the first years the Heeren XVII were in sole charge of the affairs of the VOC, but it was soon discovered that it was impossible for them to control successfully the daily administration in Asia. The distances were so great that an exchange of messages between Amsterdam and Indonesia could require two or three years. It is not possible to say whether the VOC made a profit in these early years, for the Netherlands parliament (States-General) allowed the Company not to make the first ten-year financial report called for in its charter. Certainly the company won little military success against the Portuguese and Spanish (who had arrived in the Philippines from across the Pacific in 1521 and began to establish themselves on a permanent footing after 1565). The only major VOC victory was the occupation of Ambon in 1605.

The Portuguese in Ambon were hard-pressed by their local enemies in the late sixteenth century. In 1600 they won a major naval battle in the bay of Ambon, but only with great difficulty. The arrival of the Dutch sealed their fate. In 1600 the Dutch joined the Hituese in an anti-Portuguese alliance, in return for which the Dutch were to have the sole right to purchase the spices of Hitu. The Portuguese responded to their worsening situation in 1602 with a major (and last) expeditionary force from Malacca, which temporarily reimposed an appearance of Portuguese dominance in much of Maluku. But in February 1605 a VOC fleet renewed the alliance with Hitu and prepared to attack the Portuguese fort on Ambon. Now, however, the Portuguese simply surrendered. The VOC occupied the fort, renamed it 'Victoria', and shortly thereafter expelled the Catholic missionaries and began converting local Catholics to Calvinism. This occupation of Ambon was, however, an isolated success. In 1606, a Spanish fleet took both Těrnate and Tidore. Despite their success in Ambon, the Dutch were still far from achieving their goal of imposing a monopoly over all spices and, by excluding European competitors, preventing a glut on the European market. Stronger measures were obviously required.

To take firmer charge of VOC affairs in Asia, in 1610 the post of Governor-General was created. To restrain the Governor-General's potentially despotic powers, a Council of the Indies *(Raad van Indië)* was created to advise and check him. Although the *Heeren XVII* continued to have overall control and appointed and in some cases dismissed Governors-General, it was nonetheless true that from 1610 VOC activities in Asia were largely determined by the Governor-General.

Under the first three Governors-General (1610–19) the VOC centre was Ambon, but this was not very satisfactory as a headquarters. Although it was in the heart of the spice-producing areas, it was far from the main trade routes of Asia and therefore far from VOC activities elsewhere from Africa to Japan. The Dutch began to seek a better place for a 'rendezvous', a safe port where they could have offices, warehouses and facilities for their navy. Their thoughts turned naturally to the western archipelago, somewhere near the crucial Straits of Malacca or the Straits of Sunda (which had become more important as a trade route, carrying ships up the west coast of Sumatra, since insecurity in the Straits of Malacca had followed the arrival of the Portuguese). The first permanent VOC trading post had been founded in Banten in 1603, but this was obviously unsuitable for a headquarters. There was strong competition there from Chinese and English traders, and it was under the control of a wealthy and powerful ruling house.

The need for a permanent headquarters in the western archipelago was emphasised by the increasing threat of English competition. Sir Francis Drake had made the first English contact with Indonesia in his westward circumnavigation of the world in 1577–80. He had stopped at Těrnate and returned home with a cargo of cloves. The English, like the Dutch, were under pressure to become directly involved in the spice trade. The Dutch-Spanish war disrupted the flow of spices through Antwerp, and English trade with Syria was disrupted by Spanish and Portuguese harassment at the Straits of Gibraltar. In 1591 Elizabeth I authorised the first English attempt to become directly involved in the spice trade. Sir James Lancaster (who had some experience in Lisbon) and George Raymond set sail in that year. Their voyage was a catastrophe. There was great sickness and mortality on board, and Raymond went down with his ship at sea. Lancaster did reach Aceh and Penang, but on his return home he was marooned in the West Indies and only reached England through the hospitality of a French privateer in 1594. Not surprisingly, the English were uncertain of the benefits to be had from such undertakings. But then news came of the first Dutch profits, and the doubts were abandoned.

In 1600 Elizabeth I granted a charter to the (English) East India Company, and the English advance in Asia began. The hapless Sir James Lancaster was given command of the Company's first voyage. He arrived in Aceh in June 1602 and went on to Bantěn, where he was allowed to build a trading post. This rich pepper port was to remain the centre of English activities until 1682. Lancaster returned to England with such an enormous load of pepper that some of it could not be sold, and investors had to be repaid partly in pepper. Lancaster's reputation had been restored.

In 1604 the second English East India Company voyage under Sir Henry Middleton reached Těrnate, Tidore, Ambon and Banda. But here VOC hostility was encountered, and fierce Anglo-Dutch competition for access to the spices began. The VOC was attempting to force monopoly agreements upon the rulers of the spice-producing islands, and bitterly resented what it saw as English 'smuggling' in Maluku. In the period 1611–17 the English were also setting up trading posts elsewhere in Indonesia, at Sukadana (southwest Kalimantan), Makasar, Jayakěrta and Jěpara (in Java), and Aceh, Pariaman and Jambi (in Sumatra). Anglo-Dutch conflict grew in intensity as the Dutch saw their goal of monopoly slipping through their fingers.

There was a brief episode of cooperation with the English, imposed upon an unwilling VOC by diplomatic considerations in Europe in 1620. The English were allowed to have a trading post in Ambon, but in 1623 there occurred the 'Amboyna (Ambon) Massacre', which put an end to any ideas of cooperation. The twelve English trading agents on Ambon were arrested and, under torture, confessed to a conspiracy against the VOC. Ten Englishmen (as well as ten Japanese and one Portuguese) were executed and a diplomatic fracas blew up in Europe as a result. But nothing came of it. By now English interest was in any case turning more to other areas of Asia, and in Indonesia they quietly withdrew from most of their activities except for their trade in Bantěn.

Although the English did not again challenge the predominant role of the Dutch until the late eighteenth century, and indeed in the early seventeenth century were less of a military threat to the VOC than the Portuguese and Spanish, their activities had nonetheless increased VOC anxiety to find a 'rendezvous'. They also impressed upon the VOC the necessity for rigorous measures if its aim of monopoly of the spice trade was to be achieved. In 1619 Jan Pieterszoon Coen became Governor-General (1619–23, 1627–9), and it was he who placed the VOC on a firm footing. If his predecessors had had any scruples about the use of force, Coen certainly had none. In 1614 he had told the *Heeren XVII* that they could have neither trade without war nor war without trade. From Coen's time onwards, the VOC in Asia saw clearly that there was only one way to establish its power: by destroying everything which got in its way.

Whether the policies established by Coen and pursued by his immediate successors (culminating in the events described in Chapter 6) were any more wise than gentle is open to question. In Maluku, the VOC certainly made progress towards its goal of a spice monopoly. There the local populations could hardly challenge VOC naval supremacy. In the end, the only form of resistance available to them was smuggling in defiance of VOC regulations. To attempt to control one source of this smuggling, virtually the whole population of Banda was deported, driven away, starved to death or massacred in the 1620s, and an attempt was made to replace it with Dutch colonists using slave labour. As Dutch supplies of spices into Europe grew in volume, the Asian spice network languished for want of a market. But whether such policies actually produced a profit for the VOC is not clear. VOC book-keeping methods do not allow reliable calculation of profit and loss in this period. But it is reasonable to guess that the financial costs of these policies in Maluku were at least equal to the benefits.

Coen also found the VOC's 'rendezvous', and in doing so he may have laid the seeds of its ultimate bankruptcy. The VOC had been trading in Bantĕn since 1603, and since 1611 had also had a post at Jayakĕrta (contemporary Jakarta). Coen preferred Jayakĕrta as the site for the VOC's permanent headquarters. It had an excellent harbour, which Tomé Pires had praised a century earlier as one of the finest in Java, and Coen thought that the VOC could take full control there. Jayakĕrta was ruled by a Muslim prince named Pangeran Wijayakrama, who was a vassal of Bantĕn. There were tensions between Jayakĕrta and Bantĕn, in which both the Dutch and English now got involved.

In December 1618, Bantĕn decided to deal with Jayakĕrta and the VOC. The English Admiral Thomas Dale was encouraged to go there to expel the Dutch. In the harbour he encountered Coen with a small fleet and compelled him to retire. Coen sailed to Maluku to collect a larger fleet while Dale and Wijayakrama jointly besieged the VOC fortress. When at the end of January 1619 the VOC personnel decided to surrender, Bantĕnese forces suddenly appeared to prevent this. Bantĕn apparently did not wish to replace a bothersome VOC post with a bothersome English one. Thomas Dale fled to his ships and shortly thereafter the Bantĕn troops drove Pangeran Wijayakrama into the hills. The VOC remained in their fortified post and Bantĕn troops now occupied the town. For two months nothing much happened, except that the VOC personnel, spending their time in a mixture of debauchery and prayer, decided on 12 March 1619 to rename the place 'Batavia' after an ancient Germanic tribe of the Netherlands.

In May 1619 Coen sailed back into the harbour with seventeen ships. On 30 May he stormed the town, reduced it to ashes, and drove the Bantĕn forces out. The VOC trading post of Batavia, standing amidst the ashes of Jayakĕrta, was now to be the headquarters for the VOC's vast trading empire. The conquest of Batavia was the most significant step taken by the Dutch since their first ship set sail for the East. The VOC could now develop a military and administrative centre in a relatively safe site for the warehousing and exchange of goods, located in the western archipelago with access to the trade routes to East Indonesia, the Far East and the West. This site was under the sole control of the VOC, with no major Indonesian state close enough to threaten it.

But there were less happy implications for the VOC as well. The permanent occupation of Batavia carried with it the costs of running such an establishment. Although the number of Europeans in its population was always small, the city grew rapidly as Indonesians and especially Chinese moved there to take advantage of the commercial prospects Batavia offered them. This population must be fed, which meant importing food supplies, the closest source of which was the north coast of Java. Timber had to be imported to build ships and houses. Although the city was never conquered by an Indonesian power, it had from time to time to be defended against Bantĕn in the west and Mataram in the east, both of which were hostile. All of these considerations meant heavy expenses. And they would also almost inevitably lead the VOC into its catastrophic involvement in the internal affairs of the kingdoms of Java. Batavia was a major cause of the VOC's financial decline. It was also the foundation from which Dutch rule in Java would later grow, but only after much bloodshed and hardship.

4 The Rise of New States, c. 1500–1650

New Islamic states were arising in Indonesia when the Europeans first arrived, but much of their history is poorly documented. There is, however, sufficient evidence to reconstruct with some confidence the histories of three areas: Aceh, Java and South Sulawesi. The first of these was deeply involved with the Malay Peninsula, for in the western archipelago three major powers confronted one another in the early sixteenth century: Aceh, Portuguese Malacca and Johor. In the early seventeenth century, Aceh was to emerge for a time as the most powerful, wealthy and cultivated state of the area.

Sultan Mahmud of Malacca left his defeated capital and after many moves of residence eventually re-established the Malacca dynastic line at Johor in 1518. The Portuguese attacked Johor in 1518, 1520, 1521, 1523, 1524, 1526, 1535, 1536 and 1587. Johor, Aceh and Jĕpara (in north Java) also attempted to destroy the new European port: the years 1513, 1537, 1539, 1547, 1551, 1568, 1573, 1574, 1575, 1587, 1615 and 1629 all saw major assaults on Malacca, all of which the Portuguese withstood. The most crucial battle for the history of the Malay Peninsula was probably the Portuguese attack on Johor in 1536, when Sultan Alauddin Riayat Syah I (r. 1529–64?) lost so many forces that he was obliged to come to terms with the Portuguese. There was thereafter an uneasy alliance between Johor and Portuguese Malacca, who shared Aceh as their greatest enemy. Conflicts in fact continued, and Asian ships were obliged to call at Johor and pay duties, thus reducing Malacca's income. In 1551 Johor again besieged Malacca, and in 1587 the Portuguese sacked Johor's capital. But after 1536 such hostilities were no longer the normal state of affairs. The Portuguese did not always discourage Johor's growth as a trade centre, and the Governors of Malacca themselves found it profitable to trade there sometimes. In due course, the arrival of the VOC would lead to a VOC-Johor alliance against the Portuguese, which ultimately resulted in the VOC conquest of Malacca in 1641.

On the Indonesian side of the Straits of Malacca, Aceh was emerging as a major power just as the Portuguese arrived. Indeed, had the Portuguese not conquered Malacca in 1511 the Acehnese might have attempted to do so themselves for Indonesians, too, were tempted by the wealth of Malacca. Before c. 1500 Aceh was of little consequence. The first Sultan of the expanding empire was Ali Mughayat Syah (r. ?1514–30). During his reign, a substantial part of the Asian trading community dispersed by the Portuguese conquest of Malacca settled in Aceh. In 1520 Ali Mughayat Syah began his campaigns. In that year he took Daya on the northern part of the west coast of Sumatra, which according to Tomé Pires was not yet Islamised. Then Ali Mughayat Syah began his conquests down the east coast, taking control of pepper- and gold-producing areas. As he did so, he began to create an empire subject to internal tensions. The Aceh court was a military and imperial centre whose economic survival depended on its being able to function as a central port for the region; its interests naturally conflicted with those of producer ports who wished to conduct their own independent trade. Ali Mughayat Syah first conquered Děli; in 1524 he took Pědir and Pasai, where he expelled a Portuguese garrison. Then he attacked Aru. He also encountered and defeated a Portuguese fleet at sea in 1524. Two wars had now begun, with Aceh challenging Portuguese power at sea and Johor's claims to districts in Sumatra. From about 1540 Aru became a battleground between Acehnese and Johorese power, and it was only in 1613 that Sultan Iskandar Muda took the area finally for Aceh. But the greater contest which lay behind these wars, the contest for the mantle of Malacca as the sole entrepôt of the western archipelago and the dominant power in the Straits, was to be won by no one.

Ali Mughayat Syah's eldest son and successor Salahuddin (r. 1530–c. 1537/9) is thought of as a weaker ruler. In 1537 an Acehnese assault on Malacca failed and about this time Salahuddin was deposed in a coup. The relationship between these two events is not clear. Djajadiningrat believed that Salahuddin was deposed by his brother Alauddin Riayat Syah al-Kahar before the attack on Malacca, while Lombard believes that it was Salahuddin who carried out this attack and that he was only deposed by his brother c.1539.

Sultan Alauddin Riayat Syah al-Kahar (r. c. 1537/9–71) was one of Aceh's greatest warriors. He is believed to have attacked the Batak people to the south of Aceh in 1539 when the Batak ruler refused to embrace Islam. (The conversion of Batak groups to Islam and to Christianity in fact began only in the nineteenth century.) Then he attacked Aru but was expelled by a Johor force, and Johor held Aru for twenty-four years thereafter. In 1547 he personally joined an attack on Malacca, which was repulsed. After a period of quiescence, in the 1560s Alauddin returned to the attack, this time with rather more success. In 1564 or 1565 he sacked Johor, brought Sultan Alauddin Riayat Syah I to Aceh where he was killed, and took power over Aru. In 1568 he again attacked Malacca, again without success. Aceh was never able to establish a permanent foothold across the Straits of Malacca in this period. When the Johor Sultan (a son of the murdered king) whom the Acehnese had placed on the throne in 1564/5 was deposed, Alauddin al-Kahar again sent a fleet to bring Johor to heel in 1570; Johor was, however, so well defended that the Acehnese quietly withdrew. Alauddin al-Kahar is remembered in Acehnese tradition not only as a warrior king, but also as the ruler who instituted the division of Acehnese society into administrative lineage groups (kaum or sukeë) but it is not clear whether this tradition is correct.

Throughout the later sixteenth century, Aceh remained a significant military force in the Straits. It was, however, often handicapped by internal dissension. Between 1571 and 1607 there were eight Sultans of Aceh, two of them, 1579–89, not of Acehnese descent but from the kidnapped royal house of Perak in the Malay Peninsula. One of these rulers had a reign of fifteen years (Alauddin Riayat Syah al-Mukamil, 1589–1604), but several ruled for only a few months or years. This was a period of assassinations, coups and failed military adventures. In Aceh as in any other Indonesian state, the successful exercise of military power depended on a powerful central ruler who could keep alive a consensus among the elite; in the absence of such a ruler, internal conflicts quickly arose.

A word is required about the role of Islam in these battles in the western archipelago. Some writers have wished to see the wars against Portuguese Malacca as partly wars of religion. Some have found it strange that, in such wars, Indonesian Muslims did not stand united against the Christian enemy. Such interpretations seem to reflect much later European perceptions of Islamic-Christian conflicts. In the sixteenth century the Christian Portuguese were only one of three major forces in the Straits of Malacca. The other two, Aceh and Johor, were both Islamic. In the various understandings which existed during this period of warfare, religious identity was not a determining factor. The consistent enemies were Johor and Aceh, the two Islamic states. Johor and the Portuguese were not prevented by religion from some degree of cooperation and tolerance, both in war and in trade. When the VOC arrived, Johor built up a friendly association with the Protestant Dutch, and the Portuguese attempted, albeit unsuccessfully, to forge an alliance with Aceh. Religion cannot explain the warfare in the Straits of Malacca, the true roots of which were to be found in the clash among three powerful states for commercial and imperial hegemony in the area. At the end of the sixteenth century, there was still no clear victor in this struggle. No state had emerged as a 'new Malacca', and the smooth flow of trade upon which any such emporium must be founded continued to be disrupted by the warfare and by the very absence of a single trading centre. The Asian trading community which had been the basis of Malacca's success was still dispersed among several ports of the Malay-Indonesian area.

In the early seventeenth century, the greatest of Aceh's rulers came to the throne. Sultan Iskandar Muda (r. 1607–36) established Aceh for a short time as the major power of the western archipelago. His successes were based upon impressive military power, including a navy dominated by heavy galleys which carried 600–800 men, a cavalry force which included Persian horses among its mounts, an elephant corps, substantial artillery, and conscript infantry forces. In 1612 he took Děli, and in 1613 Aru. In 1613 he also attacked and defeated Johor, carrying away to Aceh Johor's Sultan Alauddin Riayat Syah II (r. 1597–1613) and other members of the royal family, as well as a group of VOC traders. Iskandar Muda's attempt to maintain permanent Acehnese control over the Johor Sultanate was, however, frustrated when the Johorese managed to reassert their independence and expel the Acehnese garrison shortly after 1613. Thereafter Johor constructed an alliance among Pahang, Palembang, Jambi, Indĕragiri, Kampar and Siak against the Acehnese. But Iskandar Muda's aggressive campaigns continued. In 1614 he defeated a Portuguese fleet at Bintan; in 1617 he took Pahang and carried off its Sultan Ahmad Syah; in 1620 Kĕdah was conquered; in 1623 he again sacked the Johor capital; in 1624/5 he took Nias.

But in 1629 the expansionist campaigns of Iskandar Muda were brought to a halt by the Portuguese. It will be seen below that Java's greatest empire-builder, Sultan Agung, also received a setback at European hands in the same year. Iskandar Muda sent an expedition of several hundred ships against Malacca in 1629, and it was entirely devastated. It was reported by the Portuguese that all his ships and 19,000 men were lost. Thereafter Iskandar Muda launched only two more seaborne expeditions, in 1630/1 and 1635, both against revolts in Pahang. After 1629, Johor began to rebuild its influence in the Malay Peninsula and the southern Straits, free of the threat of Acehnese attack. Iskandar Muda had established Aceh as the paramount power over the major trading ports of northern Sumatra. He had not, however, attempted to conquer the pepper-producing Lampung district in the south of Sumatra, which was under Bantĕn (see below), nor had he been able to establish Acehnese hegemony in the Straits of Malacca.

The state of Aceh under Iskandar Muda, in the period thought of as its 'golden age', rested on fragile foundations. It faced precisely the same fundamental problem as the Malacca Sultanate, Portuguese Malacca, VOC Batavia or any other state which aspired to be a major coastal trading power: how to feed the non-agricultural population which was essential to its success in war and commerce. Aceh's hinterland was not easily or willingly controlled, nor could it easily produce a sufficient surplus of food to support the city of Aceh. Indeed the capital city was only tenuously linked to the Acehnese hinterland. Malay was the predominant language of the city, and its population was international. It was to a large degree a Malay-governed cosmopolitan trading state which happened to be located on the coast of Aceh, but which was not greatly different from other Malay states. Because the capital was constantly at the mercy of its hinterland, the acquisition of prisoners-of-war who could be set to work as agricultural slaves near the capital was one of the aims of Iskandar Muda's campaigns. Lombard has described the decline of Aceh in the later seventeenth century as partly a function of its earlier success, for the city grew to a size which was greater than it could feed.

There were also political reasons for Aceh's later decline. As was the case elsewhere, below the Sultan were elite groups whose support was essential to the Sultanate, but who often required rigorous persuasion to give that support, or rigorous suppression. The elite of Aceh, known as *orang kaya* (powerful men), were kept in check in Iskandar Muda's reign. He watched them carefully, and through the imposition of a royal monopoly over trading rights the Sultan kept himself wealthy and others dependent upon his favour. He created a new nobility of 'war leaders' (in Malay *hulubalang* and in Acehnese *uleëbalang);* these were given districts (*mukim*) in feudal tenure. In Iskandar Muda's reign, these members of the elite were successfully forced or persuaded to support the Sultan's cause. But subsequent Sultans had less success. The elite of Aceh, both those in the capital and its immediate hinterland and the dignitaries of other subordinate ports, had been hard pressed by Iskandar Muda's costly campaigning and draconian rule. To prevent a recurrence of such centralised tyranny, they sought an opportunity to restrict royal power.

Iskandar Muda had his own son killed and named as his successor Iskandar Thani Alauddin Mughayat Syah (r. 1636–41), a son of Sultan Ahmad of Pahang. He had been brought to Aceh with his father in 1617 and had thereafter become son-in-law to Iskandar Muda. In his reign the aggressive campaigns were no more and the court was most noted as a centre of Islamic learning (see Chapter 5). Iskandar Thani appears to have been a worthy ruler, but his reign was short. Upon his death the elite of Aceh asserted their influence and self-interest and prevented the emergence of another powerful ruler in Aceh until the nineteenth century. They placed Iskandar Thani's widow (Iskandar Muda's daughter) on the throne as queen Taj ul-Alam (r. 1641–75), and came to an agreement with Johor that henceforth each would mind its own business. Johor now entered its period of greatest influence and prosperity, for in 1641 not only was the Acehnese threat definitively removed, but Johor and the VOC also expelled the Portuguese from Malacca.

Aceh entered a long period of internal disunity and ceased to be a significant force outside the northern tip of Sumatra. Four queens ruled between 1641 and 1699, and royal authority became restricted to the capital city itself The *uleëbalangs* developed into hereditary rulers of the outlying districts and the religious leaders (*imam* or *ulama*) emerged as the only source of challenge to their power. The Sultanate became a weak symbolic institution. From 1699 to 1838 there were eleven inconsequential Sultans, including three Arabs (1699–1726), two Malays (both in 1726) and six Bugis (1727–1838).

While Aceh was rising to prominence in the western archipelago, new Islamic states were being created in Java. At first there were several influential states, but by the beginning of the seventeenth century three major political centres were consolidating their power: Bantĕn in West Java, Mataram in the interior of Central Java, and Surabaya in East Java. For the sixteenth century the evidence consists primarily of a few contemporaneous Portuguese records (among which Tomé Pires's *Suma Oriental* is the best informed) and later Javanese historical traditions which are a complex mixture of myth and history. Many important events in this period are therefore imperfectly known. It is only in the early seventeenth century that the historical record becomes clearer with the beginnings of VOC documents.

The most important Islamic state on Java's north coast in the early sixteenth century was Dĕmak. This was at the time a good seaport, although extensive silting of the coast in later centuries has now left Dĕmak some distance from the sea. Its origins are very uncertain. It was apparently founded in the last quarter of the fifteenth century by a foreign Muslim, probably a Chinese who was perhaps named Cek Ko-po. His son was perhaps the man whose name was given by the Portuguese as 'Rodim', probably meaning Badruddin or Kamaruddin; he seems to have died c. 1504. Rodim's son, or perhaps younger brother, was the founder of Dĕmak's temporary hegemony in Java. He was known as Trĕnggana, and later Javanese traditions say that he used the title Sultan, although this may be anachronistic. Trĕnggana appears to have ruled twice, c. 1505–18 and c. 1521–46; the period between these two reigns was filled by his brother-in-law, King Yunus of Jĕpara. Trĕnggana oversaw the expansion of Dĕmak's influence to the east and west, and it was during his second reign that the last Hindu–Buddhist state of East Java fell, c. 1527.

What had happened in Majapahit since the later fifteenth century is also unclear, and unless new sources are discovered will probably never be known with certainty. It seems that sometime prior to 1486 Majapahit had been conquered either by another non-Islamic power, or by an opposing branch of the royal family of Majapahit. By 1486 the Majapahit royal line (or the branch of it which had previously ruled) had been re-established by a predecessor of a king named Girīndrawardhana Raṇawijaya (who left inscriptions in 1486). Sometime between 1486 and Tomé Pires's time (1512–15), the centre of the Hindu–Buddhist kingdom was for some reason moved to Kĕdiri; whether it was still under the Majapahit dynasty is uncertain. Whatever the case, the Hindu–Buddhist state was by this time in an advanced state of collapse, rent by internal conflict and threatened by the new states arising on the coast.

During Děmak's military expansion, the Hindu–Buddhist state (at Kědiri) was conquered c. 1527. Later Javanese court chronicles describe the conquest in various ways, but all show some concern to establish that Děmak now succeeded to the legitimacy of Majapahit (these chronicles ignore the possibility that at the end the dynasty of Majapahit no longer ruled). Děmak is pictured as Majapahit's direct successor and the first 'Sultan' of Děmak, Raden Patah, is depicted as the son of Majapahit's last king by a Chinese princess, Putri Cina, who had been sent away from the court before her son was born. The fall of Majapahit in such texts is conventionally placed at the end of the fourteenth Javanese century (Ś 1400 / AD 1478–9). The turn of the century was later regarded as a time when changes of dynasties or courts normally occurred. Such legends can tell little about the actual events, but they tell much about the concern of later courts to see dynastic continuity and legitimacy as elements which transcended Islamisation.

Děmak's conquests compelled the submission of other major ports and reached to many inland areas of East Java which were probably not yet Islamised. The sources do not allow certainty about these campaigns, but the following conquests seem to have occurred. Tuban was conquered c. 1527. This was a very old port of Majapahit mentioned by Chinese sources as early as the eleventh century; it was already Islamised before 1527, but nonetheless had remained loyal to the Hindu–Buddhist ruler in the interior. Madiun was taken c. 1529–30; in the 1530s Surabaya (already an Islamic port) recognised Děmak's authority and Pasuruan was conquered or occupied; in 1543 Mount Pěnanggungan (a holy area for the Hindus of East Java) was conquered; in the 1540s or 1550s Kědiri was again raided; c. 1545 Malang was taken. During an expedition against Panarukan in 1546, 'Sultan' Trěnggana was apparently murdered.

In the west of Java, Děmak sponsored the growth of Bantěn and Cirěbon. Cirěbon was apparently occupied by Muslims late in the fifteenth century, but its florescence is traditionally associated with one of the nine walis, Sunan Gunungjati (d. c. 1570). He is said to have been born in Pasai in North Sumatra, but when the Portuguese occupied that port (1521–4) he travelled as a pilgrim to Mecca. On his return from Mecca he went to Děmak and married a sister of Trěnggana. He set off c. 1523–4 with Děmak forces to establish a strategic and trading base in West Java. In Bantěn he drove off the local ruler, a former vassal of the Hindu–Buddhist state of Pajajaran in the inland Sundanese area who had taken advantage of Pajajaran's decline to make himself independent. In 1522 the Portuguese had agreed with Bantěn that they might establish a post on its eastern border as a barrier to the Muslim forces from the east; on their return in 1527 this agreement was of course rejected by the new Muslim rulers. Pajajaran's second main port, Sunda Kalapa (now Jakarta), was also taken by the Muslims. They renamed it Jayakěrta or Surakarta (synonymous Javanese names of Sanskrit origin meaning 'Victorious and Prosperous'). Bantěn was ruled by Gunungjati as a vassal of Děmak, but his descendants were later to become independent of Děmak's overlordship. Sometime after 1552, Gunungjati moved to Cirěbon and established another royal line which was also to rule independently.

The identity and activities of Sunan Gunungjati are known largely from semi-legendary tales, and much uncertainty remains. It is not impossible that the military conquests ascribed to him were more the efforts of another man known to the Portuguese as 'Tagaril' and 'Falatehan' (perhaps Fadhillah Khan or Fatahillah), who may be confused with Gunungjati in some legends. A manuscript called *Purwaka Caruban Nagari* has been found in Cirĕbon which distinguishes between Gunungjati and Fadhillah; it was supposedly written in 1720, but there is reason to doubt its authenticity. Even if the date 1720 is correct, this would still be two centuries after the events, and this text's ostensible solution of the problems concerning Gunungjati must be regarded with caution.

The second ruler of Bantĕn, Hasanuddin (r. *c.* 1552–70), spread Bantĕn's authority to the pepper-producing district of Lampung in South Sumatra, which had long-standing connections with West Java. He thereby laid the foundations of Bantĕn's prosperity as a pepper port. The third ruler, Molana Yusup (r. *c.* 1570–80), was the conqueror of Pajajaran *c.* 1579. With the fall of Pajajaran the last significant Hindu–Buddhist state disappeared in Java, although there was still a smaller pre-Islamic state in the Eastern Salient *(Oosthoek)* and small non-Islamised communities remained in several areas. Upon the conquest of Pajajaran, the Sundanese elite is said to have embraced Islam.

In the latter half of the sixteenth century Dĕmak's claims to overlordship in Java disintegrated. The fourth ruler of Dĕmak, traditionally called Sultan Prawata (r. *c.* 1546–61 ?), appears not to have attempted campaigns like those of his predecessor Trĕnggana. It is hard to know what the hegemony of Dĕmak had amounted to even in its 'golden age', during Trĕnggana's second reign (*c.* 1521–46). This was apparently a period of confusion and fragmentation, and Dĕmak's 'empire' is unlikely to have been more than a loose federation of states. It is doubtful if there was ever any centralised administrative control, and Dĕmak's conquests may have been more in the nature of punitive (and population-gathering) raids. The geographical factors described in Chapter 2 would have limited Dĕmak's authority as much as that of any other state in Javanese history.

Several other states were important in the early sixteenth century, but none competed with Dĕmak's attempt at expansion throughout the island. Kudus was something of an Islamic holy city. It is the only place in Java which permanently acquired an Arabic name *(al-Quds,* Jerusalem). Its emergence as a centre of Islamic learning is associated with Sunan Kudus, one of the nine *walis*, who is said to have been the fifth *imam* (head) of the mosque of Dĕmak and a major leader of the campaign of 1527 against 'Majapahit' before moving to Kudus. The mosque of Kudus, which is notable both for the perseverance of pre-Islamic architectural forms such as Old Javanese split doorways and for its name *al-Manar* or *al-Aqsa* (like the mosque of Jerusalem), has the date AH 956 (AD 1549) inscribed over the *miḥrab* (niche indicating the direction of Mecca for prayer).

Jĕpara was another important port. In early 1513 its king, Yunus, led an attacking force said to contain one hundred ships and 5000 men from Jĕpara and Palembang against Portuguese Malacca, but he was defeated. Between *c.* 1518 and 1521, he apparently ruled as king over Dĕmak. Jĕpara's influence was, however, greatest in the latter part of the sixteenth century when it was ruled by a queen called Ratu Kalinyamat. In 1551 Jĕpara aided Johor in its unsuccessful attack on Malacca, and in 1574 Jĕpara again besieged Malacca for three months.

According to Chinese records the port of Grĕsik was founded by Chinese in the fourteenth century. In 1411 the ruler of Grĕsik, who was originally a native of Canton, sent a mission to the Chinese emperor. Grěsik became a major international trading centre in the fifteenth century. To Tomé Pires it was 'the jewel of Java in trading ports' (*Suma Oriental*, 193). It also became a major centre of Islam, as the nearby site of Giri became the headquarters of the first Sunan Giri, regarded as one of the greatest of the nine *walis*. He founded a line of spiritual lords of Giri which lasted until 1680, whereas the other *walis* had no successors to their authority. Sunan Giri is said in some traditions to have played a leading role in the conquest of 'Majapahit' and to have ruled Java for forty days after its fall to purify Java of pre-Islamic remnants. Until 1680 Giri was to remain a major opponent of the inland empire-builders, and the spiritual power associated with Giri would come to be feared and hated by the rulers of Mataram. The first Sunan and his successors are credited with a leading role in the spread of Islam to Lombok, Makasar, Kutai (East Kalimantan) and Pasir (Southeast Kalimantan), through conquest, marriages or the mission work of former students. There were clearly links between Giri and Maluku. Zainal Abidin, the ruler of Těrnate in 1486–1500, is said to have been a student of Sunan Giri in his youth, as late as 1618 Ambonese continued to send tribute in cloves to Giri, and the Hituese leader Kakiali (d. 1643) studied there.

Surabaya was a major trading port by the early sixteenth century as well, but it was only in the early seventeenth century that it emerged as the leading coastal power. Madura was still being Islamised in the sixteenth century. In Tomé Pires's time (1512–15) it was not yet converted, but shortly after the fall of the Hindu–Buddhist state in Java c. 1527, the Madurese (that is, probably the elite of Madura) are said to have adopted Islam; according to local traditions this occurred in 1528.

In the Eastern Salient of Java, Pasuruan was the only significant Islamic power in the sixteenth century. The other districts were under Hindu rule. There was apparently a wave of conquests by Pasuruan in the later sixteenth century, but the sources allow little confidence about the sequence of events. There may have been fighting against Hindu Balambangan in the 1540s, 1580s and 1590s. C. 1600–1 the capital of Balambangan was apparently conquered. Although the Balambangan area was not yet converted to Islam, successor Hinduised rulers were squeezed between expanding Javanese powers to the west and invading Balinese from the east, and never again had more than brief moments of power and influence.

In the second half of the sixteenth century, two new powers emerged in the interior of Central Java, which had not been the site of a major kingdom since the tenth century. The districts of Pajang and Mataram (where are located the present-day cities of Surakarta and Yogyakarta respectively) were extremely rich agricultural territories. From the late sixteenth to the early nineteenth centuries these two regions became the main political centres of Central and East Java, the land of the ethnic Javanese. With the re-emergence of courts in the interior of Java, the dominant role of coastal states in Javanese politics was coming to an end. A period of bitter warfare between coast and interior would, however, be necessary before interior dominance was established. This dominance was to have important implications both for economic and for religious affairs, for the interior of Java was less involved in seaborne commerce and less accessible to external Islamic influences.

The kingdom of Pajang was apparently the first to emerge. In Javanese historical tradition it is seen as the next successor in the line of legitimacy which leads from Majapahit through Děmak to Pajang, and culminates in the dynasty of Mataram. In the fifteenth century a shadowy Hindu state called Pěngging, about which nothing reliable is known, was located in the area of Pajang; according to some traditions Sunan Kudus conquered the area for Islam, perhaps in the 1530s. Legends say that a son-in-law of 'Sultan' Trěnggana of Děmak named Jaka Tingkir, who was from the house of Pěngging and about whom several magical stories are told, was sent to rule Pajang as a vassal of Děmak. In the period following Trěnggana's death (1546), Jaka Tingkir expanded his authority in Central Java. He is supposed to have been formally installed as king by Sunan Giri in Ś 1503 (AD 1581-2) with the agreement of the other important Islamic states of Central and East Java. Jaka Tingkir now became 'Sultan' of Pajang, but the ascription of this title in the legends may be anachronistic. He is the only ruler of Pajang described in these texts, and may have died *c.* 1587. These later chronicle stories are the sole sources for the history of Pajang; more reliable contemporaneous evidence is entirely lacking.

Mataram was the region which produced the most powerful and the longest of modern Javanese dynasties. Javanese legends say that one Kyai Gědhe Pamanahan did Jaka Tingkir of Pajang a great service by killing his main opponent, Arya Pěnangsang of Jipang, perhaps in the 1540s or 1550s. Pamanahan was promised the land of Mataram as his reward, but Jaka Tingkir failed to fulfil this promise until Sunan Kalijaga intervened and persuaded him to do so. Perhaps in the 1570s Pamanahan occupied the Mataram district, and he is thereafter called Kyai Gědhe (or Ki Agěng) Mataram in the legends. He may have died *c.* 1584. Pamanahan is said in later Mataram chronicles to have been a descendant of the last king of Majapahit, but this probably reflects a greater concern to establish legitimacy than to record a correct genealogy. Mataram is said to have been deserted when Pamanahan occupied it. This may be an exaggeration, but it does seem probable that it was only in the later years of the sixteenth century that substantial population began to return to the rich rice lands of Mataram, which over six centuries before had supported the kingdom that built Barabudhur, Prambanan and the other great temples of Central Java.

Pamanahan's son Paněmbahan Senapati Ingalaga (r. *c.* 1584-1601) is described in Javanese chronicles as the founder of Mataram's imperial expansion. In the middle of the seventeenth century, the VOC ambassador to Mataram, Rijklof van Goens, was told that it was Senapati who had actually conquered the Mataram district itself. He says that *c.* 1576, after the Mataram ruler had refused to embrace Islam, Senapati conquered the area, wiped out the local ruling house, imposed the new religion and established his own court. Many historiographical problems surround Senapati's reign. Most of it is known only from later Mataram chronicles, and C.C. Berg has argued that these are unreliable as historical records. In his view, the Mataram chroniclers attempted to create false antecedents for the man whom he sees as the real first ruler of Mataram, Sultan Agung (r. 1613-46), who is discussed below. Therefore, he argues, chroniclers created a mythical character called Senapati and ascribed to him activities which were really those later undertaken by Agung. His analysis is based upon a comparison of these two reigns as they are described in a Javanese chronicle; in these descriptions there is indeed evidence of some confusion between the two reigns.

The historiographical questions raised by Berg concerning Senapati cannot be answered with complete certainty. It is undeniably the case that chronicle accounts of the sixteenth century which were composed or recopied two or more centuries later contain inaccuracies and myths. In the absence of contemporaneous evidence, it is often impossible to assess the contents of these chronicles. It is, however, also the case that for the early seventeenth century, when contemporaneous VOC records become available, a few Javanese chronicles can be shown to have a considerable degree of historical accuracy. It is also clear that, whether or not Senapati's reign is accurately described in the chronicles, by the time the first Dutchmen reached Java at the end of the sixteenth century Mataram was already a major and expanding power. It is clear beyond reasonable doubt, therefore, that Sultan Agung was not the first ruler of the Mataram line. But it is also true that most of the chronicle accounts for Mataram history before c. 1600 cannot be verified from other sources. These chronicles must therefore be regarded with caution.

According to the chronicle accounts, Senapati decided to renounce Mataram's vassalage to Pajang. He concentrated his spiritual powers through meditation and asceticism. A falling star descended above his head as he slept on the holy stone of Sela Gilang (at Lipura, still a dynastic holy site) and prophesied both Mataram's greatness and its future fall under Senapati's great-grandson (Amangkurat I; see Chapter 7). Then Senapati sought the support of the Goddess of the Southern Ocean (Kangjĕng Ratu Kidul, or Nyai Lara Kidul), who was to become the special protectress of the House of Mataram. According to Mataram tradition, she was a princess of Pajajaran who had been driven from the court when she refused a marriage arranged by her father. He laid upon her a curse: she was made queen of the spirits with her palace beneath the waters of the Indian Ocean, and would only become a normal woman again on the Day of Judgement. She is supposed to have encountered Raden Susuruh, whom *Babad Tanah Jawi* texts inaccurately depict as the founder of Majapahit, and to have told him that she would serve him and all his descendants who ruled in the area of Mataram. After Senapati had spent three days with her in her underwater palace, the Goddess promised him the support of her spirit army. On his return to land, he encountered Sunan Kalijaga, who told him to fortify his court: Pajang would take no action, for Sunan Giri had said that the rise of Mataram was the Will of God. Senapati's reliance upon both Sunan Kalijaga and the Goddess of the Southern Ocean in the chronicle accounts nicely reflects the Mataram dynasty's ambivalence towards Islam and indigenous Javanese beliefs.

These stories obviously reveal little of the process by which a military base was created. The expansion of Mataram was nonetheless a matter of military power. C. 1587–8 Senapati apparently defeated Pajang, and Jaka Tingkir (Sultan Pajang) died. Senapati took to himself the holy regalia (*pusaka*), the symbols and supernatural accessories of sovereignty. Then he began to expand his power northwards to the coast and eastwards down the Sala and Madiun river basins. There is some logic in the chronicle accounts of the conquest of Dĕmak in 1588, of Madiun in 1590 or 1591, and of Kĕdiri in 1591. In 1591 there may also have been raids on other Sala and Madiun river sites such as Jipang (a crucial site for access to the east coast), Jagaraga and Panaraga. In 1595 there seems to have been further fighting in the Madiun river valley, and in 1600 Mataram apparently put down a rebellion in Pati. Dutch voyagers reported an unsuccessful Mataram expedition against Bantĕn c. 1597.

Now Senapati was approaching areas under the influence of Surabaya, which was emerging as the most powerful of the coastal cities. The bitter conflict between Surabaya and Mataram for hegemony in East and Central Java was not to be resolved until 1625. In 1598 and 1599 Senapati is supposed to have attacked Tuban, but without success. On Surabaya's southern flank, Senapati is said to have attacked Pasuruan in 1591 and 1600. The Pasuruan episodes seem unlikely, however, for it is unclear how Mataram could have marched an army or sent a seaborne expedition (via Dĕmak) to Pasuruan, passing through areas under Surabayan control. It may be that Pasuruan was anxious to salvage as much independence as possible from the emerging conflict between Surabaya and Mataram, and chose to declare allegiance to the more distant of the two powers. Pasuruan could reasonably suppose that the main battles would in any case be fought on the north coast and in the lower Sala and Brantas valleys.

About 1601 Senapati died and was buried at his court in Kuta Gĕde. Although the documentation for his reign is not satisfactory, one can accept that the military expansion of Mataram had begun. Mataram had been established as the major power in the interior of Central Java. Senapati was far from being sovereign over Java: Surabaya and its allies on the eastern north coast were still powerful and independent, as were Cirĕbon and Bantĕn in West Java. The power base of Java's last great dynasty had, however, been created.

For the reign of Senapati's son, Panĕmbahan Seda ing Krapyak (c.?1601–13), some VOC documentation is available and the events are therefore rather clearer. In 1602 the king's half-brother Pangeran Pugĕr, who had been sent to rule over Dĕmak, arose in rebellion. Eleven VOC sailors were captured by Dĕmak forces in 1602, and the reports of the five who escaped confirm the warfare between Mataram and Dĕmak. In 1602 Krapyak was forced to withdraw, but by about 1605 Pangeran Pugĕr had been defeated; Mataram chronicles say that he was sent to live as a religious student (santri) in Kudus, suggesting that this holy city was now firmly under Mataram control. Another half-brother rebelled c. 1607–8 and was defeated in Panaraga, and c. 1608 Kĕdiri apparently rebelled and was again brought to heel.

Krapyak's most powerful enemy was Surabaya. A VOC description of 1620 pictures Surabaya as a rich and powerful state. It was some five Dutch mijlen in circumference (approximately twenty-three miles/thirty-seven kilometres), surrounded by a canal and fortified with cannon. It was said in that year to have 30,000 men in the field against Mataram, yet there was no noticeable shortage of men in the city (this may, however, be an exaggeration). In 1622 Surabaya was overlord of Grĕsik and Sidayu. It is also said in Javanese chronicles and by the early-eighteenth-century writer Fr. Valentyn to have been lord of Pasuruan and Balambangan, but these statements seem doubtful. Its influence may have extended down the Brantas valley to Japan and Wirasaba, into areas where Mataram power was being established. It was recognised as overlord by Sukadana (Southwest Kalimantan), and Surabayan trading ships were seen throughout the archipelago, from Malacca to Maluku. A VOC trading post existed at Grĕsik from 1602 to 1615; its reports are the most reliable evidence for the early stages of the Mataram-Surabaya struggle. In 1610, Krapyak began direct assaults on Surabaya. Down to 1613 annual

Mataram campaigns brought terrible destruction to Surabaya's rice crops, thereby weakening its economic foundations. In August 1613 the VOC trading agents were obliged to flee when Grĕsik and nearby Jortan were burned.

Krapyak also made the first contacts between Mataram and the VOC. In 1613 he sent an ambassador to Governor-General (1610–14) Pieter Both in Maluku, asking for an alliance. Krapyak probably assumed that he and the VOC shared a common enemy in Surabaya. The VOC proceeded to set up a trading post in Jĕpara, under Mataram's control, but it still retained its post at Grĕsik, under the control of Surabaya.

Krapyak died in 1613 and was succeeded by his son, Sultan Agung (r. 1613–46), the greatest of Mataram's rulers. He did not in fact take the title of Sultan until 1641; at first he was apparently called Pangeran (prince) or Panĕmbahan (honoured lord) and after 1624 Susuhunan (honoured lord; often abbreviated to Sunan, the title also given to the nine *walis*). He is nonetheless called Sultan Agung (the Great Sultan) throughout his reign in Javanese chronicles, and this convention is usually accepted by historians. He was the greatest of Java's warrior kings. Not all the battles described in Javanese chronicles can be confirmed in VOC sources, but the general picture of Mataram's conquests seems accurate.

In 1614 Agung assaulted Surabaya's southern flank: the Eastern Salient, Malang and perhaps Pasuruan. Surabayan forces apparently attempted to attack the Mataram army on its homeward march, but were defeated. In 1615 Agung took Wirasaba (near the present-day town of Maja Agung); this was of great importance strategically, for it dominated the entrance to the lower Brantas, and perhaps also psychologically, for Agung now held the area where Majapahit had been located. The victory at Wirasaba was of such importance that Agung personally led his forces there. The chronicles say that the Surabayan alliance was weakened in this crucial battle by mutual suspicions between Surabaya and Tuban. But the clear threat posed by Agung's advance pushed the Surabayan allies together again. They now attempted a long march from the north coast to Pajang, where they expected the local lord to join them. Agung secured the temporary loyalty of Pajang, a Mataram spy in Tuban apparently managed to mislead the coastal forces about the best route to follow, and at Siwalan in Pajang the Surabayan army found itself surrounded and without local support. In January 1616 Agung defeated the Surabayan expedition.

Agung now swept on to victories at Lasĕm in 1616 and Pasuruan in 1616 or 1617. Pajang finally attempted a rebellion in 1617, but it was now too late. Agung destroyed the city and moved its population to Mataram; the lord of Pajang escaped to Surabaya. In 1619 Agung took Tuban, one of the main components of the Surabayan alliance. This also gave him unchallenged control of the main coastal areas producing timber for ship-building. Now a Mataram navy appeared, threatening Surabaya's supremacy at sea. By 1620, Surabaya alone stood in the way of Agung's aims in East Java.

From 1620 to 1625, Agung periodically besieged Surabaya and destroyed its crops. Finally the River Brantas was dammed and the city's water supply cut off. During this period, Agung's forces were engaged in other related conquests. In 1622 Surabaya's ally across the Java Sea, Sukadana, was subdued, thereby cutting off one source of supplies to the city. In 1624, after a difficult campaign and heavy losses, Agung's forces conquered Madura, severing Surabaya's other main source of supply. Madura had previously been divided among several local rulers, but now Agung ordered the island's government to be unified under one Madurese princely line, with its capital at Sampang. After 1678 these princes were to have the name Cakraningrat, and they would play a crucial role in Javanese dynastic politics until the 1740s. Finally, in 1625 Surabaya itself was conquered, not by assault but by starvation. Its ruler, known in Javanese tradition as Jayalĕngkara, is said to have been allowed to stay on as Agung's vassal in Surabaya, while his son Pangeran Pĕkik was ordered to take up an ascetic life at the holy grave of Sunan Ngampel-Dĕnta near Surabaya. Jayalĕngkara is said to have died shortly thereafter.

Coastal and East Javanese resistance to Agung was now effectively at an end. Balambangan was not under his control, and although Cirĕbon had apparently declared allegiance to Agung, Bantĕn remained independent in West Java. Agung had, however, successfully established his sovereignty over all the Javanese-speaking heartland of Central and East Java, as well as Madura. But his devastation of coastal military power could not end the very deep animosities between coast and interior, which would arise again in the reign of his successor. These animosities arose from conflicting dynastic loyalties and from the differing economic interests of the two areas. The coastal ports were never to be wholly convinced that their prosperity, which rested primarily on seaborne trade, could be served by paying taxes and obedience to an inland dynasty. By 1625 there was a new force on Java as well, the VOC at Batavia. Agung clearly gave his Javanese enemies priority over the VOC, but he would soon turn to deal with the Europeans as well.

Agung's authority in Central and East Java rested primarily, but not exclusively, on military power. The factors analysed in Chapter 2 had to be lived with: permanent garrisons and direct rule from the centre were extremely difficult to maintain. Agung naturally turned to the methods all other Javanese rulers had available to deal with this. He brutally crushed opposition when it existed, but also relied upon a cult of glory and wealth about himself to attract the loyalty of other powerful men. Agung appears to have differed from most of his successors in maintaining a balance between centralised legitimation and dispersed administration, resting on a foundation of military power, rather better than most other kings. During c. 1614–22 he built a new court complex, a visible expression of his legitimacy, at Karta (about three miles / five kilometres south of Kuta Gĕde). After his conquest of Madura in 1624 he adopted the imperial title of Susuhunan. Javanese traditions say that, like Senapati, he established a liaison with the Goddess of the Southern Ocean. The series of conquests which had begun in Senapati's reign had brought into Mataram hands courtiers and literati of much older centres, who probably exercised a civilising influence on the parvenu dynasty. The Mataram rulers had by now learned how to rule like emperors in the Javanese tradition.

In the years 1625–7 Agung was at the height of his power. But the damage caused by his rise to eminence must have been great. Much of the coast had been devastated; populations had been deported. How many people had died in the fighting and as a result of the sickness and starvation caused by the disruption of agriculture cannot be guessed. In 1625–7 there were serious epidemics, and VOC documents claim that two-thirds of the population died in some areas. But Agung did not rest. Indeed, he could not. His empire ultimately rested upon his military superiority. Agung's invincibility must be demonstrated over and over again, lest regional interests and powerful men attempt to behave too independently. In 1627 Pati attempted a rebellion and Agung crushed it with heavy losses. The one thing which could shake his fragile empire was a defeat; this he must avoid at any cost. But Agung was soon to suffer a devastating defeat at the hands of the VOC.

Agung's relations with the VOC had been delicate from the start. In 1614 the Dutch sent an ambassador to greet him upon his accession, and Agung warned him that the friendship which they both desired would be impossible if the VOC made any attempt to conquer the land of Java. The VOC had great need of Javanese rice, and therefore hoped that trade with the coastal rice exporters would be possible. But Agung's wars disrupted rice cultivation, and in 1618 when rice was short he forbade its sale to the VOC altogether. VOC-Javanese personal relations were poor. Dutchmen are said to have compared Sultan Agung to a dog, and to have relieved themselves against the Jĕpara mosque; there were accusations of VOC piracy upon Javanese ships. Finally, hostilities erupted. In August 1618 the Gujerati who governed Jĕpara for Agung attacked the VOC trading post there. Three Dutchmen were killed and others were taken prisoner. In November 1618 the VOC retaliated by burning all the Javanese ships in the harbour and much of the town. In May 1619, Jan Pieterszoon Coen paused on his way to the conquest of Batavia to burn Jĕpara again (and with it the English East India Company's post).

Coen's conquest of Batavia in 1619 was the final turning point. The Dutch had now done precisely what Agung had warned them not to do: they had conquered a part of the island which he intended to govern himself as sole ruler. For ten years Agung gave priority to subduing his Javanese opponents closer to home. For his part, Coen briefly considered an alliance with Surabaya in 1619–20, but abandoned the idea. While concentrating on Surabaya, Agung made some overtures towards the VOC. In 1621 captured VOC personnel were returned to Batavia and some rice was supplied. The VOC sent embassies to Agung in 1622, 1623 and 1624, but his requests for VOC naval assistance against Surabaya, Bantĕn or Banjarmasin were refused. Since the VOC would not give him naval support, there was no reason whatsoever for Agung to tolerate its presence in Java.

After the fall of Surabaya in 1625, Agung prepared to deal with the Dutch. His army finally set off in 1628. A march of some 300 miles (500 km) from the court brought the first Javanese contingents to Batavia in August; in October a second Javanese force arrived. In various clashes the Javanese suffered heavy losses, but on more than one occasion the VOC fortress was in real danger of falling. Agung's army attempted to dam the River Ciliwung, but without success. Finally, in December the Javanese withdrew after executing their failed commanders. The VOC found 744 unburied Javanese bodies, some of them beheaded. In 1629 Agung tried again, but this second siege was a débâcle. His forces (including artillery) began marching at the end of May, but in July VOC ships found and destroyed stockpiles of rice and boats at Tĕgal and Cirĕbon, thereby probably sealing the fate of Agung's army before it reached Batavia. The siege of 1629 lasted just over one month (21 August–2 October); the Javanese suffered greatly from disease and starvation, and the army disintegrated on its homeward march. VOC losses were few, although on 20 September Jan Pieterszoon Coen died of illness within the fortress.

Agung's ambition had exceeded his military and logistical capacities and had led him to a devastating defeat. Never again did a Mataram army attack Batavia, and Bantĕn was now substantially freed of the threat of Mataram, being protected by the intervening VOC position. Mataram chroniclers, or perhaps Agung himself, tried to disguise the extent of the failure of 1628–9 by announcing a prophecy that an age would now come in which the VOC and Mataram would become allies. For several years hostilities between Agung and the VOC along the coast continued on a smaller scale, and Agung tried to maintain trade and diplomatic relations with the Portuguese in Malacca and India. In 1635–6, however, he apparently concluded that the Portuguese would not be strong enough to defeat the Dutch, and moved to establish more amicable relations with the VOC. Mataram warships stopped harassing VOC shipping, but a formal restoration of peace was made impossible by Agung's refusal to release the eighty or so Dutchmen whom he held captive at the court. Nonetheless, VOC-Mataram hostilities now ceased. The reasons for this are to be found in Agung's analysis of the forces surrounding him: the VOC could not be ejected from Batavia, the Portuguese were too weak to help, and, above all, indigenous enemies had again arisen and must be given priority.

Agung's defeat at Batavia shattered the myth of his invincibility, and his fragile empire had to be patched together again with military force. In 1631–6 he crushed centres of opposition at Sumĕdang and Ukur in West Java, but the greatest threats came from Central and East Java. In 1630 a rebellion broke out which seems to have been led by religious teachers from the area of Tĕmbayat (the grave-site of the *wali* Sunan Bayat); Agung massacred the rebels. In 1633 he undertook some form of pilgrimage to the holy site at Tĕmbayat, perhaps in an attempt to subdue the spiritual as well as the military power of the opposition. He erected a ceremonial gateway there which still stands, and legends tell of him receiving supernatural powers from the spirit of Sunan Bayat. It was also at this time that Agung officially abandoned the use of the Indian Śaka era for court purposes and adopted a hybrid Javanese-Islamic calendrical system *(Anno Javanico)*. All this suggests that Agung felt his legitimacy and sacral authority to be in need of renewal, just as his military predominance required demonstration.

The holy site of Giri, near Surabaya, was the primary source of opposition based upon religious legitimacy. About 1636 Agung crushed this centre. He first brought to his court Pangeran Pĕkik, the son of the last ruler of Surabaya, who was related to the line of Sunan Ngampel-Dĕnta, an even more senior *wali* than the first Sunan Giri. Around 1633 Pĕkik was given a sister of Agung as his wife, and he was then placed in charge of an army to attack Giri. Pĕkik's spiritual ancestry may have given legitimacy to Agung's campaign; it would have had real military implications as well, for there are several cases known in which Javanese soldiers were reluctant to attack or kill holy men or princes unless led by men of greater holiness or princely standing. The date of the conquest of Giri is uncertain, but it was probably in 1636. The captured ruler was allowed to return as a vassal after paying obeisance to Agung.

The frenzy of campaigning did not stop with the conquest of Giri. By 1633 Agung was already raiding in the east, in Balambangan, Panarukan and Blitar. In the 1620s and 1630s the Hindu lord of Balambangan appealed to the VOC for aid but was refused; his only remaining support was his suzerain the Dewa Agung (king) of Gelgel in South Bali. Gelgel was expanding overseas in this period into Lombok and Sumbawa as well, but in the end it was to prove no match for Mataram's forces in Balambangan. In 1635 the first major Mataram campaign was launched to conquer Balambangan. After devastating the area, Agung's forces were driven out by the Balinese, but they returned to the attack and in 1636–40 Agung at last conquered the Eastern Salient. His hold on the area was probably tenuous, however, and its inhabitants still did not adopt Islam.

Now Agung took his final symbolic step. In 1638 the ruler of Bantěn Pangeran Ratu (r. 1596–1651) had been the first king in Java definitely known to have taken the title Sultan, with the Arabic name Abulmafakhir Mahmud Abdulkadir. Agung probably did not wish to be outdone by Bantěn, and in any case his impending conquest of Balambangan may have seemed to call for a new title. In 1639 he sent an ambassador to Mecca who returned in 1641 with authorisation for a new title, Sultan Abdullah Muhammad Maulana Matarani. At last Agung rested, and enjoyed the only significant period of peace in his reign.

Now Agung prepared for his end. Around 1645 he began the construction of a new grave-site on the top of a tall hill at Imagiri, some three miles (five kilometres) to the south of his court. This was to become the burial ground for almost all his successors and for prominent members of the royal family. It is still a holy place today. The chronicles say that two years before his death the Goddess of the Southern Ocean came to Agung and prophesied the hour of his dying. Epidemic diseases were prevalent in the 1640s, and one of these may have caused Agung's end. In early 1646, apparently sometime between early February and early April, Sultan Agung died. The entrances to the court were sealed to prevent a coup, and his son was declared his successor as Susuhunan Amangkurat I (r. 1646–77).

At the time of his death Sultan Agung was the greatest conqueror in Indonesia since the time of Majapahit. He was overlord of all of Central and East Java, including the Eastern Salient, and of Madura. The only permanent defeat of his career was his failure to take Batavia, and the only kingdom on the island of Java which had remained independent was Bantěn in the far west. Nor was his influence limited to Java and Madura. In 1622 he had conquered Sukadana; until c. 1636 Palembang regarded him as overlord, after which relations were more uncertain; Banjarmasin was an ally in the period after 1637; embassies were exchanged with Makasar in 1630 and 1632. Agung's navy was not a major overseas conquering force except at Sukadana, but its existence gave Mataram something of the influence in the archipelago of the Majapahit 'empire'. This was, however, only a shadow of what Majapahit's influence appears to have been. The VOC was rapidly becoming the strongest naval force in the Indonesian archipelago, even though Agung's navy could still make the entrances to the harbour of Batavia unsafe.

The inward-looking tendency of Agung's empire was in any case clear. He did not move his court to the north coast, where trade could be encouraged and supervised, but stayed in Mataram, which has neither access by river to the north coast nor any ports of its own, and where the sea offers access only to the Goddess of the Southern Ocean's domain. His wars had devastated the coastal areas to such an extent that the export of Javanese rice was affected, at least in some years. For trade and traders he had only contempt, as he explained to the first VOC ambassador in 1614. The dynasty of Mataram had conquered the coast at enormous cost; the crucial question for the future of this fragile empire was whether the coastal districts could be governed from the interior in such a way as to encourage the prosperity of all. If this could be done, Java would become a unified economic and military force of enormous potential. But events were to show that this was not to be.

Outside Java and Sumatra there were no conquerors to be compared with the kings of Aceh and Mataram who have been described in this chapter. There were important things happening in many areas, of course, but much of the history of this period in other areas has not been studied or is inadequately documented. The internal history of the Balinese kingdom of Gelgel during its golden age of the sixteenth century cannot be reconstructed with confidence. Legends tell of the greatness of king Dalĕm Baturenggong and his priest Nirartha. Gelgel apparently dominated all of Bali and districts elsewhere from the Eastern Salient of Java to Lombok and Sumbawa, but in the present state of knowledge little more can be said with confidence. Nor is the confrontation between expanding Balinese and Makasarese powers in Lombok and Sumbawa in the seventeenth century known in detail because of the absence of adequate sources. How this new power had emerged in Makasar (South Sulawesi) is, however, rather clearer.

South Sulawesi was the site of several small states, divided between two related ethnic groups, the Makasarese and Bugis. These two groups gained a reputation for being among the most fearsome warriors of the archipelago. They were also among the most professional. There exist manuscripts containing Bugis and Makasarese translations of Spanish and Portuguese treatises on gunnery; there are no such translations in other Indonesian languages. In the sixteenth century Sulawesi had not yet been converted to Islam. About 1530 the Makasarese state of Gowa began to expand its power over its neighbours by conquest. By the mid-sixteenth century Gowa had established itself at the head of a loosely united empire and had emerged as a major trading power in eastern Indonesia. The Portuguese arrived there in the 1540s and after brief attempts at Christianisation soon settled down to participate in the trade in spices and slaves. Christianisation ceased to be of interest to the Portuguese and Indonesians alike, and the Portuguese presented no barrier to the adoption of Islam by South Sulawesi rulers in the first decade of the seventeenth century.

In 1605 the king of Gowa adopted Islam. Apparently his invitation to the Bugis state of Bone and other states to adopt the new faith was rejected. Gowa responded with a series of campaigns in 1608–11, as a result of which Islam was imposed throughout the Bugis-Makasarese area. At the end of these wars Gowa was the predominant state of South Sulawesi. Its 'empire', like other Indonesian states, was founded on military supremacy but was not a tightly centralised system of domination. The constituent states retained their identities and considerable autonomy. Gowa's victory also did not mean the end of opposition. Its main rival was Bone, which would reverse the power relationship between itself and Gowa in the later seventeenth century by allying with the VOC.

The VOC set up its first trading post in South Sulawesi in 1609, but soon found Gowa to be a considerable challenge. Its importance as a trading centre for eastern Indonesia attracted European merchants whom the VOC was increasingly successful in excluding from Maluku. Sultan Alauddin Tumenanga ri Gaukanna (r. 1593–1639) cooperated with the English, French, Danish, Spanish, Portuguese and Asian traders in evading the VOC's attempts at a spice monopoly. The VOC concluded that stern measures were needed to stop this 'smuggling' and to end the support being given by Gowa to the VOC's enemies in South Maluku. In 1615 the VOC post was withdrawn and limited warfare between Gowa and the VOC began. Treaties of peace were concluded in June 1637, December 1655 and August-December 1660, but these did not end Gowa's importance as a centre of international trade and opponent to the VOC. By 1660, however, the Dutch and Bugis had decided to ally against their common Makasarese enemy, which would lead to the fall of Gowa (see Chapter 6).

5 Literary, Religious and Cultural Legacies

The early Islamised states of Indonesia produced not only new dynasties and empires, but also a rich cultural heritage. Some of this heritage was truly new, insofar as it was inspired by Islam, but much of it had roots in pre-Islamic culture as well. It is appropriate to regard this heritage as classical, in the sense that it provided authoritative cultural standards and frames of reference for the pre-twentieth-century civilisations of Indonesia. Because much of the documentary evidence for these classical cultures derives from the eighteenth century or later, one cannot always be certain that one's picture of pre-eighteenth-century cultural activities is either complete or precisely accurate. Nonetheless, a general description of these classical cultures is possible.

In this period, there was not a unified 'Indonesian' culture. There was instead a series of related regional cultural traditions belonging to specific linguistic and ethnic groups which were to become part of the modern Indonesian nation. There were many shared features among these regional cultures, but only the seafaring commercial groups, speaking Malay and Portuguese as lingua francas, transcended linguistic boundaries to a significant degree. The major cultural traditions are therefore to be seen in terms of the linguistic and ethnic groups to which they belonged. These were many, but in this chapter it will be possible only to look at the best-known written traditions, those of the Malay-speaking areas in the western archipelago, of Java, of Bali and of South Sulawesi. In all of these cases, one is dealing with court rather than folk traditions, although these were not entirely exclusive categories. Many other cultural traditions still await scholarly investigation. In all areas there were communities with distinctive traditions but without written literatures, which of course imposes a considerable handicap upon historical studies.

In the western archipelago, a classically Malay culture with strong Islamic influences embraced most of the coastal states of Sumatra and the Malay Peninsula. Malacca in many ways set the cultural standards for these states. Works such as *Sĕjarah Mĕlayu* ('Malay History') established literary norms and provided images of the ideal courtly life and of the proper relationship between subject and master. The Malay-speaking courts of western Indonesia consequently looked back to Malacca as their model not only in political affairs, but in cultural affairs as well. The only court in the area of present-day Indonesia to make a major original contribution to Malay literature was Aceh. From there came several classics, especially of religious literature. Four early-seventeenth-century authors were particularly important: the three Sumatrans Hamzah Pansuri (d. *c.* 1590), Syamsuddin of Pasai (d. 1630) and Abdurrauf of Singkil (*c.* 1617–90), and the most prolific of the four, the Indian Nuruddin ar-Raniri (d. 1658) from Gujerat.

Hamzah and Syamsuddin wrote works of Islamic mysticism which ar-Raniri later denounced as heresy. The boundary between orthodoxy and heresy in Islamic mysticism is not easily defined, and is a source of argument among modern scholars just as it was among the mystics of seventeenth-century Aceh. All these major Malay authors shared many fundamental ideas. In particular, Syamsuddin, Abdurrauf and ar-Raniri all employed the mystical doctrine of seven stages of emanation (*martabat*) by which God manifests Himself in the phenomenal world, culminating in the Perfect Man. This doctrine was taught widely throughout Indonesia. The theological complexities need not be considered here, but the central issue was this: if this doctrine was understood to imply that God partook of the plurality of the visible world and that the soul of man was in some sense a part of God, then it offended the fundamental Islamic belief that although God created the world, He did not enter into His creation and was unchanged and untouched by it.

Hamzah's *Sharab al-'ashiqin* ('The Lovers' Beverage') and *Asrar al-'arifin* ('The Secrets of the Gnostics'), and Syamsuddin's *Nur ad-daqa'iq* ('Light on the Subtleties') are among the major works of the 'heretical' Malay Islamic tradition. These writers' influence extended to other Indonesian cultures, and some of their works were translated into other Indonesian languages. In the reign of Iskandar Muda (1607–36) these authors enjoyed the favour of the Acehnese king.

In 1637 Nuruddin ar-Raniri arrived in Aceh, and with the patronage of Sultan Iskandar Thani (r. 1636–41) he persecuted the mystics whom Iskandar Muda had favoured. The books of Hamzah and Syamsuddin were ordered to be burned, and from ar-Raniri's prolific pen poured works which established literary as well as what he insisted were orthodox religious standards. The greatest of his works, and one of the greatest books in Malay literature, is his *Bustan as-Salatin* ('The Garden of Kings') which he began writing in 1638, and which was based upon Arabic sources. This encyclopaedic work consists of seven books, covering the creation, the prophets of Islam and the early Muslim kings of the Middle East and the Malay area, just kings and counsellors, pious kings and the saints of Islam, unjust kings and incompetent counsellors who deceive them, noble men and the heroes of the campaigns of the Prophet Muhammad, and intelligence and various sciences such as physiognomy and medicine. Ar-Raniri's works were also translated into other Indonesian languages. In 1644 he left Aceh after he lost the favour of Iskandar Thani's successor, and died in India fourteen years later.

Under queen Taj ul-Alam (r. 1641–75), Abdurrauf was the major writer in the court of Aceh. He wrote works of Shafi'i jurisprudence as well as mysticism. After this time, as Aceh entered the political decline described in Chapter 4, it also appears to have lost its role as a religious and literary centre of Malay culture.

A considerable number of other Malay works in addition to *Bustan as-Salatin* were inspired by, or translated from, texts in other Islamic languages. One of these was the *Mahkota Sĕgala Raja-raja* or *Taj as-Salatin* ('The Crown of Kings'), adapted from Persian sources in 1602–3. It is probable, although not certain, that this version was done in the court of Aceh. The text consists of orthodox teachings on man and God, and extensive advice upon various aspects of statecraft; *Taj as-Salatin* was also translated into Javanese. Many specifically religious texts were produced in Malay versions, including Qur'anic commentaries and works of juris-prudence. Legendary tales from the Islamic world are also found. *Hikayat Iskandar Dhulkarnain* ('The story of Alexander the Two-horned') concerns the legends of Alexander the Great, and *Hikayat Amir Hamzah* ('The Story of Amir Hamzah') is a romantic tale based upon Persian legends concerning the uncle of the Prophet Muhammad.

Malay literature was not, however, wholly dominated by works of Islamic inspira-tion. Hindu stories survived Islamisation and were preserved in such classics as the *Hikayat Sĕri Rama* ('The Story of the Lord Rama', based upon the *Rāmāyana*) and the *Hikayat Pandawa Jaya* ('The Story of the Victorious Pandawas', based ultimately on the Sanskrit *Mahābhārata,* but apparently taken directly from the Old Javanese *Bhāratayuddha).* Hindu stories also form the basis for the plots of the shadow-play (*wayang*), in which flat parchment puppets are moved against an upright screen with illumination from behind. There are also Malay shadow-plays based upon Javanese stories concerning the legendary pre-Islamic heroes Panji and Damar Wulan (in Malay called Damar Bulan).

Chronicles were a major genre of Malay literature. *Hikayat Aceh* ('The Story of Aceh') appears to have been written in the reign of Iskandar Muda (1607–36). It describes his predecessors and praises Iskandar Muda in his youth, and was apparently inspired by the Persian *Akbarnama* written in praise of the Mogul emperor Akbar (r. 1555–1606). There are many other Malay chronicles which concern the histories of other states in Indonesia and the Malay Peninsula.

Most of the Malay works described above are in prose, although verse passages are found within them. There was also a tradition of writing in verse. There were two main poetic forms in Malay, the *syair* and *pantun.* The antiquity of these two forms is not known because of the scarcity of early manuscripts. The name *pantun* is of Indonesian (perhaps Javanese) origin, while the term *syair* derives from Arabic (*shi'r,* poetry; *sha'ir,* poet). Both forms use four-line stanzas usually consisting of four words each, but their rhyme schemes differ (a-b-a-b in *pantun,* a-a-a-a in *syair).* The main difference between them is that the *pantun* also uses extensive internal rhyming and a quatrain is usually complete in itself, having two initial lines that allude to the second couplet in which the poet's meaning is made clear. *Syair* quatrains, on the other hand, normally form part of much longer verse works. *Syairs* cover many subjects, including historical epics. Several are Malay versions of Javanese epics, including *syair* versions of the Damar Wulan (Damar Bulan) and Panji stories mentioned above. The earliest known examples of Malay *syair* are in the works of Hamzah Pansuri, the Acehnese author described above. Both *syair* and *pantun* were sung aloud.

Javanese classical literature is clearly distinguished from Malay, although they exerted mutual influences upon each other. As well as indigenous Indonesian traditions, two general strands of external influence are discernible in Javanese literature: Old Javanese Indianised traditions and Islamic traditions. The most striking distinction between Malay and Javanese is the lesser influence of Islam in the Javanese tradition. On a superficial level, this is reflected in the choice of scripts. Malay literature was written in the Arabic script (except for a few examples from South Sumatra), whereas in Javanese the Arabic script was used much less frequently than the Javanese, which was ultimately derived from an Indian syllabary. Another important distinction is the dominance of verse over prose in classical Javanese literature. Javanese authors wrote their major works in *macapat* verse, which consists of about twenty different metres defining the number of syllables per line, the final vowel of each line and the number of lines per stanza (varying from three to ten). About seven of these metres were commonly used, the others more rarely. This verse was then chanted aloud. These verse forms are apparently of indigenous Javanese origin, although probably inspired by the Indian metres found in Old Javanese literature.

The history of Old Javanese literature in Java after the end of the last Hindu–Buddhist state *c.* 1527 is obscure. What is clear is that the Old Javanese heritage was transmitted into the Islamic period. Some of the greatest works in Javanese (or 'Modern Javanese') are adaptations of Old Javanese works, especially *Sěrat Rama* (from the Old Javanese *Rāmāyaṇa*), *Sěrat Bratayuda* (from the Old Javanese *Bhāratayuddha*), *Sěrat Mintaraga* (from the Old Javanese *Arjunawiwāha*), and *Sěrat Arjuna Sasrabau* or *Lokapala* (from the Old Javanese *Arjunawijaya*). When the Old Javanese versions ceased to be copied and read in Java is difficult to know. It is reasonably clear, however, that Old Javanese was still studied in the Javanese courts into the eighteenth century. Among the more important pieces of evidence in support of this view is an extant Old Javanese manuscript *(Dharmaśūnya kakawin)* which was copied by a prince of Kartasura in 1716. It is therefore not surprising that a substantial part of Javanese literature can be seen to be directly influenced by pre-Islamic ideas. Not only those works which were directly adapted from Old Javanese, but also many others, abound in Hindu–Buddhist influences and in allusions to pre-Islamic stories.

The Javanese shadow-puppet *(wayang)* theatre was a major means of preserving the Hindu–Buddhist heritage in Islamised Java. The main *wayang* form is the *wayang kulit,* in which flat parchment puppets are used. The stories of the *wayang kulit* are based upon the Hindu epics *Rāmāyaṇa and Bhāratayuddha.* Panji and Damar Wulan stories, concerning legendary pre-Islamic heroes, are also performed in the *wayang. Wayang golek* (round wooden puppets with moveable heads and arms) are usually used for Menak stories, which are highly elaborate romances inspired by Islamic legends concerning the Prophet Muhammad's uncle Amir Hamzah. It is only in this last case that an Islamic inspiration of a sort can be seen. There is reason to think that in court circles at least, the Menak stories were less popular than the Hindu classics. This does not mean, however, that Javanese were necessarily very conscious of the pre-Islamic origins of their cultural heritage. As strange as it may seem, although the survival of pre-Islamic culture is clearly demonstrated in the *wayang,* Javanese tradition usually ascribes the creation of the *wayang* to the nine *walis,* the semi-legendary apostles of Islam in Java.

Direct Islamic inspiration is seen in Javanese translations of Arabic or Malay religious works. In this genre the Arabic script and prose were sometimes employed, but the Javanese script and verse were also common. An exclusive commitment to Islamic sources of inspiration appears to have applied only to a minority of literate Javanese. Even devout writers of religious texts often turned to Hindu–Buddhist ideas for illumination or illustrative examples. Islamic culture also inspired numerous Javanese romances, including *Menak Amir Hamsa, Yusup, Ahmad Hanapi* and other texts. But the non-Islamic Panji and Damar Wulan romances were also an important part of Javanese literature.

A conflict within religious circles like that which occurred in seventeenth-century Aceh seems never to have taken place in pre-nineteenth-century Java. Although many Javanese religious texts have not yet been studied, it appears that the prevailing form of Islam among literate Javanese was a mysticism in which Man and God were identified. Given the apparent absence of any conflict on orthodox-heterodox lines, it seems probable that even learned and devout Javanese Muslims believed that their faith was a true understanding of the message of Islam. There are signs of tension concerning the observation of the *sarengat* (Arabic *shari'ah*: Indonesian *syari'at*),the holy law of Islam. Javanese texts describe the martyrdom or condemnation of five teachers of heretical mysticism: the *wali* Sitijěnar and Sunan Panggung in the time of Děmak, Ki Běběluk of Pajang, Seh Amongraga in the reign of Sultan Agung and Ki Cabolek in the early eighteenth century. Whether these stories are true is unknown. It is significant, however, that in these stories the teachers are not denounced for the content of their teachings (that Man and God are one), but rather because they reveal this secret doctrine to the uninitiated and/or tell the masses that daily prayer, attendance at the mosque, and so on, are not necessary, thereby threatening the observance of Islamic law. The truth of their doctrines is not disputed.

Chronicles *(babad)* were an important part of classical Javanese literature. The origin of this genre is not known, for chronicles of the voluminous length and detail found in Modern Javanese are not known in Old Javanese. One cannot rule out the possibility that Arabic chronicles inspired Javanese to begin composing *babads*, but there is no evidence that this was so. Indeed, Islamic religious concerns receive little attention in Javanese chronicles, which concentrate on kings, heroes, battles and romantic interludes. Some are encyclopaedic works which begin with both Adam and the Hindu gods, describe the legendary pre-Islamic period of Javanese history, and culminate in the seventeenth or eighteenth century; these are usually called by the generic name *Babad Tanah Jawi* ('History of the Land of Java'). These texts are rarely less than several hundred pages in length; a Surakarta version of 1836 is eighteen volumes in manuscript. Other chronicles concern the history of specific kingdoms, heroes or incidents. Javanese chronicles vary with regard to their historical accuracy, but some at least are considered to be quite accurate and important historical sources.

It is a curious fact of Javanese cultural history that although many major literary works survive in thousands of manuscripts, only a few pre-nineteenth century authors are known by name. It is often difficult to be certain whether the works traditionally ascribed even to these few writers were actually written by them. The earliest author whose identity can be established from VOC records as well as Javanese traditions is Carik Bajra (also known as Tirtawiguna), who was active at the court of Kartasura from about 1718, became a major adviser to the king in the 1730s and 1740s, then *patih* until his death in 1751. He is credited with a chronicle *(Babad Kartasura),* Panji stories, a version of the didactic text *Yudanagara Wulang* ('The Teachings of Yudanagara', on statecraft) and other works.

In the latter half of the eighteenth century Yasadipura 1 (1729–1803) was active at the court of Surakarta. If all the works attributed to his pen are correctly ascribed, he was the greatest of the pre-nineteenth-century authors. He is credited with having produced the four major classics adapted from Old Javanese which were described above: *Sěrat Rama, Sěrat Bratayuda, Sěrat Mintaraga* and *Sěrat Arjuna*

Sasrabau or *Lokapala*. He is also said to have produced a version of *Sĕrat Menak*, which is an adaptation of the Malay *Hikayat Amir Hamzah*, although it is clear that a Javanese version or versions of the text existed before his time. To Yasadipura I are also ascribed a version of *Dewa Ruci* (a story based upon the *Bhāratayuddha*, teaching Hindu mystical doctrines), *Sĕrat Panitisastra* (a text on ethics based on the Old Javanese *Nītiśāstra kakawin)*, the Javanese version of the *Taj as-Salaṭin* called *Sĕrat Tajusalatin*, and *Anbiya* or *Tapĕl Adam* (the lives of the prophets of Islam). Finally, he is credited with having written two books of a historical nature, *Sĕrat Cabolek* ('The Book of Cabolek', concerning a religious dispute of the late 1720s or early 1730s), and one of the finest of Javanese chronicles, *Babad Giyanti* ('The History of Giyanti', covering the period 1746–60). This last text is not only an accurate historical record so far as can be judged, but an excellent example of a major work of Javanese *macapat* verse.

The literature of Bali can be divided into three groups on linguistic grounds: Old Javanese, Middle Javanese (or 'Javanese-Balinese', 'Javano-Balinese' or 'Balino-Javanese') and Balinese. The first of these reflects the crucial role played by Bali in preserving the literary heritage of pre-Islamic Java after Java became Islamised. Although some manuscripts of Old Javanese texts survived in Java, the vast majority are known only in copies from Bali or the adjacent island of Lombok. The Balinese resisted Islam and kept alive the literary and religious heritage which in Java was altered (but never entirely abolished) by Islamisation.

Middle Javanese literature is a problematical subject. Most of these texts are called *kidung* (song). They consist primarily of romanticised legends concerning the age of Majapahit in Java *(Harṣawijaya, Rangga Lawe, Sorāndaka, Sunda)*, the prince Panji of a preceding period (concerning whom there are many *kidungs)*, or more popular, less courtly, heroes (*Sudamala, Sri Tanjung, Calon Arang*). A few *kidungs* are adaptations of Old Javanese works with an Indian theme, but the vast majority are set in Java. There are also Middle Javanese works on religion, and the chronicle *Pararaton* (which also concerns Java). These texts are known only in manuscripts from Bali, and a question therefore arises whether they should be seen as a part of the heritage of pre-Islamic Java which, like Old Javanese, was preserved in Bali, or on the other hand as indigenous products of the Javanised literati of Bali. Scholarly opinion has, in recent years, inclined somewhat towards the view that Middle Javanese literature is properly seen as an indigenous part of Balinese culture, but the evidence on this is insufficient to support any certain conclusions.

The Balinese also wrote in their own tongue, especially for the history of their own kingdoms. Although there are verse texts, the most common chronicle form is written in prose, and is called *babad*, as in Java. Balinese chronicles have so far received limited study. While some appear to be so mythological and devoid of chronological order that they are of little value as sources of political history, despite their literary interest, others have proved to be valuable historical sources. The main purpose of many texts was apparently to establish the ancestry of noble families, thereby facilitating ancestor-worship, and to verify the legitimacy of kingdoms. Other types of literary works were written in Balinese as well, often strongly influenced by Old or Middle Javanese stories and literary norms.

Balinese *wayang* (shadow-theatre) has much in common with that of Java, especially in its dependence upon *Rāmāyaṇa* and *Bhāratayuddha* stories for many of its plots. Calon Arang and Panji plays are also performed. The general principles of performance are the same, in that normally flat parchment puppets are played against an upright screen illuminated from behind. There are, however, various differences in the artistic conventions of the two traditions, and the Balinese puppets lack the intricate artistry of the Javanese. The coarser appearance of the Balinese puppets may reflect an older form once found also in Java, for East Javanese Hindu temples from the thirteenth and fourteenth centuries have bas-reliefs in a similar style.

The Bugis and Makasarese of South Sulawesi had closely related literatures in both prose and verse. An indigenous script was used which differs markedly from both the Arabic and Javanese scripts, although it has similarities with some Sumatran scripts and ultimately derived from an Indian prototype. These two groups only adopted Islam in the early years of the seventeenth century, but were soon noted for a selfconscious and firm commitment to their new faith. Their literature has many examples of translations from Arabic and Malay religious works, including the writings of Nuruddin ar-Raniri. A lengthy indigenous epic *La Galigo* contains mythological material about a legendary king of Sulawesi which is still regarded as sacred by many contemporary Bugis and Makasarese.

For historians, Bugis and Makasarese literature had two genres which are particularly important. Chronicles exist in both languages, called *patturioloang* in Makasarese and *attoriolong* in Bugis (both meaning 'Histories of the People of Olden Times'). What most distinguishes these chronicles from those in Malay, Javanese and Balinese is their avoidance of mythological or legendary elements except for introductory foundation myths. They appear therefore to be potentially more valuable as historical sources, but their use is often made difficult by the great rarity with which dates are given. This omission, however, is more than compensated by the existence of detailed diaries in both languages kept by kings and high officials, beginning in the early seventeenth century. This tradition of diary-writing was unknown among other Indonesian peoples. The detailed entries and numerous marginal annotations in Bugis and Makasarese diaries are rich (although as yet largely untapped) sources of historical knowledge.

There were, of course, other literary traditions than those described above. Many of these were influenced to some extent by the major traditions already mentioned, and especially by Malay and Javanese literature, the two most influential literary cultures of the archipelago. Malay literature influenced that of the Minangkabau people of Sumatra, those of many Malay-speaking coastal groups throughout the Malay-Indonesian area, and Bugis and Makasarese. Javanese influence can be seen in Madurese literary traditions and in Sundanese. Influences from both Javanese and Malay can be seen in each other. Balinese, Bugis and Makasarese literatures were much less influential outside their own linguistic groups.

The visual and performing arts were also highly developed in classical Indonesian cultures and have remained popular down to the present. The *wayang,* perhaps the most typical art form of Indonesia, has been mentioned above. Weapons, especially the ornately patterned *kris* (dagger), book-illumination, architecture, *batik* (an intricately dyed fabric) and many other objects reveal a refined artistic tradition. Dance had long been performed in the courts of Indonesia, and is depicted on the bas-reliefs of the ancient Hindu temples of Java. In the Islamic

period the continuance of dance performances is documented, but it is not possible to describe precisely the form of these dances before the twentieth century,
when detailed descriptions and photographs were made. It is clear, however, that
the visual and performing arts of Indonesia were often predominantly sacral in
nature. *Wayang* puppets, *krises*, *batik* and specific dances had spiritual personalities
and released supernatural energies; they could only be employed with due regard
to supernatural forces. Elaborate rituals and rules therefore surrounded the arts
of Indonesia.

Closely connected with dramatic performances was the classical music of
Indonesia. Musical traditions are of course found throughout the archipelago,
but particular significance attaches to those of Java. Because of the survival of
some quite old instrumental ensembles (some reputedly from the seventeenth
century or even earlier) it is possible to learn something of Java's musical traditions
before the twentieth century. It seems possible that in prehistoric times Java was
the centre of the gong-chime musical culture found throughout Southeast Asia.
Indeed, the word *gong* is one of the very few Javanese words to have found its way
into even the major languages of Europe. Two basic types of gong are found in the
Javanese *gamělan* orchestra. The *bonang* is a bronze kettledrum with a raised knob
for striking, of which several are suspended horizontally in a wooden frame. The
other basic type is the vertically suspended gong which varies in size; the *gong agěng*
(great gong) is a large, thick gong with a deep flange, three feet (one metre) or
more in diameter, which produces the deep sonorous tone typical of the Javanese
orchestra.

The Javanese gamělan orchestra consists largely of percussion instruments,
including primarily *bonang, gong,* other gong-chimes, and instruments similar to
xylophones; a complete orchestra has a total range of seven octaves. The gamělan
also normally includes one or more spike fiddles (*rěbab*), zithers (*cělěmpung*), end-
blown flutes (*suling*) and vocalists, and is led by a drummer with a double-headed
horizontal drum. A modern gamělan orchestra may have up to eighty instruments
and require some twenty-five instrumentalists and several singers. The instruments
of the *gamělan* are tuned to two different scales – *pelog* (seven unequal intervals per
octave) and *slendro* (five nearly equal intervals per octave) – and each instrument
is duplicated in both scales, although there are some *gamělan* which use only
one or other of the two. The combination of *pelog* and *slendro* in one orchestra
may be an innovation of the late nineteenth century. The music produced by the
gamělan orchestra defies description. The sound of gong-chimes of varying pitches
producing nuclear melodies, variations upon these melodies at double tempo,
elaborations on the theme, all within controlled phrases, makes it possible even for
foreigners to understand why Javanese felt that supernatural forces were moving
in the sound. *Gamělan* orchestras have spiritual identities and personal names,
are given offerings, and some may only be played on particular occasions. The
melodies of the *gamělan,* too, were bound by rules and regulations of a sacral
nature.

The *gamělan* traditions of Sunda (West Java), Bali and Madura are readily distinguished from those of Java, but the general principles and the basic percussion
instrumentation are similar. Gongs are also found in the music of other areas of
Indonesia and the rest of Southeast Asia. In addition, there were of course folk
traditions in music as in all the arts throughout Indonesia. There was presumably

mutual influence between court and folk traditions, but little is known of the older folk traditions because the surviving evidence is so overwhelmingly of courtly origin.

This chapter can only give a superficial survey of the cultural traditions of precolonial Indonesian states. It is, however, important to understand from even such a survey that behind the war, intrigue and hardship dominating so much of the history of these states, there thrived a rich cultural tradition. At its base was a profound sense of the spiritual, a deep religiosity which was often significantly influenced by Islam but sometimes by other ideas. This spiritual sense influenced the perceptions and responses of Indonesians. There was, therefore, a cultural dimension to the conflict which resulted from the first major phase of Dutch intervention, which is described in Part II. This cultural dimension is as yet little understood, but it may be that some Indonesians felt that they were facing a spiritual as well as a military, political and economic confrontation.

II
Struggles for Hegemony,
c. 1630–1800

6 Eastern Indonesia,
c. 1630–1800

By about 1630 the Dutch had made much progress towards laying the military foundations for commercial hegemony over the seaborne trade of Indonesia. They were established on Ambon, in the heart of the spice-producing islands, and had their headquarters at Batavia in the west of the archipelago. In 1641 Portuguese Malacca fell into VOC hands, and in 1648 the Eighty Years' War ended in Europe, bringing to a close the state of hostility between the Netherlands and Spain. It became clear in the middle years of the seventeenth century, however, that VOC hegemony could not be established merely by peace treaties, the erection of fortresses and the maintenance of naval supremacy. Both major and minor Indonesian powers were still able to frustrate the VOC's plans. The VOC was therefore obliged to adopt an even more aggressive military policy, with direct intervention into the internal affairs of several Indonesian states. Thus were laid the foundations for what may be called the first Dutch empire in Indonesia. Among the Governors-General who presided over this more expansionist phase Antonio van Diemen (1636–45), Joan Maetsuycker (1653–78), Rijklof van Goens (1678–81) and Cornelis Janszoon Speelman (1681–4) stand out, not usually as paragons of virtue, but as architects of the VOC's military expansion.

The first phase of this more aggressive period began in the east of Indonesia, in the spice-growing islands of Maluku. The Dutch had been established there for some time, but their efforts to impose a monopoly over the production of nutmeg, mace and above all of clove had only had limited success. Now a local alliance was emerging against them, consisting primarily of the Muslims of Hitu (the northern portion of Ambon) and the Tĕrnaten forces in Hoamoal (the western peninsula of Seram), with the support of the Makasarese state of Gowa.

The anti-VOC alliance was led by the Hituese Muslim Kakiali (d. 1643), who as a youth had been a student of Sunan Giri in Java. In 1633 he had succeeded his father as 'Kapitein Hitoe', the leader of the Hituese community under the VOC's auspices. While feigning friendship with the Dutch, he immediately supported anti-VOC plots. The Hituese began to build fortresses in the interior, and marauding Muslim warriors were soon plundering Christian villages. The smuggling of cloves in defiance of VOC regulations grew. The VOC on Ambon had the military means neither to wipe out the widespread resistance nor to control the clove trade. In 1634 the VOC tricked Kakiali on board a VOC ship and arrested him, which led the Hituese to flee to their fortresses and prepare for war. Resistance to the VOC grew and even began to be suspected among Christian communities.

In 1637 van Diemen personally attacked the Tĕrnaten forces based in Hoamoal with a large force and drove them from their fortress. Then, in an attempt to regain the support of the Hituese, van Diemen released Kakiali and restored him to the position of 'Kapitein Hitoe'. Peace was ostensibly restored and Kakiali swore to uphold the VOC's monopoly. But hatred of the VOC was by now too deeply rooted to be so easily removed. Upon van Diemen's departure, Kakiali took steps to forge an alliance among Hitu, the Tĕrnatens of Hoamoal, and Gowa, and he encouraged the 'illegal' spice trade. Sultan Alauddin Tumenanga ri Gaukanna of Gowa remained cautious, however, for fear of the VOC's naval power.

In 1638 van Diemen returned and attempted to reach an understanding with the king of Tĕrnate. The VOC would recognise Tĕrnaten sovereignty over Seram and Hitu, and pay the king 4000 *reals* annually, but at the price of an agreement to end the clove 'smuggling' and to allow the VOC *de facto* authority in South Maluku. Kakiali and the Tĕrnaten governor of Hoamoal both refused to take part in these negotiations, and they came to nothing. The king of Tĕrnate clearly did not have it in his power to give what the VOC required. Minor hostilities meanwhile continued and Kakiali, as 'Kapitein Hitoe', continued both to deal with the Dutch and to lay plans for their destruction.

In 1641 Kakiali abandoned his guise of friendship. He attacked a village which was friendly to the VOC and then a VOC fortress. Makasarese warriors were now joining Kakiali, a factor which would ultimately contribute to the Dutch conviction that Makasar must also be dealt with. Kakiali and his allies had timed their bid for power very badly indeed, for with the fall of Malacca to the VOC in 1641 the Dutch could now spare more forces to deal with their problems in the east.

A VOC force drove the Makasarese from their fortifications in Hitu in 1643 but was unable to take Kakiali's fortress. Then, in August, the Dutch paid a Spaniard who had defected from Kakiali to return and murder him. Thereafter Kakiali's fortress was conquered, but many Hituese continued their war against the VOC from a new location, Kapaha in the north of Hitu. By 1645 three VOC expeditions had failed to wipe out Hituese resistance. But in July 1646 Kapaha was finally taken. The leader of this final stage of Hituese resistance, Telukabesi, surrendered and offered to become a Christian. The VOC, however, executed him in Ambon in September 1646.

This was the end of effective resistance to the VOC in Hitu. There were attempts at anti-VOC plots in later years, but none of them offered the real threat to the VOC which the Hituese had offered before 1646. The VOC position in South Maluku was not yet secured, however, for the Makasarese and Tĕrnatens were still trading actively in spices in defiance of VOC pretensions to monopoly. Largely under the leadership of Arnold de Vlaming van Outshoorn, who was Governor of Ambon from 1647 to 1650 and Superintendent over Ambon, Banda and Tĕrnate from 1652 to 1656, a solution to the Tĕrnaten problem was soon to be found. De Vlaming was a controversial figure throughout his career, partly because his parents were Catholics and he was suspected of never truly making the conversion to Calvinism which he professed. During his Governorship of Ambon, he acted against pervasive corruption among VOC merchants and promoted Christianity among the Indonesian population. It was his second period in Maluku which saw the strenuous military measures that earned him both fame and notoriety.

In 1650 King Mandarsyah of Těrnate was deposed in a palace coup. He fled to the VOC fortress on Těrnate and begged for VOC support. De Vlaming was sent to deal with this situation, and upon his arrival the usurper surrendered and Mandarsyah was restored to his throne. A small group who resisted this restoration sailed to the Těrnaten outpost on Hoamoal, and there began full-scale war on the VOC. Within a week they murdered 131 Dutch men, women, children and slaves. The VOC was caught entirely unprepared.

In this situation de Vlaming saw an opportunity to deal finally with the problem of overproduction of cloves. First he took the Těrnaten king Mandarsyah to Batavia, where in January 1652 a contract was signed which prohibited the cultivation of cloves in any areas except Ambon or other districts controlled by the VOC. Ambon could by this time produce more cloves than the entire world consumption, and the VOC's aim was not to monopolise but to destroy clove cultivation elsewhere.

Then de Vlaming moved against the Těrnaten opponents based on Hoamoal and their Makasarese and Malay allies, in one of the bloodiest series of campaigns in VOC history. With the VOC sailed the Ambonese Christians in their war-prauws. From 1652 to 1658 the battles continued around Hoamoal. In the end the VOC was victorious. De Vlaming wanted to carry on to chastise Gowa for supporting the Hoamoal enemy, but Batavia overruled him. Hoamoal and its spice-trees were now dealt with finally. In 1656 the population which remained was deported to Ambon. All spice-trees on Hoamoal were destroyed, and thereafter it was devoid of human habitation except for passing *hongi* (war-fleet) expeditions looking for any wild cloves requiring destruction. The final steps in establishing VOC predominance in Maluku soon followed. In 1663 the Spanish gave up their remaining posts in Těrnate and Tidore, and in 1667 Tidore formally accepted VOC overlordship. The VOC now carefully policed the agreements to prohibit clove cultivation outside its own areas. Thereafter, the VOC monopoly of cloves was more secure, although smaller-scale smuggling always existed.

Only one major opponent to Dutch military and commercial hegemony now remained in the east: the Sultanate of Gowa in South Sulawesi. Here was a major military force which the VOC was obliged to regard even more seriously than its enemies in South Maluku, who had indeed been made harder to defeat by Makasarese support. Gowa was still a major centre of what the Dutch regarded as 'illegal' trade in spices. The Portuguese had been particularly active there since their loss of Malacca in 1641. Events were occurring within South Sulawesi, however, which would make it possible for Gowa to be subdued. As was always the case in the VOC's wars, if the object was a major state the VOC could act successfully only when a significant party within that state was allied to it. In this case, the Dutch found an ally in the Bugis prince La Těnritatta toUnru' (1634–96), more commonly known as Arung Palakka, one of the most famous Indonesian warriors of the seventeenth century.

Gowa's overlordship over other South Sulawesi states had left them much autonomy, but was nonetheless resented. There had been considerable fighting between Gowa and the Bugis state of Bone. In 1660 Arung Palakka was among a group of perhaps 10 000 Bugis from Bone who rebelled and were crushed by the

Makasarese. Thereupon he and a small band took refuge on the island of Butung. In 1663 the VOC granted their request to settle instead at Batavia. There they took service as soldiers for the VOC and impressed the Dutch with their martial skills. Arung Palakka and his Bugis warriors now became an essential part of the VOC's plan to subdue Gowa.

Conflicts between the VOC and Gowa had continued almost unbroken since 1615. A large VOC fleet of thirty-one ships attacked Gowa in 1660, destroyed Portuguese ships in the harbour, and forced Sultan Hasanuddin Tumenanga ri Balla'pangkana (r. 1653–69) to accept the peace of August-December 1660. But this agreement brought no end to the disputes. The fact that Arung Palakka and his followers were being protected by the VOC further exacerbated the tensions. In 1665 a VOC ship ran aground and was plundered; when a VOC official went to inspect the wreck he and his crew were attacked and killed. After a last abortive attempt at negotiation, in 1666 Governor-General Maetsuycker and the Council of the Indies decided to deal finally with Gowa. An expeditionary force of twenty-one ships was put together, carrying 600 European troops, Ambonese soldiers and Arung Palakka and his Bugis. The commander of the fleet was Cornelis Speelman, later to become Governor-General himself. The VOC hoped that the Bugis of South Sulawesi would rally to Arung Palakka and help to destroy the Makasarese state of Gowa.

In December 1666 the VOC fleet reached Makasar. As the Dutch had hoped, the return of Arung Palakka to his homeland after six years of exile encouraged the Bugis of Bone and Soppeng to arise in rebellion against Makasarese overlordship. The war against Gowa involved nearly a year of hard fighting both on land and at sea. Off Butung Speelman devastated the Makasarese fleet, while Arung Palakka commanded a difficult overland campaign. In the end, the VOC and its Bugis allies were victorious and Sultan Hasanuddin was forced to sign the Treaty of Bungaya (18 November 1667). But this treaty, too, proved at first to be meaningless. Hasanuddin resumed fighting and a second major campaign against him was necessary from April 1668 to June 1669. This time the defeat of the Makasarese Sultan and his nobility was final.

The Treaty of Bungaya was now implemented, bringing about a major reversal of South Sulawesi politics. The state of Bone and other Bugis states were relieved of their allegiance to Gowa. The Makasarese fort of Ujungpandang was turned over to the VOC and Speelman renamed it 'Rotterdam' after his own birthplace. Gowa's power was now broken, and in its place Bone arose as the supreme state of South Sulawesi. Makasarese claims to the surrounding areas of Minahasa, Butung and Sumbawa were abandoned, and European traders other than the VOC were expelled. The VOC had already established a fortress at Mĕnado (the northeastern extremity of Sulawesi) in 1658 to counteract Spanish and Tĕrnaten influence there. After 1677 the VOC also established itself in Gorontalo, Limboto and other small Minahasan states, and in the Talaud and Sangihe islands.

Arung Palakka was now the most powerful man in South Sulawesi, and remained so until his death in 1696. He was given special consideration by his ally the VOC, but at first he was merely commander-in-chief of Bone. Not until 1672 did he formally become king (arumpone, i.e. the arung of Bone). He was a man of extraordinary courage, tenacity and ambition, who created for himself a position which no previous ruler in this area had had. He ignored the consultative system of government which had previously existed and ruled without the customary advice of a council of notables. Instead he relied upon the martial skills of the band of refugees who had accompanied him throughout his years of exile. He appointed men of his own choice to the thrones of subordinate states, including Gowa. Although the Dutch themselves found Arung Palakka to be a troublesome ruler at times, his value to them as a military ally and his personal ties with Speelman always outweighed their objections. Thus a more authoritarian form of government than had been known before was made possible by the events which surrounded the VOC intervention in Sulawesi. This unusual situation did not long survive Arung Palakka's death, however, for it depended ultimately upon his unique personal position.

Arung Palakka's campaigning did not end with the victory over Gowa. He waged a series of campaigns against recalcitrant states, which brought much hardship to the people and damage to the lands of South Sulawesi. He also took an army to Java to aid the VOC during the Trunajaya war (see Chapter 7). It was largely because of these devastating campaigns and Arung Palakka's authoritarian rule that large numbers of Makasarese and Bugis fled from South Sulawesi in his reign. They took to their ships like marauding Vikings in search of honour, wealth and new homes. They intervened in the affairs of Lombok, Sumbawa, Kalimantan, Java, Sumatra, the Malay Peninsula and even Siam. Well into the eighteenth century these fierce warriors were the scourge of the archipelago.

By the 1670s, then, the VOC position in East Indonesia had been consolidated. The Dutch still faced intrigues and resistance, but there was no longer any major Indonesian power opposing them in this area. Tĕrnate, Tidore and Gowa were all finished as major military powers. Spice-trees which the VOC could not control had been cut down; Hoamoal had been depopulated; large numbers of Bugis and Makasarese had abandoned their homelands; unknown numbers had died among the Europeans, their allies and their enemies. This had all happened ostensibly because of the VOC's aim of monopolising the spices of Maluku. Ironically, however, just when control of these spices was becoming more certain, they were becoming less and less central to the VOC's profits. In the first place, it was not easy to ensure profits from the spices, for the Dutch naturally found it difficult to forecast supply, demand and prices accurately. There were therefore major changes of policy as trees were planted, then cut down, then more planted, in an effort to produce the right volume. And secondly, these spices were declining in their relative importance in VOC trade. Pepper was a larger element in the seventeenth century, by 1700 textiles were the most important item, and coffee and tea became major trade items in the eighteenth century.

In fact the wars in East Indonesia had not been fought solely in the cause of commerce. The VOC was well on its way to becoming an imperial power. The actual profits and losses involved in this process were both unclear, because of the VOC's accounting system, and of only secondary interest to the empire-builders and adventurers who determined VOC policy in Indonesia, whose personal profits seemed to them to be more important.

The VOC in the seventeenth century had two main foci of interest. In the first, Maluku, its predominance was now relatively firm. In the second, Java, events were occurring which would also lead to a Dutch interventionist policy. This is the subject of the following chapters.

What followed the establishment of Dutch power in East Indonesia down to the nineteenth century has yet to receive serious study, except for South Sulawesi and the peripheral area of Nusa Těnggara. The VOC was active in Nusa Těnggara in the seventeenth century, but on a less flamboyant scale. The island of Timor was still a source of sandalwood, but Flores, Sumba, Savu and Roti were of little commercial interest. The Portuguese established a fortress at Kupang (Timor) but abandoned it. The VOC arrived in Timor in 1613 and occupied Kupang in 1653. But the VOC faced serious competition for control of the sandalwood from the 'black Portuguese' or 'Topasses', a Portuguese-speaking Christian mestizo group based on Flores. There was a virtual stalemate between them until 1749 when a 'black Portuguese' attack on Kupang was decisively defeated. The Portuguese themselves had by now withdrawn to insignificance in East Timor, so the handful of VOC officers in Kupang and their local allies were left as the main force in West Timor. But by the end of the century there was little sandalwood to be had and the VOC was in the general state of decline described in Chapter 9.

The most surprising developments which are known to have arisen from Dutch intervention in Nusa Těnggara took place in Roti, which held little commercial interest for anyone. There the Dutch allied themselves with local factions. In 1681 a bloody VOC campaign established the dominance of its local allies and Roti became mainly a supply base for Kupang and a source of slaves. There was, however, no substantial VOC fortification on Roti.

In the eighteenth century the Rotinese themselves began to take advantage of the circumstances of the VOC presence. They slowly began adopting Christianity, which offered higher social status, freedom from slavery and potential VOC favour. When a lengthy legal case of 1724–9 established the precedent that a Rotinese Christian was not subject to the authority of his pagan ruler, conversion accelerated. In 1729 the first Rotinese ruler converted. Then began a remarkable development. Rotinese Christian rulers asked the VOC to provide them with schoolmasters. By 1765 local Rotinese themselves were able to take over the running of these Malay-language schools. The Rotinese produced a local form of Christianity buttressed by their own school system, both of which they successfully defended from the reforming instincts of nineteenth-century European missionaries. The Rotinese thus became an educated elite in the region, which was to give them a leading regional role in the twentieth century.

Events in eighteenth-century South Sulawesi were dominated by the continuing military rivalry among the Bugis and Makasarese states. The VOC could do little more than defend its own position in Makasar and that of its ally Bone. The most dramatic figure of the period was Arung Singkang (La Ma'dukěllěng, ?1700–65), a descendant of the Bugis royal family of Wajo. He began his career as a pirate. In 1726 he conquered Pasir and then Kutai in East Kalimantan, both areas of Bugis settlement. In 1733 his chief commander failed to take Banjarmasin. Arung Singkang then returned to Sulawesi in 1735 and began his effort to wrest power over the Bugis and Makasarese states from Bone.

Arung Singkang was no welcome guest in Sulawesi, and immediately upon his arrival warfare began which was to last intermittently until his death. He succeeded in winning control of Wajo itself in 1737 and in building a shaky alliance of several states against Bone and the VOC. Early in 1739 he and his allies marched against Makasar. Although the court of Bone was burned, the VOC withstood a series of attacks and then went over to an offensive which drove Arung Singkang into retreat to Wajo.

The VOC then launched a punitive expedition against Wajo at the end of 1740. When its troops returned to Makasar three months later after experiencing heavy fighting, bad weather and much illness, Wajo had been punished but not broken. Arung Singkang soon taught those of his allies who had failed to support him against the VOC that they had made a serious mistake. Wajo's power was vigorously reimposed in the area. But Arung Singkang faced competitors for power in Wajo, which consequently became embroiled in a civil war that seems to have lasted from 1747 to 1751. By 1754 the people of Wajo had had enough of campaigning and refused to support Arung Singkang in war against Sidenreng. In that year he stepped down as ruler of Wajo but continued his private war against Bone until his death in 1765. The Dutch continued to govern Makasar in alliance with Bone, but exercised no significant influence over the Wajo area until the later nineteenth century.

Seventeenth- and eighteenth-century Bali was free of direct VOC interference, but was nevertheless influenced by the VOC presence. This period is not well documented and only the kingdom of Měngwi has so far received serious historical research. The general pattern of events and their causation is, however, becoming clearer. Before c. 1650 Bali was still subject to the overlordship of the king of Gelgel. It was less involved in maritime commerce than some other parts of Indonesia, but exported significant quantities of cotton, rice, pigs, cattle and poultry. Then, however, the authority of Gelgel collapsed and Bali became a collection of fluid and warring kingdoms. At the same time, the VOC presence at Batavia after 1619 created a major new market for slaves. This new human export enabled rival Balinese lords to grow rich by selling off their criminals, their debtors and, above all, their prisoners of war. The slave trade thus facilitated the political disintegration of Bali by providing the economic resources for war and consuming its human spoils. It should be remembered, however, that the economic foundations of all Balinese kingdoms still primarily rested upon wet-rice agriculture. The royal families took an active interest in the construction and maintenance of irrigation works and political alliances among them often flowed in the same directions as the irrigation water.

In the 1660s Ki Gusti Ngrurah Panji Sakti (d. c. 1704) established Buleleng in North Bali as a leading kingdom of the island. In 1697 he conquered Balambangan in Java's Eastern Salient, perhaps in alliance with the Balinese adventurer Surapati (see Chapter 8). The line of Gelgel meanwhile carried on in the kingdom of Klungkung, whose lords adopted the title Dewa Agung and were recognised by the other kings of Bali as the senior royal line. In the east of Bali, Karangasěm expanded overseas from the 1680s, battling Sumbawa and Sulawesi forces for control of Lombok. Not until 1740 was Karangasěm's control of Lombok secure. It thereupon established six Balinese kingdoms in western Lombok which became major patrons of Balino-Javanese culture. In the last quarter of the eighteenth century Karangasěm totally defeated Buleleng and replaced it as the principal kingdom of North Bali.

Měngwi emerged as a major power in South Bali c. 1700 under its king Gusti Agung Anom (d. 1722). He took advantage of succession disputes in Buleleng following the death of Gusti Panji Sakti to win Balambangan to his side and to play the Buleleng competitors off against each other, emerging as Bali's most powerful lord. His authority was, however, under constant challenge. He had to make repeated forays to Java's Eastern Salient to maintain his suzerainty over Balambangan. Local Balinese lords also tested him. In particular, from 1713 to 1717 Měngwi was at war against Sukawati (Gianyar), from which conflict Měngwi emerged victorious. At his death Gusti Agung Anom was precariously lord over much of central and southern Bali, a status reflected in the new royal title he took in 1717, Cokorda Gusti Agung.

As was normal in kingdoms such as these, when Gusti Agung Anom's son Gusti Agung Made Alěngkajěng (d. c. 1740) succeeded, he faced repeated challenges to his authority, to which the main response was war. He spent much of his time in Balambangan attempting to maintain Měngwi's overlordship there. In 1733 he and his allies won a great battle in Buleleng against Dewa Anom of Sukawati, in which as many as 12 000 men may have been involved. Intrigues within the Měngwi royal family, however, threatened Gusti Agung Made Alěngkajěng's power. He had to return from one of his expeditions to Balambangan in 1739 to put down a coup by a brother. When he died shortly after 1740, further conflicts followed. By the 1770s Gusti Agung Made Munggu (d. c. 1770–80; also known as Cokora Munggu) of Měngwi was again one of Bali's most powerful kings. He had, however, lost control of Balambangan to the VOC (see Chapter 9) while parts of Buleleng were lost to Karangasěm. The loss of Balambangan was particularly significant culturally, for it severed Balinese kings' foothold in Java, whence they believed their families to have come after Islamic powers succeeded Majapahit. During the repeated campaigns in Balambangan, three times (1714, 1726, 1729–30) there were attempted Balinese expeditions to the old site of Majapahit in East Java. On the third occasion, Gusti Agung Made Alěngkajěng of Měngwi was accompanied by the Dewa Agung of Klungkung, the king of Tabanan and an entourage of 4000. All of these pilgrimages were, however, aborted because of the threat or actual outbreak of war at home.

At the end of the eighteenth century there was no prospect of any single Balinese lord reimposing the central authority exercised by Gelgel in the sixteenth and early seventeenth centuries. Bali was poised for further violent upheavals which would eventually culminate in the bloody Dutch conquest described in Chapter 12.

7 Java, c. 1640–82

The creation of the states of Mataram and Bantĕn is described in Chapter 4 above. In the middle and later years of the seventeenth century both experienced serious internal conflicts, which the VOC at Batavia could not ignore. In terms of VOC interests, Bantĕn was in some ways similar to Maluku. It was a major source of pepper, which was becoming of even greater commercial importance than the spices of Maluku; it harboured foreign European competitors; it was accessible by sea; and resistance there could disturb Batavia just as Ambon had been threatened in the east. Mataram, however, was a very different affair. It was a far larger state than any the VOC had yet invaded and it had a vast interior where VOC naval power was meaningless. Its importance arose not because any of the VOC's major exports came from there or because it was a centre of 'smuggling', but rather because it supplied rice, without which the Dutch and their allies could not live, and timber, without which they could not build their ships or buildings. It also posed a potential threat to the security of Batavia. VOC commercial interest was limited almost entirely to the north coast of Java, but events there were so inextricably involved with the interior that the Dutch were obliged in the end to march into the heart of Java.

Sultan Agung's son and successor as ruler over the Mataram empire was Susuhunan Amangkurat I (r. 1646–77). The main theme of his reign was his attempt to consolidate the Mataram empire, to centralise its administration and finances and to destroy all opposition. He hoped to turn the empire which Agung had based upon military might and the ability to win or compel a consensus into a unified kingdom whose resources were monopolised for the benefit of the king. Had he succeeded, he would have revolutionised Javanese politics, but his efforts were doomed to failure; the facts of geography, communications and population, which determined that administrative authority in Java must be decentralised, could not be changed by royal fiat. As a result of his policies, Amangkurat I alienated powerful people and important regions and in the end produced the greatest rebellion of the seventeenth century; this brought about the collapse of the dynasty and the intervention of the VOC.

Amangkurat I revealed his nature at the very beginning of his reign. In 1637, while still crown prince, he had been involved in a scandal involving the wife of a senior official, Tumĕnggung Wiraguna. In 1647 the new king sent Wiraguna to the Eastern Salient, ostensibly to expel Balinese forces, and there, away from his family and supporters, he was murdered. Then Wiraguna's family in Mataram and others involved in the scandal of 1637 were killed. The king's brother Pangeran Alit had sided with Wiraguna in 1637 and, seeing his associates being killed, he seems to have sought support among Islamic leaders. Apparently they actually attacked the court but were repulsed and Pangeran Alit was killed in the fighting. Now Amangkurat I turned against this Islamic leadership. A list of prominent religious leaders was compiled and they were all assembled together at court. Then, according to the VOC ambassador Rijklof van Goens, between 5000 and 6000 men, women and children were slaughtered.

In 1647 Amangkurat I moved to a new court at Plered, just northeast of Karta. This was constructed of brick, rather than of wood like the old court, a token perhaps of the greater permanence and solidity which Amangkurat I hoped to see throughout his empire. Work at Plered continued at least until 1666. While the new court complex grew, so did the Susuhunan's tyranny. His father's old associates steadily disappeared, some probably because of old age, but many because they were murdered upon the king's orders. In 1648 van Goens remarked upon this 'strange manner of government . . . whereby the old are murdered in order to make place for the young' (*Gezantschapsreizen*, 67). Among the most distinguished of the king's victims was his own father-in-law, Pangeran Pěkik of Surabaya, who was murdered along with most of his family in 1659. Even the life of the king's uncle Pangeran Purbaya, the only surviving brother of Sultan Agung, was threatened but saved by the intervention of the king's mother.

Amangkurat I was hard at work destroying the consensus of notables which was essential to Javanese kingship. At court and throughout his empire, he murdered those whom he suspected of opposing him, and naturally caused anxiety and alienation among those who managed to survive. On the outer fringes of the state, disintegration was becoming evident. By demanding a subservience he could not in fact enforce, Amangkurat I encouraged allies and vassals to desert him. In 1650 he ordered Cirěbon forces to attack Bantěn, and in late 1657 another Mataram force marched for Bantěn. Both campaigns were failures, and not only confirmed Bantěn's hatred of Mataram but very possibly led Cirěbon to question the wisdom of vassalage to Amangkurat I. His single attempt to control the Eastern Salient in 1647 failed, and this area remained free of Mataram influence thereafter. Balinese raided the east coast, and Mataram could do nothing. Outside of Java, only Palembang continued to profess loyalty, in a forlorn hope that Mataram would support it first against their mutual enemy Bantěn and then in its war with the VOC (1658–9). Jambi definitively rejected Mataram suzerainty after 1663 and chose to cooperate with the VOC. Kalimantan was also completely free of Mataram influence after about 1659. During his struggles with the VOC, Sultan Hasanuddin of Gowa sent embassies to Mataram in 1657 and 1658–9. But Amangkurat I demanded that Hasanuddin come to his court in person to submit, which he would not of course do. Mataram-Gowa relations consequently became decidedly cool.

The reasons for this disintegration on the fringes of the empire were fundamentally military. Amangkurat I was unable to launch the kind of expeditions which Sultan Agung had mounted. And this was a direct result of his tyrannical rule. He dared not leave his guarded court and place himself in the midst of commanders whom he could not trust with his life. Equally, he dared not entrust the command of a major army to anyone else. His tyranny had thus led to a collapse of the consensus of notables, which isolated the monarchy and made it impossible to construct a large army, to command it or to entrust its command to another dignitary. A favourable environment therefore arose for outlying allies and vassals to renounce their allegiance. Amangkurat I was meanwhile providing ample reasons for powerful men to conclude that their self-interest could best be served by independence.

The king's relations with the VOC at first seemed amicable. In 1646 he accepted a treaty of friendship by which captives were exchanged and the VOC returned a substantial sum of money which it had captured from an emissary of Agung en route to Mecca in 1642. Amangkurat I seems to have viewed this treaty as a token of Batavia's submission to his authority, and the VOC was not troubled to point out any different interpretation. Between 1646 and 1654 a series of VOC missions visited the court, and in 1651 the VOC trading post at Jĕpara was reopened. VOC trade with the coast began to flourish anew.

The revival of Javanese-VOC trade on the coast produced a new internal crisis in Java. The products which the Dutch required – primarily rice and timber – were coastal products. The producers, traders and officials of the north coast probably gained most of the profits from this revival of trade, while the king received less than he desired. Amangkurat I therefore moved to take firmer control of the coast, thereby reviving the deep-seated antagonism between coast and interior.

In 1651 Amangkurat I ordered a census, probably to facilitate the collection of taxes. He also decreed that none of his subjects could travel outside of Java, thereby attacking directly the interests of coastal traders, and appointed two coastal governors, one to control the western segment and one for the eastern. In 1652 he forbade the export of rice and timber altogether. He informed the Dutch that this was a measure directed not against them but against Bantĕn, and that they might acquire rice by sending an ambassador to him to negotiate the amount and price. In other words, he was attempting to ensure that the profits from VOC trade were channelled directly into the royal treasury. The Dutch objected to the restrictions, but Amangkurat I was adamant. His coastal subjects meanwhile suffered from royal demands for their cash and royal disruption of their trade.

In 1655 Amangkurat I ordered the ports closed entirely. In theory, not even fishermen were to put to sea. Officials were sent to requisition all large craft and to destroy all small ones. It seems that these measures were designed to facilitate the collection of a major tax, but behind them lay the king's obvious willingness to destroy the coast if he could not control it. In 1657 the ports were suddenly reopened, but in 1660 again they were closed to all traders, and this time the VOC trading post at Jĕpara was also broken up. This second closure was said to be, at least in part, a retaliation for the VOC destruction of Palembang in 1659. The VOC had been interested in Palembang as a source of pepper for some time, and in 1642 had won a treaty which gave it monopoly rights. But conflicts had continued and in 1657 VOC ships were attacked there. The result was a VOC attack in 1659 which burned Palembang and led to the re-establishment of the VOC post. Amangkurat I was said to be shaken by this destruction of his only remaining ally outside of Java. But there was clearly more to the closure than this, for all traders, not just the VOC, were forbidden to trade at the ports. In 1661, however, they were again reopened.

Amangkurat I's attempts to control the coast and his desire to monopolise trade with the VOC were of course intimately connected. He seems to have had four primary objectives: (1) to ensure that the revenue of coastal trade was channelled directly to the court; (2) to re-establish the 'vassal' relationship of the VOC which he believed the 1646 treaty had established; (3) to acquire VOC gifts which could enhance the pomp and glory of his court, such as Persian horses, etc.; and (4) to acquire VOC money to alleviate the chronic shortage of cash in his kingdom. These goals could be achieved by destroying the autonomy of the coast and compelling the VOC to arrange all its purchases directly with the court. Amangkurat I continued to press the VOC to send ambassadors to him, threatening that otherwise the ports would be closed again. VOC missions were sent to Plered in 1667, 1668 and 1669, but little progress was made towards creating stable and amicable trading arrangements, and the last of these missions was in fact refused permission to complete its journey to Plered. As will be seen below, the court was by this time near to collapse.

Meanwhile the VOC was advancing in East Indonesia. Just as the destruction of Palembang in 1659 had shocked Amangkurat I, so the conquest of Gowa shook him ten years later. He now began to see the VOC not only as a source of cash, but of danger as well. This only increased his frenetic determination to control the coast. The two coastal governors appointed in 1651 had been replaced by four such governors in 1657. In 1669 their powers were reduced and direct representatives of the court called *umbuls* were sent out to oversee the administration. The economic and administrative life of the coast descended further into chaos, and storm clouds began to gather.

It is difficult to know how much active opposition to the king existed before the late 1660s. There must have been widespread, perhaps nearly universal, latent opposition, but few men of sufficient influence to lead a coup or rebellion can have escaped the constant killing. But the 1660s saw the rise of one man whose own position and control of troops would have been sufficient to ensure him some prospects of both survival and success. This was the king's own son, the crown prince, later Susuhunan Amangkurat II (r. 1677–1703).

The crown prince was Amangkurat I's son by a Surabayan princess, the daughter of Pangeran Pĕkik. It seems likely that he was actually raised by his mother's family and that he was therefore deeply alienated by his father's murder of that family and of Pĕkik in 1659. Little is known of his character as a young man, except that he had a weakness for beautiful women which produced conflict with his father, who had similar tastes. In 1660 the Dutch heard rumours that Amangkurat I intended to kill his son, and in 1661 that he had done so. This soon proved to be untrue, but in 1663 further rumours were heard of a failed attempt by the king to poison the crown prince. There is some evidence suggesting that the crown prince's party failed in a coup attempt in 1661, which resulted in the murder of many of his supporters. If this is true, the crown prince himself clearly escaped his father's revenge, perhaps because his personal entourage was too strong.

In 1668–70 another conflict broke out between the crown prince and his father over a woman. The estrangement between father and son seems by now to have been complete, if it had not in fact already been so for a decade. As early as 1660 the crown prince had begun trying to make independent contacts with the VOC. Between 1667 and 1675 he sent nine missions to Batavia, asking for everything from Dutch chickens to Persian horses and Makasarese maidens. His real aim was probably to discover whether he could count on VOC support. The six other princes at the court also had their own armed entourages and defended residences, among them Pangeran Pugěr, who was later to become Susuhunan Pakubuwana I (r. 1704–19). Plered had now become a collection of armed camps, the princes divided by their jealousies and ambitions within a political environment in which the price of a false step was murder.

The crown prince had for some time been in contact with a man who was to play a crucial role in the impending chaos. This was Raden Kajoran, also called Paněmbahan Rama, a holy man reputed to have magical powers. Kajoran was a place some sixteen miles (twenty-six kilometres) northeast of the court, in the area of the holy site Těmbayat. In the 1630s this region had apparently been the centre of resistance to Sultan Agung and in 1633 Agung had undertaken some form of pilgrimage to the grave of Sunan Bayat there. Raden Kajoran was descended from the family of Sunan Bayat and had marriage connections with the house of Mataram. Even more significantly, his eldest daughter was married to a disaffected prince of Madura named Raden Trunajaya (?1649–80). Had it not been for the intervention of the VOC, Trunajaya would almost certainly have become the founder of a new dynasty in Java. He had ample reason for hating Amangkurat I, for his father had been murdered at court in 1656, and his own life had been threatened by a court intrigue some time thereafter. He had then fled to Kajoran and become Raden Kajoran's son-in-law.

Raden Kajoran introduced Trunajaya and the crown prince to each other in about 1670, and the outcome was a fateful conspiracy against Amangkurat I. Trunajaya was to launch a rebellion and when the king was defeated the crown prince would become the new Susuhunan. Trunajaya would receive control of Madura and, apparently, a part of East Java, and was perhaps also to be the chief administrative official (patih) for the entire kingdom. Raden Kajoran prophesied that Trunajaya would be a great hero and that Mataram would fall. The crown prince returned to court to await events and Trunajaya went to Madura to create a base for the rebellion. There he gathered troops and took control of Paměkasan in southern central Madura. From this base he succeeded in taking control over the whole of Madura in the course of 1671.

The vanguard of this rebellion was to be non-Javanese. First the Madurese forces were assembled, then those fierce warriors of East Indonesia, the Makasarese. Having fled their homeland after the defeat of Gowa in 1669 and because of the oppressive rule of Arung Palakka, bands of Makasarese sailed to Java, living largely by piracy and plunder. A group had gone to Bantěn, but when relations there became strained they left and in 1674 came to Jěpara with the intention of asking Amangkurat I for land on which to settle. They were refused permission to go to court, but it seems that the crown prince authorised them to settle on the coast of East Java at a place called Děmung (now Běsuki). More Makasarese joined them and in 1675 they entered into a pact with Trunajaya and began raiding Javanese ports. The prospect of sharing the spoils of a major war in Java must have greatly lifted the spirits of these exiles.

Now the Mataram empire began to disintegrate. The king was old and ill, but his tyranny and murders continued. There was a famine in 1674–6, and much sickness. Inauspicious omens were seen: Mount Měrapi erupted in 1672, there were earthquakes and lunar eclipses, and the rains fell out of season. Moreover, the end of the century was approaching. Javanese court tradition posited a cycle of centuries which saw the fall of courts at the end of each. As the Javanese year AJ 1600 (beginning in March 1677) approached, prophecies spread that the end of Mataram was imminent. Such ideas, in a state as fragile as that of Amangkurat I, could only increase the likelihood that when the challenge to the king finally arose, resistance would seem futile.

In 1675 the rebellion broke out in earnest. The Makasarese attacked and burned the ports of East Java as far west as Tuban. These ports had had their fortifications broken up by Sultan Agung after he had conquered them, and were hardly able to defend themselves. VOC naval forces also encountered the Makasarese and had only limited success against them. Trunajaya's Madurese army now landed in Java and took Surabaya. Coastal loyalties were divided. The ports from Juwana to the east appeared to favour the rebellion, while the ports farther west (especially Cirĕbon) seemed still loyal to Amangkurat I, although there were suspicions aroused about the attitudes of all the coastal lords. The court, too, was split. One party favoured asking the VOC for aid. Another, influenced apparently by the Panĕmbahan of Giri, argued on religious grounds that there should be no cooperation with Christians. The crown prince's position was extremely delicate. He remained at court, trying to promote the rebellion which he believed to be in his favour without revealing the extent of his involvement. The rebellion mean-while spread as Trunajaya's forces and the Makasarese gained further victories on the coast. The rebels called upon the Javanese to support them in the name of Islam and found a favourable response. The Panĕmbahan of Giri now gave them his blessing, saying that Mataram would never prosper so long as the VOC was present in Java. This portended a growing anti-VOC as well as anti-Amangkurat I element in the rebellion, which was a problem for the crown prince who seems to have been favourably disposed towards the VOC.

The crucial military turning point came in 1676. The crown prince's role in the rebellion was suspected at court, but it is unclear whether Amangkurat I believed the accusations or thought he was in a position to do anything about them. Whatever the case, he put the crown prince at the head of an army which was sent to destroy Trunajaya's forces. Other princes were sent along, including the crown prince's brother and arch-enemy Pangeran Singasari. It may be that the king intended to have the crown prince murdered during the campaign. It may also be that the crown prince hoped to stage a fake battle against Trunajaya, but was prevented from doing so by the presence of the other princes. Instead, the royal army eventually encountered Trunajaya at Gogodog on the northeast coast in October 1676. There the Mataram army disintegrated before the rebels. Among the Mataram dead was the aged Pangeran Purbaya, the only brother of Sultan Agung to have lived long enough to see the collapse of Agung's empire.

After Gogodog the rebellion spread even faster. Many Javanese dignitaries ceased to recognise Amangkurat I as their king and joined the rebels. By the beginning of 1677 rebel forces controlled all the ports. Even Cirĕbon submitted to the rebels, but Bantĕn warships soon appeared there to impose Bantĕnese influence instead.

Trunajaya's aspirations were now increasing. In 1676 he had taken the titles *panĕmbahan* (honoured lord) and *raja* (king). He began to claim descent from Majapahit and a right to the throne of Mataram. In other words, the crown prince had lost control of the rebellion he had encouraged. But Trunajaya was equally losing control of his unruly allies the Makasarese, whose immediate interests had little to do with the question of who governed Java.

The Dutch were, of course, intimately interested in the course of events, and had already been engaged in hostilities against the Makasarese. Both the crown prince and Trunajaya asked the VOC for cannon, gunpowder and other equipment. The VOC needed stability on the coast so that trade was possible and had now to decide what, if anything, it could do to promote such stability. At the end of 1676, Batavia decided upon a limited intervention, designed to mediate some sort of settlement. The man who was given this task was Admiral Speelman, the victor of Makasar. He was provided with some 1500 troops but was ordered not to march into the interior. Batavia did not wish to be involved in a major campaign in Java, for its troops might be needed elsewhere: Malacca was being harassed by the Malays of Johor and it was clear that Bantěn and other states were also plotting against the VOC. There were also general doubts about the wisdom of fighting a war in Java, for some believed that the VOC could only subdue Java at the cost of ruining the island and involving the VOC in heavy expenditure. The logic of intervention would, nonetheless, shortly lead the VOC deep into the interior.

In February 1677 Amangkurat I and the VOC renewed the treaty of 1646, which had long since become a dead letter. The Dutch promised to aid the king against his enemies, but the king was to pay all the costs of such aid and to give the VOC economic concessions such as freedom from tolls. After this alliance was created, the rebellion only accelerated. Islamic self-consciousness seems to have been strong among the rebels, and prophecies were spread that God would not bless Java so long as the Christians were present. In May 1677 the VOC intervened on the coast. They drove Trunajaya from Surabaya, thereby forcing his army farther inland and inducing even more Javanese to join him.

Now the rebellion reached its high point. The court of Plered was attacked and fell to Trunajaya's forces. The date of its fall is not certain, but it must have been between late May and late June 1677. Javanese chronicles say that as the enemy approached, the king's forces assembled before the court, but he told them not to resist the will of God: the end of the century had come, and with it the time for Mataram to fall. Javanese tradition also says that, nearly a century before, the falling star of Sela Gilang had prophesied to Senapati that Mataram would fall in the time of his great-grandson, who was Amangkurat I. The king fled the court before his enemies reached it. He turned it over to his son Pangeran Pugěr and took the crown prince with him northwestwards towards the coast. The crown prince, who had survived so many years amidst his enemies within the royal family, would have had little prospect of survival in the hands of his former protégé Trunajaya. Pugěr was unable to resist the rebels, and was himself forced to flee and abandon the court to them. Trunajaya looted Plered and then withdrew eastwards to Kĕdiri, taking the Mataram treasury with him. Pugěr then reoccupied the court and took the royal title Susuhunan Ingalaga, thereby beginning a long period of tension between himself and his brother the crown prince.

Amangkurat I did not survive the hardships of his flight. In July 1677 he died; on 13 July his son buried him at Tĕgal-Wangi (Tĕgal) on the north coast. The king had had to leave behind his treasury and the heavier regalia (*pusaka*), but the regalia he had managed to carry off were now the property of the crown prince. Thus, with holy regalia but without a treasury, an army, a court or a kingdom, Susuhunan Amangkurat II (r. 1677–1703) began his reign. He had only one possible means of establishing himself as ruler of Java: he must get the VOC to fight his war for him.

The VOC-Amangkurat II alliance was confirmed in July 1677, on the basis of the February 1677 treaty. But from the beginning the king seemed reluctant to trust his allies entirely, and not until September did he agree to go from Tĕgal to Jĕpara, where Speelman had established his headquarters after expelling rebel forces from the central part of the coast. By this time the royal debt to the VOC for its military costs was already considerable, and the king had no treasury from which payments could be made. In October 1677 and January 1678 he therefore entered into new agreements. Now the VOC was promised the incomes of the coastal ports until its costs were repaid, monopolies over the purchase of rice and sugar, monopolies over the import of textiles and opium, freedom from tolls, a direct cession of Sĕmarang and a recognition of Batavia's boundaries which were now to reach southward to the Indian Ocean, so that the whole of the Priangan highlands became VOC territory. Only later would the VOC learn that most of these promises were meaningless (see Chapter 8).

Speelman was anxious now to march into the interior, but Batavia was reluctant. Personnel changes in Batavia, however, soon made a more active policy possible. Governor-General Maetsuycker died in January 1678 and was replaced by the former Director-General Rijklof van Goens, who was replaced as Director-General by Speelman himself. Speelman's command at Jĕpara was eventually turned over in June to Anthonio Hurdt, who had little military experience and knew nothing of Java, but who was to be the agent of Batavia's new aggressiveness.

In September 1678 Hurdt marched into the interior of Java with Amangkurat II to destroy Trunajaya's stronghold at Kĕdiri. The force endured many hardships. Its European officers knew nothing of the interior and were sometimes misled by their guides. The troops suffered from disease and food shortages. Eventually, however, Kĕdiri was reached, and on 25 November it was taken. Trunajaya fled as the Javanese and European troops plundered the city, in the course of which the Mataram treasury was looted by the victors. Captain François Tack discovered an object described as the 'golden crown of Majapahit', a piece of regalia which is no longer known in Java. He was presumptuous enough to sell it to Amangkurat II for 1000 reals; the king was later unwilling to pay up and eventually repaid Tack for his effrontery by having him killed at court in 1686.

The rebellion now rapidly disintegrated. At the end of 1679 Trunajaya was captured in East Java and taken to the king. In January 1680 Amangkurat II personally stabbed him to death. In November 1679 the Makasarese were expelled from their main stronghold at Kĕpĕr in East Java. Here the VOC had the assistance of a force which knew better than any other how to fight the Makasarese: Arung Palakka of Bone and his Bugis troops. A VOC force under Captain Jan Albert Sloot marched to Pajang and in September 1679 this force killed Raden Kajoran. In April 1680, in what the Dutch described as the most furious battle of the war, the Panĕmbahan of Giri was killed and most of his family were executed. As the victories of Amangkurat II and the VOC multiplied, more and more Javanese declared allegiance to the king.

There remained, however, the unresolved issue of the central districts of Java. The king's brother Pangeran Pugĕr held the court of Mataram and was clearly unwilling to recognise Amangkurat II as king. Other princes had also opposed him, but the two principal ones had died in 1678 and Pugĕr therefore remained as the main obstacle between Amangkurat II and his throne. In September 1680 Amangkurat II went to Pajang and established a new court which he called Kartasura. He was unable, however, to convince his brother to submit. In November his and the VOC's forces attacked and drove Pugĕr from the old court at Plered. But by August 1681 Pugĕr had rebuilt his forces to about 10 000 men and reconquered the Mataram district. He then launched an attack on Kartasura and nearly took the new court before being repulsed by the VOC. In November 1681 the VOC again defeated him, and finally Pugĕr submitted. He went to Kartasura and recognised his brother's sovereignty; his personal safety was to be guaranteed by the VOC. Other lesser rebels were meanwhile being defeated and killed; some simply melted away into the hills. The king was restored to his throne at last.

The rebellion which was now over had roots deep in the past and several themes which arose in the years of fighting would remain of importance well into the eighteenth century. The conflict had been in part regional, with Madura and the northeast coast opposed to Central Javanese authority. This opposition reached back to the late sixteenth century when the Mataram empire began to be created, and had been exacerbated by Amangkurat I's tyrannical rule. The war had also been a dynastic struggle involving the king and princes, and their conflicting ambitions. Perhaps it was partly religious as well, for the leaders and areas which supported the rebellion, and the Makasarese as well, were known as self-consciously Muslim. Islamic appeals appeared frequently on the rebel side. This may also have been expressed in the anti-Dutch attitude of the rebels, although religion is not necessary to explain why those who were trying to topple the dynasty disliked the VOC's intervention. Perhaps even more fundamentally, this had been a conflict concerning the legitimacy of the dynasty, for by his tyrannical rule, his murders, his attempts to destroy regional autonomy and his inability to exercise military power, Amangkurat I had destroyed the consensus of notables which was essential to legitimacy and effective rule.

The role which the VOC had now adopted was also to remain relatively constant for many decades. Here was a powerful military force, better trained, better armed, more disciplined than most of its enemies. But its difficulties were many. It was often isolated in the midst of much larger enemy forces, ignorant of the terrain, poorly supplied, beset by illness, misled or deserted by its Indonesian allies, and weakened by incompetence and incessant internal conflicts among its commanders and the VOC's top officials. Its campaigns entailed heavy losses and enormous expense. Victories against large enemy forces were possible only because there were substantial Indonesian forces on the same side as the VOC. Basically, the VOC's military capacity was limited to winning and holding selected lowland areas. Mountainous regions were often beyond the VOC's reach, except for occasional raiding columns, and they harboured rebellious groups sometimes for generations. The VOC's strategy was therefore essentially defensive. It could defend a ruler in return for payment and concessions; it could destroy major rebel parties and hold strategic points, but it could not police all of Java.

VOC intervention had now made it possible for a king who lacked sufficient Javanese support to rule effectively and to claim legitimacy, nonetheless to stay on his throne. The VOC could defend him but could not make him legitimate or give him the means to rule. The VOC always believed that legitimacy consisted of little more than being the son of a previous king. It further believed a king's authority to be more absolute than Javanese traditions and circumstances allowed. Therefore, in the VOC's search for stability, it supported rulers whom Javanese notables frequently believed to have no legitimate right or ability to rule. The Dutch thereby exacerbated rather than resolved this source of instability. The VOC in 1680 wanted nothing more than to withdraw its military forces from Central and East Java, but it was to find that the results of its own policies would require a constant state of military preparedness. They would also require high levels of expenditure on the military and in this lay part of the cause of the financial decline of the VOC through the eighteenth century.

In the west of Java, the state of Bantĕn also underwent a crisis which ended in VOC intervention. The reign of Sultan Agĕng (also known as Sultan Tirtayasa) of Bantĕn (r. 1651–83) was that kingdom's golden age. He had an impressive fleet constructed on European models. Ships sailing with his passes carried on an active trade within the Indonesian archipelago. With the help of the English, Danes and Chinese, the Bantĕnese traded with Persia, India, Siam, Vietnam, China, the Philippines and Japan. Here, indeed, were the last remnants of the long-distance traders of Java. Sultan Agĕng was a firm opponent of the VOC. For their part, the Dutch were desirous of monopoly over this port's rich supply of pepper, and worried about a wealthy and powerful state so close to their own headquarters at Batavia, some forty-five miles (seventy-five kilometres) to the east.

The Bantĕn-VOC hostilities which attended the conquest of Batavia in 1619 are described in Chapter 3. In 1633–9 another war was fought, ending in a vague agreement to cease hostilities. In 1645 a treaty was signed to regulate VOC-Bantĕn relations. But with the accession of Sultan Agĕng in 1651, conflict quickly resumed. In 1656 war broke out, with the Bantĕnese raiding Batavian districts and VOC ships, while the VOC blockaded the port. In 1659 a new peace settlement was reached. The necessity for some more final solution of the Bantĕn problem was, however, becoming clear to Batavia. The occasion for such a solution came in a form common throughout the archipelago: an internal conflict within the royal house of Bantĕn.

The crown prince of Bantĕn, later Sultan Haji (r. 1682–7), exercised considerable power in Bantĕn, and was indeed referred to by the VOC as the 'young Sultan', while his father was called the 'old Sultan'. The ambitions of father and son led to conflict and relations with the VOC naturally became involved in their disagreements. The court split into two factions, with the crown prince's party being willing to seek the support of the Dutch. Sultan Agĕng's party opposed the VOC and the more militant Muslim elite took this side. In 1671 bands of Makasarese, with ample reason for hating the VOC, arrived in Bantĕn. Among them was a famous Makasarese teacher called Shaikh Yusup. Sultan Agĕng and the Makasarese soon clashed over his treatment of Makasarese women and their own unruly behaviour, and these warrior bands who might have won the day for Agĕng left Bantĕn for East Java in 1673–4. Shaikh Yusup, however, remained in

Bantĕn. By 1671 Agĕng had already withdrawn to a residence outside the town itself, accusing his son of an intention to usurp all power.

During Trunajaya's rebellion, Sultan Agĕng declared himself for the rebels, sent them ammunition and harassed VOC ships and Batavian districts. In 1678 he wrote to Amangkurat II and accused him of being neither a Muslim nor a Christian but something in between, and no longer a king but a common subject of the VOC. When Mataram collapsed in 1677, Agĕng's forces moved into Mataram's westerly dependencies of Cirĕbon and the Priangan highlands. They seemed ready to attack Batavia itself as soon as Trunajaya's victory was certain. With Batavia surrounded by Bantĕn's forces to the west, south and east as well as at sea, the VOC naturally informed Bantĕn as quickly as possible of its victory at Kĕdiri in 1678. Sultan Agĕng did not make his move.

In 1680, with the fighting in Central and East Java nearing its end, Sultan Agĕng finally declared war when Bantĕn merchants were mistreated by the VOC. What might have happened had he done so two or three years before cannot be guessed, but certainly by 1680 the moment for such a move had passed. But before hostilities could begin, in May 1680 the crown prince took over the government and confined Agĕng to his residence. The prince's position was, however, weak: he had carried out a palace coup, but had offended the strong Islamic sentiments in Bantĕn by doing so. The more he appeared to turn to the VOC for help, the more he lost Muslim support. The VOC, meanwhile, would come to his aid only on certain conditions: that runaway slaves and deserters from Batavia be turned over even if they had converted to Islam, that 'pirates' be punished and the VOC indemnified, that claims to Cirĕbon be abandoned, that involvement in Mataram's affairs be renounced, and, most importantly of all, that the VOC's European competitors be excluded from the port. Thus, the VOC was promising to rescue the crown prince if he abandoned Bantĕn's independent foreign policy and the basis of its prosperity. As his position grew more desperate, the prince was finally obliged to accept all of this.

In March 1682 a VOC force commanded by François Tack and Isaac de Saint-Martin sailed to Bantĕn. By this time the crown prince was besieged in his palace, Sultan Agĕng's supporters having retaken the town and set it afire. The prince's submission to the VOC was complete and it therefore recognised him as Sultan. The Dutch now went to war on his behalf. The Europeans trading in Bantĕn were expelled; the English withdrew to Bĕngkulu (Bencoolen) in South Sumatra, which was their only remaining permanent post in Indonesia. Dutch artillery drove Sultan Agĕng from his residence and, after being pursued into the highlands, in March 1683 he surrendered. For a time he was kept in Bantĕn, but he was then transferred to Batavia where he died in 1695. Shaikh Yusup was eventually captured and exiled to the Cape of Good Hope. Bantĕn's independence was at an end.

Cirĕbon and the Priangan highlands now also came under VOC influence. Mataram did not have the means to govern Priangan, and in any case Amangkurat II had signed this area over to the VOC in October 1677. With Bantĕn's power broken as well, VOC domination of this area was possible. Amangkurat II still desired Cirĕbon's vassalage, but the princes there were unenthusiastic about loyalty to Mataram. In 1680–1 they were taken under VOC protection. Cirĕbon was supposed to remain friendly to Mataram, but the VOC was now the dominant external power in Cirĕbon. It had monopolies on the import of textiles and opium, freedom from tolls and a monopoly over the purchase of pepper there. Amangkurat II was not happy, but could do nothing about the detachment of Cirĕbon from his domains.

By about 1682, the VOC's main opponents in Java thus seemed to be crushed. But, as will be seen in the following chapter, it soon became clear that in the vast empire of Mataram, VOC intervention had exacerbated more problems than it had solved.

8 Java, Madura and the VOC, c. 1680–1745

The fates of the VOC and the Javanese were now entwined. For the VOC, events in Java were a primary concern, for it had invested men and money in the restoration of the Mataram dynasty and hoped now to win profit from this investment. For the Javanese there were other priorities to be considered, but no longer could any major change take place without the possibility of the VOC becoming involved. The Madurese involvement in Javanese affairs which had brought about VOC intervention was also far from being over. Down to the middle years of the eighteenth century this intermingling of Dutch, Madurese and Javanese affairs caused much misfortune.

At the start of his reign, Susuhunan Amangkurat II (r. 1677–1703) seemed wholly a creation of the VOC. In 1680 there were even rumours among the Javanese that he was not the former crown prince at all, but rather a son of Speelman in disguise. Under the treaties of 1677–8 the VOC indeed seemed to be in a very strong position. But these agreements were only as good as the king's willingness to fulfil them. As various minor rebels were eliminated in the early 1680s and relative tranquillity returned to Central Java, Amangkurat II began to feel more secure. As his need for VOC arms decreased, his deference to the VOC vanished.

The king's relations with the VOC rapidly deteriorated. The payments due for VOC military expenses were not made; the supply of rice, timber and sugar was frustrated; the costs of the VOC garrison at court were not met; jurisdictional and boundary disputes arose concerning the cession of Sĕmarang to the VOC, which continued to employ Jĕpara as its coastal headquarters. The VOC stopped adding interest charges to the king's debt in 1682, in the hope that this would encourage him to pay some of it. But the debt had already reached 1 540 000 *reals*, five times the sum thought to have been in the Mataram treasury when Trunajaya took it in 1677. VOC monopolies over the import of opium and textiles also proved to be virtually without value, for the Javanese were so impoverished after the years of tyranny and war that they could not pay the VOC's prices. Indeed, while VOC warehouses swelled with these unsaleable goods, the indigenous Javanese textile industry underwent something of a revival. The coast of Java was meanwhile made unsafe by the activities of pirates, with whom some Javanese officials seem to have been involved. The king himself was harbouring Makasarese and Balinese fugitives who had escaped VOC service or slavery.

The VOC itself was now entering a long period of troubles. When Governor-General Speelman died in 1684 the extent of his corruption and abuse of power was revealed. It was alleged that he had governed virtually without the advice of the Council of the Indies, had arrested over a hundred men of whom all but one were now declared innocent, had sold free men as slaves, had authorised payments for nonexistent soldiers and for work not done, and had underpaid Indonesian pepper suppliers. During his time (1681–4) textile sales had dropped by ninety per cent, the opium monopoly was ineffective and private traders had been allowed to infringe VOC monopolies. He had also embezzled large sums. In 1685 his entire estate was confiscated by the VOC, but it was believed that an even larger amount had been smuggled to the Netherlands in the form of jewels. He had, in addition, been well known for his general debauchery.

VOC personnel in general did not have the opportunities which Speelman had enjoyed, but most took such chances as they had to emulate his style. This frequently resulted in inefficiency, debauchery, corruption and a vulgarity and brutality towards Indonesians which contributed to their dislike of the VOC. For instance, the commandant of the VOC garrison at Kartasura in 1682 reported that VOC soldiers were assaulting Javanese women in their houses, and that both his Indonesian and his European troops were smoking opium and drinking 'unwholesome' rice wine. In an agreement regulating VOC-Bantĕn relations in February 1686, it was necessary for Batavia to undertake that VOC servants in Bantĕn would not take goods by violence from market traders before the price was agreed and paid, would not enter mosques without permission or act in an 'unseemly' fashion in them, would not make indecent approaches to Bantĕnese women in their houses or on the streets, and would not stare at the Sultan or his women when they were bathing in the river. Such behaviour was in fact hardly amenable to control from Batavia. Behind the large-scale problems which are discussed in this chapter, there were therefore endless small-scale, personal causes for animosity towards the VOC. VOC personnel also had little reason to think that they found themselves in a tropical paradise. If they were not killed in a brutal war or a local quarrel, they faced the near-certainty of an early death from disease or alcoholism. In 1620 Coen had observed that 'our nation must drink or die'; in practice, very many VOC servants did both. With their prospects so poor, it is not surprising that most sought refuge in immediate pleasures and maximum avarice.

In the court of Kartasura, anti-VOC sentiments continued to grow. The court was, however, cautious about a full-scale break, for it had ample experience of the VOC's military capabilities. But in 1684 more violent options began to be considered when there arrived a man who was to become the most hated of all the VOC's Indonesian enemies. This was Surapati, a Balinese slave who had lived in Batavia. Like many other slaves, he had escaped to the highlands south of Batavia and become the leader of a band of brigands. In 1683 he unexpectedly surrendered and was enrolled in the VOC's military service. He then helped to capture a fleeing son of Sultan Agĕng of Bantĕn. But in January 1684 he attacked a VOC force, killed twenty out of thirty-nine European troops, and then escaped eastwards after a VOC counterattack inflicted heavy losses among his men. In Kartasura the anti-VOC party, led by the *patih* (1682–6) Anrangkusuma, persuaded the king to give refuge to Surapati and his band of eighty men. They were given women and quarters near the court, and settled down. The anti-VOC party believed that they had found just the man they needed.

By 1685 Batavia had concluded that a special embassy to the court was necessary to resolve all the issues outstanding. Captain François Tack, the saviour of Sultan Haji of Bantĕn and the man who had sold the golden crown of Majapahit to Amangkurat II in 1678, was made ambassador. There were few Dutchmen whom the king disliked more. Tack was instructed to deal with a long list of grievances. He was to regulate the affairs of Cirĕbon as a VOC vassal, the boundaries of Batavia, the supply of timber and rice, and so on. Most importantly, he was to renegotiate the king's debt, which he was authorised if necessary to reduce to sixteen per cent of the required sum in order to induce the king to pay. And he was to lay his hands on Surapati, by whatever means necessary. In November 1685 Tack left Batavia, and on 4 February 1686 he departed from Semarang for Kartasura.

As the date of Tack's arrival at court neared, the king faced a dilemma. He would not surrender Surapati, yet he feared the VOC too much to show open resistance. On 8 February 1686 a faked assault was therefore launched on Surapati's quarters by the king's troops. At this moment Tack arrived, thought he saw the king's forces attacking Surapati, and set out in pursuit himself. He then heard cannonfire behind him and concluded that Surapati had doubled back to attack the VOC post at the court. Tack hastened back, and in front of the court was attacked by Surapati and Amangkurat II's own troops disguised as Balinese. Tack was cut down; twenty wounds were later counted on his body. When the day's fighting was done, seventy-four other Dutchmen were dead. Javanese sources say that the court had carefully plotted this assault, and indeed go so far as to say that it was Pangeran Pugĕr, whose safety the VOC had made its special concern, who actually killed Tack. The 248 surviving Europeans withdrew to the VOC garrison post, where they remained until 20 March when they were allowed to withdraw unmolested to Jĕpara. The VOC no longer had a garrison at court

Immediately after the attack Surapati left for Pasuruan in East Java, where Anrangkusuma later joined him. There Surapati proceeded to build up an independent domain. He and his descendants were to govern much of East Java south of the Brantas river for over eight decades. In cooperation with Balinese princes, Surapati even exercised considerable influence in the Eastern Salient. As Surapati's dominance spread in the east, it became clear that the price Amangkurat II had paid for his revenge on the VOC was a partial dismemberment of his empire. In 1690 he sent an army against Surapati which was completely defeated. Javanese levies could not stand against Surapati, who used his experience of European military techniques to good advantage. Surapati's links with the court seem never to have been entirely severed, however, for various dignitaries apparently maintained contacts with him.

Amangkurat II sent letters to Batavia claiming that he was innocent of the assault on Tack and the VOC at Kartasura. No one believed him. In fact, evidence soon came to light of attempts by the king to build up an anti-VOC alliance with anyone available. In 1686 the VOC discovered letters written before the attack which linked the king to the Minangkabau adventurer Raja Sakti (Ahmad Syah ibn Iskandar), who was threatening both Bantĕn and the VOC in Sumatra. Amangkurat II also sent letters to Cirĕbon in 1686 and to Siam in 1687, and contacts were apparently also made with Johor and Palembang. It was later said that he had also attempted to contact the English East India

Company for assistance before the attack. In the years 1686–9 rumours spread of an impending general uprising against the VOC throughout much of the archipelago. The Dutch attributed Islamic xenophobia to their enemies, but the apparent willingness of several of their opponents to solicit English or Siamese support, and the involvement of Balinese bands in several places, suggest that the antagonisms were specifically against the VOC rather than generally against non-Muslims.

In 1689 a plot was discovered which terrified the VOC. Since 1665 the head of the Ambonese in Batavia had been a Muslim called Captain Jonker. He had fought for the VOC against the Portuguese in Timor and Ceylon, against the Makasarese, against the Bantĕnese near Batavia, against the Minangkabau in Sumatra, and in Java he had not only fought Trunajaya but had personally arrested him at the end of 1679. In August 1689 it was discovered that Jonker had joined with other opponents of the VOC in plotting a massacre of the Europeans in Batavia. He was believed to have had contacts with both Raja Sakti and Amangkurat II, and men, horses and money were said to be on the way from Kartasura to assist him. Upon discovering the plot the VOC attempted to arrest Jonker, but he broke into open plunder and murder and was only caught and killed after a pursuit. His followers then fled to Kartasura, where they at first found refuge. A few months later, however, Amangkurat II turned over some fifty of the conspirators to the VOC, which executed them. Jonker was replaced as head of the VOC Ambonese by his Christian nephew Zacharias Bintang (d. *c*. 1730).

Both the VOC and Amangkurat II were apprehensive. With troubles on all fronts, the VOC did not want a new war in Central Java, and with mounting financial worries it could ill afford one. Its forces were weak. The VOC maintained trading posts at Jĕpara, Sĕmarang, Surabaya, Rĕmbang, Dĕmak and Tĕgal in order to acquire such products as it could, but in 1702 the total military strength of these posts was 869 European troops. The VOC administration was also chaotic. In 1691 Governor-General (1691–1704) Willem van Outhoorn was in conflict with the Council of the Indies and especially with the Director-General Joan van Hoorn. This was solved by van Hoorn marrying van Outhoorn's daughter. The *Heeren XVII* in Amsterdam feared the effects of nepotism, however, and in 1701 ordered van Outhoorn to retire and van Hoorn to become Governor-General. Van Hoorn refused, and over two years of confusion ensued. The *Heeren XVII* persisted and now named a new Director-General as well, so that there were now two Governors-General (one who refused to retire and another who refused to take his post) and two Directors-General. Finally van Hoorn gave in; he became Governor-General in July 1704 and held this post until 1709.

For Amangkurat II, the prospect of a war against the VOC was unattractive. His kingdom was failing apart. Surapati's power was growing in the east and by 1699 it reached as far as Madiun. Coastal areas also revealed little enthusiasm for Amangkurat II. His court was splitting into factions, with the party of the crown prince (later Amangkurat III) opposed to another surrounding Pangeran Pugĕr (later Pakubuwana I). In his search for allies, the crown prince was apparently in friendly contact with Surapati. In 1702 the king sent an emissary to a secret meeting with the VOC at Sĕmarang, at which his desperate situation and his hopes for a reconciliation with the Dutch were expressed. But the VOC, quite understandably, would not trust him.

In 1703 Amangkurat II died and was succeeded by his son Amangkurat III (r. 1703–8). Conflicts with his uncle Pangeran Pugĕr and the latter's family led Pugĕr to flee from the court in March 1704. He went to Sĕmarang and there told the VOC that Amangkurat III was their joint enemy and an ally of Surapati. He claimed that most Javanese preferred him to the new king and asked the VOC to recognise him as monarch. The Dutch were greatly influenced by Panĕmbahan Cakraningrat II (r. 1680–1707), the lord of West Madura, whom they regarded as a reliable ally. He supported Pugĕr's claims and convinced the VOC that Pugĕr had the support of the Javanese.

It is unclear why Cakraningrat II should have endorsed a man whom he later seems to have disliked intensely. It is probable, however, that a primary consideration was the threat which was posed to Cakraningrat II's own designs in East Java by an alliance between Amangkurat III and Surapati. By this time, Cakraningrat II was quietly extending his dominance over the Javanese coast from Surabaya in the east to Juwana and Pati in the central north coast, and had perhaps also gained control of the toll gates along the Sala river. He may therefore have preferred to see a ruler in Kartasura whom he expected to be weaker and less likely to frustrate his plans. He may also have looked forward to the prospect of a new war in Central Java, which would present the Madurese with the first opportunity for intervention there since the defeat of Cakraningrat II's own nephew Trunajaya.

In June 1704 the VOC recognised Pugĕr as Susuhunan Pakubuwana I (r. 1704–19), and the conflict known as the First Javanese War of Succession (1704–8) began. The coastal areas whose support Pakubuwana I had claimed soon proved to have little interest in him. Several asked to be made dependants of the VOC, as was Cirĕbon, thereby sparing themselves from the coming conflict and the burdens of rule by the Mataram dynasty. This the VOC was unwilling to accept. The main coastal resistance to Pakubuwana I came from Dĕmak, which was conquered in October and November 1704. The coastal areas now fell into line, and in August 1705 a force of Javanese and Madurese, with VOC Europeans, Bugis, Makasarese, Balinese, Malays, Bandanese, Ambonese and *Mardijkers* (free Portuguese-speaking Indonesian soldiers) marched for Kartasura. Amangkurat III's main force changed sides as Pakubuwana I and his allies approached, leaving Amangkurat III little option but to flee. In September Pakubuwana I entered Kartasura without encountering resistance, and occupied the throne.

Amangkurat III fled eastwards and joined Surapati. He took with him all the holy regalia (*pusaka*) of the kingdom. In 1706, 1707 and 1708 furious campaigns were fought by the VOC, Madurese and Kartasura forces in East Java. Heavy losses were suffered from both battles and disease, and the VOC's commerce and its finances were seriously affected. In 1706 Surapati was killed at Bangil, but the campaign was otherwise a failure. In 1707, however, Pasuruan was conquered and Amangkurat III and Surapati's sons fled to Malang.

In 1708 Amangkurat III finally agreed to negotiate with the VOC, on the understanding that he would be allowed some part of Java to govern and would not have to submit to Pakubuwana I. The VOC, however, was better at fighting wars than keeping promises. Amangkurat III was arrested and exiled to Ceylon, where he died in 1734. There followed a desperate search for the missing *pusakas*. It appeared that Amangkurat III had either distributed them among his followers, hidden them in East Java, smuggled them into exile with him or melted them down. Some of the regalia were brought back to Java in 1737 when Amangkurat III's sons were allowed to return from Ceylon, but there is room for doubt whether the whole set of *pusakas* was ever in fact reassembled. Over the years various regalia were said to have come to light in the hands of rebels. As late as 1762 a great-grandson of Amangkurat III named Raden Mas Guntur apparently had a *pusaka kris* (dagger).

In October 1705 a new contract was agreed between Pakubuwana I and the VOC. The Dutch abolished the dynasty's accumulated debts before 1705 in return for Pakubuwana I making large concessions to the VOC. The main concessions were: (1) renewed recognition of Batavia's boundaries including Priangan; (2) recognition of Cirěbon as a VOC protectorate; (3) cession of the eastern half of Madura; (4) confirmation of VOC control of Sěmarang (where the VOC finally moved its coastal headquarters in 1708); (5) a right to construct fortifications anywhere in Java; (6) a right to purchase as much rice as it desired; (7) confirmation of the monopolies of opium and textile imports; (8) 800 *koyan* (approximately 3 million lbs/1300 metric tons) of free rice annually for twenty-five years; (9) the restoration of a VOC garrison at the court at the king's expense; (10) a prohibition on Javanese sailing farther east than Lombok, farther north than Kalimantan or farther west than Lampung (South Sumatra). In 1709 further agreements were made concerning the delivery of rice, timber, indigo and coffee (the cultivation of which the VOC had introduced into Java from 1696). The VOC appeared to have secured its dominance in Java. Pakubuwana I's policy was clearly to agree to anything the VOC demanded and then to tell his subjects to pay it.

But Java could not be exploited by pieces of paper. The burdens apparently led to population movements from several areas and, with the cultivators moving away, deliveries became more difficult. The north coast was badly deforested and could not supply timber except from far-distant stands. Pakubuwana I made a serious effort to pay what he owed, but this was beyond his capacity. In three years of his reign his total payments actually exceeded one year's due, but he was never able to dispose of the arrears accumulated in 1705–9. By 1717/18 he had paid sixty-nine per cent of his total debt, but then his payments began falling behind again as his kingdom fell apart. Regional officials naturally disliked both the burdens and the king who ordered their payment. By imposing heavy burdens on Java, the VOC merely lessened the likelihood that its own candidate for the Mataram throne would be able to rule in tranquillity.

The VOC had serious financial problems. Of its twenty-three offices in Asia in the period 1683–1710, only three (Japan, Surat and Persia) normally showed profits. Nine showed losses in every year, including Ambon, Banda, Těrnate, Makasar, Bantěn, Cirěbon and the coast of Java. The VOC was now committed to an enterprise which could hardly be profitable. Its enormous expenses led it to demand more and more of the Javanese, which led to further rebellion and resistance, and thus to yet more expense.

Intrigues and animosities grew at the court of Kartasura and in the outlying regions. In 1709 Jangrana II of Surabaya was murdered in the court at the desire of the VOC for his treachery in the 1706 campaign. This completed the alienation of his brothers, who succeeded him in Surabaya. Pangeran Cakraningrat III

(r. 1707–18) of West Madura began to lay plans for the expansion of his own influence. By 1712 Cakraningrat III, and by 1714 Jayapuspita of Surabaya, were refusing to come to court. Surapati's descendants and Balinese forces naturally became involved in these and other intrigues. Regional officials were clearly revealing their lack of enthusiasm for the king, while the princes and dignitaries at court split into factions. The VOC commandant at Kartasura since 1715, Lieutenant Jochum Frederikse, was meanwhile so often drunk that he was unreliable.

In 1717 Surabaya rebelled and called in Balinese troops as allies. Thus began six years of brutal fighting. The VOC reconquered the city of Surabaya in 1718, but the rebel forces were not destroyed. In 1718 Panaraga, Madiun, Magĕtan and Jagaraga rebelled. In the same year the king's son Pangeran Dipanagara was sent to attack the rebels, and himself rebelled. Cakraningrat III's position was unclear to the VOC, to which he continued to profess a dubious loyalty. In January 1718 he boarded a VOC ship, where a misunderstanding led to fighting and to his death. Balinese then plundered West Madura, but after a difficult campaign they were expelled by Madurese and European troops in the course of 1718.

In the midst of this collapse in the east of his kingdom, Pakubuwana I died in February 1719. He was succeeded by his son Amangkurat IV (r. 1719–26), whom the VOC described at the start of his reign as a ruler who was deserted by all of his people and had acquired virtually the whole of the Javanese world as his enemy. In June 1719 his brothers Blitar and Purbaya with the sympathy of his uncle Pangeran Arya Mataram attempted an assault on the court but were repulsed by the VOC garrison. Thus began the Second Javanese War of Succession (1719–23). Yet again only the VOC could save the king.

In November 1719 the VOC took the offensive and drove the rebel princes from their stronghold in Mataram. In 1720 they fled eastwards into the heart of the areas already in rebellion, and the main VOC effort now moved to these eastern regions. As VOC victories accumulated, at the usual heavy cost to all involved, the various rebellious forces in the east coalesced. But under the heavy toll taken by disease and battle, the rebellions began to disintegrate. In October 1719 Pangeran Arya Mataram had already surrendered, and had then been strangled at Jĕpara. Among the Surabaya family, Jangrana III died in 1718 and Jayapuspita in 1720. Pangeran Blitar died in 1721. Finally, in May and June 1723 the remaining rebels surrendered, including several of Surapati's descendants, Surengrana of Surabaya and Pangerans Purbaya and Dipanagara. Purbaya was kept at Batavia, but the others were exiled to Ceylon. Remnants of the Surapati family and Balinese forces remained involved in eastern Java and the Eastern Salient for many more years, but the main rebellions were now broken. The cost of these wars was now added to the royal debt to the VOC.

Despite the crushing of the rebels, the last years of Amangkurat IV's reign were far from tranquil. Pangeran Cakraningrat IV (r. 1718–46) of West Madura resisted the king's authority as much as had his predecessors. It was his desire to stand under the VOC rather than Kartasura, but neither the king nor the VOC would agree to this. Personal animosity between himself and the king contributed to his refusal on several occasions to come to court, where he feared he would be poisoned. As court intrigues grew, the VOC found that there was no opportunity to renegotiate its contracts with the court. Regular payments seem, however, to have been made in accordance with the arrangements of 1705–9. In March 1726 the king fell ill. Before he could decide which of his relatives and dignitaries to accuse of poisoning him, he died on 20 April. He was succeeded by his son Pakubuwana II (r. 1726–49), whose reign is distinguished from the others described in this chapter by being an even greater catastrophe.

Pakubuwana II was only sixteen years old when he became king, and in the early years of his reign he was dominated by his mother Ratu Amangkurat and the *patih* Danurĕja, who had been the chief official of the kingdom since 1709 (until 1720 with the name Cakrajaya). Relations with Cakraningrat IV were restored and he was given one of the king's sisters in marriage. Thereafter Cakraningrat IV and his mother-in-law Ratu Amangkurat seem to have had a sympathetic understanding. The VOC was also pleased by Pakubuwana II's promise to pay off the royal debt. The statistical record is incomplete, but it seems that Pakubuwana II kept pace with his burdens under the old treaties and that by 1733 the remaining arrears consisted largely of the debt of 1705–9 which Pakubuwana I had never paid, plus the arrears for 1718–23. Nonetheless, the VOC had not yet been paid for approximately one-third of its costs in putting Pakubuwana I on the throne and maintaining a garrison at the court since then, nor had it received anything at all towards the costs of the wars of 1717–23. It was therefore anxious to have a new contract to regulate the payment of these debts.

Despite the apparently promising beginning of the reign, the court very rapidly became a centre of intrigue, with powerful individuals manoeuvring for wealth and influence. Yet again, relations with the VOC were involved, for it was both the main military guarantee of the dynasty's rule and the main drain on the kingdom's wealth. Two major parties emerged, with Ratu Amangkurat favouring amicable relations with the VOC and Danurĕja opposing this. Danurĕja's power grew rapidly. The king's brother Pangeran Arya Mangkunĕgara, who had been in rebellion with the other princes but had surrendered in 1723 and been allowed to return to Kartasura, was popular and influential. He and Danurĕja hated each other and in 1728 Danurĕja engineered a trap for him. He was accused of attempting an affair with one of the wives of the king, who asked the VOC to exile him. The VOC disbelieved the charges but feared that Mangkunĕgara would rebel and that many dignitaries would join him. It felt compelled, therefore, to send him into exile, first to Batavia, then to Ceylon and finally to the Cape of Good Hope.

Dutch suspicions of Danurĕja were now growing. He was clearly ill-disposed towards the VOC and was suspected of having contacts with the descendants of the hated Surapati who still held out in East Java. Javanese dignitaries were also more and more anxious to be rid of Danurĕja's burdensome rule. Many were deeply worried by his treatment of Mangkunĕgara, whose son Raden Mas Said was to inherit much of the respect which his father had enjoyed, becoming one of the most able and popular rebels of the 1740s and 1750s. Cakraningrat IV distrusted both Danurĕja and the king, and began again to say that he desired to be a subject of the VOC.

In 1732 Pakubuwana II began to turn against his *patih*. In 1733 he announced that he was taking personal charge of affairs of state and asked the VOC to exile Danurĕja, which it gladly did. He then appeased Cakraningrat IV and excused him from appearing personally at court. At last the treaty revision also took place. After lengthy negotiations, the king promised to pay 10000 *reals* annually for twenty-two years to cover arrears and interest, 15 600 *reals* annually for the costs of the VOC garrison at Kartasura and 1000 *koyan* (approximately 3.8 million lbs/1700 metric tons) of rice annually for fifty years. These rice deliveries were 1.15 times the highest delivery ever made before, and the cash payments were 1.52 times the best previous payment. What is truly extraordinary is that Pakubuwana II appears to have kept up with these payments until his break with the VOC in 1741.

The domestic impact of these payments seems to have been significant. They probably increased the reluctance of regional officials to accept the king's authority. Significant population movements appear to have taken place to escape the burdens, and robber-bands spread. Thus, the VOC relationship was placing strains upon the kingdom which soon proved intolerable. The Dutch believed, however, that in 1733 their goal of a stable, malleable king had at last been achieved. They kept their garrison post at Kartasura, but they withdrew the detachment on the raised terrace in front of the court *(Siti Inggil)*, which had commanded the palace itself.

But intrigues only proliferated as the 1730s passed, and anti-VOC sentiments grew. By 1738 Cakraningrat IV was refusing to come to court, despite the king's order that he should again do so, and for a time he even refused to send his wife (the king's sister) or his son as his representative. Cakraningrat IV's power in East Java was growing and he was challenging Balinese power in the Eastern Salient; he again insisted that he be relieved of his loyalty to Kartasura and be made a VOC vassal. Ratu Amangkurat apparently supported his cause, but the VOC opposed giving him or his sons control of any more lands on the northeastern coast. The *patih* (1733–42) Natakusuma was forming an anti-VOC party and influencing the king. In 1737 a second *patih*, Pangeran Arya Purbaya, was appointed whose anti-VOC sentiments were unmistakeable. In 1738 the VOC persuaded Pakubuwana II to exile Purbaya, an act which gave great offence to many dignitaries. Natakusuma was pardoned, however, and allowed to remain as *patih*. Pakubuwana II clearly faced a deadly dilemma: how to avoid being blamed for the burdens imposed by his dependence on the VOC, without at the same time offending the Dutch. This dilemma may go some way towards explaining the inconstancy and vacillation that marked the whole of his reign.

The VOC was still in a state of crisis as well. Batavia, with its cramped Dutch houses and pestilential canals, was struck by severe epidemics; in 1734 a general day of prayer and fasting was declared to urge God to lift this plague from the city. The pleas of Batavia's populace, generally conceded to be a debauched and irreligious rabble, went unanswered. Sickness continued and carried away Governor-General Dirk van Cloon (1732–5). The high administration of the VOC was splintered by conflicts and could agree on little except that it was fortunate not to be facing another war in Java, for which it was unprepared. The Council of the Indies was unable to agree on who should succeed van Cloon, and resorted to drawing lots. The draw was won by the aged and decrepit Abraham Patras (the only Frenchman to become Governor-General). Before the *Heeren XVII* could act on his urgent request to be relieved of the job, he too died in 1737. Meanwhile, the VOC accounts for Bantĕn and the coast of Java showed constant heavy losses. Exports were small and market calculations wrong. In 1738, for instance, too much sugar and too little coffee were sent to the Netherlands, and the Governor-General and Director-General were ordered to cover the resulting losses out of their own pockets.

The mounting crises within the court of Kartasura, the outer districts of the kingdom, the VOC generally, and the city of Batavia coalesced in 1740. The catalyst was provided by the presence of large numbers of Chinese at Batavia. Chinese had been present in Indonesia as traders for centuries, and since 1619 they had been an important part of Batavia's economy. They were active there as traders, skilled artisans, sugar millers and shopkeepers. By 1740 there were 2500 Chinese houses within Batavia's walls, and the total Chinese population of the city and its surroundings was probably no less than 15000. This would have been at least seventeen per cent of the total population at this point. It is possible that in fact the Chinese were an even larger element of the population, for in a census of 1778 approximately twenty-six per cent of the population of the city's environs (outside the walls) was Chinese, and in the British period (1811–16) approximately twenty-four per cent of the population within the city and its immediate suburbs was Chinese. In 1740 there were also Chinese in the Javanese ports and at Kartasura, although their numbers seem to have been small.

The *Heeren XVII* in Amsterdam admired the industry of the Chinese, but the local population of Batavia disliked and distrusted them. Other developments contributed to the Europeans' sense of insecurity in Batavia. In December 1721 the VOC discovered what it thought to be an Islamic plot to massacre the Europeans in Batavia, with support from Bantĕn, Cirĕbon, Bali, Balambangan and Kartasura. The ringleader was supposed to be a wealthy Batavian mestizo named Pieter Erbervelt. Forty-nine people, including three women, were brutally executed. From 1722 the treatment of Chinese in Batavia was also typified by excessive brutality and corruption. Nonetheless, their numbers were growing rapidly. The VOC imposed a quota system to cut down immigration, but Chinese ship captains were able to evade it, often with the help of corrupt VOC officials. Many of the Chinese who arrived could find no employment and large numbers joined criminal gangs around Batavia.

In October 1740 mutual suspicions led to violence. The VOC concluded that the Chinese were plotting a rebellion, for which there was some evidence. The Chinese believed that the VOC was going to ship excess Chinese out of Batavia and throw them into the sea as soon as they were over the horizon. On 7 October Chinese bands outside the city attacked, killing several Europeans. The VOC feared that Chinese inside the city would join the attackers, so a curfew was imposed and a search of Chinese houses for weapons was ordered. Precisely what happened next is unclear, and was later hotly debated. But it seems that Governor-General Adriaan Valckenier (1737–41) hinted that a massacre of the Chinese would not be unwelcome. The search of Chinese houses soon got out of hand, shots were fired and on 9 October a general massacre of the Chinese began. Europeans and slaves did most of the killing and in the end something like 10000 Chinese were killed. The Chinese quarter burned for several days and the looting was only stopped by paying a premium to VOC troops to return to duty. This slaughter had important repercussions within the VOC, as will be seen below. It also had great significance in Java, for it was the beginning of the last series of wars of the eighteenth century.

The fighting which now began in Java was to last, almost without interruption, for seventeen years. The Chinese who escaped the slaughter in Batavia headed eastwards along the coast and joined compatriots who had already begun hostilities there. They overran the VOC post at Juwana in May 1741. The VOC's coastal headquarters at Sĕmarang was besieged and other posts threatened. The post at Dĕmak was withdrawn in May 1741. An attempt was made in June to withdraw the VOC post at Rĕmbang, but it was completely cut off and in July the VOC personnel there were massacred. The Dutch at Sĕmarang were deeply divided among themselves and short of men and military supplies. They told Batavia that they had little chance of holding out, but in the end they proved able to do so.

Pakubuwana II was now faced with the most difficult decision of his reign. According to a Javanese source, his court split into two main groups. One group, which was led by the *patih* Natakusuma, favoured joining the Chinese against the VOC. The other, led by powerful coastal lords, reasoned that the VOC was bound to win in the end; the king should therefore wait until the VOC's situation was more desperate and then come to its aid at the price of a complete revision of VOC-Javanese relations, getting rid of payments, garrisons, etc. This coastal view was, with hindsight, probably a correct estimation of how to grasp a golden opportunity. Typically, Pakubuwana II made the wrong choice and decided to break with the VOC. He sent an army and artillery to Sĕmarang ostensibly to relieve the VOC, but in fact his forces joined the besieging Chinese. By November 1741, the VOC post at Sĕmarang was surrounded by an estimated 20 000 Javanese and 3500 Chinese with thirty cannon. Cakraningrat IV was now convinced that Pakubuwana II was heading for disaster and that alliance with the VOC was more essential than ever.

The VOC already suspected that Pakubuwana II was close to a final break. In July 1741 any lingering doubts were removed when the king's forces in Kartasura attacked the VOC garrison post there. The commandant Captain Johannes van Velsen and several others were eventually killed. The survivors were offered the choice of conversion to Islam or death, and most chose conversion.

In these desperate circumstances, the VOC turned to the only significant military force which was offering itself as an ally: Cakraningrat IV and his Madurese. Cakraningrat IV said that he would come to the VOC's aid if it was agreed that he should become free of Kartasura and rule independently under VOC protection, and have a free hand in East Java. In June–July 1741 the VOC formally accepted his offer of aid, but postponed any commitment concerning East Java. Cakraningrat IV, however, proceeded to conquer much of it. Reinforcements were meanwhile reaching Sĕmarang, which by November had over 3400 VOC troops in the fortress. The VOC now went over to the offensive. It drove the attackers from Sĕmarang and massacred all Chinese in the area. In late 1741 and early 1742 the VOC retook other threatened areas, while Cakraningrat IV continued his sweep through East Java.

Pakubuwana II now saw what a terrible mistake he had made. His Chinese allies were losing the war, many of his dignitaries were unenthusiastic about his policies, and the eastern part of his kingdom was rapidly falling to Cakraningrat IV. He and his mother Ratu Amangkurat now contacted the VOC and begged forgiveness. The VOC was, of course, deeply suspicious, but felt that it had little option but to respond favourably. A small Dutch force of seven soldiers under Captain

Johan Andries Baron von Hohendorff undertook the dangerous trip to the court in March 1742 and began negotiations. In mid-June 1742 the king sent his *patih* Natakusuma to Sĕmarang; the VOC arrested him there with the king's approval and sent him into exile.

The king had now detached himself from the anti-VOC war. But this war had very deep roots. The Javanese who had already joined with the Chinese in their thousands were not only motivated by hatred of the VOC, but by suspicions of the monarchy as well. These suspicions were now confirmed by the renewed, if shaky, friendship between Pakubuwana II and the Dutch. As the rebellion gathered force, the rebels named a new Susuhunan early in 1742, a twelve-year-old grandson of the exiled Amangkurat III named Raden Mas Garĕndi (Sunan Kuning). The war was now as much anti-Pakubuwana II as anti-VOC, and the main forces were now more Javanese than Chinese. Several major princes were with the rebels.

At the end of June 1742 the rebellion reached its peak with the conquest of Kartasura itself. Pakubuwana II and von Hohendorff fled eastwards and the king addressed a desperate plea to the VOC. If he could be restored to his throne, he would repay the Dutch by giving them the coast and letting them choose the *patih*. The VOC decided to accept this offer. The rebellion rolled on, however, and the VOC found that while it could hold a stalemate on the coast it could not attack the rebel armies in the interior. Pakubuwana II had no troops of his own, so the only offensive force was that of Cakraningrat IV.

In December 1742 Cakraningrat IV's forces conquered Kartasura and expelled the rebels. For nearly seven decades Madurese lords beginning with Trunajaya had been intervening in Java and for the second time the great prize, the court itself, had fallen to one of them. Cakraningrat IV told the VOC that Pakubuwana II should be killed as an example to disloyal rulers. But the VOC decided that stability was still to be sought in alliance with a malleable king of the Mataram dynasty, and no king could be more malleable than Pakubuwana II in 1742. To avoid a breach with the VOC, Cakraningrat IV was therefore obliged to hand the battered court back to Pakubuwana II. The VOC was now beginning to worry about the ambitions of its Madurese ally.

The rebellion now began to collapse. In October 1743 Garĕndi surrendered, followed by many others. By the end of 1743 the main rebels remaining were the king's brothers Pangeran Singasari and Pangeran Mangkubumi (later Sultan Hamĕngkubuwana I, r. 1749–92), and his nephew Mas Said (later Pangeran Adipati Mangkunĕgara I, r. 1757–95). In 1744 Mangkubumi returned to the court. The others remained in rebellion, but their forces were dwindling.

The VOC relationship was reconstructed in a treaty of November 1743, by which Pakubuwana II was formally restored to his throne. This restoration can safely be called the sole success of his reign. In addition to other commitments, the king ceded to the VOC full sovereignty over West Madura, Surabaya, Rĕmbang, Jĕpara and the Eastern Salient (where his claims were, in any case, empty pretensions), and a part of the incomes of all the other ports. The VOC was further given an option to take a narrow strip along the entire coast and along all rivers flowing into the Java Sea, if it desired. The king was also to turn over 5000 *koyan* (approximately 18 million lbs/8600 metric tons) of rice annually forever, as well as other crops. The *patih* could be chosen only with VOC approval and there was to be a VOC garrison at court. Javanese were to sail nowhere outside Java, Madura and Bali.

Once again it looked as if the VOC was 'the master of Java', or so Batavia assured the *Heeren XVII* in 1745. Yet again, this proved untrue. Nor was the VOC entirely the master of itself. The Chinese massacre of 1740 had become caught up in the bitterest of all the VOC's internal feuds. Gustaaf Willem Baron Van Imhoff had been picked by the *Heeren XVII* to restore the VOC's fortunes, and since his arrival in Batavia in 1740 he had led the party opposed to Governor-General Valckenier. What roles these two men actually played in the Chinese massacre is not entirely clear, but van Imhoff blamed Valckenier for the whole affair. In December 1740 Valckenier arrested van Imhoff and sent him to the Netherlands under military arrest. Ignorant of these events, the *Heeren XVII* had meanwhile named van Imhoff Governor-General (1743–50) and when he arrived in the Netherlands they promptly sent him back to Batavia. When the appointment of van Imhoff was learned of in Batavia late in 1741, Valckenier retired and sailed for home. In May 1743 van Imhoff's ship reached Batavia and he immediately took over from the interim Governor-General Johannes Thedens (1741–3). An order had already been sent to the Cape of Good Hope to arrest Valckenier when he called there. He was brought back to Batavia in November 1742 and was jailed in the fortress, where he remained until his death. He was accused of every conceivable offence and sentenced to death after a trial which was rigged by van Imhoff. He avoided decapitation by appealing. His friends in the Netherlands also brought a suit on his behalf which was not settled until 1760, after both protagonists had died, van Imhoff in 1750 and Valckenier in 1751. Valckenier's son won the suit.

While this bitter episode was being played out in Batavia, yet more war was breaking out in Java. Cakraningrat IV believed that he had won a right to much of East Java. The VOC, however, denied his 'exorbitant pretensions'. The VOC had concluded, quite wisely, that a Madurese domain in East Java was unlikely to bring much tranquillity. Cakraningrat IV therefore forged links with the family which governed Surabaya and with the descendants of Surapati, brought in Balinese troops, and stopped the payments of rice and port-duties from East Java to the VOC. In July 1744 the VOC attempted negotiations with him, to no avail. In February 1745 they declared that he was deposed and to be treated as a rebel. Cakraningrat IV went to war and conquered East Madura. Fighting now took place throughout Madura and along the coast of Java from Pasuruan to Rĕmbang. A VOC force in Madura found itself surrounded for six months, but as 1745 passed, VOC victories began to accumulate. Finally Cakraningrat IV saw that his cause was lost and at the end of the year he fled to Banjarmasin in Kalimantan. There he took refuge on an English ship, where he was robbed. The Sultan then betrayed him to the VOC, which took him to Batavia and thence exiled him to the Cape of Good Hope in 1746. His son succeeded him as the VOC's vassal in West Madura.

Madurese intervention in Java was at an end and Pakubuwana II was back on his throne. But, as will be seen in the following chapter, there was still no peace in Java.

9 Java and the VOC, c. 1745–92

The military advance which has been discussed since Chapter 6 had won no stability and little profit for the VOC. In Java, it had been attended by a series of brutal wars and permanent instability. In the second half of the eighteenth century the pace of the VOC's advance would halt, and this first Dutch attempt at empire would end in partial withdrawal. The VOC was to restrict its activities largely to west and north coastal Java and Maluku, and a partial restoration of the Javanese state would become possible. However, the Javanese elite would still have to face the problem which had given rise to so much turbulence and bloodshed: their own disunity. Their solution was to be the partition of the kingdom. But before all this could take place, there were still more battles to be fought.

In 1743 Pakubuwana II decided to abandon the battered court of Kartasura. Some seven miles (twelve kilometres) to the east, on the Sala river, he built the new court of Surakarta, which is still occupied by his descendants. This was virtually completed in 1745, and the formal move seems to have taken place early in 1746. VOC administrations were meanwhile being set up in Surabaya, Rĕmbang and Jĕpara, and of course Sĕmarang remained in VOC hands.

The new court was as unstable as the old. Mas Said, Pangeran Singasari and at least four other princes were still in rebellion. Pangeran Mangkubumi had returned to the court in 1744, but in 1745 again went into the hills for a time. To subdue the rebels, the king announced that whoever could drive them from Sokawati, a district to the northeast of the court, would be paid with an appanage of 3000 households. The fiery Mangkubumi accepted the challenge. In 1746 he defeated Mas Said and claimed his reward. But then his arch-enemy at court, the *patih* (1742–55) Pringgalaya, persuaded Pakubuwana II to withhold the appanage. Into this delicate situation came the indelicate Governor-General van Imhoff. This was the first time a serving Governor-General had ever appeared at court; van Imhoff had no experience to enable him to understand Javanese kingship or to guide him through the treacherous maze of court intrigue. His visit precipitated an eleven-year war.

Van Imhoff's main concern was to deal with the problem of the coast. Under the 1743 treaty the VOC had an option for a narrow strip along the entire coast and all rivers which led into the sea. But what van Imhoff wanted was the complete cession of all the coastal ports not already ceded, with their inland dependencies. To him, this was a potential source of profit. To the king he presented it as a solution to the inability of the Mataram court to govern the coast, which had been amply demonstrated for a century. The inconstant Pakubuwana II hardly knew how to react. But van Imhoff pressed, so the king gave in. The coast was leased to the VOC in return for an annual rent of 20 000 *reals*.

When Pakubuwana II informed his closest advisers of the leasing of the coast, Pangeran Mangkubumi objected. The sum of 20 000 *reals* was too little, he said. (It may be noted here that in 1744 coastal *syahbandar*-ships were farmed for a total of 94 176 *reals* per year; all of this and much other income would now fall to the VOC.) More fundamentally, Mangkubumi saw that under VOC pressure the king had offended a basic principle of Javanese kingship. He had taken a major decision, indeed he had signed away one of the richest parts of his kingdom, without consulting his dignitaries. In such an environment, powerful dignitaries like Mangkubumi naturally doubted whether their self-interest would be served by further loyalty. What the future of the kingdom might be without the coast was also a source of worry. Mangkubumi's alienation was complete when van Imhoff intervened in the dispute concerning the 3000 households. The Governor-General persuaded the king that this would give Mangkubumi too much power and that the reward should be withheld. Before a court gathering van Imhoff then personally reprimanded Mangkubumi for being too ambitious.

Mangkubumi had had enough. In May 1746 he went into rebellion, and the Third Javanese War of Succession (1746–57) began. Mangkubumi now joined with Mas Said, and these two rapidly attracted a large following. By 1747 Mangkubumi commanded an army estimated at 13 000 men, including 2500 cavalry. The VOC's army was in a poor state by this time, and although yet again it could maintain a stalemate in its coastal areas, it could not defeat the rebels farther inland. In 1748 Mangkubumi and Mas Said attacked Surakarta and for a time threatened the court itself.

In the midst of this threat, Pakubuwana II fell ill late in 1749. The VOC Governor of the Northeast Coast, Baron von Hohendorff (1748–54), therefore went to Surakarta to oversee the succession. He was the man who had engineered Pakubuwana II's reconciliation with the VOC in 1742, and had remained at the court as VOC commandant until 1748. When he now returned to Surakarta, Pakubuwana II seized upon him as a source of salvation for the kingdom. He proposed that von Hohendorff himself should take charge of the state. Although initially taken aback, von Hohendorff soon agreed with the proposal. A contract was drawn up and signed on 11 December 1749 by which sovereignty over the entire kingdom was ceded to the VOC. Nine days later the king died. The treaty he had signed was not, however, the landmark which it may seem, nor was it the final step in the VOC conquest of Java. Like so many treaties before, it was only a piece of paper. In 1749 the VOC was in the midst of the last major Javanese war of the eighteenth century, and no document could win that war. In fact, until the early nineteenth century this treaty was a dead letter. The VOC did not again refer to it, and by the time the fighting ended the Dutch had neither the means nor the will to exercise sovereignty in the interior of Central Java.

On 15 December 1749 von Hohendorff announced the succession of the crown prince as Susuhunan Pakubuwana III (r. 1749–88), but even before this could be done Mangkubumi had been declared king by his followers. In his rebel headquarters at Yogya in Mataram, on 12 December 1749 Mangkubumi also took the title Susuhunan Pakubuwana. Thus began the long reign (1749–92) of the most able ruler from the Mataram royal family since Sultan Agung. In 1755 he became the first ruler since Agung to take the title Sultan, and he then adopted the name Hamĕngkubuwana (I), which all of his successors have used. Thus, from the end of 1749 Java was again divided between a rebel king and a monarch supported by the VOC. The difference this time was that the rebel was so strong, and the VOC was growing so much weaker financially and militarily, that the rebel could not be destroyed.

As the 1750s passed, the rebellion grew in strength. In 1750 Mas Said, now Mangkubumi's *patih,* again attacked Surakarta and inflicted heavy losses on the VOC. Pakubuwana III was being deserted by more and more dignitaries; in 1753 even the crown prince of Surakarta joined the rebels. But there was no final victory for either side, and both began to conclude that such a victory was not likely. The VOC could defend Pakubuwana III but could not subdue his kingdom for him. The rebels could win victories, but could not eliminate the king in Surakarta. By 1752 a split was also developing between Mangkubumi and Mas Said and Mangkubumi may have feared losing his dominance over the rebel armies. The VOC decided to attempt to negotiate a settlement, in order to extricate itself from the wars in Java which were bankrupting it. By 1754 Mangkubumi was also ready to attempt negotiations.

In 1754 the new Governor of the Northeast Coast, Nicolaas Hartingh (1754–61), was authorised to placate Mangkubumi by offering him a part of Java. Through a Turkish intermediary named Seh Ibrahim contact was made and indirect negotiations began in April 1754. By September they had progressed sufficiently for a personal meeting to take place between Hartingh and Mangkubumi. Mangkubumi was by this time desirous of VOC military support against Mas Said. Although there were substantial initial differences between him and the VOC, the negotiations ended in a settlement on Mangkubumi's terms. He was to receive one-half of the kingdom, with his capital in Mataram; he seemed reluctant to recognise VOC rule on the coast, but in the end accepted it as the price of an alliance, and he would also receive half of the 20 000 *reals* paid annually for its lease. The VOC and he were to be allied against Mas Said. Batavia was not entirely happy with these arrangements, but felt obliged to ratify them. Pakubuwana III had not been consulted about this dismemberment of his kingdom, but he too had no choice but to agree.

On 13 February 1755 the Treaty of Giyanti was signed and the VOC recognised Mangkubumi as Sultan Hamĕngkubuwana I, the ruler of half of Central Java. This formalised the defeat of VOC policy in Java. Since their first military intervention nearly eighty years before, the Dutch had sought stability by maintaining a king on the throne of Mataram who would rule all of Java in their interest. They had found that instead of enjoying the profits of stability, they were constantly fighting wars on behalf of the kings whom they supported, at a crippling cost to themselves. In 1743–6 they had taken the first step away from this policy by deciding that direct VOC rule over the coast was preferable to rule by the court. Now they also admitted that they could not maintain the unity of the kingdom under a single malleable monarch. Instead, they had to recognise the most powerful rebel they had ever faced as ruler over half of it. This defeat of one policy, however, soon gave rise to another which had somewhat more promise of success. The VOC soon learned that the partition of the kingdom made possible a policy of divide-

and-rule. By the second half of the eighteenth century, however, the VOC was in such an advanced state of incompetence, corruption and financial difficulty that this possibility was only rarely used to success. Hamĕngkubuwana I was therefore in a more advantageous position than any monarch for many generations, and he made good use of his opportunities.

In 1755 Hamĕngkubuwana I moved to Yogya. In 1756 he built a court there and renamed the town Yogyakarta. But the new Sultan faced formidable obstacles. There was still another king, Pakubuwana III, in Surakarta. The problems posed by the presence of two kings for Javanese theories of legitimacy, which were posited upon the rule of a single king who had supernatural sanctions, were not to be solved for several decades. Hamĕngkubuwana I may have thought that Paku-buwana III would not last long, for in 1755 he had hardly any supporters left at court. But after the Giyanti settlement, many dignitaries who had previously fled returned to Surakarta. For the first time Pakubuwana III became a serious contender for elite support, which gave the partition between the two courts the beginnings of an air of permanence.

But the war was not yet at an end. The main contender had now become a Sultan, but many other rebels were still at large. Mas Said was the most important and his army was still formidable, although desertions were increasing. In October 1755 he defeated a VOC force and in February 1756 he nearly burned the new court at Yogyakarta. The forces of Surakarta, Yogyakarta and the VOC were unable to capture Mas Said, but he was also clearly unable to conquer Java against such a combination of enemies. He therefore began negotiations in 1756. In February 1757 he submitted to Pakubuwana III and in March at Salatiga he formally swore allegiance to Surakarta, Yogyakarta and the VOC. In return he received an appanage of 4000 households from Pakubuwana III, but nothing from Hamĕngkubuwana I. Mas Said now became Pangeran Adipati Mangkunĕgara I (r. 1757–95); he had his own princely domain under Surakarta, but the status of this domain and whether his descendants would succeed to it were not yet clear. Hamĕngkubuwana I had wanted to destroy Mangkunĕgara, not appease him, and was scornful of the settlement. The continuing animosity between them remained a major theme of Javanese history for many years.

After 1757 the main warfare was over. There was no major war in Java from 1757 to 1825, the longest period of peace at least since the early sixteenth century. The rebels who still remained, or those who attempted new rebellions in coming years, had relatively small followings. They were either defeated and killed or took refuge in inaccessible areas, especially in Malang, where Surapati's descendants still ruled. As peace returned, Javanese agriculture began to flourish again. Dignitaries now enjoyed a more settled life and more regular incomes, and it seems that the idea generally took hold that Java need not always be at war. A determination began to grow among the elite that the peace should be preserved. Although the partition of the kingdom was not yet accepted as a permanent arrangement, warfare ceased to be an acceptable means of overturning it. With great relief, the VOC now paid off most of its Indonesian troops and settled down to administer the coast; at last it could withdraw its armies from the interior of Java (except for token garrisons at the courts), as it had wanted to do since 1680.

Having abandoned warfare as a means to reunite the kingdom, Sultan Hamĕngkubuwana I, Pangeran Mangkunĕgara I and Susuhunan Pakubuwana III now engaged in a complex game of marriage diplomacy. The prize to be won was the succession in Surakarta, for Pakubuwana III had no sons. A marriage to one of his daughters could therefore legitimise succession in Surakarta by either Hamĕngkubuwana I's or Mangkunĕgara I's line. Mangkunĕgara had already married Hamĕngkubuwana I's eldest daughter in the period when they were allies, and although the Sultan had sons, this marriage might be of use in Yogyakarta as well. There followed several years of complicated manoeuvrings, with marriages proposed and refused, and minor outbreaks of violence. This was all complicated by the fact that Pakubuwana III had none of the strength of will or political skill of Hamĕngkubuwana I, so that the Surakarta court remained a spider's web of intrigue throughout his reign.

In 1762 Mangkunĕgara I's eldest son was married to Pakubuwana III's eldest daughter, which appeared to place him in a powerful position with regard to the succession. But Mangkunĕgara I's potential claim through marriage in Yogyakarta as well came to an end in 1763, when his wife Ratu Bĕndara (Hamĕngkubuwana I's daughter) left him and returned to Yogyakarta. For a time it seemed as if full-scale war would break out, but in the end Ratu Bĕndara divorced Mangkunĕgara I. He remained bitter about this to the end of his life, believing that Hamĕngkubuwana I had forced his daughter to divorce him against her will. But he did not go to war. At the end of August 1768 the whole game of marriage diplomacy collapsed when Pakubuwana III finally had a son, who lived to rule as Pakubuwana IV. Now that there were heirs in both courts, another step had been taken towards a permanent partition.

There were still rebels who had not yet accepted the authority of Hamĕngkubuwana I, Pakubuwana III or Mangkunĕgara I. These included a few who posed a potential threat of some significance, but as the 1760s passed they were eliminated. In 1762 Raden Mas Guntur, a great-grandson of Amangkurat III and son-in-law of Mangkunĕgara I, was killed after attempting rebellion. Thus ended the attempts by the line of Amangkurat III, which had been bypassed by the installation of Pakubuwana I, to regain power in Java. These attempts had included several lesser episodes as well as those of Raden Mas Garĕndi in the Chinese War and Raden Mas Guntur. The Amangkurat III line had represented an alternative, and perhaps more legitimate, branch of the dynasty since 1708, but was now finished. In 1763–5 a rebel named Abdul Kadir and his two sons won considerable success in the areas to the west of Sĕmarang, perhaps with clandestine support from Hamĕngkubuwana I. But the sons were killed by Pakubuwana III's troops; Abdul Kadir himself disappeared and perhaps died in 1764.

Finally attention shifted to Pangeran Singasari, Hamĕngkubuwana I's brother and Pakubuwana III's uncle. He was at Malang with Surapati's descendants. Attempts had been made by both Surakarta and Yogyakarta to cajole him into submission, but to no avail. Then the VOC decided to wipe out resistance in the Eastern Salient, which it had acquired in the 1743 treaty. With both the Dutch and the Javanese ignorant of precise longitudes in East Java, it was wrongly believed that Malang was on the VOC's side of the line established in 1743. In 1767 and 1768 the VOC sent a series of expeditions into these eastern areas, at a time when the Balinese were distracted by civil war. In July 1768 Pangeran Singasari was captured. Hamĕngkubuwana I and Pakubuwana III both asked that he be exiled from Java, but he died in imprisonment in Surabaya before this could be done. Surapati's descendants were defeated, and the last of his line was finally captured in 1771. Although by this time the VOC had discovered that Malang was not on its side of the 1743 line, both Javanese rulers were quite willing to let the VOC have it.

The whole area of Malang and the Eastern Salient was nearly devoid of population after so many years of turmoil. As their vassal rulers in the Eastern Salient the VOC recognised two Balambangan princes who abandoned Hinduism and embraced Islam. The VOC hoped thereby to detach them from the Balinese. But in 1771–2 a further war was necessary against Balinese and local resistance. Thereafter the VOC was less insistent upon Islamisation, but Hinduism was nevertheless rapidly losing ground in the Eastern Salient. It is one of the curiosities of VOC history that in the Eastern Salient, where it faced the threat of Hindu Balinese intervention, the VOC encouraged the spread of Islam, which elsewhere in Indonesia it greatly feared.

By the late 1760s the political situation in Central Java had acquired a fairly stable form. Alternatives to the partition of the kingdom had been progressively eliminated. The VOC, too, had settled into its new role as sovereign of the coast. Its interference in court affairs had now lost most of its military sanction. Hamĕngkubuwana I even prevented the VOC from constructing a defensible fortress in Yogyakarta until very nearly the end of his reign. Nonetheless, behind the growing durability of the partition of the kingdom lay the potential power of the VOC. Anyone who went to war could assume that he would find the VOC among his enemies, a prospect that was far from attractive. Pakubuwana III was far too timid to offend the VOC and was easily influenced by it (indeed, he was easily influenced by almost anyone). Hamĕngkubuwana I knew well that the VOC could be a dangerous enemy, although he knew equally well that it was far from invincible and could be manipulated. He managed to keep the VOC out of court affairs, and generally had his own way. Among the three principals of Javanese history in this period, only Mangkunĕgara I seems to have been contemptuous of the VOC, but he never had an opportunity or perhaps sufficient recklessness to express his contempt in battle.

In the early 1770s, the partition of Java acquired still greater permanence and the need for the VOC as a mediator between the courts was further reduced. Disputed boundaries arising from the 1755 division had caused much argument and some violence. In 1773–4 a new census and an agreed division of territories between Surakarta and Yogyakarta were achieved and procedures for settling further disputes were established. New law codes were also jointly agreed, ending the complex jurisdictional problems which the partition had created and formally regulating relations between the subjects of the two courts. The Anggĕr-Agĕng ('Great Law Code') and Anggĕr-Arubiru ('Law on Disturbing the Peace') were agreed in 1771 and 1773 respectively, and regularly renewed thereafter by the two patihs. The system of partition was thus becoming more regularised and stable, because the Javanese principals agreed to make it so. As this happened, the roots of many conflicts between Surakarta and Yogyakarta were removed and with them the need for VOC mediation.

Although the partition was becoming more regularised, it was not yet seen to be legitimate. In the essentially fragile kingdoms of Java, a sense of legitimacy, with its supernatural sanctions, was one of the prime pillars of kingship. This was particularly true after the mid-eighteenth century, for the military function of kingship was rapidly losing its relevance. The Javanese high and low had had enough of inconclusive civil war. It was therefore essential that legitimacy be sought, especially by Hamĕngkubuwana I, for his new court of Yogyakarta clearly stood outside the line of courts which led to Surakarta and lent it a form of legitimacy.

Javanese historical traditions now both presented a crisis of legitimacy and offered a solution to it. Court chronicles depicted the rise and fall of courts in a rigid cycle of centuries. According to several of these texts, Majapahit fell in Ś 1400 (AD 1478), Dĕmak was founded in Ś 1403 (AD 1481) and ended in Ś 1500 (AD 1578) and Pajang was founded in Ś 1503 (AD 1581). Pajang and Mataram were regarded as a single stage in this cycle, so that the next event was the fall of Plered in AJ 1600 (AD 1677), followed by the foundation of Kartasura in AJ 1603 (AD 1680). The fall of Plered and the foundation of Kartasura actually took place in these years. These events may therefore have been the model for the entire theory, but there is evidence to suggest that the theory in fact predated these events and, therefore, presumably influenced their occurrence. In the eighteenth century, as the partition of the kingdom more and more gained an air of permanence, the end of the century approached again. AJ 1700 began in March 1774. It may have been apprehension about the approach of this year, when a court was expected to fall, which moved both Surakarta and Yogyakarta to conclude the land settlements and legal codes of 1771–4, by which the stability of both courts was enhanced.

At the beginning of AJ 1700 (March 1774) the crown prince of Yogyakarta, later Sultan Hamĕngkubuwana II, wrote a remarkable book entitled Sĕrat Surya Raja ('The Book of the Sun of Kings'). This enormous work was later to become one of the holy regalia of the Sultanate. It prophesied the resolution of Yogyakarta's problems in a thinly disguised allegorical form. Fictitious kingdoms and characters represented the main actors in Yogyakarta's future. According to the Surya Raja scenario, the divided kingdom would be reunited and the Dutch converted to Islam after a series of horrific wars in which the Goddess of the Southern Ocean and eventually God would come to the aid of the hero, who evidently represented none other than the crown prince himself. Whether, or how, this was to come about in the real world is unclear. But it would appear that Surya Raja was an attempt to surmount the crisis of AJ 1700. Sultan Hamĕngkubuwana I apparently contemplated abdicating in favour of his son at this point, so as to produce a new ruler, if not a new court, for the new century. Yet this attempt at a literary solution to the crisis seems not to have been sufficient. The difficulties of translating it into real events may have seemed insoluble – at least, in the face of VOC reluctance to recognise the crown prince's right of succession, Hamĕngkubuwana I did not abdicate. But the historical theory remained to be faced. Now, however, the political environment was such that no major force existed which dared to initiate full-scale war and thereby make a court fall in accordance with the theory.

In AJ 1703 (AD 1777), when a new court should have been founded, another book was written by a son-in-law of the Sultan. This was a chronicle called Babad Kraton ('Chronicle of the Courts'). Unlike Surya Raja, it looked backwards rather than forwards. It presented a view of the past which made Yogyakarta seem to be that which it was not: the direct successor to Kartasura. It took two tries to select the correct point at which to end the chronicle, but finally it was concluded with the fall of Kartasura (1742). The implication appears to have been that Kartasura, the last court to have been founded in accordance with the historical theory, could be regarded as equivalent to the court which should have fallen in AJ 1700/AD 1774 (the point at which, according to the theory, Kartasura should indeed have fallen). Yogyakarta could therefore be regarded as its legitimate successor of AJ 1703/AD 1777. The elite of Yogyakarta were thus taking refuge in a contrived picture of the past in an effort to avoid the hard, and potentially bloody, implications of the turn of the Javanese century.

A kind of legitimacy had been found, and with its discovery the partition of the kingdom can be said to have achieved permanence. But this legitimacy was founded on a fiction. Each king was legitimate to his supporters, each was the protégé of the Goddess of the Southern Ocean, each set of regalia was the true set, but only if the existence of the other court was ignored. The legal agreements and land settlement of 1771–4 made it possible for the two kings to ignore one another, for conflicts between the two courts diminished and any new disagreements were to be settled by the *patihs*. The rulers took refuge in the fiction that the other did not exist, and were thereby spared the necessity of going to war to reunify the kingdom. Yet there were two courts, and an inherent dislike of the partition never entirely disappeared. By the 1770s, however, the system was so regularised, and so many dignitaries were committed to it for their own benefit, that it was never to be overturned. The legitimacy which each could claim in the new Javanese century was based upon a fiction, but it was sufficient for the senior dignitaries, who had by now concluded that there was no real alternative to partition.

The permanent division of Central Java between two courts was thus at last accomplished. Both Hamĕngkubuwana I and Pakubuwana III could proceed without fear of challenge from each other. Problems persisted, but now they were predominately internal to each ruler's domain. Only the continuing animosity between Hamĕngkubuwana I and Mangkunĕgara I caused tensions which crossed the borders of Yogyakarta and Surakarta. But Mangkunĕgara I's position, too, was changing. He seems to have abandoned any serious designs upon the throne of either court, and instead concentrated on an attempt to make his princely domain permanent. Although the status of his holdings was still not clarified, the institution of a permanent, inheritable, but subsidiary principality in Surakarta was beginning to take form.

As the years passed, the older generation which had engineered the permanent partition of the kingdom began to be challenged by rising younger men. In Yogyakarta the crown prince (b. c. 1749–50) won ever greater authority, occasionally in the face of his father's displeasure. His later reign as Sultan Hamĕngkubuwana II (see Chapter 10) was hardly successful, but as his power first began to grow in the 1770s and 1780s he appeared to be a man of considerable talent. He recognised the VOC's military weakness, and as his influence grew at court the VOC was taken less and less seriously. Much of the later tragedy of his reign as Sultan resulted from his failure to recognise the sudden change in European power which occurred in the early nineteenth century. It was the crown prince's influence which led to the sudden construction of massive European-style fortifications around the court in 1785, and the Sultan may have formally turned over much of his authority to his son at this point.

Hamĕngkubuwana I himself was also growing less concerned about maintaining friendly relations with the Dutch. The main aim of his alliance with the VOC, the destruction of Mangkunĕgara I, had never been achieved. After 1757 the VOC refused requests from the Sultan to exile Mangkunĕgara I on several occasions. The Sultanate was meanwhile growing progressively more powerful, prosperous, and stable, and was clearly the predominant military power in Central Java. Hamĕngkubuwana I maintained his alliance with the VOC, but he revealed his growing dissatisfaction with it on several occasions. For instance, from 1777 to the end of his reign he refused to send missions of felicitation to new Governor-Generals because he would not accept a VOC change of protocol which he found demeaning. Pakubuwana III, by contrast, accepted the new arrangements.

In Surakarta, internal problems continued to grow. Pakubuwana III's general incompetence, court intrigues and behaviour by VOC officials which was poor even by the standards of the age, began to threaten security and stability there. The Dutch placed complete trust in Pakubuwana III's loyalty, but began to worry about the obviously volatile state of his kingdom. They had never trusted Mangkunĕgara I and tended to blame him for much of the tension in Surakarta. Mangkunĕgara I, however, began to display greater loyalty and cooperation towards both Pakubuwana III and the VOC in the 1780s, apparently in the hope that they would arrange for his descendants to inherit his position.

The first major test of the durability of the partition occurred when Pakubuwana III died in 1788 and was succeeded as Susuhunan of Surakarta by his nineteen-year-old son Pakubuwana IV (r. 1788–1820). He brought unrealistic aspirations and a consistent inability to assess his political environment to a tense and intrigue-ridden court where some of the VOC's most corrupt and incompetent officers served. Early in 1789, Pakubuwana IV began to appoint a new group of favourites to high positions. These men were inspired by religious ideas which were not necessarily Islamic; they were at least opposed by the established religious hierarchy in Surakarta. They encouraged the new king to think that Surakarta could become the senior court of Java, thereby overturning the equality which underlay the permanent partition between Surakarta and Yogyakarta. The court of Yogyakarta believed that Pakubuwana IV was planning a war of conquest to reunify the kingdom. In fact, military measures do not seem to have been contemplated; instead, Pakubuwana IV's aims were to be achieved by persuading the VOC to recognise Surakarta's dominance.

Rumours began to spread. Mangkunĕgara I feared for his and his descendants' futures; Yogyakarta worried about the stability of the partition; displaced Surakarta notables feared for their fortunes and for that of the kingdom. These people all began trying to manipulate the VOC into joining them against Pakubuwana IV. The VOC was slow to recognise the existence of a threat, although the Governor of the Northeast Coast knew that the corrupt and extortionate practices of the Surakarta Resident (1784–8) W. A. Palm had contributed to an aversion to Europeans on the part of the new king. The Dutch were suddenly shocked, however, in July 1789 when it was rumoured that Pakubuwana IV and his new advisors were planning a general massacre of Europeans in Java. Then in September 1789 the VOC Resident (1788–90) in Surakarta, Andries Hartsinck, was discovered going to a secret conference in the court at night, clad in Javanese dress. The VOC now began to fear that treachery reached even to within their

Surakarta fortress. In fact, the rumours of a massacre of Europeans were probably false, and Hartsinck's role was never wholly clarified. The VOC, however, began to panic. By this time, Haměngkubuwana I was both old and sometimes ill; the Dutch feared that he would die and that a succession crisis in Yogyakarta would lead to military intervention by Surakarta.

The court of Yogyakarta fed ever wilder rumours to the VOC and in the end convinced the Dutch that military measures were necessary to stop Pakubuwana IV's designs. The threat of his plans was believed by both Haměngkubuwana I and Mangkunĕgara I to be so great that for the first time in nearly forty years they acted together. From the VOC Mangkunĕgara I now got 4000 *reals* annually to relieve him of his dependence on Pakubuwana IV and to ensure his support of VOC actions. Later, in 1792, the VOC also decided that Mangkunĕgara I's descendants should inherit his domain of 4000 households; the Mangkunĕgaran principality thereby became a permanent institution.

In November 1790 Pakubuwana IV's enemies began the encirclement of the court. Several thousand troops from Yogyakarta and Mangkunĕgara I's lands took up positions around Surakarta. The VOC sent several hundred Madurese, Bugis, Malay and European troops to its fortress within the city. The senior princes and officials of Surakarta increased their pressure upon Pakubuwana IV to abandon his advisers and their schemes before they brought the kingdom to ruin. Sultan Haměngkubuwana I began to think that the absorption of Surakarta might now be possible; he asked the VOC whether his own son, the crown prince, might have the throne there if Pakubuwana IV were deposed. The VOC rejected this, however, having already secretly decided to recognise Mangkunĕgara I as king of Surakarta if it came to a deposition.

Finally Pakubuwana IV saw the hopelessness of his position. On 26 November 1790 he surrendered his advisers to the VOC and they were promptly exiled. He begged the VOC's pardon, which was quickly granted. The VOC was relieved to have been spared the expenses of war and the older generation was again dominant in Surakarta. The permanent partition of Central Java had been vindicated: the vested interests which supported it were such that even a king's closest relatives and courtiers would oppose his attempt to overturn it. For Yogyakarta the outcome of the crisis was only a partial success. It had successfully manoeuvred the VOC into action, but it had failed to bring about a reduction of Surakarta's status.

From the crisis of 1790 emerged a new treaty which formalised the constituent elements of the permanent partition of Central Java. This was signed upon VOC urgings by Pakubuwana IV, Haměngkubuwana I, Mangkunĕgara I, and the VOC Governor of the Northeast Coast (1787–91) Jan Greeve in September-November 1790. It was, of course, a dead letter until after Pakubuwana IV's submission in late November. This new treaty was an advance on previous agreements in that it explicitly admitted Mangkunĕgara I as a signatory, thereby acknowledging his special standing above other princes, and formally recognised that the VOC was the final court of appeal for otherwise insoluble disputes among the Javanese signatories. Just as the military intervention of the VOC from 1677 had been partly responsible for the partition of the kingdom, so now its continued presence was recognised as essential to the functioning of that partition on a permanent basis.

Having made Yogyakarta a prosperous, permanent and powerful state, Hamĕngkubuwana I died in March 1792, at about eighty years of age. He left behind a tradition of greatness which his son, now Sultan Hamĕngku-buwana II (r. 1792–1810, 1811–12, 1826–8), hoped to emulate. But already intrigues were developing among this younger generation of Yogyakarta dignitaries. And their conviction that the Europeans were a factor which could be ignored or manipulated at will was soon to lose its basis in fact. Nevertheless, by 1792 a restoration of a kind had been completed. Yogyakarta was the most powerful and independent Javanese state since the seventeenth century, and Hamĕngkubuwana I had been the greatest monarch of the Mataram dynasty since Sultan Agung. The Javanese kingdom was, however, permanently divided, and it was therefore unable to stand united against the European threat which was to rise from the VOC's ruins early in the nineteenth century.

In Bantĕn, the other main kingdom of Java, troubles had also arisen in the mid-eighteenth century, but the outcome there was very different from that in Central Java. Bantĕn was much closer to Batavia and much smaller than Surakarta and Yogyakarta. For the military security of Batavia and Priangan, and because of Bantĕn's financial importance as a source of pepper, the Dutch could not afford to ignore instability in Bantĕn. The dominance which the VOC established in Bantĕn in 1682 (see Chapter 7) began to be undermined by palace intrigues in the reign of Sultan Zainul Arifin (1733–48). His Arab wife Ratu Sarifa engineered a conflict between Zainul Arifin and his son the crown prince which resulted in the prince being exiled and Sarifa's nephew being named as the new crown prince in 1747. This new prince was too young to rule, however, and Zainul Arifin was showing signs of insanity. In November 1748 the VOC, with the agreement of Ratu Sarifa, therefore arrested the Sultan and exiled him to Ambon. Then she was made regent in the name of the VOC, which announced its direct control of Bantĕn until a further agreement concerning the institution of the Sultanate could be arrived at.

Sarifa's regency soon provoked domestic opposition. The elite of Bantĕn complained that she ignored them in decision-making, while her extortionate rule brought protests from both commoners and aristocrats. In October 1750 a full-scale rebellion broke out under the leadership of a religious teacher named Kyai Tapa. The VOC's army was in a poor state and was already deeply involved in the Third Javanese War of Succession. In November 1750 a combined force from Ratu Sarifa and the VOC, totalling 800 men, collapsed in the face of the Bantĕnese rebels. Shortly thereafter a VOC force of 460 men (including over 300 Europeans) was driven to flight by an enemy force estimated at 7000 men, with the loss of over thirty European officers and soldiers. The VOC held its two fortresses in the city, but most of Bantĕn fell to the rebels. They also began to threaten Batavia's boundaries and forced the VOC to abandon its post at Tulang Bawang in Lampung. The VOC saw that more vigorous measures were necessary if it was not to be defeated both in Mataram and in Bantĕn.

In November 1750 Batavia ordered the VOC commander in Bantĕn to arrest and exile both Ratu Sarifa and her nephew the crown prince. In March 1751 Ratu Sarifa died on the island of Edam in the bay of Batavia. The throne was offered to Pangeran Arya Adi Santika, a brother of the exiled Sultan Zainul Arifin. Adi Santika accepted the position of 'Sultan-Regent' only until the lawful successor, the crown prince who had been exiled in 1747, was brought back. Adi Santika's elevation did not induce Bantĕnese to desert the rebellion. Batavia sent such forces as it could spare to Bantĕn, and by January 1751 had over 1000 European and 350 Indonesian (mainly Balinese) troops there. Although most of these soldiers were ill, the remainder managed to drive the rebels from the city. Then Kyai Tapa began to burn, plunder and murder in Batavia's highlands; virtually every European plantation was destroyed. But his main stronghold was finally taken in September 1751. Kyai Tapa and the pretender he had supported, Ratu Bagus Buang, fled. Bagus Buang simply disappeared. Kyai Tapa continued desultory attacks on the VOC for some time on the Sunda Straits and near Bandung and Bogor (Buitenzorg). Then he went eastward into the battles of the Third Javanese War of Succession and he, too, disappeared.

In 1753 the exiled son of Sultan Zainul Arifin was brought back from Ceylon and declared to be Sultan Zainul Asyikin (r. 1753-77). Thereafter Bantĕn was formally a fief of the VOC. Peace returned to Bantĕn, but it was unlike the peace enjoyed in Central Java. In Bantĕn, this peace came with submission to VOC dominance. Problems of course continued, and dislike of the VOC was never far from the surface, but VOC influence in Bantĕn was never again seriously challenged.

The Bantĕnese experience was unusual. Outside of Java, the later eighteenth century saw a general retrenchment of VOC positions comparable on a smaller scale to its withdrawal to the coast in Central and East Java. The VOC no longer faced serious competition in Indonesia from other Europeans, except for the English in South Sumatra. Outlying posts such as those at Timor, Makasar, Palembang, Padang and South Kalimantan were essentially being reduced to mere symbols of a VOC presence. Even the VOC clove monopoly in Ambon was collapsing; in 1769-72 two French expeditions captured clove plants there and introduced the clove to Mauritius, and soon to other French colonies. VOC finances were in decline. The VOC was exhausted by its wars, and wanted no more. Its main efforts now went into the production of tea and coffee in the Priangan highlands. In the midst of corruption, inefficiency and financial crisis, this first Dutch empire in Indonesia was gently going to sleep.

III
The Creation of a Colonial State, *c.* 1800–1910

10 Java, 1792–1830

In the last decade of the eighteenth century, the Javanese kingdoms of Surakarta and Yogyakarta faced many problems, but they were more independent of European pressure than any Javanese state since the late seventeenth century. The aristocratic elite were still in control, and in Yogyakarta in particular a substantial restoration of the state had been accomplished. Soon, however, internal conflicts would bring crisis to Yogyakarta, just at a time when the European threat was suddenly renewed. The result would be the utter destruction of Javanese independence within less than forty years of the death of Haměngkubuwana I, and the beginning of the truly colonial period of Javanese history.

Peace had reigned since the 1750s, and the population of Java was beginning the substantial growth which was particularly notable later in the nineteenth century. Although all of the statistics for this period are doubtful, it seems that in 1755 the population of Surakarta and Yogyakarta was no more (and probably less) than about 690 000 to 1 million, while by 1795 it was about 1.4 to 1.6 million. The area under cultivation seems to have expanded rapidly, and there was still land available for further development.

The Javanese were prospering in many ways, and Yogyakarta was an especially powerful kingdom. For instance, the professional standing troops of Sultan Haměngkubuwana II *c.* 1808 amounted to 1765 men and at least in theory he had a potential troop levy of over 100 000 men from his subordinates. The Dutch situation was very different: in 1803 the Dutch garrison at Yogyakarta totalled a mere 89 men, most either very young or very old and afflicted by varying degrees of disease and debauchery. There were, however, internal problems in both Javanese states. Pakubuwana IV of Surakarta (r. 1788–1820) was a mercurial man who disliked the existence of the court of Yogyakarta and desired revenge for the humiliation he had suffered in 1790 (see Chapter 9). Haměngkubuwana II of Yogyakarta (r. 1792–1810, 1811–12, 1826–8) bears the greatest responsibility for the decline of Yogyakarta in this period, and will be discussed below.

The north coastal territories under VOC rule since 1743–6 have been little studied. They appear, however, to have been prospering. Again, all population figures are doubtful, but it seems that the coastal regions and Madura had no more than about 380 000 to 490 000 people in 1755, while by 1795 the population was perhaps as much as 1.5 million. The rate of population growth was thus very much greater than in the Javanese kingdoms, the difference presumably representing internal migration to the coast.

The VOC itself was on its last legs. During the Fourth English War (1780–4) the VOC in Indonesia was isolated from the Netherlands. It not only had to request the loan of about 2300 troops from Surakarta and Yogyakarta to defend Batavia against an expected British attack (which never occurred), but also turned to the Dutch government at home for financial support. The government then began an investigation of the affairs of the VOC and revealed bankruptcy, scandal and mismanagement in all quarters. In December 1794-January 1795 the French successfully invaded the Netherlands and a new French-dominated regime was established. In 1796 the *Heeren XVII* were dismissed and replaced by a new committee, and then the VOC was formally dissolved on 1 January 1800. Its territorial possessions now became the property of the Netherlands government. There was little immediate change in Indonesia, however, for the same personnel remained in their jobs and pursued their old ways.

Relations between the Dutch and the Javanese were fairly stable by 1792. On the north coast, the Dutch ruled directly in theory, but in practice local lords *(bupati)* acted as their agents. In the interior, the treaty of 1749 which had given sovereignty over the Mataram empire to the VOC was a dead letter, and Dutch relations with the Javanese courts in fact took the form of an alliance. Dutch Residents at the courts functioned as ambassadors, not as colonial rulers. The Javanese had created a mythological justification for their relationship with the Dutch, which is found primarily in texts called *Sĕrat Baron Sakendher* ('The Book of Baron Sakendher'). These pictured the Dutch as being the legitimate heirs to the sovereignty (and supernatural powers) of Pajajaran in West Java, and natural senior allies of the Central Javanese kings, but not a sovereign power in Central Java. The military weakness of the Dutch and the military strength of the Javanese states, especially Yogyakarta, meant that there could be no Dutch pretensions to sovereign authority in the interior.

The military predominance of Yogyakarta was, however, being threatened by the rule of Hamĕngkubuwana II, which began to destroy the elite consensus which was essential to strength and stability. The Sultan was at odds with his brothers, especially with Pangeran Natakusuma (1764–1829), who was intelligent, capable and influential in the court. Many of Hamĕngkubuwana I's advisers and officials were already dead or of advanced age, and Hamĕngkubuwana II rapidly replaced them with his own, less capable, favourites. His father's able *patih* (1755–99) Danurĕja I was succeeded by his grandson Danurĕja II (1799–1811); he was inefficient and soon became closely allied with a court clique surrounding the crown prince (later Hamĕngkubuwana III). The Sultan's taxation and corvée system was rapidly growing more oppressive. His building projects at the court placed a particularly heavy labour burden upon the population of the outer districts *(mancanĕgara)*. His contempt for the VOC's weakness contributed to a rapid deterioration of his relations with the Dutchmen at his court. And his three wives became increasingly influential as the arbiters of court intrigue. Out of all of this, uncertainty and disaffection grew.

In Surakarta, both Pakubuwana IV and Pangeran Adipati Arya Mangkunĕgara II (r. 1796–1835; at the start of his period known as Pangeran Prangwadana) were attempting to isolate Yogyakarta and turn the Dutch against the Sultan. Mangkunĕgara II had good reason to dislike the Dutch, for on his accession the whole of his inheritance was confiscated by the Dutch Resident (1790–6) in Surakarta, J. Fr. Baron van Reede tot de Parkeler. This man probably has the distinction of being the most corrupt ever to serve in the VOC, a status requiring truly colossal dishonesty. Not until 1809 did Mangkunĕgara II regain his inheritance after lengthy litigation. He nevertheless had decided that his future was best secured by cooperation with the Dutch, his only defence against the hostility of both the Susuhunan and the Sultan. In 1808, upon the order of Daendels (see below), Mangkunĕgara II organised his military retainers into the 'Mangkunĕgaran Legion' with Dutch financial aid. He was given the rank of Colonel and over 10000 *ryksdaalders* annually as a salary and support for a Legion of 1150 men. His Legion was to see much service in alliance with colonial governments in the coming years, including the storming of Yogyakarta in 1812, the Java War of 1825–30, and the·Aceh War in 1873–4. Pakubuwana IV also attempted to ingratiate himself with the Dutch, but at the same time pretended friendship and courtesy towards Hamĕngkubuwana II. His aim was to engineer Yogyakarta's destruction. As Hamĕngkubuwana II's relations with the Dutch deteriorated and opposition grew within his own domain, he was clearly playing into the hands of his enemies.

In 1808 a new age in Javanese-European relations began. The Netherlands had been under French domination since 1795. In the interests of greater centralisation of power, Napoleon Bonaparte placed his younger brother Louis Napoleon on the throne of the Netherlands in 1806. In 1808 the Napoleonic regime sent Marshal Herman Willem Daendels to be Governor-General in Batavia (1808–11) and to fortify Java as a base against the British in the Indian Ocean. Daendels was an admirer of revolutionary principles of government. He brought to Java a combination of reforming zeal and dictatorial methods which achieved little but offended many. He attempted to clean up the inefficiency, abuses and corruption which pervaded the European administration, but many of his reforms had little effect. Towards Javanese lords *(bupati)* in Dutch-controlled regions he felt a distaste arising from his anti-feudal instincts. He treated them not as lords over their society but as officials of the European administration, and reduced their powers and incomes.

Daendels approached the Central Javanese rulers as if they were vassals of Batavia. In law he was correct, for the 1749 treaty had surrendered sovereignty to the VOC. But never before had Batavia attempted to exercise sovereignty in the interior. The Residents at the courts were now redesignated 'Ministers'. They were to be regarded not as ambassadors from one ally to another, but as the local representatives of the sovereignty vested in the European government and represented in Batavia by the Governor-General. In all matters of protocol they were to be the equals of the Javanese kings. This was a direct assault upon the relationship which had existed since the 1750s. Consistent with their personalities and policies, Pakubuwana IV accepted the changes but Hamĕngkubuwana II rejected them. A long period of conflict now began which was to end in the Java War.

Daendels had brought no new troops with him but he rapidly built up the mainly Indonesian forces in Dutch service from 4000 to 18000 men. These troops were poorly disciplined and performed badly on several occasions. Nonetheless, the European side of the military equation in Java was growing less contemptible; Hamĕngkubuwana II, however, continued to be contemptuous. He resisted all that Daendels stood for: a new age in European attitudes, in which the exercise of sovereignty over all the Javanese and the reform of Javanese society were seen as necessary and proper objects of government.

Pakubuwana IV's more astute responses persuaded Daendels that he was cooperative, but Haměngkubuwana II appeared to be preparing for war. In fact, he seems not to have contemplated full-scale war at this stage, but Daendels' suspicions contributed to the dangers of Yogyakarta's position. In 1810 the Sultan's chief administrator of the outer regions *(mancaněgara)*, Raden Rangga, launched a revolt against the European government. He was the Sultan's brother-in-law and had the tacit support of the Sultan and the Yogyakarta aristocracy. The rebellion was easily crushed and Rangga was killed, but his son Sěntot survived to play a leading role in the Java War. The growing tensions within the court meanwhile led Haměngkubuwana II to bypass the *patih* Danureja II (whose post was by treaty a joint Javanese-Dutch appointment) and to give his powers to Pangeran Natadiningrat, a son of the Sultan's brother Natakusuma.

The rebellion of Raden Rangga provoked an ultimatum from Daendels to Haměngkubuwana II. He must accept the revised court ceremonial regarding the position of the European Minister, restore Danurěja II to full authority, and accept responsibility for Rangga's rebellion. The Sultan resisted, so in December 1810 Daendels marched upon Yogyakarta with 3200 troops and compelled Haměngkubuwana II to step down in favour of his son, who now became 'prince regent' (Haměngkubuwana III, r. 1810–11, 1812–14). About 500000 guilders in prize-money was taken. Haměngkubuwana II was, however, allowed to remain in Yogyakarta at the insistence of the 'prince regent'.

In January 1811 Daendels imposed new treaties on both Surakarta and Yogyakarta, which involved extensive annexations to Dutch government territory. Consistent with the assumption of sovereignty, the rent for the coast which Batavia had paid since 1746 was now cancelled. At a stroke, Daendels thereby abolished the main financial incentive for the Javanese courts to tolerate European rule of the coast, and removed a significant source of court income. He then exiled Pangeran Natakusuma and his son Natadiningrat to imprisonment in Cirěbon because he believed them to have been intimately involved in Rangga's rebellion. Although he did not order their execution, he let it be known that he would be glad to learn of their deaths. They survived only by luck. On all sides there were now deep and bitter hatreds, for Haměngkubuwana II suspected Danurěja II of denouncing the two princes, while Natakusuma never forgave Haměngkubuwana III for his exile and near-death.

The Napoleonic wars in Europe now spilled over into Indonesia. When William V of the Netherlands fled from the French armies to England in 1795, he took up residence at Kew and issued what are known as the 'Kew letters'. These instructed Dutch colonial officials to surrender their territories to the British, in order to keep them out of the hands of the French. Armed with this authority, and with more ships, men and firepower than the Dutch possessed in Indonesia, the British proceeded either to conquer or to be given several Indonesian posts. In 1795 they occupied Padang (which in fact they had earlier occupied in 1781–4) and Malacca, and in 1796 Ambon. From 1795 the British mounted blockades of Batavia which seriously affected the Dutch administration's income by disrupting the export of coffee. With the fall of the main French base on Mauritius late in 1810, the British were ready to conquer the heart of Dutch possessions, the island of Java.

In May 1811 Daendels was replaced as Governor-General by Jan Willem Janssens, who had already suffered the humiliation of surrendering the Cape Colony to the

British in 1806. He lasted just long enough in Java to do the same. On 4 August 1811, sixty British ships appeared before Batavia and the city and its surroundings were in British hands by 26 August. Janssens retreated to Sĕmarang, where the Mangkunĕgaran Legion and troops from Yogyakarta and Surakarta joined him. The British drove them back and on 18 September Janssens capitulated near Salatiga.

The British conquest was followed by a period of confusion. Hamĕngkubuwana II grasped this opportunity to retake the throne of Yogyakarta. His son was reduced to his former status as crown prince and then the Sultan had the *patih* Danurĕja II murdered. But he had misjudged the nature of the times and there rapidly followed a series of disastrous events. Thomas Stamford Raffles was appointed Lieutenant-Governor of Java (1811-16; there was no post of Governor-General in Java under the British), and if Hamĕngkubuwana II thought that his government would differ from Daendels', he was soon proved wrong. Raffles was as much a reformer and opponent of 'despotism' as Daendels. At first he tolerated Hamĕngkubuwana II's measures, but it was soon clear that the Sultan was a hard and determined man from whom the British could expect no cooperation. It began to seem as if the life of the crown prince (Hamĕngkubuwana III), whom the British favoured, was in danger at his father's court. Pakubuwana IV, on the other hand, seemed pliant and reasonable.

In November 1811 John Crawfurd arrived in Yogyakarta as the new Resident (1811-14, 1816). He was a man of inflexible opinions, one of which was that Hamĕngkubuwana II could not be tolerated. He both gave and received slights and insults at court until finally concluding that only the firmest measures would suffice. Raffles urged caution until sufficient troops were available, but did not substantially differ in his view of the Sultan. When Raffles visited the court in December 1811 he personally encountered the Sultan's hostility and replied with belligerence which on one occasion nearly led to armed combat in a crowded room. Meanwhile, Pangeran Natakusuma had been released from imprisonment. As an enemy of Daendels he naturally became an ally of the British; as an enemy of both Hamĕngkubuwana II and his son, he exerted every effort to achieve an independent status in the court.

Pakubuwana IV now joined the conflict. He entered into a secret correspondence with Hamĕngkubuwana II which led the latter to believe that Surakarta would stand by him in armed resistance to the European government. The Susuhunan's true aim was to encourage the Sultan to a boldness which would bring about the destruction of the Sultanate at European hands. The British were soon informed of the Surakarta-Yogyakarta correspondence. They began secret negotiations with the Yogyakarta crown prince (Hamĕngkubuwana III) and Natakusuma, and prepared for the destruction of Yogyakarta.

In June 1812, 1200 European troops and Indian Sepoys, supported by 800 men of the Mangkunĕgaran Legion, conquered the court of Yogyakarta after an artillery barrage. Pakubuwana IV did nothing but put his troops across the British lines of communication. The court of Yogyakarta was plundered, its library and archives were looted, large sums of money were taken, and Hamĕngkubuwana II was deposed and exiled to Penang. He was replaced as Sultan by his son Hamĕngkubuwana III. Natakusuma was rewarded for his assistance to the British by being given an independent inheritable domain of 4000 households in Yogyakarta lands and the name Pangeran Pakualam I (r. 1812–29). The Pakualaman thus became the Yogyakarta mirror-image of the Mangkunĕgaran in Surakarta, and the division of the kingdom of Mataram into two senior and two junior principalities was complete. A Pakualaman Corps of 100 cavalry (later 50 cavalry and 100 infantry) was also established. But unlike the Mangkunĕgaran Legion, it was never of much significance and was eventually disbanded in 1892.

The impact of the conquest of Yogyakarta cannot be overestimated. This was the only time in Javanese history when a court was taken by storm by the forces of a European government. The humiliation of the Yogyakarta aristocracy was profound. No one could any longer doubt that a new era had dawned in Java.

Pakubuwana IV soon learned that he had failed in his scheme to reduce Yogyakarta while leaving Surakarta intact. All European governments in Java followed a policy of equality towards both courts in order not to upset the balance in Javanese politics, so what was done to one court was invariably done to the other. In any case, the devious Surakarta correspondence with Yogyakarta had been discovered and had compromised Pakubuwana IV. Indeed, Raffles nearly decided to march on Surakarta and depose him, too. Instead, he annexed many regions from the outer districts of both Yogyakarta and Surakarta whereby many dignitaries lost their appanage lands. The British also took over the administration of toll gates and markets. These were then farmed out to Chinese, who had run the toll gates since the previous century, but now their administration was marked by increasing abuse and extortion at the expense of the Javanese. As reward for his assistance, Mangkunĕgara II received another 1000 households from the lands of Pakubuwana IV.

In 1814–15 Pakubuwana IV entered into the last and most unlikely of his major conspiracies. He plotted with disaffected Indian Sepoys stationed in Java to destroy both the European government and Yogyakarta. The plot was discovered, however, and nearly seventy Sepoy ringleaders were court-martialled; seventeen were shot and the remainder sent back to India in irons. Raffles decided not to depose Pakubuwana IV for his part, but exiled the main prince involved in the plot. This was the third time since 1788 that Pakubuwana IV had only narrowly escaped deposition.

Raffles stands in the annals of colonial history as a great reformer. Bastin points particularly to his enunciation of 'native welfare' as a concern of government, his introduction of the 'land rent' (land tax) system which laid the foundations for the later growth of a money economy, his emphasis on the village as a primary unit of colonial administration and his perseverance in Daendels' principle of treating Javanese officials as part of the governmental bureaucratic machine. Many of his reforms, like those of Daendels, were never put into effect, but several of his principles were taken up by his successors. The idea that the welfare of Indonesians should be a primary concern of the colonial government, however, was only a theory in Raffles's time and rarely as much as that thereafter, at least until the later nineteenth century. Daendels and Raffles together are most important for Indonesian history as the originators of a colonial revolution, a new policy which called for European assumption of sovereignty and administrative authority throughout Java and which aimed to use, reform or destroy indigenous institutions at will. In 1816 Java and other Indonesian posts were returned to Dutch authority as part of the general reconstruction of European affairs after the Napoleonic wars.

Raffles had already left Java to return to England; he was ultimately to achieve his greatest fame as the founder of Singapore in 1819.

From 1812 to 1825, discontent grew in Java as a result of several continuing problems. Europeans continually interfered in court affairs generally, and especially in the succession in Yogyakarta. Corruption and intrigue grew at both courts. Europeans and Chinese were leasing ever-larger tracts for sugar, coffee, indigo and pepper plantations in Central Java, especially from aristocrats in need of funds. On these plantations Javanese villagers and their customary law (adat) were treated with contempt. As farmers were increasingly obliged to pay their government taxes in money rather than kind, they were forced into the hands of moneylenders, most of whom were Chinese. Chinese entrepreneurs and tax-farmers also played an increasingly prominent role in rural society, all of which exacerbated ethnic tensions between them and the Javanese. In territories remaining to the Javanese rulers, the administration of taxes and toll-gates was extortionate; indeed, the European government's revenue from Yogyakarta toll gates trebled from 1816 to 1824. In territories newly annexed to the colonial government, conditions for tax-paying peasants were, if anything, even worse. The proliferation of toll-gates meanwhile threatened to choke off rural commerce. Hardship led to social dislocation, and robber-bands grew in number and daring. The use of opium spread among the Javanese population as a consequence of such dislocation, much to the profit of the European government, nearly twelve per cent of the revenues of which came from its monopoly of opium in the years 1827–33.

Into this increasingly turbulent picture stepped one of the most famous figures of Indonesian history, Pangeran Dipanagara (1785–1855). The eldest son of Sultan Hamĕngkubuwana III, he grew up amidst the intrigues and troubles of Hamĕngkubuwana II's reign. During his childhood and adolescence he lived with his grandmother the Ratu Agĕng (d. 1803) at Tĕgalrĕja, an isolated residence some miles from the court of Yogyakarta. There he meditated and studied Islamic religious texts as well as Javanese classics and history. He moved in pĕsantren (religious school) circles and resisted appearing at the court, which he disliked for its intrigue, decadence, immorality and corrupting European influence. His links with the rest of Javanese society were perhaps unique. As a senior prince he had access to the aristocracy, as a mystic to the religious community, and as a rural dweller to the masses of the countryside. As a critic of the state of affairs in Central Java, he became a focus of loyalty for the discontented.

About 1805–8 Dipanagara underwent a religious experience which convinced him that he was the divinely appointed future king of Java. He went on a pilgrimage to holy sites associated with the Mataram dynasty, in which he had a series of visions. The Goddess of the Southern Ocean came to him and promised him her aid, thereby confirming his status as a future king. A disembodied voice finally made it known that he was to initiate a period of devastation which would purify the land.

For nearly twenty years Dipanagara bided his time, while the situation in Java deteriorated and his following coalesced. In the 1820s small uprisings began. In 1821 there was a poor rice harvest and cholera spread to Java for the first time. In 1822 Hamĕngkubuwana IV (r. 1814–22) died amidst rumours that he had been poisoned, and there were heated disputes over the appointment of guardians for his three-year-old son Haměngkubuwana V (r. 1822–6, 1828–55). At the end of 1822 a major eruption of Mount Měrapi occurred and was taken as an omen of impending chaos. The seeds of war planted since 1808 now rapidly grew to maturity.

In 1823 Governor-General G. A. G. Ph. van der Capellen (1816–26) decided to end the abuses surrounding the private leasing of land in Central Java. He ordered that such leases should be abolished. The aristocrats who had leased their lands now not only lost this source of revenue, but were obliged to repay advances (which in most cases had already been spent) and to compensate the Chinese and European leaseholders for capital improvements on the lands (most of which were valueless to the aristocrats, who did not intend to run their appanages as plantations). This was the final step in pushing many aristocrats towards rebellion.

In May 1825 a new road was to be built near Těgalrěja. As the stakes for the roadway were being placed, a clash occurred between retainers of Dipanagara and those of his enemy the *patih* (1813–47) Danurěja IV. A period of considerable tension followed. On 20 July the Dutch sent forces from Yogyakarta to arrest Dipanagara. Open fighting broke out, Těgalrěja was captured and burned, but Dipanagara fled and raised the banner of rebellion. The Java War (1825–30) had begun.

The rebellion rapidly spread throughout Central and East Java, but its heart was in the Yogyakarta area. There fifteen out of twenty-nine princes joined Dipanagara, and forty-one out of eighty-eight *bupatis* (senior courtiers). Surakarta remained aloof, but the court seems to have been ready to go over to the rebel cause if its success appeared certain. The religious community rallied to Dipanagara, among them Kyai Maja, who became the spiritual leader of the rebellion. Villagers fought for Dipanagara and supported his battalions when they were unable to fight themselves. Troops which the ambivalent court of Surakarta sent to help the Dutch achieved little against the rebels. The Dutch also received troops from the Sultan of Yogyakarta: Dipanagara's animosity was, after all, directed at the court as well as the Europeans. Many Yogyakarta soldiers, however, deserted to the rebels. Troops from the Mangkuněgaran Legion showed both ability and loyalty to the anti-rebel cause. The princes of Madura and most regional Javanese officials also opposed Dipanagara.

As the rebel attacks on Chinese and Europeans spread, Dutch government authority was threatened throughout Central and East Java. By the end of 1825 it was clear that the rebels would not, however, be able to drive the Dutch out of Java easily. The Dutch were short of troops, but with the assistance of their Indonesian allies they withstood the first onslaughts. By 1826 Dutch government troop strengths were adequate, but they were poorly used. Large formations of government forces were able to achieve little against the rebels' mobile guerilla tactics. Dipanagara suffered a major defeat in October 1826 when he was pushed back from Surakarta. Nevertheless, by the end of 1826 the government forces seemed at a standstill and Dipanagara controlled much of the countryside in the interior of Central Java. In August 1826 the Dutch brought the aged Sultan Haměngkubuwana II back from exile in Ambon and placed him on the throne of Yogyakarta (1826–8), but this failed utterly to win Javanese support away from the rebellion.

By 1827 the Dutch were learning how best to use their troops. They adopted the *benteng-stelsel* (fortress-system), by which small mobile columns operated independently from an ever-growing network of strategic fortified posts and permanently policed the local population. Rebel parties were offered battle before they could grow to significant numbers and were prevented from establishing themselves for long in any district. As 1827 passed, Dipanagara and his forces found themselves more and more pursued and harassed. Cholera, malaria and dysentery claimed many on both sides, but by 1828 the war had clearly turned in favour of the Dutch and their allies.

Desertions and captures from the rebel side increased. In November 1828 Kyai Maja surrendered to the Dutch along with many other Islamic leaders; their abandonment of Dipanagara's cause arose largely from a growing conflict between their religious goals and the more secular aims of Dipanagara's aristocratic advisors. In September 1829 Dipanagara's uncle Pangeran Mangkubumi surrendered; he was allowed to return to Yogyakarta where he became one of the most senior and respected princes. In October 1829 Dipanagara's main commander, Ali Basa Prawiradirja, better known as Sěntot, also surrendered. Sěntot was thereupon given the rank of Lieutenant Colonel in the colonial army. He went to West Sumatra in 1831 to fight on the Dutch side against the Padris (see Chapter 12). But his anti-Dutch sentiments were never far from the surface. Indeed, Sěntot perceived in Sumatra an opportunity to become an autonomous king of the Minangkabau highlands. His machinations were, however, obvious to the Dutch, who placed him under strict control at Běngkulu in 1833, where he lived until his death in 1854. Finally, in March 1830 Dipanagara entered into negotiations in Magělang. What he expected to come of this conference is unclear, but it was inevitable that he would be arrested. The Dutch exiled him to Měnado and then Makasar, where he died in 1855. The rebellion was finished. It had cost the government side the lives of 8000 European and 7000 Indonesian soldiers. At least 200000 Javanese had died, and the population of Yogyakarta was reduced by about half.

After the end of the Java War, the government held Yogyakarta responsible and all of its outer districts *(mancanĕgara)* were annexed. To maintain the principle of equality which all European governments in Java followed, the outer districts of Surakarta were also annexed. Pakubuwana VI (r. 1823–30) was so disturbed by this apparent injustice that he left Surakarta and set out for the Indian Ocean to confer with the Goddess of the Southern Ocean. Fearing yet more rebellion, the Dutch brought him back and exiled him to Ambon, where he died in 1849.

The Java War was the last stand of the Javanese aristocratic elite. It had been a conservative movement, a vain effort to turn back the colonial tide which had been rising since 1808. The breadth of the social movement of protest which supported the war effort clearly reveals in retrospect how deeply the colonial revolution had already disrupted Javanese society, and in this respect the Java War prefigured the anti-colonial movement of the twentieth century. Dipanagara and his senior followers, however, may not have comprehended just how revolutionary were the changes which the renewed European threat had brought. Armed with ideas and traditions that were increasingly irrelevant, Dipanagara went down to defeat.

Many local lords and princes had found themselves on the Dutch side in the war. After 1830, almost all of the aristocratic elite took this course. Thus the mass protest which had fuelled the rebellion was left without access to aristocratic leadership. The Central Javanese courts, now without most of their territories, became ritual establishments and generally docile clients of the Dutch, although a dislike of their subservient position was often just below the refined surface of court affairs. For his services, Mangkunĕgara II was decorated and his estates increased.

The support which many Javanese aristocrats had given the Dutch and the deeply rooted social malaise which had caused the war, together led the Dutch to a major revision of policy. The dangers of tampering with institutions which were perceived as traditional and the value of holding the allegiance of the aristocracy seemed clear. The anti-feudal instincts of Daendels and Raffles were therefore rejected by the Dutch. For many years thereafter, Dutch rule would be based upon an alliance with the indigenous aristocracy. In a partial sense, the conservative Javanese aristocracy thus collectively won the peace, although the most dynamic part of it had lost the war. The aristocracy had, however, lost its last chance for any independent control of its environment.

11 Java, 1830–1900

In 1830 the truly colonial period of Javanese history began. For the first time, the Dutch were in a position to exploit and control the whole of the island, and there was not to be any serious challenge to their dominance until the twentieth century. Their position was, however, a curious one. For over 200 years they had been involved in Java, and for over 150 years directly involved in the interior. The Java War had been their last great investment of men and money in the struggle for hegemony. In 1830, political dominance throughout Java was at last achieved, but on balance this effort had been a financial failure. If there was profit to be had out of involvement in Central and East Java, for over two centuries no one had succeeded in extracting it, except for the benefit of individuals who corruptly acquired personal fortunes. Only the coffee plantations of Priangan (West Java) had ever looked like being consistently profitable ventures. But in Central and East Java, profits had been wiped out by military and administrative overheads. The question which therefore faced the Dutch in 1830 was whether the dominance they had at last achieved could be made profitable.

Profit from Java was essential. Not only must it cover the costs of the administration in Java, but it was also needed to bolster the deteriorating financial position in the Netherlands. In the aftermath of the Napoleonic wars, the Dutch domestic debt and interest payments upon it rose sharply. The position grew still worse when the Dutch-Belgian union created by the Congress of Vienna in 1815 collapsed in the Belgian revolt of 1830. The Dutch attempt to reconquer Belgium was defeated in 1831–2, and in 1839 the Netherlands recognised Belgian independence. The Netherlands thus lost a part of the state, and invested yet more money in a fruitless attempt to regain it.

During the Java War, the Dutch contemplated various proposals for Java. All shared a general aim of somehow procuring tropical produce at the right volume and price to make a profit, an aim which had been central to Dutch thinking since the first voyage set sail in 1595. In 1829 Johannes van den Bosch (1780–1844) submitted proposals which were to become the so-called *cultuurstelsel* (cultivation system, sometimes less accurately called culture system). The king accepted the proposals, and in January 1830 van den Bosch arrived in Java as the new Governor-General (1830–3).

Van den Bosch's thinking on the *cultuurstelsel* was never very explicitly formulated, but it was apparently founded on a simple general principle. The Javanese villages owed a land tax (the 'land rent') to the government, normally calculated as 40 per cent of the village's main crop (usually rice). In fact, the actual assessment was often below this figure, and collection of the tax (largely to be paid in cash) had often been difficult because of inadequate administrative resources and shortages of currency. Van den Bosch's idea was that each village should set aside part of its land to produce export crops (especially coffee, sugar and indigo) for sale at fixed prices to the colonial government. The village would thereby be able to cover its land tax commitment, and van den Bosch estimated that the produce of 20 per cent (later 33 per cent) of the village land should be sufficient for this purpose. If the village earned more by the sale of crops to the government than its land tax obligation, it would keep the excess payment; if less, it must still pay the difference from other sources. By 1833, a link between land tax and crop payments was less clear in van den Bosch's statements, and he spoke instead of the production of export crops as being more profitable to the village than growing rice. In any case, the principle was clearly that for the village there should be a trade-off between land tax based on rice production and export crop sales to the government.

In theory, everyone was to benefit from this system. The village would be left with more land for its own use and would acquire a cash income. Instead of an uncertain land tax revenue the government would acquire tropical produce so cheaply that, in van den Bosch's estimate, it could even compete on the world market with West Indies sugar produced by slave labour. The crops would then be shipped to Europe by the Netherlands Trading Company (NHM: *Nederlandsche Handelmaatschappij*), set up in 1824–5 upon the Dutch king's initiative. This would break British and American dominance of shipping in the Malay-Indonesian area and bring transportation revenues to the Netherlands.

In practice, there was never a 'system' at all. There were wide variations in the application of van den Bosch's ideas from one area to another in Java. His concept of procuring benefit for all turned into one of the more purely exploitative episodes of colonial history. Local officials, both Dutch and Indonesian, set both the land tax assessment and the level of export crop production for each village, then compelled the village to produce. As the payment for the crops rose, officials used this as a justification for increasing the land tax assessment, so that much of the excess crop payment was brought back into the hands of government. In fact, the *cultuurstelsel* amounted to compulsory delivery of export crops to the government, and was to a very large extent like the system of compulsory deliveries which the VOC had imposed for coffee in Priangan in the eighteenth century. Indeed, just as before van den Bosch's arrival, coffee was consistently the most profitable crop; it was also the last to be abolished when the *cultuurstelsel* came to an end.

The administrative structure of the *cultuurstelsel* was consistent with the new conservatism of Dutch policy after 1830. Previous experiments in dealing with individual cultivators were abandoned, and the village became the basic unit of administration. The village headman was the link between the cultivator and higher levels of Indonesian officials, culminating in the aristocratic Regency head, the *bupati* (called regent by the Dutch). The *bupati* was responsible to the European administration, but European officials were also involved at lower levels. The officials, both Dutch and Indonesian, who were charged with implementing the new scheme were paid percentages upon crop deliveries. This was a fruitful source of corruption and a stimulus to extortionate demands upon the villages. Indeed, corruption and abuse were rife. Yields were underestimated, a private trade in government crops grew up, and shady deals proliferated among indigenous officials, Dutchmen and Chinese entrepreneurs. The colonial government in Batavia was never in a position to monitor and control the implementation of its directives, except in a most general way.

The main input into this 'system' was Javanese and Sundanese labour. Only a small portion of the cultivated land was involved. Excluding areas for coffee (which was grown on land not usable for rice agriculture), for all of Java only 6 per cent of cultivated land was involved in 1840 and 4 per cent in 1850. There were major regional variations, but the highest official figures were for Bagĕlen and Pĕkalongan, where 15 per cent of the land was committed to government crops in 1840. But the labour investment was clearly massive. The statistics for the *cultuurstelsel* are not reliable in detail, for there was substantial under-reporting. Fasseur's unadjusted figures show that in all of Java 57 per cent of the population was involved in production of government crops in 1840, and 46 per cent in 1850. Allowing for under-reporting, Van Niel concludes for the period of 1837–51 that over 70 per cent of agricultural families were producing export crops, over half of them in coffee. The distribution of this enormous burden was very uneven. Fasseur's unadjusted figures show that in some areas considerably less than half the population was involved; in 1840, however, the figure for Bantĕn was 92 per cent, and in 1845 for Kĕdu it was 97 per cent.

These percentages probably represent a continually growing exploitation in terms of number of people, for throughout the nineteenth century the population of Java maintained the steady increase that had begun in the eighteenth century. There are serious and probably insoluble problems surrounding population figures, but at the end of the eighteenth century the population may have been as high as 5 million and by 1830 it was around 7 million. By 1850 it had reached 9.5 million, by 1870 16.2 million, and by 1890 23.6 million. There was thus at least a fivefold increase over a century. It was this steady growth of available labour which made the *cultuurstelsel* a success. Possible causative links between the *cultuurstelsel* and this high rate of population growth have been a subject of considerable historical controversy. Boomgaard argues that opportunities for paid non-agricultural employment encouraged couples to marry earlier and to have more children. In the second half of the nineteenth century, when birth rates may have declined somewhat, this was more than offset by a decline in mortality (especially infant mortality) through successful vaccination against smallpox and the decreasing virulence of cholera and typhoid epidemics.

The impact of the *cultuurstelsel* upon the Javanese and Sundanese varied widely over Java, and is still disputed. Pending further research, certain suppositions seem reasonable. For the aristocratic elite throughout Java this was a time of apparent benefit. Their positions became more secure and hereditary succession to official posts became the norm, especially after the Constitutional Regulation of 1854. They often made great profits from the percentages paid on crop deliveries. They were, however, directly dependent upon Dutch rule for their positions and incomes, and had to organise the compulsion which proved necessary for the *cultuurstelsel* to function. They were increasingly subject to supervision or interference from Dutch officials. They were being detached from their own society, relieved of pressure from the former indigenous sanctions upon the abuse of power, and not encouraged to modernise in any way. Indeed, it was a prime aim of Dutch rule to employ the 'traditional' prestige of the aristocracy in the cause of cheap administration. The aristocratic clients of Dutch rule were thus slowly moving away from their position of leadership within the society, although their prestige was still high among many in the villages.

It is impossible to arrive at definitive generalisations about the impact of the *cultuurstelsel* on lower levels of Javanese society for two reasons. Firstly, the statistical evidence from this period is voluminous but often of doubtful reliability. Secondly, these questionable sources are nevertheless sufficient to demonstrate that there were substantial variations from one part of Java to another. It is, however, possible to say that for the majority of Java's indigenous population this was a time of hardship.

The impact of the compulsory cultivation of government crops was complex. The development of sugar and indigo plantations took land, labour and water away from rice cultivation (to the detriment of the local people) but provided opportunities for paid employment (to their benefit). In some areas, notably Pasuruan, local people developed a symbiotic relationship with the sugar industry to the benefit of both sides. Everywhere government payment for crops and greater opportunities for wage labour increased the amount of money in circulation. Growth in production encouraged labour specialisation in non-agricultural activities associated with the plantations and factories in the countryside.

If there were benefits to be seen, particularly after the 1840s, there were also very serious burdens laid upon most local people. In the first place, while the distribution of benefits is difficult to see in the extant evidence, it was certainly inegalitarian. Those who were in the best position to take advantage of the *cultuurstelsel's* opportunities were the village and supravillage elites through their control of land and local authority, non-indigenous entrepreneurs (mainly Chinese, but also some Arabs) through their control of capital and tax farms (notably the opium farm), and European officials and entrepreneurs through their control of capital and influence over the machinery of government. Shared interests often linked these three groups in arrangements of dubious legality. There is reason to believe that the local social order grew less egalitarian, more stratified, as elites grasped opportunities to increase their land-holdings and incomes while more of their compatriots became landless labourers. In some areas there may have been a trend towards communal land-holding c. 1830–50 so as to share the burden of taxation and labour which attended land-holding, but this, too, enhanced the position of the village elite who determined the distribution of land under communal rotation arrangements. For the poorest people of Java, the landless labourers, new opportunities for paid labour may have meant significant improvement in their material circumstances. The peasantry of Java appears to have been quite mobile in this period, with significant numbers moving considerable distances to escape burdens or to seek employment. This was true of areas which were heavily committed to government crops and of those with little or no such commitment, which suggests that many of the problems experienced by the people of Java arose more from the general circumstances of Dutch rule than from specific arrangements under the aegis of the *cultuurstelsel*.

The results of the *cultuurstelsel* for the Dutch are quite clear: at long last, steady and immense profitability was achieved. Already by 1831 the colonial Indonesian budget was balanced, and thereafter the old debts of the VOC were paid off.

Enormous remittances were sent to the Netherlands; from 1831 to 1877 the Dutch home treasury received f. 832 million. Before 1850, these remittances accounted for about 19 per cent of Dutch state revenues, in 1851–60 for about 32 per cent and in 1860–6 for about 34 per cent. These revenues kept the domestic Dutch economy afloat: debts were redeemed, taxes reduced, fortifications, waterways and the Dutch state railway built, all on the profits forced out of the villages of Java. Ironically, the funds were also used to pay compensation to slave-owners to emancipate the slaves of Surinam (Dutch Guiana). Amsterdam again became a major world market-place for tropical produce, especially coffee and sugar.

It had been demonstrated that Java was capable of producing a substantial surplus, at least under coercion. This surplus was, however, used to support the Dutch colonial administration in Java, its conquests in the outer islands (see Chapter 12) and the Dutch home economy. The main investment was Javanese and Sundanese labour, and both the agricultural and administrative techniques were of a traditional kind. The Dutch succeeded in milking the economy of Java, while returning significant benefits to only a small stratum of the indigenous society.

By the 1840s, however, the *cultuurstelsel* was already encountering problems. Signs of hardship among the Javanese and Sundanese began to appear, particularly in sugar areas. Sugar cane was grown on the same land as rice, and the time required for the growth and harvesting of sugar, followed by preparation of the fields for rice, made it difficult to achieve a steady rotation of the two crops. Sugar mills also competed with rice agriculture for water supplies. Indigo also produced problems. For example, there is reason to believe that in the vast areas committed to indigo in Pěkalongan, nutrients in the soil were so depleted as to cause a series of bad rice harvests several years after indigo planting was cut back. Rice shortages appeared, and the price of rice fluctuated widely, with some sharp rises in the 1840s. The famines which broke out in Java were, however, caused more by the poverty of the peasants and the avarice of those who held power over them than by actual shortages of rice, for there was often rice available (not infrequently warehoused by local elites and Chinese traders seeking higher prices) but the peasants could not pay for it. In 1843 there was a major famine in Cirěbon. Epidemics, particularly typhoid, broke out in 1846–50, and famines spread in Central Java around 1850. The government meanwhile imposed drastic increases in land tax and other impositions. Mass flight from villages led to even more rice land falling out of production. Financial crises also occurred in both the Netherlands Trading Company and the Java budget. The extension of the *cultuurstelsel* was reaching its limits, and in 1845–50 exports of coffee, sugar and indigo fell. After 1850, however, profits from coffee and sugar again rose rapidly as the world prices for these crops rose. Indeed, in 1851–70 the Netherlands treasury received twice the amount of remittances it had received in 1831–50. In the colonial budget itself, however, a major escalation in military expenditures (see Chapter 12) produced a deficit by 1858, which could only be made good from the profits of the *cultuurstelsel*. The financial surplus from the Indies finally came to a definitive end in 1877.

Opposition to the *cultuurstelsel* now grew in the Netherlands. Government opinion began to doubt whether the system was tenable any longer, despite its renewed profitability. In 1848 a liberal constitution gave the Dutch parliament (States-General) for the first time a position of influence in colonial affairs. In parliament, opposition coalesced. Dutch middle-class interests, grown wealthy on the profits which the Dutch economy had derived from Java, pressed for change. They urged a 'liberal' reform: a drastic reduction of the role of government in the colonial economy, a freeing of the restrictions on private enterprise in Java and an end to forced labour and oppression of the Javanese and Sundanese. In 1860 a former colonial official, Eduard Douwes Dekker (1820–87), published a novel entitled *Max Havelaar* under the pseudonym 'Multatuli'. This was a devastating exposure of the oppressive and corrupt state of Dutch rule in Java. This book became an influential weapon against the nineteenth-century colonial regime in Java. The liberals faced a dilemma, however, for they wanted to be rid of the *cultuurstelsel* but not of the profits which Dutchmen gained from Java.

The result of this political debate in the Netherlands was the piecemeal dismantling of the *cultuurstelsel,* as the colonial government abolished compulsory state crops throughout its Indonesian territories. The first to go were the least profitable, or those which were not profitable at all: pepper in 1862, clove and nutmeg in 1864 (this being truly the end of an era, after over 250 years), indigo, tea and cinnamon in 1865, and tobacco in 1866 (tobacco soon proved, however, to be profitable for private growers; see Chapter 13). Coffee and sugar, the latter having been a particular source of scandals, were the most profitable and the last to be abolished. In the Sugar Law of 1870 it was decreed that the government would withdraw from sugar cultivation over 12 years, beginning only in 1878. Compulsory coffee cultivation was abolished by even slower stages from the 1870s. It finally came to an end in Priangan – where it had begun in the early eighteenth century – at the beginning of 1917, and in areas of the north coast of Java in June 1919.

The Agrarian Law of 1870 opened Java to private enterprise. Freedom and security were provided for entrepreneurs. Only Indonesians could own land, but foreigners were allowed to lease it from the government for up to seventy-five years or from indigenous holders for maximum periods of between five and twenty years (depending upon the conditions of tenure). Private estate agriculture could now develop in Java as well as the outer islands. The opening of the Suez Canal in 1869 and the development of steam navigation (largely in British hands) from about the same time further encouraged private development by improving communications with Europe. In 1860 private and government exports from all of Indonesia were roughly equal in value, but by 1885 private exports were ten times those of government. The total value of state and private exports in 1885 was twice that of 1860. The number of European civilians in Java increased rapidly, from 17 285 in 1852 to 62 447 in 1900. The 'liberal' period (*c.* 1870–1900) represented a major intensification in the exploitation of Java's agricultural resources, as well as those of the outer islands (see Chapter 13).

The impact of the 'liberal' period upon the people of Java requires further investigation. In general it can be said that the hopes of liberal reformers were frustrated insofar as they had believed that the new economic arrangements could both benefit indigenous people and continue to extract an agricultural surplus from Java to the benefit of the Netherlands economy and private entrepreneurs. Chinese entrepreneurs seem to have prospered from the 1870s to the turn of the century, but the incomes of Indonesian entrepreneurs, artisans and wage employees fell in real terms. Rice consumption per capita also fell, particularly after 1885, but an expansion in production of other foodstuffs (notably maize and cassava) meant that the supply of food was usually sufficient to prevent starvation, although famines occurred in Banten in 1881–2 and in Central Java, especially Sĕmarang, in 1900–2.

The 1880s saw a major crisis which affected both Java's indigenous people and those who so successfully exploited them. From the 1870s coffee leaf disease began to spread and coffee production fell. Still more importantly, in 1882 a sugar blight hit Cirĕbon and thence spread eastward across Java, reaching its eastern tip by 1892. The Java sugar industry was then dealt a further blow when beet sugar flooded the European market. In 1884 sugar prices plummeted. Sugar's domination of Java's economy meant that the impact of the crisis was widespread. A general rural depression ensued which reached its nadir in 1887–8. Trade stagnated and bankruptcies among traders and planters led many enterprises to fall into the hands of banks and large trading companies. Even Java's wealthy Chinese opium-farmers felt the pinch; by 1889 only four of Java's nineteen opium farms had escaped bankruptcy. Peasants whose livelihoods had depended on employment in the coffee and particularly the sugar industry were now thrown out of work. Having become dependent upon export crop sales, the peasants had also become exposed to their risks. The sugar industry eventually survived. After lengthy and difficult experiments in hybridisation the Dutch finally produced cane which resisted the blight. The industry also increased output. The area under cane was expanded but greater growth in production came from improvements in technology. In 1885 sugar production from Java was 380 400 metric tons and in 1890 just under 400000 metric tons, but by 1895 it has risen to 581 600 metric tons and by 1900 to 744 300 metric tons. The industry also increased its profitability by cutting both the wages and the rents paid to peasants for their lands, so while it survived Javanese peasants continued to suffer.

The gradual freeing of the cultivator from compulsory production of export crops brought little amelioration, for the land tax and other substantial payments were still due to government but the source of income to pay these was being abolished. Van Deventer's 1904 report estimated that the average household in Java owed 23 per cent of its cash income and 20 per cent of its total (cash and kind) income to government. The hardship was felt especially in coffee districts, for coffee land could not be turned to other cash crops. In the wake of the coffee leaf disease from the 1870s onwards, and without either the compulsion of forced labour or attractive wages and prices, coffee production fell. To pay their taxes and meet other expenses, cultivators were obliged to turn to money lenders, among whom local *hajis* (those who had made the pilgrimage to Mecca) were prominent. These were legally 'natives' and were thus able to own land; their foreclosures on mortgages led to increasing landlessness. Chinese, being classed as 'foreign orientals', could not own land and were thus obliged to work through indigenous middlemen, but they were in a strong position because of their simultaneous control of pawnshops and opium dens. Government sale of opium farms was abolished in stages from 1894, finally being replaced by a state-run Opium Administration throughout Java at the beginning of 1904. The pawnshop farm was abolished in stages shortly thereafter. In van Deventer's view, however, Arabs were the most rapacious usurers of all.

The royal elite of Java were now removed from political affairs. Rebellion was virtually abandoned after 1830. There were several disturbances in the royal domains, but only rarely were members of the royal families involved. In 1842 five members of the Surakarta royal house left the court and attempted to cause trouble, but were captured within five days. In Yogyakarta a rebellion in favour of a weakminded prince named Pangeran Suryengalaga was plotted by his mother in 1883. This affair worried the Dutch and the Yogyakarta royal establishment, but in the end it was quickly suppressed. Both Suryengalaga and his mother were on their way to exile in Měnado within a week of their attempted rebellion. Suryengalaga's name was, however, invoked in several later conspiracies. Dislike of the Dutch seems to have continued in some court circles, but it led to no serious resistance to Dutch rule. In theory the four princely Houses (the senior houses of the Sultanate of Yogyakarta and the Susuhunanate of Surakarta, and the subsidiary Mangkunĕgaran and Pakualaman houses) ruled their own territories (the *vorstenlanden*), and Dutch rule was indirect. In fact the Dutch Residents exercised real control there, although there were differences between the principalities and directly ruled areas because of the different legal standing of Dutch authority. The *cultuurstelsel*, for instance, did not in theory apply to these principalities, although similar arrangements for producing export crops existed. At the end of 1872 the population of these principalities was about 1.1 million.

With little room for political manoeuvre, the royal elite turned much of its energy towards cultural affairs. Pakubuwana V (b. 1785, r. 1820–3), while still crown prince, had ordered the compilation of *Sĕrat Cĕnthini* ('The Book of Cĕnthini'); this is a major work which imparts Javanese mystical knowledge through the story of a wandering student of religion named Seh Amongraga in the time of Sultan Agung. Pakubuwana V's successors were also supporters of literary activity. With royal patronage, Raden Ngabei Ronggawarsita (1802–73) was active in Surakarta as an author of both prose and verse works in Javanese. Conventionally seen as the last of the great court poets, his monumental prose work *Pustakaraja Purwa* ('The Book of Kings of Ancient Times') and its prologue *Paramayoga* ('The Exalted Age'?) covered the mythical past of Java, beginning with Adam and Indian gods and ending in the year 730. He also wrote several moralistic works in verse and prose. Mangkunĕgara IV (r. 1853–81) was a major poet, and collaborated with Ronggawarsita. Among the works attributed to him, the poem *Wedhatama* ('Exalted Wisdom') is the most famous; this teaches moral values consistent with the Javanese mystical variant of Islam, and is critical of the more selfconsciously Islamic community in Java.

The royal elite of Yogyakarta were also patrons of literature. Pakualam II (r. 1829–58) and Pakualam III (r. 1858–64) were considerable authors themselves, and the house of Pakualam patronised much literary activity. Sultan Hamĕngkubuwana V (r. 1822–6, 1828–55) also enthusiastically encouraged the writing of literary works, and may have composed some personally. Thereby the library of the Sultanate, which had been looted by the British in 1812, was gradually rebuilt. Royal patronage of the arts also led to much activity in music and *wayang* in both Surakarta and Yogyakarta. In general, the subsidiary principalities of the Mangkunĕgaran and Pakualaman seem to have been more lively and experimental than the two senior courts.

The cultural activity of the courts after 1830 did not, however, produce much real innovation. It was largely an attempt to express the ideals of an aristocratic ethos which was increasingly irrelevant in an age of peace, but which the royal elite found reassuring and the Dutch found useful as part of their policy of using 'traditional' authority in the cause of tranquillity. There was very little which was comparable to the development of more modern ideas and literary forms which can be discerned among Filipino, Vietnamese, Japanese, Indian or Arab writers in the nineteenth century.

In the visual arts there were some signs of the arrival of new ideas. Raden Saleh (? 1814–80), a descendant of the family which ruled Sĕmarang under the VOC, spent over twenty years in Europe where he was influenced by Delacroix and became a well-known court painter. After his return to Java in 1851 he painted at the courts of Yogyakarta and the Mangkunĕgaran for a time. A few (mostly anonymous) Indonesians also became skilled draughtsmen and a few of their illustrations appear in nineteenth-century European publications concerning Indonesia. This was largely a matter of individuals adopting wholly European styles. The traditional Javanese arts were, however, marginally influenced. For instance, a few Javanese manuscripts superimpose *wayang* figures upon more naturalistic watercolour backgrounds or provide rather crude European-style illustrations. This somewhat greater innovation in the visual, as opposed to the literary, arts was probably made possible by the absence of a significant indigenous tradition of painting or illustration (except for manuscript illumination or the rigidly stylised *batik* patterns) to challenge the new styles.

Of all the royal courts, the Mangkunĕgaran was the most successful in adjusting to the new circumstances of Dutch rule. It may be significant that this was the only court where the military traditions of the Javanese aristocracy lived on, albeit under Dutch control. The Mangkunĕgaran Legion, consisting of infantry, cavalry and artillery, continued to be maintained with Dutch financial support. The Mangkunĕgaran also developed extensive estate agriculture, especially in coffee and sugar. The foundations of this economic activity were laid in the reign of Mangkunĕgara IV (r. 1853–81), when Europeans were employed in introducing European techniques of estate management and exploitation, but with the important difference that the profits were reinvested in the prince's domains rather than being sent abroad. Twice, in 1857 and 1877, Mangkunĕgara IV failed to regain control over lands which had been leased to European planters. But he was successful in slowly replacing the appanage system for his retainers and officials with one of salaries. Although serious burdens were laid upon the village population, migration into his domains suggests that these burdens were less than in some other districts. Mangkunĕgara IV had, however, created a typically 'underdeveloped' economy, in which revenues depended upon the world price for a few crops. After his time, the spread of coffee diseases and the rise of sugar beet in Europe produced an extended financial crisis in the Mangkunĕgaran, as they did in the rest of Java. This resulted in the Residents of Surakarta taking direct control of Mangkunĕgaran finances from 1888 to 1899, during which time the principality's financial position was restored.

As European-style gilt chairs, Italian marble, crystal chandeliers and Dutch military uniforms and decorations appeared, the courts probably became more splendid than they had ever been before. Their cultural prestige among the masses seems to have been high. The combination of their political impotence and cultural prestige perhaps explains why the royal elite were not major targets of criticism for the nationalist movement which arose in the early twentieth century. But there was little substance left to court life: the royal elite were knights with no more battles to fight. The courts therefore degenerated into an effete formalism, an elaborate and antiquated artificiality.

The higher elite, the main foundation of Dutch rule outside the principalities, found their positions changing under 'liberalism', as a renewed zeal for social reform crept into colonial policy. During the *cultuurstelsel*, the *bupatis* and higher administrative elite had profited greatly in both incomes and security. But their abuses, especially in the use of compulsory labour, had produced both animosity from their own society and increasing criticism from their Dutch masters. From the 1860s onwards the Dutch took steps to reform the haphazard administrative structure and to create a more regularised indigenous administration to parallel the Dutch administration. The *bupatis* (of whom there were seventy-two in 1900) remained in theory the supreme indigenous officials and leaders of their society. Increasingly, however, Dutch practice bypassed them and placed greater reliance on their assistants, the *patihs*. The *wĕdana* (district head, of whom there were 434 in 1900) also grew in importance, and the centre of gravity in the indigenous administration came to rest upon the *patih* and *wĕdana*, whose tasks and posts tended to merge as the years passed.

The highest level of the aristocratic regional elite thus began to be bypassed. The *bupatis'* wealth and opportunities for abuses were also eroded. In 1867 they were deprived of appanages and were given salaries instead, which were often said to be inadequate. In the same year, the payment of percentages on government crops to European civil servants was abolished, but these percentages continued to be paid to indigenous officials until 1907. As the *cultuurstelsel* was progressively abolished, however, their incomes from this source declined. In 1882 all indigenous officials lost the right to personal services from their subjects, and in the following twenty years many other forms of compulsory labour on public works were abolished. Although this considerably reduced opportunities for abuse by indigenous officials, it brought little improvement for villagers. Their obligation for services was converted into a head-tax in cash, which may have been an even greater burden.

The Dutch had never before been interested in 'modernising' the *bupatis*, for they were most useful for their 'traditional' status. Their level of education was poor; in 1900 only four out of the seventy-two *bupatis* were said to know the Dutch language. The colonial government had used the *bupatis* for its own purposes, abusing their status and encouraging them to abuse it. When the abuses became clear and the *bupatis* ceased to be so useful, the government began to bypass them. By 1900 even the outward displays of aristocratic status were under attack. The *hormat circulaire* (etiquette circular) of 1904 ended official Dutch encouragement of 'outmoded' displays, such as parasols, large groups of retainers, regalia, etc.

In the 'liberal' period the government not only acted to abolish the feudal attributes of the aristocratic elite, but also attempted to instil a new spirit in its younger generation. Beginning in 1878 *hoofdenscholen* (chiefs' schools) were established for the sons of the higher elite. From about 1893 these took on a more vocational character, with courses in law, bookkeeping, surveying, etc. But the demoralisation within the *bupatis'* families was already such that many sons did not wish to succeed to their fathers' positions. Increasingly, the government had to fill high administrative posts with the sons of lower officials or even from outside the ranks of the indigenous aristocracy.

The higher aristocratic elite of Java was, by 1900, at a low point in prestige, authority and self-assurance. There were, of course, individual exceptions, such as the *bupati* of Majakĕrta who in 1896 established a fund to loan seed rice free of interest to farmers, using mosque funds as finance. But many others seem to have responded less positively to changing and difficult times. Many of the younger generation left administrative service and sought careers in law or medicine. Others produced intellectual movements which had a clearly anti-Islamic content, and which were linked to Theosophy. Such movements attributed Java's unhappy state to the spread of Islam, and sought revitalisation through a union of *budi* ('intellect', here meaning Western scientific thought) and *buda* (pre-Islamic Javanese culture). At about the same time, Islamic circles were beginning to conclude that a revitalisation and purification of Islam was needed. Thus, as Java entered the twentieth century, a distinction between two conflicting ideologies as the basis for national rejuvenation was already emerging.

The higher aristocratic elite also found itself challenged by a growing group of new officials. The administrative upper classes of Java are collectively called *priyayi*, and this new group can be loosely called the 'new' or 'lesser' *priyayi*. The emergence of this group reflects an ambivalence in late-nineteenth-century colonial policy about the need for 'traditional' forms of authority. Their tasks were wholly new, being the jobs which new administrative services required. But they were formally defined into the *priyayi* class and accorded titles and forms of display associated with that class, in order to give these new roles a clear status in indigenous society. In 1861, for instance, government school teachers were given the rank of *mantri-guru* (teaching officer) and the right to appear in public with a parasol, a pike, a mat, a betel-nut set and an entourage of four. A vaccination service had begun on a small scale in 1811, and in 1851 the 'Doktĕr-Jawa' school was established in Weltevreden (a suburb of Batavia, now Gambir). In 1875 the vaccinator course was reformed, and thereafter it consisted of a course of five to six years taught in Dutch. Other new *priyayi* emerged in the irrigation, forestry, railway, telegraph and other services. After the 1904 *hormat circulaire* this process began to be abandoned, the last group to be defined into the *priyayi* class being government pawnshop clerks in 1906.

The new *priyayi* differed from the old aristocratic elite less in their social origins (for many came from families which were at least among the better-off) than in the basis of their status. The new *priyayi* achieved their standing through individual talent, whereas the old had ascribed status due to their birth. Conflicts and tensions naturally developed between these two groups. In the twentieth century, the new *priyayi* were destined to play a crucial role. Those who remained in the bureaucracy joined the older *priyayi* to become the backbone of first Dutch, then Japanese, then Indonesian administrations. Those who turned their backs on government service led the anti-colonial movement and created the independent state.

With the royal and bureaucratic elites of Java so tied to the colonial administration, centred in urban areas, or reduced to political impotence, rural peasant protests found little leadership. They broke out often, especially from the 1870s onwards. Indeed, these protests or small-scale rebellions were often directed specifically against the indigenous administration, as well as against Chinese or against European officials and entrepreneurs. They sought inspiration in messianic ideas, both Islamic and Javanese nativist in origin. Such leadership as existed often came from rural Islamic leaders. But none of these movements seriously threatened colonial rule. Mass discontent was deeply rooted by the end of the nineteenth century, but it lacked effective direction or coordination.

Meanwhile, a new leadership group was slowly emerging within Islamic circles. Religious revival movements were to play a major role in the twentieth century, but the nineteenth-century background in Java is still little known. It is clear that the number of *hajis* (pilgrims) from Indonesia to Mecca, most of them from Java, rose significantly. This was especially true after the opening of the Suez Canal in 1869, which diverted the main South East Asia-Europe sailing routes to the Red Sea. In the 1850s and 1860s, an average of approximately 1600 Indonesian *hajis* left annually, but in the 1870s it was 2600, in the 1880s 4600, and by the end of the century it was over 7000. Several Indonesians became important figures in Mecca, notably Syaikh Muhammad al-Nawawi (1815–98) from Bantĕn. *C.* 1884 he published a lengthy Arabic commentary upon the *Qur'an*, thereby becoming the first major Indonesian commentator since Abdurrauf of Singkil in the seventeenth century. While al-Nawawi's commentary is in many respects a conservative one, Johns argues that its approach was consistent with the reformism then arising in the Islamic world.

Indonesian pilgrims were naturally exposed to new reform and revival movements in Middle Eastern Islam in the nineteenth century. *Hajis* returning to the rural countryside of Java figured not only as usurers and landowners, but also as leaders of some protest movements. They appear also to have challenged the social positions of established rural teachers of religion *(kyai)*, thereby producing tension within selfconsciously Islamic circles. The mystical brotherhoods, the Sufi *tarekats*, also underwent a significant revival. In particular, the Naqshabandiyya brotherhood spread, particularly among the elite in West and Central Java, from the 1850s. Its rather upper-class orientation in most areas of Java prevented it from becoming the anti-colonial force which it was in some other parts of the Islamic world. Another mystical order which combined elements of the Naqshabandiyya and the Qadiriyya orders, and was thus called Qadiriyya wa Naqshabandiyya, was founded by Ahmad Khatib from the Kalimantan state of Sambas, who died in Mecca *c.* 1878. This order had a more popular following and played an important role in the peasant uprising in Bantĕn in 1888. The more devoutly Islamic sectors of Java were thus emerging out of the rather heterodox religious world of previous centuries into an age of both conflict and renewal. As this happened, those circles which were less committed to Islam faced an unaccustomed challenge, and some responded with hostility. The nature of this fluid situation in the late nineteenth century is not yet very clear, but its outcome was to be significant social and religious divisions in the twentieth century.

By 1900, an older order had been definitively destroyed in Java. The advantageous ratio of population to agricultural land, the vitality of the old elite, the easy religious tolerance, and the previous structure of power and authority had all disappeared or were rapidly disappearing. The rise of reformist Islamic movements in the Middle East and the growth of population in Java played their part in these developments, but much of the causation is to be ascribed directly to Dutch colonial policy and practice. In 1900 Java was in a state of transition, with an old age dead but the form of the new age not yet clear.

12 The Outer Islands, *c.* 1800–1910

By about 1910, most of the regions which now comprise the Republic of Indonesia were brought under Dutch rule. Governor-General van den Bosch (1830–3) had established profitability as the main principle of government, and believed that the Dutch should therefore restrict their attentions to Java, Sumatra and Bangka (a source of tin). Nonetheless, from about 1840 onwards Dutch involvement increased throughout the outer islands. There were many reasons for this. Often there were economic motivations, including the protection of inter-insular trade. (The economic developments which followed Dutch expansion are described in Chapter 13.) Often local Dutch officials intervened out of ambition for glory or promotion, despite Batavia's official policy of avoiding further extensions of Dutch authority. Two general considerations applied everywhere. First, to protect the security of areas they already held, the Dutch felt compelled to subdue other regions which might support or inspire resistance movements. Second, as the European scramble for colonies reached its height in the later nineteenth century, the Dutch felt obliged to establish their claims to the outer islands of the archipelago in order to prevent some other Western power from intervening there, even where the Dutch initially had no great interest themselves.

In the last quarter of the nineteenth century, the equation of military power shifted decisively against independent Indonesian states, and this made the final stage of Dutch expansion possible. In the days of wooden sailing ships and muzzle-loading muskets, the gap in military technology between Indonesians and Europeans had not been insuperable. But as the expanding colonial power began to adopt breech-loading rifles, repeaters, steam-powered gunboats, and the other military byproducts of an industrialised society, most of the pre-industrial states of Indonesia could resist only with determination and outmoded firearms. A few independent rulers attempted to redress the balance by purchasing modern armaments, but they could rarely equal the military power of the colonial forces for long.

The extension of Dutch power to the outer islands was quite different from its expansion in Java, for in most of the outer islands there had never been any permanent or serious pretensions to authority by the Dutch. There were some areas where the Dutch had long had contacts, but very few in which they had previously been the predominant power. In districts where the VOC had earlier established trading posts, by 1800 these were rarely more than powerless tokens of Dutch interest; some, indeed, had ceased to exist altogether. Even where the

Dutch presence had been significant, the British occupation of Dutch posts during the French Revolutionary wars had severed the Dutch connection. In the outer islands, Dutch expansion in the nineteenth century essentially represented the creation of a new empire, not the culmination of long and intensive involvement. In all areas, it was intimately connected with indigenous Indonesian events. It is unfortunately true, however, that for many of these regions the Indonesian side of developments has so far received inadequate historical attention.

Madura, off Java's northeast coast, did have a long tradition of involvement with the Dutch. This did not arise out of direct Dutch interest in Madura itself, but rather because of Madurese involvement in Java from the seventeenth century onwards. East Madura was ceded to the VOC in 1705 and West Madura in 1743. The island was not very fertile, and was initially of little economic value to the Dutch. Its primary product was people, who migrated in significant numbers to East Java in search of a better life. Madura was also a source of colonial troops, and this was its main value to the Dutch. In the second half of the nineteenth century (especially after 1870), however, Madura acquired greater economic value as the main supplier of salt to Dutch-governed areas of the archipelago, where salt was a profitable monopoly of the colonial government.

There were various arrangements for governing Madura, with authority divided among the lords of Bangkalan, Pamĕkasan and Sumĕnĕp. In 1817 the whole island became a single Residency, and in 1828 it was made a part of the Residency of Surabaya. Thereafter, Java and Madura were viewed together as a single administrative entity by the Dutch. Prior to the restoration of Dutch authority (after the British interregnum) in 1816, the Madurese lords had remained largely independent in internal affairs. After that time the Dutch took a more direct interest in the administration of Madura, and both the titles and prerogatives of the Madurese lords were reduced. Daendels and Raffles had favoured the Cakraningrat line of Sumĕnĕp and Bangkalan with the title of Sultan, but in the second half of the nineteenth century the Dutch refused to give this title as new Madurese lords succeeded. By 1887, the lords of Bangkalan, Pamĕkasan and Sumĕnĕp were reduced to the same status as *bupatis* in Java: they were merely aristocratic regency heads, under direct Dutch rule.

The experience of Bali was very different from that of Madura. The Dutch had encountered Balinese troops in Java in the eighteenth century and were also the principal purchasers of Balinese slaves, many of whom served in the VOC and colonial armies. But the Dutch had not become directly involved in this turbulent island. The British administration of Java went to war with the kings of Buleleng and Karangasĕm in 1814 in an attempt to end the slave trade. The Balinese submitted but the slave trade continued nonetheless. After 1816 the Dutch colonial government made several attempts to persuade the Balinese *rajas* (of whom there were about ten in 1839) to accept Dutch authority, but without success. Although the king of Badung agreed to provide soldiers for the colonial army, the Dutch had no significant influence on the island.

During the nineteenth century, Bali experienced a series of tragedies of natural, cultural, economic and political origin which give its history a wider significance and a pervasive grimness. The drama opened with the greatest natural explosion ever known, the consequence of which Bali shared with neighbouring islands. From April to July 1815, Mount Tambora on the island of Sumbawa erupted,

killing more people than the better-known eruption of Krakatau in 1883. Twelve
thousand were killed directly, an estimated 44000 died as a result of famines which
followed the eruption and the total death toll may have been up to 96000. At least
25000 died in Bali. The island was covered with 20 cm or more of volcanic ash
which destroyed its rice fields. This tragedy was accompanied by one of several
mouse plagues which devastated food supplies and by famine and epidemics.
A further major epidemic hit Bali in 1817 and a smallpox epidemic raged in
1828. Between 1850 and 1888 there were seven epidemics of smallpox and five
of cholera, four mouse plagues, outbreaks of dysentery and finally, in 1888, an
earthquake. The worst death toll was that of the smallpox plague of 1871 which
left 15000–18000 dead.

Bali's economy at the start of the nineteenth century still depended heavily on
the export of slaves, about two thousand being sold by the Balinese aristocracy
each year. In return they imported primarily copper coins, weapons and particularly opium, which was widely consumed in Balinese society. From the time of
the British interregnum, colonial governments in Batavia sought to restrict and
eventually to abolish the slave trade. This threatened the incomes of Balinese
aristocrats just when Mount Tambora was working its devastation upon Bali's
agricultural economy. But more positive ecological and political developments
then produced an economic transformation. Mount Tambora's ash deposits soon
enhanced soil fertility while the British colony of Singapore created a new market
for Balinese exports (and a British interest in Bali which the Dutch regarded with
much suspicion). Bali was transformed within two decades from an exporter of
slaves to an exporter of crops, particularly rice, coffee and indigo, and pig meat.
Rather than selling their people, Balinese lords now needed to keep them at work
in the fields. The Balinese aristocracy remained in control of this new enterprise,
as it had been of the slave trade. This was in sharp contrast to Minangkabau where,
as will be seen below, the development of new products in the late eighteenth
and early nineteenth centuries undermined the dominance of the old elite. But
competition among Balinese *puris* (courts) was enhanced by these new sources of
wealth, as was true also among the 'pepper *rajas*' of North Sumatra, as will be seen
below.

By about 1840, two factors had convinced the Dutch that Bali must be brought
under their influence: Balinese piracy and plundering of shipwrecks, and the
possibility of some other European power becoming established there. There was
little real reason to fear intervention by another European nation, for the Balinese
sense of independence was so strong that they could be expected to resist any
outside power. But the problem of Balinese piracy and plundering persisted. In
1841 a Dutch ambassador persuaded the *rajas* of Badung, Klungkung, Karangasĕm
and Buleleng to sign treaties recognising the sovereignty of the Dutch colonial
government. It was not the primary intention of the colonial government actually
to administer Bali, but merely to create a legal basis for the exclusion of any
other Western power. The Balinese *rajas* were told that these agreements would
not limit their own exercise of internal sovereignty, and they accepted them in
the hope of Dutch assistance in an attack against the kingdom of Mataram in
Lombok. Such military support was apparently promised by the Dutch emissary,
contrary to his instructions, and to that extent these agreements rested upon
deception.

In 1842–3 these *rajas* and those of Tabanan and Lombok (which was governed by a line of kings from Karangasěm) signed further treaties designed to end the more immediate problem of the plundering of shipwrecks. These proved to be ineffective, and plundering continued. The king of Buleleng now became angry when the Dutch seemed to place a wider interpretation upon his surrender of sovereignty, and in 1844 he refused to ratify the agreements. The king of Karangasěm also refused. Tensions mounted while the Balinese *rajas* prepared for war. Late in 1845 Buleleng and Karangasěm allied in an attempt to conquer other Balinese states. The Dutch felt obliged to act. In 1846 they successfully attacked Buleleng, but this was merely the first step in a long and bitter struggle. The senior king of Bali, the Dewa Agung of Klungkung, along with most of the other *rajas*, secretly supported the attempts of Buleleng and Karangasěm to resist the Dutch, and began to construct a military coalition. The Dutch attacked again in 1848, but faced greater resistance than they had expected and were defeated. In 1849 they attacked for the third time. This campaign was successful in North Bali. When, however, the colonial forces turned their attention to South Bali, they found themselves facing formidable difficulties. The Danish trader Mads Lange intervened and made it possible for the Dutch government forces to avoid a decisive battle there.

From 1849 to about 1882, the colonial government watched over, but did not significantly interfere in, the internal affairs of South and East Bali (Klungkung, Badung, Tabanan, Gianyar, Měngwi, Bangli and Karangasěm). After a domestic rebellion in Buleleng in 1853, however, the Dutch took more direct control of North and West Bali (Buleleng and Jěmbrana). Dutch administrators were introduced there in 1855–6 for the first time, and Dutch control grew thereafter despite isolated outbreaks of Balinese resistance. In 1882 Bali and Lombok were united as a single Residency of the Netherlands East Indies, and North Bali came under direct Dutch rule.

The kings of South and East Bali were shocked by the announcement of this new Residency of Bali, which appeared to assert a degree of colonial authority over the whole island to which they had never assented. The Dutch assured them, however, that no alteration in their status was intended and confirmed this by adopting a policy of non-interference in their affairs. This area of Bali meanwhile turned into a vast battlefield after 1883 as internecine conflicts and intrigues spread. In 1885 the king of Gianyar offered his land to the colonial government as a means of saving himself from attacks launched by Klungkung, Bangli and Měngwi. But Batavia refused him. This clear evidence that the Dutch would not intervene undermined Klungkung's attempt to forge a united front among the *rajas* and encouraged further conflict. In 1891 the king of Měngwi was defeated and killed and his kingdom taken over by Badung. Now the main combatants in South Bali were Klungkung and Karangasěm. Because the Balinese kingdom on Lombok was the overlord of Karangasěm, the civil war now involved Lombok as well.

While Balinese lords ruled Lombok, its population was partly Hindu Balinese and partly indigenous Sasak Muslims. The various Dutch attempts to impose influence in Bali also involved Lombok, and in 1843 the Balinese *raja* of Lombok accepted Dutch sovereignty. He subsequently showed himself to be willing to agree to various Dutch demands. Indeed, in 1849 he supported the colonial campaign in Bali by attacking Karangasěm; thereafter Karangasěm was ruled by a line of the Lombok dynasty. But the colonial government sought a pretext for more direct rule over Lombok. From 1877 onwards, the Dutch desire to control opium-smuggling and slavery, and to maintain Dutch prestige in the area, made the imposition of colonial rule nearly inevitable.

When in 1891 the Balinese king of Lombok levied his Sasak subjects to fight in Bali, he precipitated a Sasak uprising led by a religious teacher of the Naqshabandiyya order. This provided Batavia with a justification for intervention. The Dutch imposed a blockade, which proved ineffective, so in 1894 they invaded. Their first expeditionary force was badly defeated by a Balinese counterattack and reinforcements had to be brought in. The fighting was bitter, but finally the *raja's* capital of Mataram was conquered and after it the last Balinese stronghold at Cakranĕgara. There the Balinese went down in a *puputan*, a final battle, a horrific end to resistance of a kind which would soon follow in South Bali as well.

As a consequence of the Dutch conquest of Lombok, Karangsĕm in East Bali became a Dutch dependency, which was called a 'government land' (*gouvernements-landschap*.) This status provided Gusti Gĕde Jĕlantik, the lord of Karangasĕm, Dutch protection from his enemies. This seemed so attractive to the beleaguered lord of Gianyar that he offered to become a Dutch dependant in 1900 and was accepted. By anticipating Dutch dominion as inevitable, these two lords employed the new political realities of the Indonesian archipelago to protect themselves. The Dewa Agung of Klungkung protested at this extension of Dutch authority, to no avail.

By the turn of the twentieth century, the Dutch were adopting the Ethical policy, which is discussed in Chapter 13. In the case of Bali – which remained of little economic value to Batavia – the Dutch were particularly concerned to suppress arbitrary rule, slavery and opium smuggling, the last not in order to abolish opium usage but in order to bring it within the government's own very profitable opium arrangements. The rarely practised but culturally significant custom of burning widows alive at the cremation of their royal husbands also greatly offended the Dutch. Indeed, Governor-General W. Rooseboom (1898–1904) was so angry at being unable to prevent a widow-burning at Tabanan in 1903 (probably the last to take place) that he submitted his resignation to the Minister of Colonies, but was refused. The government pressured Balinese lords on this issue and by 1905 all had agreed to the abolition of widow-burning.

Balinese independence finally ended in a horrific fashion. The plundering of a shipwreck in 1904 provided the Dutch with an occasion for military intervention. They attacked in 1906. The two *raja* families of Badung responded in a way that has haunted Indonesian history ever since. First at Den Pasar and then at Pamĕcutan, they ritually purified themselves for death, dressed in white, and, armed only with lances and *krises*, stormed out to their final battle (*puputan*). As Dutch guns cut down the *rajas* and their families, including women and children, the Balinese royalty paused only to kill their wounded, and then marched forward again until virtually all were dead. Probably over a thousand died in these *puputans*. The colonial forces moved on to Tabanan, where the *raja* surrendered but then committed suicide with his son. Karangasĕm, Klungkung, Bangli and Gianyar were also forced to accept more direct Dutch authority. The last act in Bali's tragedy occurred in 1908. The senior king of Bali, the Dewa Agung of Klungkung, objected to the introduction of the government's opium administration in April 1908 and launched a final and futile attempt to resist Dutch rule. This precipitated the last Dutch expedition of conquest to Bali. The Dewa Agung and his followers were cut down in the last *puputan*. Bali's independence was at an end. The royal families who survived Dutch conquest with some of their status and prerogatives intact were those who had anticipated colonial rule and sought an accommodation in advance of conquest.

Farther east, the remaining islands of Nusa Těnggara (Lesser Sunda Islands), a term which includes Lombok, were brought under effective Dutch rule only in the first decade of the twentieth century. The main islands are Sumbawa, Flores, Sumba, Savu, Roti, Timor and the Solor and Alor groups. Flores was the main target of Dutch activity in the nineteenth century. Slave-trading and the plundering of shipwrecks in this area led to expeditions against Flores in 1838 and 1846. The Portuguese still governed East Timor and laid claim to other areas, but in 1859 they recognised Dutch claims to Flores. In 1890 a further Dutch military expedition was sent there to protect a tin-exploration mission. A rebellion in 1907 led to a colonial expeditionary force sweeping through the whole of Flores in 1907–8, putting down resistance everywhere, but not ending local animosity towards Dutch rule. The other areas of Nusa Těnggara were also brought under definitive Dutch rule in the years 1905–7. The Portuguese, however, remained in control of East Timor.

The cultural, economic and demographic character of Nusa Těnggara was significantly affected by Dutch expansion. Except for providing soldiers for the VOC, Savu had remained relatively isolated before the nineteenth century, resisting both Islam and Christianity, although there had been some movement of Savunese to Sumba. From about 1860 Savu was forced open to the outside world. One of the first consequences was a smallpox epidemic which killed between one-third and one-half of the population of Savu in 1869. Christian missionary work also began there. Christian converts were rejected by Savunese society, quite unlike the circumstances on Roti, and these Christian Savunese were now encouraged to settle in larger numbers on Sumba in an effort to counteract the spread of Islam there, and on Timor (but in smaller numbers). At the same time Christian Rotinese were being encouraged to settle on Timor. The palm-tapping economies of the Rotinese and Savunese were thus transported to Sumba and Timor. On both of the islands the immigrants formed a favoured and educated elite, whom the Dutch defended from local attacks. In the twentieth century Rotinese and Savunese Christians were to dominate both government service and the anti-colonial movements on Timor. Important changes also followed the introduction of horse-raising for export in Sumba from the 1840s and of Balinese cattle in Timor from about 1910; these developments are analysed in detail by Fox.

South Sulawesi was a great challenge to the Dutch. As the main ally of the VOC, Bone had become the most powerful state in the area. In 1814 and 1816 Bone and other South Sulawesi states attacked the British, but were defeated. When the Dutch returned in 1816 the hostilities ceased, but tensions grew between the Dutch and Bone. Many South Sulawesi rulers believed that their previous relations with the Dutch had been cancelled by the Dutch surrender to the British in 1811, and that the Treaty of Bungaya (1667) no longer had legal force. In 1824 Governor-General van der Capellen visited the region and persuaded the other states of South Sulawesi to renew the Treaty of Bungaya, but Bone refused. Upon van der

Capellen's departure, the queen of Bone led the Bugis states into war, conquered Dutch-governed districts and slaughtered two Dutch garrisons.

In 1825 the Dutch and the Makasarese forces of Gowa defeated Bone, but when the Java War (1825–30) broke out, all but an absolutely essential minimum of colonial troops were withdrawn to Java, thereby enabling Bone to resume its hostile posture. Not until 1838 did Bone renew the Treaty of Bungaya. This did not, however, establish Dutch supremacy. Rebellions continued to break out, both because of indigenous conflict and because of opposition to Dutch rule. Colonial forces again fought major campaigns in 1858–60, but the final and decisive conquest occurred only in 1905–6, when the resistance of the Bugis and Makasarese states was broken. In 1905 the Dutch also extended their power over the animist and head-hunting Toraja people of Central Sulawesi, in the face of bitter resistance.

The Dutch faced problems after the British interregnum even in Ambon, the oldest of their directly governed districts in Indonesia. The Ambonese had been pleased by the two periods of British administration (1796–1803, 1810–17), and had lost much of their awe for Dutch power. When the Dutch administration returned in 1817, it seemed unwilling to support the Protestant church to the extent which Ambonese thought proper. This was a major cause of the violence which immediately erupted. An Ambonese Christian soldier named Thomas Matulesia (?1783–1817), also known as Pattimura, led a rebellion on Saparua, took the Dutch fortress there and repelled the colonial force sent against him. After the Dutch Resident on Saparua and his family (except for one small child) were murdered, the Dutch sent reinforcements from Batavia. The rebels were then defeated and Matulesia surrendered. In December 1817 he was hanged in Ambon with three others. Ambon gradually returned to its role as the most loyal of all Dutch territories in Indonesia. In the later years of the nineteenth century, the ending of the government clove monopoly created an economic crisis in Ambon. For the more educated Ambonese – who were overwhelmingly Christian rather than Muslim – the main opportunity for economic advancement now lay in service with the expanding colonial government, either as bureaucrats or as soldiers. The special role which they thus came to play elsewhere in the Indonesian archipelago was to make Ambonese Christians the objects of suspicion in the eyes of twentieth-century nationalists.

The eastern extremity of contemporary Indonesia, Irian Jaya (West New Guinea), was the last area to fall under Dutch jurisdiction. In 1828 Fort Du Bus was established at what is now Lobo, solely to prevent any other power from settling there. It was soon concluded that, so far as could then be seen, there was nothing to attract anyone on this vast and remote island, populated by bands of Stone Age peoples. Fort Du Bus was located in a malarial region and took a great toll in men and money; it was abandoned in 1836. Irian was in fact only brought under permanent Dutch occupation after 1898, especially in the period 1919–28.

The Aru and Tanimbar island groups to the west of Irian were of little interest to the Dutch. Only Aru had much economic value as a source of pearls and mother-of-pearl, as well as birds of paradise. The VOC had monopolised the trade between Banda and Aru from the 1620s, but in the general VOC withdrawal in the late eighteenth century this trade had been taken over by Bugis and Makasarese. Only after 1882 were Aru and Tanimbar brought under regular Dutch administration.

In Kalimantan (Borneo) there emerged a more direct competition between expanding imperial interests. In the early nineteenth century, both Britain and the Netherlands had interests there which were fairly clearly defined. For the British the main issue was strategic: Kalimantan itself was of little interest, but because it flanked the sailing routes between India and China, the British could not ignore the possible establishment of any other European power there, especially in West and North Kalimantan. The Dutch interest was in principle more colonial: Kalimantan lay on the north side of the Java Sea and was a centre for pirates and anti-Dutch Chinese. Although the interior was unknown and apparently of little value, the Dutch had some interest in controlling the south and west coasts.

By the late 1820s and 1830s the Dutch had concluded treaties with Pontianak, Měmpawah, Sambas and other small west-coast states. But Dutch operations there were on a very small scale. In 1834, for instance, the entire Dutch garrison at Měmpawah consisted of one Indonesian officer and four policemen. In some areas, after the treaties of the 1830s were signed the Dutch had no further relations until the 1840s. At Banjarmasin in southeast Kalimantan there had been VOC posts, but in 1809 Daendels had withdrawn the post. In 1817 the Dutch returned and the Sultan of Banjarmasin signed several districts over to Dutch rule, including Kotawaringin (but the Dutch did not bother to open an office there). In 1826 further Banjarmasin coastal districts were signed over to the colonial government, but the Sultan remained sovereign in his own lands. Down to 1840, Dutch interest was wholly restricted to the coast of Kalimantan, and even there little reality attached to Dutch claims of predominance.

Dutch imperial interest in Kalimantan was suddenly stimulated by the intervention of the Englishman James Brooke (1803–68) in Sarawak. Brooke used his modest inheritance to buy an armed yacht, and in 1839 he sailed to Singapore and thence to Sarawak in search of adventure. He intervened in a civil war there in support of a Brunei prince, and in 1841 he was rewarded (after some difficulty with the prince) by being made governor of the area of Kucing, which became the First Division of Brooke's extraordinary private empire. The expanding territorial authority of James Brooke and his two successors, the three 'white rajahs' of Sarawak, caused embarrassment in London and much anxiety in Dutch circles. The spectre of intervention by other Europeans had suddenly turned into reality, and the lackadaisical Dutch attitude towards Kalimantan was converted into a more active policy of imperial expansion. In the 1840s and 1850s the Dutch intervened in several areas, putting down internal disputes and regulating relations with new treaties. From 1846 on, coal mines began to be opened in South and East Kalimantan, whereby the island acquired greater economic value to the colonial regime.

In West and Southeast Kalimantan the new Dutch attitude produced significant resistance. The Chinese *kongsis* (associations) which controlled the gold mines of the Pontianak-Sambas area were in bitter dispute with each other over control of the declining gold resources. Despite Dutch intervention, this rivalry persisted, sporadic hostilities breaking out from 1850 to 1854. In the end the Dutch colonial forces were victorious, but disturbances continued in this area thereafter.

Banjarmasin was the scene of a more familiar form of Indonesian resistance. When Sultan Adam (r. 1825–57) died in 1857, the Dutch elevated his grandson Tamjidillah to be Sultan (r. 1857–9). The Crown prince Abdul Rakhman, Sultan

Adam's son and Tamjidillah's father, had died in 1852 and since then it had not been clear who would succeed the old Sultan. Tamjidillah was Abdul Rakhman's eldest son, but he was not popular in Banjarmasin, both because his mother was Chinese rather than a Banjarese aristocrat and because he had a taste for alcohol, which offended Islamic sensibilities. Prince Hidayatullah, a younger son of Abdul Rakhman by an aristocratic mother, was a more popular candidate. But Tamjidillah was preferred by the Dutch because he promised them greater concessions; their determination to install him as Sultan in the face of popular discontent precipitated tensions which shortly led to the Banjarmasin War (1859–63).

In April 1859 a major rebellion broke out in Banjarmasin led by a prince from a line of the royal family whose power had been usurped in the eighteenth century, Pangeran Antasari, and two peasant leaders. They attacked a Dutch coal mine and European missionary stations, killing Europeans whom they encountered there. The Dutch brought in reinforcements and had regained the military initiative by the end of 1859, but the war took a heavy toll of Dutch finances and manpower as rural Islamic leaders led a courageous and determined resistance. In June 1859 the Dutch forced Tamjidillah to abandon his throne and exiled him to Bogor in West Java. In 1860 they declared the Sultanate of Banjarmasin to be 'lapsed' and announced direct colonial rule. Hidayatullah joined the side of the resistance but surrendered early in 1862 and was exiled to Cianjur in West Java. After his exile, Antasari became the principal focus of loyalty for those who wished to resist Dutch conquest, until his own death from smallpox in October 1862. Major hostilities carried on until 1863, with more sporadic resistance thereafter. The descendants of Antasari allied with those of a major Muslim Dayak leader named Surapati (d. 1875) and together they maintained resistance for many years in an attempt to preserve the Sultanate from colonial conquest. Finally, in 1905 Sultan Muhammad Sĕman of the Antasari family was killed, ending the line of royal leadership. The last resistance to Dutch rule ended in 1906.

Some of the most protracted warfare associated with the new phase of Dutch expansionism occurred in Sumatra. This great island had long been of interest to the Dutch. It occupied a crucial strategic position, was an area of rivalry with the British and had pepper and other valuable products. The VOC had been active in several areas of Sumatra. It was nonetheless true there, as elsewhere, that the decline of the VOC in the eighteenth century and the subsequent British interregnum meant that the Dutch had to rebuild and extend their influence in Sumatra after 1816 virtually from nothing.

In South Sumatra, the Sultanate of Palembang had long had contacts with the Dutch. It was important for its strategic position, its pepper and its sovereignty over the islands of Bangka and Bĕlitung. Tin had been discovered in Bangka at the beginning of the eighteenth century. After the decline of the VOC later that century, the tin mines had acquired renewed importance and higher productivity early in the nineteenth century. Bĕlitung also had tin, and was occupied by the Dutch in 1817 over British protests. The main actor in the drama of Palembang, Sultan Mahmud Badaruddin (r. 1804–12, 1813, 1818–21), was no friend of the Dutch. In the confusions surrounding the British conquest of Java in 1811, he attacked and slaughtered the eighty-seven men (twenty-four of them Dutch) at the Dutch garrison in Palembang. Nor was he more cooperative towards the British.

Consequently, in 1812 the British attacked Palembang, sacked the court, and installed Badaruddin's younger brother as Sultan Ahmad Najamuddin (r. 1812–13, 1813–18). Badaruddin fled but in 1813 he submitted and again occupied the throne for just over one month, until Raffles rejected this arrangement (which had been made by the Resident of Palembang) and put Najamuddin back on the throne. The tensions between these two brothers persisted until after the Dutch returned in 1816. The Dutch were then unable to exercise any real control, and the British complicated matters by interfering in Palembang affairs from their post at Běngkulu (Bencoolen).

In 1818 a Dutch expedition was sent against Palembang and Najamuddin was exiled to Batavia. When this did not end Palembang's independence, a further expedition was dispatched in 1819, but it was defeated by Badaruddin. In 1821 the Dutch put together a large force of over 4000 troops which was, however, repelled in its first attack. Its second assault succeeded, and Badaruddin was sent into exile on Těrnate. Palěmbang was now near the end of its independence. Najamuddin's eldest son was made Sultan, also with the name Ahmad Najamuddin (r. 1821–3). In 1823 the Dutch placed Palembang under their direct rule and the Sultan was given a pension. He and his courtiers were dissatisfied. In 1824 they first attempted to poison the Dutch garrison, and their subsequent attack upon it was easily repulsed. The Sultan fled but surrendered in 1825 and was exiled to Banda, whence he was moved in 1841 to Měnado. There was a last rebellion in 1849, which the Dutch suppressed.

Jambi had had relations with the VOC since the seventeenth century, but in 1724 the VOC post there had been abandoned. Dutch involvement began anew in 1833 when Sultan Muhammad Fakhruddin (r. ?1833–41) sought and received Dutch help against pirates, but then invaded districts of Palembang. He was driven back by Palembang forces, and the Dutch used this opportunity to impose a treaty upon the Sultan recognising Dutch sovereignty (1834). A colonial garrison was established downriver at Muarakumpe. In 1855 Sultan Abdul Rahman Nasiruddin (r. 1841–55) was succeeded by Ratu Taha Saifuddin (r. 1855–8), whose refusal to sign a treaty precipitated a Dutch attack in 1858. Taha fled into the interior, taking the most important regalia with him. His Dutch-supported successors recognised Dutch sovereignty, but Taha and his supporters controlled much of the interior and inspired resistance for many decades. He was finally killed in the interior by a government patrol in 1904. In 1899 the last Sultan recognised by the Dutch, Ahmad Zainuddin (r. 1885–99), retired. The Dutch and the elite of Jambi were unable to agree upon a successor, so the Dutch Resident of Palembang was placed in charge of Jambi in 1901. Fresh resistance broke out, which military expeditions into the interior districts of Jambi failed to suppress until 1907.

In the west coast Minangkabau districts, Dutch expansionism clashed violently with the first major Islamic revival movement of Indonesia. Minangkabau has been a centre of social, religious and political change since the late eighteenth century, and consequently has a significance for the rest of Indonesia which is greater than that of many other regions of the outer islands.

A system of royal government had been imposed in Minangkabau by Adityavarman (r. c. 1356–75), a protégé of Majapahit. Minangkabau began to be Islamised in the sixteenth century, and a system of three kings then emerged: Raja Alam (king of the world), Raja Adat (king of customary law) and Raja Ibadat (king of the Islamic religion). Royal authority rested primarily upon the control of gold. The villages supporting royal interests occupied the main gold-producing areas (in the Tanah Datar district) and the main export routes, and followed the system of customary law called *Kota Piliang*. By the 1780s, gold supplies were running out and the old order of Minangkabau society was threatened by the rise of new sources of prosperity, especially coffee, salt, gambier and textiles. These were centred in the hill areas of Agam and Limapuluh Kota districts, in villages which followed a different customary law system called *Bodi Caniago* and which traded primarily with the Americans and the British (whose establishment of Penang in 1786 greatly stimulated this commercial revolution).

Out of this new commercial activity arose an Islamic reform movement, which began in Agam in the 1780s. After about 1803–4, this became known as the Padri movement because of the leadership of the *orang Pidari*, the 'men of Pĕdir' who had made the pilgrimage to Mecca via the Acehnese port of Pĕdir. The reform movement derived its impetus from Agam and Limapuluh Kota, from hill districts, from *Bodi Caniago* villages, and from merchants who sought protection in a revitalised Islamic law from the prevailing violence and insecurity which threatened their contracts, their goods and their persons. Sufi teachers, especially of the Shattariyya order, played important roles, although in later stages of the movement there were signs of anti-Sufi sentiments.

A group of three *hajis* (pilgrims) who returned to Minangkabau in 1803 or 1804 were inspired by the conquest of Mecca (early in 1803) by the puritanical Wahhabi reformers, and were similarly willing to use violence to reform Minangkabau society. The Padri movement opposed gambling, cockfighting, aspects of the local matriarchal customary law (especially concerning inheritance), the use of opium, strong drink, tobacco and betel nut, as well as the generally lax observance of the formal ritual obligations of Islam. They did not, however, share all the puritanism of the Wahhabi movement in Arabia, for they did not oppose reverence for saints or holy places.

The main Padri leaders were accorded the Minangkabau title of respect for religious teachers, *tuanku;* the most prominent among them was Tuanku Imam Bonjol (1772–1864). Dutch observers tended to see the conflict in terms of Islam versus *adat* (customary law), or of *tuanku* (religious leaders) versus *pĕnghulu* (clan heads, the *adat* or 'secular' leaders). This assumption later became a principle of Dutch administration here as elsewhere in Indonesia, as will be seen below. This does not, however, adequately depict the complex social and theological issues involved in the Padri movement, as preceding paragraphs show. Indeed, *tuankus* were in dispute among themselves about both the aims and the methods of the reform movement, and *pĕnghulus* existed who were supporters of it.

In the course of the civil war which grew out of the attempts at reform, the Padris faced greatest resistance in Tanah Datar and in plains areas, i.e. in those regions least involved in the commercial revolution. But the reformers won victory upon victory. In 1815 most of the Minangkabau royal family was murdered in Tanah Datar, and the Padri victory was nearly complete. Now the Padris spread into South Tapanuli and began the Islamisation of the pagan Bataks there. But the military success of the Padris was soon threatened by the return of the Dutch (after the British interregnum) to Padang in 1819. Anti-Padri *pĕnghulus* and the remnants of the royal family turned to the Dutch for support. In February 1821 they signed a treaty surrendering Minangkabau, over which they no longer held any real authority, to Dutch sovereignty. The first Dutch attack upon the Padris followed shortly thereafter, and the Padri War (1821–38) began.

The colonial forces found that they faced a formidable enemy. Their victories were mixed with failures, including a serious defeat in Lintau in 1823. During the Java War (1825–30) the Dutch were unable to act decisively, but reinforcements later became available. By this time Imam Bonjol had Acehnese support, but nonetheless by 1832 the Padris seemed to be subdued. In 1833, however, the war resumed and renewed colonial offensives were required. The economic lifelines of Minangkabau resistance were progressively cut as the Dutch sealed off the west coast and then the east coast outlets for Minangkabau trade. In 1837 the fortified town of Bonjol was finally taken. Tuanku Imam Bonjol fled but then surrendered. He was exiled first to Priangan, then to Ambon, and finally to Měnado, where he died in 1864. The Padri War ended with a final colonial victory at Daludalu at the end of 1838.

Dutch rule was now imposed throughout Minangkabau. The colonial government relied upon the 'adat chiefs' (the pěnghulus) to counteract what it saw as Islamic fanaticism. The Dutch thereby artificially enhanced the distinction between customary law (adat) and Islam in Minangkabau society, and contributed to a decline in the prestige of the pěnghulus. The colonial government did not allow Minangkabau royalty to regain any autonomous power, but treated them as mere regents (bupatis), on the Javanese model.

Despite their military defeat, the Padris had left a deep and lasting mark upon Minangkabau society. A strong commitment to Islamic orthodoxy remained. In the fluid balance between adat and Islam, the role of Islam as a part of the whole set of rules which governed Minangkabau society had been greatly increased. Under Dutch rule, there was indeed a further wave of reform in the mid-nineteenth century, when the Qadiriyya and especially the Naqshabandiyya orders of Sufism, with a greater concern for orthodox ritual, forced the Shattariyya order to lose its predominant position in the area.

The Dutch advance in Sumatra now seemed to be moving inexorably up to the boundaries of Aceh. A treaty was signed with Indĕragiri in 1838, Singkil and Barus were occupied in 1839–40, and in 1840 a protection treaty with Siak was near completion. As a result of the Padri War, Dutch influence also permeated the Batak areas to the north of Minangkabau. The Bataks were a fierce and violent pagan people whose religious life was a combination of animism, magic and old Hindu (or Hindu-Javanese) influences. The Padris had supported the spread of Islam among the Bataks, and from the 1850s the Dutch encouraged Christianisation and began to suppress cannibalism. The Bataks had no higher political organisation, except for a certain loyalty to a divine king called Si Singamangaraja at Bangkara. Resistance to the Dutch was therefore not unified, but the colonial army was obliged to fight several fierce campaigns. In 1872 occurred what is known as the Batak War, which ended in victory for the Dutch and their local allies, but Batak resistance was not finally crushed until 1895.

The apparently inexorable Dutch advance was, however, halted temporarily by the same factor which had in part encouraged it: the threat of British influence in the area. Throughout the nineteenth century, the British rather than the Dutch were the most powerful naval and commercial force in the Malay-Indonesian area.

The British were vitally interested in anything which happened in the Straits of Malacca, through which the China-India trade routes passed. With the foundation of Penang (1786) and Singapore (1819) British commercial contacts with Sumatra expanded greatly. To avoid Anglo-Dutch conflict in the Straits, in March 1824 the Treaty of London defined British and Dutch spheres of interest. In essence, the British sphere contained the Malay Peninsula and the Dutch contained Sumatra. Dutch Malacca and Dutch posts in India were turned over to the British and British sovereignty over Singapore was recognised; Běngkulu in Sumatra was surrendered to the Dutch. There were two particularly important aspects of this Treaty for future events. First, British trade with Sumatra was not to be restricted irrespective of Dutch political dominance there. And second, the independence of Aceh was guaranteed, but the Dutch were supposed to exercise an ill-defined moderating influence over Aceh.

As the Dutch seemed about to subdue all of Sumatra up to the borders of Aceh, the merchants of Singapore and Penang objected that Dutch tariffs were restricting their trade, contrary to the Treaty of London. The Dutch gave in, being anxious not to offend the British. In 1842–4 they withdrew their posts on the east coast north of Palembang and broke off negotiations for a treaty with Siak. Their garrison near Jambi remained on the grounds that it was essential for the defence of Palembang, but the discriminatory tariffs there were suspended. For several years Dutch expansionism was restricted to Bali, Nusa Těnggara, Kalimantan and Sulawesi, the areas described earlier in this chapter. In the west of the archipelago, they extended their influence only to the pagan island of Nias, which was of little commercial interest to the British. A treaty had been signed there in 1825 to end slave trading, which nevertheless continued, most of the slaves being sold in Padang and Singapore (despite Raffles's official abolition of slavery there). In 1840 a Dutch office was opened at Gunungsitoli. Military expeditions were required in 1847, 1855 and 1863 to establish Dutch authority over Nias.

Aceh was now expanding as a commercial and political power. By the 1820s it produced over half of the world's supply of pepper. The spread of pepper production meant independent sources of wealth for many lords of small ports who were nominally vassals of Aceh. As Europeans and Americans competed for access to this pepper, the northern part of Sumatra became a centre of political disintegration. The 'pepper rajas' acted independently and American, British and French gunboats went into action as a result of various violent incidents. But a vigorous and capable new Acehnese leader, Tuanku Ibrahim, began to restore order and the authority of the Sultanate, for the first time since the great days of the seventeenth century. During the reign of his brother Sultan Muhammad Syah (r. 1823–38), Tuanku Ibrahim emerged as the most powerful force in the Sultanate. In 1838 he became guardian to the heir Sulaiman (nominally Sultan from 1838 to his death in 1857), and from 1838 to 1870 Tuanku Ibrahim in fact ruled Aceh, taking the title of Sultan Ali Alauddin Mansur Syah. His able rule was threatened only by Sulaiman's abortive attempts to claim his throne in 1850–7.

Tuanku Ibrahim played the 'pepper rajas' off against each other, and in 1854 sent an expedition down the east coast which imposed his authority in Langkat, Děli and Sěrdang. Aceh was thus moving south just when the Dutch had temporarily suspended their northward advance. A clash between these two imperial powers was inevitable. Aceh was too powerful and wealthy for the Dutch to allow it to continue as an independent state. Dutch fears of intervention there by another European power were also growing. Various rumours and incidents suggested that Aceh might allow such an intervention. In 1852 it was reported that an Acehnese emissary had been received by the French Emperor Napoleon III (r. 1852–70). In 1869 it was learned that the Acehnese had appealed to the Turks for protection. The Dutch now realised that the Treaty of London, by ruling out British involvement in Aceh and obliging the Dutch to respect its independence, effectively reserved Aceh for intervention by any power other than Britain or the Netherlands. Not surprisingly, expansionist pressures began to grow again in Dutch circles.

In 1857 the suspended negotiations with Siak were resumed and resulted in a treaty in 1858 by which Siak became Dutch territory. The second article of this treaty defined the boundaries of Siak in an exaggerated fashion, reaching as far north as Alas and Langkat and thus including pepper ports which were both under Aceh's jurisdiction and important to British trade. The British objected and in 1863–5 sent gunboats to these pepper ports. Several Sumatran states, most importantly Aceh, concluded that the British (their main trading partner) would be willing to defend them against the Dutch. In Batavia the Council of the Indies realised that the Siak treaty infringed upon Aceh's territory, but felt that they could not afford to back down and reveal again the weakness which the withdrawal of the 1840s had shown. The die was cast.

British policy towards Aceh now changed. Dutch commercial policy had grown more liberal since 1848, and by the late 1860s it no longer seemed essential, or indeed feasible, to insist on independence for Aceh. As the European competition for colonies accelerated, London decided that it would be better to let the Dutch have Aceh than a stronger power such as the French or the Americans. The result was the November 1871 Anglo-Dutch Treaty of Sumatra which, with two related treaties, represented one of the greatest trade-offs of the imperialist age. The Dutch surrendered the Gold Coast in Africa to the British, the British allowed the shipment of Indian contract labourers to Dutch Surinam in South America, the Dutch were given an entirely free hand in Sumatra with British approval, and British and Dutch commerce were to have equal rights there from Siak to the north. This treaty represented a public pronouncement that the Dutch intended to take Aceh, a pronouncement which in this imperialist age had to be acted upon with haste. For both the British and the Dutch this trade-off meant war: by mid-1873 the British were involved in the Ashanti War in Africa and the Dutch in the Aceh War.

Early in 1873, the American Consul in Singapore had discussions with an Acehnese emissary about a possible Acehnese-American treaty. The Dutch saw this as a justification for intervention; in March they bombarded the Acehnese capital Banda Aceh (Kutaraja) and in April they landed a force of 3000 men. But they had misjudged the opposition; their force was beaten into a withdrawal by the Acehnese with the loss of its General and eighty men. The Dutch now resorted to a blockade and the Acehnese gathered to do battle; estimates of their numbers varied from 10000 to 100000. The colonial advance had now encountered its wealthiest, most determined, most organised, best armed and most fiercely independent opponent. In his last months of formal independence, Sultan Mahmud Syah (r. 1870–4) appealed to the Turks, the British, the Americans and the French for support. He got nothing but pious sentiments from the Turks (who were in any case powerless to help), a flat rejection from the British, encouragement from the American Consul but rejection by Washington, and no reply at all from the French. The Acehnese were on their own.

A second Dutch expedition was dispatched late in 1873. This was the largest they had ever assembled in Indonesia: 8500 troops, 4300 servants and coolies, with a further reserve of 1500 troops soon added. Both the colonial force and the Acehnese suffered greatly from cholera and other diseases. Between November 1873 and April 1874, 1400 men died in the colonial army. The Acehnese decided to abandon Banda Aceh, and the Dutch moved in in January 1874, believing that they had thereby won the war. They announced that Aceh was annexed and the Sultanate abolished. While this was sufficient to prevent other foreign powers from intervening, it did nothing to abate Acehnese resistance. Sultan Mahmud and his followers withdrew to the hills, where Mahmud died of cholera. A young grandson of Tuanku Ibrahim named Tuanku Muhammad Daud Syah was proclaimed by the Acehnese to be Sultan Ibrahim Mansur Syah (r. 1875–1907).

The Sultanate and Acehnese resistance continued for many decades after the Dutch annexation. The colonial forces were now, in effect, besieged in Banda Aceh, losing some 150 men each month from cholera. The rulers of Acehnese ports quickly made nominal submissions to the Dutch in order to be freed from the blockade, but then used their incomes to support the resistance forces in the interior. The Dutch hoped that they might finalise their dominance by a treaty of the kind they had won elsewhere in the archipelago, but their abolition of the Sultanate made negotiations impossible. Since the Acehnese refused to surrender, outright conquest was the only option remaining to the Dutch.

The Aceh War was a long and bitter struggle. As the Dutch advanced, bombarding and burning villages, the population fled to the hills and maintained their resistance. In 1881 the Dutch declared the war to be over, one of the most fanciful pronouncements of colonialism. The guerrilla resistance came to be dominated by religious leaders, the *ulamas,* among whom the most famous was Teungku Cik di Tiro (1836–91), and the resistance assumed the nature of a Holy War of Muslims against unbelievers. The Dutch found that they had won nothing except what was permanently occupied by their garrisons. The costs of this war were so huge that major economies were required in other areas of the colonial budget and taxes on Indonesians had to be increased. In 1884–5 a retrenchment was ordered, and much of the countryside relapsed to Acehnese control.

The Dutch finally found a solution to their dilemma in the policies of two men: Dr Christiaan Snouck Hurgronje (1857–1936) and Joannes Benedictus van Heutsz (1851–1924). Snouck Hurgronje was the foremost Dutch scholar of Islam; from 1891 to 1906 he was principal adviser to the colonial government on Islamic and indigenous Indonesian matters, and he ended his days as a professor of Leiden University. He maintained that nothing could be done to appease the fanatical resistance of the *ulamas,* so they should be utterly crushed and reliance placed upon the *uleëbalang* (seen as the *adat* or 'secular' chiefs). This would, however, be a very expensive policy. But by now economic considerations were playing a role in determining Dutch policy alongside imperial motivations. Before about 1880, few believed North Sumatra to have much economic potential, but from that time onwards these views began to change. Meanwhile – as will be seen in

Chapter 13 – the Netherlands East Indies oil industry was developing. In 1898 the future of 'de Koninklijke' (see Chapter 13) seemed threatened by both rising American competition and declining output from its existing oil field. Oil had meanwhile been discovered further north in areas involved in the Aceh fighting. 'De Koninklijke' promptly mobilised its very considerable political connections in The Hague and Batavia to press for military measures which would secure access to these more northerly reserves. Vigorous military action followed, under the command of van Heutsz, a soldier who had served in Aceh for long periods since 1874. He was appointed Governor of Aceh (1898–1904) and thereupon carried out the campaigns which gave Aceh at last a semblance of pacification, with Snouck Hurgronje at his side until 1903. The Dutch sought out amenable *uleëbalangs*, whom they perceived to be the equivalent of Javanese *bupatis* or Minangkabau *pĕnghulus*: *adat* leaders who would counterbalance Islamic political influence. And slowly the *uleëbalangs* compromised with the Dutch, thereby creating a deep and eventually bloody division between them and much of Acehnese society. Snouck Hurgronje also proposed a new form of political agreement with local potentates, the so-called Short Declaration (*Korte Verklaring*), which was first introduced in Aceh in 1898 and thereafter became the standard form of agreement throughout the archipelago. It replaced long and cumbersome contracts with individual rulers with a standard short agreement whereby an Indonesian ruler recognised the authority of the Netherlands East Indies government and agreed to accept its orders.

By about 1903 a fairly stable government, resting upon an alliance with cooperative *uleëbalangs*, was established. In 1903 the Sultan, Tuanku Daud Syah, surrendered, but he maintained his contacts with the guerrillas. In 1905 he contacted the Japanese Consul in Singapore, and in 1907 he plotted an attack upon the Dutch garrison of Banda Aceh which failed. The Sultan was then exiled. Panglima Polem Muhammad Daud (1879–1940), the main military leader of the later stages of the war, also surrendered in 1903 and became a major official under Dutch rule. The *ulamas*, however, carried on their resistance for another decade or so. It is a matter of judgement as to when the Aceh War actually ended. Several of the leading *ulamas* were killed in battle in 1910–12. In the minds of some Acehnese, however, the war never came to an end. It is significant that after World War II, when the Dutch attempted to reconquer Indonesia, Aceh was the only Residency they did not try to re-enter. In their absence, the leading *uleëbalangs* were imprisoned or murdered in 1946.

Van Heutsz went on to become Governor-General (1904–9), in which capacity he presided over the final conquests throughout Indonesia which have been described in this chapter. Dutch possessions in the west of the archipelago were rounded off by military occupation of the Mĕntawai islands, despite prolonged local resistance, from about 1905. By about 1910, the boundaries of the present state of Indonesia had been roughly drawn by colonial armed forces, at a great cost in lives, money, devastation, social cohesion and human dignity and freedom. But a dislike of colonial conquest and exploitation should not blind one to the more positive consequences of Dutch expansion. Feudal political systems, slavery, widow-burning, internecine wars, head-hunting, cannibalism, piracy and other unacceptable practices were being abolished under Dutch rule. New and more modern abuses replaced them, of course, as an industrialised coloniser proceeded with its exploitation of subject peoples. But in important respects many Indonesians had been forced into a more modern age. The peoples of Indonesia had also been given a potential common enemy. The foundations had been laid for the eventual creation of a new nation, united by centuries of related cultural and political traditions and by the recent experience of Dutch conquest and rule. The Dutch did not create Indonesia, but they did define its territorial extent and create an environment in which nationalist forces could ultimately develop.

It is wise to consider, however, the means with which this new colonial state had been created. Because Indonesians were still divided from one another, they were not only subdued by relatively small colonial forces but actively assisted in the subjugation of each other. In 1905 the indigenous population of Indonesia was estimated to be about 37 million. Europeans serving in the colonial army and navy in Indonesia at that point totalled only 15 866 officers and men. But at their side fought 26 276 Indonesians. Most of these were in the army (24 522), and of these 68 per cent were Javanese, 21 per cent Ambonese, and the rest Sundanese, Madurese, Bugis and 'Malays' (mostly from Timor). A sense of a common Indonesian identity or of common goals simply did not yet exist. Most Javanese, for instance, neither knew nor cared about what happened in Aceh, except for those who were fighting beside the Dutch to destroy its independence. The growth of a shared Indonesian identity had to await the tumultuous events of the twentieth century.

IV
The Emergence of the Idea of Indonesia, *c.* 1900–42

13   A New Colonial Age

As the twentieth century began, Dutch colonial policy underwent the most significant change of direction in its history. Its authority was acquiring a new territorial definition as the conquests described in the preceding chapter were being completed. It also now adopted a new aim. The exploitation of Indonesia began to recede as the main justification for Dutch rule, and was replaced by professions of concern for the welfare of Indonesians. This was called the 'Ethical policy'. The period during which this policy emerged saw such fundamental changes in the colonial environment that Indonesian history in the early twentieth century cannot be understood without reference to it. There was more promise than performance in Ethical policies, and the fundamental facts of exploitation and subjugation were not in fact altered, but this does not lessen the importance of understanding this new colonial age.

The Ethical policy had roots both in humanitarian concern and economic advantage. The denunciation of Dutch rule presented in the novel *Max Havelaar* (1860) and in other exposés began to bear fruit. Voices were raised in favour of relief for the oppressed peoples of Java, and by the late nineteenth century new colonial administrators were on their way to Indonesia with *Max Havelaar* in their baggage and its message in their minds. During the 'liberal' period (*c.* 1870–1900) private capitalism came to exert a preponderant influence upon colonial policy. Dutch industry began to see Indonesia as a potential market, which required a raising of living standards there. Capital, both Dutch and international, sought new opportunities for investment and extraction of raw materials, especially in the outer islands. A need for Indonesian labour in modern enterprises was felt. Business interests therefore supported more intensive colonial involvement in the causes of peace, justice, modernity and welfare. The humanitarians justified what the businessmen expected to be profitable, and the Ethical policy was born.

In 1899 C. Th. van Deventer, a lawyer who had spent 1880–97 in Indonesia, published an article in the Dutch journal *de Gids* entitled 'Een eereschuld' ('A debt of honour'). He argued that the Netherlands owed the Indonesians such a debt for all the wealth which had been drained from their country. This was to be repaid by giving primacy in colonial policy to the interests of Indonesians. Until his death in 1915 van Deventer was one of the foremost champions of the Ethical policy, as an adviser to government and a member of the States-General. In 1901 Queen Wilhelmina (r. 1890–1948) announced an enquiry into welfare in Java, and the Ethical policy was thereby officially endorsed. In 1902 Alexander W. F. Idenburg became Minister of Colonies (1902–5, 1908–9, 1918–19). In this post, and as Governor-General (1909–16) Idenburg more than any other single individual put

Ethical ideas into practice. The Dutch enunciated three principles which were thought of as typifying this new policy: education, irrigation and emigration. For such projects funds were necessary. The colonial government's debt of some f. 40 million was therefore taken over by the Netherlands government, so that Batavia could increase expenditure without further indebtedness. The Ethical policy was on its way.

All this was occurring within a rapidly altering economic environment. The conquests in the outer islands brought new areas under Dutch rule, and these islands rather than Java became the main focus of new economic development. The production of tropical crops expanded rapidly in the hands of private enterprise. From 1900 to 1930 sugar production rose nearly four times, tea nearly eleven times. Tobacco developed rapidly from the 1860s, especially on the east coast of Sumatra. Pepper, copra, tin, coffee and other products expanded, and now were largely developed in the outer islands. Two new products were particularly important for placing Indonesia at the forefront of world economic interest in the twentieth century: oil and rubber. Both were predominantly, although not exclusively, outer island products.

Since the 1860s the existence of petroleum deposits in the Langkat area of North Sumatra had been known. This was a troubled region throughout the Aceh War. In 1883 A. J. Zijlker received government approval for a concession from the Pangeran of Langkat, and test drilling began. After many problems of personnel, finance, terrain, climate and a well fire in 1888, oil at last began to flow in promising quantities. In 1890 Zijlker set up the Koninklijke Nederlandsche Maatschappij tot Exploitatie van Petroleum-bronnen in Nederlandsch-Indië (Royal Dutch Company for Exploitation of Petroleum Sources in the Netherlands Indies), usually known simply as 'de Koninklijke'. In 1892 production began. By 1900 'de Koninklijke' was exporting oil to other parts of Asia, from Chinese ports in the east to Indian ports in the west. In 1901 it expanded its activities to Kalimantan.

Oil was initially used primarily for lamp-oil. It is one of the coincidences of modern history that just as the electric light bulb, commercially developed from the 1880s, threatened to destroy the oil industry, the petrol-engined motor car opened vast new opportunities for it from about 1900 onwards. Other companies were soon attracted to Indonesian oil deposits, and by the 1920s there were some fifty companies at work in Sumatra (along the east coast from Aceh to Palembang), Java (at Sĕmarang, Rĕmbang and Surabaya) and Kalimantan (on the east coast). Exploration continued in other areas, but offered little promise of success. To finance drilling in East Kalimantan, in 1897 a company was set up in London with British capital which became the Shell Transport and Trading Company. In 1907 Shell and 'de Koninklijke' merged to become one of the great oil multinationals, Royal Dutch Shell. By 1930 Royal Dutch Shell was producing about 85 per cent of the total oil production of Indonesia. American companies began taking up major concessions from the 1920s; the most important among them were Caltex (California Texas Oil Corporation) and Stanvac (Standard Vacuum Oil Co.). In 1930 the Japanese entered the Indonesian oil business with their Borneo Oil Company, which operated at Kutai in East Kalimantan.

Rubber was the other new product which rode, literally, on the wheels of the booming car industry. The native rubber tree *Ficus elastica* was tried as a plantation crop in West Java and the east coast of Sumatra from 1864. But it was the first government experiments with the imported *Hevea brasiliensis* in 1900 which pointed the way to success. The colonial government encouraged the spread of the new product (as it encouraged other products) by providing advice, scientific research, general regulation, and so on. From about 1906 *Hevea brasiliensis* spread rapidly, especially in Sumatra. When the first trees reached sufficient maturity for tapping (after about five years), rubber began to be exported in 1912. The internationally agreed Stevenson Rubber Restriction Scheme of 1922 did not apply to Indonesia, but restricted production in British Malaya. There followed a rubber boom in Indonesia. By 1930, 44 per cent of the acreage devoted to the principal plantation crops in Indonesia was planted with rubber. By this time, Indonesia was producing nearly half the world's rubber supply. The Depression, however, brought a major crisis to the rubber industry in 1930, as well as to other enterprises.

It was not only Dutch entrepreneurs who were active in Indonesia. The creation of Royal Dutch Shell in 1907 reflected a general internationalisation of investment. In agricultural development, Dutch capital was predominant overall. But about 70 per cent of Dutch capital in 1929 was invested in Java, about half of it in sugar. The outer islands were a more international operation. In East and South Sumatra over 40 per cent of agricultural investment in 1929 was non-Dutch, over 18 per cent of it British. The oil industry was even more international. Indonesians were active in agriculture as well, especially in the outer islands. In 1931 small-scale Indonesian producers accounted for 35 per cent of rubber production, 79 per cent of tobacco, 57 per cent of coffee, 19 per cent of tea, and nearly all coconut, pepper and kapok production.

All of this activity meant that the outer islands surpassed Java both as a field of investment and as a source of exports. Java's main exports were coffee, tea, sugar, rubber, cassava and tobacco. In most of these, the outer islands surpassed Java. There were considerable fluctuations, but overall the value of Java's coffee exports fell by nearly 70 per cent from 1880 to 1930; by 1930 coffee exports from the outer islands were about twice the value of Java's, exports of outer island rubber were nearly twice the value of Java rubber, and outer island tobacco exports were nearly four times the value of Java tobacco (very large amounts of tobacco were also grown by Indonesians in Java and the outer islands for the domestic market). Among major exports, Java exceeded the outer islands only in tea and sugar, the latter being almost exclusively a product of Java. The value of Java sugar exports reached a peak in 1920, but fell by 75 per cent in the following decade because of lower prices (production actually rose in volume). Java tea exports grew in value, but in 1930 they were worth only half the value of outer islands rubber exports. Cassava exports came almost exclusively from Java, but in 1930 the value of these was only about one-eighth of outer islands rubber exports. In 1925, 99 per cent (by value) of the oil exports came from the outer islands. In 1930, the main exports (cassava, coffee, copra, rubber, sugar, tea, tobacco, tin, oil) amounted to about f. 930.5 million, of which 55.3 per cent came from the outer islands. Java produced 44.7 per cent, but over 60 per cent of this represented sugar exports, of which Java (especially East Java) was one of the world's major producers. The drop in sugar prices and the need to use sugar land to grow rice for Java's increasing population threatened even this main export.

The shift of economic activity to the outer islands introduced a major complication into government policy, a complication which has persisted ever since. The major fields of investment and the major earners of export revenues were now the outer islands. The main welfare problems, the main claims upon a 'debt of honour', however, were in Java. In theory, welfare programmes in Java could have been financed by requiring the outer islands to subsidise them, thereby avoiding increases in the already very heavy levels of taxation in Java. This would have required substantial taxation upon the fortunes being made in outer island enterprises. Not surprisingly, this did not happen. The outer islands were not taxed to the degree which would have been necessary to raise living standards in Java. The humanitarian and economic interests whose alliance created the Ethical policy in practice went their separate ways, while subscribing to the same rhetoric. As welfare measures were introduced in Java, the Javanese and Sundanese found that both money and labour were demanded of them to pay for the new programmes. When colonial finances were threatened after World War I, taxation upon Indonesians was substantially increased, demonstrating that in practice welfare was subordinated to a balanced budget.

Thus the distinction between Java and the outer islands which had roots in the past was now further accentuated. The outer islands were the areas of deeper Islamic commitment, greater entrepreneurial activity, more valuable export products, greater foreign investment, more recent Dutch subjugation and lesser population pressure. Java was the land of more uneven Islamisation, less entrepreneurship, declining value as a source of exports, lesser new economic development, longer and more fundamental colonial interference, and overpopulation. Such generalisations of course conceal much variety and many changes, but nonetheless the history of twentieth-century Indonesia has been shaped to a considerable degree by this distinction.

Economic development and the concern for indigenous welfare were linked only in infrastructure projects. There was, for instance, a major expansion of railways and tramways. In 1867 there were only about 15 miles / 25 km of railway in the whole of the Netherlands East Indies, and in 1873 only about 160 miles / 260 km. But then a rapid expansion followed. By 1930 there were 4614 miles / 7425 km of railway and tramway. Even more directly linked to welfare were the irrigation projects which were attempted, not always with success. A major scheme to irrigate the Sala River valley was abandoned after about f. 17 million had been wasted upon it. Nevertheless, between 1885 and 1930 the area of irrigated rice land went up by about 1.8 times. The significance of this can be seen against the perspective of population, which also increased by about the same factor in the same period.

The Dutch contributed to food production by experimenting with new seeds, encouraging the use of fertilisers, and so on. These efforts met with considerable success, but not enough to keep pace with population. The consumption of rice per head of population in Java and Madura seems to have fallen somewhat between 1913 and 1924, although this was partly compensated by an increase in the consumption of other, but less nourishing, foods.

Population growth overshadowed all the events of this new colonial age, as it has overshadowed Indonesian history ever since. In brief, Java (especially Central and East Java) was becoming seriously overpopulated, while in the outer islands there were still vast unpopulated or underpopulated tracts. Not until 1930 was there a census which can be said to give reliable figures for the whole of Indonesia, but the general trends are nonetheless clear. In 1900 the indigenous population of Java and Madura was already about 28.4 million, a dramatic increase over the 5 million which was suggested in Chapter 2 as a maximum estimate for the period before 1800. By 1920 the indigenous population of Java and Madura had reached 34.4 million, and the definitive figures for the 1930 census place it at 40.9 million. The outer islands were estimated to have 7.3 million indigenous inhabitants in 1905, 13.9 million in 1920, and the final 1930 figures give 18.2 million. The total indigenous population of Indonesia in 1930 was 59.1 million (plus 1.6 million Europeans and 'Foreign Orientals', 1.2 million being Chinese, giving a total of 60.7 million).

Thus, nearly 70 per cent of the Indonesian population in 1930 was living in Java and Madura, which comprise about 7 per cent of the total land area of Indonesia. Java, once the rice bowl of the archipelago, had by now become a deficit food area. Ironically, however, it would again became a net rice exporter after 1936 when the effects of the Depression (especially the exclusion of Java sugar from some of its principal markets) led to much sugar land reverting to rice agriculture; this was not, of course, an indicator of general prosperity but one of the many anomalies caused by the Depression. In general, it is difficult to avoid the suspicion that the race with population in Java was already lost before the Dutch or anyone else realised it had begun.

Java's growing population was of fundamental relevance to its low level of welfare, but the Dutch had no policy which could solve the problem. Indeed, it is difficult to see what could have been done in any case. Except for limited and unsuccessful experiments in agrarian reform, the only answer offered by the Dutch was emigration from Java to the outer islands, a policy which continued after Indonesian independence under the label of 'transmigration'. In 1905 the first colonies of Javanese were placed in Lampung (South Sumatra) and other areas were subsequently opened for colonisation. In 1930 the population of these colonies totalled about 36000. Many inhabitants of Java also left their island to work as contract labourers on the plantations of East Sumatra and elsewhere (in 1931 there were over 306000 such labourers), and some left to seek other work or trading opportunities. But the total number of such people amounted only to several hundred thousand. Between 1905 and 1930 the population of Java meanwhile increased by about 11 million.

The Dutch increased their expenditures on public health projects nearly tenfold between 1900 and 1930. But set against the massive poverty and overpopulation of Java the results were of marginal benefit. Various immunisation programmes, anti-malaria campaigns and hygienic improvements may have contributed to a lowering of the mortality rate (and thus to the growth of population as well), although the statistics are open to question. Whatever the case, mortality still remained at high levels. The most lasting result of hygiene reform was the general adoption of tiles rather than thatch for house roofs. This was a measure designed to cut down infestation by rats and other vermin, which gave particular cause for concern after the first outbreak of bubonic plague in 1911. Professional medical provision, however, remained generally inadequate. In 1930 there were only 1030 qualified doctors in Indonesia (667 of them in Java), representing one for every 62.5 thousand inhabitants (of all races) in Java and one for every 52.4 thousand in the outer islands. These doctors were largely to be found in the cities and towns, on plantations and so on; professional medical care for villagers was nearly nonexistent. There were in addition medical and other welfare services provided by Indonesian organisations, which are discussed in Chapter 14.

The village was to be the main instrument of government welfare efforts. The 1906 Village Regulation and subsequent Dutch practice aimed to increase democratic popular involvement in village affairs, to increase social cohesion, and to allow the Dutch Resident and Controleur in conjunction with the village headman to direct the village towards necessary welfare measures. These efforts failed. Poverty and overpopulation might have been sufficient by themselves to destroy the autonomous and semi-democratic life of the villages of Java. In any case, the heavy hand of Dutch paternalism ensured this outcome. The Dutch found the Javanese village to be an inefficient administrative unit. To produce a more rational administrative structure and to guarantee larger incomes to village headmen, a policy of amalgamating villages was introduced. In 1897 there were 30 500 villages recorded in Java with an average population of 800 each. In 1927 only 18 584 amalgamated villages remained, with an average population of 1800 each. These new administrative units often had no indigenous basis and failed to grow into the autonomous welfare organisations the colonial government sought. Village banks, rice-stores and other projects were encouraged, with mixed results. There was considerable corruption and maladministration. Population pressure led to ever-decreasing field sizes, and poverty and unemployment encouraged violence and criminality. Many villagers were also caught up in the political turmoil and violence described in the following chapter. Not surprisingly, Dutch and Indonesian officials of the colonial government in fact directed such welfare measures as were introduced, rather than the villagers themselves.

A great deal of effort was put into education, and the results were often pointed to with pride by Dutch officials. All supporters of the Ethical policy favoured an increase in education for Indonesians, but there were two distinct schools of thought about what kind of education and for whom. Snouck Hurgronje and the first 'Ethical' director of education (1900–5), J. H. Abendanon, favoured an elitist approach. They wanted more European-style education in the Dutch language for a Westernised Indonesian elite which could take over much of the work of Dutch civil servants, thus producing a grateful and cooperative elite, cutting administrative expenses, restraining Islamic 'fanaticism' and ultimately creating an inspiring example for lower levels of Indonesian society. Idenburg and Governor-General van Heutsz (1904–9) favoured more basic and practical education in vernacular languages for these lower levels. The elitist approach was intended to produce leadership for the new Dutch-Indonesian age of enlightenment, the mass approach to contribute directly to welfare. Neither policy was pursued with sufficient resources, and neither succeeded in doing what its supporters wanted.

Under Abendanon the elitist approach was favoured. In 1900 the three old *hoofdenscholen* (chiefs' schools) at Bandung, Magĕlang and Prabalingga were reorganised to become schools clearly designed for the production of civil servants, and were renamed OSVIA (Opleidingscholen voor inlandsche ambtenaren, Training schools for native officials). The course was now five years long, in Dutch, and open to any Indonesian who had finished the European lower school. It was no longer necessary for an entrant to be from the aristocratic elite. In 1927 the course was reduced to three years. In 1900–2 the 'Doktĕr-Jawa' school at Weltevreden was turned into STOVIA (School tot opleiding van inlandsche artsen, School for training native doctors). Its course was also taught in Dutch. Since 1891 the European lower schools which were a necessary prerequisite for admission to OSVIA and STOVIA had been open to Indonesians, but the fees could be afforded only by the wealthy. Abendanon widened the opportunities for non-aristocratic Indonesians to attend and abolished the fees for parents with incomes below f. 50 per month.

Abendanon faced opposition in these reforms from many directions, including the more conservative *bupatis*. He persevered, however, and was defeated only in his desire to increase educational opportunities for upper-class Javanese women. His hopes were shared by Raden Ajĕng Kartini (1879–1904), the daughter of Raden Mas Adipati Arya Sasraningrat of Jĕpara, one of the most enlightened of Java's *bupatis*. Kartini had attended the European lower school in Jĕpara at a time when most *bupatis* found the idea of female education entirely unacceptable. This remarkable young woman hoped to contribute to the enlightenment of the women of her class. She married another progressive *bupati*, Raden Adipati Arya Djajaadiningrat of Rĕmbang, but tragically died at the age of twenty-five a few days after giving birth to their first child.

The cause of women's education so desired by Kartini and Abendanon was never taken up as a government priority. Conservative *bupatis* and sceptical colonial officials ensured that this was so. In 1911 Abendanon paid personal tribute to Kartini by publishing the moving letters which she wrote to his wife and others between 1899 and 1904 under the title *Door duisternis tot licht* ('Through darkness into light'). Women's education did, however, receive attention from non-governmental organisations. Indonesian activities in this field are mentioned in Chapter 14. In the Netherlands, a private foundation called the Kartini Fonds (Kartini Fund) was established in 1913 to provide Dutch-language education for Javanese women, and the colonial government then provided a subsidy. The 'Kartini schools' which this foundation set up in Java played an important role in subsequent years, and Kartini is remembered as an early representative of female emancipation and the national awakening which is the subject of following chapters.

During van Heutsz's period as Governor-General (1904–9), during most of which Dirk Fock was Minister of Colonies (1905–8), the idea of mass education received more encouragement. Fock favoured technical and vocational schools. Snouck Hurgronje and his followers argued that the products of these schools would not, as Fock hoped, stimulate indigenous enterprises, but would only be able to find employment in European concerns. Fock, however, insisted. Various vocational schools had been opened by Christian missions since 1881 in Minahasa, the Batak regions of Sumatra, and Java. In 1909 the first government vocational schools were opened in Batavia, Sĕmarang and Surabaya. Eventually they taught courses for metal- and woodworkers, electricians, car repairers, etc. Their graduates did sometimes stimulate indigenous enterprises, but most became employees of European firms. The sceptics were proved right.

The most significant educational reforms were in the old two-class primary school system which had been available on a very small scale to Indonesians since

1892–3. First Class schools were designed for the upper classes, while Second Class schools were for the general population. To relieve pressure on the European lower schools, the only institutions where an Indonesian could learn Dutch adequately and proceed to OSVIA and STOVIA, the First Class schools were reformed in 1907. They now provided a five-year course in which Dutch was taught, with a sixth year in which Dutch was the medium of instruction (a seventh year was added in 1911). Dutch teachers now appeared in these schools (mostly women, since their male colleagues were reluctant to teach 'natives'). At the indigenous teacher-training schools (*kweekscholen*), the first of which was opened in 1852 with several others following especially after 1870, Dutch was reintroduced as a subject after some twenty years during which it had been removed from the course of study; shortly thereafter it became the language of instruction.

Indonesians now had greater access to Dutch-language instruction, but a structural problem remained. The First Class schools were in the 'native' educational system; there was no way for an Indonesian to leap from this system to the parallel European system, which alone led to secondary education. In 1914 the First Class schools were therefore turned into Hollandsch-Inlandsche (Dutch-Native) schools (HIS). Although these remained schools for the Indonesian upper classes (there was still a minimum income requirement for parents), they were now formally a part of the European school system in Indonesia. The Hollandsch-Inlandsche schools, the Hollandsch-Chineesche (Dutch-Chinese) schools which were begun in 1908, and the European lower schools, although in principle ethnically distinct, now all led to the secondary levels of European education and thence to higher bureaucratic employment. Dutch was the language of instruction in all of them.

Above the HIS level, ethnic separation in education ended. In 1914 MULO (Meer uitgebreid lager onderwijs, More extended lower education, a sort of junior high) schools were created for upper-class Indonesians, Chinese and Europeans who had finished their respective primary schools. In 1919 AMS (Algemeene middelbare scholen, General middle schools) were established to carry pupils to university entrance level. Up to this time, there had been no university-level education available in Indonesia. The minuscule number of Indonesians who had access to university education were those who went through the European system to HBS (Hoogere burgerschool, Higher middle-class school) and thence to university in the Netherlands. In 1905, only thirty-six Indonesians entered HBS. In 1913 Hoesein Djajadiningrat (b. 1886), from one of the most distinguished *bupati* families of West Java, became the first Indonesian to gain a doctorate with his Leiden University thesis on *Sĕjarah Bantĕn*. In 1920 university-level education, without regard to ethnicity, at last became available in Indonesia with the opening of the Technische Hoogeschool (technical college) at Bandung. In 1924 a Rechtshoogeschool (law college) opened in Batavia, and in 1927 STOVIA was turned into the Geneeskundige Hoogeschool (medical college).

The reform of the First Class schools and the further educational developments described above had nothing to do with lower-class Indonesians, for whom the Second Class schools had been designed. Broadening education for the masses was an awesome financial problem, and a cause for which there was far from unanimous support even among followers of Ethical ideas. In 1918 it was estimated that it would cost f. 417 million per year to provide Second Class schools for all Indonesians; this was considerably more than the colonial government's total expenditure. Initial plans for expanding the Second Class schools were greatly delayed for financial reasons.

In 1907 van Heutsz found the answer. Village schools (*desascholen*, also called *volksscholen*, people's schools) were to be opened with the villagers themselves bearing much of the cost, but with government subsidies where necessary. As with so many other Ethical reforms, the government decided what was good for the Indonesians and then told them how much they must pay for their betterment. These schools were to have a three-year course taught in the vernacular offering basic literacy, numeracy and practical skills. Fees were to be charged. The villages proved to have little enthusiasm for the village school idea, so the Dutch proceeded by exerting *pĕrintah halus,* the 'gentle pressure' from above which typified the Dutch approach to village welfare measures. By 1912 there were over 2500 village schools. By the 1930s there were some 9600 and of Indonesian children between the ages of six and nine over 40 per cent attended a school of some sort at some time, most of them at government village schools and many of them more or less unwillingly. In 1915 Inlandsche Vervolgscholen (native senior schools) were created to carry pupils to a higher level of education.

The old Second Class schools became Standaardscholen (standard schools) in 1908, and were now intended for those engaged in trade or otherwise removed from the agrarian life of the villages, which the village schools were to provide for. Chinese were now admitted to the Standaardscholen, which theoretically became 'middle-class' schools, between the lower-class village schools and the elite First Class schools. They were really an anomaly within the educational system and when the effects of the Depression hit after 1930, they were converted into village schools and attached Vervolgscholen.

The complex school system now seemed to provide for everyone except a village child who wished to proceed from his village school to the secondary level, which existed only in the European system. In 1921 the first Schakelschool (link school) was opened, with a five-year course which proceeded from the level of the village school to that at the end of HIS. Thence the student could proceed to MULO. These link schools were of little importance. Most upper-class Indonesians sent their children to HIS or the European schools; villagers had little interest in higher education and could rarely pay the fees. In 1929 many of the link schools were closed.

The high point of educational reform, as of other Ethical reforms, was reached about 1930, after which time the Depression ended any major new development, although the number of school places continued to grow. The absolute increase in educational opportunities was great. In 1900, there were only 265 940 Indonesians in private or government schools in the whole of Indonesia. In 1930–1 there were over 1.7 million Indonesians in such Western educational institutions. But when these figures are set against the terrible facts of population size, it can be seen how marginal all of this effort was. In 1930–1, about 1.66 million Indonesians were in the vernacular primary schools designed for them: 2.8 per cent of the total population, or 8 per cent of the population group between infants who could not yet walk and adults. In the European school system (including HIS, MULO, AMS, vocational schools, but excluding kindergarten) below university level, there were 84 609 Indonesians: 0. 14 per cent of the total population. At university level, there were 178 Indonesians: 3 ten-thousandths of 1 per cent of the population.

In vocational agriculture and forestry schools, a sector where one might have expected much to be done, there were 392 Indonesians: 7 ten-thousandths of 1 per cent of the population.

In the 1930 census, the literacy rate for adult Indonesians throughout the archipelago was only 7.4 per cent: 13.1 per cent in Sumatra, 6 per cent in Java and Madura, and only 4 per cent in Bali and Lombok. Much of this literacy was due to indigenous educational institutions, both the old *Qur'an* schools and the more modern schools described in the following chapter. The highest literacy rate (50 per cent) was in Christian areas of South Maluku, where Christian missions were active in education. The literacy rate in the Dutch language among Indonesians in 1930, however, was only 0.32 per cent (but reaching 13 per cent in the city of Ambon). This makes for a poor comparison with the most ambitious public education programme in a colonised country, that of the United States in the Philippines, where by 1939 over a quarter of the population could speak English. The Dutch never made a commitment to public education like that of the Americans, and even had they done so the size of the problems they faced might have proved insuperable.

Education produced neither a grateful and cooperative new elite nor a buoyant new spirit among the masses; welfare measures in general did not produce welfare. Although all the welfare surveys of the Ethical period produced doubtful statistics, there is no evidence of increasing general prosperity before 1930, and some evidence of declining living standards after 1914. After 1930, there is no dispute about the decline of welfare. Education produced some able and loyal officials, but it also produced a tiny dissatisfied elite who led the anti-colonial movements described in subsequent chapters. A similar story attends Ethical political reforms.

Decentralisation was a main aim of Ethical supporters: decentralisation from the Hague to Batavia, from Batavia to the regions, from Dutchmen to Indonesians. Despite various reform measures, however, the Hague remained in control of Indonesia. Local councils began to be set up in 1905 for the main towns, and by 1939 there were thirty-two urban councils (nineteen of them in Java). These urban councils were reasonably successful, but all had a Dutch majority and the franchise was extended only to literate male residents with high levels of income tax payments, thus excluding all but a handful of Indonesians. Councils were also set up for each of the seventy-six Regencies (*kabupaten*) in Java, but the Indonesian members were largely officials while the *bupati* was chairman. The *bupatis* were indeed the main group of Indonesians to benefit from these reforms. As political agitation increased (see Chapter 14), from about 1915 the government lost much of its suspicion of *bupatis* and began again to push them forward as leaders of their society. These councils were all basically advisory, and there was little real delegation of power from Batavia. The *bestuurshervormingwet* (government reform law) of 1922 called for Indonesia to be split into large regions with local councils. West Java was made such a region in 1926, East Java in 1929, Central Java in 1930, and in 1934 three governmental regions were established covering the outer islands. But the whole scheme was the object of much criticism. The majorities in the councils were Dutch and 'others' (mainly Chinese), and the Indonesian members were primarily officials. Government in Indonesia in practice remained centralised.

The most obvious gesture towards decentralisation and increasing popular involvement in government was the creation of the Volksraad (People's Council), which first met in 1918. The origins of this body were associated with the *Indië weerbaar* (defence of the Indies) agitation described in the following chapter. The Volksraad was established as a unicameral body with advisory powers only, but it had to be consulted by the Governor-General on matters of finance. Initially it had nineteen elected members (ten of them Indonesians) and nineteen appointed members (five of them Indonesians), plus a chairman. The electorate, however, consisted of the conservative and official-dominated local councils. More radical Indonesians found themselves in the Volksraad only when the Governor-General appointed them to it. With about 39 per cent of the membership initially Indonesians, this grew to 40 per cent when the Volksraad was expanded to forty-nine members in 1921, to 42 per cent when it was expanded to 60 members in 1927, and to 50 per cent when the balance among European, Indonesian and other (mainly Chinese) members was altered in 1931. The number of elected members came to exceed the appointed members, but the electorate still consisted of the conservative local councils. In 1939 the Volksraad electorate totalled only 2228 individuals in the whole of Indonesia, the population of which was then about 70 million.

In its early days, the Volksraad was a source of considerable criticism and pressure upon the colonial government. A new *staatsinrichting* (constitution) for Indonesia introduced in 1925 reduced the Council of the Indies to an advisory body and gave the Volksraad limited legislative powers. The budget and other internal legislation now required its assent and it could initiate legislation. In fact, however, the States-General in the Hague remained as much in control of the colonial budget as before. The Governor-General and the heads of the various administrative departments were not responsible to the Volksraad and could not be removed by it. The Volksraad never developed into a true parliament. Through its various phases, it remained what it was always intended to be: a gesture towards popular involvement in what was still a colonial state resting upon economic and military dominance, in which a small European nation governed a large Asian territory. But, not surprisingly, from its very beginning the Volksraad was caught up in the political awakening discussed in the following chapters.

A major question about the Ethical period upon which many scholars have disagreed is when it ended. Several points have been suggested. The period of the conservative Minister of Colonies Simon de Graaff (1919–25) and of Dirk Fock as Governor-General (1921–6) has been suggested. In an effort to balance the colonial budget, many services were cut back and the already heavy tax burdens upon Indonesians were increased. Those who emphasise political aspects (see Chapter 14) also point to the period from 1919, when rising political activism and violence led to the arrest, imprisonment and exile of several Indonesian leaders, or to 1927, when the Communist rebellion ushered in a period of still greater political repression. Those who look at economics prefer 1930, when the Depression destroyed export prices and government revenue and expenditure, and pushed welfare levels to new lows. Those who emphasise the existence of a general, if unrealised, commitment to Indonesian welfare as a principle of government point to 1942, when the Japanese put an end to Dutch rule.

If one considers the general shape of this new colonial age, however, the question of when it ended becomes still more complex. Throughout the period described in this chapter, there was a general distinction between proclaimed principles and actual performance. Welfare was proclaimed, but set against the perspective of population the results were few. The semi-democratic village was to be the basis of all, but in fact it was only treated as a passive and malleable tool in the hands of officials who wished to direct its development. The populace was to be associated with its rulers, but only as grateful and cooperative followers of a conservative elite. There was no real attack on population growth. The nation's wealth was used for the interests of foreign enterprises and indigenous industries were not developed. The main economic development took place in the outer islands, while the main welfare problems grew in Java. Education was to be the key to a new age, but the number of school places provided was small when set against the size of the population. Token concessions of political authority were made to legitimise an authoritarian government. Token welfare measures were meant to show that it was good. These features will be seen to recur throughout Indonesian history in the twentieth century, even after the Dutch were gone from the scene. In some senses the Ethical policy set patterns, not for two decades, or three, or four, but for much of the rest of the century.

14 The First Steps towards National Revival, *c.* 1900–27

The first three decades of the twentieth century witnessed not only a new territorial definition of Indonesia and the proclamation of a fresh colonial policy. There was also a transformation of indigenous Indonesian affairs which was so profound that in political, cultural and religious affairs Indonesians were set upon novel courses. Rapid change occurred in all the areas recently conquered by the Dutch. But with respect to the anti-colonial and reform movements which first emerged in this period, Java and the Minangkabau area of Sumatra attract particular attention. There the changes were such that the history of modern Indonesia moved into a new age and acquired a new vocabulary. The reasons for Java and Minangkabau to be the leaders in this sudden transformation are reasonably clear. The degree of social disruption and change in Java has been described in previous chapters. Minangkabau had undergone the first major Islamic reform in Indonesia under the Padris, had experienced great changes since the imposition of Dutch rule, and had traditions of mobile external contacts which opened it to new ideas. While Balinese kings and Acehnese *ulamas* were still fighting to defend an older order against colonial conquest, Minangkabaus and the people of Java were already laying the foundations for a new order.

The key developments in this period were the emergence of novel ideas of organisation and the arrival at more sophisticated definitions of identity. The former involved new forms of leadership and the latter involved a deeper analysis of the religious, social, political and economic environment. By 1927 a different kind of Indonesian leadership and a new awareness of self were established, but at a considerable cost. These leaders found themselves bitterly opposed to each other, and greater self-awareness split this leadership along religious and ideological lines. The Dutch moved to a higher level of repression in response to these developments. This period saw no solution of problems, but it did irrevocably change the Indonesian leadership's view of itself and its future.

The 'new' or 'lesser' *priyayi* of Java, the upwardly-mobile officials who saw education as the key to advancement, were the first to seize the initiative. This group represented a major social and cultural stream in twentieth-century Indonesia. They were predominantly *abangan* (literally, the brown or red ones), a Javanese term used to describe those Muslims whose adherence to Islam is seldom more than a formal, nominal commitment. *Abangan* are the majority among Javanese; they tend to be mystical in their religious ideas, relatively unconcerned about the demanding ritual obligations of Islam (five daily prayers, fasting, giving alms, etc.), and culturally committed to Javanese art forms such as *wayang* (shadow theatre) which are largely pre-Islamic in inspiration. In the early twentieth century, Western education seemed to offer to the administrative upper classes (*priyayi*) among the *abangan* a key to a new synthesis which they saw as the basis for a rejuvenation of their culture, class and people. Among this group, most were prepared to regard Islam with at least a friendly neutrality, but as Islamic pressures grew some became hostile to it.

The idea of emancipating Indonesians through the education of the *priyayi* was encouraged from an early stage by the journal *Bintang Hindia* ('Star of the Indies'), first published in the Netherlands in 1902. This was edited by a Minangkabau graduate of the Doktěr-Jawa school at Weltevreden (after 1900 called STOVIA) named Abdul Rivai (b.1871) and a Dutchman who subsequently found Rivai's ideas to be too progressive for his taste. The journal was distributed in Indonesia and was very widely read among the Indonesian elite before it ceased publication in 1906.

Dr Wahidin Soedirohoesodo (1857–1917) was the inspirer of the first recognisably modern organisation for Javanese *priyayi*. He was also a graduate of the Doktěr-Jawa school and worked as a government doctor in Yogyakarta until 1899. In 1901 he became editor of the periodical *Retnadhoemilah* ('Luminous jewel'), printed in Javanese and Malay for a *priyayi* readership and reflecting *priyayi* concern for their problems and status. Wahidin was a gifted performer of classical Javanese music (*gamělan*) and *wayang* as well as a product of Western-style education. He saw Javanese culture as being primarily Hindu–Buddhist in inspiration, hinted that the decline of the Javanese was at least partly to be blamed upon the coming of Islam, and sought restoration of the Javanese through Dutch education.

Wahidin attempted to set up scholarships to provide Western education for Javanese *priyayi*. But few of the older generation of officials or those of the *bupati* class were enthusiastic; this hereditary elite in fact tended to fear the competition they faced from the rising lower *priyayi*. In the highest levels of Javanese society, only a prince of the Yogyakarta lesser royal house of Pakualam supported him. Indeed, several scions of the Pakualaman played significant roles in the new developments of this period.

In 1907 Wahidin visited STOVIA and there, in one of the most important institutions producing the lesser *priyayi* of Java, he encountered an enthusiastic response from the students. It was decided to create a student organisation to further the interests of the lesser *priyayi* and in May 1908 a meeting was held at which Budi Utomo was born. This Javanese name (properly spelt *budi utama*) was translated by the organisation as *het schoone streven* (the beautiful endeavour), but in the rich connotations of the Javanese language it also carried the meanings of superior intellect, character or culture. At the initial meeting students of STOVIA, OSVIA, teacher-training schools and agriculture and veterinary schools were represented. Branches were set up in these institutions and by July 1908 Budi Utomo had 650 members. Non-students also joined, and as they did so student influence began to diminish and the organisation grew into a party of the Javanese lesser *priyayi* in general.

Budi Utomo was always primarily a Javanese *priyayi* organisation. It officially defined its area of interest as including the peoples of Java and Madura, thus

reflecting the administrative union of these two islands and including the Sundanese and Madurese whose cultures were related to the Javanese. Malay rather than
Javanese was adopted as the official language. But Javanese *priyayi*, and to a much
lesser extent Sundanese, were the heart of Budi Utomo's support. The Javanese
sense of cultural superiority was rarely far from the surface; in Bandung there
were even separate chapters for Javanese and Sundanese members. Budi Utomo
never acquired a true mass base among the lower classes and reached a peak
membership of just 10000 at the end of 1909. It was also primarily a body with
cultural and educational interests; as will be seen below, it rarely played an active
political role.

In October 1908 Budi Utomo held its first congress in Yogyakarta. Wahidin was
by now becoming a mere father-figure and new voices arose to direct the organisation. A minority was led by the radical Tjipto Mangunkusumo (1885–1943), also
a medical doctor. He wanted Budi Utomo to become a political party working for
the uplifting of the masses rather than just the *priyayi*, with its activities throughout
Indonesia rather than restricted to Java and Madura. Tjipto also did not share the
general admiration for Javanese culture as the basis for rejuvenation. Dr Radjiman
Wediodiningrat (1879–1951), another Doktĕr-Jawa, also put forward his ideas. He
was influenced by Javanese culture, by the dialectics of Hegel, the subjectivism of
Kant and the anti-rationalism of Bergson, and had already embraced the mystical
doctrines of Theosophy as a synthesis of East and West. Theosophy was one of
the few movements which brought elite Javanese, Indo-Europeans and Dutchmen
together in this period, and was influential among many Budi Utomo members.
But neither Tjipto nor Radjiman carried the day. The former seemed a dangerous
radical and the latter a stuffy reactionary. A board of directors was elected which
was dominated by an older generation of officials who favoured greater education
for *priyayi* and the encouragement of Javanese entrepreneurial activity. Tjipto
was elected to the board, but resigned in 1909 and eventually joined the radical
Indische Partij.

Governor-General van Heutsz welcomed Budi Utomo, just as he had welcomed
the publication of *Bintang Hindia*, as a sign of the success of the Ethical
policy. It was, indeed, just what he wanted: a moderately progressive indigenous
organisation controlled by enlightened officials. Other Dutch officials suspected
Budi Utomo or simply thought it a potential nuisance. But in December 1909 it
was declared a legal organisation. The welcome it received from government led
many of the more dissatisfied Indonesians to suspect it. Throughout its life (it was
formally dissolved in 1935) Budi Utomo often seemed in fact to be a quasi-official
government party.

In general, Budi Utomo stagnated almost from the very beginning, being short
of both money and dynamic leadership. It pressed government for more Western
education, but this pressure played only a minor role in the reforms described
in Chapter 13. Many of the senior *bupatis* of Java and Madura looked down
upon Budi Utomo's lesser *priyayi* origins and feared that their own influence
upon government might be threatened by it. In 1913 they formed their own
Bupatis' Union (Regentenbond), which did virtually nothing for several years.
The bureaucratic elite of Java were too concerned about their careers and too
divided by social distinctions from each other and the masses to play a dynamic
role.

More active and significant organisations were soon formed. Some of these were religious, cultural and educational, some political, and several both. These organisations functioned at lower levels of society and for the first time built links between villagers and new elites. The lesser *priyayi* class was important in several of these movements, but this was a different branch of the lesser *priyayi* from that which was active in Budi Utomo. Whereas Budi Utomo members were largely making their careers in government service, those who led these more activist movements were almost entirely those who had gone through Dutch schools but had then either resigned or been dismissed from government jobs. A new religious leadership also appeared, as Indonesian Islam was launched on the most significant period of reform in its history.

In Javanese society, the minority which tried to adhere strictly to the obligations of Islam in their daily lives were called variously *wong Muslimin* (the Muslims), *putihan* (the white ones) or *santri* (students of religion). Two groups could be distinguished within this community: the rural Muslims grouped around teachers of Islam *(kyai)* and their religious schools *(pĕsantren,* the place of the *santris)* and, on the other hand, urban groups who were often engaged in commerce. These urban groups lived in separate districts in Javanese towns called *kauman* (the place of the pious), usually near the main mosque. In the early twentieth century, these urban Muslims were open to ideas of reform and progress. They found themselves increasingly in conflict with locally domiciled Chinese. The latter were in commercial competition with Javanese entrepreneurs and their relations with Javanese society in general were strained by increased Chinese displays of arrogance and pride in the wake of the 1911 revolution in China.

In 1909 a graduate of OSVIA named Tirtoadisurjo, who had left government service and become a journalist, founded Sarekat Dagang Islamiyah (Islamic Commercial Union) in Batavia. In 1910 at Buitenzorg (Bogor) he set up another such organisation. Both were designed to support Indonesian traders. In 1911 he encouraged a successful *batik* trader in Surakarta named Haji Samanhudi (1868–1956) to found Sarekat Dagang Islam as a Javanese *batik* traders' cooperative. Other branches were soon set up. In Surabaya H. O. S. Tjokroaminoto (1882–1934) became a leader of the organisation. He, too, was a graduate of OSVIA who had turned his back on government service. He was a charismatic figure who became known for his belligerent attitude towards those in authority, whether Dutch or Indonesian, and was soon to become the most prominent leader of the early popular movement.

In 1912 the organisation changed its name to Sarekat Islam (Islamic Union, SI). Tirtoadisurjo and Samanhudi fell out with one another, so Samanhudi, whose time was committed to business affairs, turned to Tjokroaminoto to lead the organisation. The Islamic and commercial origins of the organisation were soon obscured, and the term Islam in its title now reflected little more than a general awareness that its Indonesian members were Muslims while the Chinese and Dutch were not. Tjokroaminoto himself seems to have had no very profound knowledge of Islam, at least when compared to the learned men discussed below who founded the true religious reform movement.

From 1912 SI grew rapidly, and for the first time a mass base appeared, albeit an unruly and ephemeral one. By 1919 SI claimed 2 million members, but the true number probably never exceeded half a million. Unlike Budi Utomo, SI spread from Java to the outer islands, but Java remained the centre of its activities. Membership involved secret oaths and membership cards which villagers sometimes regarded as amulets. Tjokroaminoto was sometimes taken to be the *Ratu Adil*, the 'just king' which Javanese messianic traditions prophesied, who would be named Eru Cakra (i.e. the same name as *Cakra*-aminata, Tjokroaminoto). Even some members of the Javanese court elite, resentful of Dutch intrusion into their affairs, supported SI.

SI proclaimed loyalty to the Dutch regime, but as it spread in the villages violence erupted. Villagers seem to have perceived SI less as a modern political movement than as a means of self-defence against an apparently monolithic local power structure, in the face of which they felt impotent. It thus became an expression of group solidarity, united and apparently motivated by dislike of the Chinese, the *priyayi* officials, those who did not join SI, and the Dutch, approximately in that order. In some areas SI became virtually a shadow administration which the *priyayi* officials were obliged to accommodate. A boycott of Chinese *batik* traders in Surakarta rapidly grew into mutual Chinese-Indonesian insults and violence across Java. In 1913–14 there was a particularly severe outburst of violence in towns and villages, with local SI branches playing a leading role.

Governor-General Idenburg was cautiously favourable to SI, and in 1913 he granted it legal recognition. He did not, however, recognise it as a national organisation controlled by its headquarters (Centraal Sarekat Islam, CSI), but rather as a collection of autonomous branches. In doing this, Idenburg may have intended to help the leaders of the new organisation by not burdening CSI with legal responsibility for the activities of all SI branches. The consequence of his decision was that in practice it became even more difficult for CSI to exercise control. Other Dutchmen thought that Idenburg was wrong to recognise SI at all, and it began to be said that SI actually stood for *salah Idenburg* (Idenburg's mistake).

A more idiosyncratic form of rural protest also reached a peak in 1914. In the southern Blora area (north-central Java), an illiterate Javanese peasant named Surantika Samin (?1859–1914) had built up a following among peasants who rejected any form of outside authority, and who especially disliked the new forestry regulations being introduced in this teak-forest region. Saminists followed a nativist religion which Samin called *elmu nabi Adam* (the science of the prophet Adam) which, despite its Arabic terminology, owed nothing to Islam. Nor does it seem to have been Hindu–Buddhist in inspiration. Rather, it was a body of religious and ethical doctrine which stressed the importance of agricultural labour and sexuality, passive resistance and the primacy of the nuclear family, while rejecting the money economy, non-Saminist village structures and any form of external authority. Saminists refused to pay their taxes, to perform corvée labour or to use government schools. In 1907 the government feared that revolt was imminent, quite wrongly so far as can be seen, and it therefore exiled Samin to Palembang, where he died. But his movement carried on, and Saminist passive resistance reached a peak in 1914 when the Dutch demanded an increased head-tax. Infuriated *priyayis* could not break the Saminist movement, which indeed survived into the 1970s in this region.

Throughout Indonesia, the period after about 1909 saw an extraordinary proliferation of new organisations among the educated elite, most of them based on ethnic identities. Sarekat Ambon (Ambonese Union, 1920) and its predecessors since 1909 aimed to protect the interests of Ambonese; Jong Java (Young Java, 1918) was the first students' body; Pasundan (1914) was to be a sort of Budi Utomo for Sundanese; Sarekat Sumatra / Sumatranen Bond (Sumatran Union, 1918) was a Sumatran student group; Jong Minahasa (Young Minahasa, 1918) was for Minahasans; Timorsch Verbond (Timorese Alliance, 1921) was founded by Rotinese and Savunese to defend the interests of the peoples of Timor; Kaum Bĕtawi (The People of Batavia, 1923) promoted the claims of the 'original' Indonesian citizens of Batavia; Pakĕmpalan Politik Katolik Jawi (Political Association of Javanese Catholics, 1925) served the interests of that minority group. These and many other groups reflected the new enthusiasm for organisation, but also the continuing strength of ethnic and communal identities. The concept of an all-Indonesian identity had as yet hardly any following at all.

Even trade unions came to Indonesia in this burst of organisation-building. The first union was established in 1905 for European employees of the state railways, but Indonesians soon joined and by 1910 formed the majority of the membership, albeit a majority without voting rights. In 1908 was founded the Vereeniging voor Spoor- en Tramweg Personeel (Union for Railway and Tram Workers, VSTP); membership was open to Indonesian employees on an equal footing with Europeans from the beginning. Thereafter more unions were founded for teachers in government schools, customs officers, government pawnshop employees, government opium-monopoly workers, public works employees, treasury workers, sugar factory workers, and for peasants and workers in general. Organised labour was generally weak, however, for there was an abundance of labour available, and the employers (both government and private) were rarely restrained either by law or by sentiment from the use of any available means to break strikes. In the years 1918–21, however, a shortage of skilled labour placed trade unions in an unusually strong position, as will be seen below.

An even more profound sign that a new age was dawning was the birth of the Islamic reform movement. The background to this reform movement must be sought both in Indonesia and in the Middle East. Indonesian Islam was notable for its considerable diversity. All Indonesian Muslims were in principle Sunnis (Orthodox, as opposed to Shi'is) and were followers of the Shafi'i school of law, founded in the Middle East in the late eighth and early ninth centuries AD. Many pious Indonesians were also involved in Sufi mysticism, notably the Shattariyya, Qadiriyya and Naqshabandiyya orders and a popular combination of the last two founded by Ahmad Khatib of Sambas (West Kalimantan) (d.c.1878) called Qadiriyya wa Naqshbandiyya. But behind this superficial uniformity lay much diversity, heterodoxy and ignorance. As in any place where one of the great world religions is found, Islam in Indonesia had been influenced by many local customs (adat) and ideas. Learned Indonesian Muslims consequently observed all around them a widespread need for reform; their feelings were strengthened by Dutch domination, which they felt had been made possible by the decline of Islam.

Some Middle Eastern Muslims had already come to similar conclusions in the nineteenth century. Jamal ad-Din al-Afghani (1839–97), Muhammad Rashid Rida (1865–1935) and above all Muhammad 'Abduh (1849–1905) produced a reform movement which came to be called Modernism, with its centre in Cairo. Modernism had a dual thrust. On the one hand, it wanted to break free of the domination of the four medieval schools of law and to return to the original sources of Islam: the *Qur'an,* the Word of God transmitted to His Prophet Muhammad, and the *Hadith* or *Sunnah,* the traditions of the Prophet's life. These alone should be the basis of law *(shari'ah)* and doctrine. The four Orthodox schools had arisen through a process of reasoning *(ijtihad)* by learned scholars who had arrived at consensus *(ijma')* concerning the interpretation of the sources of law. *Ijma'* had led to the establishment of the four schools of law, after which time they believed that no Muslims had been sufficiently learned to become new interpreters of the law. Modernists said that *ijma'* could not close the *bab al-ijtihad* (the gate of reasoning), and that new circumstances called for reinvestigation of the eternal truths of the *Qur'an* and *Hadith.* Islam must be purified of all the illegal innovations *(bid'a)* which had crept into it over the centuries. This first thrust was, thus, scripturalist, fundamentalist, and in spirit puritanical. The second thrust was what justified the term Modernism. This new *ijtihad* must make use of the scientific advances of modern (i.e. Western) learning which, Modernists believed, could be combined with a purified Islam to raise Islamic civilisation out of its centuries of ignorance, superstition and decline (as they saw it.) Scripturalist, fundamentalist, opposed to medieval elaborations of doctrine and open to the advances of science, Modernism was a combination of the progressive and the conservative.

The British colony of Singapore played a major role in spreading the Modernist analysis to Indonesia. The Dutch distrusted Islam and attempted to restrict the pilgrimage traffic to Mecca until about 1902, when Snouck Hurgronje succeeded in altering this policy on the grounds that as a religious doctrine Islam should be free of interference although as a political force it should be destroyed. In the late nineteenth and early twentieth centuries, many Indonesian *hajis* (pilgrims) therefore travelled via Singapore, where the British did not restrict them and, in any case, where places on ships were both more numerous and cheaper. Indonesians often lived in Singapore for extended periods in connection with their pilgrimages.

In Singapore there was a substantial community of Arabs (mostly Hadhramis) and locally born Indian Muslims. Both groups often had Malay mothers. The Singapore Muslim community was in contact with the Middle East, heavily engaged in trade throughout the Indonesian archipelago, largely untouched by the local traditions which influenced Malay Islam, and deeply conscious of its religious identity because of direct competition and daily contact with the Chinese. In the later nineteenth century Singapore Muslims established lithograph presses which produced a stream of religious texts and newspapers reflecting Modernist ideas. A part of this material was printed in Malay. In terms of the religious reform movement, Singapore was much more influential in Indonesia than in Malaya, where the conservative religious establishments dominated by the Sultans kept out Modernist ideas, and where such ideas in any case seemed to evoke little response.

Minangkabaus played a leading role in the early reform movement. In 1906 the Malay-language paper *al-Imam* ('The Religious Leader') began to be published in Singapore, with the first really serious presentation of the Modernist analysis of social, religious and economic issues. Among the Muslims involved in *al-Imam* was the Minangkabau scholar Shaikh Tahir bin Jaluddin (Muhammad Tahir bin

Jalaluddin al-Azhari, 1869–1957). He had lived for twelve years in Mecca, where he stayed with his Minangkabau cousin Shaikh Ahmad Khatib (c.1855/60–1916). The latter had risen to be head (imam) of the Shafi'i school of law at the mosque of Mecca (Masjid al-Haram) and many of the reformist leaders of Indonesia were his students there. Ahmad Khatib of course defended the Shafi'i school, but allowed his pupils to read Modernist works. Tahir Jalaluddin went on to study in Cairo for four years, where he was influenced by 'Abduh's ideas and became a close friend of Rashid Rida. Ahmad Khatib supported the idea of reform and disapproved of Sufism, which was so influential in Indonesia. In 1906–8 he wrote three tracts which particularly denounced the practices of the Naqshabandiyya order on the grounds that they constituted bid'a. Modernists in Indonesia had to come to terms with Sufism: some were willing to tolerate it as a pious way of life, others were suspicious of it as an exaggeration of Islam, and others were entirely hostile to it, seeing Sufism as a haven of heresy.

In 1903 Shaikh Muhammad Djamil Djambek (1860–1947) returned to Minangkabau from Mecca, and in 1906 Haji Rasul (Haji Abdul Karim Amrullah, 1879–1945) returned. Both had been students of Ahmad Khatib, and both had become Modernists. Haji Rasul was particularly known for his belligerent opposition to adat or to any who opposed him. In 1909 the first Modernist school, the Adabiyah school, was opened in Padang, but when it received a government subsidy and a Dutch head in 1915 it fell outside the religious reform movement. The Thawalib School of Padangpanjang was more important, as Haji Rasul and others developed it into a model of Modernist educational reform. Arabic was stressed so that students could have independent access to the sources of Islam. In 1916 a system of graded classes was introduced and in 1919 desks and a more developed curriculum were introduced. Egyptian textbooks began to be used and subjects such as geography and history were added to the religious subjects. In 1915 Islamic women's education began when the Diniyah School was opened in Padangpanjang. In 1911 a fortnightly paper entitled al-Munir ('The Illuminative') began to be published in Padang (later in Padangpanjang), the first Modernist journal in Indonesia.

The Modernist movement in Minangkabau provoked opposition. A group of aristocrats and officials who favoured the kind of progress that seemed to be represented by Dutch education and social styles, and who were suspicious of the influence of religious teachers, was led by Datuk Sutan Maharadja. This group wanted reform of the adat and thus found itself in opposition to many of the older generation of officials as well. Sutan Maharadja favoured women's education, reflecting the high status of women in Minangkabau adat. In 1909 he set up the first weaving school for women in Padang, and in 1911 he opened a newspaper called Soenting Melajoe ('The Malay Ornament'), one of the first publications for women in Indonesia.

The religious reform movement also spread to Java. The first initiatives were taken by the Arab community of Batavia, who in 1905 established Jam'iyyat Khair (Union for the Good) there. This opened a modern school taught in Malay, to which in 1911 a Modernist teacher from Sudan named Shaikh Ahmad Surkati (1872–1943) was invited. Surkati soon fell out with his employers and in 1915 he set up al-Irshad (Jam'iyyat al-Islah wal-Irshad, Union for Reformation and Guidance). Al-Irshad established coeducational schools taught in Malay, Arabic and Dutch, most of them in Java. Although most of its students were Arabs, some Indonesians also attended.

In 1911 the first cautious steps for reform were taken by Indonesian Muslims in West Java. The Pĕrsyarikatan Ulama (Union of Religious Scholars) was set up by Orthodox teachers, but they entertained some of the Modernist ideas of reform and had little contact with old-fashioned *pĕsantren* circles. Pĕrsyarikatan Ulama opened a school (1916), set up an orphanage run largely by its own women's branch, and engaged in economic activities such as printing, weaving and agriculture.

The most significant Modernist organisation of Indonesia was established in Yogyakarta in 1912. Kyai Haji Ahmad Dahlan (1868–1923) was from the religious establishment of the Yogyakarta Sultanate. In 1890 he went to Mecca and studied with Ahmad Khatib and others. He returned with a determination to reform Islam and to resist the Christianising efforts of Western missionaries. In 1909 he joined Budi Utomo in the hope of preaching reform among its members, but his supporters urged him to establish an organisation of his own. In 1912 he established Muhammadiyah (the Way of Muhammad) in Yogyakarta. Muhammadiyah threw its energies into educational and welfare efforts, and into a missionary programme of its own to counteract Christianity and local 'superstitions'. In 1917 Dahlan formed a women's section named Aisyiyah, after a wife of the Prophet, which was to play an important role in the modernisation of the life of Indonesian women.

At first Muhammadiyah grew only slowly. It faced opposition or indifference from officials, from the old-fashioned Islamic teachers of the countryside, from government-recognised religious hierarchies, and from pious communities who rejected Modernist ideas. In its purification efforts it criticised many customs which pious Javanese had believed for centuries to be the true Islam. In its early years, Muhammadiyah thus brought much hostility and bitterness to the religious community of Java. By 1925, two years after Dahlan's death, Muhammadiyah had only 4000 members, but it had established fifty-five schools with 4000 pupils, two clinics in Yogyakarta and Surabaya, one orphanage and one poorhouse. It was introduced into Minangkabau by Haji Rasul in 1925. Once it was linked to the dynamic Islamic world of Minangkabau, it grew rapidly. In 1930 it had 24000 members, in 1935 43000, and in 1938 it claimed a remarkable membership of 250000. By 1938 it had spread throughout the main islands of Indonesia, ran 834 mosques and prayer houses, 31 public libraries and 1774 schools, and had 5516 male and 2114 female proselytisers *(muballigh)*. The history of Islamic Modernism in Indonesia after 1925 is to a very large extent the history of Muhammadiyah.

Two contending streams of thought had emerged as a basis for national rejuvenation, and now a third was added. To the upper-class Westernising (and at least potentially anti-Islamic) stream represented most clearly by Budi Utomo and the Modernist Islamic stream typified by Muhammadiyah, radical socialist ideas were now added. In 1911 a political party called the Indische Partij (Indies Party) was founded by the radical Indo-European E. F. E. Douwes Dekker (1879–1950, also known as Setiabuddhi), a distant relative of E. Douwes Dekker (Multatuli). It proclaimed an 'Indies' nationalism and called for independence. Two prominent Javanese, Tjipto Mangunkusumo and Suwardi Surjaningrat (later called Ki Hadjar Dewantara, 1889–1959), joined Douwes Dekker. The government refused recognition to the party, and in 1913 all three of these leaders were exiled to the Netherlands (Tjipto until 1914, Douwes Dekker until 1918, and Suwardi until 1919).

In 1913 H. J. F. M. Sneevliet (1883–1942) arrived in Indonesia. He had begun his career as a Catholic mystic but had then turned to social-democratic revolutionary ideas and trade union activism. He was later to act as the Comintern's agent in China under the alias G. Maring. In 1914 he founded the Indische Sociaal-Democratische Vereeniging (Indies Social-Democratic Association, ISDV) in Surabaya. This small leftist party was shortly to become the first Communist party in Asia outside the Russian sphere. ISDV was almost entirely Dutch in membership, but it desired a base among the Indonesian masses. In 1915–16 it allied with Insulinde (Indies Archipelago), a party which had been founded in 1907 and which had absorbed most of the radical Indo-European membership of the Indische Partij after 1913. Insulinde had 6000 members, including some leading Javanese, but it was clearly not the ideal means of access to a mass base. So ISDV's thoughts began to turn to Sarekat Islam, the only organisation with a large following among the Indonesian masses.

World War I (1914–18) initiated a period of hectic political activity in Indonesia. Shipping between Indonesia and Europe was disrupted by the hostilities, communications were hampered, the colonial military budget was raised and the welfare budget cut, prices rose and Indonesian welfare declined. With imports disrupted, some local import-substitution industries grew up, only to be wiped out when imports resumed at the end of the war. In the midst of this uncertain time, there arose a major political issue in which the new Indonesian parties played a significant role.

The *Indië weerbaar* (defence of the Indies) issue began as a defence question but soon became entangled with proposals for the creation of a Volksraad (People's Council). The idea of a part-time militia composed of Indonesians had been considered and rejected by the government in 1913–14. But when World War I broke out in August 1914 it was taken up again, for this would be a cheaper defence force than an enlarged professional army. Budi Utomo, which had branches among Javanese serving in the colonial army, was awakened from its general lethargy and began to campaign for such a militia. Critics hinted that Budi Utomo had been put up to this by the government. Sarekat Islam took the view that the peoples of Indonesia could be expected to defend the colonial regime only if they were represented in its government. In 1915 Budi Utomo also endorsed this view. The *Indië weerbaar* campaign had thus quickly shifted to the issue of popular representation. In 1916–17 a delegation consisting of representatives from Budi Utomo, SI, the Bupatis' Union and similar organisations for the four Javanese principalities, visited the Netherlands. They petitioned Queen Wilhelmina and toured the country giving lectures. When the Dutch States-General acted on the issues, the bill to create an indigenous militia failed, but in December 1916 the bill to establish the Volksraad passed.

The Indonesian parties now prepared for the Volksraad elections. Budi Utomo quickly revealed its limitations. It was proposed to make Islamic appeals a part of its platform in order to attract a mass following, and to spread its sphere of activity beyond Java and Madura. The anti-Islamic potential in the ideas of Radjiman and others carried the day, however, and there was not enough support to launch

Budi Utomo out of its Java-centric thinking either. Budi Utomo now began to split between moderates and conservatives. With Governor-General J.P. Count van Limburg Stirum (1916–21) still in favour of further political reform, Budi Utomo was in some danger of finding itself to the right of the colonial government.

Sarekat Islam was undergoing increasing leftist influence, as ISDV sought its mass base. In 1914 a young Javanese railway worker named Semaun (1899–1971) joined SI's Surabaya branch. In 1915 he moved to Sĕmarang, where Sneevliet was active in the Railway and Tram Workers' Union (VSTP). Semaun now joined ISDV as well. The Sĕmarang SI grew rapidly to 20000 members in 1917, and under Semaun's influence it adopted a strongly anti-capitalist line. It opposed SI's participation in the *Indië weerbaar* campaign, opposed the idea of sitting in the Volksraad, and bitterly attacked the Central Sarekat Islam (CSI) leadership. In the 1917 SI congress the radicals seemed to have considerable support. Tjokroaminoto feared to start an internal battle with them and agreed to a condemnation of 'sinful' capitalism, thereby apparently condemning foreign and Chinese capital but not capital in the hands of Indonesian *hajis* and others. Abdul Muis (1890–1959), a Minangkabau who had been SI's representative on the *Indië weerbaar* delegation to the Netherlands, went so far as to say that if the Volksraad proved to be a failure, SI would revolt.

SI was now splitting into several segments, although the full significance of these was not yet clear. The leftists led by the Sĕmarang branch were working for control. In West Java a secret revolutionary branch called 'Afdeeling B' (Section B) or 'Sarekat Islam B' was being set up by Sosrokardono of CSI and some other activists, beginning in 1917. CSI was meanwhile looking towards legal political activity in the Volksraad. The unruly mass membership was still inclined to disorganised violence. And finally, since 1915 a new force had been rising within SI. In that year a Minangkabau employed as a police informer named Haji Agus Salim (1884–1954) went to a SI meeting, was converted to SI's cause, and brought with him a commitment to Pan-Islam and Modernism as the proper basis for political activity.

At the beginning of 1918 the results of the Volksraad elections became known. Abdul Muis of CSI and Abdul Rivai, who was a member of Insulinde, were elected, but the rest of the elected Indonesian members were mostly *bupatis* or other officials. Governor-General van Limburg Stirum was disappointed by this outcome. He used his powers of appointment to name, among others, Tjipto Mangunkusumo (now back from exile) from Insulinde and Tjokroaminoto from SI, in the hope of involving the more radical forces and bringing them to a cooperative approach. The elected European members were more progressive than the majority of Indonesian members. Dutchmen opposed to Ethical reforms had largely ignored the elections, so the Ethically-inclined Nederlandsch Indische Vrijzinnige Bond (Netherlands Indies Liberal Alliance), along with the Dutch socialists (Sociaal Democratische Arbeiderspartij, Social Democratic Workers' Party) and the more liberal Indonesians formed a majority of elected members. The ISDV now began to fear that the Volksraad might prove to be a success and thereby lead progressive Indonesians away from the extreme left.

In November 1918 the political excitement of the World War I period reached a peak when it seemed as if the social-democratic revolution in Germany would overflow into the Netherlands. The attempt failed. But while uncertainty about the outcome persisted in Indonesia, van Limburg Stirum – who probably already knew that the Dutch monarchy was safe and merely used the occasion to support further reform – issued his 'November promises', agreeing to further transfer of power to the Volksraad and other unspecified social reforms. The Volksraad looked increasingly promising.

But during 1919 the colonial government withdrew from its apparent liberalism, as even van Limburg Stirum began to feel that things were getting out of hand. He turned first to ISDV. Since the Russian Revolution of 1917, ISDV had become an even more clearly Communist body. Late in 1917 it had gathered 3000 soldiers and sailors into soviets, mainly in the port city of Surabaya. During 1918 and 1919 the government crushed these soviets, exiled Sneevliet and arrested or exiled most of the other Dutch leaders of the party. As the Dutch radicals disappeared, however, ISDV fell to Indonesian leadership, which would shortly enable it at last to acquire its mass base. Insulinde was the next to be hit. Early in 1919 there were rural troubles in Surakarta led by Haji Misbach (d.1926), a man whose preaching of the doctrine that Islam and Communism were the same thing earned him notoriety as the 'red *haji*'. Other Insulinde leaders also seemed to be involved, so Misbach and Douwes Dekker were arrested and Tjipto Mangunkusumo was banished from all Javanese-speaking areas. Next it was SI's turn.

In May 1919 a Dutch Controleur was murdered at Tolitoli (North Sulawesi) just after Abdul Muis of CSI had made a speaking tour in the region. CSI was blamed and Muis was arrested. Then in June 1919 a shooting incident at Garut (West Java) led to the discovery of the secret Section B. Sosrokardono of CSI was arrested along with some Indonesian ISDV members. In 1921 Tjokroaminoto himself was arrested for perjury in the Section B trials. Moderate members of SI now began to worry about the organisation and its mass base began to wither as villagers feared that SI membership cards were passports to trouble. The Javanese *priyayi* administrators became even more consciously opposed to the popular movements, and the Dutch expanded their intelligence and police organisations.

The political environment was turning against radicalism, but ironically this left ISDV in a position to take command of the popular political movement. ISDV was now in the hands of Semaun and a young Javanese aristocrat named Darsono (b. 1897). It was still very small (269 members in 1920), but it was now predominantly Indonesian. In May 1920 it changed its name to Pĕrsĕrikatan Kommunist di India (the Communist Association in the Indies); in 1924 it was changed to Partai Komunis Indonesia (the Indonesian Communist Party). PKI was born.

PKI propaganda now revealed how thoroughly Indonesian the party had become. Rather than emphasise the theoretical doctrines of Marx and Lenin, PKI spoke in a vocabulary which appealed to Indonesians, especially to Javanese *abangan* (nominal Muslims). The classless society was presented as a reincarnation of a romanticised Majapahit, seen as a great egalitarian age before the Dutch had come and, significantly, before Islam. The heroes of PKI were Dipanagara, Kyai Maja and Sĕntot from the Java War. The messianic prophesies of the *Ratu Adil* (just king) were also harnessed to PKI appeals. And there was an Islamic Communist variant of all this. Between his release from prison late in 1922 and his arrest the following year, Haji Misbach spread Islamic Communism in the Surakarta area. Islamic Communism also spread in Minangkabau and in West

Java. It is important to note that although students from Modernist schools were often attracted to Islamic Communism, it was mostly led by Sufi teachers and other representatives of more traditional forms of Islam. Modernist leaders, with their dedication to strict scriptural orthodoxy, were the main opponents to Islamic Communism.

Between 1918 and 1921, Indonesian trade unions had considerable success in improving conditions and wages for their members. This was primarily because those years saw a combination of price inflation, shortage of skilled labour and successful organisation of labour by political parties, mainly SI and PKI. Unions' successes naturally encouraged people to join them. As they attracted members, the unions played a significant role in politicising workers and contributing to the development and organisation of Indonesian anti-colonialism. In December 1919 an attempt was made to create a federation of PKI and SI unions, containing twenty-two unions and 72000 members. Semaun chaired this federation, while the vice-chairman was the CSI union leader Surjopranoto, nicknamed 'raja mogok' (the strike king), who soon disputed Semaun's leadership. The federation was permanently crippled by such internal conflicts. Meanwhile employers were becoming more organised and effective in resisting strikes, the government was growing more repressive towards Indonesian trade unions and economic conditions were turning against them as the shortage of skilled labour turned into a surplus by 1921. Thus the context in which unions tried to operate was becoming more hostile.

Now SI and PKI came into open and irreconcilable conflict. In November 1920 the PKI's Dutch-language newspaper *Het vrije woord* ('The Free Word') published Lenin's theses on the national and colonial questions, which included denunciations of Pan-Islam and Pan-Asianism. SI was now more and more under the influence of Haji Agus Salim and others who supported Pan-Islam. The ensuing public battle was bitter, and no matter what contortions PKI attempted it could not avoid the charge of being anti-Islamic. The bitter personal rivalries that were splitting the political movement had now achieved an ideological definition. As the public battle raged in meetings and newspapers, the mass base that SI claimed was even more inclined to abandon political organisations altogether.

Attempts by some leaders to patch up the quarrels failed. At the October 1921 SI congress, 'party discipline' was adopted. This made it impossible for a SI member to belong to another party (although some exceptions were allowed, such as Muhammadiyah). PKI members were now driven out of CSI, but the battle remained to be fought out in each SI branch. The result was that SI began to split into 'Red SI' and 'White SI' branches. Semaun left Indonesia to go to the Soviet Union, and Tjokroaminoto was now in jail. In their absence a Minangkabau named Tan Malaka (1897–1949) made some fruitless efforts to restore PKI-SI cooperation. In 1922 the first really large-scale strike broke out in the pawnshop workers' union led by Abdul Muis of CSI. PKI felt obliged to announce its support. The strike was broken by the government, which simply fired the strikers, and Muis and Tan Malaka were both exiled.

In May 1922 Semaun returned to a scene of apparent catastrophe. He immediately set to work to rebuild PKI unions and PKI influence in SI branches and schools. Tjokroaminoto was released from jail in May 1922 (he was formally acquitted of perjury in August); by now he was determined to be rid forever of

PKI, which among other things had been calling him a dishonest drunkard. At the February 1923 SI congress he set up Partai Sarekat Islam (Islamic Union Party) with party discipline, and determined to establish a branch of this party wherever there was a 'Red SI' branch. The 'Red SI' branches were now renamed Sarekat Rakyat (People's Union) and the battle was on.

In mid-1923 Semaun was exiled to Europe after the government crushed a strike by his railway and tram workers' union (VSTP). Darsono became PKI leader. Salim's influence in CSI now led it to adopt a policy of non-cooperation (it withdrew its Volksraad members), which it called *hijrah* (migration) in remembrance of the Prophet Muhammad's *hijrah* from Mecca to Medinah in AD 622. CSI was now withdrawing from any significant political action. As CSI slowly faded into inactivity, PKI began its last drive to take control of the dying popular movement. The main scene of the contest was now in what remained of the unruly rural SI branches.

While the political movement was disintegrating, the religious and cultural debate was also producing deeper divisions. In 1916 SI had already split along doctrinal lines in Minangkabau. Modernists called themselves 'white card SI' while the more old-fashioned religious groups led by Sufis were called 'red card SI'. The party of progressive *adat* leaders under Datuk Sutan Maharadja meanwhile reconciled its differences with the older aristocrats. In 1916 they formed the Sarekat Adat Alam Minangkabau (Adat Union of the Minangkabau World); this became a pro-government political party opposed to the reformist religious leaders. In 1918 the traditionalist religious leaders and the *adat* party moved closer together in their shared opposition to Modernism. In 1919 Sumatra Thawalib (General Organisation of Students of Sumatra) was formed for Modernist students and by 1922 political activism was strong among them. Until his arrest in November 1923 Haji Datuk Batuah (b. 1895) spread Islamic Communism among the students, against the bitter opposition of Haji Rasul and the Modernist teachers. As noted above, in 1925 Haji Rasul brought Muhammadiyah to Minangkabau, apparently having lost hope in the Sumatra Thawalib.

In Java, an article appeared in the Surakarta newspaper *Djawi Hisworo* ('Javanese of the King') in January 1918 which slandered the Prophet Muhammad as a drunkard and opium smoker. Muslims were incensed and in February they set up a committee called Těntara Kangjěng Nabi Muhammad (Army of the Prophet Muhammad). Anti-Islamic sentiment among some Javanese was so strong that a Comité voor het Javaansch Nationalisme (Committee for Javanese Nationalism) published a pamphlet condemning Islamic fanaticism; although these people, too, disapproved of the style of the *Djawi Hisworo* article, Islam as it was now being taught by the reformists seemed to them to be an unwelcome foreign import.

A more positive and significant reaction to the rising tide of Islamic reform came from the former Indische Partij radical Suwardi Surjaningrat. Suwardi was from the Yogyakarta royal house of Pakualam and a brother of the CSI union leader Surjopranoto. During his exile in the Netherlands (1913–19) he had taken an interest in new educational movements. On his return he joined a Javanese mystical group in Yogyakarta, where Muhammadiyah was based. This mystical group felt that a truly indigenous (i.e. non-government and non-Islamic) educational system was needed. In 1922 Suwardi, now renamed Ki Hadjar Dewantara, therefore set up the first Taman Siswa (Garden of Pupils) school in Yogyakarta, combining modern European-style education and traditional Javanese arts. By 1924 its school took students up to the level of MULO and teacher training school. Taman Siswa did not, however, adopt the government's curriculum and therefore received no government subsidy (nor did it want one, preferring its independence). Here was the logical outcome of the feeling among many Javanese that Islam, and certainly Modernist Islam, was not an acceptable basis for national revival. Taman Siswa soon spread outside of Yogyakarta. By 1932 it had 166 schools and 11000 pupils.

Modernism was meanwhile reaching new extremes. In 1923 a group of merchants set up Pĕrsatuan Islam (Islamic Union) in Bandung. In 1924 a Singapore-born Tamil with a Javanese mother named A. Hassan (b. 1887) joined the organisation. His biting defence of Modernist doctrines, his denunciation of anything that smacked of superstition (that is to say, much of what was accepted as proper Islam by local Muslims), his vehement opposition to nationalism on the grounds that it divided Muslims in one land from another, all justified the organisation's nickname 'Pĕrsis' (a pun on the Dutch *precies:* precise, punctilious). This resulted in the exodus of more moderate members of the group; in 1926 they formed Pĕrmufakatan Islam (Islamic Agreement).

The strict Islamic community of Indonesia was now becoming as split as the political movement. The adoption of the *hijrah* policy of non-cooperation by the declining SI even led it into conflict with the expanding but largely non-political Muhammadiyah, which accepted government subsidies for its schools. In 1929 SI eventually adopted party discipline towards Muhammadiyah, thus driving its members out. But the strongest reactions came from within the ranks of the Orthodox Shafi'i Muslims who objected to Modernism's purifying efforts and its denial of the authority of the four Orthodox schools of law. The arguments were extremely bitter, with accusations flying back and forth that those on the other side were *kafirs* (infidels). A crisis in the Middle East finally brought a formal split between Orthodox and Modernist Indonesians.

In 1924 Turkey abolished the position of Caliph, the spiritual head of all Muslims which the Ottoman Sultans had claimed to be for some six decades. Egypt planned an international Islamic conference to discuss the caliphate question. But further confusion ensued when in 1924 Ibn Sa'ud captured Mecca, bringing with him puritanical Wahhabi ideas of reform and a claim that he was Caliph. He, too, invited all Muslims to a caliphate conference. During 1924–6 Indonesian Muslims set up committees to attend these conferences but the representatives were predominantly Modernist, and Tjokroaminoto appeared prominently.

The Orthodox Shafi'i leaders in Java had had enough. They disliked Modernism, which in any case they equated with Wahhabism (a puritanical movement which accepted only the authority of the Hanbali school of law), they had a low opinion of Tjokroaminoto, and they feared that the interests of the Shafi'i school of law would be ignored in Mecca and Cairo as they were being attacked in Indonesia. In 1926 Kyai Haji Hasjim Asjari (1871–1947), the head of an Orthodox *pĕsantren* (religious school) at Jombang in East Java, therefore set up Nahdlatul Ulama (the Rise of the Religious Scholars, NU) to defend the interests of Orthodox Muslims. Other rural Orthodox teachers *(kyais)* in East Java joined him, the leaders being mainly people who had family connections to Hasjim Asjari. NU spread in other areas, but East Java always remained its heartland. It supported the improvement of Orthodox religious schools, care for the needy, and economic enterprises. By 1942 it had 120 branches in Java and South Kalimantan, much of its membership being traders.

The government was now trying to get some control over the proliferating Islamic educational establishments, which it saw as a potential threat to the colonial regime. In 1905 it had proclaimed a *goeroe ordonnantie* (teacher ordinance) for Java, which required written permission from the authorities before religious instruction could be given, and the keeping of pupil lists. Many *pěsantrens* with teachers who did not know the Western alphabet but only the indigenous and Arabic scripts, and which had floating student populations, were unable to meet these requirements. But in those days before the religious and political turmoil had begun, there was no organised protest. This *goeroe ordonnantie* appears to have had only a limited impact. In 1925 a new *goeroe ordonnantie* was proclaimed. This time it applied to all of Indonesia and was in some ways milder: it only required written notification of an intention to give religious instruction, but student lists and curriculum details had to be submitted on standard forms. In Minangkabau the protest at this interference in religious affairs was now so great that the Governor-General decided it was wiser to suspend the *goeroe ordonnantie* there. In both Minangkabau and Java the effect of this new ordinance was to increase politicisation and anti-government sentiment among devout Muslims.

With animosities growing on all sides, the Indonesian political parties moved towards catastrophe. The competition for a rural following between SI and Sarekat Rakyat branches led PKI into a violent and anarchic milieu. The PKI leadership was uncertain about its course, its ideology or its appeals, as it found itself with a growing non-proletarian following. SI split up still further as Salim and other Pan-Islamic leaders gained in influence. Sosrokardono (released from prison in 1923) broke with SI and joined PKI in 1924. Two other Javanese who had also been involved in the Section B affair, Alimin Prawirodirdjo (1889–1964) and Musso (1897–1948), both of whom had been ISDV members but had been loyal to Tjokroaminoto at the Section B trials, joined PKI on their release. Surjopranoto also leaned towards the Communists.

In early 1924 violence in rural Java increased with the appearance of groups called *sarekat hijau* (green union), especially in Priangan. These were gangs of thugs, policemen and *kyais*, encouraged by the Dutch administration and *priyayi* officials. By early 1925 there were about 20000 members who attacked PKI and SI meetings and intimidated their members. Government surveillance was greater, and what remained of the PKI leadership often found itself under arrest.

Unable to decide finally whether it should abandon the Sarekat Rakyat in order to preserve a proletarian character, PKI stumbled towards rebellion. In December 1924 it was decided to prepare for insurrection. The PKI leadership in Java found itself criticised by the Comintern and by its own leaders in exile, notably Semaun and Tan Malaka, but it stood firm. An attempt to foment a major strike wave in 1925 was a disaster. Thereafter, the government thoroughly suppressed what remained of the trade unions and PKI was virtually driven underground as the police broke up its meetings and carried off individual leaders. In September 1925 Darsono and many others were arrested; Darsono was allowed to travel at his own expense to the Soviet Union the following year. Alimin fled to Singapore where he joined Tan Malaka. As the confusion mounted, PKI appeared in an exotic array of local styles, few of which had much to do with theoretical Communism. In Bantĕn it became hyper-Islamic. As it grew more and more attractive to the anarchic elements of rural society, PKI grew rapidly in Sumatra and Java, with little central coordination.

In December 1925 the remaining PKI leaders decided to rebel. The government attempted to arrest most of the central leadership in January 1926 but many succeeded in escaping. The only remaining leader of any stature was Musso, who fled to Singapore. With its leaders in exile and their heirs in Java thoroughly split over the proper course, PKI was fast disintegrating. The police had penetrated its chaotic lines of communication and, before the insurrection could break out, in November 1926 many branch leaders were arrested, including those along the north coast of Java where the insurrectionary urge had been strongest. When the moment came, these branches did nothing. On the night of 12 November 1926 the PKI uprising broke out in Bantĕn, Batavia and Priangan. It was put down in Batavia by the next day, and throughout Bantĕn and Priangan by December. One European was killed. After the revolt had been utterly crushed in Java, it broke out in Sumatra on 1 January 1927. The fighting here was heavier, but the insurrection was crushed by 4 January. Another European was killed by the rebels.

PKI was dead, and was not to be resurrected for nearly twenty years. About 13000 people were arrested; some were shot. Some 4500 were imprisoned, and 1308 were sent to the notorious prison camp at Boven Digul in Irian, which was specially constructed in 1927 to house them. With PKI's destruction two other things came to an end for the duration of the colonial period. Never again until World War II did the rural masses play an active role in political agitation. And never again did the Dutch tolerate radical anti-colonial movements for more than brief periods.

The first stage of national revival came to an end as the shock of the PKI rebellion and its utter failure spread throughout Indonesia. Indonesian life, especially in Java and Minangkabau, had been truly transformed. It was not yet clear, however, whether it had progressed. Some important patterns had emerged, but they had only increased the sense of disunity among Indonesians. Instead of a vague sense of a shared Islamic identity, it now mattered what kind of Muslim one was or, indeed, whether one wished to be a Muslim at all. Instead of an unspecified opposition to Dutch rule, it was now a question of what kind of anti-colonial doctrine one supported or, indeed, whether one's interests really lay with the colonial regime. Instead of a general belief that Indonesians had something or other in common, regional identities were even clearer as a result of the growth of ethnically based organisations. Instead of an assumption that various classes in each region were brothers of a sort, the bureaucratic elites and their subjects were very clearly warned of the interests that divided them.

There were, however, some promising signs. The next generation of Indonesian politicians would include some who were more realistic, Islam was undergoing a true reform, and the nature of the enemy had been perceived. Eventually Indonesian leaders would find that there were things which united them, and that these things could be regarded as more important than the issues which divided them, at least as a temporary expedient. Out of this discovery nationalism would shortly be born. This would be a new step, for among the major organisations described in this chapter the influence of religious reform, of Pan-Islam, of international Marxist categories or of regional and communal identities was such that none was truly nationalist. But soon some leaders would begin to think of all the indigenous peoples of Indonesia as their constituency and an Indonesian national state as their goal. On this, at least, many would eventually be able to agree.

15 Repression and Economic Crisis, 1927–42

Between 1927 and the destruction of the Dutch colonial state by the Japanese in 1942, the Indonesian national revival proceeded in a less flamboyant fashion. In political affairs, the anti-colonial movement went through a series of false starts which ended in nothing. The Dutch regime entered the most repressive phase of its twentieth-century history. The rural masses no longer played an active political role, being both disillusioned by their experience with SI and PKI in preceding years and, from 1930 onwards, more immediately occupied with surviving the hard years of the Depression.

There were, however, several aspects of this period which set the stage for the events which were to follow after 1942. Firstly, any hopes of progress in cooperation with the Dutch were utterly dashed, so that opposition to the Dutch became the only possible tactic for the future. Secondly, the deep divisions within the tiny Indonesian elite were generally subordinated to an understanding that some form of autonomous or independent Indonesian state was the prime goal of political effort; thus nationalism was established as the dominant ideological position. Thirdly, in the interest of maximum unity among Indonesia's cultural, religious and ideological streams, this nationalist idea rejected the Pan-Islamic and reformist instincts of the urban Islamic leadership, adopting a position which is conventionally called 'secular' but which in practice was often seen as anti-Islamic by Muslim leaders; Islam was thus pushed into the isolated political position which, with rare exceptions, it has occupied ever since. Fourthly, the awareness that they faced many common challenges and shared a common commitment to their faith lessened the bitter arguments between Modernist and Orthodox Muslims and brought these two wings closer together. And finally, the individuals who emerged as Indonesian leaders in this period were significant, for, despite all appearances at the time, they were destined to be the first generation in Indonesian history to preside over the entire archipelago as a unified and independent nation.

Among the new leaders who emerged after the destruction of PKI, particular interest attaches to the man who was eventually to become the first President of independent Indonesia. Sukarno (1901–70) was the son of a Javanese teacher in the government school system and his Balinese wife. His father was from the nominal Muslim (*abangan*) community of Java and a Theosophist. After finishing his studies in his father's school in Majakěrta (East Java), Sukarno went into the European school system, finishing the European Lower School there in 1916. Then he was sent to the European HBS (Higher middle-class school) in

Surabaya, where he boarded with Tjokroaminoto of SI, who was a friend of his father.

In Surabaya, Sukarno met many of the early political leaders: Tjokroaminoto himself, Salim, Sneevliet, Semaun, Musso, Alimin and Ki Hadjar Dewantara among others. He began to read widely, exploring European and American history and absorbing many new ideas. His resentment at the petty discrimination he suffered at HBS, the things he heard from the political leaders and his studies and private reading all began to move him towards an anti-colonial political position. In 1918 he joined the youth movement Jong Java, started to write for the SI newspaper *Oetoesan Hindia* ('Indies Messenger') and began to speak impressively at SI meetings. In 1920 or 1921 he sealed his status as a protégé of Tjokroaminoto by taking the latter's fifteen-year-old daughter in a 'hung marriage' *(kawin gantung)*, a form of matrimony in which the consummation of the marriage is postponed, often because of the young age of one or both of the partners.

In 1921 Sukarno finished HBS and proceeded to the recently opened Technical College in Bandung. When Tjokroaminoto was arrested for perjury in the Section B trials in August 1921, Sukarno left his studies and returned to work as a railway clerk in Surabaya in order to support the family. When Tjokroaminoto was released in 1922 Sukarno returned to Bandung. But in Bandung new influences were beginning to weaken his links with Tjokroaminoto. His new landlord's wife Inggit Garnasih began to hold a great attraction for him. In 1922 he divorced Tjokroaminoto's daughter and the following year he married Inggit, thus ending his personal tie to Tjokroaminoto. Bandung was also a centre of new kinds of ideas which contributed to the increasing sophistication of Sukarno's outlook. Here Modernist Islam took its most extreme form in Pĕrsatuan Islam. Here also PKI was active.

Most significantly, in Bandung Sukarno met and was deeply impressed by Douwes Dekker and especially Tjipto Mangunkusumo, and grew much closer to Ki Hadjar Dewantara. Before their exile in 1913 these three had led the radical Indische Partij, the membership of which had been largely Indo-European and which had been the only party to think in Indonesian nationalist terms rather than in Islamic, Marxist or narrowly ethnic categories. All three were now back from exile. Their influence was revealed repeatedly in Sukarno's subsequent career. In their ideas he found justification for a form of nationalism which was devoid of any specific Islamic commitment, theory of class struggle or formal link to a particular ethnic group. Dewantara's Taman Siswa school system, begun in 1922, rejected reformist Islam and adopted Javanese culture as the philosophical basis for a new national character. This struck a responsive chord in Sukarno's thinking. The way in which Javanese *abangan,* and especially the upper-class *priyayi* among them, had absorbed Hindu, Buddhist, Islamic and Western ideas into a unique synthesis which they found satisfactory seemed to Sukarno to be a model for the Indonesian nation as a whole.

In Sukarno's hands, appeals to nationalism and to unity in the cause of nationalism meant that other doctrines must be subordinated to a set of ideas which denied the need for Islamic reform or dominance, for social struggle within Indonesian society or for anything other than a vaguely radical rejection of colonial rule. This political philosophy was, and remained, almost wholly devoid of positive prescriptions for what should follow once independence was won.

Sukarno's main contribution to this nationalism was the injection of a romantic streak, a belief that he could be like the great men of history of whom he had read: Washington, Lincoln, Garibaldi and others. Throughout his career, Sukarno believed so strongly in his own historical destiny that many others began to believe in it, too.

In November 1925, during his final year at the Technical College, Sukarno helped to found the Algemeene Studieclub (General Study Club) among the students. This was inspired by the Study Club set up in Surabaya in 1924 by Dr Sutomo (1888–1938), one of the founders of Budi Utomo, who had won notoriety for his view that Islam detracted from proper nationalistic sentiments. Sukarno's Study Club was overtly political, with independence for Indonesia being its goal. In the deeply divided anti-colonial movement of the day, Sukarno saw evidence that above all else unity must be achieved.

When he finished his engineering degree in Bandung in 1926, Sukarno was still uncertain whether to go into government service or political activity. He was now one of the most highly educated Indonesians of his time, but to what use should he put his status and learning? His dilemma was, of course, that of the lesser *priyayi* as a whole. His feeling that the anti-colonial movement needed to be unified, and that he was the man to achieve this, meanwhile continued to grow. Later in 1926 he published a series of articles which argued, as others had argued before, that Islam, Marxism and nationalism should be united in the cause of independence. In practice, he implied that the first two of these should be subordinated to the third. By assuming that the real differences among these ideologies did not exist, and by resisting involvement in the bitter controversies of the day, Sukarno's Study Club managed to maintain friendly contacts with all other factions. When the PKI rebellion was crushed in late 1926 and early 1927, by which time SI had largely faded into inactivity, fate seemed to have made Sukarno's choice of careers for him. With Communism destroyed and Islam increasingly impotent as a political force, the time for nationalism seemed to have dawned.

On 4 July 1927 Sukarno and his Bandung Study Club took the initiative in founding a new political party, the Persěrikatan Nasional Indonesia (Indonesian Nationalist Association), with Sukarno as chairman. In May 1928 its name was changed to Partai Nasional Indonesia (Indonesian Nationalist Party, PNI). PNI's aim was independence for the Indonesian archipelago, to be achieved by non-cooperative methods and mass organisation. This was the first major political party in which the membership was ethnically Indonesian, the goal was simply political independence, the territorial vision encompassed the present boundaries of Indonesia, and the ideology was 'secular' nationalism. By May 1929 PNI had branches in the main cities of Java and one in Palembang, and claimed 3860 members (most of them in Bandung, Batavia and Surabaya); at the end of 1929 it had 10000 members.

By the end of 1927, Sukarno appeared already to have achieved a united front of the main Indonesian political organisations. The Partai Sarekat Islam leader Sukiman Wirjosandjojo (b. 1896) gave Sukarno crucial support in creating this ephemeral unity, over the objections of Salim who disapproved of 'secular' nationalism and disliked the influence of the new generation of Westernised intellectuals. Partai Sarekat Islam, Budi Utomo, the Surabaya Study Club and the main regionalist and Christian organisations joined with PNI in a body known as PPPKI (Pĕrmufakatan Pĕrhimpunan-pĕrhimpunan Politik Kĕbangsaan Indonesia, Agreement of Indonesian People's Political Associations). The idea of an all-Indonesian nationalism as a common denominator was now growing. The intellectual leaders of ethnic and regionalist groups were adopting the concept partly as a means of defence against potential Javanese domination, and Christian groups saw it partly as a defence against Islamic domination. Some sections of the Chinese and Arab communities also endorsed Indonesian nationalism on a multi-racial basis. But the growth of nationalism had more positive roots as well, for many leaders were convinced that there was such a thing as an Indonesian nation and that this nation had a right to a life of its own.

Real differences of aims, ideology and personalities still divided the movements, however, and the unity achieved by PPPKI was superficial. The Partai Sarekat Islam (in 1929 renamed Partai Sarekat Islam Indonesia, PSII) withdrew from PPPKI in 1930 because the other groups refused to give Islam the recognition that the urban Islamic leaders thought it deserved. The 'secular' nationalists tended, indeed, to look admiringly at Egypt, Persia, Iraq and especially Turkey, where religion and the state were being separated in the name of modernity. The Indonesian Islamic leadership could not accept such ideas. The loose unity represented by PPPKI confirmed the idea that a nationalism devoid of regional or religious ties was a possible basis for joint action, but this implied that joint action would almost certainly bypass the Islamic groups who would therefore find themselves isolated from the main stream of political leadership. This did not yet, however, bring Muslims closer together. The urban PSII leaders continued to stress Modernist ideas which the rural Orthodox leaders of NU found unacceptable.

In the Netherlands, too, a new leadership group was emerging among Indonesian students. This group was shortly to produce the main alternative to Sukarno's style of religiously neutral nationalism. In 1922 the old organisation for Indonesian students in the Netherlands, the Indische Vereeniging (Indies Association, est. 1908) was renamed Pĕrhimpunan Indonesia (Indonesian Association) and became more involved in political questions. The exiled PKI leaders Tan Malaka and Semaun, among others, spoke to its meetings and the organisation moved in a radical direction. Two of its main leaders were Minangkabaus: Mohammad Hatta (1902–80) and Sutan Sjahrir (1909–66). Hatta was to become both Vice President and Prime Minister of Indonesia and Sjahrir was to become Prime Minister. Two other future Prime Ministers, the Javanese Ali Sastroamidjojo (1903–75) and Sukiman Wirjosandjojo, were also prominent. These were, in general, the most intellectual of the Indonesian leaders; they had attended Dutch universities and had an informed and generally unromantic view of the outside world, of the Dutch and of imperialism, but they often lacked empathy with their less favoured countrymen at home. Hatta was the dominant personality among them. In ideology they were mostly socialists who accepted much of the Marxist interpretation of imperialism. Later, in 1931, Pĕrhimpunan Indonesia was to split when Moscow-oriented Communists gained control; both Sjahrir and Hatta were then expelled.

In September 1927 Hatta, Ali and others were arrested on a charge of encouraging armed resistance to Dutch rule in Indonesia. After over five months in prison they were tried in the Hague in March 1928 and were acquitted, much to the embarrassment of the authorities. Hatta had used his defence speech to make a sweeping denunciation of Dutch rule and justification of Indonesian nationalism. In Indonesia as well the government moved against the new leaders. The Dutch community was turning even more to the right in this period, and was greatly worried and offended by large public meetings where Sukarno and others deliberately insulted colonial authority. The Ethically-inclined Governor-General (1926–31) Andries C. D. de Graeff was still reluctant to endorse general repression. Nevertheless, he sent Tjipto Mangunkusumo into exile on Banda in 1928 (until 1941) and presided over the destruction of the last remnants of the leftist labour union movement when the leadership of the Sarekat Kaum Buruh Indonesia (Indonesian Workers' Union, est. 1928) was arrested in 1929.

In 1929 the government finally acted against PNI by arresting Sukarno and other leaders. Despite the fiasco of the trials in the Hague, it was eventually decided to send Sukarno for public trial in Bandung late in 1930. He made a resounding defence speech which echoed the commitment if not the intellectual rigour of Hatta's speech in the Hague. Sukarno was convicted of being a threat to public order and sentenced to four years in Sukamiskin prison in Bandung. PNI was paralysed by the arrest and imprisonment of its leader and suspended its activities. With Sukarno's removal PNI seemed to amount to very little.

The idea of a national Indonesian identity devoid of specific religious or regional ties had nonetheless begun to be widely accepted among the elite, and by now was being supported by developments in the cultural field. A new literature was growing, based upon the Malay language, which had been used for centuries as a *lingua franca* in the archipelago and was therefore essentially neutral in ethnic terms. More specifically, it was not Javanese, and therefore carried no implication of Javanese dominance. As this literature developed, Indonesian intellectuals stopped calling the language Malay and instead referred to it as the Indonesian language *(Bahasa Indonesia)*. The linguistic vehicle of national unity was thereby born.

All branches of writing expanded rapidly in Indonesia. In 1918 there were already about 40 newspapers published, mostly in Indonesian; by 1925 there were about 200; by 1938 there were over 400 dailies, weeklies and monthlies. A modern literature also evolved, in which Minangkabau writers played a leading role. They were products of a dynamic society whose role in the modernisation of Indonesia has already been discussed in the preceding chapter, and of all the regional languages of the archipelago Minangkabau was the closest to Malay/Indonesian. Muhammad Yamin (1903–64), who was to become one of the most radical of Indonesian political leaders, abandoned the *pantun* and *syair* forms and published the first truly modern poems in 1920–2. In 1922 Marah Roesli (b. 1898) published the first modern novel *Sitti Noerbaja* ('Miss Nurbaya'), dealing with a tragic love affair which arises from the clash between traditional and modern values. The Batak writer Sanusi Pane (1905–68) was also writing modern poetry by 1921, and after spending 1929–30 in India began to urge that cultural inspiration be sought in Indonesia's pre-Islamic past, despite the fact that he was himself a Muslim.

Much of this modern Indonesian literature was published by the government printing house Balai Pustaka (Office for Literature; in Dutch: Commissie – after 1917 Kantoor – voor de Volkslectuur, Committee/Office for Popular Literature), which was established in 1908. This performed three main functions: the publication of older classical works and popular stories in regional languages, the translation of Western literature into Indonesian and the publication of the new Indonesian literature. At one and the same time it thus helped to keep regional cultures alive, opened Indonesia to more universal literary values and contributed to the creation of an all-Indonesian culture. In the literary field it thus maintained some of the high ideals of the Ethical policy long after they were dead in political affairs.

In October 1928 the cultural and political trends towards Indonesian unity were formally joined at a Youth Congress held in Batavia. In its 'Youth Pledge' *(sumpah pěmuda)* the Congress adopted three ideals: one fatherland, Indonesia; one nation, Indonesia; and one language, Bahasa Indonesia, the language of unity. In celebration of this Congress, Yamin wrote a collection of poems which were published in 1929 under the title *Indonesia tumpah darahku* ('Indonesia, land of my birth'). These reflected the self-conscious conviction among young intellectuals that they were Indonesians first, and only secondly Minangkabaus, Bataks, Javanese, Christians, Muslims or whatever.

The economic context within which Indonesians lived was suddenly altered by the world-wide economic Depression of the 1930s. Just as there were signs of an impending crisis in the industrialised world before the Wall Street Crash of October 1929, so also in Indonesia there were indications that the apparent prosperity of the late 1920s would not last. Prices for some of Indonesia's products were already on a downward trend and the market for sugar exports was contracting as beet sugar production expanded elsewhere, particularly in Great Britain and Japan. Yet no one was adequately prepared for what was to follow after October 1929. Indonesia was heavily dependent on its exports, particularly oil and agricultural products. In 1930, 52 per cent of these exports went to the industrialised nations of Europe and North America. The economic crisis in these lands followed by the widespread adoption of protectionism, coupled with falling prices, suddenly plunged Indonesia into an economic crisis from which it never fully recovered before the Japanese conquest in 1942.

Price fluctuations were a common phenomenon, but now the prices for all of Indonesia's main exports fell simultaneously and disastrously. Beginning in 1929 the average price for Indonesia's exports plummeted. By 1935, the value of Indonesia's exports was about 32 per cent of that in 1929. The volume of exports also fell as markets contracted and protectionism spread. The impact upon various sectors differed widely. The oil industry expanded production to cope with falling prices, as did rubber producers. But rubber, sugar, coffee and tobacco – products which employed large numbers of Indonesians as labourers and small-scale producers – faced disaster. In 1932 the price of rubber was 16 per cent of the 1929 price. Sugar contracted dramatically. The area under cane was reduced as rapidly as possible: in 1934 there were 200000 hectares under cane; in 1939 there were only 90000. Workers were dismissed and the sugar industry's wage bill was thereby cut by 90 per cent. The Depression in fact brought an end, after over a century, to the domination of Indonesia's exports by sugar and coffee. Javanese workers on the plantations of East Sumatra began to flow back home as work opportunities disappeared there. On balance, Indonesian incomes appear to have dropped more in the outer islands than in Java, but the crisis was severe everywhere.

As exports fell it was necessary also to reduce imports, including food items. Government revenues derived largely from trade levies and taxes upon income and expenditure, so Batavia found itself facing a revenue crisis. The land taxes paid primarily by Indonesians also declined, but less slowly than did the price of rice, the principal domestic crop, so the real tax burden on Indonesians rose. Government revenue was necessarily cut back. Civil service recruitment was almost entirely halted, salaries were cut (although, given falling prices, real incomes frequently rose) and non-essential government employees were laid off. This only exacerbated the problem of unemployment among graduates of the modern school system. There was, however, simultaneously some tendency in the opposite direction as firms dismissed higher-paid European, Indo-European and Chinese employees and replaced them with lower-paid Indonesians.

The Dutch colonial government abandoned its *laissez-faire* economic instincts in an attempt to mitigate the scale of the disaster. For example, it restructured the production of rubber, employing restriction schemes and excise tax which hurt Indonesian smallholders most and large plantations least. One of Batavia's greatest difficulties arose from sudden Japanese penetration of the Indonesian economy. In 1929–30 Japan accounted for 10 per cent of the value of all imports into Indonesia. Whereas the Dutch clung to the gold standard until September 1936, the Japanese devalued the yen in December 1931 and thereafter rapidly displaced the Dutch in Indonesia's imports. The availability of cheap Japanese goods was important in mitigating the impact of the Depression upon Indonesians. By 1934, the peak of Japan's success in this regard, Japanese imports represented 32.5 per cent of the value of all Indonesian imports, nearly two-and-one-half times the value of Dutch imports into the colony. Negotiations with the Japanese to restrict their import penetration failed in 1934, so Batavia introduced a system of licences and quotas which had the effect of restricting Japan's imports alone. By 1936 Batavia and Tokyo shared an informal understanding on trade matters. Japan's imports fell to 25.4 per cent of the value of Indonesia's imports in 1937 and finally were surpassed again by imports from the Netherlands in 1938, when Dutch imports were 22 per cent while Japanese imports were 14.4 per cent of the value of all imports. As the Japanese were pushed out of markets they had previously penetrated, Indonesians found lower-priced Japanese goods replaced by costlier Dutch products. The Japanese retail network had employed Indonesian workers, but they now lost their jobs as the European importers again turned to their customary Chinese middlemen.

The impact of this crisis upon Indonesians was clearly very serious. While it is true, as some Dutch observers said at the time, that Indonesian labourers could often return to subsistence agriculture, it is also true that many did not have this option at all. As land fell out of sugar production some of it returned to rice production, but the increase in rice production could not keep pace with the growing population's need for food and employment. In fact per capita availability of foodstuffs declined from 1930 to 1934. Indeed, there is no serious doubt that at least until the late 1930s Indonesian welfare was in decline. By 1937 per capita income had probably recovered to 1929 levels, but such figures reveal nothing about the distribution of income. Undoubtedly for many Indonesians times were still very hard indeed on the eve of the Japanese conquest. Indonesian welfare organisations such as Muhammadiyah and some political parties set up village-level support activities. Some unions were still functioning sufficiently to support retrenched workers, notably the pawnshop workers' union. For Indonesians who managed to retain salaried jobs in the urban formal sector, these were much less difficult times, for salaries fell less than prices, but their hours of work and other conditions worsened.

Just as there was no cause for optimism in economic affairs in the 1930s, so also was there none in political affairs as the Dutch administration moved decisively to the right. From 1931 to 1936 the Governor-General was Bonifacius C. de Jonge, a former Minister of War and director of Royal Dutch Shell. He was opposed to any form of nationalism and unwilling even to see the Volksraad play any significant role. Political meetings were frequently broken up by the police and speakers arrested. His successor Alidius W. L. Tjarda van Starkenborgh Stachouwer (1936–45) was a rather more flexible man, but brought no great change. The Minister of Colonies in the Hague from 1933 to 1937 was Hendrikus Colijn, a bitter opponent of Ethical ideas and sometime director of Shell. In this environment, it is hardly surprising that nationalism made little progress. In the 1930s the Dutch were firmly in control of Indonesia and determined to remain so.

Political leaders reacted to the arrest of Sukarno and the changing economic and political climate in various ways. Within the Volksraad Muhammad H. Thamrin (1894–1941), the leader of Kaum Bĕtawi, set up a National Party (Nationale Fractie) in January 1930, based upon both Java and outer islands members. Its aim was to work for some form of Indonesian autonomy in cooperation with the Dutch. In Surabaya, Sutomo reorganised his Study Club in October 1930 and turned it into the Pĕrsatuan Bangsa Indonesia (Indonesian People's Union), which was viewed with considerable suspicion by the government. This turned to economic and social activities in East Java such as setting up clinics, student houses, village banks, advice bureaux, etc. It therefore paralleled similar activities by Islamic organisations, and is to be seen as the social and economic equivalent to Taman Siswa's challenge to Islam in the educational field.

PNI itself was dissolved in April 1931. Its leaders had received clear warnings from the Dutch authorities in January 1930 that PNI would not be allowed to pursue political activities while charges against its leaders were pending; after Sukarno's conviction PNI's leaders felt that the party had in effect become a prohibited organisation. In its place was created Partindo (Partai Indonesia, Indonesian Party), which had the same goal as PNI of achieving independence through non-cooperation and mass action. But many former PNI members were now deeply discouraged. As a consequence, in February 1932 Partindo had only 3000 members. Several Indonesian leaders criticised this decision to dissolve PNI, most notable among them being Hatta, who was still in the Netherlands.

In December 1931 a rival to Partindo was created by Sjahrir who had just returned from the Netherlands. This was Pĕndidikan Nasional Indonesia (Indonesian Nationalist Education) which, because of its initials, was called PNI-Baru (New PNI). This party was led by men whose style differed from Sukarno's, but whose ideas were initially quite similar to his. From 1933 onwards, however, as Dutch political repression intensified, PNI-Baru was to develop tactics which distinguished it from the old PNI. PNI-Baru's leaders then developed the view that mass action was difficult if not impossible in the current environment, and reliance on a single leader could lead to the paralysis of a party if he was arrested. Therefore, PNI-Baru aimed to create a cadre of leaders who could step into the shoes of arrested politicians. Marxist influences were also evident in PNI-Baru, which believed in the necessity for struggle against the indigenous bourgeoisie and thus distanced itself from both Islamic commercial circles and the administrative *priyayi*. The religiously neutral nationalist movement thus came to be split between the mass-action model and the cadre-formation model. Neither in fact had any prospect of success in the 1930s.

While the urban intellectuals were seeking new forms of political organisation in the face of Dutch opposition, the largest political movement in Indonesia was being built by a very different kind of leader. In June 1930 a charismatic, very traditional and poorly educated prince of Yogyakarta named Pangeran Surjodiningrat established PKN (Pakěmpalan Kawula Ngayogyakarta, Association of the Subjects of Yogyakarta). The many grievances of the peasantry during the Depression and the appeal of a princely leader combined to give PKN a potential shared by none of the urban intellectual movements. In May 1931 it claimed over 100000 members in Yogyakarta and in August 1939 it claimed nearly 260000. Its membership within the Yogyakarta area was thus comparable to that of Muhammadiyah throughout Indonesia. By actively defending the interests of the peasants PKN came to be a virtual shadow administration and many peasants were attracted to it in the faith that Surjodiningrat was the messianic *Ratu Adil* (just king); in these respects PKN was more truly a successor to Sarekat Islam in its early days than were any of the urban parties. But it also earned the animosity of the bureaucracy and the Dutch. After 1934 government pressure and police harassment forced Surjodiningrat to restrict PKN's activities to social and economic affairs, especially the promotion of cooperatives. Nor were the urban nationalists willing to link themselves to such an apparently feudal kind of organisation, one which also embarrassed them by being far more successful in winning mass support than their own efforts. PKN nevertheless survived until the Japanese occupation and was revived in 1951 as a local Yogyanese party under the name Gěrinda (Gěrakan Rakyat Indonesia, Indonesian People's Movement), still under the absolute authority of Surjodiningrat.

One of Governor-General de Graeff's last acts in office had been to reduce Sukarno's jail sentence. In December 1931 he was freed and immediately attempted to reunify the nationalist movement. He failed in this and in August 1932 joined Partindo, which seemed to share his style and instinct for mass action. By July 1933 Partindo claimed 20000 members. In August 1932 Hatta returned after eleven years in the Netherlands and took over the leadership of PNI-Baru. The contrast between Sukarno and Hatta now symbolised the divisions within 'secular' nationalism just as their later cooperation after 1942 would symbolise the burying of differences; on the one hand a romantic Javanese nominal Muslim with populist instincts, and on the other a highly intellectual and elitist Minangkabau, a devout Muslim who was nonetheless committed to secular socialist political doctrines.

The reaction of the Islamic leadership to the growth of 'secular' nationalism was generally hostile. Another future Prime Minister, the Minangkabau Mohammad Natsir (b. 1908), emerged in this period as a leading Islamic polemicist. He had been educated in the European school system but also attended Islamic schools in Minangkabau. In 1927 he was sent to the General Middle School (AMS) in Bandung. There he became associated with the extreme Modernist thinking of Pěrsatuan Islam and in 1932 he took charge of its new school system. Since 1925

Salim had already been warning devout Muslims that Sukarno's idea of 'mother Indonesia' threatened their sole devotion to God. A. Hassan of Pĕrsatuan Islam equally denounced nationalist ideas. By 1931 Natsir was writing articles which argued that only Islam could be the basis of an Indonesian nationality, but for Muslims independence itself could not be the ultimate goal; rather, they must struggle for a state which would serve Islam and in which Islamic law and Muslim leaders would be dominant.

Modernist Islamic leaders disapproved of nationalism because it was an idea of men whereas Islam was a revelation of God, because it divided the international community of Muslims, and also because it was of European origin and had brought war and imperialism to the West. They were fundamentally unable to see how, in a country where the majority was Muslim, anything other than Islam could seriously be proposed as the basis of unity. The fact that it was Modernist leaders who most opposed 'secular' nationalism, and particularly that the extreme Pĕrsatuan Islam took this position, only tended to confirm the suspicion among those who did not accept Modernist ideas that Islam was a dangerous and divisive political force. This contributed further to the political isolation of Islam. It also contributed to the isolation of the nationalist elite from the masses, for at this time only Islam could offer potential organisational links between educated urban leaders and rural society. The only significant Islamic political body, Partai Sarekat Islam Indonesia (PSII), meanwhile continued under the influence of Salim and Tjokroaminoto to favour Pan-Islam as well as to decline in political influence.

Only in Minangkabau was there a serious attempt to unite Islam and nationalism. Minangkabau students in Cairo began to doubt the value of Pan-Islamic ideas, and were confirmed in this doubt by the failure of the Caliphate conferences in Cairo and Mecca in May and June 1926. Iljas Jacub (b. 1902) and Muchtar Lutfi (b. 1901) returned to Minangkabau in 1929 and 1931 respectively. They took charge of Pĕrmi (Pĕrsatuan Muslim Indonesia, Indonesian Muslims' Union), which was founded in May 1930 upon a slogan of *Islam dan kĕbangsaan* (Islam and [Indonesian] nationality). This combination was attractive to many younger Minangkabaus, including some who were Orthodox rather than Modernist. By August 1933 Pĕrmi claimed 10000 members, about 40 per cent of them women. But Pĕrmi also provoked much opposition.

By late 1932 all the main political streams were represented in Minangkabau. Pĕrmi had established links with Partindo, and PNI-Baru had been introduced into the area. PSII was attempting to establish its own credentials as a radical movement and bitterly attacked the nationalist doctrines of the other parties. Then the government presented these parties and those in Java with a highly emotive issue which drew them together, and thereby brought about their destruction.

In September 1932 the government announced a 'wild schools ordinance' *(wilde scholen ordonnantie)*, which required permission from the authorities before any private school without a government subsidy (which put a school under government supervision) could be established. There was a national outcry at this interference in private schools, just at a time when the government school system was being restricted for financial reasons. Ki Hadjar Dewantara of Taman Siswa led a national campaign in alliance with Islamic groups. Every significant Indonesian organisation, including even Budi Utomo, joined the opposition. Even the Volksraad disapproved and in 1932 rejected the government's education budget in protest. In February 1933 Governor-General de Jonge backed down and suspended the ordinance.

The government now perceived a dangerous potential for united action among the Indonesian movements. Its concern was increased by a brief mutiny of Dutch and Indonesian sailors aboard the naval ship *Zeven Provinciën* in February 1933, which de Jonge partly attributed to the political agitation of the nationalist parties. He reacted firmly. On the basis of existing legislation the government turned against the schools in Minangkabau, where protest against the ordinance had been strongest. Schools were searched, political literature seized, some schools were closed and many teachers banned from teaching. Then the government went over to a general repression of political leaders. Beginning in late 1932 and extending into 1934 (but primarily in the course of 1933), the leaders of Pĕrmi and PSII in Minangkabau were arrested and exiled to Boven Digul, among them both Muchtar Lutfi and Iljas Jacub.

In August 1933 Sukarno was arrested. He was much disturbed by this second arrest. During the following weeks, he wrote four letters to the Dutch authorities, offering to refrain from political activity in return for his freedom, but to no avail. This time there was no public trial; he was exiled to Flores but in 1938 was moved to more comfortable circumstances in Bĕngkulu (South Sumatra). In February 1934, Hatta, Sjahrir and other PNI-Baru leaders were arrested and then exiled to Boven Digul (in 1936 Hatta and Sjahrir were moved to Banda). Bereft of their leaders and subject to increased police harassment, the 'secular' nationalist movements of Partindo and PNI-Baru and the Islamic anti-colonial movements of Pĕrmi and PSII withered. With the death of Tjokroaminoto in December 1934 the Islamic political movement lost its original and foremost leader, and proceeded to disintegrate into yet more factions.

After 1934 radical anti-colonialism on a non-cooperative basis was effectively dead, but cooperative methods had not yet been entirely discredited. In December 1935 the moderate and essentially Javanist bodies Pĕrsatuan Bangsa Indonesia and Budi Utomo merged to form Parindra (Partai Indonesia Raya, Greater Indonesian Party). Its aim was eventual independence in cooperation with the Dutch. Sutomo was its chairman, and Thamrin and others joined. This was essentially a body of religiously neutral or anti-Islamic conservatives, and some of its leaders began to look to Japan as a model. In 1937 it had over 4600 members and at the end of 1939 about 11 250, most of them in East Java. By May 1941 it claimed about 19 500 members. With the rise of fascism in Europe and Japan, many Indonesian leaders with leftist sympathies also began to feel that they should join with the Dutch against the common fascist enemy.

But even those who were in favour of cooperation with the Dutch were beginning to have some doubts about its value. The degree to which nationalist ideas and dissatisfaction had penetrated even those groups which were closest to the government was revealed in 1936. Soetardjo Kartohadikocsocmo (b. 1892) was a Javanese member of the Volksraad with a career in the colonial bureaucracy. He was, therefore, from outside the mainstream of nationalist politicians. But he and his colleagues had grown increasingly dissatisfied with the salary cuts, redundancies, restriction of educational opportunities, and the generally suspicious, interfering and parsimonious policies of the government since about 1930. In July 1936 Soetardjo submitted a petition to the Volksraad which called for a conference to arrange Indonesian autonomy within a Dutch-Indonesian union over a period of ten years. This was essentially what the United States had given the Philippines in 1933, resulting in the establishment of the Philippine Commonwealth government in November 1935. Soetardjo and his supporters were aware of, and inspired by, the Philippines case. The main Indonesian nationalist parties were divided by this proposal, but Christian, Arab, Chinese and Indo-European representatives in the Volksraad supported it, and it was passed in September 1936 primarily because most European members also desired greater autonomy from the Hague.

A public discussion of the Soetardjo petition ensued. Parindra was suspicious, and did not like the idea of Soetardjo succeeding where recognised leaders of the anti-colonial movements had failed. PSII split at this point. In November 1936 Salim, who had decided that the *hijrah* policy of non-cooperation was a failure, set up a cooperative faction called Barisan Pĕnyadar PSII (Awareness Front of PSII). In 1937 the Pĕnyadar faction was formally expelled from PSII. The radical wing also reorganised itself. In November 1936 Partindo was dissolved and in May 1937 Gĕrindo (Gĕrakan Rakyat Indonesia, Indonesian People's Movement) was formed. This included such radicals as Yamin and another future Prime Minister, the leftist Batak Christian Amir Sjarifuddin (1907–48). Gĕrindo's aim was a full parliament for Indonesia, but on the basis of cooperation with the Dutch against the joint threat of fascism, especially Japanese fascism. None of these parties, however, showed any conspicuous support for the Soetardjo petition.

With the clear dominance of cooperative methods among the Indonesian elite (those who rejected such methods either kept their heads down or were quickly removed by the police) and the moderate proposals embodied in the Soetardjo petition, the loftier ideals of those who had initiated the Ethical policy might have been realised. The Dutch authorities had, however, come a long way since the opening decades of the twentieth century, mostly in a backward direction. In November 1938 a royal decree finally pronounced upon the petition: it was rejected. There was little reaction in Indonesia, for by then few had expected it to succeed. Most Indonesian nationalists concluded that since non-cooperation was merely a passport to prison or exile, moderate and evolutionary methods alone could be pursued. But the attitude of the government consistently led them to doubt whether the Dutch would respond favourably or in good faith.

Meanwhile Indonesian literature continued to stimulate and shape an ideal of Indonesian nationality that was devoid of any specific Islamic character. In July 1933 there began to be published the most influential literary journal of the prewar period, *Poedjangga Baroe*, ('New Poet'). Under the editorship of the Minangkabau Takdir Alisjahbana (b. 1908) and the Batak Armijn Pane (1908–70) literary and linguistic standards for the language of Indonesian unity were established. The most important poet of the age, Amir Hamzah (1911–46), was published in *Poedjangga Baroe*. A cultural debate was also pursued in its pages with Takdir urging modernisation (i.e. the adoption of Western ideas) as the essential part of the new Indonesian identity, while Sanusi Pane (Armijn Pane's brother) looked to pre-Islamic Asian cultural values. No one seriously argued for an Islamic basis to this new culture. Balai Pustaka also continued to publish major new novels, including *Salah asuhan* ('Wrong upbringing') by Abdul Muis in 1928, and *Lajar terkembang* ('Unfurled sails') by Takdir in 1936. Armijn Pane's *Belenggoe* ('Shackles') was rejected by Balai Pustaka because it was felt to fall below accepted moral standards by describing an extramarital love affair; it was, however, published in *Poedjangga Baroe* in 1940.

As the Islamic leadership found itself progressively isolated from both political and cultural developments, and facing an increasingly hostile colonial regime, the bitter controversies between the Orthodox and Modernist wings at last declined. The Modernists began to accept that the purification they desired would take a long time, and the Orthodox accepted that the Modernists were a permanent feature of the environment. Orthodox groups also began to adopt many of the reforms introduced by Modernists which did not threaten the dominance of the Shafi'i school of law or Orthodoxy's somewhat more flexible interpretation of the faith. By 1928 Nahdlatul Ulama had already begun to use Javanese as well as Arabic in the Friday sermon, and Orthodox schools in Java and Minangkabau soon began to introduce formal curricula and a system of graded classes. Both wings began to accept that, whatever their differences, they were united in their devotion to Islam.

In September 1937 leaders of Nahdlatul Ulama and Muhammadiyah took the initiative in creating the Majlis Islam A'laa Indonesia (Supreme Islamic Council of Indonesia, MIAI). Pĕrsatuan Islam, al-Irshad and virtually every other Islamic organisation throughout Indonesia soon joined. MIAI was not intended to be a political body but rather a forum for discussion, and many controversies continued within it. There were fundamental issues of Islamic law which were, after all, irreconcilable. But the desire for unity among the Islamic leadership was genuine. They were still unable, however, to convert this into a meaningful role in either political or cultural developments.

PSII continued to split into factions. In 1933 Surjopranoto and Sukiman Wirjosandjojo had set up Partai Islam Indonesia (Indonesian Islamic Party, PII) after they had been expelled from PSII, but the organisation had languished. In 1938 Sukiman, Wiwoho Poerbohadidjojo and others revived PII and expanded it rapidly in Java and the outer islands. This was the last serious effort before World War II to establish Islam as a basis for political unity among Indonesians. But in many ways the battle was already lost.

All hopes for political progress were by now destroyed by the lengthening shadow of fascism. In 1931 Japan invaded Manchuria; two years later Hitler became Chancellor of Germany; in 1936 the Spanish Civil War broke out and in July 1937 the Sino-Japanese war; in March of the following year Hitler absorbed Austria and in September the Munich Conference dismembered Czechoslovakia; in March 1939 Hitler invaded its remnants. As war loomed in Europe and the Pacific, Dutch and Indonesian perceptions polarised. Indonesians felt that their willingness to cooperate against fascism and the drain on Dutch strength which a war would bring should inspire the Netherlands to grant Indonesia some form of autonomy. The Dutch felt that this was no time to undertake any new political experiments, which could only increase instability and uncertainty and which, in any case, most Dutchmen now strongly opposed. Towards Indonesian organisations they grew even more restrictive. Meetings were disbanded and local leaders arrested. Parindra, with its sympathies for Japan, was a particular target.

In May 1939 the main Indonesian nationalist organisations except PNI-Baru formed GAPI (Gabungan Politik Indonesia, Indonesian Political Federation) which called for a full parliament for Indonesia. In December GAPI staged an

Indonesian People's Congress (Kongres Rakyat Indonesia) in Batavia which was judged to be a great success. But within the Volksraad the Indonesian leadership continued to be split. On 1 September 1939 Hitler invaded Poland and World War II began in Europe. GAPI pressed the Dutch to grant autonomy, so that joint Dutch-Indonesian action against fascism would be encouraged. The Dutch would not, of course, respond. In February 1940 the Netherlands government announced that so long as it held ultimate responsibility for Indonesia there could be no question of Indonesian autonomy or parliamentary government.

On 10 May 1940 Hitler invaded the Netherlands and the Dutch government fled to exile in London. Thereafter it would, naturally enough, make no change in Indonesia's status while the war was in progress. On the same day, martial law was declared in Indonesia and all public political meetings were banned. Indonesian leaders in the Volksraad still hoped to win some concessions from the Dutch, but were continually disappointed. They received only vague replies from Governor-General van Starkenborgh that some changes might follow when the war was over. He cannot have guessed how great the changes were to be.

Three motions in the Volksraad sponsored by Thamrin, Soetardjo and Wiwoho asked the government to use the term 'Indonesian' rather than *inlander* (native) in official documents, to define an Indies nationality and to inquire into a reform of the Volksraad to turn it into a quasi-parliament. These received a generally negative response from the government in August 1940 and were withdrawn by their sponsors. In the same month GAPI began its final effort when it called for a Dutch-Indonesian union of equality, with the Volksraad to be turned into a bicameral legislature based on a fair electoral system. MIAI supported GAPI but, consistent with the general inflexibility of the Islamic leaders in such matters, it added that the head of this new system and two-thirds of the cabinet must be Muslims and there must be a Ministry for Islamic Affairs. But there was no time left for the Dutch even to make a formal rejection.

The war in Asia now approached. Indonesia's resources of oil, rubber, bauxite, tin and other strategic materials had long been important in Japanese eyes. As was pointed out above, during the Depression Japan's peaceful economic penetration proceeded rapidly and with it Japanese intelligence activities expanded. The Japanese gained considerable sympathy from Indonesians, who welcomed cheap Japanese goods and courteous treatment in Japanese shops and admired Japan's strength. In the later 1930s, Japan's share of Indonesia's trade dropped significantly. The United States abrogated its commercial treaty with Japan in July 1939 and proceeded to embargo strategic supplies to Japan and to freeze Japanese assets in the USA. This made access to Indonesia even more essential to the Japanese.

In September 1940 the Tripartite Pact sealed the Japanese-German-Italian alliance. France had fallen in June 1940 and the collaborating Vichy government allowed Japan to have military bases in French Indochina in September. By now Japanese leaders were talking publicly about liberating Indonesia. In the Hague before the fall of the Netherlands, and in Batavia after it, the Japanese pressed the Dutch for access to Indonesia such as they were granted in Indochina, but these negotiations collapsed in June 1941. In July Indonesian exports to Japan were stopped and Japanese assets in Indonesia frozen. In the same month, Japanese armed forces in Indochina were strengthened.

The Dutch took two more significant steps in preparation for war. The first was to remove some potential trouble-makers. In January 1941 the police arrested Thamrin, who was fatally ill, for being in contact with the Japanese, along with Douwes Dekker, who had become secretary of the Japanese Chamber of Commerce. Five days later Thamrin died in custody. There is no suggestion that the Dutch mistreated him, but this event meant the loss of an important leader and even deeper suspicions of the Dutch. Haji Rasul, now sixty-two years old but still a very active leader of Modernist Islam and a continuous source of irritation to the government, was arrested and exiled from Minangkabau at the same time. Most Indonesian organisations protested, but to no avail.

Then the defence issue which had inspired Indonesians to call for the creation of the Volksraad in 1914–18 brought the history of the Volksraad to a close. The government was expanding its military forces. Among the new recruits to the professional colonial army was the future second President of Indonesia, a young Javanese named Soeharto (b. 1921) who entered the military school in Gombong (Central Java) in June 1940. The Dutch also wanted to create a militia of up to 6000 Indonesians. Indonesian nationalists in the Volksraad took the view that there should be no militia without a full parliament. In July 1941 the militia proposal nonetheless passed the Volksraad through the support of the appointed and European members.

But Dutch rule was now in its final days. On 8 December 1941 (7 December in Hawaii) the Japanese attacked Pearl Harbor, Hong Kong, the Philippines and Malaya. The Netherlands immediately joined its allies in a declaration of war upon Japan. On 10 January 1942 the Japanese invasion of Indonesia began. On 15 February the supposedly impregnable British base at Singapore surrendered. At the end of that month the Japanese destroyed a combined Dutch, British, Australian and American fleet in the battle of the Java Sea. The Indonesian masses, hardly surprisingly, gave little support to the beleaguered colonial forces and sometimes gladly turned against Dutch civilians and soldiers. On 8 March 1942 the Dutch in Java surrendered and Governor-General van Starkenborgh was arrested.

Dutch rule in Indonesia was at an end. It left behind few friends among Indonesians. Even those among the elite who had hoped for evolution through cooperation by now had grave doubts about Dutch goodwill. And in detention throughout the archipelago was a generation of leaders to whom Dutch colonialism represented a burden which must never again be tolerated.

V
The Destruction of the Colonial State, 1942–50

16 World War II and the Japanese Occupation, 1942–5

The three and a half years of Japanese occupation constitute one of the most crucial episodes of Indonesian history. Before the Japanese invasion, no serious challenge to the Dutch existed. By the time the Japanese surrendered, there had been so many extraordinary changes that the Indonesian Revolution was possible. The Japanese contributed directly to these developments. Especially in Java and to a lesser extent in Sumatra, they indoctrinated, trained and armed many of the younger generation and gave older leaders opportunities to forge links with the masses. Throughout the archipelago they politicised Indonesians down to village level both by intention and by subjecting Indonesia to the most oppressive and devastating colonial regime in its history. The villages were thus rudely shaken out of the lethargy and political isolation of the later Dutch period. In the end, the most helpful thing the Japanese did was to lose the war, for had they succeeded in their intentions for a 'Greater East Asia Co-Prosperity Sphere' there would have been little prospect of real Indonesian independence.

Indonesia was divided into three regions by the Japanese. Sumatra was placed under the 25th Army, while Java and Madura were under the 16th Army; both of these were under the 7th Area Army with its headquarters in Singapore. Kalimantan and East Indonesia were controlled by the navy. Policies differed markedly among these regions. In general, Java was perceived as the most politically advanced and least economically important area, its main resource being people. Japanese policies there stimulated nationalism very much more than in the other two regions, and the greater political sophistication of Java over other areas was thereby enhanced. Because of the significance of these developments for the future, Java has also received greater scholarly attention than the other islands. Sumatra was important for its strategic resources and only when Japan was on the brink of defeat were nationalist ideas encouraged there. The area under naval control was regarded as politically primitive and economically essential to Japan; it was governed in the most repressive manner of all.

Mopping up Dutch and Allied troops and taking over the administration required many months. Dutch military forces collapsed, and only a very few bodies of troops held out in some isolated regions. Most Indonesians gave them no support. In some areas they attacked Dutch troops and civilians, whose only means of salvation became surrender to the Japanese. The Japanese intended to intern all Europeans (except nationals of Japan's allies, most notably Germans), but in some cases their skills were needed to keep industries running. Over a year elapsed before almost all were interned. Estimates of the final number of internees total about 170 000, of whom 65 000 were Dutch military, 25 000 were other Allied troops, and 80 000 were civilians (including 60 000 women and children). Conditions in the internment camps were poor. About 20 per cent of Dutch military internees, 13 per cent of civilian women and 10 per cent of children died. The highest death toll was in the male civilian camps, where 40 per cent died.

One of the first tasks of the Japanese was to stop the revolutions which threatened to attend their conquest. In Bantĕn, Cirĕbon, Surakarta and many smaller cities and towns of Java, outbreaks of looting and personal violence seemed to betoken a revolutionary surge. In some places these actions were led by local Islamic figures. Europeans and their property, Chinese shops and traders, and in some places Javanese Christians were subjected to violent and occasionally fatal attack. Similarly, in Aceh and in East and West Sumatra the indigenous tensions of the Dutch period began to explode in violence. Acehnese religious leaders *(ulama)* had formed PUSA (Pĕrsatuan Ulama-ulama Sĕluruh Aceh, All-Aceh Union of Ulamas) in 1939 under the leadership of Mohammed Daud Beureu'eh (1899–1987) to defend Islam and to encourage the modernisation of Islamic schools. It soon became a focus of opposition to the Dutch-supported *uleëbalang* administrators. PUSA had contacted the Japanese and laid plans to assist their attack. On 19 February 1942, three weeks before the Japanese landed in the area, Acehnese *ulamas* began a campaign of sabotage against the Dutch and by early March Aceh was in general revolt. Most *uleëbalangs* decided to shift with the wind, and the Dutch had no choice but to evacuate southward. The PUSA leaders expected the Japanese to reward them for their efforts by removing the *uleëbalangs* from power. In East Sumatra, Karo Bataks with nationalist Gĕrindo leadership aided the Japanese in the hope of seeing the Dutch-backed aristocracy ousted from power. They began to occupy land which they claimed as their own and to attack their opponents, especially in the Dĕli area in June-July 1942. In Minangkabau, too, the *ulamas* hoped to see the *pĕnghulu* leaders ousted from power.

But the Japanese had a war to fight, and their priorities did not include revolutions in conquered territories. They quickly intervened wherever revolution threatened and put a stop to it, if necessary by arresting, shooting or beheading the leaders of local movements. Like the Dutch, the Japanese had to administer Indonesia and had little option but to rely upon experienced local men: the *rajas* of East Sumatra, the *pĕnghulus* of Minangkabau, the *uleëbalangs* of Aceh, the *priyayi* administrators of Java, and similar groups elsewhere. Although their propaganda had long been aimed at winning the sympathy of Islamic leaders, the Japanese were aware that a group which had largely refused cooperation to the Dutch might also be troublesome for them. They did give Islamic leaders opportunities they had been denied by the Dutch, as will be seen below. But it was only later, when defeat became inevitable, that the Japanese decided to let the revolutionary surge roll on in the hopes of frustrating an Allied reconquest.

A primary Japanese aim was the restructuring and redirection of the Indonesian economy in order to support Japan's war effort and its plans for long-term economic domination of East and Southeast Asia. New regulations to control and redirect Indonesia's main products and the severing of contact with traditional export markets together produced chaos and hardship which made the worst years of the Depression seem mild. Japan could not absorb all of Indonesia's export products, and Allied submarines soon inflicted such damage upon Japanese shipping that even products which Japan required could not be shipped in sufficient volume. By 1943 rubber production was about one-fifth of 1941 levels (in Java and West Kalimantan rubber production was almost completely suspended), and tea was about one-third. Japan and Formosa (Taiwan) were to be the main suppliers of sugar for the Greater East Asia Co-Prosperity Sphere, so this crop which was a major source of income (especially for landless wage-labourers) in East and Central Java was to be reduced. Japanese began to take over the sugar estates in August 1943, and it was only then that their European managers were interned. Similarly, considerable tobacco land in East Sumatra was converted to food production.

The military government meanwhile flooded Indonesia with occupation currency, which contributed to rising inflation particularly from 1943 onwards. By the middle of 1945 this currency was worth about 2.5 per cent of its face value. Compulsory food requisitioning and labour recruitment along with the general chaos led to outbreaks of famine, especially in 1944 and 1945. Mortality rates increased and fertility dropped; the Japanese occupation was the only period in two centuries when population failed to grow significantly, so far as is known. Like other occupied areas, Indonesia became a land of extreme hardship, inflation, shortages, profiteering, corruption, black markets and death.

Japanese policy towards Indonesians had two priorities: to wipe out Western influences among them and to mobilise them in the interests of Japanese victory. The Japanese, like the Dutch, intended to control Indonesia for their own interests. They faced many of the same problems as the Dutch and employed many of the same solutions (indeed, Dutch colonial law remained in force except where it conflicted with Japanese military law). But the Japanese, in the midst of an enormous war requiring maximum utilisation of resources, decided to control through mobilisation (especially in Java and Sumatra) rather than by imposing an orderly quiet. As the war progressed, their increasingly frenetic efforts to mobilise Indonesians laid the groundwork for the Revolution which was to follow.

It needs to be remembered how rapidly the Japanese military advance was stopped. In May 1942 a thrust towards Australia was halted in the battle of the Coral Sea. A similar thrust towards Hawaii was stopped at Midway in June. In August 1942 the Americans landed on Guadalcanal (Solomon Islands) and by February 1943 the Japanese had been expelled with heavy losses. From 1943 the Americans took the offensive in the Pacific. Japanese policy in Indonesia therefore evolved within a steadily worsening military context. It was only very late in the war that the Japanese fully accepted that defeat was inevitable, but from an early stage of their occupation of Indonesia they had to contemplate the possibility of an eventual Allied invasion. In the end, however, the Allied advance was to bypass most of Indonesia.

To destroy Western influences, the Japanese banned the use of Dutch and English and promoted the use of Japanese. The banning of Dutch and English books made higher education virtually impossible for the duration of the war. The Japanese calendar was introduced for official purposes, European statues were pulled down, streets were renamed, and Batavia was again called Jakarta, a name which had never entirely died in Indonesian usage. An intensive propaganda campaign was begun to convince Indonesians that they and the Japanese were brothers-in-arms in the great struggle for a new order in Asia. The Japanese employed Indonesians to implement their propaganda aims, particularly schoolteachers, artists and literary figures with anti-Dutch records. Muhammad Yamin, Sanusi Pane and Armijn Pane were among those engaged in such work. Movies, drama, *wayang* and especially radio were used to spread Japanese messages. Because of a shortage of radio sets, much radio propaganda was broadcast through loudspeakers erected in public places. This propaganda effort was, however, often frustrated by the realities of the occupation: the economic chaos, the terror of the Military Police (Kenpeitai), the forced labour and rice requisitions, the arrogance and cruelty of the Japanese in general, the beatings and rapes, and the obligation to salute every Japanese. Those who had welcomed the Japanese as liberators were often quickly discouraged. This anti-Western campaign did, however, stiffen anti-Dutch sentiments throughout Indonesian society and contribute to the spread of the idea of Indonesia among the masses. Since the Japanese language was little-known, Indonesian became the major linguistic vehicle for propaganda and its status as the national language was thereby enhanced.

Until August 1942 Java remained under provisional administrative arrangements, but then an administration headed by a Military Governor (Gunseikan) was inaugurated. Many Indonesians were promoted to fill the places of interned Dutch officials, but large numbers of Japanese administrators were also brought in. Many of these new Indonesian officials were former school teachers, whose removal from the educational system contributed to the precipitous decline of educational standards.

Along with new administrators to help them run the country, the Japanese in Java sought popular leaders to help mobilise the masses. They first wiped the political slate clean. In March 1942 all political activities were banned and then all existing associations were formally dissolved and the Japanese began to build up new organisations. Islam seemed from the start to offer a primary avenue for mobilisation. By the end of March 1942 the Japanese in Java had already set up an Office for Religious Affairs (Kantor Urusan Agama; in Japanese: Shumubu).

In April 1942 the first attempt at a mass movement, the 'Triple A Movement' (Pĕrgĕrakan Tiga A), began in Java. This name derived from the slogan of Japan as the leader of Asia, the protector of Asia, and the light of Asia. Within the movement an Islamic subsection called Preparatory Union of the Islamic Community (Pĕrsiapan Pĕrsatuan Ummat Islam) was set up in July under Abikoesno Tjokrosoejoso (b. 1897), the brother of Tjokroaminoto and his successor as chairman of PSII. Abikoesno was briefly regarded by the Japanese as the natural leader of Indonesian Islam. But it was not long before the Japanese (like the Dutch) began to be uncertain about the politically active Modernist leaders, as will be seen below. In general the Triple A Movement did not achieve its objectives. Indonesian administrators gave it little support, no major Indonesian nationalist was involved in it, and its propaganda was so heavy-handed that even in these early days of the occupation few Indonesians took it seriously.

The Japanese began to accept that if they were to mobilise the masses of Java they would have to use the leading figures of the pre-war nationalist movement.

Sjahrir and Hatta had been returned to Java by the Dutch just before the Japanese victory. Both were opposed to fascism and had offered the Dutch their support. These two men were close to each other and decided to adopt complementary strategies in the new circumstances of Japanese rule. Hatta would cooperate with the Japanese, attempting to mitigate the harshness of their rule and to manipulate events in the interests of the Indonesian nation. Sjahrir would stay aloof and build up an 'underground' network based largely on former PNI-Baru members, and would attempt to make contact with the Allies. Sjahrir and Hatta kept in close touch with each other throughout the war.

On 9 July 1942 Hatta and Sjahrir were joined in Jakarta by Sukarno, whom the Japanese in Sumatra had sent there at the request of the 16th Army. Sukarno was less interested in the theoretical distinctions between fascism and democracy and saw the war primarily as a contest between empires. He joined Hatta in cooperating with the Japanese in the interest of the greater goal of independence. Sukarno and Hatta immediately began to press the still-reluctant Japanese to create a mass political organisation under their leadership.

Only one major pre-war leader attempted active underground or resistance activity in Indonesia as these terms are understood in the context of occupied Europe (although there were some Indonesians in the Netherlands who were associated with the Dutch underground). Just before the Japanese victory, Amir Sjarifuddin accepted a substantial amount of money from a Dutch official to set up an anti-Japanese resistance movement. But armed resistance now was even more futile than it had been under the Dutch. The Japanese Military Police penetrated Amir's organisation and in January 1943 he and fifty-three others were arrested. In February 1944 several of his lieutenants were executed, but Amir's sentence was commuted to life imprisonment upon the intercession of Sukarno and Hatta. The Japanese dared not offend the tiny intellectual elite in Java by executing one of its prominent members.

In the outer islands there was some resistance from groups not connected with the pre-war urban politicians. A peasant uprising against the Japanese in Aceh was led by a young *ulama* in November 1942, but was crushed with the loss of over a hundred Acehnese and eighteen Japanese lives. In South and West Kalimantan the Japanese suspected plots against them among Chinese, officials and even the Sultans. Any such conspiracies were destroyed by arrests in South Kalimantan in July 1943 and the imprisonment of at least 1000 people, including twelve Sultans, in West Kalimantan between September 1943 and early 1944. An attempt to set up an Islamic state in the area of Amuntai in South Kalimantan was crushed in September 1943. By late 1944 the Dayaks of West Kalimantan had begun killing Japanese. But none of these forms of popular resistance seriously threatened Japanese rule, and all met with terrible consequences.

In Java there was no serious popular resistance until 1944. In the meantime the Japanese sought leaders to help them mobilise the masses in the interest of the war effort. In September 1942 a conference of Islamic leaders was held in Jakarta which produced disappointing results for the Japanese and pushed them towards other leadership groups. The Japanese had hoped to replace the pre-war MIAI with a new organisation under their direction. The Islamic leaders, however, not only decided to retain the organisation but also elected a new leadership which was dominated by PSII figures rather than the basically non-political

Muhammadiyah and NU leaders. The Japanese were already having doubts about the urban Islamic politicians. They were beginning to realise that an avenue to the masses through Islam could only be produced by Muhammadiyah and NU, which had schools, welfare activities and informal links reaching out from urban areas into smaller towns and villages, and which lacked any clear political demands. Clearly some new approach to mobilisation was required.

In October 1942 a meeting of the heads of occupied areas in Tokyo was told that, with the military advance halted, mass mobilisation in occupied territories must be given priority. Colonel Horie Choso, head of the Office for Religious Affairs in Jakarta, toured Java late in the year meeting with rural religious teachers (*kyai*), whose *pěsantren* schools seemed to be ideal tools for mobilising and indoctrinating young men. In December 1942, Horie arranged for thirty-two *kyais* to be received in Jakarta by the Gunseikan, a distinction unthinkable in Dutch days. The Japanese were now discovering a viable channel for mobilisation. In December they opened another by promising a Jakarta mass meeting that a new political party would soon be created.

Early in 1943 the Japanese began to throw their efforts into mobilisation. New youth movements were given high priority, and were kept under close Japanese supervision. In August 1942 training schools for new officials and teachers had already been opened in Jakarta and Singapore, but now youth organisations were greatly expanded. A semi-military Youth Corps (Seinendan) was begun in April 1943 for youths between fourteen and twenty-five (later twenty-two). It had branches down to larger villages, but was primarily active in urban areas. For young men of twenty-five to thirty-five a Vigilance Corps (Keibodan) was set up as an auxiliary police, fire and air-raid organisation. In mid-1943 Heiho (Auxiliary Forces) was created as a part of the Japanese army and navy. By the end of the war about 25 000 Indonesian youths were in Heiho, where they received the same basic training as Japanese soldiers. Various other organisations were also created, some of which will be discussed below. In all of them there was intensive indoctrination and strict discipline. Over two million young Indonesians were said to be in such organisations at the end of the war, about 60 per cent of them in the Keibodan.

In March 1943 the promised political organisation also appeared in Java and the Triple A Movement was abolished. The new body was called Putěra (son, prince), an acronym derived from the full name Pusat Těnaga Rakyat (Centre of People's Power). This was under close Japanese control, but four leading Indonesians were placed at its head: Sukarno, Hatta, Ki Hadjar Dewantara and Kyai Haji Mas Mansur (1896–1946), a pre-war chairman of Muhammadiyah. The Japanese were thus linking the two leading urban nationalist figures to leaders of two major educational systems. But this new organisation again achieved little support, partly because the Japanese were still unwilling to unleash such potentially powerful popular forces: there was, for instance, no question of giving Putěra any control over the youth movements. Dewantara in fact returned to Yogyakarta early in 1944 to concentrate on seeing his Taman Siswa schools through the difficult times, and Mansur gradually withdrew from active involvement, perhaps because of ill health.

The Japanese were by now trying to develop the rural Shafi'i teachers as their main link to the masses of Java. There were many difficulties between the Japanese and Islamic leaders in general, but especially between them and the urban

Modernists. Haji Rasul led the Islamic opposition to bowing towards the Emperor in Tokyo, which appeared to conflict with a Muslim's obligation to pray towards Mecca and to submit only to God. Eventually the Japanese agreed that there need be no bow towards the Emperor on religious occasions. The Japanese also wanted World War II to be declared a Holy War, which Muslims adamantly refused since the Japanese, like the Allies, were *kafirs* (unbelievers) and a war on their behalf could hardly be designated a Holy War. By the end of 1942 the Japanese also had to abandon their wish to ban the use of Arabic, but did so only on condition that Japanese also be taught in Islamic schools and that their curriculum for non-religious subjects be accepted. The Japanese maintained the 1925 Teacher Ordinance (*goeroe ordonnantie)*, and the Indonesian officials administered it even more strictly, out of both opposition to Islamic elites and fear of Japanese disciplinary measures if they seemed too lenient. Modernist schools were particularly affected by these policies.

While urban Modernist politicians and the Japanese were thus growing disenchanted with one another, the less sophisticated *kyais* of Java's countryside seemed more amenable to Japanese designs. The Japanese combination of physical, martial and spiritual disciplines struck responsive chords in *pĕsantren* communities. In July 1943 the Japanese started bringing groups of about sixty *kyais* to Jakarta for training courses of about one month's duration. By May 1945 over 1000 *kyais* had gone through these courses, where they heard some lectures on religious questions but were mainly indoctrinated with Japanese propaganda. They appeared to be so valuable for Japanese purposes that all attempts by the MIAI itself to organise the *kyais* were frustrated by the Japanese. The MIAI leadership wanted to build links with rural Islam, but the Japanese preferred to deal directly with those who already had them.

To stimulate support of the worsening war effort, the Japanese also began to promise some Indonesian involvement in the affairs of government in Java. In August and October 1943 first Burma and then the Philippines were granted puppet independence. Java was felt not to be ready for this, but a series of councils was set up to give an appearance of participation. The number of Indonesian advisors *(sanyo)* to the Japanese administration was increased, a Central Advisory Board (Chuo Sangi-in) was set up in Jakarta with Sukarno as chairman, and regional councils (Shu Sangi-kai) were established. These were all, however, purely advisory. Even less significant gestures towards popular involvement began in Sumatra in late 1943. The navy took no such steps at this stage in its area except to allow some consultation in municipal administration.

The Japanese 16th Army in Java wanted to move faster in the area of Indonesian participation than did the 25th Army in Sumatra, the navy in East Indonesia, or Tokyo. It may have been for this reason that Sukarno, Hatta and the chairman of Muhammadiyah, Ki Bagus Hadikusumo (b. 1890), were flown to Tokyo in November 1943 to be decorated by the Emperor. This was the first time that Sukarno had been abroad or seen an industrialised country. The impression this trip made on him may have been great, but his efforts to get more Japanese support for Indonesian nationalism failed. The Prime Minister, General Tojo Hideki (1941–4), refused his request to allow the use of the Indonesian anthem 'Indonesia Raya' (Greater Indonesia) or the red and white Indonesian flag (Dwiwarna, the Bicoloured; or Sang Merah-Putih, the Holy Red-and-White).

The Japanese still needed Indonesia's resources for the war, and all else was secondary. Indonesian labour now began to be exploited in a more ruthless fashion than ever before. In October 1943 the Japanese ordered the recruitment of 'volunteer labourers' (romusha), primarily peasants drafted from their villages in Java and put to work as labourers wherever the Japanese needed them, as far away as Burma and Siam. It is not known how many men were involved, but it was probably at least 200000 and may have been as many as half a million, of whom not more than 70000 could be found alive at the end of the war. Their families were left behind in pitiable circumstances. At the same time the Japanese introduced new regulations for the compulsory sale of rice to the government at low prices, in effect a system of requisitioning to supply the Japanese military. The Indonesian officials who had to administer romusha recruitment and rice requisitioning earned much hatred from the villagers.

In October 1943 the Japanese began the most significant of their youth organisations, the Peta (Pěmbela Tanah Air, Protectors of the Fatherland). This was an Indonesian volunteer army which by the end of the war had 37000 men in Java and about 20000 in Sumatra (where it was usually known by its Japanese name Giyugun, volunteer soldiers). Unlike the Heiho, Peta was not formally a part of the Japanese military but was intended to be an auxiliary guerrilla force to resist an Allied invasion. Its officer corps included officials, teachers, kyais and Indonesian soldiers of the former Dutch colonial army. Among them was an Islamic schoolteacher named Soedirman (?1915–50), who was to become one of the leading military figures of the revolution. Peta discipline was intense and Indonesian nationalist ideas were used in indoctrination.

The Japanese also created their new organisation for controlling Islam in October 1943. MIAI was dissolved and replaced by Masyumi (Majlis Syuro Muslimin Indonesia, Consultative Council of Indonesian Muslims), with branches in every Residency of Java. The Japanese thoroughly bypassed the urban Modernist politicians who had succeeded in dominating MIAI; Masyumi leadership was placed in the hands of Muhammadiyah and NU figures. Hasjim Asjari, the founder of NU, was made its head but he stayed at his pěsantren in Jombang and the effective head was his son Kyai Haji Wachid Hasjim (1913–53).

In January 1944 Putěra was replaced by a new mass movement in the search for a more satisfactory umbrella organisation for mobilising the people of Java. The Jawa Hokokai (Java Service Association) was set up for everyone over fourteen years of age. The Gunseikan was head of the association but Sukarno and Hasjim Asjari were made his principal advisers and the management was assigned to Hatta and Mansur. The Japanese of course intended to use the Indonesian leaders to further their own aims, but the latter were now taking advantage of the Japanese. Sukarno was particularly successful in using propaganda tours for the Hokokai to enhance his own standing as the primary leader of popular forces. The priyayi administrators were directly tied to the new body by being made heads of it at each level of administration. The Hokokai also had an organisational means of penetrating even the villages. Neighbourhood Associations (Rukun Tětangga; in Japanese: Tonari Gumi) were set up to organise the whole population into cells of ten to twenty families for mobilisation, indoctrination and informing. Lower-level administrators and village headmen had responsibility for these cells. By February 1944 village headmen, too, were undergoing indoctrination courses.

But the Japanese began to realise that they were both losing the war and losing control of the popular forces they were unleashing. In February 1944 the first serious peasant resistance in Java to rice requisitioning broke out in a village in Priangan and was brutally crushed. Leadership had been assumed by a local NU *kyai* and his students, representatives of precisely that group which the Japanese had most hoped to use. Further revolts led by local *hajis* broke out in West Java in May and August, and from this time onward isolated peasant protests became more common. The Japanese tried to get a firmer grip on rural Islam by setting up branches of the Office for Religious Affairs throughout Java, and in August they appointed Hasjim Asjari (in fact represented by his son Wachid Hasjim) as head of the Office. But the revolutionary potential of rural Islam, once stimulated, could not easily be controlled. In the cities, especially Jakarta and Bandung, educated youths were beginning to establish their own underground networks, in many cases under the influence of Sjahrir. They knew that the war was going badly for the Japanese, and began to lay plans for seizing national independence out of the impending Japanese defeat.

In February 1944 the Americans expelled the Japanese from Kwajalein in the Marshall Islands, and B-29 bombing raids on Japan started in June. In the same month the Japanese suffered a crushing naval defeat in the battle of the Philippine Sea. In July the Japanese lost their naval base at Saipan (Mariana Islands), which led to a cabinet crisis in Japan. Tojo resigned and General Koiso Kuniaki replaced him as Prime Minister (1944–5), bringing with him a greater inclination to consider puppet independence for Indonesia. Meanwhile, the Allied invasion of northern Europe had begun in June and Japan's allies in Europe were crumbling. In September the Americans landed on Morotai, off Halmahera in the east of Indonesia. In the same month American planes began to bomb Manila.

On 7 September 1944 Prime Minister Koiso promised independence for the 'East Indies' *(To-Indo,* a term the Japanese continued to use officially until April 1945). But he set no date for independence, and it was clearly expected that Indonesians should respond to this gesture with grateful support for Japan. The 16th Army in Java was now told to stimulate nationalist forces and the Indonesian flag was allowed on Jawa Hokokai offices. The navy generally remained unenthusiastic about the whole idea. Since March 1944 it had set up some consultative committees in its area, but they had no authority, consisted only of indigenous officials and aristocrats, and met only a few times before the Japanese surrender. The 25th Army in Sumatra, however, announced a consultative Central Advisory Board (Sumatra Chuo Sangi-in) for the island in March 1945. But this body met in Bukittingi only once before the end of the war.

While the navy still resisted any attempts at promoting nationalism in its administrative area, a remarkable naval officer stationed in Java now took an active role. Vice-Admiral Maeda Tadashi was in charge of the army-navy liaison office in Jakarta, and was a man of progressive views regarding Indonesian nationalism. He now began to use naval money to finance speaking tours by Sukarno and Hatta, sending them even to Makasar in April 1945 and to Bali and Banjarmasin in June. In October 1944 he also established the Asrama Indonesia Mĕrdeka (Free Indonesia Dormitory) in Jakarta, either to train new youth leaders for an independent state or to find a means of infiltrating the existing underground youth networks. Maeda became a confidant of many leading Indonesians of all ages, and contributed to the process by which the younger and older generations of leaders came to know and understand (if not always to respect) each other in Jakarta.

New youth and military groups were now created. Jawa Hokokai was for the first time given a youth organisation of its own, the Barisan Pělopor (Vanguard Column), which at the end of the war was said to have 80000 members. This was initially to be used for propaganda purposes, but in May 1945 it began guerrilla training. Educated urban youth leaders were linked to lower-class youths of the towns and cities, and they in turn were formally linked to the Hokokai figures led by Sukarno. In December 1944 Masyumi was also given a military wing called Barisan Hizbullah (God's Forces), which began training in February 1945 and was said to have 50000 members at the end of the war. Its leadership was dominated by Muhammadiyah figures and members of Salim's cooperative faction of the pre-war PSII. Again the main pre-war non-cooperative Islamic politicians were bypassed.

More Indonesian officials were now promoted. In November 1944 Indonesian Vice-Residents began to be appointed. The advisers (sanyo) were gathered into a sort of upper chamber (Dewan Sanyo, Council of Advisers) of the Central Advisory Board, with rather wider advisory competence. These higher officials were enrolled in indoctrination courses in January 1945, an experience which both encouraged nationalist thinking among them and enhanced their dislike of the Japanese for requiring them to undergo what seemed to be a demeaning exercise.

The Japanese were finally required to give substance to their promise of independence by the rapid disintegration of their military position. In October 1944 what remained of the Japanese fleet was nearly wiped out in the Leyte Gulf; with its demise even the defence of Japan itself was hardly feasible any longer. In January 1945 the American invasion of Luzon in the Philippines began and in February Manila was taken. After the loss of the Philippines the Japanese navy abandoned its opposition to puppet independence for Indonesia, since it no longer had much hope of retaining control in any case and thus recognised the need to win Indonesian goodwill. But in practice the navy itself did little to encourage this. The difficulty of maintaining such goodwill was meanwhile becoming clearer. In February 1945 the Peta detachment at Blitar (East Java) attacked the Japanese armoury and killed several Japanese soldiers. Sixty-eight Peta soldiers were court-martialled (of whom eight were executed) and four senior Indonesian administrators there were forced to resign. The Japanese now began to fear that they could not control the Indonesian military forces they had created. These fears were strengthened in March when comparable forces in Burma turned against them and joined the invading Allies.

As they saw that they were losing control, the Japanese decided to release the remaining restraints upon Indonesian popular forces. The 16th Army pressed more cautious elements within the Japanese hierarchies to act speedily, since it knew well that the seeds of revolution were deeply planted in Java. In March 1945 the Japanese announced the formation of an Investigating Committee for Preparatory Work for Indonesian Independence (Badan Pěnyělidik Usaha Pěrsiapan Kěměrdekaan Indonesia), which met in late May in the old Volksraad building in Jakarta. Its membership represented most of the surviving middle-aged leaders of Java from all the main schools of thought. Radjiman Wediodiningrat was in the chair, while before him sat Sukarno, Hatta, Mansur, Dewantara, Salim, Soetardjo Kartohadikoesoemo, Abikoesno Tjokrosoejoso, Ki Bagus Hadikusumo, Wachid Hasjim, Muhammad Yamin, and others. The Japanese were naturally determined that when independence came it would be in the hands of older leaders whom they felt they could deal with rather than the unpredictable younger generation.

In July 1945 the Japanese in Java tried to unify the youth movements, Masyumi and Jawa Hokokai into a single Gĕrakan Rakyat Baru (New People's Movement). But the attempt collapsed when youth leaders insisted upon dramatic nationalistic gestures which most of the more timid (and more realistic) older generation would not undertake. The initial meeting ended in acrimony and the Movement was stillborn. The Japanese arrested Yamin, whom they believed to have inspired the young activists, but events were now moving too rapidly for the Japanese to make a second attempt at uniting the older and younger leaders.

In the Investigating Committee in Jakarta, Sukarno urged that his version of religiously neutral nationalism should be adopted. Since this was indeed the only basis upon which the other leaders could agree, Sukarno carried the day. In his speech of 1 June he laid out his doctrine of Pancasila, the 'five principles' which were to become the official philosophy of independent Indonesia: belief in God, nationalism, humanitarianism, social justice and democracy. While these principles were sufficiently unobjectionable and ambiguous to receive general acceptance, Islamic leaders were unhappy that Islam seemed to play no special role. Eventually they accepted a compromise called the Jakarta Charter (Piagam Jakarta) which said that the state was to be based upon 'belief in God, with the obligation for adherents of Islam to carry out Islamic law'. What this implied for the relationship between Islamic law and the state was to be a source of bitter disagreements in coming years. The Committee finished its work by drafting Indonesia's first constitution, which called for a unitary republic with an extremely powerful Presidency, and by deciding that the new state should include not only Indonesia but Malaya and British territories in Borneo (Kalimantan) as well.

By July 1945 all elements among the Japanese were agreed that independence must be granted to Indonesia within a few months. In March the Americans had taken Iwojima and begun to use it as a bomber base for raids on Japan. Koiso resigned as Prime Minister in April and was replaced by Admiral Suzuki Kantaro, who favoured a negotiated peace. In May Germany surrendered, leaving the Allies free to concentrate on the Pacific war. In the same month Rangoon fell. Okinawa fell in June and truly massive bombing of Japan began. Late in July at Potsdam the Allied leaders issued a demand for Japan's unconditional surrender. Japan could no longer think of victory or of retaining its conquered territories. In Indonesia its aim now was to create an independent state in order to frustrate the restoration of rule by the Dutch enemy. At the end of July the Japanese army and navy held a meeting in Singapore to plan the transfer of the economy to Indonesian hands. They decided that Java should be given independence by early September and the other areas soon after.

On 6 August the first atomic bomb was dropped on Hiroshima, killing at least 78000 people. The war in Asia was nearing its horrific end. The following day in Jakarta, the membership of a new Preparatory Committee for Indonesian independence (Panitia Pĕrsiapan Kĕmĕrdekaan Indonesia) was announced, and news of this Committee was given throughout Indonesia. It had both Java and outer islands representatives, was dominated by the older generation, and was scheduled to meet on 19 August. On the 7th, the parallel committee of Japanese which was to take the real decisions met. The Soviet Union declared war on Japan on 8 August. On the following day the second atomic bomb was dropped on Nagasaki and the Soviets invaded Manchuria. On that day, with surrender looking inevitable to leading Japanese, Sukarno, Hatta and Radjiman were flown to Saigon to see the Commander of the Southern Area, Field Marshal Terauchi Hisaichi, whom they met in Dalat on 11 August. Terauchi promised them independence for the whole of the former Netherlands East Indies, but vetoed the inclusion of Malaya and British areas of Borneo. Sukarno was appointed chairman of the Preparatory Committee and Hatta vice-chairman. On 14 August Sukarno and his colleagues arrived back in Jakarta.

On 15 August Japan surrendered unconditionally, and thereby presented Indonesian leaders with a formidable problem. Because there had been no Allied reconquest of Indonesia, there was now a political hiatus: the Japanese were still in control but had surrendered, and no Allied forces were present to replace them. Plans for orderly Japanese-sponsored independence seemed now to have come to a halt, and by the following day the Gunseikan had received specific orders to hold the status quo until Allied forces could arrive. Sukarno, Hatta and the older generation were uncertain what to do and feared to provoke conflict with the Japanese. Maeda wanted to see a quick transfer of power to the older generation, fearing both the volatile youth groups and the demoralised Japanese forces. The youth leaders wanted a dramatic declaration of independence outside of the framework set up by the Japanese, and were supported in this by Sjahrir. But no one dared move without Sukarno and Hatta.

On the morning of 16 August Hatta and Sukarno were not to be found in Jakarta. During the night they had been taken by youth leaders to the Peta garrison at Rěngasdengklok, a small town well off the main road to Cirěbon, on the pretext of protecting them when a rebellion of Peta and Heiho broke out. There was no uprising, and Sukarno and Hatta soon realised that this was an attempt to force them to declare independence outside of the Japanese arrangements, which they refused to do. Maeda sent word that if they were brought back safely he could arrange for the Japanese to look the other way when independence was declared. By that night Sukarno and Hatta were in Maeda's house in Jakarta. During the night the declaration of independence was drafted. The young activists wanted dramatic and fiery language, but to avoid offending the Japanese or encouraging violence a calm and simple statement devised by Sukarno was adopted.

On the morning of 17 August 1945 Sukarno read the declaration of independence before a relatively small group outside his own house:

Proclamation:

We the people of Indonesia hereby declare
the independence of Indonesia.
Matters concerning the transfer of power, etc., will be carried out
in a conscientious
manner and as speedily as possible.

Jakarta, 17 August 1945.

In the name of the people of Indonesia,
[signed]   Sukarno Hatta

The red and white flag was raised and 'Indonesia Raya' was sung.

The Republic of Indonesia was born. Meanwhile the victorious Allies, almost entirely ignorant of what had transpired within Indonesia during the war, were hastily planning their arrival to accept the Japanese surrender and to restore the colonial regime. But the Japanese period had created conditions of such chaos, had so politicised the masses, and had so encouraged both older and younger Indonesian leaders to take the initiative, that the Allies were to find themselves confronted by a revolutionary war of independence.

17 The Revolution, 1945–50

The Revolution by which independence was won is not only a central episode of Indonesian history but a powerful element in the Indonesian nation's perception of itself. All the uncertain gropings for new identities, for unity in the face of foreign rule, for a juster social order, seemed to come to fruition in the years after World War II. For the first time in the lives of most Indonesians, the artificial restraints of foreign rule were suddenly lifted. It is not surprising that the result was not the appearance of a harmonious new nation, but a bitter struggle among contending individuals and social forces. Yet behind these often violent struggles lay a commitment to independence. The subsequent national myth that Indonesians stood shoulder-to-shoulder during the Revolution has little historical foundation. But the conviction that it was the nation's most triumphant hour, that Indonesia's right to independence was demonstrated by the sacrifices made in the name of the Revolution, has much to support it.

Academic studies of the Revolution have done their best to impose order upon a period which was essentially one of disorder. Concerning those Indonesians who supported the Revolution, contrasts have usefully been drawn between the forces of armed struggle (*pĕrjuangan*) and those of diplomacy, between those in favour of social revolution and those against it, between the younger and the older generations, between the left and the right, between Islamic and 'secular' forces, and so on. These distinctions are helpful, but it needs to be remembered that they did not always coincide. They are not different labels for the same basic distinction; they are all partial pictures of a period in which the divisions within the nation were multiform and constantly shifting. At the beginning of the Revolution, none of the basic divisions among Indonesians had been resolved except insofar as there was agreement on independence as the immediate goal; for the revolutionaries, anything seemed possible but defeat. By the end, defeat had come very near and the possibilities were drastically limited. The forces of armed struggle and diplomacy, while distrusting each other, jointly won independence. The forces favouring social revolution, the younger generation, the left and Islamic dominance all faced sharply limited prospects.

Both the Dutch and the Indonesian revolutionaries saw the Revolution as a time of continuity with the past. For the Dutch, the aim was to destroy a state run by collaborators with the Japanese and to restore a colonial regime which they believed they had built out of 350 years of effort. For the Indonesian revolutionary leaders, the aim was to complete and perfect the process of national unification and revival which had begun four decades before. Each believed destiny and righteousness to be on its side. Both views had some justification, but both were also misleading.

In fact, this was the third time the Dutch had set out to conquer Indonesia. Their first effort, in the seventeenth and eighteenth centuries, had ended in partial withdrawal in the face of Indonesian resistance and their own inadequacies, and finally in their defeat by the British. The second, in the nineteenth and early twentieth centuries, had ended in their defeat by the Japanese. They were now to try for a third time, and now they faced the problem of conquering the whole archipelago at once. For their part, the Indonesians were facing unprecedented circumstances. For the first time since the sixteenth century they were in occupation of virtually the whole of their national territory and were more united than ever before in facing the Dutch, whom they greatly outnumbered. But full national unity was still a long way from being achieved. Poor communications, internal divisions, the weakness of the central Indonesian leadership and ethnic diversity meant that in practice the Revolution was a highly fragmented phenomenon. Largely for this reason, the Dutch conquest nearly succeeded. In the end it was defeated by Indonesian resistance and the support of sympathetic powers, especially the United States of America. This near-victory of the Dutch, however, did much to weld the diverse Indonesian nation into a unitary republic, in considerable agreement on what it opposed, if not always on what it supported. Thus, in the end the Dutch would have to abandon their empire-building attempt in Indonesia, leaving behind a precious legacy of unity.

A central Republican government was quickly established in Jakarta in late August 1945. It adopted the constitution which had been drafted by the Preparatory Committee for Indonesian Independence before the Japanese surrender. The Japanese navy warned, however, that Christian Indonesians in its area would disapprove of any special role for Islam, so the Jakarta Charter and a condition that the head of state must be a Muslim were dropped. Sukarno was made President of the Republic (1945–67) and Hatta Vice-President (1945–56), since the Jakarta politicians were convinced that only they could deal with the Japanese. Pending elections, which in the event were not to be held for ten years, a Komite Nasional Indonesia Pusat (KNIP, Central Indonesian National Committee) was appointed to assist the President and similar National Committees were to be established at provincial and residency levels.

An administrative structure was also easily defined. Incumbent Indonesian administrative advisors *(sanyo)* and Vice-Residents were named as Republican officials, so that the administration could be peacefully and discreetly turned over to them by the Japanese without too obvious violation of the terms of Japan's surrender to the Allies. The Jawa Hokokai, which had proved useful to Sukarno and the Republican leaders, was also to be carried on as a state party. It was given the name of Sukarno's pre-war party, Partai Nasional Indonesia (Indonesian Nationalist Party), but it soon collapsed. Sjahrir and his supporters objected to such an obvious extension of a Japanese organisation and, of course, to the continued dominance of the collaborating elite which it was intended to ensure. The Jawa Hokokai had, in any case, been a forced fusion of elites whose interests were often far from identical, and without Japanese compulsion the Jawa Hokokai / PNI was internally incoherent. At the end of August 1945 it was suspended, leaving the KNIP and lower-level National Committees as the main political organs.

While administrative arrangements seemed to be proceeding smoothly in Java, a disruption occurred in the Republic's military forces. Between 18 and 25 August the Japanese in Java and Sumatra disarmed and disbanded the Peta/Giyugun and Heiho, most of whose members did not yet know of the declaration of independence. They thereby dismantled the command structures and membership of the forces which the Republican leadership had looked upon as the basis for a national army. Rather than the Republic inheriting a trained, armed and hierarchically structured army (albeit one that lacked higher command levels), the armed forces which began to be formed in early September often grew out of local initiatives by able, and usually younger, leaders with charisma and/or access to arms. One of the major problems of the revolutionary period and after was to create from this disorganisation a rational military structure obedient to central authority.

As news spread of the declaration of independence, many Indonesians far from Jakarta disbelieved it. On 22 August the Japanese finally made a public announcement of their surrender, but it was well into September 1945 before the fact that independence had been declared was known in remoter regions. Once it was known, the question of allegiance immediately arose. The four rulers of the Central Javanese principalities declared their support of the Republic early in September. But many *rajas* of the outer islands who had been supported and enriched, and hence compromised, by the Dutch were unenthusiastic. They disliked the apparently radical, non-aristocratic and sometimes Islamic nature of the Jakarta leadership as well as the local Republican youth who most directly represented the cause of independence. In South Sulawesi, however, the king of Bone (Arumpone) La Mappanjuki, who still recalled the battles against the Dutch early in the century, declared his support. Most of the Makasarese and Bugis *rajas* joined him in accepting the authority of G. S. S. J. Ratulangie (1890–1949), a Měnadonese Christian who was appointed by Jakarta as Republican governor there. Similarly, several Balinese *rajas* accepted Republican authority. But in many other regions the *rajas* chose to oppose the Revolution and thereby often became its victims, as will be seen below.

For the Indonesian masses there was a sense of freedom which led most of them to regard themselves as pro-Republican, but without any very clear knowledge yet of what this commitment would entail. Indonesian bureaucratic administrators, however, faced unprecedented circumstances with the sanctions of foreign rule removed for the first time in their careers. Many simply had no idea what to do. Javanese *priyayi* officials were often quite unable to respond positively; they were both compromised by their service to foreign rulers and deprived of the precolonial military skills of their class. The initiative thus fell to others who were not reluctant to embrace violence.

The euphoria of revolution soon began to sweep the country, and Indonesian youths in particular responded to the excitement and challenge of independence. Local Japanese commanders often abandoned urban areas and withdrew their troops to perimeter positions to avoid confrontation. Many discreetly allowed young Indonesians to acquire arms. Between 3 and 11 September, Republican youths in Jakarta took over control of the railway stations, tram system and radio station without encountering Japanese resistance. By the end of September major installations in Yogyakarta, Surakarta, Malang and Bandung were also in the hands of Indonesian youths. Despite the worries of older leaders about provoking the Japanese, mass rallies were held in Surabaya on 11 and 17 September and in Jakarta on 19 September, where some 200000 people are said to have filled the square now called Medan Měrdeka (Independence Square). On these occasions Japanese forces, including tanks, stood in position around the rallies, but violence was avoided. On 19 September Sukarno turned his oratorical gifts to convincing the Jakarta crowd to disperse without challenging the Japanese. His success in this confirmed the impression that only Sukarno could prevent massive violence.

In literature and the arts as well as in politics a revolutionary spirit was seen. Republican newspapers and journals sprang up in many places, especially in Jakarta, Yogyakarta and Surakarta. A whole generation of writers is loosely referred to as the 'Generation of 45' (angkatan 45), men whose creative skills came to fruition in the revolutionary period. Among them was the poet Chairil Anwar (1922–49), the prose writer Pramudya Ananta Tur (b. 1925), much of whose writing was done in a Dutch prison in 1947–9, the journalist Mochtar Lubis (b. 1922) and others. Many of these men believed that their art could be a part of the revolutionary events. There was still little specifically Islamic writing, except for Bahrum Rangkuti (1919–77), who was much inspired by the Pakistani writer Muhammad Iqbal. Modern painting also came to maturity in the Revolution as artists such as Affandi (1910–90) and Sudjojono (b. 1913) not only captured the spirit of the Revolution in their paintings but also gave more direct support by producing anti-Dutch posters.

Many youths joined armed struggle groups (badan pěrjuangan). In Sumatra they had a virtual monopoly of revolutionary authority since established nationalist leaders there were few in number and uncertain what to do. Former Peta and Heiho soldiers formed the best disciplined groups, but many badan pěrjuangan were very undisciplined, in response both to the circumstances of their formation and to what was perceived as the revolutionary spirit. The army of Masyumi, Barisan Hizbullah, took in many new fighters, and was now joined by another loose group of Islamic forces generally called Barisan Sabilillah (Forces in the Path of God), mostly led by rural Islamic teachers (kyai).

Violence between the Revolution and its perceived enemies soon began. After the Japanese surrender many Dutch internees simply walked out of their camps and went home. By September brawls had begun in the streets of Surabaya between Indonesian youths and Europeans, and tensions were mounting elsewhere. In all these matters Java was more advanced than the outer islands where there were more Japanese troops (especially in the navy areas), less sympathetic Japanese commanders and fewer Republican leaders and activists. So far, however, the Revolution had not yet faced serious resistance. But it was soon to do so.

As the Allies began arriving to accept the Japanese surrender, the first serious challenges to the Revolution emerged. The American advance through the Pacific had left Allied enclaves in Kalimantan (Tarakan and Balikpapan), on Morotai and in parts of Irian Jaya. Dutch administrators had already returned to these areas. At the end of June 1945 small commando units (mostly Dutch, but with some British officers) had also been parachuted into North Sumatra. The Allies had decided early in 1945 that American forces would concentrate upon the Japanese home islands. Responsibility for Indonesia thus fell at the last moment to the British Southeast Asia Command under Lord Louis Mountbatten. The Dutch were naturally anxious to reoccupy Indonesia and to punish those who had collaborated with the Japanese, but they were in no position to do so themselves in 1945, so their hopes now rested upon the British. Mountbatten was to demonstrate, however, that he had no intention of conquering Indonesia for the Dutch; nor, indeed, did he have enough soldiers to do so. He defined his aims narrowly: to release European internees and accept the Japanese surrender. The rest was up to the Dutch; in practice Mountbatten treated Republican administrations as the *de facto* authority in areas where they were found.

In the Japanese navy area the Revolution was nipped in the bud when the Allies moved in. Australian troops took the Japanese surrender there (except for Bali and Lombok) and with them came Dutch troops and administrators. Between mid-September and mid-October 1945 the Australians occupied the major cities of East Indonesia, in most cases before Republican administrations had been established. Demonstrations were put down and some pro-Republican officials arrested. The pro-Republican rajas of South Sulawesi decided that it would be unwise to fight the Australians and therefore grudgingly allowed the return of the Dutch.

British troops, most of them Indian, were meanwhile moving into Java and Sumatra. The first reached Jakarta in the latter half of September 1945, and in the course of October they arrived in Medan, Padang, Palembang, Sěmarang and Surabaya. The British commander for Indonesia, Lieutenant General Sir Philip Christison, hoped to avoid clashes with the Indonesians. He therefore diverted soldiers of the former Dutch colonial army and newly arriving Dutch troops to East Indonesia, where the Dutch reoccupation was proceeding rapidly. The Dutch Lieutenant-Governor Hubertus J. van Mook (1942–8; there was no Governor-General appointed after the war) was in favour of the Dutch concentrating initially on East Indonesia, which was of considerable economic value and where the population was expected to be less anti-Dutch.

As Allied troops began to appear, tensions mounted in Java and Sumatra. Street fights developed in October between young Republicans on the one hand and former Dutch prisoners, Dutch colonial troops (including Ambonese), Chinese, Indo-Europeans and Japanese on the other. The Japanese were in a particularly difficult position, for it was no longer possible for them to ignore their obligations to the Allies and maintain a laissez-faire attitude toward the revolutionaries.

In October 1945 the Japanese attempted to recover authority in the towns and cities in Java where they had recently allowed the Indonesians to take over, thereby initiating the first stages of warfare. On 3 October the Japanese Military Police (Kenpeitai) massacred Republican youths in Pěkalongan. On 10 October Japanese troops pushed the Republicans out of Bandung and a week later turned the city over to the British. On 14 October they began to retake Sěmarang. The Republicans there retaliated by murdering at least 130, and perhaps as many as 300, Japanese whom they were holding. The British arrived in Sěmarang six days later, by which time the Japanese had nearly won control of the city, leaving some 500 Japanese and about 2000 Indonesians dead. The British decided to evacuate Indo-European and European internees as quickly as possible from the volatile interior of Java. Detachments went into Magělang and Ambarawa to bring out some 10000 detainees (mostly women and children), but they encountered so much Republican resistance that air-strikes had to be used against the Indonesians. On 2 November a ceasefire was arranged by Sukarno at the request of the British, but by late November fighting had resumed and the British withdrew to the coast.

Surabaya became the site of the heaviest battle of the Revolution and thereby a national symbol of resistance. The senior Japanese commander there, Vice-Admiral Shibata Yaichiro, favoured the Republic and gave Indonesians ready access to Japanese arms. When a Dutch navy Captain reached Surabaya as the first Allied representative, Shibata surrendered to him on 3 October and then, recognising the reality of Indonesian control of the city, ordered his forces to surrender their few remaining weapons to the Indonesians who would be responsible for turning them over to the Allies (which, of course, they neglected to do). In late October and early November the leaders of Nahdlatul Ulama and Masyumi declared that war in defence of the Indonesian fatherland was Holy War, an obligation laid upon all Muslims. From the *pěsantren* schools of East Java *kyais* and their students began to pour into Surabaya. The fiery Soetomo (1920–81), better known as 'Bung Tomo' (Brother Tomo), used the local radio to encourage an atmosphere of fanatical revolutionary enthusiasm throughout the city.

Into this explosive city some 6000 British Indian troops came on 25 October to evacuate internees. Within three days fighting had begun. Some 10–20000 Indonesian armed regulars of the recently formed People's Security Army (Tĕntara Kĕamanan Rakyat) and mobs of 70–140000 people killed many of the Indian troops and seemed poised to wipe out the entire force. The British flew in Sukarno, Hatta and Amir Sjarifuddin (now Minister of Information in the Republican government) and a ceasefire was arranged on 30 October. Fighting broke out again, however, and the local British commander, Brigadier-General A. W. S. Mallaby, was killed. During a subsequent lull in the fighting the British brought in reinforcements and evacuated the internees. At dawn on 10 November, a day now commemorated as Heroes' Day (Hari Pahlawan), the British troops began a bloody punitive sweep through the city under cover of air and naval bombardment, in the face of fanatical resistance. In three days about half the city was conquered but it was three weeks before the fighting was over. At least 6000 Indonesians died and thousands more fled the devastated city.

The Republicans lost much manpower and many weapons in the battle of Surabaya, but their sacrificial resistance there created a symbol and rallying-cry for the Revolution. It also convinced the British that wisdom lay on the side of neutrality in the Revolution. The battle of Surabaya was a turning-point for the Dutch as well, for it shocked many of them into facing reality. Many had quite genuinely believed that the Republic represented only a gang of collaborators without popular support. No longer could any serious observer defend such a view.

The central leadership in Jakarta had little contact, influence or sympathy with the violence which was now spreading. The earlier and more substantial Allied presence in Jakarta meant that there was little revolutionary violence there, and the central leadership was committed to an orderly revolution which would win diplomatic recognition and support. But Sukarno, who had seemed to be indispensable within Indonesia, was clearly an international liability. Van Mook was told by the Dutch government that he must have no dealings with this arch-collaborator. Although Sukarno continued to demonstrate his ability to sway a crowd, his cautious role since the declaration of independence and especially his intervention at the request of the British to arrange ceasefires at Magĕlang and Surabaya had also led many young revolutionaries to distrust him.

Sutan Sjahrir thus began to emerge within the manoeuvres of the Jakarta elite, partly because he had not collaborated with the Japanese and was therefore more acceptable to the Allies (which was true), partly because he was believed to have special influence among Republican youths (which was true only to a limited extent). His pamphlet *Perdjuangan kita* ('Our struggle'), published in November 1945, showed Sjahrir to be committed to the idea of an international socialist revolution which would be democratic, anti-aristocratic and anti-fascist (and hence opposed to those like Sukarno who had found things to admire in Japanese ideas). But it also reflected the deeply Europeanised cast of Sjahrir's mind, which made it difficult for him to grasp the influence of invulnerability cults and millenarian traditions, the depth of indigenous social tensions or the appeal of violence for many Indonesians. Furthermore, it revealed a basis for distrust between him and the Republic's military forces, many of which had their roots in the Japanese occupation.

On 16 October 1945 Sjahrir and Amir Sjarifuddin (who had not only refused to collaborate with the Japanese but had been imprisoned and nearly executed by them) engineered a takeover within the Central Indonesian National Committee (KNIP). The period of extraordinary Presidential powers was ended. The Committee was given legislative powers, to be carried out through a Working Party (Badan Pĕkĕrja KNIP) which Sjahrir and Amir selected. Political parties were now to be formed, thereby beginning a process which institutionalised the conflicts among Indonesians. On 11 November the cabinet was made responsible to the KNIP rather than the President. Finally, on 14 November a new cabinet was formed. Sjahrir became Prime Minister (1945–7) as well as Minister for Foreign Affairs and the Interior; Amir became Minister for People's Security (i.e. Defence) and Information. Thus, after less than three months, the 1945 constitution was suspended in practice, although in theory it remained in force. Sukarno, Hatta and the other leaders whom the Japanese had used were now pushed into the background, while Sjahrir, Amir and their followers in the former Jakarta youth undergrounds gained power at the centre. Neither group had much influence over the Revolution in the countryside, but at least from this point onward it became more difficult for the Dutch to claim that the republic was a government of collaborators. Discussions soon began between Sjahrir and van Mook.

By November and December 1945 the Revolution in the countryside was entering a phase commonly known as the 'social revolution'. This label is, however, somewhat misleading if considered in terms of class conflict: a subordinate social class rarely overturned the power of a dominant social class. Most of the 'social revolutions' resulted from competition between alternative elites, ethnic and communal groups or generations; social class structures were of secondary importance. Most were also of only temporary significance except in some areas of Sumatra, as will be seen below.

The arrival of the first Allied forces only increased the tension in Sumatra and Java, and impelled those who were whole-heartedly in favour of the Republic to turn against those whose commitment was doubted. In the name of 'the people's sovereignty', young revolutionaries intimidated, kidnapped and sometimes murdered administrators, village headmen and policemen whose loyalty was suspect, or who were accused of corruption, profiteering or oppression during the Javanese occupation. In Java, artificial amalgamation of villages by the Dutch had brought firm Muslim (*santri*) and nominal Muslim (*abangan*) communities together under a single headman. *Abangan-santri* tension within these villages had grown throughout the century as a result of heightened pressures for religious orthodoxy, but foreign rule had prevented any serious conflict between the two sides. Now, as the revolutionary spirit rose, members of one or the other of these communities often overthrew the headman if he was from the other community and replaced him with a man from their own side, all in the name of 'the people's sovereignty'. In the confusion, actions in the name of the Revolution were sometimes difficult to distinguish from simple robbery, looting, extortion and the settling of old scores.

Social tension on the north coast of Java reached a peak in December 1945. In the three regencies (*kabupaten*) of Brĕbĕs, Pĕmalang and Tĕgal, all of them part of the residency of Pĕkalongan, there occurred what is known as the 'three regions affair'. Here peasant social protest and a wish to avenge oppression suffered during the Japanese occupation fuelled widespread violence. By early October actions against village headmen in this area were already under way, the initiative being taken by young activists from the Orthodox Islamic community, survivors of the 1926 PKI uprising and pre-war underground Communists. By the end of November the Bupatis of Brĕbĕs, Tĕgal and Pĕmalang had been replaced by supporters of this 'social revolution'. On 12 December the social revolutionaries overthrew the Resident of Pĕkalongan himself and replaced him with a former secret PKI member and underground leader who had been imprisoned by the Japanese. Now the local opposition swung into action. Local Republican army units and youths who supported them swept through the three regencies and arrested over 1000 supporters of this 'social revolution', which thus ended in defeat. Many of the new *santri* headmen in the villages, however, remained in office.

In the principality of Yogyakarta, more enduring social change took place, this time from the top down. In 1939 Sultan Hamengkubuwana VIII (1921–39) ordered his son to come back from the Netherlands, where he was studying at Leiden University. Shortly after his return the old Sultan died and the young man (b. 1912) became Sultan Hamengkubuwana IX (1939–88). During the Japanese occupation he made some gestures towards reform of his principality, but it was only after August 1945 that this effort could be pursued with success. At the start of that month his chief administrator (*patih*) died and the Sultan appointed no successor, thereby taking personal control of affairs. When the Japanese surrendered and independence was declared, the Sultan had both an opportunity to realise his hopes for change and – because of his personal popularity, direct control of his administration and the prestige of the Sultanate – the means to do so. When the *patih* of the subsidiary prince Pakualam VIII (1938–) died, he followed the Sultan's example by appointing no successor; Pakualam VIII now became the Sultan's lieutenant in reforming Yogyakarta.

By early 1946 laws had already been promulgated in Yogyakarta which increased the electorate for village councils and headmen and abolished the head tax. Yogyakarta village administration was now probably the most enlightened in Indonesia. The old court bureaucracy was rapidly reduced in power and its incomes, already much reduced by inflation, were allowed to dwindle. In this way the Sultan overturned Dutch practice and gave the court elite a more restricted but more meaningful role. Rather than social atavisms in the countryside they became custodians of royal traditions within the court itself. Indonesian replaced Javanese as the language of official communication, thereby reducing the influence of the subtle hierarchical social levels of Javanese among administrators. The Sultan also formed a *lasykar rakyat* (people's army) loyal to himself. Indeed, he so consciously adopted a military role like that of pre-colonial rulers that he regarded himself as an army officer and was recognised as such by Republican army commanders.

By January 1946 the Dutch reoccupation of Jakarta had proceeded so far that it was decided to remove the Republican capital to Yogyakarta, which remained the capital of independent Indonesia for the duration of the Revolution. Dutch occupation of Bandung as well as Jakarta also meant the loss of Indonesian control over the only universities in the country. In 1946, therefore, Gajah Mada University was opened in Yogyakarta, with the Sultan offering the front portion of his court to house it. Thus, as one of the Sultan's closest advisers has observed, in Yogyakarta 'the Revolution could not possibly smash the palace doors, because they were already wide open' (Selosoemardjan, *Social changes*, 365).

In Sumatra there were violent 'social revolutions' which opposed the aristocratic elites. In Aceh the bitter animosity between religious leaders *(ulama)* and aristocratic administrators *(uleëbalang)* led to a permanent change at elite level. Many *uleëbalangs* expected the Dutch to return and were left exposed when they did not. In August 1945 a Dutch force arrived in Sabang to repatriate labourers whom the Japanese had transported there. A small Dutch group was in Kutaraja (Banda Aceh) from early October to early November, but withdrew to Medan as the atmosphere grew more hostile. Acehnese now began attacking Japanese, or allowing them food only in exchange for weapons. In mid-December the Allies began to evacuate the Japanese from Aceh, except for over one hundred who joined the Republican forces as instructors. Civil war then broke out.

The *uleëbalangs* failed to put up a united opposition to the pro-Republican forces led by *ulamas*. Between December 1945 and March 1946 the leading *uleëbalangs* of Aceh and their families were imprisoned or killed. The violent social division which had roots in the Aceh war and in conflicts over the control of land, the judiciary and administrative authority – conflicts which the Japanese had temporarily halted in 1942 – were thus resolved by the permanent displacement of the *uleëbalang* aristocracy by Islamic leaders. For the duration of the Revolution the Dutch left Aceh untouched. After 1946, the established dominance in Aceh of a coherent elite and a single ideology (Islam) made it the most stable area of Indonesia during the Revolution. But it also placed Aceh at a distance from the rest of the country, for while others were to argue in subsequent years about whether Islam should dominate the nation, in Aceh it already did.

In East Sumatra armed groups consisting largely of Bataks and led by leftists attacked the Malay, Simalungun Batak and Karo Batak *rajas* in March 1946, as they had in 1942. Arrests and robberies of the *rajas* soon turned into a slaughter in which hundreds of East Sumatran aristocrats died, among them the poet Amir Hamzah. The Jakarta leadership, local Republican politicians and local army units all opposed this violence, and by the end of April the most notorious leaders of this bloody 'social revolution' had either been arrested or gone into hiding. The authority of the *rajas* of East Sumatra, however, had been irrevocably weakened. The divisions within the revolutionary forces in East Sumatra were clearly revealed by the suppression of the 'social revolution'; the Dutch would soon be able to profit from this disunity. Similar violence broke out in Tapanuli (North Sumatra), where about 300 people were killed in May 1946 in fighting between Toba Bataks and Karo Bataks, an ethnic conflict which was reinforced by the presence of Christianity among the Toba and Islam among the Karo.

The divisions among the revolutionary elite in Java were meanwhile becoming more rigid as political parties came into being. While some of these represented ideological streams, many were merely the personal followings of particular leaders. An informal group formed around Tan Malaka, the former PKI leader who returned secretly from exile in 1942. In August 1945 he revealed his identity in Jakarta and immediately attracted a large following. Tan Malaka had by now abandoned Stalinist ideas and thus founded what is known in Indonesia as 'national Communism', a generally leftist stance founded on the idea that Indonesia must seek its own path to and formulation of the socialist state. Tan Malaka never formed his own political party, but became the acknowledged leader of a group of organisations and individuals opposed to the elite then in the Republican government.

By the early months of 1946 the main political parties of the revolutionary period could be identified. The Communist Party (PKI) was reconstituted in October 1945, and after considerable internal conflict and a clash with Republican army units in February 1946, by April 1946 it was controlled by orthodox internationally oriented older leaders, many of them former activists from the 1920s now released from detention. In November 1945 Amir Sjarifuddin's followers in the former youth undergrounds formed Pěsindo (Pěmuda Sosialis Indonesia, Indonesian Socialist Youth); as Minister of Defence Amir also built up the military police as a force loyal to him. Amir's followers merged with those of Sjahrir to form Partai Sosialis (Socialist Party) in December 1945; in early 1947 they split again along these original lines. The Socialists formed the main pro-government force so long as Sjahrir and Amir held power. The main Islamic political party was Masyumi, within which Nahdlatul Ulama and Muhammadiyah functioned as corporate members. In November 1945, urban Modernist politicians led by Sukiman Wirjosandjojo, Natsir and others regained control from the Muhammadiyah and Nahdlatul Ulama leaders whom the Japanese had favoured. The Indonesian Nationalist Party (PNI) was revived in January 1946, but Sukarno was not made its chairman since as President he was theoretically above politics. PNI's main constituency was still found among the Javanese *abangan* and especially among the Javanese bureaucracy, but it also gained much influence in Sumatra. Although PNI was now a new party, free of the taint of Japanese influence which the involvement of Sukarno would have implied, much of its appeal undoubtedly derived from the facts that it carried the name of Sukarno's old party and was led by pre-war PNI and Partindo figures.

The army was also emerging as a political force, but a far from united one. A general distinction can be drawn between two groups. On the one hand, those among former Peta and Heiho soldiers and irregulars who had no pre-Japanese military training were imbued with a revolutionary spirit and trained primarily for guerrilla warfare. This group was best typified by Soedirman, whom the army elected as its own supreme commander in November 1945. On the other hand, former Dutch colonial army soldiers (who took the view that the Dutch surrender in 1942 had released them from their oath of loyalty to the Dutch queen) were better trained for staff work and had a generally more professional, less populist, view of the military role. This group included such men as the Batak Muslim A. H. Nasution (b. 1918) and the Batak Christian T. B. Simatupang (1920–90). The central Republican government profoundly distrusted Soedirman and tended to favour the 'professionals', who soon dominated the general staff and Ministry of Defence. In May 1946 Nasution took command of the West Java Siliwangi Division, which became the major pro-government element within the regular army. Amir's and Sjahrir's distaste for anything tainted by Japanese fascism, and Amir's hopes of politicising the Republican forces along Marxist lines, meanwhile helped to push Soedirman and his followers into greater opposition to the Republican government.

In the first months of 1946, pressures began to increase on both the Republican and Dutch sides. In December 1945–January 1946 the Dutch relieved the Australians in East Indonesia. They arrested Ratulangie, six of his aides and the *rajas* of Bone and Luwu in April 1946. The Revolution was thus deprived of its senior leadership in South Sulawesi, and Republican youths either went underground or set sail for Java. Early in 1946 the Dutch also occupied Bangka, Bĕlitung and Riau. The British turned Bandung over to the Dutch in April, and on 13 July 1946 the Southeast Asia Command formally handed all of Indonesia over to Dutch authority except for Java and Sumatra. As the Dutch occupation proceeded, the British pressed the Dutch to come to some agreement with the Republic. The Indonesia issue was also raised in the United Nations for the first time in January 1946, the beginning of UN involvement which would, in the end, prove to be important.

Sjahrir was meanwhile under increasing domestic pressure. Opponents of his government, especially followers of Tan Malaka, argued that Sjahrir's willingness to negotiate with the Dutch would inevitably lead to the demise of the Republic. In January 1946 a Struggle Union (Pĕrsatuan Pĕrjuangan) was created under Tan Malaka's influence. Youth leaders (including the future Vice-President Adam Malik, 1917–84), radicals such as Yamin, and most of the armed irregulars supported the Union's demand for '100 per cent independence' as the Republic's basis of negotiation. Sjahrir and his followers were seriously threatened by this coalition.

As the pressure mounted, Sukarno found himself emerging from the peripheral position he had occupied for several months. Being the only Javanese among the major Republican leaders and hence the only one who could appeal directly to the masses of Java, and a man capable of adopting the rhetoric of the radicals while quietly supporting the policy of diplomacy, he was becoming essential again as an arbiter of conflict to whom all could turn for legitimacy in the name of the Revolution.

In March 1946 Sjahrir and Amir pulled their followers, especially the Pĕsindo armed units, out of the Struggle Union. At the Union's conference in Malang in that month, Pĕsindo and military police units arrested its leaders. Tan Malaka was held for over two years while awaiting trial, but the opposition's attack on the government was not yet at an end. With the Republican capital situated in Yogyakarta, the rival court city of Surakarta naturally became the centre of the opposition.

In Surakarta the feckless ruler Pakubuwana XII (r. 1944–) and the subsidiary prince Mangkunegara VIII (r. 1944–87) showed few of the skills of their opposite numbers in Yogyakarta, nor were they able to cooperate with one another. They fumbled opportunities to play a positive role in the revolution and thus never gained control of events. The Surakarta radicals were led by Dr Muwardi (1907–48), who commanded armed groups known as Barisan Banteng (Buffalo Column). In January 1946 they kidnapped Pakubuwana XII briefly to demonstrate the people's displeasure, and by April the only real authority in Surakarta was exercised by Barisan Banteng. Soedirman and the local army commanders successfully protected Barisan Banteng against the government's wish to quell it and restore central authority over Surakarta. Finally on 1 June 1946 the prerogatives of the Surakarta princes outside the walls of their courts were formally abolished by the government under pressure from Soedirman and the radicals; Sjahrir's government was obliged to watch Surakarta fall entirely into the hands of the opposition, both military and political.

Negotiations with the Dutch were now at a delicate stage. In March 1946 Sjahrir had secretly agreed with van Mook to negotiate on the basis of *de facto* Republican sovereignty in Java, Madura and Sumatra alone, a recognition of Dutch sovereignty elsewhere, and a cooperative Dutch-Republican effort to create a federal Indonesia within a Dutch-Indonesian union. In April two Indonesian cabinet ministers attended further talks in the Netherlands which broke down because the Dutch government was facing an election on 17 May and dared not appear willing to make concessions to the Republicans. This convinced many Republican leaders that the Dutch would not act in good faith, an impression which was soon strengthened when van Mook decided unilaterally to set up a federal Indonesia under Dutch control.

On 27 June 1946 Hatta made a speech in Yogyakarta which revealed the limited nature of the government's negotiating position. The opposition forces saw this as a betrayal of '100 per cent independence'. That same night, when Sjahrir and several others stopped in Surakarta on their way back from a trip to East Java they were arrested by local army units who hoped that this action would leave Sukarno, Soedirman and '100 per cent independence' in control of the Republic. Instead, Sukarno proclaimed martial law and demanded that the Prime Minister be released. Soedirman, however, refused to have him set free. On 30 June Sukarno broadcast over the radio, saying that the arrest of Sjahrir endangered the unity of the nation. This appeal by Sukarno, as so often in his career, shook the confidence of the opposition. Sjahrir was released that night and returned immediately to Jakarta.

The government now arrested several of its leading opponents. Yamin got away, but Malik and thirteen others were captured. Then it was the army's turn to demand the release of these prisoners. On 3 July 1946, army units freed them from jail and sent a delegation to Sukarno in Yogyakarta which demanded that he dismiss the cabinet and put Soedirman in charge of security affairs. This delegation, however, was now arrested and then about one hundred others were captured by government supporters (this time Yamin did not escape). This 'July 3rd Affair' was crucial. All realised how dangerous their domestic rivalries were, how close in fact they had come to civil war in Central Java. The government blamed Tan Malaka, who was still under arrest, for the whole affair. Soedirman decided in the interest of the Revolution and of his supporters to adopt a more flexible stance. And, yet again, Sukarno had emerged as the only man capable of preventing chaos. Sjahrir's domestic support was clearly seen to be small, but in the interest of the Republic's diplomacy he could not yet be replaced.

Meanwhile the Dutch proceeded with their attempt at a federal solution. In July 1946 they organised a conference at Malino (South Sulawesi) where thirty-nine Indonesian representatives of the *rajas*, Christians and several ethnic groups of Kalimantan and East Indonesia supported the idea of a federal state and some form of continuing Dutch connection. The Dutch were surprised, however, to find that the Indonesians also expected some measure of genuine autonomy. Plans were laid for the formation of a state in Kalimantan and another for East Indonesia.

In November 1946 the Dutch finally concluded their first diplomatic agreement with the Republic. The British had insisted on some agreement before withdrawing all their forces from Java and Sumatra in December. In October negotiations had begun and a ceasefire was agreed in Java and Sumatra. On 12 November, at Linggajati (near Cirĕbon), the Dutch recognised the Republic as the *de facto* authority in Java, Madura and Sumatra, both sides agreed to cooperate in the creation (by 1 January 1949) of a federal United States of Indonesia in which the Republic would be one of the states, and the Dutch queen was to become the symbolic head of a Dutch-Indonesian union of sovereign states. This peace agreement was to have but a brief lifespan. Both sides distrusted each other deeply and in both countries ratification of the agreement provoked bitter political controversies over the concessions which had been made.

The Dutch were discovering that federalism was not necessarily an easy solution. By November 1946 their position in South Sulawesi was being seriously threatened by local Republican youths returning from Java, where they had received further military training. The Dutch responded in December by unleashing one of the most infamous figures of the Revolution, Captain Raymond 'Turk' Westerling. His methods of using arbitrary terror were soon emulated by other anti-Republicans in South Sulawesi. In three months at least 3000 Indonesians are estimated to have been killed by these methods. Among them was the pro-Republican Datu of Supa who was killed by Westerling's troops in February 1947. The Republican youth groups were decimated.

The Dutch pushed forward with their plans for federal states as best they could. A state of East Indonesia was created at a conference in Den Pasar (Bali) in December 1946. This was called Nĕgara Indonesia Timur (State of East Indonesia) and abbreviated NIT; opponents joked that these initials stood for *nĕgara ikut tuan* (the state which goes along with the master, i.e. the Dutch). But despite continuing Dutch control, even at Den Pasar nationalist ideas were strong: 'Indonesia Raya' was adopted as the NIT anthem and a pro-Republican Bugis was very nearly elected President. It proved impossible to set up a state for all of Kalimantan, as the Muslims of the south and east coasts were too strongly pro-Republican. In May 1947 a separate state for West Kalimantan was established under Sultan

Abdul Hamid II (r. 1946–50) of Pontianak. Sjahrir protested ineffectually at the unilateral creation of these two states.

These developments only deepened Republican distrust of the Dutch and dislike of the Linggajati agreement. In order to have a better chance of getting the agreement ratified by the KNIP, it was necessary to increase its members from 200 to 514 by packing it with pro-government figures, who had formed themselves into a coalition called the Left Wing (Sayap Kiri) in December 1946. Ratification was nevertheless not assured. But when it became clear that Hatta and Sukarno would resign if Linggajati were not accepted, the KNIP ratified it in February 1947. The expansion of the Left Wing coalition in the KNIP, however, spelled the end of Sjahrir's dominance, for other leftist groups were now the equal of his followers within the Socialists. In June 1947 Amir Sjarifuddin and most of the Left Wing withdrew their support of Sjahrir, who now went abroad to represent the Republic at the UN. In July Amir became the new Prime Minister (1947–8), just in time to face the first major Dutch offensive against the Republic.

By about May 1947 the Dutch had already decided that they must attack the Republic directly. The cost of keeping a largely inactive force of about 100 000 soldiers in Java was a serious financial drain which the war-torn Netherlands economy could ill afford. If they were to maintain this force, the Dutch needed access to the products of Java (especially sugar) and Sumatra (especially oil and rubber). The Dutch military believed that Republican-held cities could be conquered in two weeks and the whole of Republican territory in six months.

At midnight on 20 July 1947 the Dutch launched their first 'police action'. Major columns swept out from Jakarta and Bandung to occupy West Java (excluding Bantĕn), and from Surabaya to occupy Madura and the Eastern Salient. Smaller troop movements secured the Sĕmarang area. The Dutch thus gained control of all the deep-water ports in Java. In Sumatra, plantations around Medan, oil and coal installations around Palembang, and the Padang area were secured. Republican forces retreated in some confusion, destroying what they could. In some areas last-minute acts of revenge took place: Chinese in West Java and imprisoned aristocrats in East Sumatra were murdered. Some Dutchmen, including van Mook, wished to carry on to conquer Yogyakarta and install a more malleable Republican government, but American and British dislike of the 'police action' led the Dutch to stop short of complete conquest of the Republic.

The United Nations now became directly involved in the conflict, an involvement which would eventually trap the Dutch in an impossible diplomatic position. India and Australia were particularly active in supporting the Republic's cause in the UN, where the Soviet Union also lent its support. But the most crucial role was eventually played by the United States. Those who determined Dutch policy, even the more progressive among them, were convinced that both history and common sense gave them the right to determine the development of Indonesia, but this right could only be exercised by first crushing the Republic. The Netherlands' main allies – especially the British, Australians and Americans (upon whom the Dutch primarily relied for post-war reconstruction aid) – did not recognise such a right unless the people of Indonesia did, which was clearly not the case if the Dutch had to rely upon military conquest. They began to press the Netherlands to adopt a less rigid stance, and the UN became a public forum for examining

Dutch actions. This only increased the Dutch inclination to seek a quick solution in Indonesia.

At the end of July 1947 the Dutch felt that they must accept a UN call for a cease-fire, which was ordered by the Dutch and Sukarno on 4 August. The UN then allowed Sjahrir to speak for the Republic, but refused admittance to representatives from Dutch-held areas. In October a UN Good Offices Committee with American, Australian and Belgian representatives was established to assist Dutch-Republican negotiations for a new ceasefire. Since August the Dutch had continued mopping-up operations behind their advance points where many Republican fighters remained. In particular, the Siliwangi Division was still behind Dutch lines in West Java.

In January 1948 a new agreement was reached aboard the American ship USS *Renville* in Jakarta harbour. This recognised a ceasefire along the so-called 'van Mook line', an artificial line which connected up the most advanced Dutch points despite the fact that many Republican-held areas remained in the rear. Although this looked like a considerable Dutch negotiating victory, the apparent reasonableness of the Republicans in accepting it (a course dictated partly by shortages of ammunition on the Republican side) won them crucial American goodwill.

The humiliations of the first 'police action' and the subsequent *Renville* agreement led to the fall of Amir Sjarifuddin's government. PNI and Masyumi members in his cabinet resigned when the *Renville* agreement was signed, and Amir then resigned as Prime Minister on 23 January 1948. He may have expected a new leftist cabinet to follow him, but Sukarno turned in another direction. He appointed Hatta to head an emergency 'presidential cabinet' (1948–9), responsible not to the KNIP but to Sukarno as President. Its membership was of a broadly centrist nature, consisting mainly of PNI, Masyumi and non-party individuals. Amir and the Left Wing now went into opposition. Sjahrir's followers formalised their split with Amir's by creating their own Partai Sosialis Indonesia (Indonesian Socialist Party, PSI) in February 1948 and giving their support to Hatta's government.

The Dutch meanwhile pushed ahead with their federal solution in the conquered areas but with limited success, for what goodwill they had enjoyed was running out. In December 1947 they set up an East Sumatra state, in February 1948 a Madura state and a West Java state called Pasundan, in September 1948 a South Sumatra state, in November 1948 an East Java state, and so on until in all there were fifteen federal states in the areas they had conquered. In March 1948 van Mook announced the creation of a provisional government for a federal Indonesia, of which he himself was to be President. In July the Dutch established an Assembly for Federal Consultation (Bijeenkomst voor Federale Overleg) consisting of the leaders of the federal states. They intended to create a federal United States of Indonesia with or without the Republic's agreement by the end of the year. But within these federal states there was significant pro-Republican sentiment among the elite and little support for federalism among the masses. The Dutch were therefore pushed farther towards the contemplation of some final military solution.

Conditions within the Republic in Java were chaotic in 1948. It was effectively reduced to the overpopulated and rice-deficient interior of Central Java, where hardship was increased by the Dutch blockade and an influx of perhaps as many as six million refugees and Republican soldiers. The Republican government printed more money to meet its costs and inflation soared. This was not, however, without beneficial effects. As inflation and rice prices rose, peasants' incomes increased and many of their debts were wiped out, while wage-earners' incomes fell. The result was a levelling effect which improved the relative lot of the peasantry and thereby also reduced pressures from below for major social change. Chaos also descended in Tapanuli (North Sumatra), where retreating Republican units gathered and a virtual civil war among rival Republican forces ensued.

The leftists who were out of the Republican government now began a fateful effort to regain power, under the leadership of Amir Sjarifuddin. In February 1948 the Left Wing coalition renamed itself People's Democratic Front (Front Demokrasi Rakyat) and denounced the *Renville* agreement, which Amir's government itself had negotiated. The Front attempted to build up peasants' and workers' organisations, but with only limited success. A strike at a state textile factory in Dĕlanggu (Central Java) began in May 1948, and in the violence which followed it became evident that the Front's base in the countryside was less a matter of social class or ideology than of communal identity. The *abangan* (nominal Muslim) workers who supported the Front found themselves under attack from *santri* (strict Muslim) followers of Masyumi, who were supported by Hizbullah units. In July the strike was settled on terms favourable to the strikers, but by then there was evidence that central political manoeuvres were becoming entangled in the communal tensions of Javanese villages.

A critical military move had meanwhile taken place. In accordance with the *Renville* agreement, Colonel Nasution led the 22 000 men of the Siliwangi Division out of Dutch-held West Java into Republican Central Java in February 1948. This had important consequences both in the region they left and in the one they entered.

In West Java there remained many militant Islamic guerrillas led by a Javanese mystic named S. M. Kartosuwirjo (1905–62). He had been expelled in 1927 from medical school for radical political ideas and had then lived with Tjokroaminoto, his foster-father, until 1929. He then fell seriously ill and during his convalescence studied Islam with various mystical teachers. Thereafter he was active in Partai Sarekat Islam Indonesia until being expelled in 1939 over policy disagreements. In 1940 he set up the Suffah Institute in the Garut region of West Java, where young militants were given religious and general education and imbued with personal loyalty to Kartosuwirjo. The Japanese closed the Suffah Institute but Kartosuwirjo maintained his contacts in the area and became head of the local Hizbullah guerrillas. He expanded his forces in the early stages of the Revolution and became active in Masyumi. But by this time he disliked leftist ideas, and hence distrusted many of the Republican leaders.

When the Siliwangi Division withdrew, Kartosuwirjo felt that West Java had been abandoned by the Republic. His response was to launch what became the first regional rebellion against the Indonesian Republic, while continuing to fight against the Dutch in West Java. In May 1948 he proclaimed himself *imam* (head) of a new state called Nĕgara Islam Indonesia (Indonesian Islamic State), more commonly referred to as Darul Islam (Arabic *dar al-Islam*, territory or house of Islam). Darul Islam government was based upon Islamic law and administered by *kyais*. Much of its local support came, however, from devotion to the charismatic

Kartosuwirjo, whose followers ascribed supernatural powers to him. As the years passed, Darul Islam became progressively more difficult to distinguish from simple banditry, extortion and terrorism on a grand scale. It was to survive as a regional rebellion, controlling much of the countryside of West Java, until Kartosuwirjo was captured and executed in 1962. While the Revolution continued the Republican government could only ignore Darul Islam; some Masyumi leaders were in any case sympathetic towards it.

Siliwangi's march into Central Java had consequences there which were important to the final achievement of independence. Nasution and his largely Sundanese soldiers formed a force loyal to the Hatta government, and soon found themselves in opposition to local Javanese units who looked to Soedirman's leadership or to Amir Sjarifuddin's People's Democratic Front. The Hatta government wanted to reduce the massive armed forces for which it was responsible, roughly estimated at some 350000 regular troops and 470000 irregulars. Nasution, too, favoured a smaller army with higher professional standards, but the losers in such a rationalisation scheme would obviously be the fighters who supported the government's opponents. As the military split into factions over the rationalisation proposals, kidnappings, murders and armed clashes began in the Yogyakarta-Surakarta area. By the end of August 1948 civil war again seemed possible. There was now an explosive mixture of elite political manoeuvres, military politics and communal tensions in Central Java, while Dutch forces stood in positions on the West, North and East.

Suddenly Musso, the PKI leader of the 1920s, arrived in Yogyakarta from the Soviet Union on 11 August 1948. Except for a secret visit in 1935 to establish an underground PKI organisation, Musso had not set foot in Indonesia since 1926. Amir and most of the other Central and East Java leaders of the People's Democratic Front immediately accepted his authority, and Amir announced that he had been a member of the underground PKI since 1935. Musso adhered to Stalinist thinking in insisting that there could be only a single party of the working class. By the beginning of September the major leftist parties in the Front had dissolved themselves to merge into PKI. A new PKI politburo was formed on 1 September which included several younger men who were more eager to accept Musso's authority than the existing PKI leaders; these new figures included the future PKI leadership group of D. N. Aidit (1923–65), M. H. Lukman (1920–65), Njoto (1925–65) and Sudisman (1920–68).

PKI now encouraged demonstrations and strikes by workers and peasants. The peasantry were encouraged to take over their landlords' fields in the Surakarta area and then elsewhere. Masyumi denounced the Communist actions and *santri* peasants refused to support the strikes. Musso's pro-Soviet pronouncements meanwhile threatened the Republic's main diplomatic strategy of gaining the sympathy of the United States. Landlords (many of them *santri*), village headmen, bureaucrats, the central Republican leadership and pro-government military forces all realised that they faced a serious challenge. In September the government released Tan Malaka in the vain hope of winning leftists away from Musso.

By mid-September 1948 open warfare had broken out in Surakarta between pro-PKI and pro-government armed forces. On 17 September the Siliwangi Division drove PKI supporters out of the city. They withdrew to Madiun and were joined there by other pro-PKI units which left their positions along the van Mook line to face the expected government attack on Madiun.

On 18 September the PKI supporters took over strategic points in the Madiun area, killed pro-government officers, and announced over the radio that a new National Front government had been formed. Musso, Amir and other PKI leaders hastened to Madiun to take charge of this premature attempt at a coup. Soedirman was caught in a difficult position. He sympathised with the pro-PKI units' opposition to demobilisation and had little affection for the Republican government's actions, but he was equally opposed to any attempt by Musso and PKI to gain influence over the Republican government, which would lead to attempts to impose PKI control over the army. Nor did he want civil war. Soedirman hoped to negotiate a solution which would involve only the arrest of the Madiun ringleaders but Sukarno, Hatta and Nasution seized the initiative for a more drastic solution.

On 19 September about 200 PKI and other leftist leaders remaining in Yogyakarta were arrested. That evening Sukarno denounced the Madiun rebels over the radio and called upon Indonesians to rally to himself and Hatta rather than to Musso and his plans for a Soviet-style government. Musso's lack of recent experience in Indonesia probably made him unable to gauge the power of such an appeal from Sukarno. He made the fatal error of replying over Madiun radio that he would fight to the finish. Faced with an irreconcilable choice between Musso and Sukarno, many military units which were basically sympathetic to the anti-government side decided to remain aloof. The People's Democratic Front organisations in Bantĕn and Sumatra announced that they had nothing to do with Madiun.

Pro-government forces spearheaded by the Siliwangi Division now marched on Madiun, where there were some 5000–10000 pro-PKI soldiers. As the rebels were pushed back they began killing Masyumi and PNI leaders and officials, and in the villages killings began along *santri-abangan* lines. On 30 September the rebels abandoned Madiun town and were pursued through the countryside by pro-government troops. Aidit and Lukman fled the country for China and Vietnam. On 31 October Musso was killed while attempting to escape from captivity, ending his eighty-day career as PKI leader. Amir and a body of 300 soldiers were caught by Siliwangi troops on 1 December; Amir was later to be shot along with other prominent PKI leaders. In the arrests which followed Madiun about 35000 people were picked up. How many died during the affair is unknown, but is thought to have been at least 8000. In its aftermath, *santri* peasants in Surakarta turned upon and killed *abangan* supporters of PKI there.

Madiun was one of the crucial turning points of the Revolution. PKI was removed as a threat to the established Republican leaders until the 1950s, and was tainted forever with treachery against the Revolution. The left in general was discredited and many of its leaders were imprisoned or dead. With the removal of the Stalinists, the 'national Communists', who followed Tan Malaka's thinking and opposed the PKI rebellion at Madiun, joined together to form Partai Murba (Proletarian Party) in October 1948; they were now the main leftist group among the revolutionaries. A tradition of army-PKI hostility was established by Madiun and the antagonism between Masyumi and PKI was strengthened, as was the *santri-abangan* communal tension which it reflected. The alliance between the more professional army officers and the Hatta government was sealed. The army itself was more battle-hardened and unified, and a purge of the officer corps and demobilisation of many irregular units followed rapidly.

Perhaps most importantly, the Republic's defeat of a Communist rebellion turned vague American sympathy based upon anti-colonial sentiments into diplomatic support based upon global strategy. The year 1948 saw the beginnings of the Berlin blockade by the Soviet Union, the Communist *coup d'état* in Czechoslovakia, the start of the Communist insurrection in Malaya, the rebellion of the Red Flag Communists in Burma (the White Flags had been in rebellion since 1946), continuing Communist insurrection in the Philippines, continuing advances by the Communist side in China, and evidence from elsewhere which contributed to an image of rapid political advances by Communism. American strategic thinking was now dominated by the idea that a 'cold war' was under way between an American-led 'free world' and a Soviet-led bloc. Within this framework, the Indonesian Republic had shown itself to be anti-Communist and hence worthy of American support. When the Dutch now made their last bid for conquest, they found the weight of the United States thrown onto the diplomatic scales against them.

While the Dutch proceeded unilaterally with their federal solution, negotiations between them and the Republic were at a standstill. Hatta refused to accept the Dutch demands that they be responsible for internal security during the transition to independence or that the Republican army be integrated within a federal army. Minor hostilities meanwhile continued on the Dutch side of the van Mook line, and increased when part of the Siliwangi Division began to infiltrate back into West Java after the Madiun affair. In November–December 1948 the Dutch decided on a final military push to crush the Republic.

On 18 December 1948 the Dutch launched their second 'police action', which proved to be both a military and a political catastrophe for them despite the appearance of being an easy victory. On 19 December Yogyakarta was taken. The Republican government allowed itself to be captured in the hope that world opinion would be so offended that the Dutch military victory would be turned into a diplomatic defeat. Sukarno, Hatta, Agus Salim (Foreign Minister) and all the cabinet except for the few who were away were captured, as also was Sjahrir. The Republican army, however, was generally unable to understand the reason for the civilian politicians' surrender to the Dutch while soldiers were laying down their lives for the Republic. The army now looked upon itself as the only saviour of the Revolution.

Republican forces withdrew to the countryside and began full-scale guerrilla war on both sides of the van Mook line. The army killed Amir Sjarifuddin and over fifty other imprisoned leftists as it withdrew from Yogyakarta in the night of 19/20 December, rather than take the risk that they might be set free. By the end of December all the major Republican towns of Java and Sumatra were in Dutch hands. The only region which remained under the sole control of the Republic was Aceh, where Daud Beureu'eh was in charge. The Dutch felt it was wiser not to touch Aceh.

In the UN Security Council there was the outrage which the Republican government had hoped for. The UN Good Offices Committee had actually been only a few miles from Yogyakarta at the hill resort of Kaliurang when the Dutch struck, and the dignity, authority and good offices of the UN appeared to have been treated with contempt. American opinion was also angered. On 22 December the United States suspended further transfers of aid funds to the Netherlands which were intended for expenditure in Indonesia, while pressure mounted in the American Congress for the suspension of all economic aid to the Netherlands. Indonesian Republican leaders, however, still hoped for more decisive American support.

The Dutch soon discovered that their military advance merely created problems in the rear. Indonesian civilians gave them next to no cooperation and Republican guerrilla operations reduced many Dutch positions to virtual siege conditions. Nor could the Dutch get any Indonesian political support. Reflecting an extraordinary inability to understand how much circumstances had changed, they attempted to persuade Sultan Hamengkubuwana IX to become leader of a new Javanese state, but he refused to discuss their offer. He resigned as head of the Yogyakarta district in January 1949 and his court became a primary channel of communication between the city and Republican units in the countryside. The cabinets of both East Indonesia and Pasundan created major embarrassment for the Dutch by resigning in protest at the 'police action'.

The Dutch accepted a UN call for a ceasefire on 31 December 1948 in Java and 5 January 1949 in Sumatra, but the guerrilla fighting continued. Soedirman was now dying of tuberculosis; although still the symbol of army unity he was hardly able to exercise command. Nasution was effectively in charge as deputy commander and on 22 December he proclaimed a military government for Java. In practice, most units operated autonomously during this guerrilla period. In addition to their many smaller victories against the Dutch, Republican forces under Lieutenant-Colonel Soeharto struck a major blow when they recaptured and held Yogyakarta for six hours on 1 March 1949.

The only civilian politician of the first rank still alive and at large was Tan Malaka, who was in East Java when the Dutch struck. He issued a call for total resistance but he no longer had any large following of his own. In February 1949 he was with an army unit in East Java which was defeated in a clash with another Republican unit. Tan Malaka was captured and executed.

The UN and the United States began to adopt more resolute stances against the Dutch which, in conjunction with Republican military pressure, finally forced the Netherlands to abandon its final attempt at empire in Indonesia. Late in January 1949 the Security Council demanded the release of the Republican cabinet, the establishment of an interim government, and a full transfer of sovereignty by 1 July 1950. The United States publicly condemned the Dutch in the UN and threatened to cut off the reconstruction aid upon which the Dutch domestic economy heavily depended. By April the Dutch accepted that they must give in, but insisted on preliminary talks with the Republican government. On 7 May it was agreed that Sukarno and Hatta would order a ceasefire upon their return to Yogyakarta, that the Dutch would accept the Republic at a Round Table conference, and that they would create no more federal states.

On 6 July 1949 the Republican government was returned to Yogyakarta, which Dutch troops had already evacuated by the end of June. Soedirman and other army leaders were reluctant to accept the authority of the civilians who seemed to have deserted the Republic, but they did so when Sukarno threatened otherwise to resign. A conference was held in Yogyakarta and Jakarta in July, where the federal states proved to have many of the same interests as the Republic, largely because of their respect for the Republic's resistance and their disappointment at the failure of the Dutch to transfer any significant powers to them. The conference agreed that the Republican army would form the core of the military for a new Republic of the United States of Indonesia (RUSI) and that Sukarno and Hatta would be President and Vice-President of that state.

On 1 August a ceasefire was announced, to take effect in Java on 11 August and Sumatra on 15 August. Just before it was implemented, Republican forces recaptured most of Surakarta and held their gains for two days. Further isolated clashes continued into October. But gradually the handing over of military authority from Dutch and irregular forces to regular Republican units and the creation of an integrated military authority for the new RUSI state were arranged by Hamengkubuwana IX as Coordinator of Security. There were, however, some turbulent areas such as South Sulawesi, East Sumatra, South Kalimantan and West Java where this process encountered resistance from local irregular forces.

From 23 August to 2 November 1949 a Round Table conference was held at the Hague. Hatta dominated the Indonesian side of the negotiations and won the admiration of all participants. A loose union of the Netherlands and RUSI was agreed, with the Dutch queen as symbolic head. Sukarno was to be President of RUSI and Hatta Prime Minister (1949–50) as well as Vice-President. Various guarantees were provided for Dutch investments in Indonesia and it was agreed that there would be consultations on some financial matters; many Indonesians saw these arrangements as unreasonable restrictions upon their sovereignty. On the two most difficult issues the Indonesians were obliged to make concessions. The Netherlands retained sovereignty over Irian Jaya until there could be further negotiations on the status of that area. And RUSI accepted responsibility for the Netherlands East Indies debt, a figure which after much haggling was fixed at f. 4.3 billion; much of this in fact represented the costs of the Dutch attempt to crush the Revolution.

On 27 December 1949 the Netherlands formally transferred sovereignty over Indonesia, excluding Irian Jaya, to RUSI, a federal state which survived intact for only a few weeks. There was much pro-Republican sentiment in the federal states created by the Dutch, sentiment which had been strengthened by the release of some 12000 Republican prisoners from Dutch jails between August and December 1949. Federalism was generally suspect because of its obvious origins as a Dutch stratagem; it was now finally discredited by 'Turk' Westerling's last flamboyant effort to alter the course of events.

On 23 January 1950 Westerling and about 800 troops captured key points in Bandung, but the Dutch High Commissioner and the commander of the Dutch garrison still in Bandung persuaded him to withdraw that same day. The following day it was discovered that Westerling planned to attack the RUSI cabinet and assassinate several ministers. Westerling's troops had infiltrated Jakarta after leaving Bandung, but they were driven out and in February Westerling fled the country in disguise. There was widespread shock at these events.

The arrest of several Pasundan leaders for suspected complicity in Westerling's plot led the parliament of that state to ask on 27 January 1950 that Pasundan be dissolved. By the end of March most of the smaller federal states had followed this precedent by deciding to dissolve themselves into the Republic. The Hatta cabinet found itself swept along in a unitarist tide and was forced to make hasty legislative arrangements to cope with it. Early in April Sultan Abdul Hamid II of Pontianak, head of state in West Kalimantan and minister without portfolio in the RUSI cabinet, was arrested as a major instigator of Westerling's plot. Thereupon authority over West Kalimantan was taken over by the RUSI government.

The greatest opposition to the unitarist movement came from the East Sumatra and East Indonesia states. In the latter, many Ambonese who were Christian, pro-Dutch and had fought against the Revolution resisted the demise of federalism. They looked upon the Republic as a state dominated by Javanese, Muslims and people whom they regarded as leftists. In April 1950 colonial soldiers (mostly Ambonese) and Republican units clashed in Makasar (Ujungpandang), as a result of which the East Indonesia government was compromised. A new East Indonesia cabinet was formed in May with the intention of dissolving the state into a unitary Indonesia. On 25 April, however, the former Minister of Justice in the East Indonesia government, the Ambonese Dr. Soumokil, proclaimed a Republic of South Maluku in Ambon. After tough campaigns from July to November this new state was crushed by Republican troops. Faced with the collapse of the other federal states, East Sumatra had little option but to go along.

Finally, on the occasion of the fifth anniversary of the declaration of independence, on 17 August 1950, the whole constitutional structure of the revolutionary years was formally swept away. The Republic of the United States of Indonesia, the Republic of Indonesia as a constituent element within it, and the states of East Sumatra and East Indonesia were replaced by a new Republic of Indonesia with a unitary (but provisional) constitution. Jakarta was made the capital of this new state.

The political revolution was now complete. Many questions remained, but the revolutionary years appeared to have resolved some issues. It seemed reasonable to suppose that Indonesia was not to be several things: neither a federal state, nor an Islamic state, nor a Communist state, nor above all a Dutch colony. But the coming years were to reveal that these things were not as certain as they seemed in 1950. Nor was it clear what the implications of independence would be for the many social, religious, communal, ethnic, cultural and economic questions which remained.There were still fundamental issues which, in the years of anti-colonialism, war and revolution, Indonesians had not had the time or the opportunity to confront. As they now came to confront them, it became evident that – beyond victory over the Dutch – the Revolution had not resolved so many issues after all.

VI
Independent Indonesia

18 The Democratic Experiment, 1950–7

Indonesia was at last independent, at least in a formal legal sense, and now faced the prospect of shaping its own future. In a country still typified by poverty, low educational levels and authoritarian traditions, much depended upon the wisdom and good fortune of the Indonesian leadership. The history of the nation since 1950 has, however, been partly a story of the failure of successive leadership groups to meet the high expectations generated by the successful struggle for independence. In 1950 the older urban nationalists of the leading 'secular' and Islamic parties were in charge of governmental affairs. There was a general consensus that democracy was desirable and that these were the men to create a democratic state. But by 1957 the democratic experiment had collapsed, corruption was widespread, the territorial unity of the nation was threatened, social justice had not been achieved, economic problems had not been solved, and the expectations generated by the Revolution were frustrated.

Given the circumstances facing Indonesian governments in the years 1950–7, it is not surprising that the democratic experiment foundered, for there were few foundations upon which representative democracy could be built. Indonesia inherited from the Dutch and Japanese the traditions, assumptions and legal structure of a police state. The Indonesian masses – mostly illiterate, poor, accustomed to authoritarian and paternalistic rule, and spread over an enormous archipelago – were hardly in a position to force politicians in Jakarta to account for their performance. The politically informed were only a tiny layer of urban society and the Jakarta politicians, while proclaiming their democratic ideals, were mostly elitists and self-conscious participants in a new urban super-culture. They were paternalistic towards those less fortunate than themselves and sometimes simply snobbish towards those who, for instance, could not speak fluent Dutch. They had little commitment to the grass-roots structure of representative democracy and managed to postpone elections for five more years. A plant as rare as representative democracy can hardly grow in such soil. It must be said, however, that because of the elite commitment to the idea of democracy, the years 1950–7 stand as the freest period of Indonesian history for the politically articulate.

The economic and social issues facing the nation after the Japanese occupation and the Revolution were enormous. Plantations and industrial installations throughout the nation had been badly damaged. Perhaps most fundamentally, population growth accelerated. In 1950 the population was estimated at 77.2 million, in 1955 at 85.4 million, and in the 1961 census it was 97.0 million.

Food production increased, but not enough. In Java rice production per capita actually declined slightly from 1950 to 1960. So substantial food imports were still necessary. Agriculture absorbed much of the new labour force by dividing the work among an ever-increasing number of workers. But as the average size of land holdings declined, many farming families no longer had sufficient land for their subsistence and had to find much or most of their income from wage labour. Many people flocked to the booming cities. In 1930, 3.8 per cent of the population was classified as urban; in 1961 it was 14.8 per cent. Between 1945 and 1955 Jakarta's population doubled to 1.8 million and then grew further to 2.9 million by 1961. By that time two other cities were around one million (Surabaya and Bandung) and three were around half a million (Sĕmarang, Palembang and Medan). The cities and larger towns became the natural focus of political activity, and the problems of rural areas were often ignored.

Since Java had the capital city, most of the other large cities, the vast majority of the civilian politicians and the majority of the nation's population (61 per cent in 1961), the outer islands in general tended to be neglected. In an effort to subsidise the net-importing economy of Java, the Indonesian Rupiah (a currency first introduced during the Revolution) was maintained at an artificially high exchange rate. This imposed difficulties on the net-exporting economies of the outer islands and encouraged black markets and smuggling. Most commercial and industrial interests suffered. Although many of the civilian politicians believed that foreign enterprises were essential to economic development, it was never politically wise to support them too publicly. The locally domiciled middle class was politically weak and divided by antagonism between the Chinese, who had substantial commercial networks but no political support, and the largely Islamic Indonesian bourgeoisie, who had less extensive commercial networks and only limited political support.

Education was given high priority and the number of educational institutions expanded dramatically. Between 1953 and 1960 the number of entrants to primary schools rose from 1.7 million to 2.5 million, but around 60 per cent of these consistently dropped out before completing school. State and private (mostly religious) high schools and university-level institutions sprang up everywhere, but especially in Java, and many achieved high standards. Two substantial benefits from this educational expansion were soon evident. In 1930 the adult literacy rate had been 7.4 per cent, while by 1961 it was 46.7 per cent for those over the age of ten (56.6 per cent in Sumatra, 45.5 per cent in Java). For males between ten and nineteen the rate was over 76 per cent. These figures demonstrate the vast achievement since the Dutch period. And the use of the Indonesian language throughout the educational system, as well as in all official communications and the mass media, established it firmly as the national language. Increasing Indonesian literacy was reflected in daily newspaper circulation which, however, remained small for a nation of such size. Daily circulation nearly doubled from just under 500 000 in 1950 to over 933 000 in 1956, while other periodicals trebled to over 3.3 million in the same period. But by the time these hopeful developments were bearing fruit, the system of constitutional democracy which they might have supported was already discredited.

Many more people sought employment now, including those from the expanding educational institutions, former guerrilla fighters, and former federal and Republican officials. The governments of the 1950s gave many of them positions in the bureaucracy, and continued to swell its ranks by making government jobs one of the prime spoils of political power. In 1930 the colonial civil service totalled about 145000, representing approximately one official for every 418 inhabitants. In 1950 the bureaucracies of the former federal states (approximately 180000) and the Republic (approximately 240000) were amalgamated. Then many former guerrillas were given office jobs, the students came in, and the politicians paid off their supporters. In the nation as a whole there were nearly 807000 permanent civil servants in 1960, representing about one for every 118 inhabitants. Salaries were low and were badly affected by inflation. Inefficiency, maladministration and petty corruption became normal, and this cumbersome bureaucracy became increasingly incapable of doing much of anything.

The recovery of Indonesia's exports was slow. Oil, the second largest foreign-exchange earner after rubber, was the most hopeful for the long term. By 1957 oil production was twice the level of 1940, but part of this increase was consumed domestically. During 1950–6, domestic demand for petrol rose by 64.5 per cent and for kerosene by 200.5 per cent. In general, government infrastructure programmes which were essential to the export sector (such as roads, ports, flood control, irrigation, forestry) deteriorated, and the artificial exchange rate discriminated against exporters.

In the economy generally non-Indonesian interests remained important. Shell and the American companies Stanvac and Caltex were strong in the oil industry, and most inter-island shipping was in the hands of the Dutch KPM line (Koninklijke Paketvaart Maatschappij, Royal Mail Steam Packet Company). Banking was dominated by Dutch, British and Chinese interests, and Chinese also controlled much of the rural credit. It was clear to informed observers that Indonesians were not independent economically, a fact which was to contribute to the radicalism of the late 1950s.

Given the slow economic recovery and the expansion of government expenditures, it is not surprising that the inflation of the war and revolutionary periods continued. The general cost of living rose by about 100 per cent over 1950–7, but this figure conceals larger fluctuations in particular areas, periods and commodities. All sectors of society suffered in some degree from erratically rising prices. Salaried officials and wage-labourers were particularly affected, while landowners, village officials who were given land in lieu of salaries, and peasant rice-producers gained relatively. Compared with the Japanese occupation period and the revolutionary years, conditions were better for most Indonesians in 1950–7, but independence did not bring the general prosperity many had expected.

Among the problems facing the new nation was what to do with the army. This was the source of issues which dominated much of Indonesian history after 1950: who controlled the army, how was it to be structured, and what was its role in the life of the nation? In 1950 the civilian politicians took the view that theirs was the right to determine military affairs. At independence the government had about 250–300000 soldiers and an unknown number of irregulars to deal with, and had to absorb some 26000 Dutch colonial army troops. By November 1950 the army was said already to be down to 200000 men, a level which was to be maintained until about 1960. The army commanders were divided among themselves, uncertain of their own proper role, less educated than the leading politicians and for the most part at least ten years younger than they.

It was to be some time before the army found its feet in the swell of national politics.

The divisions within the army reflected its origins in the Dutch, Japanese and revolutionary periods. The central command was in the hands of Nasution, Simatupang and others who insisted on military professionalism, a stance favourable to men of their kind and hierarchical structures which they could control. Against them were pitted regional commanders who favoured a revolutionary spirit, military decentralisation and minimum hierarchy. The army was, however, fairly coherent ideologically, having been shorn of its left wing at Madiun and of its Islamic elements by demobilisation and the Darul Islam rebellion. Its deepest commitment was to the spirit of the Revolution, although what this spirit entailed was not clearly defined beyond the idea that the army was somehow its supreme embodiment. The factions were also united in their suspicion of civilian politicians, whom they regarded as having made a minimal contribution to the winning of independence.

The civilian politicians created a large number of political parties, but only a few had real significance in Jakarta. Sjahrir still led the Socialist Party (PSI), backed by Jakarta intellectuals but with little popular support elsewhere. Sjahrir himself, however, never sat in a cabinet again. PSI was influential among higher civil servants and had supporters among the central army command. The 'national Communists' who had admired Tan Malaka were in Partai Murba (Proletarian Party); they were bitter opponents of the Communists for left-wing support, but had little strength outside Jakarta. Christians had both an Indonesian Christian (i.e. Protestant) Party (Parkindo: Partai Kristen Indonesia) and a Catholic Party (Partai Katholik); their significance was increased by the substantial over-representation of Christians in higher levels of the civil service and the military because of their superior educational qualifications.

Masyumi represented Islamic political interests and was presumed to be the largest party in the country, although until elections were held this could only be a presumption. It was loosely organised, with a primary internal division between Orthodox and Modernist religious leaders. In 1952 these wings were to split. At the top Masyumi was led by the Modernist politicians Sukiman Wirjosandjojo and Mohammad Natsir. There was, however, some tension between the followers of these two men, with Sukiman's support coming largely from Javanese and Natsir's from non-Javanese. Masyumi's political base consisted of committed Muslims, including a substantial part of the indigenous bourgeoisie, as well as religious teachers and scholars *(kyais* and *ulamas)* and demobilised Hizbullah and Sabilillah guerrillas. But the party never officially placed the idea of an Islamic state among its priorities in the 1950s. While its national leaders were devoted to God in their private lives, in politics their devotion was to Indonesia. They avoided doctrinaire stances which could threaten national unity or appear to associate the party with the Darul Islam rebellion. Those who were opposed to Masyumi, however, suspected it of latent religious fanaticism.

The Indonesian Nationalist Party (PNI) was presumed to be the second largest. Its primary base was in the bureaucracy and among white-collar workers. In the countryside of Java it had considerable appeal to the nominal Muslim *(abangan)* community, partly because it was thought of as the party of Sukarno (which formally it was not, since the President joined or led no party) and partly because it was thought to be the main counterbalance to Islamic political pretensions. Similarly, PNI had much support in Christian areas of the outer islands and in Hindu Bali, where also anti-Islamic feelings existed.

Finally, the Indonesian Communist Party (PKI), which was decimated but not outlawed in 1948, was on the verge of making the most spectacular comeback of its chequered history. In an internal contest which ended in January 1951, the youthful leadership of Aidit, Lukman, Njoto and Sudisman took control of the Politburo from older survivors of Madiun. From the beginning Aidit insisted that Marxism was a guide to action, not an inflexible dogma. His leadership brought a new pragmatism to PKI which enabled it shortly to become one of the largest political parties. PKI's initial base was primarily among urban and agricultural estate workers, who were organised through the union federation SOBSI (Sentral Organisasi Buruh Sĕluruh Indonesia, All-Indonesia Workers' Organisation Centre), which was wholly controlled by PKI. Later the party was to expand to other sectors of society, including the peasantry, which led it to lose much of its proletarian character.

Aidit argued that Indonesia was a semi-colonial and semi-feudal country, and that the first target of the party must be the remnants of colonialism. The party should therefore seek cooperation with non-Communist but anti-colonial forces. In practice, he initially looked for support from PNI. The party's strategy was cloaked in Marxist-Leninist terminology which concealed a departure from conventional Marxist-Leninist theory. Rather than social class determining political orientation, in Aidit's arguments political orientation became a determinant of social class. Thus, he argued that the Communists could collaborate with the petit bourgeoisie and national bourgeoisie against the compradore bourgeoisie and the feudal classes. But the main political party supported by the indigenous bourgeoisie was Masyumi, whose leaders were anti-Communist. Masyumi was therefore castigated, along with PSI, as a party of the compradore bourgeoisie. PNI, which was bureaucratic (and in some senses 'feudal') more than bourgeois, proved more amenable to PKI wooing and it was therefore PNI which Aidit identified as the party of the national bourgeoisie. When Nahdlatul Ulama split from Masyumi in 1952, Aidit was relieved to be able to regard NU as a bourgeois party, which in some senses it was. Aidit's strategy of seeking allies among other political streams meant that in practice PKI adapted itself to a social structure in which cultural, religious and political allegiances were vertical or communal (the so-called *aliran*, currents or streams) rather than horizontal, as in a class-conscious society. By adapting itself in this way, PKI largely forestalled any attempt to stimulate a greater class-consciousness that would cut across existing communal and party loyalties.

Aidit's strategy was defensive, for PKI was widely distrusted by many in the political elite and the military. His main aim was to protect the party from those who hoped for its destruction, whatever theoretical adjustments or political alliances this might require. Aidit defended PKI with remarkable success for nearly fifteen years, but this endeavour took the party along strange paths. In the end, what was at stake was less the future of the working class or of Communism as a political ideology than the future of PKI as an organisation. Most of the party's opponents, however, viewed it in terms of its exclusive ideological positions and the threats which they believed Communism posed to religion and the dominance of the established military and political elite. To be fair to these opponents, it must be admitted that no one can know what measures PKI would have imposed had it ever come to power.

It is important to note that the civilian politicians who dominated Indonesia in this period were still largely from the lesser *priyayi* class, the group which had taken the lead in the nationalist movement. They were an intelligentsia with backgrounds in political activism and government service. Few had business contacts or landed wealth. Politics was what they knew and their only significant source of status and reward. Much the same was true of the military leadership, for whom the military life was all that they knew or could benefit from. These facts explain much of the bitterness of the conflicts of 1950–7, for the price of failure in politics was not only a loss of power but a loss of income and status as well. During the 1950s some politicians and military men began to acquire business interests, but it was only after 1957 that these circumstances changed significantly (see Chapter 19).

In 1950 the Jakarta politicians naturally constructed a parliamentary system like the one they knew best: the multiparty democracy of the Netherlands. The cabinet was responsible to a unicameral parliament (Dewan Pĕrwakilan Rakyat, People's Representative Council) of 232 members which reflected what were presumed to be party strengths. Masyumi had 49 seats (21 per cent), PNI 36 seats (16 per cent), PSI 17 seats (7.3 per cent), PKI 13 seats (5.6 per cent), Catholic Party 9 seats (3.9 per cent), Christian Party 5 seats (2.2 per cent), and Murba 4 seats (1.7 per cent), while over 42 per cent of the seats was divided among the remaining parties or individuals, none of them with more than 17 seats. This was hardly a structure to support strong governments, but it was generally believed that the party structure would be simplified when elections were held. Sukarno as President had no real power except to appoint *formateurs* to construct new cabinets, a task which often involved complex negotiations.

The first cabinet (September 1950-March 1951) was formed by Natsir and based upon Masyumi with PSI support after an attempt at a Masyumi-PNI coalition failed. Natsir's foreign policy was independent and neutralist while remaining sympathetic to the Western powers. In September 1950 Indonesia was admitted to the United Nations. Natsir's government faced the most favourable economic circumstances of the period of constitutional democracy, for the Korean War boom in commodity prices increased export earnings and government export duties until mid-1951. As the scramble for spoils began in Jakarta, the Minister of Finance, Masyumi's Sjafruddin Prawiranegara (1911–89), was criticised for refusing to use these revenues to dole out patronage.

Sjafruddin's policies were consistent with the Natsir cabinet's concentration on the sober necessities of reconstruction of the economy and restoration of security. The Ambonese rebellion was ended by November 1950, but no progress was made towards negotiations with Kartosuwirjo in West Java. Early in 1951 a solution was finally achieved for those Ambonese soldiers of the colonial army who refused to be demobilised in Indonesia. They and their families, a total of some 12 300 persons, were transported to the Netherlands where they found new problems of integration. But discussions with the Dutch about sovereignty over Irian produced no progress. Nor did the government succeed in its hopes of reducing the size of the bureaucracy. The cabinet did, however, inspire the first signs of opposition to the infant political system. Natsir insisted, entirely correctly, that Sukarno confine himself to the role of figurehead President. Sukarno cared little for such a role and found himself increasingly in agreement with PNI and radical views that winning sovereignty over Irian should not be given low priority merely because of the needs of economic development. Natsir's cabinet resigned after less than seven months in office, having failed to move much in any direction or to build a base of support either in or outside the parliament.

The next Prime Minister (April 1951-February 1952) was Sukiman Wirjosandjojo, who succeeded in building the Masyumi-PNI coalition which many thought to be the natural form of government. Sukarno was happier with this arrangement, not least because the cabinet gave him a larger budget and a freer hand in speech-making. No one from Natsir's following within Masyumi was included, nor was any PSI leader, so the groups which had most sympathy with the central army command were excluded. The absence of Hamengkubuwana IX from a cabinet for the first time since 1946 particularly weakened army-cabinet relations.

Almost immediately a conflict with the army occurred. The non-party radical Muhammad Yamin was Minister of Justice in the new cabinet. At this point there were some 17000 prisoners, many not yet charged, who had been arrested by the army since 1949 for involvement in rebellious or bandit groups. Early in June Yamin released 950, including several leading leftists. Immediately the army rearrested them except for those who went into hiding. Yamin resigned and an early skirmish between civilian government and the armed forces was thus won by the latter.

The Sukiman cabinet is most notable for the only serious attempt in this period to suppress PKI. The Communists had been angered by PNI's willingness to join in a coalition with Masyumi, since their strategy depended on these two parties remaining opposed to one another. In June-August 1951 a series of strikes broke out, a hand grenade was thrown into a crowd at Bogor, and an armed gang with hammer-and-sickle emblems attacked a police station. The government decided that PKI was to blame, a charge which the Aidit leadership denied to no avail. Without consulting the army, the government ordered large-scale arrests. On 11 August PKI leaders in Medan were arrested. A few days later there followed a major wave of arrests in Jakarta, including sixteen members of parliament (among them Aidit's father who was a member for a minor party). It is unclear how many were arrested at this time, but in late October the government put the figure at 15000. None was ever brought to trial and all were released by the later Wilopo cabinet. Aidit, Lukman and Njoto went into hiding and reconsidered their strategy.

PKI leaders concluded from this episode that the Jakarta politicians would not let them play politics on an equal footing with the other parties. Therefore they adopted a more long-term strategy to build an independent mass base so large that the party could neither be ignored nor immobilised by the arrest of its leaders, while at the same time working for at least the neutrality of non-Communist forces. Thus the policy of the 'national united front' was adopted and nationalist slogans took precedence over class demands. A membership drive now began, primarily in Java. By the end of 1952 claimed party membership rose from 100000 (in May) to 126 671; by March 1954 it reached 165 206.

Being uncertain of PNI as an ally, PKI also began to court Sukarno's favour. For all their private dislike of the President, from this time on PKI leaders no longer called him a Japanese collaborator or fascist, and no longer blamed him for provoking Madiun; their rationalisation of that episode now laid all blame on Hatta, Sukiman and Natsir (all of them members of the cabinet at the time). In order to reassure potential allies, the party adopted a less partisan role, informing SOBSI in March 1952 that striking for higher pay was 'sectarianism' which threatened the national united front strategy. As will be seen below, PKI's subsequent growth was spectacular, but much of this growth was undoubtedly because the party abandoned its militancy in the interest of survival.

Security problems were meanwhile reviving, after considerable success in 1950–1 in several areas. In South Sulawesi delicate negotiations were in progress over the reduction and incorporation of army units commanded by Lieutenant-Colonel Kahar Muzakkar (1921–65), a leading Republican commander in the Revolution. In July 1950 Kahar joined some 20 000 troops who refused to be demobilised. After further negotiations failed, in August 1951 he took to the mountains in open rebellion. In January 1952 Kahar contacted Kartosuwirjo and formally made his rebellion a part of the Darul Islam movement, which carried on unabated in its West Java homeland. The Sukiman cabinet's failure to deal successfully with Kahar greatly weakened its authority.

Finally the cabinet fell over a foreign policy crisis. It had followed a more actively pro-Western line, and in January 1952 the Masyumi Foreign Minister secretly signed an aid agreement with the United States which committed Indonesia to the defence of the 'free world'. As soon as this commitment became known a political uproar resulted. In February the Foreign Minister and then the whole cabinet resigned. The following cabinet abandoned the American agreement and sought aid with fewer strings attached. Some people were already beginning to ask themselves whether the kind of politics seen in Jakarta was the cause for which the Revolution had been fought.

Another PNI-Masyumi coalition followed, this time with PNI's Wilopo (b. 1909) as Prime Minister (April 1952–June 1953). The two parties were, however, unenthusiastic partners from the start. A general realignment of political forces was now under way. PNI was growing suspicious of the Islamic motivations of some Masyumi leaders and was looking for allies to help it postpone elections, which it feared might be won overwhelmingly by Masyumi. PKI, with its national united front strategy, was willing to offer PNI its support and did not denounce this cabinet as it had its predecessor. All those arrested in the anti-Communist sweep of 1951 were now released. Both PKI and PNI being parties with their main support among *abangan* Javanese, their alliance was perhaps a natural one, although it contained the seeds of competition.

Hatta and Sjahrir, who had been expelled from Pĕrhimpunan Indonesia in 1931 by Communists, saw PKI as a reviving threat. Their followers and admirers in Masyumi and PSI therefore became even more implacably anti-PKI and the two parties drew closer together, being united also by their similarity in having largely Dutch-educated Sumatran intellectuals as national leaders.

Meanwhile the Orthodox and Modernist Muslims within Masyumi split. There were many reasons for the schism, including basic doctrinal differences, but the immediate occasion was a dispute over the post of Minister of Religion, which went to a Modernist rather than to Wachid Hasjim for the first time since 1949. Between April and August 1952, Nahdlatul Ulama withdrew from Masyumi and turned itself into a separate political party led by Wachid Hasjim until his death in 1953. The split left great bitterness. It was soon evident that NU, primarily based in Central and especially East Java, found it easier to cooperate with the other Java-based parties, PNI and PKI, than with Masyumi. For their part, PNI and PKI were pleased that they could deal with an Islamic party without having to deal with Masyumi. A political divide was now emerging between the Java-based and outer islands-based parties.

Economic conditions were worsening now, with the Korean War boom over. Between February 1951 and September 1952 the price of rubber, the leading national export, fell by 71 per cent. Government revenues of course fell. In an effort to correct the unfavourable balance of trade and the drain on gold and foreign-exchange reserves, the government imposed surcharges of 100 to 200 per cent on luxury imports and cut expenditure. These measures did ameliorate the worst effects of the economic crisis, but they hit PNI's main supporters hardest. Masyumi supported the policies, thereby increasing PNI-Masyumi tension. The cabinet also planned reductions in the size of the bureaucracy and the military. PNI was unhappy about any attempt to cut the bureaucracy, and the planned reductions in the military precipitated a crucial conflict within the army.

Sultan Hamengkubuwana IX was again Minister of Defence in the Wilopo cabinet and close cooperation with the 'professionals' of the army central command was restored. Although the Sultan, Nasution, Simatupang and most of their closest supporters in Jakarta were non-party individuals, they had strong informal links with Sjahrir and PSI. Nasution himself, however, was primarily committed to the army rather than to any civilian faction. These men now set about a centralisation and demobilisation scheme to reduce the army from 200000 to 100000 troops. These proposals pitted this central group against regional army commanders, many of whom were sympathetic to PNI and to Sukarno. Critics of the scheme claimed that PSI intended to reduce the army to an organisation loyal only to itself, and then use it for a coup. Military coups took place in Thailand in November 1951 and Egypt in July 1952; some Indonesians wondered whether their country was next.

Regional commanders attempted to resist the scheme and were supported by their political allies in Jakarta. In parliament it was demanded that the central army leadership be dismissed and the Ministry of Defence reorganised. Faced with this challenge, the central army group attempted a show of force, fatally miscalculating the forces around them. On 17 October 1952 they brought army tanks and artillery and many civilian demonstrators, said to total about 30000 in the end, to the Presidential palace to demand the dissolution of parliament. Sukarno himself cared little for the demobilisation scheme, which would remove many of the revolutionary leaders with whom he sympathised, and, although he shared Nasution's distaste for parliamentary politicking, he had no wish to be manipulated by the army high command. He spoke to the assembled crowd, who dispersed at his command; yet again Sukarno saw himself, and others were obliged to see him, as the man who could speak directly to the people. Then he received an army delegation and promised them vaguely that their interests would be satisfied. They, like the crowd, dispersed at Sukarno's word.

The show of force had come to nothing. Sukarno went on the radio to appeal for calm, making it clear that attempts to coerce the President were unacceptable.

Now central army supporters were rapidly displaced. Throughout October and November commanders who had been newly installed by the central leadership over regional forces were overthrown by the former commanders. In December 1952 Nasution was suspended and for three years he remained on the inactive list. During this time he matured (he was thirty-three at the time of the '17 October affair', as it came to be called, whereas Sukarno was fifty-one) and reconsidered his tactics, concluding that it was better to have Sukarno as an ally than an opponent. In January 1953 Hamengkubuwana IX resigned as Minister of Defence. In March the Secretary-General of the Ministry was replaced. In November Simatupang was removed when his post as armed forces chief of staff was abolished. None of these men was charged with an attempted coup, but the power of the central army command was broken.

The army was now left in a highly decentralised state and even more open to civilian interference. Its bargaining power in Jakarta was devastated, with the result that government budgeting for the military fell and regional commanders began to search for more unorthodox sources of funds. Eventually even they were forced to realise that there were advantages in a strong central command. As factional conflicts developed within the army, its effectiveness against rebels and bandits declined. The Wilopo cabinet, for its part, was discredited by the collapse of its demobilisation scheme. Sukarno was encouraged by his success in the affair and began to adopt a more assertive public role as a critic of the politicians.

The dissolution of parliament having been an issue in the 17 October affair, it was no longer easy for the politicians to postpone elections indefinitely. In April 1953 an election bill was finally passed. The date for parliamentary elections was later fixed for September 1955 and elections for a Constituent Assembly (Konstituante) to draft a permanent constitution were fixed for December 1955. The Jakarta politicians now began to work for the first time at building mass support which would deliver votes. In their search for popular support they used broad ideological appeals which contributed to communal tensions in the villages. Islamic party activists at lower levels called for a state based on Islamic law. The 'secular' parties, most notably PNI and PKI, attempted to associate Masyumi with Darul Islam and turned Pancasila into a partisan anti-Islamic slogan rather than the umbrella philosophy Sukarno thought it to be. For over two years political turbulence and violence increased, and all hopes rested upon the elections producing a clear mandate for the future.

The PNI-Masyumi coalition had never been very cordial and by the early months of 1953 there was little substance left to it. In March police killed five peasants near Medan while removing squatters from foreign-owned estate lands. PKI had been active among the squatters and now allied with PNI in parliament to demand that the cabinet resign. Before a vote of no confidence could be taken in parliament, the cabinet returned its mandate to Sukarno.

After over six weeks of bargaining and five attempts at various party combinations, a PNI cabinet supported by NU and minor parties was formed by Ali Sastroamidjojo (July 1953-July 1955). Masyumi and PSI were excluded, while two figures sympathetic to PKI were included. Yamin was back as Minister of Education and he and several others, including Ali, were thought of as left-wingers. In fact, however, there was little change of policy. Indeed, policy was of declining importance to governments as more attention was directed to winning and holding power, and sharing its spoils. The Ali cabinet expanded the bureaucracy with more PNI supporters, partly because control of the bureaucracy was expected to be crucial in the coming elections. The cabinet also pressed for Indonesianisation of the economy, with encouragement for indigenous businessmen. In practice, however, many new firms were bogus fronts for arrangements between government supporters and Chinese – the so-called 'Ali-Baba' firms, in which an Indonesian ('Ali') was front man for a Chinese ('Baba') entrepreneur. Instances of corruption and scandals involving PNI figures became more common.

After relative price stability in 1952–3, inflation accelerated again. During the period of the Ali cabinet the money supply was increased by 75 per cent and the free market exchange rate fell from 44.7 per cent of the official rate to 24.6 per cent. Exporters, among them many Masyumi supporters in the outer islands, were badly affected and smuggling increased. Impoverished army units joined in the smuggling. As the price of PNI protection, PKI muted its criticisms of corruption and economic problems. In May 1955 SOBSI members even helped to break a strike by a PSI union. The economy, the political system and the country were falling apart while Jakarta politicians manoeuvred for advantage.

The militant Muslims of Aceh had had enough of high-living, irreligious, incompetent Jakarta politics. In 1949 Aceh had been made an autonomous province of the Republic but in 1950 it was amalgamated with the province of North Sumatra. The membership of the All-Aceh Union of Ulamas (PUSA) included both Modernist Islamic teachers and scholars (*ulama*) and devout lay Muslims (*zuama*). The former grew dissatisfied with the course of national developments largely on religious grounds, while the latter were particularly concerned about Aceh's loss of provincial autonomy. This combination formed a potential base for resistance to Jakarta. In 1950 PUSA's leader Daud Beureu'eh, Aceh's strongman and bulwark of the Republic in the Revolution, refused to take a job in Jakarta and sat in Aceh watching developments. So long as Masyumi figures were prominent in the cabinets he took no action. In May 1953, however, evidence was found that he had been in contact with Kartosuwirjo of Darul Islam. When the Ali cabinet was formed Daud became suspicious; rumours spread that the cabinet intended to arrest prominent Acehnese.

On 19 September 1953, Daud and his followers in PUSA rebelled openly against Jakarta, with the support of many Acehnese civil servants and military men. Daud declared that there was no more Pancasila government in Aceh, which was now part of Darul Islam. The Ali government sent in troops to drive the rebels from the main towns. PKI supported cabinet policy and denounced the Aceh rebellion as colonial, militarist, feudal and fascist, mostly epithets which the Acehnese thought more appropriately applied to Jakarta. Daud withdrew to the hills and a military stalemate ensued which lasted until 1959. In West Java, Darul Islam activity also increased during the Ali cabinet. Darul Islam, now comprising the hinterlands of Aceh, West Java and South Sulawesi, had become an even greater challenge to the government and a major drain upon its funds.

Public attention was temporarily diverted from domestic problems in 1955 by a grand diplomatic event, the Asian-African Conference at Bandung. Ali wished Indonesia to be an active leader of an Afro-Asian bloc of nations, an aim warmly endorsed by Sukarno. In April-May 1954 a meeting of the Prime Ministers of India, Pakistan, Ceylon (Sri Lanka), Burma and Indonesia – the so-called

'Colombo Powers' – was held in Colombo. There Ali proposed a large conference of Afro-Asian states; others soon began to endorse the idea, and a conference was scheduled for April 1955, by which time other diplomatic developments had occurred.

The People's Republic of China was now abandoning its hostility to the non-Communist and neutralist states of Asia. Indonesia sent its first ambassador to China in May 1953. In December the Ali government signed the first small Chinese-Indonesian trade agreement. Relations between the two nations grew progressively more friendly and culminated at the Bandung conference, where a dual nationality treaty was signed. China traditionally claimed that all overseas Chinese were citizens of China, which left this community with an ill-defined dual citizenship status in Indonesia. The 1955 dual nationality agreement obliged Indonesian Chinese to choose either Chinese or Indonesian citizenship, but under terms which made it difficult for them to choose the latter.

Diplomatic efforts towards the acquisition of Irian Jaya had meanwhile broken down again. Negotiations with the Dutch resulted in a protocol of August 1954 which envisaged the abolition of the Netherlands-Indonesian Union (a nonentity in any case) and some adjustment of the Round Table agreements, but there was no progress on the Irian issue. Indonesia failed to get a moderate resolution on Irian adopted by the UN in the same month. In the Indonesian parliament, Masyumi used these setbacks to propose a motion of no confidence in the government's Irian policy in December. This vote failed, but it revealed that the opposition could muster so many votes that only the parliamentary cooperation of PKI guaranteed the government's survival.

In April 1955 the Bandung conference was held and represented a triumph for the Ali government. Twenty-nine states were present. Of the major nations of Africa and Asia only the two Koreas, Israel, South Africa and Outer Mongolia had not been invited. Many of the major leaders of Asia attended, including Zhou Enlai (Chou En-lai), Nehru, Sihanouk, Pham Van Dong, U Nu, Mohammad Ali and Nasser. Sukarno and Ali Sastroamidjojo derived great satisfaction and domestic prestige from being seen as leaders of the Afro-Asian world, and the conference's final communiqué endorsed Indonesia's claim to Irian Jaya. It was clearly possible for Indonesia to play a leading role in the world, and Sukarno began to make such a role his personal responsibility.

Once the Bandung conference was over, the politicians threw their energies into the coming elections. But the forces which would ultimately topple the whole parliamentary system were already forming. The growth of PKI during Ali's cabinet, when it was free from repression, was spectacular. Between March and November 1954 claimed party membership trebled from 165 206 to 500 000, and by the end of 1955 it was 1 million. PKI was now beginning serious recruitment of peasant members. Its Indonesian Peasant Front (BTI: Barisan Tani Indonesia) claimed 360 000 members in September 1953 but over nine times that number (3.3 million) at the end of 1955, nearly 90 per cent of the membership in Java, and nearly 70 per cent in Central and East Java. Pěmuda Rakyat (People's Youth), the successor to Pěsindo of the Revolution, trebled from 202 605 members in July 1954 to 616 605 at the end of 1955, 80 per cent of its members being peasant youths and the vast majority in Java. The PKI newspaper *Harian Rakjat* ('People's Daily') more than trebled in circulation between February 1954 (15 000) and

January 1956 (55000), by which time it had the largest circulation of any party-affiliated newspaper. PKI was also the wealthiest of the political parties, with income from membership fees (collection of which, however, was often erratic), fund-raising campaigns and other sources. Much of its money probably came from the Chinese business community, either willingly or through pressure from the Chinese embassy.

But as PKI expanded into rural Central and East Java, its class identity and potential militancy were virtually submerged. Many poor peasants joined because PKI promised to defend their interests, but many joined for other reasons. PKI teams repaired bridges, schools, houses, dams, public lavatories, drains and roads; they eradicated pests and set up literacy courses, organised village sports and musical groups, and offered members support in times of hardship. As a community organisation PKI surpassed all others, and because it seemed non-violent and moderate, villagers flocked to it. Often it was led in the villages by teachers, headmen, middle and rich peasants, and even some landlords, who brought whole communities or groups of dependants into PKI with them. These communities were almost exclusively nominal Muslim *(abangan)*. *Santri* villagers were largely NU supporters. This political distinction at village level thus reflected a communal distinction, and hardened it by politicising it. During the election campaign, however, NU, PKI, and PNI restrained their criticism of one another in Java and turned their joint fire upon Masyumi. Masyumi's anti-Communist diatribes meanwhile probably pushed even more *abangan* into the PKI fold.

As it grew in this way, PKI acquired a mass base which enabled it to pressure other political forces and shortly to make an impressive showing in the elections. It was unlikely, however, that this could ever be a base for revolution. The Aidit leadership was obliged to organise general literacy and basic education courses before it could think of exposing most of its rapidly expanding following to Marxist-Leninist ideas. The strategy of seeking a peaceful parliamentary path to power by building an enormous mass membership was now so successful that it would be difficult for PKI to contemplate any other path.

Meanwhile one of PKI's main enemies, the army, was putting its own house in order. Its factions were realising that they must settle their differences if they were to stand against the civilian politicians and PKI. In mid-1954 the two main factions from the 17 October affair began to reconcile themselves. In February 1955 a conference of 270 officers at Yogyakarta adopted a charter of unity and agreed to regard the affair as a thing of the past. The new unity of the officer corps was, however, very fragile. Nasution was not present, being inactive, and he still had many opponents within the army.

Then the army challenged the government over who should be installed as its chief of staff. The officers refused to recognise the man installed by the cabinet on 27 June 1955, and the opposition parties supported them. The issue was not resolved until after the elections. As yet another political crisis loomed, Sukarno left (18 July) on a pilgrimage to Mecca and a state visit to Egypt. NU had long been dissatisfied with the cabinet's personnel, economic and security policies, and on 20 July decided that the government must resign. Having insufficient support left in parliament, Ali's government resigned four days later.

After more complex bargaining, Burhanuddin Harahap (b. 1917) of Masyumi put together a cabinet based on Masyumi with PSI and NU support (August

1955–March 1956). The army was not entirely happy since it believed many of the new cabinet members to be as corrupt as their predecessors. But it was pleased at the opportunity to arrest several PNI figures for corruption, as well as the Minister of Justice in the previous cabinet (who was convicted and sentenced to a year's imprisonment in January 1956 but pardoned by Sukarno in July). As the political disputes in Jakarta became more acrimonious and tension grew in the villages, the long-awaited elections at last took place.

There was a high turnout in the September 1955 parliamentary elections. Over 39 million voted, representing 91.5 per cent of registered voters. Although many undoubtedly voted as they were told to vote by religious leaders, headmen, officials, landlords or other patrons, these were nevertheless the most important national elections in Indonesian history. They offered the freest choice among an unrestricted range of parties, all of which campaigned vigorously; the election results can therefore tell much about political allegiances at the time. The most important results are given below.

party	valid votes	% valid votes	parliamentary seats	% parliamentary seats
PNI	8434653	22.3	57	22.2
Masyumi	7903886	20.9	57	22.2
NU	6955141	18.4	45	17.5
PKI	6176914	16.4	39	15.2
PSII	1091160	2.9	8	3.1
Parkindo	1003325	2.6	8	3.1
Partai Katholik	770740	2.0	6	2.3
PSI	753191	2.0	5	1.9
Murba	199588	0.5	2	0.8
others	4496701	12.0	30	11.7
TOTAL	37785299	100.0	257	100.0

The elections produced several disappointments and surprises. The number of parties was increased rather than reduced, with twenty-eight gaining seats whereas only twenty had seats before. But only four parties had more than eight seats: PNI, Masyumi, NU and PKI. Among these 'big four' parties there was nearly a stalemate. The largest could command only 22 per cent of the parliamentary seats. Some Masyumi leaders felt that Islam's progress to national power was now blocked and that their attention should turn to an intensification of Islam at grass-roots level. NU leaders, however, were elated at a result which increased their parliamentary seats from eight to forty-five. The showing of PKI was a considerable shock to the Jakarta elite, and increased PNI's worries about the potential threat posed by its junior partner.

Perhaps the most ominous pattern was the clear party split between Java and the outer islands. Masyumi was by far the strongest party in the outer islands, winning between a quarter and a half of the votes in all regions except Bali and Christian areas, and three-quarters in Aceh; it was also the largest party in strongly Islamic West Java, although there PNI was not far behind whereas both PKI and NU were weak. In Central and East Java, there was a fairly even balance among PNI, NU and PKI. Looking only at the votes cast in Central and East Java for the 'big four', PNI won 32 per cent, NU 30 per cent (being the largest party in its heartland of East Java) and PKI 27 per cent, while Masyumi won only 12 per cent. Rather than resolving political issues, the elections merely helped to draw the battle-lines more precisely.

The elections had produced no solutions and thereby represented a further step in discrediting the whole parliamentary system. The Constituent Assembly elections in December were something of an anticlimax and produced similar overall results. The Assembly was not convened until November 1956 and, as will be seen in the following chapter, was dissolved almost three years later without having drafted a new constitution.

The Burhanuddin cabinet hung on as long as it could, resisting pressure to make way for the elected parliament and a new government. As rapidly as possible it promoted PNI bureaucrats upwards to powerless positions and put PSI and Masyumi supporters in their places. The cabinet also reached a settlement with the army. In August 1955 it accepted the army's proposal to forget about the 17 October affair, so that officers suspended then (among then Nasution) could return to active duty. After lengthy bargaining, Nasution emerged as the army's leading candidate for chief of staff, and the cabinet appointed him in October. Nasution took up his duties in November 1955 and was promoted to Major-General. The government also renewed negotiations with the Netherlands at the end of 1955, to no avail. In February 1956 it announced the unilateral dissolution of the meaningless Netherlands-Indonesian Union and promised further unilateral steps regarding the Round Table agreements. But the cabinet had no life left in it after NU withdrew its support in January 1956, and it finally resigned early in March.

Again Ali Sastroamidjojo formed a cabinet (March 1956–March 1957). He was determined to have a PNI-Masyumi-NU coalition so that he need not rely upon PKI. He succeeded, but at the price of a cabinet so internally divided that it could hardly function. On 26 March the new parliament was assembled, the only parliament in Indonesia's history which could claim to reflect a free choice by universal adult suffrage from a full range of parties. It was to last four years before being dissolved. But neither the new parliament nor the new government displayed much authority, and by this time few Indonesians expected that they would. In his opening speech to the parliament, Sukarno expressed hopes for a truly Indonesian form of democracy, one based on consensus rather than the divisive '50 per cent plus one' democracy of the West with its parliamentary contest between government and opposition. He was now beginning to call for a 'guided democracy', echoing the views of his old friend Ki Hadjar Dewantara who described the governance of his Taman Siswa schools in these terms.

Relations with the Netherlands continued to worsen, primarily because of Dutch refusal to negotiate the surrender of Irian to Indonesian control. On 4 August 1956 the Ali cabinet unilaterally repudiated f. 3.661 billion of the nation's debt under the Round Table agreements, 85 per cent of the figure agreed in 1949, on the grounds that this represented the costs of the Dutch war against the

Revolution. This repudiation was warmly welcomed in Indonesia. But there were few other achievements credited to this government. It arranged for elections to regional assemblies to be held in 1957, but for the rest much of its attention went to handing out patronage. More and more scandals became public knowledge.

In the largest opposition party, PKI, Aidit's leadership weathered two internal problems in 1956 and emerged upon its same course. While Aidit was on a visit to the Soviet Union in March, his leadership was challenged by Alimin, who had twice seen the downfall of PKI and was now an elderly man in his late sixties. He circulated a statement that the Aidit leadership group was soft, opportunist and deviationist, and was leading PKI to become an ordinary bourgeois party by stifling class-consciousness. He was largely correct, but it is hard to see how PKI could have survived in any other way. Alimin found no support, was forced to recant, and withdrew to a lonely and embittered old age. He died in 1964 before having to witness the third and bloodiest destruction of PKI.

The unilateral abrogation of the Netherlands-Indonesian Union in February 1956 and the repudiation of the Round Table debt agreement in August presented another minor problem by removing PKI's main evidence for Indonesia's semi-colonial status. Aidit changed course slightly and now emphasised the Dutch retention of Irian, which was an increasingly important public issue, and the presence of internal reactionaries (implying Masyumi above all) who were conniving with foreign imperialists to restrict the nation's independence. Increasingly, PKI's issues and enemies were Sukarno's issues and enemies.

The social and political fabric of the nation was now fraying at the edges. The Jakarta politicians who had shown how easily the rule of law could be ignored were obliged to watch in impotence as others followed their example in more violent ways. Economic problems tended to be blamed on the Chinese, and soon mobs were attacking this community, particularly in the outer islands and more strongly Islamic areas of Java. Ethnic and regional sentiments became increasingly obvious, encouraged by the regional distinctions revealed in the 1955 elections. The Sundanese of West Java protested their irritation with the Javanese, who by weight of numbers dominated many aspects of national life. Outer islanders were also dissatisfied with the number of Javanese appointed to government posts. In East Sumatra the Toba Bataks were particularly objects of hostility, and there were some deaths in public brawls. In the outer islands generally the frustrations at the overvalued Rupiah and Jakarta's general neglect came to a head.

By now regional interests were closely linked to army affairs. In the years since 1952 many regional commanders had forged unorthodox links with outer island interests as a means of financing their units and their personal incomes. These circumstances held little appeal for Nasution and his supporters, who aimed for a cohesive, centrally controlled army free of civilian entanglements. By late 1954 and early 1955 large-scale smuggling operations were underway from Sulawesi (especially Minahasa). In June 1956 the government ordered the main smuggling port of Minahasa to be closed, but local leaders returned an ultimatum that the order must be rescinded within seven days. Jakarta gave in. By early 1956 there had come to light a rubber-smuggling operation run by the commander in North Sumatra, Colonel Maludin Simbolon (b. 1916), a Toba Batak Christian, one of the army's most respected officers and a rival to Nasution. In July he came to an amicable agreement with Jakarta and was never charged.

Finally a protracted internal military crisis brought the political system crashing down. With the political parties increasingly polarised along a Java-outer islands division and the bureaucracy being so ineffectual, the army was virtually all that held the national administration together; as it divided, the nation divided. Upon becoming army chief of staff in November 1955, Nasution announced another plan for large-scale transfers of officers, many of whom were by now well entrenched in private business arrangements. As transfers began to be carried out in the face of procrastination by many officers in 1956, the army and civilian interests associated with it split into two main factions. But these groupings did not replicate those of the 17 October affair. Now Nasution and his army supporters worked in alliance with Sukarno, Ali and PNI; this faction included several officers who had opposed Nasution in 1952. Against them stood Simbolon and the deputy chief of staff Lieutenant-Colonel Zulkifli Lubis (b. 1923), also an opponent of Nasution in 1952; they were allied to Masyumi and PSI figures and largely supported by non-Javanese, anti-Jakarta officers. As will be seen in the following chapter, this was the alignment of factions that underlay the Sumatran rebellion of 1958.

In August 1956 tensions mounted in Jakarta. One of Lubis's supporters attempted to arrest the PNI Foreign Minister Roeslan Abdulgani (b. 1914) for alleged corruption, but the order was countermanded by Nasution. Then Lubis, who ceased to be deputy chief of staff on 20 August, plotted a coup with the support of officers of the Siliwangi Division of West Java, the best-equipped and best-trained division within the army. Sukarno was out of the country (28 August-16 October 1956) on a state visit to China, the Soviet Union and other Communist states, and the plotters hoped to be rid of Nasution and the cabinet before the President's return. They failed. On 11 October and again on 16 November pro-Lubis troops failed to enter Jakarta, on the first occasion being stopped by pro-Nasution units and on the second being thwarted by Nasution's superior organisational manoeuvres. There was no shooting, but the arrest of Lubis was ordered; he went into hiding, later to re-emerge in the Sumatran rebellion.

Nasution now rapidly arrested or transferred his opponents within the Siliwangi Division and turned it into his most reliable division. When Mochtar Lubis, a highly regarded journalist in Jakarta and a novelist of great moral courage, alleged corruption involving Foreign Minister Roeslan, he was arrested and brought to trial in December 1956 for libel. He was to remain in jail or under house arrest for nine years. Roeslan was ultimately found guilty of unintentional violation of exchange control regulations and fined Rp. 5000 in April 1957.

A political impasse seemed to exist in Jakarta, with many people feeling that the constitutional system could not survive but not knowing what should follow. Some called for a new Hatta cabinet, but by now the old cooperation between Hatta and Sukarno was dead. On 20 July 1956 Hatta submitted his resignation as Vice-President, to take effect on 1 December. This removed the most admired outer island figure from the centre of government. He made no flamboyant gestures, but was clearly discouraged by the nation's course. In his final speech he criticised the narrow self-interested behaviour of the parties. On this he and Sukarno were in agreement, but on little else. Hatta would have preferred to improve the parties; Sukarno wanted to be rid of them.

Sukarno increasingly took the initiative in public. Around him gathered a group of non-party radicals, several of whom had been admirers of Tan Malaka during the Revolution. In a speech on 28 October 1956 Sukarno called for the parties to be buried. Two days later he said that he had a notion, an idea *(konsepsi)*, of a new system of 'guided democracy'. Natsir and other Masyumi leaders opposed any such ideas. Murba, with little possibility of access to power under the parliamentary system, praised them and tied itself increasingly closely to Sukarno. PNI and NU, attracted by Sukarno but with much to lose if the parliamentary system were abolished, were ambivalent. PKI, seeking protection before all things, supported the President but with the hope that political parties would not be abolished. Outer islanders worried about a Sukarno-Murba-PKI-PNI-NU government system, a government of Java and radicals against themselves and Masyumi. Within the army, outer island commanders saw a similar system forming, run by Jakarta against themselves.

In December 1956, army officers in Sumatra, many of them veterans of the former Banteng Division of the revolutionary period, decided to make their stand against Jakarta with local civilian support. On 20 December the regimental commander in West Sumatra took over civil government. On 22 December Simbolon announced a takeover in North Sumatra. Two days later the commander of South Sumatra forced the civilian governor there to begin introducing autonomy measures. The army councils in Sumatra rapidly acquired popular support by introducing reforms, repairing schools and roads and cutting down corruption. They appeared to have the sympathy of foreign enterprises in the island, including the American oil companies. They also began arresting members of PKI, which was therefore among the first to denounce the coups.

Jakarta could not ignore the loss of control over the richest island of the nation. The exports of North Sumatra (which included the former East Sumatra residency of Dutch times) earned about half of the nation's foreign exchange in 1956. This encouraged Sumatran civilians to demand much greater autonomy from Jakarta. But the Sumatran military had less far-reaching ambitions, for their primary concern was the nature of their relationship to the central army command. Within the army, it was clear that no one desired civil war at this stage. Jakarta reacted by blockading Medan and then announcing new army appointments in North Sumatra, which precipitated complex internal moves. On 27 December Simbolon was overthrown in Medan by a group of Karo Batak officers and fled to Tapanuli.

The escalating political crisis in Sumatra had meanwhile impelled Jakarta to attempt to end the resistance in Aceh. The Ali cabinet decided to reestablish a province of Aceh, to which parliament agreed in October 1956. Sukarno was slow to approve this, however, only doing so after (and perhaps because) Simbolon's moves to detach North Sumatra from Jakarta had become clear. With the reestablishment of a province of Aceh under an ethnic Acehnese governor, the grounds for Acehnese *zuama* (devout lay Muslims) to support resistance to Jakarta were greatly attenuated. They therefore pressed the *ulamas* to end hostilities. Eventually Daud Beureu'eh agreed to a ceasefire in April 1957 and talks then began with Jakarta for a permanent solution to Aceh's grievances.

The Sumatran crisis led to renewed calls for the Ali cabinet to step down for a non-parliamentary cabinet led by Hatta, who was thought to be the only man who could satisfy Sumatra. When PNI and NU refused to resign, Masyumi withdrew from the cabinet on 9 January 1957. While negotiations between the Sumatra and Jakarta army factions continued, more councils of officers sprang up in Kalimantan, North and South Sulawesi and Maluku to join the clamour for greater autonomy from Jakarta. In many cases they became linked to local leaders of Masyumi, the only one of the 'big four' parties to view regional dissatisfaction with sympathy.

Sukarno meanwhile kept the details of his *konsepsi* secret, if indeed he had worked them out. By early 1957 it was clear that the abolition of political parties was not essential, and PKI therefore gave Sukarno its full support. Aidit hoped to preserve some form of the parliamentary system within which PKI had done so well, but in the interests of the party's defence he stayed close to Sukarno. Sukarno himself was now happier with PKI than PNI, for the Communists were untainted by corruption scandals (never having had access to government and the means of corruption) and had adopted a revolutionary posture which appealed to him. Given the hostility of the army and the other parties to the Communists, Sukarno calculated that PKI would be dependent upon his protection and hence an amenable means of organising the mass support that he felt to be naturally his.

On 21 February 1957 Sukarno lifted the veil of secrecy. His new 'guided democracy' would, he proposed, be a form of government more suited to the national character. It would be based upon a 'mutual cooperation' *(gotong royong)* cabinet of the major parties, including PKI, advised by a National Council (Dewan Nasional) of functional groups (youth, workers, peasants, religions, regions, etc.) rather than political parties. He did not, however, propose the abolition of parliament. The idea of a Hatta cabinet, the only step which might have mollified regionalist interests, was obviously not in Sukarno's mind. PNI, PKI, Murba and some other small parties approved the proposals. Masyumi and the Catholic Party did not. NU, PSI and the others appeared not to be in favour, as far as could be discerned from the qualifications and obscurities of their replies.

While mass demonstrations supported Sukarno's ideas, the regional crisis grew more serious. On 2 March 1957 the commander for East Indonesia, Lieutenant-Colonel H. N. V. Sumual (b. 1923), proclaimed martial law in the whole of his region from his headquarters in Makasar (Ujungpandang), thereby theoretically taking over all civil authority from Bali through Nusa Těnggara, Sulawesi and Maluku. Then a long 'Universal Struggle Charter' (Pěrmesta: Piagam Pěrjuangan Sěmesta Alam) was read out to Sumual's officers, who pledged themselves to complete the Indonesian Revolution. The Pěrmesta rebellion had begun. On 8 March the South Sumatra regional assembly voted no confidence in the governor and the army took over authority in that region.

With the nation literally falling apart, Nasution seized the initiative to end parliamentary democracy. There were still many calls for a Hatta cabinet, a solution endorsed also by NU on 11 March 1957. Nasution attempted to arrange a meeting between Hatta and Sukarno but the latter refused. So he proposed that Sukarno should proclaim martial law over the entire nation. This would place the military in charge throughout the country and give it the means to deal with its own internal divisions, while technically removing the challenge posed by regional military coups by simply legalising them. The proposal was accepted. On 14 March the Ali cabinet resigned and Sukarno proclaimed martial law. Parliamentary democracy, such as it had been in Indonesia, was dead. No one yet knew how the regional challenge would be resolved. Nor was it known what new form of government would follow, except that it would not be the kind of multiparty democracy which was perceived as having failed the nation.

Despite the shortcomings of the political system down to 1957, however, the people of Indonesia had achieved one extraordinary victory. Indonesia was a single nation. Even the dissident regional movements and Darul Islam did not dispute this: they protested at the way the nation was structured and governed, not at its existence. It is never easy to see how such mass commitments emerge, but several elements appear to have encouraged a clearly Indonesian sense of identity. The fact of political independence, the rapid spread of the Indonesian language, the discrediting of regional political identities by the Dutch attempt at federalism during the Revolution, the growth of more cosmopolitan urban centres, Sukarno's constant hammering at the theme of national unity, the agitation over Irian, the political parties' insistence upon their role as national organisations, the symbolism of the national elections of 1955, the military's dedication to the spirit of the Revolution, the aspiration of all contenders to gain power at the centre rather than in some part of the country, and the widespread popular feeling that the sacrifices of the Revolution should not have been in vain – all contributed to this development.

The ultimate irony of the years 1950–7 was that as the nation fell apart, it also became one. Rarely was there more truth in the national motto *bhinneka tunggal ika* (officially but slightly inaccurately translated as 'unity in diversity'). There were still many divisions and conflicts within the nation, some of them ultimately irreconcilable. But by now they were clearly divisions and conflicts within a single nation.

19 Guided Democracy, 1957–65

In the midst of the crisis of 1957, the first steps were taken towards a form of government which Sukarno called 'guided democracy'. This was a fluid system, born of crisis and constantly changing through the most disturbed period of Indonesian history since the revolution. Guided democracy was dominated by the personality of Sukarno, although he shared the initiative for its introduction with the army leadership. At the time some observers saw Sukarno as a dictator and as his posturing grew more flamboyant some were inclined to see him as an aging caricature. He was neither of these things. Sukarno was a skilled manipulator of men and of symbols. He could harangue a crowd or charm a potential adversary with equal ease, although he was also very adept at hating his enemies. He offered Indonesians something to believe in, something which many hoped would give them and their nation dignity and pride. Other powerful forces turned to him for guidance, legitimacy or protection. Having thrust himself forward in the crisis of 1957, he was joined by others in maintaining his central position. But this was all in support of a political balance which not even Sukarno could maintain, one which represented a compromise among irreconcilable interests and was therefore satisfactory to no one. Although Sukarno had a vision of his own future, he had none (or at least none which others could in the end accept) for the future of his nation and its people. The promise of guided democracy was an empty one.

Attempts have been made to characterise guided democracy as a system of government, a process rather similar to describing the shape of an amoeba. Some scholars accept Sukarno's view that this was a return to something more in keeping with Indonesia's, and specifically Java's, past. Sometimes such analyses have the flavour of a psycho-cultural determinism, as if the spirit of Sultan Agung whispered in Sukarno's ear. It is true that some aspects of guided democracy would have seemed familiar to Sultan Agung, for Sukarno was in some ways like a pre-colonial Javanese king. He represented a centre of legitimacy which others needed. Conspicuous display was the outward expression of legitimacy; stadiums, statues and great public occasions were perhaps similar in function to the court ceremonial and buildings of an older age. Sukarno had little organised power of his own and was obliged to manipulate, threaten and cajole other powerful men. Intrigue and conspiracy became the common fare of politics. The political elite became a complex of cliques around influential men. The financial and legal systems became increasingly arbitrary and irregular as bureaucratic norms disintegrated. Local government relied increasingly upon unpaid labour from the peasantry.

Although these are interesting parallels with the pre-colonial past, they explain little, nor were they uniquely Indonesian. There can have been little conscious or even subconscious reliance upon genuine pre-colonial state principles. Javanese political traditions had been so severely distorted by Dutch colonialism that by the 1950s nothing remained but romanticised legends, the stylised images of the *wayang* theatre and the impotent establishments of the courts themselves. That villagers could understand Sukarno in terms of *wayang* models merely reflects the subtlety and richness of that art form and Sukarno's own love of *wayang* and skill in the manipulation of symbols. The personal military role of Indonesian kings was missing in guided democracy. Instead of small bodies of professional soldiers and vast armies of peasant levies, there was now a large standing army under its own commanders. Sukarno's lack of personal military experience and power was equalled only by his catastrophic ignorance of economics. He hated stability, order and predictability, the goals of any pre-colonial ruler. He wanted continuing revolution and mass mobilisation, and here one sees the impact of the nationalist movement, the Japanese occupation and the Revolution, influences more fundamental than what little Sukarno may have known about Javanese kingdoms.

The circumstances of the twentieth century had little that was comparable to the pre-colonial past. Indonesia was part of a competitive international order and was influenced by other nations in a way entirely unlike the ancient kingdoms. The population explosion and the revolution in communications and technology meant a much higher potential for an authoritarian domestic order. The population could be watched, informed, mobilised or coerced more successfully than in any of the old kingdoms. The Japanese, even more than the Dutch, had shown how these things could be done. As Sukarno and other political forces felt their way towards a more authoritarian order, they did in some ways return to something older. But they returned to the ideas of the Dutch and especially Japanese repressive states more than to those of the old Javanese kingdoms, of which they knew next to nothing. Dutch and Japanese colonialism represented forms of government with which the elite was familiar and which, for all their faults, seemed at least to have been more effective than the multiparty system of 1950–7.

The political parties were clearly on the defensive in 1957, but their mutual antagonisms were too great for them to work together in defence of the parliamentary system. In April 1957 Sukarno announced a 'business cabinet' (Kabinet Karya) under the non-party politician Djuanda Kartawidjaja (1911–63) as Prime Minister. Djuanda had been in almost every cabinet since 1945 and was respected as an able and sensible man with an understanding of economics. One of Sukarno's closest confidants, Chaerul Saleh (1916–67), entered the cabinet as Minister for Veterans' Affairs. He was among the youth leaders who had pressed Sukarno and Hatta to declare independence in 1945, and had followed Tan Malaka in the Revolution; he was arrested by the army, released by Yamin in June 1951 and then rearrested by the army. He went to the Netherlands in 1952 only to be expelled in 1953. After his return to Indonesia in 1955 he became one of Sukarno's circle of radical advisers and now began to build up his position at the head of an influential, and profitable, clique. The Minister for Foreign Affairs was Dr Subandrio (b. 1914), a former ambassador to London (1947–54) and Moscow (1954–6). He, too, was to become a central figure in the intrigues and conflicts of these years. Three Deputy Prime Ministers were appointed: PNI's Hardi (b. 1918), NU's Kyai Haji Idham Chalid (b. 1921), and Dr Johannes Leimena (1905–77) of the Christian Party.

Although the cabinet was theoretically non-party, at heart it was a coalition of PNI and NU. There were no PSI or PKI members in it, but the Communists could count several sympathisers. Two Masyumi members joined but the party expelled both for accepting their posts. Sukarno and Djuanda said that the cabinet was still responsible to parliament and the various parties in it added up to a parliamentary majority, but this was little more than a gesture to a dying system.

In May 1957 a National Council was created, consisting of forty-one 'functional group' representatives (youth, peasants, workers, women, intellectuals, religions, regions, etc.), plus various *ex officio* members. Most political parties, including PKI, were indirectly represented through functional group members, but Masyumi and the Catholic Party were not. Sukarno was chairman but the Council's affairs were directly in the hands of its vice-chairman Roeslan Abdulgani, who emerged as an elaborator of guided democracy ideology.

As the new governmental system evolved, PKI and the army took steps to strengthen their positions. At least by 1957 (and perhaps already in 1955) an undercover PKI member had begun infiltration of the military through contacts with intelligence officers who were themselves seeking to infiltrate PKI. This was the mysterious figure 'Sjam' (Kamarusaman bin Ahmad Mubaidah, d. 1986). He is said to have come from an Orthodox *santri* family on the north coast of Java and to have been born sometime around 1920. His life and career are very unclear, however, as is his relationship with Aidit. While this work was beginning, PKI was also having its first real success among intellectuals. In October 1956 Pramudya Ananta Tur was so impressed by a visit to Beijing (Peking) that he began to take up the PKI cause among intellectual circles. He became a leading figure in the PKI artists' and writers' organisation Lekra (Lĕmbaga Kĕbudayaan Rakyat, People's Cultural Institute, est. 1950), which was shortly to become a major instrument of intellectual repression. PKI members were also becoming influential within the Taman Siswa school system, where they were assisted by the close parallels between Taman Siswa and guided democracy ideology.

The army was working to ensure that the new fashion of relying upon functional groups would enhance the army's role. The parties had various functional groups affiliated to them and in June 1957 Nasution began establishing army-civilian cooperation bodies to detach these from the parties. Over the next two years such bodies established links with NU's youth wing Ansor (est. 1934, named after *al-ansar*, 'the helpers' who supported the Prophet in Medinah), PKI's Pĕmuda Rakyat, PNI and Masyumi youth groups, and so on. But for the most part the parties were able to resist these moves. Nasution was, however, successful in uniting all veterans' organisations into a veterans' league under army control in August 1959. PKI, which had had much success among veterans, was particularly affected by this for it thereby lost its only organised body of supporters with potential military value.

Sukarno was also groping for some new means of mass organisation. In June 1957 he praised the one-party system of the Soviet Union and said that he preferred such a structure. In August he revived an idea which the Japanese had failed to implement in July 1945 when their New People's Movement (Gĕrakan Rakyat Baru) had failed. He called for a New Life Movement (Gĕrakan Hidup Baru) which was supposed, in some vague way, to revitalise the nation. PKI pledged its support but nothing happened and the Movement was soon the butt of political jokes. Sukarno continued to insist, however, that the corrupt rock-and-roll culture of the West must somehow be abandoned for a more truly Indonesian personality.

The cabinet, National Council and army were also attempting to solve the problems which had given rise to the governmental crisis. Under martial law, Nasution ordered a clean-up which led to the arrest of several politicians for alleged corruption and the flight of others. In May 1957 the PSI economist and former Minister Professor Sumitro Djojohadikusumo (b. 1917) was among the first to flee Jakarta for Sumatra. Regional commanders arrested many civilians and restricted party activities. PKI particularly suffered from such curtailment, and in July 1957 the PKI and SOBSI headquarters in Jakarta were attacked with hand-grenades. The political parties began calling for an early end to martial law, but in the event it was to last for six years and by the time it was lifted the army was so well entrenched that this made little difference.

The cabinet contacted the dissident regional military councils and even provided them with some of Jakarta's limited funds under the guise of regional development. Djuanda organised a National Conference (Musyawarah Nasional) which was held in Jakarta between 10 and 14 September 1957, followed by a National Development Conference (Musyawarah Nasional Pĕmbangunan) two months later. Hopes were high that the first conference in particular would lead to real solutions. The representatives of the regional councils seemed cooperative. But nothing was achieved and the regional stalemate continued. Renewed efforts to restore cooperation between Hatta and Sukarno foundered on their inability and unwillingness to work in partnership.

Elections for provincial councils were held in the latter half of 1957 and revealed major PKI gains. This increased the determination of the army and anti-Communist civilians that the old political system must go quickly. PKI was the only party with an active grass-roots organisation and it had campaigned for the implementation of Sukarno's guided democracy, land reform and an end to corruption. In Java its vote was 37.2 per cent higher than in 1955, most of its new support coming from former PNI voters.The 'big four' results for the Central and East Java elections in July gave PKI 34 per cent, NU 29 per cent, PNI 26 per cent and Masyumi 11 per cent. PNI was left with a majority in only one regency (kabupaten) and its Central Java leaders began to urge that the party should end all cooperation with PKI. In East Java NU remained in first place, but its vote fell and PKI was less than 3 per cent behind. Masyumi still led in the West Java elections of August, but PKI replaced PNI in second place. These results clearly reinforced Sukarno's view that PKI could not be refused a role in government.

In September and October 1957 Colonel Simbolon and the other military dissidents of Sumatra, Colonel Sumual of the Pĕrmesta movement, and Colonel Lubis held several meetings in Sumatra to coordinate their activities. They condensed their aims into a three-fold objective: an election for a new President to end Sukarno's pro-PKI activities, the replacement of Nasution and his central staff, and the outlawing of PKI. Masyumi, which glumly refused to have anything to do with guided democracy, meanwhile held an All-Indonesia Congress of Islamic Scholars (Muktamar Ulama Sĕ-Indonesia) in Palembang in September which proclaimed that Communism was forbidden to Muslims and that PKI must be outlawed. NU, seeking to defend Orthodox Islam within the emerging system, refused to send an official delegation to the Congress. In mid-November the Constituent Assembly began its deliberations in Jakarta and became bogged down in arguments between proponents of Islam or Pancasila as the philosophical basis of a new constitution.

At the end of November 1957 two events heightened political tension. On 29 November the UN failed to pass a resolution calling upon the Dutch to negotiate a settlement of the Irian issue; Sukarno had warned that Indonesia would take steps which would startle the world if the resolution failed. Then, while he was visiting his son's school in the Cikini district of Jakarta on the 30th, the first of several assassination attempts was made upon him. A group of Islamic zealots, thought to be protégés of Lubis and the regional dissidents, threw hand-grenades which claimed several lives but left Sukarno unharmed. Nasution now felt that the reasonable limits of intrigue had been exceeded and that compromise with the dissidents was no longer possible.

The failure of the UN resolution led directly to an outburst of anti-Dutch radicalism encouraged by Sukarno. On 3 December PKI and PNI unions began taking over Dutch enterprises and business offices. Neither Djuanda nor Nasution could control these events. The Dutch-owned Royal Mail Steam Packet Company (KPM) was the first to be seized, but many of its ships were at sea and simply sailed out of Indonesian waters. At a stroke the nation thus lost much of its inter-island shipping and further exacerbated regional dissatisfaction with Jakarta's actions. Hatta and Masyumi leaders condemned the poor planning of the takeovers. One of the bastions of Anglo-Dutch economic power, Royal Dutch Shell, was not nationalised but on 5 December the Ministry of Justice ordered the expulsion of about 46000 Dutch citizens in Indonesia.

Nasution took control of these events on 13 December 1957 by ordering that the army would manage the seized enterprises. PKI and SOBSI, anxious to avoid confrontation with the army, pledged their support in keeping these businesses at work. This was a crucial development, for the army now assumed the role of a major economic force; it gained patronage to dispense and independent sources of funding. This strengthened the position of Nasution and the central command against regional commanders and the army as a whole against other services and civilian government. It aligned the army with those who favoured state rather than private enterprise, the latter being primarily Masyumi and NU supporters. The community of interests between outer island commanders and Masyumi was thus threatened.

But the effects upon the economy and the army were far from being entirely beneficial. There was much mismanagement and inefficiency, particularly as a result of Nasution's inclination to place older or less able officers in charge of enterprises while more able commanders were left in charge of troops. The army's attention was directed away from purely military functions and corruption of the officer corps accelerated; neither of these developments was welcome to Nasution. But a crucial step had been taken towards a consolidation of political, military, administrative and economic power in army hands. A further step was taken on 10 December 1957 when Nasution placed his second deputy, Colonel Dr Ibnu Sutowo (b. 1914), in charge of a new oil company called Pěrmina (Pěrusahaan Minyak Nasional, National Oil Enterprise). This was the first stage of the army's move into the oil industry.

The radical surge continued throughout December 1957 and January 1958. In December Natsir and other Masyumi figures fled Jakarta in the face of intimidation by youth groups. In the same month the regional elections in South Sumatra showed that Masyumi was still by far the largest party, but even there PKI pushed PNI out of second place. PKI was now emphasising continuing Dutch control of Irian as the main evidence of Indonesia's semi-colonial status. In January Nasution moved to capture this radicalism under army management by setting up a National Front for the Liberation of West Irian (Front Nasional Pěmbebasan Irian Barat) based upon the army-civilian cooperation bodies. The parties managed to obstruct its growth, however, and Sukarno gained much influence over it.

In January 1958 PSI and Masyumi demanded a new cabinet to deal with the nation's problems. PNI and NU of course defended the cabinet. Rumours now spread of impending rebellion. While Sukarno was out of the country (6 January – 16 February) a meeting was held near Padang among Simbolon, Lubis, other Sumatra officers, the Masyumi leaders Natsir and Sjafruddin, and PSI's Sumitro Djojohadikusumo (one of the very few ethnic Javanese to join the dissidents). Nasution, the cabinet and PSI and Masyumi leaders still in Jakarta contacted their colleagues in Sumatra to try to prevent rebellion, but without success. The Sumatra figures were convinced that events in Jakarta were going in intolerably radical directions and that a stand must be made.

On 10 February 1958 the Padang dissidents sent a five-day ultimatum to the government: the cabinet must be dissolved, Hatta and Sultan Hamengkubuwana IX must be appointed to form a new business cabinet until elections were held, and Sukarno must return to his constitutional position as figurehead President (a position which Natsir had insisted upon during his Premiership). The cabinet immediately rejected the ultimatum and the main army officers involved were dishonourably discharged for promoting rebellion and attempting to assassinate Sukarno at Cikini.

On 15 February a rebel government was announced in Sumatra, with its headquarters at Bukittingi. This was known as PRRI (Pěměrintah Revolusioner Republik Indonesia, Revolutionary Government of the Indonesian Republic). Sjafruddin was its Prime Minister (1958–61) and its cabinet included Natsir, Burhanuddin Harahap, Sumitro Djojohadikusumo and Simbolon. Two days later the Pěrmesta rebels in Sulawesi joined PRRI. By now the rebels were assured of clandestine support from the United States, which was equally worried by Sukarno and PKI. But from the start the rebels faced serious shortcomings. The South Sumatra commander did not join them, being uncomfortably close to Java and worried about the large number of Javanese labourers in the oil fields who were in PKI organisations. Nor was there significant support in North Sumatra or Kalimantan. The Darul Islam rebels in Aceh, West Java and South Sulawesi continued to go their own way, although late in 1959 tenuous links between Darul Islam and PRRI would be established. The oil companies Caltex, Stanvac and Shell accepted Jakarta's assurances that their interests would be protected and maintained their payments of revenues to Jakarta. PRRI was thus reduced to a rebellion primarily based in two distant centres, West Sumatra and Sulawesi (especially North Sulawesi, which had by now become the centre of the Pĕrmesta movement).

On 16 February Sukarno returned and insisted on harsh treatment of the rebels. Djuanda, Nasution and most PNI and PKI leaders also wanted the rebellion crushed. Hatta, along with Masyumi and PSI leaders in Jakarta, urged a negotiated settlement, thus placing themselves in a compromised position. Hamengkubuwana IX, informally an ally of PSI, also favoured negotiation and refused to accept a post in a reshuffled cabinet in June 1958 because of the government's hard line against PRRI. Hereafter he played no significant public role until after October 1965. Masyumi was divided, demoralised and discredited. The Sukiman wing was willing to expel Natsir, Sjafruddin and Burhanuddin but was prevented from doing so by their supporters. Natsir in fact remained the party's chairman for over a year after the rebellion began.

The military acted decisively. The air force bombed PRRI installations in Padang, Bukittingi and Mĕnado in late February 1958. In early March the army began landing units from the Java-based Siliwangi and Diponĕgoro Divisions in Sumatra under the command of Colonel Achmad Yani (1922–65). The Americans were supplying the rebels with arms and had proposed landing a force of Marines ostensibly to protect American citizens and property in the Sumatran oil fields. The Indonesian government rejected the proposal and by 12 March had secured the Caltex fields to prevent unilateral American action. The rebels were then driven out of Medan on 17 March and a month later Padang was taken with little resistance. On 5 May Bukittingi was taken and PRRI in Sumatra was reduced to guerrilla fighting in the countryside. Then attention turned to North Sulawesi, where the fighting was heavier. Here Jakarta relied upon the East Java Brawijaya Division. Gorontalo was taken by mid-May and Mĕnado by late June. Here, too, the rebellion was now reduced to guerrilla proportions. By the middle of 1958 the PRRI rebellion was already a lost cause, even if its final collapse was still three years away.

The outbreak and rapid reduction of PRRI had a significant effect upon Indonesia's foreign relations. Several thousand lives had been lost, and no one could regard the affair as something simply to be forgotten. American sympathy and support for PRRI was obvious to Jakarta and seriously damaged Indonesia-United States relations. On 18 May an American civilian pilot was actually shot down over Ambon in a B-26 while on a bombing run in support of the rebels. The United States had already realised that it was supplying a losing cause, and within two days the American Secretary of State J. F. Dulles condemned intervention on behalf of PRRI in an effort to repair relations with Jakarta. But the episode left a sour taste, and inclined Sukarno and many others to regard the United States with even greater suspicion than was usual between developing states and great powers. PKI was quick to capitalise on anti-American feelings.

Malaya, which had become independent in 1957 and was still fighting the remnants of its own Communist 'emergency', had also supported the PRRI rebels and had been a major channel for arms supplies, as had Singapore. The Philippines, Taiwan and South Korea also sympathised with PRRI. Thus, Indonesia's desire for a neutralist foreign policy was becoming more difficult as the list of its enemies lengthened. In August 1958 the Guomindang (Kuomintang) was banned in Indonesia, shortly after which the army took over businesses of pro-Taiwan Chinese, thereby inadvertently giving PKI a monopoly of political support within the local Chinese community.

PRRI helped to simplify Indonesian military politics. Many dissident officers were now removed from army affairs, leaving Nasution as the unchallenged leader of the army. In July 1958 he was promoted to Lieutenant-General, the first to hold that rank since Soedirman. Many of those removed were from the outer islands, leaving the officer corps more heavily Javanese; by the 1960s it was estimated that 60 to 80 per cent of army officers were Javanese, whereas that ethnic group formed about 45 per cent of the population.

The psychological impact of the rebellion was considerable. It stained Masyumi with the mark of treachery as Madiun had stained PKI. It was also a major step in the consolidation of the ascendancy of Java over the outer islands and the army over other political forces. Regional rebellion was now made more difficult by the stationing of Siliwangi, Diponěgoro and Brawijaya Division officers and units in the outer islands. Nevertheless, regional commanders were still only tenuously controlled by the central command.

Success over PRRI did not make the army popular. Its heavy-handed rule under martial law was already earning it much criticism, which encouraged those who thought its power could be limited. Among these was Sukarno, whose old opponents and enemies among civilian politicians, men such as Hatta and Natsir, were now discredited. The emerging political system was becoming a competitive arrangement between Sukarno and the army. PKI, still very much in the wings, was anxious to attach itself as closely as possible to Sukarno. The President cared little for the PNI leaders Ali Sastroamidjojo and Hardi, and increasingly looked upon PKI as his primary ally against the army.

The Jakarta politicians, both civil and military, now turned to the question of how to complete the transition to guided democracy. Masyumi and PSI, who had cast themselves in the role of defenders of democracy, began to press for postponement of the parliamentary elections scheduled for 1959, for they presumed that PKI would be the victor. PNI and NU shared this view and in September 1958 Djuanda announced that elections would be postponed. But the existing political elite in Jakarta could reach no agreement on the next step to be taken. Rumours circulated that Sukarno would form a state party, or that there would be an army coup. The Constituent Assembly remained deadlocked over the philosophical basis for a new constitution.

Nasution proposed a solution in July 1958. Rather than writing a new constitution, he favoured simply restoring the constitution of 1945. This provided for a strong President responsible to an infrequently convened People's Consultative Assembly (Majělis Pěrmusyawaratan Rakyat) but needing the consent of a lower-house parliament (Dewan Pěrwakilan Rakyat, People's Representative Council). Some of its clauses could be read as authorising functional group representation, and although it did not recognise the existence of political parties they were not disallowed. The philosophical debate would be resolved by including the Jakarta Charter of June 1945, which obliged Muslims to observe Islamic law while leaving Pancasila as the philosophical foundation of the nation. This proposal slowly began to attract support, but Sukarno was not eager to have the personal responsibility imposed on the President by this constitution. He also feared that this was a means to create a system which, in practice, the army would dominate. It was by now accepted that the armed services were themselves functional groups, so lengthy debates surrounded the issue of what proportion of any new representative bodies should consist of such groups.

Nasution wanted the army to be disenfranchised and thus freed of political party interference, but to be directly represented at all levels of government as a functional group. In November 1958 he formalised this as the doctrine of the middle way: the army should neither be aloof from political affairs nor take over government itself. Others nevertheless feared the possibility of a coup, fears which were enhanced by a wave of military takeovers in Third World countries in July-November 1958 (Iraq, Pakistan, Burma, Thailand, Sudan).

In September 1958 Nasution suddenly banned Masyumi, PSI, the Christian Party and an army front organisation which had favoured his opponents (Ikatan Pĕndukung Kĕmĕrdekaan Indonesia, League of Supporters of Indonesian Independence, est. 1954) in all regions where they had supported the rebels. He then arrested a leader from Natsir's wing of Masyumi for giving a speech sympathetic to PRRI. With Nasution so obviously seizing the initiative, the political parties began to feel that they must go along with whatever Sukarno proposed or face a takeover by the army. Sukarno now began favouring re-introduction of the 1945 constitution, partly in the hope that this would revive the spirit of optimism, dedication and revolution of which it had been a part. Only Masyumi maintained its inflexible opposition to guided democracy.

PNI and PKI leaders accepted the idea of reintroducing the 1945 constitution by early 1959. In February NU agreed, partly under the pressure of threats to prosecute several of its leaders for alleged corruption, but with the understanding that the Jakarta Charter formed part of the constitution and had legal force. The cabinet then decided to propose this to the Constituent Assembly. If NU voted in favour there, the proposal would receive the necessary two-thirds majority. But again everything became bogged down in intractable conflict between the Islamic and non-Islamic parties. While the army organised demonstrations in support of the 1945 constitution and PKI and Masyumi youth groups took to the streets of Bandung, where the Assembly met, Sukarno set off on a world tour (23 April-29 June 1959) and NU's chairman Idham Chalid went on the pilgrimage to Mecca. When in May the Assembly defeated a proposal to make the Jakarta Charter a part of the constitution with legal force, NU turned against reintroducing the old constitution. On 2 June 1959 the final Constituent Assembly vote was 56 per cent in favour of reintroducing the 1945 constitution – short of the necessary two-thirds. Yet again there was deadlock.

While Islamic sentiments remained the main barrier to constitutional change at the national level, the government reached a final settlement with the most truly religious segment of the Darul Islam rebellion. Since March 1957 a ceasefire had been agreed in Aceh, but its implementation had been difficult. In May 1959, while the Constituent Assembly wrangled, the government accepted the creation of what was virtually an Islamic state within the nation by giving Aceh the status of a Special District (Daerah Istimewa). The Acehnese were given virtual autonomy in matters of religion, customary law (adat) and education. The fighting now stopped, although some guerrillas remained in the hills for two more years. Daud

Beureu'eh was given a pension as a former governor and became active in the promotion of public works projects. Such a solution was acceptable in far-off Aceh, but clearly unacceptable for West Java or the nation as a whole.

Nasution now decided that the only solution to the deadlock at national level was reintroduction of the 1945 constitution by Presidential decree. PKI and PNI agreed that this was the only way to bypass the intransigence of the Islamic parties and avoid an army takeover. NU also favoured this; its main interest was the defence and representation of Orthodox Islam in whatever regime was to emerge, but it could not be seen to vote in the Constituent Assembly for a constitution giving no special place to Islam. Masyumi's inflexibility was clearly a dead-end, so NU preferred a solution which would at least spare it acrimonious philosophical debates in public and the political impotence facing Modernist Islam. On 3 June Nasution ordered a temporary ban on all public political activities and told the press to stay calm. All now awaited the return of Sukarno.

On 29 June 1959 Sukarno returned to Jakarta, apprehensive of Nasution's growing power. He decided to adopt Nasution's proposal. On 5 July he dissolved the Constituent Assembly and restored the old constitution. The Jakarta Charter was, he said, a historical document which inspired the whole of the constitution but was not itself a legal part of it. According to this construction, the state was not obliged to oversee the implementation of Islamic law among those who called themselves Muslims, but Islamic leaders continued to take the view that it was. The decree was undoubtedly unconstitutional, but many were relieved that this part of the national impasse was ended.

On 9 July a new 'working cabinet' (Kabinet Kěrja) was announced with Sukarno as Prime Minister and Djuanda as 'First Minister'. Leimena, Chaerul Saleh and Subandrio remained in the core of the cabinet; Idham Chalid did not, but another NU figure was Minister of Religion (the Ministry which NU most wanted to control). To emphasise the non-party nature of the new government several ministers resigned from their parties, including Subandrio from PNI and Leimena from the Christian Party. There were no PKI members, but several ministers were regarded as Communist sympathisers. Sukarno wanted to weaken Nasution by bringing him into the cabinet and replacing him at the top of the army. He failed in the face of Nasution's determination, so Nasution became Minister of Defence and Security as well as army chief of staff. The chiefs of staff of the navy, air force and police also entered the cabinet as ex officio members. Several individual officers became ministers.

Further institutions of guided democracy were quickly announced. Later in July 1959 the National Council was abolished and the Supreme Advisory Council (Dewan Pěrtimbangan Agung) called for in the 1945 constitution was appointed, as was a new body called the National Planning Council (Dewan Pěrancang Nasional) of which Yamin was chairman. Masyumi and PSI were represented in neither of these; PNI, PKI, NU and the other parties were in both. Sukarno then ordered that higher civil servants and managers of state enterprises could not belong to political parties. In September 1959 regional heads were relieved of their responsibility to local elected councils, which were replaced by appointed councils in 1960–1. The parties continued to exist, but only PKI showed much vitality. Political leaders increasingly exercised influence not through formal institutions or party structures but through access to Sukarno or the army.

On independence day, 17 August 1959, Sukarno's speech set out the ideology of guided democracy, which a few months later was named Manipol (from Manifesto Politik, Political Manifesto). He called for a revival of the spirit of the Revolution, for social justice and for 'retooling' of the institutions and organisations of the nation in the name of ongoing revolution. Early in 1960 this vague creed was elaborated by having the initials USDEK added, standing for the 1945 constitution, Indonesian socialism, guided democracy, guided economy and Indonesian identity (Undang-undang dasar 1945, Sosialisme ala Indonesia, Demokrasi těrpimpin, Ekonomi těrpimpin, Kěpribadian Indonesia).

Manipol-USDEK was now the official definition of ideological orthodoxy. What precisely it meant depended upon who precisely was claiming to endorse it. It was introduced into all levels of education and government, and the press was obliged to support it. Some pro-Masyumi and pro-PSI editors refused to do so and their papers were banned. Between 1959 and 1961 newspaper circulation was cut by about one-third, from 1039000 copies for ninety dailies to 710000 copies for sixty-five dailies.

The economic chaos of the guided democracy period was now beginning. In an effort to restrain inflation, on 25 August 1959 the Rupiah was devalued by 75 per cent, a monetary purge was ordered by which all Rp. 500 and 1000 notes were reduced to one-tenth their face value and large bank deposits were frozen. This reduced the money supply from Rp. 34 billion to Rp. 21 billion at a stroke. Sukarno himself seems to have inspired these severely deflationary steps. The wealthy, the bureaucrats and especially the Chinese and indigenous businessmen were badly affected. Some regional commanders, however, refused to implement the measures in full. The liquidity crisis was so severe that the government was obliged to allow an expansion of credit, and within six months the money supply was back to its former level and inflation again crept upwards. Economic affairs were given a tragi-comic flavour by the promulgation at the end of 1960 of an eight-year development plan. It was an elaborate ritual nonsense divided into 17 parts, 8 volumes and 1945 clauses to symbolise the date of the independence declaration.

Army interference in the economy and administration was also increasing. In May 1959 it had been decreed that, with effect from 1 January 1960, aliens would be banned from rural trade. While this affected Arab and Indian traders, it was mainly an army-instigated move to hurt the Chinese, weaken Jakarta's friendship with China and embarrass PKI. Late in 1959 the army began forcibly moving Chinese from rural areas to the cities. Eventually about 119000 were actually repatriated to China. The Chinese government put very heavy diplomatic pressure upon Jakarta, while both PKI and Sukarno attempted to defend the Chinese and were at least able to prevent the army from taking even more severe measures. The exodus of Chinese from rural areas and from the country altogether, and the general fear within this crucial commercial community, led to serious economic dislocation, hoarding and a new surge of inflation. In the course of 1960 the army also increased its direct influence over civil administration when five officers became provincial governors.

In competition for power with Nasution, Sukarno was following two main tactics. He sought the support of the Java-based political parties, especially PKI, and he courted the other armed services, especially the air force. The air force chief of staff, Air Commodore Surjadi Surjadarma (b. 1912), was close to Sukarno and had poor relations with Nasution. His wife was active in leftist and PKI causes and had been arrested for a time in 1948 on Nasution's order. The air force was jealous of the predominance of the army and was now becoming the closest thing Sukarno ever had to a military force he could rely upon. But no chief of staff could actually guarantee the behaviour of his own men. This was vividly illustrated in March 1960 when an air force pilot strafed the Presidential palaces in Jakarta and Bogor while an army unit tried to move into Jakarta, apparently in some kind of abortive coup attempt. The parties, for their part, increasingly felt that they must acquiesce in their own subservience to Sukarno's will or face complete abolition by the army.

PSI and Masyumi put up their last resistance to guided democracy in 1960, and were swept away. In March the elected parliament, the last governmental institution in which they were represented, rejected the government's budget in an unexpected display of authority. Sukarno endorsed the budget by decree and dissolved parliament. He then announced that he would appoint a Mutual Cooperation People's Representative Council (DPR-GR: Dewan Pěrwakilan Rakyat – Gotong Royong). PSI, Masyumi and some allies, with the encouragement of Hatta and some military figures, formed a Democratic League (Liga Demokrasi) to resist this move.

When Sukarno returned in June from another overseas trip the League quickly collapsed and the 'mutual-cooperation' parliament of 283 seats was appointed. Masyumi and PSI had no seats. Over half the seats (154) went to functional groups, but many of these appointees were also party members. PKI was variously estimated to have between 17 and 25 per cent of the members and Lukman was a deputy chairman. The armed services were represented as functional groups. Sukarno then appointed also a 616-member Provisional People's Consultative Assembly (MPRS: Majělis Pěrmusyawaratan Rakyat Sěměntara), of which Aidit was a deputy chairman. PKI was now in every governmental institution except the cabinet; Masyumi and PSI were in none. Within Islamic circles, the political victory of Orthodoxy (NU) over Modernism (Masyumi) now seemed assured. In August 1960 Masyumi and PSI were finally banned, a formal sealing of the fate which they had ensured themselves by their leaders' enmity towards Sukarno over many years, their opposition to guided democracy, and their involvement in PRRI.

Sukarno now began emphasising a theme as old as his articles of 1926 which had argued for the unity of nationalism, Islam and Marxism. This was now called the doctrine of Nasakom (from Nasionalisme, Agama, Komunisme). What it apparently meant was that PNI (for nationalism), NU (for religion) and PKI (for Communism) should share a role in government at all levels, thus producing a system which, among other things, would rest upon a coalition of Java-based political forces. Since PNI and NU were already well represented, the only serious issue raised by Nasakom at this stage was the inclusion of PKI ministers in the cabinet. This the army was not prepared to allow.

The army acted to restrict PKI in the latter half of 1960. In July PKI launched criticisms of the cabinet, especially Subandrio who was accused of offending China, and of the army for failing to finish off the PRRI rebels. The army picked up the whole of the PKI Politburo for questioning but Sukarno successfully pressed Nasution to release them. Regional commanders in South Sumatra, South

Sulawesi and South Kalimantan banned PKI and arrested local Communists in August. Sukarno also got these bans lifted in December, except in South Kalimantan where the ban lasted for a year. In these regions PKI continued to be watched, harassed and restricted by the army. At the end of October all seven of the Politburo's magazines were suspended permanently, and from this point onwards the daily *Harian Rakjat* was allowed only a reduced supply of newsprint. Those within PKI who doubted Aidit's strategy were forced now to concede that there was no alternative to the alliance with Sukarno. And Sukarno was forced to accept that he could not yet bring PKI ministers into the cabinet.

Indonesia was now lurching into the radicalism which was to give PKI its opportunity for growth, despite the army's hostility. The Dutch were trying to create an independent state in Irian with considerable local support. Early in 1960 they announced that elections would be held there for a representative council. In August 1960 Indonesia broke off diplomatic relations with the Netherlands. A year earlier the Supreme Advisory Council had created a National Front which Sukarno hoped would supersede the army's National Front for the Liberation of West Irian. In August 1960 the leadership of the new National Front was announced; Aidit and Njoto were members, as were leaders from PKI-affiliated organisations. Small-scale military infiltration of Irian now began and PKI's considerable capacity for mobilising mass demonstrations was enlisted in the cause of winning control of Irian.

The military requirements for a campaign to capture Irian pushed the army and the government towards the Soviet Union, which was working to increase its influence in Indonesia to the detriment of both the United States and China. In January 1960 Khrushchev had visited Jakarta and extended a US $250 million credit to Indonesia. In January 1961 Nasution went to Moscow and got a Soviet loan of $450 million for arms. The army now began to grow in size for the first time since the Revolution, reaching about 300000 men in 1961 and 330000 by late 1962. An increasing amount of Indonesia's military hardware was of Soviet origin, including modern fighters and long-range bombers for the air force and new ships for the navy. Indeed, much of the new equipment went to the navy and air force, services which Sukarno found more cooperative than the army. But the Irian campaign still remained at a fairly low level of military activity. When John F. Kennedy assumed the American Presidency in January 1961, he set about countering Soviet influence in Indonesia by working for a negotiated settlement of the Irian issue.

As the military's attention was drawn increasingly towards the Irian campaign, army negotiations with the PRRI rebels since late 1958 at last bore fruit. By now the rebels were running out of ammunition and other supplies. In February-April 1961 a series of Pĕrmesta groups surrendered in North Sulawesi. Then Sjafruddin ordered his forces to surrender, and between June and October 1961 many did so. Simbolon, Zulkifli Lubis, Sumual, Sjafruddin, Natsir and the other leaders were returned to Jakarta. Sumitro Djojohadikusumo was abroad, where he remained until 1967. Many Acehnese rebels, Darul Islam fighters in West Java and followers of Kahar Muzakkar also laid down their arms. But Kahar himself remained in the hills of South Sulawesi, increasingly isolated by government forces, until he was killed in February 1965. By October 1961 some 100000 rebels had surrendered. Despite Sukarno's insistence upon harsh treatment of the leaders, the army merely placed Sjafruddin and the other leaders under loose house or city arrest and did not charge them. Although the army could not forgive rebellion, many of its leaders were sympathetic towards individuals who had joined PRRI.

Sukarno remained critical of the gentle treatment the army offered the PRRI leaders and finally won a victory over Nasution in this matter. The sense of domestic radicalism rose and the conspiratorial atmosphere was heightened by another assassination attempt on the President in January 1962 while he was visiting South Sulawesi. Sukarno now insisted that his enemies be punished. In January Sjafruddin, Natsir, Simbolon, Burhanuddin and many other senior leaders of Masyumi and PSI were imprisoned. The President's old antagonist Sjahrir, who was ill and had been little involved in politics since the Revolution, was also arrested; in 1965 he was allowed to go to Switzerland for medical treatment, too late to save his life. With the imprisonment of men who had been part of the central core of nationalist leaders since the Revolution and before, Indonesian politics were clearly growing more bitter.

The ending of PRRI freed the army to concentrate upon both its new objective in Irian and its old Darul Islam enemy in West Java. Late in 1961 a new offensive was launched against Darul Islam. Kartosuwirjo was wounded in April 1962, shattering his followers' faith in his invincibility. In June he was captured and tried both for rebellion and for an assassination attempt on Sukarno the month before. He was executed in September. Security was restored to the countryside of West Java for the first time since the Revolution.

The army and Nasution increasingly dominated affairs, despite Sukarno's efforts to gain the initiative and the army's own persistent unpopularity. Sukarno wanted the Irian campaign to be a means of galvanising Indonesia into the mass momentum that he felt to be essential to ongoing revolution and for which his leadership talents were uniquely suited. PKI also saw an opportunity to increase its national role. But there was a danger that the army would dominate events yet again. Both Sukarno and PKI therefore wanted to prevent the Irian campaign from becoming a wholly military operation.

As a basic precaution, Sukarno had to remain in control of the Irian campaign. In December 1961 a new Supreme Operations Command (Koti: Komando Opěrasi Těrtinggi) for the liberation of Irian was established. Sukarno was its commander, Nasution his deputy and Major-General Yani his chief of staff. The fighting was to be in the hands of a Mandala Command headed by Major-General Soeharto. Sukarno also acted to reduce Nasution's predominance within the military. In January 1962 an Indonesian force suffered a serious defeat off Irian in which the deputy commander of the navy and fifty others died. The army insisted on the removal of Surjadarma from command of the air force for failure to provide adequate air support. Sukarno replaced him with Air Vice-Marshal Omar Dhani, who was at first thought to be less committed to the President. But Sukarno cultivated Omar Dhani's vanity and he soon became an ally of the President and PKI against the army leaders. Sukarno also encouraged rivals to Nasution within the army. Nasution wanted to become commander of all the armed forces, but in June 1962 he was outmanoeuvred by Sukarno (with the support of Omar Dhani) and suffered a major political defeat. Sukarno made Nasution merely chief of staff of the armed forces (the first to fill this position since November 1953) with only coordinating and civil defence roles; he remained Minister of Defence and

Security. He was replaced as army chief of staff by Yani, who was as implacably anti-PKI as Nasution but more amenable to Sukarno's influence.

PKI used the Irian campaign to increase its own influence and membership. In July 1962 PKI's peasant front (BTI) claimed 5.7 million members, said to be one-quarter of all adult peasants. Later in the year SOBSI claimed nearly 3.3 million members. Early in 1963 the youth front Pĕmuda Rakyat and Gĕrwani (Gĕrakan Wanita Indonesia, Indonesian Women's Movement, est. 1954) each claimed 1.5 million members. PKI itself had over 2 million members by the end of 1962, making it the largest Communist party in any non-Communist nation. The PKI intellectuals' front Lekra claimed 100000 members in May 1963 and was by now promoting a bitter attack on the 'bourgeois' mentality of its opponents in intellectual circles. Pramudya and the leftists of Lekra were supported by the PNI intellectuals' front LKN (Lĕmbaga Kĕbudayaan Nasional, National Cultural Institute) under the leadership of Sitor Situmorang (b. 1924), a writer who staunchly endorsed Sukarno and his Manipol-USDEK. These intellectuals provided a kind of legitimacy for Sukarno's drive for orthodoxy and the repression of his opponents. In March 1962 Sukarno appointed Aidit and Njoto advisory ministers without portfolio. But this left them out of the inner cabinet and was a potential embarrassment for them since it carried the risk of responsibility without power. PKI was not any closer to power; it was merely more obvious and objectionable to its enemies.

As the economy settled into permanent hyper-inflation (which remained around 100 per cent per annum from late 1961 to 1964) and the nation drifted into radicalism, as the military became increasingly dependent on the Soviet Union and PKI grew rapidly, the United States became more deeply worried about its influence in Indonesia. In something of a replay of the diplomacy of the Revolution, the Americans belatedly pressured the Netherlands to negotiate an Irian settlement. By now the Dutch realised that the price of retaining sovereignty over Irian would probably be serious and prolonged jungle warfare. The lesson of Nehru's military occupation of Goa and two other Portuguese enclaves in India in December 1961 after negotiations had failed was not lost on the Netherlands, although of course Irian was a military problem on a very different scale. In January 1962 the Dutch said that they were willing to negotiate. In February President Kennedy sent his brother, the Attorney General Robert F. Kennedy, to Indonesia and the Netherlands as mediator. This first series of negotiations broke down in March and Indonesian infiltration of Irian was increased. But new negotiations followed with American mediation.

On 15 August 1962 a settlement of the Irian issue was at last achieved. The Dutch agreed to transfer the territory on 1 October 1962 to an interim UN administration which would turn it over to Indonesia by 1 May 1963. Before the end of 1969 Jakarta would hold an 'act of free choice' in Irian to see whether its people wished to remain within Indonesia. An exodus of Dutch citizens from Irian began immediately.

The Irian victory ushered in one of the most uncertain periods of guided democracy, one which pushed the nation on the road to chaos by making a return to stability seem even less attractive. The army feared that martial law would be lifted and military budgets cut; PKI feared that less frenetic politics would block its growth; Sukarno feared that the congenial mass emotionalism of the Irian campaign would come to an end, derailing his return to the revolutionary spirit. There was, thus, considerable ambivalence about the future.

The United States now attempted to draw Indonesia away from its apparently leftward course. After the Irian success the Americans enjoyed substantial goodwill among the non-Communist elite, but PKI understandably labelled the United States the nation's most dangerous enemy. In November 1962 a team of the International Monetary Fund visited Jakarta to consider economic reforms. Assistance from American sources would be impossible if PKI had power, so in early 1963 Sukarno told PKI that this was not the time to push for prominent places in the cabinet. After more study and discussion, the Indonesian government announced major new steps in May 1963. On the first of the month martial law was lifted. On 26 May drastic budget cuts (including military expenditures), tight credit, price increases, a *de facto* devaluation and a doubling of government salaries were announced. These measures were the price of American and International Monetary Fund aid. Urban consumers and small businessmen were particularly badly affected and there was much public protest.

But already a new foreign policy issue was emerging. In the course of 1961 Malaya, Singapore and the British worked out a solution to several mutual problems: Singapore's desire for independence, Malaya's apprehension at the size of its Chinese minority and the racial implications of any merger with Singapore and Britain's desire to make some arrangement for the future of its territories in Borneo (Sabah, Brunei and Sarawak). The solution seemed to be a merger of all of them into a new Federation of Malaysia.

Jakarta was not entirely pleased. Indonesia's relations with Malaya had been ambivalent since Malayan independence in 1957. Many Indonesian leaders regarded Malaya as somehow less truly independent since it had had no revolution, and were suspicious of the continuing British presence there, jealous of the economic successes of Malaya and deeply offended by Malayan and Singaporean support for PRRI. Now it looked as if Malaysia would be both neo-colonial, since British bases would remain, and an opening for the dynamic Chinese community of Singapore to dominate the new nation and thus (so some Indonesians reasoned) to promote Chinese influence and the growth of Communism in the region.

Nor were the Borneo territories enthusiastic about the Malaysia proposals. The strongest opposition arose in Brunei. In December 1962, Shaikh A. M. Azahari, the leader of the Brunei People's Party (Partai Ra'ayat), launched a short-lived rebellion against federation and in favour of an independent state of North Kalimantan. He had been in Indonesia during the Revolution and had maintained contact with Nasution, who sympathised with Azahari's aims. But contacts with the Brunei rebels were quickly monopolised by the Indonesian Central Intelligence Board (Badan Pusat Intelijens) directed by Subandrio. In January 1963 Sukarno said that the Malaysia proposal was unacceptable to Indonesia and Subandrio defined the Indonesian attitude as one of 'confrontation'.

The Americans were as committed to the British and Malaysia as they were to restoring relations with Jakarta. Sukarno and many others in Indonesia wanted American aid and opposed Malaysia at the same time. For several months efforts were made to reconcile these interests. The Philippines government of President Diosdado Macapagal further complicated matters by putting forward its own claim to Sabah on the basis of historic links with the Sultanate of Sulu. Indonesian-

Malayan-Filipino ministerial meetings and summit conferences among Sukarno, Macapagal and Malaya's Tungku Abdul Rahman were held in May-August 1963. For a time there was talk of a loose confederation of the three states to be called 'Maphilindo'. A compromise seemed possible in August when Malaya agreed to hold a test of opinion in Sarawak and Sabah before federation (in July the oil-rich state of Brunei had already announced that it would remain outside Malaysia). It seemed as if Sukarno and Subandrio were willing to compromise their anti-colonialism in the interest of economic stabilisation.

China was strongly opposed to Malaysia. The American commitment in South Vietnam was growing rapidly and the Chinese disliked the prospect of yet another pro-Western nation on their southern flanks, to be added to Thailand, South Vietnam, the Philippines and Taiwan. PKI was fearful of a general turn towards the United States in Indonesia itself. The Sino-Soviet split was now beyond reconciliation and the Soviet Union had clearly used the Irian campaign to increase its influence with the Indonesian government and military rather than to support PKI. When the Soviet Union signed the nuclear test ban treaty in August 1963, the Chinese feared that the Soviets were prepared to conspire with the Americans to contain China. China and PKI thus hoped for a radical anti-Malaysia policy which might frustrate the creation of Malaysia and perhaps tie down British troops there, while wrecking the economic stabilisation scheme and American influence in Jakarta. But neither desired a vast growth in a Soviet-supplied military.

There was thus a dangerous three-cornered competition of interests among the United States, the Soviet Union, and China in the international sphere, and another among Sukarno, the army and PKI in the domestic sphere. The first step towards a resolution of these competitions occurred in September 1963.

Before the results of the test of opinion in Sarawak and Sabah were reported, it was announced that Malaysia would come into existence on 16 September 1963. This appeared to be a grave insult to Indonesia, whose leaders did not pause to consider that their questioning of Malaysia had seemed even greater effrontery across the Straits of Malacca. PKI brought its members onto the streets in mass demonstrations against Malaysia. The British Embassy and twenty-one staff houses in Jakarta were burned down. The Malayan Embassy was attacked and in retaliation the Indonesian Embassy in Kuala Lumpur was attacked. On 17 September Malaysia broke off diplomatic relations and within four days Indonesia severed all relations with Malaya and Singapore, which handled nearly half the nation's exports. On 25 September Sukarno announced that he would 'gobble Malaysia raw' (*ganyang Malaysia,* usually but less accurately translated as 'crush Malaysia'). The United States abandoned its hope of remaining friendly with both Malaysia and Indonesia at the same time and the economic reform scheme was wrecked. China and the Soviet Union both praised Sukarno's policy.

Confrontation was now elevated to the prime issue of the day. Sukarno could again drive the revolutionary spirit onward, the military could look forward to increased budgets and PKI could take the lead in mass agitation. Indonesia moved rapidly into an anti-American diplomatic orbit, but the events within the nation were even more dramatic.

Sukarno was concerned that the Malaysia campaign should not become a vehicle for Nasution and the army to dominate affairs. He strengthened Yani's position in the army through a reorganisation of the Supreme Operations

Command (Koti) in July 1963. Yani remained its chief of staff but Nasution ceased to be deputy commander. Two of its five sections were under army control, but its intelligence role was now placed under Subandrio, operations were put under an air force officer and mobilisation under a civilian. Soeharto had already been given a new and eventually crucial post in May 1963, at the end of the Irian campaign, when he was put in command of the new Army Strategic Reserve Command (Kostrad: Komando Cadangan Strategis Angkatan Darat), comprising airborne, infantry, armoured and artillery units. Soeharto was now gaining a useful reputation as an able leader of troops and a simple man who resisted the extravagant corruption of other top generals.

It was PKI, however, which took the most dramatic steps to gain the initiative. Given the many influences, contacts and intrigues, both domestic and international, surrounding Indonesian affairs by this time, the precise motivation for PKI's new assertiveness is not clear. For whatever combination of reasons, the Aidit leadership attempted to break out of its domestic restraints. Late in September 1963 Aidit returned from extended visits to the Soviet Union and China. On his return, for the first time he aligned PKI unequivocally with China against the Soviet Union. It is possible that Aidit had accepted Chinese advice to mount a domestic political offensive. But he also had his own reasons for believing that the anti-Malaysia campaign had only narrowly rescued Indonesia from a turn towards the United States. The possibility of a domestic anti-PKI move was clearly present. PKI thus attempted to push for greater power, since offence seemed now to be the best means of defence.

But the difficulties facing PKI soon became clear. China shortly became so confident of its influence in Jakarta at government-to-government level that its support of PKI rural policies may have been qualified. The Soviet Union looked to the Indonesian army and anti-PKI leftists for allies. The Americans almost certainly became involved in clandestine encouragement of anti-Communists. And, most importantly, PKI's actions completed the alienation of many PNI supporters and drove NU and crucial army officers into active opposition in Java. The national united front strategy was thus endangered by PKI itself. Its amorphous mass base was not strong enough to withstand such a combination of circumstances, although at the time many observers in Indonesia and abroad believed that PKI was on the threshold of power, with Sukarno as its mentor.

Late in 1963 PKI launched a 'unilateral action' campaign to carry out land reform laws of 1959–60, the implementation of which had hardly begun. As PKI villagers began seizing land – especially in Central and East Java but also in Bali, West Java and North Sumatra – they came into violent conflict with landlords (many of whom were committed Muslims or PNI supporters), bureaucrats, army managers and particularly in East Java with *santri* supporters of NU. Brawls, burnings, kidnappings and killings spread, much of the violence upon communal lines as *abangan* supporters of PKI clashed with *santris*. In East Java, anti-PKI violence was spearheaded by the NU youth group Ansor. In some ways PKI was now reviving the assertive rural policies which followed Musso's return in August 1948, but with the crucial difference that it now had no military forces. Perhaps the Aidit leadership was as much misled by Communist membership figures and Sukarno's favour as were PKI's enemies into believing that PKI was now strong enough to withstand its opponents.

A respected voice of moderation in the cabinet was removed by the death of Djuanda in November 1963. Thereafter a triumvirate of Subandrio, Chaerul Saleh and Leimena took charge, with Subandrio increasingly the dominant figure. He now began to act as an ally of PKI, probably because he hoped to establish himself as Sukarno's ultimate successor and knew that the army would not support him. In return, the PKI leadership felt obliged to veil its dislike of Subandrio. PKI now increasingly demanded the wholesale 'retooling' of anti-PKI government officials.

On 17 August 1963 a group of intellectuals who were opposed to Lekra proclaimed a Cultural Manifesto (Manikěbu: Manifes Kěbudayaan) which, while necessarily endorsing Pancasila, failed to proclaim Manipol-USDEK or Nasakom and called for a national culture dominated by no particular political ideology. The distinguished literary critic H. B. Jassin (b. 1917) was among the inspirers of Manikěbu. PKI and Lekra, with the support of PNI's intellectual front (LKN), heatedly denounced this as a bourgeois, non-revolutionary and 'universal humanist' deviation, and Sukarno agreed. On 8 May 1964 he banned Manikěbu on the grounds that there was room for only one manifesto in Indonesia and that was Manipol. PKI and its student following now began hounding intellectual opponents even more actively in the name of 'retooling'. Shortly after, Jassin was dismissed from his lectureship at the University of Indonesia in Jakarta.

The Americans still had futile hopes of stopping the leftward swing in Indonesia. Their commitment in South Vietnam was increasingly heavy and difficult, especially after the Buddhist crisis of 1963 and the overthrow and assassination of Ngo Dinh Diem in November, and the Americans feared the prospect of Indonesia becoming a Communist or pro-Communist state. In January 1964 Robert F. Kennedy arranged a Malaysia-Indonesia ceasefire. But even as he was doing so PKI workers were taking over British plantations and businesses. Yet again the army stepped in to run them. Further efforts at Malaysia-Indonesia-Philippines negotiations followed, but broke down in March. In that same month Sukarno announced that the United States could 'go to hell' with its aid. Official American influence in Jakarta was now virtually dead. A final meeting among Sukarno, Abdul Rahman and Macapagal in Tokyo in June was a total failure.

Meanwhile the small-scale border war in the jungles of Kalimantan was clearly being won by the Malaysian and British forces. The Indonesian army was reluctant to commit too many troops in Kalimantan, for the prospect of a domestic crisis was increasing. In May 1964 Sukarno placed Air Marshal Omar Dhani in charge of a Vigilance Command (Koga: Komando Siaga) to pursue confrontation with Malaysia. The army feared that the air force would now gain control of the campaign. In August and September 1964 small-scale Indonesian incursions into peninsular West Malaysia took place, apparently without Yani's approval. PKI meanwhile took the lead in mobilising mass support for confrontation and in March 1964 chairmen of the National Front committees at all levels of government, many of them PKI, were given a voice in administrative affairs. Domestic instability was increased by a bad rice harvest in February and rising inflation, which reached 134 per cent in 1964.

As its worries about the direction of events grew, the army leadership began to obstruct confrontation and established secret contacts with Malaysia. In June Yani persuaded Sukarno to limit Koga's authority to retaliation in the event of a British attack. In October the army won an alteration in the Koga command structure. Omar Dhani remained in command, but his authority was restricted to Sumatra and Kalimantan, while army units assigned to the Malaysia campaign were first transferred to Kostrad under Soeharto, who kept many of the best troops available for action in Java.

By late 1964 the violence surrounding PKI's 'unilateral action' campaign had placed PKI on the defensive in Central and East Java and Bali, and the leadership seemed to be losing control of its cadres at lower levels. Its enemies began to conclude that PKI was not as powerful as it and Sukarno claimed. By now a domestic explosion was building up, but the conspiracies which lay behind it are naturally far from clear. In stages which have yet to be explained, an army group of which intelligence officers were crucial members apparently established links with NU and other Islamic leaders, and perhaps with anti-PKI radicals, other anti-Communists and Western intelligence agencies. Out of this emerged intrigues aimed primarily against PKI, Subandrio, Sukarno and those military officers who seemed unable or unwilling to stand against these three, either out of ideological conviction or because they found the prevalent corruption too congenial. Somewhere near the centre of these intrigues was an army intelligence organisation known as Opsus (Opěrasi Khusus, Special Operations) run by Lieutenant-Colonel Ali Murtopo (1924–84) under the general direction of Soeharto, to whom Yani gave responsibility for the army's clandestine contacts with Malaysia. Other intrigues abounded, many of them ephemeral. Within the military there was growing dissatisfaction with the extravagant corruption of some of the Jakarta generals. Several intelligence officers were by now in well-established contact with PKI's underground agent Sjam; their relationship with anti-PKI intelligence networks is unknown.

The Soviet Union was apparently working to increase its influence with the military and Murba party in 1964 in an effort to counteract Sukarno's and PKI's commitment to China. Although the Russians were a major source of economic and military aid to Indonesia, they could count on few committed friends within the army or government. Of those army officers who received training overseas, the vast majority (something like 4000 during 1958–65) went to the United States, although it must be said that many of these men were disillusioned by their personal observations of American life, especially its racism and urban slums. Some air force and navy officers had received technical training in the Soviet Union but they, too, often found daily life there unappealing. Several Murba leaders, however, were close to the Russians. This was especially true of Adam Malik, who had been ambassador to Moscow in 1959.

In September 1964 a group of anti-PKI journalists led by Adam Malik formed a Body for the Supporters (or Spreaders) of Sukarnoism (Badan Pěndukung – or Pěnyěbar – Sukarnoisme). Chaerul Saleh and Yani supported this Body in an attempt to divorce Sukarno from PKI. Sukarno recognised the aim and banned the Body on 17 December 1964; he later claimed that it had been a plot by the American Central Intelligence Agency. The army then took other steps to coordinate its allies. In October 1964 it established a body called Sekber Golkar (Sekrětariat Běrsama Golongan Karya, Joint Secretariat of Functional Groups). The army-civilian cooperative bodies and some former affiliates of the banned PSI and Masyumi joined. But the army was not yet in a position to take positive action.

By now the unity of the military itself was in doubt. This both encouraged PKI and impelled anti-PKI officers to move quickly. The air force was already close to PKI and Sukarno, and opposed to the army. The navy tended to side with the army, but the allegiance of some of its junior officers was uncertain. In March 1965 a mutiny of 'progressive' naval officers (among them a son of Leimena) in Surabaya ended in the transfer or dismissal of 145 officers. The top army leadership was divisible into at least two factions, those who looked to Yani or Nasution. Both were anti-PKI, but Yani found Sukarno too attractive and the Jakarta high-life too enjoyable for the liking of some officers. Soeharto was among the senior officers who worked to prevent these army factions becoming openly antagonistic.

Even more ominously, PKI was making inroads in the army, especially in the Diponěgoro and Brawijaya Divisions of Central and East Java. According to the later testimony of Sjam, in November 1964 PKI established a Special Bureau (Biro Khusus) under his direction to coordinate its infiltration of the military. By mid-1965, again according to Sjam, PKI had regular contacts with some 450 sympathetic officers in Central and East Java and some 200–250 elsewhere. How much of this was known to anti-PKI officers at the time is not certain, but there is no doubt that the army was making its own efforts to infiltrate PKI. The conspiratorial complexities and possibilities of this period are suggested by the fact that the head of army intelligence, Major-General S. Parman (1918–1965), was a younger brother of the PKI Politburo member Sakirman (1911–?67).

As public anti-American feelings reached a frenzy in late 1964 and early 1965, partly in response to the rapid escalation of the American war in Vietnam, China opened a diplomatic offensive in Jakarta which is still surrounded by some mystery. On 16 October 1964 China exploded its first nuclear device. This coincided with the sudden removal of Khrushchev from power in the Soviet Union, initiating uncertainty about the new Russian leadership's foreign policy aims. Three weeks later Sukarno met with Zhou Enlai in Shanghai for secret discussions. In mid-November the director of the Indonesian army arsenal said that Indonesia, too, would have an A-bomb in 1965. In late November the Chinese Foreign Minister Chen Yi (Ch'en Yi) visited Jakarta and it was announced that China and Indonesia would cooperate in foreign policy matters; reports also said that Chinese training in nuclear technology was promised. Further statements about an impending Indonesian nuclear explosion followed.

Some observers believe that China, which was increasingly confident of Indonesian governmental cooperation, offered to explode a nuclear device in Indonesian territory and let Indonesia take credit for it in order to reduce the army's hostility and weaken Soviet influence. The Chinese could not match Soviet supplies of conventional armaments, but they may have hoped to capitalise on the uncertainty surrounding the new Soviet leadership. In March 1964 China had also offered to turn the assets of the Bank of China in Jakarta over to the Indonesian government, and did so in November. This move is still not entirely explained. The Bank was believed to be PKI's main source of Chinese financial aid. That this represented a further step in the Jakarta-Beijing alliance is clear. What is not clear is whether this was intended to give the Indonesian government leverage to restrain the adventuristic rural policies of PKI before they threatened the political balance which China seemed now to be exploiting with success.

By December 1964 PKI was trying to cool down its 'unilateral actions', which were revealing that its enormous membership could be neither entirely controlled nor used as a base for constructive revolutionary action. Over the next few months its peasants' front (BTI) activists were restrained, but NU continued its counter-offensive in East Java with the support of local PNI followers. The killings were still, however, on a small scale compared to what was to follow in late 1965 and 1966. PKI continued its verbal offensive against army 'bureaucratic capitalists' and others in need of 'retooling' and, like the Chinese government, began to turn its attention again to gaining more power at the top in Jakarta rather than in the countryside. The party was now rather like a tightrope walker losing his balance who tries to run the last few steps.

Jakarta's alliance with Beijing was sealed in January 1965 when Indonesia withdrew from the United Nations after Malaysia had been given a non-permanent seat in the Security Council. This also increased Indonesia's diplomatic isolation from other Afro-Asian nations. Subandrio then visited China to confirm the friendship. At his trial later he said that Zhou Enlai offered him weapons to arm a people's militia, the only form of military force which PKI might be able to organise. It was at this point that Aidit proposed to Sukarno the creation of a 'fifth force' of armed workers and peasants, to be added to the existing navy, army, police and air force, and the appointment of Nasakom advisers (i.e. PKI cadres) to existing armed forces units. These proposals threatened the army directly, as Subandrio also appeared to do when he said in January that some former comrades-in-arms had become counter-revolutionaries and might have to be abandoned.

PKI's position in Jakarta was apparently strengthened in January 1965 when Sukarno banned the Murba party. This is evidence for those who argue that Sukarno genuinely wished PKI to come to power, for Murba leaders such as Adam Malik had had much influence with Sukarno, as did Chaerul Saleh who, although non-party, was thought of as a Murba man. Murba had long opposed PKI for leadership of the left, and was also apparently favoured by the Soviet Union. PKI now stepped up demands for the 'retooling' of Malik and Chaerul Saleh. They lost some power in a cabinet reshuffle in March but remained in the government.

In late February, twenty-one newspapers in Jakarta and Medan which opposed PKI were suspended. The army reacted by beginning to publish its own newspapers. In the same month, as anti-American sentiments increased still further in response to the bombings of North Vietnam, PKI unions and other leftists seized American business enterprises. The army took over their management. Stanvac, Caltex and Shell were placed under government supervision in March and they found it increasingly difficult to carry on normal operations. The economy was now in a state of near-chaos. In April the American Peace Corps was expelled, but discussions with the United States and other potential sources of economic aid apparently continued. Even at the height of anti-Western feelings, Indonesia's main trading partners remained the United States, Japan and West Germany.

Chinese delegations paid frequent visits to Jakarta. In April 1965 Zhou Enlai himself came. The Chinese publicly urged the creation of a 'fifth force' but the army dragged its feet. Nor did Sukarno order that a 'fifth force' be formed, which is evidence for those who believe that the President had no genuine intention of helping PKI to power but sought only to pressure the army leadership. In May the conspiratorial atmosphere was heightened by Sukarno's revelation of a telegram sent to London by the British Ambassador in Jakarta – the so-called 'Gilchrist letter' – which in Sukarno's view confirmed the existence of army-British plots against the regime.

In May Yani saw Sukarno about the 'Nasakomisation' of the army. It was never clear just what Sukarno thought this meant in practice. On this occasion he accepted the army interpretation that it amounted to a spirit of unity linking nationalism, religion and Communism rather than any formal structures which would give PKI a role in army affairs. Soon thereafter the army announced that it was already Nasakom in spirit, so that nothing further need be done.

But the 'fifth force' proposals were not dead. On 31 May 1965 Sukarno spoke of Zhou's offer to arm the people and told the four armed services to submit plans for doing so. Yani and Nasution continued to play for time by saying that all the people should be armed, not just the workers and peasants (the accepted euphemism for PKI's organised followers), and that the 'fifth force' should be controlled by the army. In June the navy appeared to give some support to the idea. The police force was factionalised, but some of its officers (especially in Central and East Java) were sympathetic to PKI. In June one such officer was appointed police commander in Jakarta. But it was the air force under Omar Dhani which acted to give substance to a 'fifth force'. On 5 July it began giving short training courses to civilians from PKI's mass organisations at Halim Pĕrdanakusumah air force base southeast of Jakarta. By late September over 2000 civilians had attended these courses.

PKI's apparent surge towards dominance in Jakarta continued. Early in August 1965, under pressure from Sukarno, PNI leaders who were opposed to cooperation with PKI and who had friends in anti-PKI army circles were purged. Hardi, Hadisubeno Sosrowerdojo (1912–71), and about 150 other PNI leaders were suspended. This left Ali Sastroamidjojo and his followers, who were at least willing to play at Nasakomisation, in charge. In the same month PKI released its last membership figures. Over 27 million Indonesians were claimed as members of PKI or its mass organisations. Allowing for multiple memberships this probably represented about 20 million individuals. How much was merely nominal or even fictitious is unclear. It is difficult to account for more than about one-quarter of this membership on the basis of the number who were later killed, imprisoned, disenfranchised for political reasons in the 1971 elections, or who would have died of natural causes by 1971. The experience of previous moves towards rural radicalism in Java suggests that PKI's rural base is more likely to have shrunk than expanded since 1963.

Much depended upon the President, for many Indonesians agreed with him in finding the idea of Indonesia without Sukarno almost unthinkable. Whom did he favour, what revolutionary step would he next announce, who could influence him? By early 1965 a new question was becoming prominent: who would succeed him? He had been suffering from a kidney complaint which some believed to be threatening his life, and the soothsayers of Indonesia increasingly predicted the fall or death of Sukarno. In the first week of August 1965 Sukarno suddenly vomited and collapsed while receiving a delegation. He soon recovered, but the intrigues now went into high gear as the President's mortality was forcibly impressed upon political leaders. Aidit hastened back from China and, according to later trial evidence (which is suspect), at this point he decided to encourage a group of 'progressive' army officers who were preparing to act against the army's top leadership. Anti-PKI forces were also drawing together.

In August 1965 Sukarno withdrew Indonesia from remaining links with the capitalist world (International Monetary Fund, Interpol, World Bank). When Lee Kuan Yew tearfully announced Singapore's separation from Malaysia on 9 August, Sukarno viewed this as confirmation of the righteousness of confrontation. But Singapore's separation also removed most of the basis for the army leaders' genuine fears of Malaysia and increased their inclination to end confrontation.

In his independence day speech of 17 August Sukarno announced an anti-imperialist Jakarta-Pnom Penh-Hanoi-Beijing-Pyongyang axis, said that the people should be armed, intimated that the army generals were obstructing him in this, and promised a decision soon. On 16–19 September Omar Dhani went secretly to China upon Sukarno's instructions to discuss, among other things, the Chinese offer of small arms, without prior notification having been given to Nasution as Defence Minister. By now China appears to have abandoned the idea of offering Indonesia a nuclear bomb (if, indeed, it had really intended to do so), probably for fear of appearing so irresponsible that the Americans or Soviets might feel justified in making a preemptive strike against China. But Chinese support of a 'fifth force' remained strong.

The social, political and economic structures of the nation were now near to collapse. Inflation was extreme, with prices rising at something like 500 per cent for the year. By the end of 1965 the price of rice was believed to be rising at an annual rate of 900 per cent. The black market rate for the Rupiah against the US dollar plunged from Rp. 5100 at the beginning of 1965 to Rp. 17 500 by the third quarter of the year and Rp. 50 000 by the fourth. In the cities, towns and villages, Communists and anti-Communists believed stories of assassination squads being prepared and lists of victims being drawn up. Prophesies, omens and violence spread. By late September, with tens of thousands of troops gathering in Jakarta in preparation for Armed Forces Day on 5 October, expectations of a coup were high. On 27 September Yani finally announced that the army opposed the creation of a 'fifth force' or Nasakomisation of the military in any structural sense.

On the night of 30 September–1 October 1965 the tensions were released by an ill-planned coup attempt in Jakarta. What happened on that night and the following days is reasonably clear. But complicated and sometimes partisan arguments continue over who masterminded the events and what manoeuvres lay behind them. The intricacies of the political scene, the contacts, friendships and hatreds which linked most of the major participants to one another, and the suspect nature of much of the evidence, make it unlikely that the full truth will ever be known. It seems improbable that there was a single mastermind controlling all the events, and interpretations which attempt to explain events solely in terms of a PKI, army, Sukarno or Soeharto plot must be treated with caution.

During the night of 30 September a battalion of the palace guard commanded by Lieutenant-Colonel Untung (formerly of the Diponĕgoro Division), another from the Diponĕgoro Division, one from the Brawijaya Division, and civilians from

PKI's Pĕmuda Rakyat, left Halim air base. They went to abduct Nasution, Yani, Parman and four other senior army generals from their houses in Jakarta. The leaders of the coup attempt included Brigadier-General Supardjo of the Siliwangi Division and the Dipongĕgro Division's head of intelligence. Untung appears to have been a pawn. They had the support of Omar Dhani, who gave them Halim air base as their headquarters and was present there himself. They also had contacts with Sjam's PKI Special Bureau and some members of the PKI Politburo were at least vaguely aware of their plans. But Aidit was the only senior PKI leader present at Halim. Njoto and Lukman were both out of Jakarta, as were Subandrio, Chaerul Saleh and Ali Sastroamidjojo.

The attempted coup was typified by extraordinary incompetence and confusion. Yani and two other generals were killed at their houses when they resisted arrest. Nasution escaped and spent the rest of the night and part of the next day in hiding, but his five-year-old daughter was shot and later died on 6 October and one of his aides was captured. This aide, the three generals' bodies and the three taken alive were brought to Halim, where Parman and the three other living captives were murdered. Gĕrwani and Pĕmuda Rakyat members took part in these killings. All seven bodies were then thrown down a disused well. With the killings of this night a new threshold of violence was crossed. They also wiped out the Yani faction among the top generals and the army thus fell to those more willing to stand against Sukarno and the army's enemies. About 2000 troops of the coup group meanwhile occupied three sides of Medan Mĕrdeka commanding the Presidential palace, the radio station and the telecommunications centre, but did not occupy the east side where the Kostrad headquarters was located.

Just before dawn on 1 October Soeharto, who was not on the coup group's abduction list, went to Kostrad upon being told of the disappearance of the generals and shooting at their houses. From there he could see soldiers occupying Medan Mĕrdeka. Nasution and Yani were missing, so Soeharto took command of the army with the agreement of those army generals he could contact, the police and the navy. He ordered all soldiers confined to barracks unless specifically ordered by him to move, and set about finding out what was happening.

Just after seven o'clock the insurgents announced over the radio that the '30 September Movement' was a military group which had acted to safeguard Sukarno from a coup plotted by a council of corrupt, high-living Jakarta generals who were tools of the American Central Intelligence Agency. About two hours later Sukarno, who had headed for the Presidential palace but turned away upon learning of the presence of unidentified troops, arrived at Halim; he later said that this was in order to be near an aircraft in case he needed to flee. What Sukarno had known about plans for a coup has never been clarified. At Halim he met with Omar Dhani and other coup figures, but apparently Aidit was in a separate building. To the air base the President summoned Leimena, the commanders of the navy and police and others for consultations. But Sukarno never publicly endorsed the coup attempt, perhaps because he learned that six generals were dead but Nasution had escaped, circumstances which placed the success of the coup gravely in doubt. His presence at Halim, however, compromised him in the view of many army officers.

The soldiers on Medan Mĕrdeka were meanwhile getting hot, tired, hungry and thirsty, and the coup leaders failed to send provisions. Soeharto persuaded the

Brawijaya troops to come over to Kostrad headquarters about four p.m. Two hours later the Diponĕgoro troops withdrew to Halim. Soeharto thus regained control of the centre of Jakarta without a shot. By this time Nasution had joined him and the events of the previous night were becoming clearer, although it was still not known that the six generals were murdered. At four p.m. Sukarno sent word that he was assuming command of the army himself but Soeharto ignored this entirely, the first evidence of the determination of this man whom the coup group had not thought to abduct.

At nine p.m. Soeharto announced over the radio that six generals had been kidnapped by counter-revolutionaries but that he was now in control of the army and would crush the 30 September Movement and safeguard Sukarno. He then sent an ultimatum to the coup group at Halim. About ten p.m. Sukarno left by car for his palace at Bogor. Then the coup leaders departed in the face of the expected Kostrad attack. Aidit flew to Yogyakarta and Omar Dhani to Madiun. Before dawn on 2 October the elite army para-commando regiment (RPKAD: Resimen Para Komando Angkatan Darat) moved in on Halim. After some skirmishes, the air force commander there ordered a ceasefire. The coup was over in Jakarta.

The Diponĕgoro Division in Central Java was the base of the military conspirators. During 1 October a series of intra-army coups left five of the Diponĕgoro's seven infantry battalions in the hands of the 30 September Movement. The PKI mayor of Surakarta announced his support and on 2 October, by which time the coup had utterly collapsed in Jakarta, PKI turned out in Yogyakarta for a march in support of the Movement. Also on 2 October, PKI's Jakarta daily *Harian Rakjat* incredibly published an editorial in praise of the Movement, which it depicted as an internal army affair. These events, in conjunction with the role of Gĕrwani and Pĕmuda Rakyat in the killings at Halim, sealed PKI's fate. Anti-PKI army officers no longer wanted to restrict or ban PKI; they now saw reason and occasion to annihilate it. Anti-PKI civilians, especially Islamic activists, were in hearty agreement.

The collapse of the coup in Jakarta demoralised the leading military conspirators in Central Java. During the night of 1–2 October they withdrew to the Mount Mĕrapi-Mĕrbabu area with two companies of soldiers. The officers they left behind realised that the cause was lost and begged forgiveness. Jakarta thus regained control in the region, but the loyalty of many of the soldiers was still doubtful. Only after more trustworthy troops were moved in after mid-October was Soeharto confident of the restoration of order.

Again Indonesia was at a crossroads; again an experimental political system had produced crisis. Sukarno and PKI, with the support of the air force, pursued a policy aimed at destroying the dominance of the army, which after the crisis of 1956–7 emerged as the single most powerful political, economic and administrative force in the nation, because it was the most powerful military force. In doing so, they ensured the army's enmity. The army leadership manipulated the chaotic system to its own advantage, but by 1965 it was clear that unless someone stood firm the army would face serious threats to its position. NU similarly tried to manipulate the system to defend its role, but was pushed into active and violent opposition even before the army, when PKI threatened the religious and economic interests of its supporters.

On the night of 30 September 1965 the house of cards came prematurely crashing down. It was months before the consequences were clear, but on that night the balance of hostile forces which underlay guided democracy came to an end. Many observers have seen tragedy in the period, especially the tragedy of Sukarno, the man who outlived his time and used his popular support to maintain a regime of extravagant corruption and hypocrisy. But a greater tragedy lay in the suffering of the Indonesian people.

20 Creating the New Order, 1965–75

For some months after the attempted coup of 1965, Indonesia's political future was in doubt. In the end, Soeharto established what is known as Indonesia's 'new order', to contrast it from the 'old order' of Sukarno's days. The new order began with much popular support from those groups which were anxious to be freed from the troubles of the past. There was talk of a new generation of young leaders and a new age in intellectual life, of a 'generation of 66' (*angkatan 66*). But within a few years the new order elite – at its heart a military faction supported by a small group of civilians – had alienated many original allies.

The period 1965–75 attracted mixed judgements from observers both within and outside the country. Rightists admired the Soeharto government for destroying PKI and adopting pro-Western policies. Leftists despised it for doing the same. Among less committed observers, there were many who admired the government's achievements in stabilising the economy, but who condemned its human rights record and corruption.

Comparisons can be drawn between the new order's policies in its first decade and those of the Ethical period of colonial rule described in Chapter 13. The new order, too, justified much of its claim to legitimacy on its promises of national economic development and of improvements to levels of education and welfare. It delivered much of the first but less of the second in the period discussed in this chapter. The government's style was paternalistic and frequently heavy-handed. It sought popular involvement as a token of legitimacy, but only in carefully controlled ways. Much of the nation's economic development was in the hands of foreign enterprises and there was little growth of indigenous industries. Snouck Hurgronje's ideas regarding Islam were also of continuing significance, for the new order, too, displayed respect for Islam as private religious practice but determination that it not become a powerful political force, once the initial period of alliance between Islamic activists and the pro-Soeharto military had succeeded in destroying PKI and ousting Sukarno.

There were other parallels between the Ethical policy and Soeharto's new order government which, however, reveal significant differences of scale. Notably, both employed political imprisonment to remove opponents, but the latter did so on a far larger scale than the former, and furthermore allowed torture of its prisoners. And the centralisation of economic, political, administrative and military power in the hands of a small elite was probably greater under Soeharto than in Dutch times.

One of the most important differences between the social setting of the new order and the colonial period concerned Islam. For many reasons, some of which will be discussed below, Indonesia experienced an intensification of religious commitment within Islam and other religions after 1965. This was not without its hazards. Because of the activities of Islamic reformers and the reactions of their opponents since the early twentieth century, Indonesian society had come to be more firmly structured along communal (*aliran*) than class lines, a pattern reinforced by the politicisation of *aliran* over the period 1950–65. As a consequence, the prospects of domestic communal conflict were greater than at the turn of the century, especially within Javanese society.

The religious environment was made more volatile by the changing perceptions of the senior generation of Modernist Islamic leaders. They had lost some of the self-confidence of the early years of the twentieth century. Rather than awaiting others' recognition of what they regarded as their natural right to lead the nation, they became bitterly accustomed to the role of political outsiders. They now saw leadership as something to be won rather than assumed. Their belief that anyone who was shown the true Islam would naturally embrace it had meanwhile been shaken by the limited (albeit very significant) progress of the Modernist interpretation of Islam and the hostile reaction it sometimes produced.

Many Modernists turned their attention from politics to mission work (*dakwah*; Arabic *da'wa*, the call to walk in God's ways), by which they hoped the Islamisation of Indonesian society would be perfected. Only in this way, they felt, would Islam one day truly govern the life of the nation. This led many devout Muslims to devote their energies to educational and welfare institutions. But this shift of attention was born partly of frustration. Modernists' political frustration was completed when they realised after 1965 that the destruction of PKI would not catapult Islam to power. To this was added religious frustration born of the unexpected growth of other religions since 1965, which is discussed below. Just when Modernists concluded that Islam's future lay in a deeper Islamisation of society, they were confronted with this new challenge in the religious field. Sometimes their frustration turned to anger.

Orthodox Islam, on the other hand, continued to adapt itself to changing political circumstances and maintained its strength and vitality in the countryside. Meanwhile a new generation of Islamic leaders was emerging which was sometimes unhappy with the leadership its elders gave and was less concerned about old issues, about the schism between Orthodoxy and Modernism, or about the difficulties of living within an increasingly multireligious society. These younger Muslims found it easier to respect younger Christian leaders, and this generation from both religious communities came to be looked upon by many Indonesians as one of the main hopes for the nation's future.

The social problems which the new order had to confront were greater than those faced by the Ethical reformers. This was partly because the Dutch failed to solve these problems decades before and partly because the passage of time and the turbulent events since the Japanese conquest had exacerbated them. The Dutch failed to meet the welfare needs of a nation of 60.7 million people in 1930. It is perhaps not surprising, given decades of neglect and the urgent need first to regain control of the nation's economy in the years after 1965, that the new order government was initially unable to make much contribution to the welfare needs of its population, which reached 119.2 million in the 1971 census and 147.3 million in 1980.

Health and education standards remained low, but significantly better than in Dutch times. By 1974 there were 6221 doctors. In Java there was one doctor for every 21.7 thousand inhabitants and in the outer islands one for every 17.9 thousand (which did not mean easier access to a doctor there, for the population was dispersed over greater distances). The 1971 census showed that for people over the age of 10, the literacy rate (in any script) was 72.0 per cent among males and 50.3 per cent among females. But the general quality of the school system had been declining since the 1950s, so these literacy figures should not be taken as evidence that there was adequate provision of formal education. By 1973, 57 per cent (11.8 million) of 7- to 12-year-olds was in primary school, leaving about 8.9 million in this group still without schooling. At tertiary education level, the Indonesian government continued to surpass the Dutch record. Yet in 1973, only about one-quarter of one percent of the population (329 300) was enrolled in state and private tertiary institutions, of whom 117 600 were at state universities or institutes of higher learning. These numbers were quite low, but nonetheless represented more graduates than the nation could absorb at its level of development, for there was a growing problem of graduate unemployment. The quality of education at this level also attracted criticism. Only from the mid-1970s was the government able to make substantial new progress in health and education.

The nation's social problems were complicated by continuing urbanisation. In 1971, 17.3 per cent of the population was classified as urban, as opposed to 14.8 per cent in 1961 and 3.8 per cent in 1930. By 1971 Jakarta had surpassed 4.5 million inhabitants. Java continued to have the majority of the nation's population (60.4 per cent in 1971) and the new order failed as the Dutch had failed to move any significant proportion of the inhabitants of Java to the outer islands, a policy now called 'transmigration'.

At the very centre of the complex and violent events which led to the inauguration and stabilisation of the new order regime stood the previously little-known General Soeharto. He was, like Sukarno, of Javanese ethnic origin (from Central rather than East Java). Indeed, in his personal life Soeharto was more truly a son of rural Java than Sukarno, and he was therefore explicable, even (as it proved) admirable, to many of the people whom Sukarno regarded as his own special constituency. As a young man Soeharto was never exposed to the urban anticolonialism or higher Western education which influenced Sukarno's views. He went no farther than a Muhammadiyah junior high (MULO level) in Yogyakarta, which he left in 1939. Nor was he exposed to the grander forms of Japanese fascism in Jakarta which Sukarno found congenial during the Second World War.

As a teenager Soeharto lived with and assisted a religious teacher (*kyai*) who was famed as a shaman (*dukun*). Here he lived in that world on the boundaries between the popular version of Orthodox Islam, with its Qur'anic recitations and mysticism, and the spirit realm of Java, with its spectres, folk remedies and magic. He became, and remained, devoted to the intense inner mysticism of rural Java, a mysticism where Islam exists only in its more esoteric form and religious legalism has little force. Here Soeharto found an inner peace which may partly explain his apparent cool-headedness throughout his years of rule. Soeharto admired Sultan Hamengkubuwana IX of Yogyakarta and desired the kind of supernatural legitimacy which Javanese rulers claimed. He is said to have brought some holy regalia (*pusaka*) from the court of Surakarta to surround him in Jakarta in 1966, and to have returned them hastily when severe floods in Surakarta were interpreted as supernatural retribution for their removal.

In addition to his Javanese roots and inner strengths, Soeharto was an able politician. By 1965 he already had a circle of close allies within the army. His support among other officers rested not only on personal respect, but also on his willingness to allow his followers to reap financial rewards for their loyalty with little regard for legality. Nasution's long opposition to the corruption of the officer corps, on the other hand, made him unpopular among those who saw changing political circumstances at least partly in terms of their potential cash payoff; Nasution in fact made no effort to seize the initiative from Soeharto. For his part, Sukarno appears to have underestimated how formidable a contender he faced in Soeharto. For many months Sukarno sought to prove that the coup attempt was a minor incident in the continuing revolution and that he was still in charge. But Soeharto proved to be an opponent too slippery and able for the aging, ill and self-indulgent Sukarno. The President ultimately lost the struggle with his successor, and his vision of ongoing revolution was lost with it.

During October 1965 the collapse of guided democracy began. On 2 October, Soeharto accepted Sukarno's order taking personal command of the army, but on condition that Soeharto himself have full authority to restore order and security. This authority was later institutionalised on 1 November with the creation of Kopkamtib (Komando Opĕrasi Pĕmulihan Kĕamanan dan Kĕtĕrtiban, Operational Command for Restoration of Security and Order). On 3 October the murdered generals' bodies were discovered at Halim and Armed Forces Day on 5 October became a massive public funeral for them. The army began publicly blaming PKI for the coup attempt, which was now called Gĕstapu (from Gĕrakan September Tigapuluh, 30th September Movement) with clear allusion to the Gestapo of Nazi Germany. PKI denials of involvement had no effect.

Anticommunist youths now took to the streets, burning the PKI headquarters in Jakarta on 8 October. In late October anti-PKI university students formed KAMI (Kĕsatuan Aksi Mahasiswa Indonesia, Indonesian Students' Action Front), with army encouragement and protection. Its core consisted of Islamic, Catholic and former PSI youth groups. A similar high school students' front called KAPPI (Kĕsatuan Aksi Pĕlajar Pĕmuda Indonesia, Indonesian Youth and Students' Action Front) and a university graduates' front KASI (Kĕsatuan Aksi Sarjana Indonesia, Indonesian Graduates' Action Front) were formed early in 1966, both with a Masyumi-PSI core. Meanwhile arrests were underway, over 10000 PKI activists and leaders having been picked up in Jakarta and West Java by December 1965; among them was Pramudya Ananta Tur.

In October 1965 the killings started. Violence against people associated with PKI took place across the country, but the worst massacres were in Java and Bali. The conflict in East Java between PKI and NU which had begun in 1963 turned into full-scale slaughter from the second week of October 1965. In mid-October Soeharto sent reliable paracommando units into Central Java; he ordered out troops whose loyalty was suspect and they went rather than resist the paracommandos. Anti-PKI slaughters were then triggered off there, with the army assisting youths in finding Communists. In Bali, with no Islamic forces involved, upper-caste PNI landlords took the lead in urging the extermination of PKI members. PKI's top national leadership was also being found and killed. Njoto was shot about 6 November and Aidit on 22 November; Lukman fell soon thereafter.

At a meeting in Jakarta on 9–11 November 1965, Muhammadiyah proclaimed that the extermination of 'Gĕstapu/PKI' constituted Holy War. Other Islamic groups endorsed this view. Whatever Islamic leaders may have meant by this, such pronouncements appeared to make the killing of Communists a religious duty and a passport to paradise for any Muslim who lost his own life in the violence. Indonesians who suspected Islam of latent fanaticism felt their suspicions to be confirmed.

Since political allegiances of the 1950–65 period had increasingly corresponded with *aliran* loyalties in Java, so did much of the killing. The army encouraged and supported zealots from the *santri* side of Javanese society in finding PKI targets among their *abangan* brothers; the gulf between *santri* and *abangan* at village level thus widened in a bloody fashion. Not only PKI supporters fell. In Java, many who were thought of as 'left PNI' were also killed. Sometimes old feuds were settled which had little or nothing to do with political conflicts. There were stories of landlords ridding themselves of squatters by simply killing them.

The killings came to an end in the first months of 1966, leaving a death toll which is never likely to be known with certainty. Most scholars accept that at least half a million died, but no one really knows, for no one counted. Indonesia had not seen domestic slaughter on such a scale in its history. These killings left an indelible mark upon many Indonesians. Some remained proud of having helped to exterminate PKI. Others felt that this was the nation's most shameful and unforgivable episode, an exercise in collective madness. Many people were also arrested, interrogated (often under torture) and held without trial. The number of these is similarly uncertain. Perhaps as many as 100000 people were still imprisoned without trial a decade after the dreadful events of 1965–6.

Sukarno was distressed by the massacres and the collapse of his threadbare revolution. In November 1965 he pathetically appealed to Muslims at least to bury the dead. In December he distorted history and offended even army officers who were sympathetic to him by praising PKI's role in the Revolution. But by this time PKI was destroyed. PKI supporters who had escaped death or arrest were now in hiding or attempting to conceal their past. The army was well on its way to unchallenged power, although Islamic political forces were still deceiving themselves that they would share in this power.

Sukarno still tried to hold centre stage, but his old magic no longer worked. In January 1966 he broadcast an appeal for all to follow him, while Subandrio called for the creation of a Sukarnoist column (Barisan Sukarno). Soeharto neutralised the latter by pledging his own loyalty to Sukarno and telling all of the President's loyal supporters to register their allegiance with the army. Although Soeharto would perhaps have preferred Sukarno to act as a legitimating figurehead for army dominance, it was becoming clear that the old President would have to be removed.

In February 1966 Sukarno made his final fumbling effort to save guided democracy. On 21 February he reshuffled his cabinet. He removed Nasution as

Defence Minister and abolished his post as armed forces chief of staff; Nasution simply refused to recognise his dismissal. Omar Dhani and Subandrio – two men whom the army much wanted in its hands – were retained as ministers. Sukarno appointed as State Minister for Security Affairs Lt. Col. Iman Sjafei, a boss of the Jakarta underworld. Anti-KAMI thugs soon began to be organised.

Soeharto's policy appears now to have been to encourage such violence in Jakarta that in the end Sukarno would have to hand power to him to restore order. Pro-Sukarnoist and anti-Sukarnoist youths now fought it out in the capital's streets. The American embassy was attacked by the Sukarnoists on 23 February. Sukarno then banned KAMI, but the students and their army mentors ignored this. Sukarno ordered the University of Indonesia closed on 3 March but the anti-Sukarnoist students occupied the campus while their army allies guarded the perimeter.

Meanwhile Extraordinary Military Courts (Mahmillub: Mahkamah Militer Luar Biasa, established in December 1965) were holding trials which both corroborated the view that PKI had masterminded the coup attempt of 30 September 1965 and raised questions about Sukarno's role. In February 1966 the former SOBSI Secretary-General Njono Prawiro was sentenced to death. On 7 March Untung received the same sentence.

The army encouraged students to demonstrate for the banning of PKI (which by this stage would be merely a reproach to Sukarno, since there was little of PKI left to ban) and for a new cabinet and economic reforms. The economy was still running wild, the cost of living index for December 1965-January 1966 having recorded a 50 per cent increase. On 5 March Soeharto presented Sukarno with a list of cabinet ministers who should be dismissed, which Sukarno rejected.

On 11 March 1966 the subtle game of manoeuvre between Sukarno and Soeharto – its subtlety backed by bloody violence in the capital – was resolved decisively in favour of Soeharto. Sukarno opened a cabinet meeting in Jakarta, with student demonstrators filling the streets. He was informed that unidentified troops (in fact paracommandos) were surrounding the palace, so he hurriedly boarded a helicopter for Bogor, taking Subandrio and Chaerul Saleh with him. That evening, three generals acting as Soeharto's emissaries went to Bogor and persuaded Sukarno to sign a document giving Soeharto full authority to restore order, to facilitate the functioning of government and to protect the President in the name of the Revolution. With allusion to Sěmar, the most powerful god-clown of the Javanese *wayang* theatre, this document was called Supersěmar (from Surat Pěrintah Sěbělas Maret, 11 March letter of instruction).

On the authority of Supersěmar, Soeharto and his supporters now overturned the remnants of guided democracy, in the face of Sukarno's impotent fury. On 12 March PKI and all its mass organisations were banned. On 18 March, Subandrio, Chaerul Saleh, Imam Sjafei and eleven other cabinet ministers were arrested; one of the army's cabinet targets, Surachman, escaped but was killed in South Blitar in 1968. Chaerul Saleh died in prison in 1967. Those who were thought of as moderate Sukarnoists were not arrested, men like Idham Chalid, Leimena and Roeslan Abdulgani, who remained in the new cabinet installed on 27 March. This was led by a triumvirate of Soeharto, Sultan Hamengkubuwana IX and Adam Malik. The latter two were emerging as the new order's most prominent civilian supporters.

Purges of the military and bureaucracy now began. About 2600 Diponĕgoro Division soldiers were discharged, suspended, retired or disciplined, and many others were arrested. By the middle of April over 300 air force officers had been arrested. Some anti-PKI but pro-Sukarno army officers were transferred from sensitive commands in May.

Guided democracy foreign policy was abandoned under Adam Malik as the new Foreign Minister. The Jakarta-Beijing axis was quickly destroyed. Chinese diplomatic and private property was attacked by anti-PKI activists from the opening stages of conflict. By early 1966 Beijing knew that there was no point in attempting to maintain its operations in Indonesia. In March it closed its Xinhua (Hsin Hua) news agency in Jakarta and then its three consulates, and in May recalled its ambassador. The Indonesian ambassador to Beijing had already been ordered to come home in February, but he had refused to do so and had been given political asylum by the Chinese. Diplomatic relations with the People's Republic were formally 'frozen' by Jakarta on 31 October 1967, after another wave of anti-Chinese riots.

One aim of the new foreign policy stances was to meet Western nations' requirements for urgently needed economic aid, requirements which included the ending of confrontation with Malaysia. In April 1966 Indonesia rejoined the United Nations and in May Malik announced it would rejoin the International Monetary Fund. Hamengkubuwana IX was in charge of economic, financial and development affairs; he announced the first economic reform measures in April. The ending of confrontation was, however, somewhat complicated by the insistence of some military men that it not be done in a humiliating fashion, so Malik found his efforts to negotiate a settlement interfered with by Ali Murtopo and his Opsus organisation, which already had clandestine links with Malaysia.

In May 1966 Soeharto endorsed the ending of confrontation and a delegation of senior officers paid a goodwill visit to Kuala Lumpur. Within days, Japan led the noncommunist embrace of the new order by offering US$30 million emergency credits. On 29 May Malik met Malaysia's Deputy Prime Minister Tun Abdul Razak in Tokyo and confrontation at last ended. This was confirmed in a treaty of 11 December, full diplomatic relations being restored in August 1967.

The domestic political scene was not, however, fully under the new order's control. A backlash by pro-Sukarnoist forces still seemed possible, perhaps relying upon PNI as a political base. Anti-Sukarno zealots among the military and Islamic groups wanted PNI banned, but Soeharto was concerned by what he regarded as Islamic fanaticism and wanted PNI as a counterweight to it. So instead of banning PNI he purged it. In April 1966 he arranged a PNI congress which removed the Sukarnoist leadership under Ali Sastroamidjojo installed the previous August. Hardi and Soeharto's old friend Hadisubeno now took charge of PNI.

Under the 1945 constitution, the President was responsible to the Provisional People's Consultative Assembly (MPRS). This was now reduced in size by the arrest of about 180 of its members and anti-Sukarno feeling was increasing among its remaining members. Soeharto judged that it was safe to convene the Assembly in June–July 1966. The Assembly ratified Supersĕmar and the banning of PKI, outlawed Marxism as a political doctrine, called for elections to be held in 1968 and demanded that Sukarno give an explanation of the immorality, corruption and economic mismanagement of guided democracy and of his own role in the

1965 coup attempt. He was stripped of the title of President-for-life which the Assembly had conferred on him in May 1963 and was forbidden to issue Presidential decisions. Sukarno refused to respond to the MPRS demands for explanations, but it was clear to everyone that the Sukarno era was drawing to a definitive end. Only in January 1967 did he finally tell the MPRS that he had no prior knowledge of the coup attempt; perhaps it was true.

The break with guided democracy was confirmed in mid-1966 by the release of those who had been arrested for their roles in the PRRI and Pĕrmesta rebellions. Sumual, Simbolon and other military men who were released found new careers in the business world. Sjafruddin, Natsir and the other civilians who had been involved found far fewer opportunities awaiting them, for they were hardly less distrusted by the new order elite than they had been by the Sukarno regime.

As the new order demonstrated its increasing control of the nation and the chances of a Sukarnoist revival receded, Soeharto's prospects of winning the massive financial support which he needed from the Western world continued to improve. One of his first problems was the heavy external debt inherited from guided democracy. At the end of 1965 this amounted to US$2.36 billion, of which 59.5 per cent was owed to Communist states (42 per cent to the Soviet Union), 24.9 per cent to Western nations, and the rest to other noncommunist sources. Japan was the largest creditor outside the Communist world (9.8 per cent of the total debt). Although this was a very large debt, it should be noted that it was much less than that subsequently acquired by the new order. Indonesia's noncommunist creditors agreed to act in concert and eventually formed themselves into IGGI (Inter-Governmental Group on Indonesia) in 1967. From July 1966 they began making arrangements to reschedule Indonesia's debt repayments. In October Adam Malik, who had long had cordial relations with the Soviets, also arranged the rescheduling of some of the debts owed to them.

In return for Western economic assistance, the Soeharto government adopted reform measures of the kind consistently favoured by the World Bank and IMF, measures which dominated economic policy into the 1970s. Open-door *laissez-faire* strategies to encourage foreign investment and maximum economic growth were coupled with strict internal economic controls. Crucial to these new policies was a group of academically trained Indonesian economists, technocrats loosely known as the 'Berkeley mafia' after the university from which several held degrees. Because they could speak the language of international economics, they gave the Soeharto government credibility with Western nations and exercised an influence over the military-dominated regime which was sometimes challenged by those who favoured greater economic nationalism, but which was to remain central to new order policy-making.

Indonesia's September 1966 report to its noncommunist creditors revealed the scale of economic disaster facing the new regime. Annual inflation was calculated to be in excess of 600 per cent, the money supply was over 800 times the 1955 figure and the government deficit was over 780 times that of 1961 (and 1.8 times the total money supply). In consultation with the IMF, the technocrats introduced budgetary restraints, high interest rates, stricter export controls and anti-corruption measures beginning in October. Confiscated British and American firms were soon restored to their owners and in February 1967 a new investment law was promulgated to encourage foreign investment.

But the technocrats were in fact in control of only a part of the economy. Drastic cuts in official military budgets were of little concern to the army, for by now its own private economy was well developed. In fact, the army's official budget probably covered no more than one-half of its expenditure, the rest coming from army-run businesses. Its oil enterprise was of particular importance. Since 1963 Pĕrmina had had profit-sharing agreements with Caltex and Stanvac, and at the end of 1965 Shell sold out altogether to Pĕrmina. Another major earner was Bulog (Badan Urusan Logistik, Logistics Affairs Board) set up in 1966 primarily to deal in rice.

Business empires run by Chaerul Saleh and other leaders of the old order were taken over by the new order elite, both the military and their bureaucratic supporters. Ever closer connections were forged between the new Indonesian leadership and the world of private capital. The elite found it useful to work with Chinese businessmen, who were attractive because of their access to capital, business acumen and political impotence. Such entrepreneurs were called *cukong* (from Hokkien words for boss and grandfather, meaning in Indonesian a financial backer). Over the years, the wealth which flowed into the hands of the Indonesian elite would create a new upper class, the primary social foundation of the Soeharto regime, while some *cukong* families would grow fabulously rich.

While economic reform was being pursued, domestic political tensions were nearing their final stages. Testimony at several Mahmillub trials implicated Sukarno in the 1965 coup attempt. Subandrio and Omar Dhani were sentenced to death in October and December 1966 respectively (neither sentence had been carried out down to the time of writing). In December 1966 Sudisman was captured; he was sentenced to death in July 1967 and executed in 1968. In January 1967 the highest military officer involved in the coup attempt, Brig. Gen. Supardjo, was found; in March he was sentenced to death. In the latter month Sjam was captured and the new order gained its most useful source on the coup plot; he was reportedly held and pumped for information regularly until finally being executed in 1986. Students, lawyers and judges now began calling for Sukarno also to be put on trial.

In November 1966, Sukarnoist officers in the East Java Brawijaya Division of the army, the East Java police and the navy plotted to kidnap Sukarno during a planned visit to East Java, intending to encourage him to make a stand against Soeharto, but their plans fell through. Sukarno, to his credit, refused to cooperate with a plot which would probably have meant civil war. Soeharto cancelled the visit and began buying off leading Sukarnoist officers with ambassadorships or other lucrative jobs.

Soeharto now took his final steps to victory in domestic politics, believing that it had become possible to dismiss the old President altogether. He appointed new members of parliament (DPR-GR) to replace purged members and then convened the MPRS in March 1967. Amidst rumours that the navy's marine corps (KKO: Korps Komando), the police and the Brawijaya Division would defend Sukarno, and with 80000 troops occupying Jakarta, on 12 March the MPRS stripped Sukarno of all powers and titles and named Soeharto Acting President. Sukarno's various ideological pronouncements were declared no longer to be the ideology of the state, which was reduced to Pancasila alone. Soeharto was authorised to decide whether Sukarno should stand trial, but he never submitted his discredited predecessor to this indignity or ran the risk of thereby mobilising

Sukarno's remaining defenders. The nation's first president retired to *de facto* house arrest and embittered isolation in Bogor, where he remained until his death in June 1970. Soeharto's political dominance was firmly established.

Economic changes were occurring rapidly, with domestic political consequences. Inflation was cut back to about 100 per cent in 1967, still a very high figure but a great improvement over the preceding chaos. The foreign exchange regime was liberalised. From 1966 to the end of 1968 the Rupiah was allowed to float (i.e. devalue) freely. This cut down export smuggling and foreign imports and encouraged foreign aid donors and investors. Naturally overseas entrepreneurs and *cukongs* with access to overseas funds sought the quickest and highest rates of return, leaving less profitable fields for Indonesian (*pribumi*) investors. The government's reliance on high interest rates to restrain inflation put *pribumi* entrepreneurs without access to foreign capital at a great disadvantage. They found themselves pushed out even of businesses which had traditionally been theirs (e.g. textiles, beverages, *kretek* cigarettes) by Chinese and foreign competitors with access to cheaper money. So *pribumi* businessmen, who tended to be anticommunist and linked to devout Islamic circles and had thus formed part of the initial coalition supporting Soeharto, began to wonder whether their interests would be served by the new order. Meanwhile unemployment and underemployment continued to grow, and knowledge spread of the corrupt use of power for personal gain by the regime's leaders. By 1967 even the students – the staunchest allies of the new order in 1965–6 – began to demonstrate against it, demanding lower prices and an end to corruption.

A new and explosive religious issue was also emerging. Throughout the twentieth century, Islamic reformers had pressed for greater adherence to the tenets of their faith. After 1965, Islam's increased assertiveness was evident in the role of Islamic activists in the 1965–6 killings, in the call to prayer being broadcast at full volume over public address systems and in repeated admonitions to believers to perfect their faith. Very many Muslims responded positively to this atmosphere of heightened religious awareness. But some Indonesians found Islam in its new, more dynamic style to be unattractive. Some even turned their backs upon Islam and embraced other faiths. Many Javanese *abangan* (nominal Muslims) turned to Kĕbatinan (literally, inwardness), a term used for indigenous mystical sects with hybrid theologies. Even more remarkably, throughout Indonesia, but especially in the cities of East and Central Java, there began an unexpected and unprecedented wave of conversion to Christianity. Conversions to Hinduism and Buddhism also took place, although on a smaller scale. Such conversions were partly for religious and partly for political reasons. In the wake of the events of 1965, not to be an adherent of an officially recognised world religion was to run the risk of being labelled an atheist and hence a Communist. Some Indonesians who were unwilling to call themselves Muslims therefore proclaimed themselves Christians, sometimes without having had prior contact with Christian proselytisers. Anecdotal evidence suggested that this was particularly true of former PKI villages, but Christianity's less onerous ritual obligations and food laws doubtlessly played a role alongside political considerations. Christian missionaries were, of course, present, and the proselytisation practices of some churches, notably the Jehovah's Witnesses and Seventh Day Adventists, attracted much criticism from the Islamic side.

The 1971 census revealed major religious changes since the last figures of the 1930s, but perhaps they were less dramatic than some Muslims had feared. In 1933, 2.8 per cent of all Indonesians were Christians (under 2 million people) whereas in 1971 the figure had grown to 7.5 per cent (nearly 9 million people). In Central and East Java the scale of increase was more dramatic. In the 1930s 0.1 per cent of the population in Central Java and 0.4 per cent in East Java were Christians; in 1971 these figures were 2.1 per cent and 1.7 per cent respectively. These are of course small percentages, but the Christians were particularly visible because of the prominence of Christian schools and because conversions were heaviest in urban areas. In 1971 Christians constituted 11.6 per cent of the population of urban Central Java as a whole; they were 14.9 per cent in Yogyakarta and 15.1 per cent in both Surakarta and Magĕlang. Some of these new Christians were Chinese, but most were Javanese.

Indonesia had always been a multireligious society, but in the past different religious communities had for the most part been based in different geographical areas or ethnic groups. Now adherents of different religions lived in proximity to one another, indeed were often from the same ethnic groups or even family. In the wake of a period of extraordinary political conflict and violence, it is not surprising that Indonesia's transition to this new form of multireligiosity was not entirely smooth. In April 1967 a series of violent incidents began when Muslims attacked Christian churches in Aceh. In October very serious anti-Christian riots broke out in Makasar (Ujungpandang) and religious violence was reported from Java and Sumatra.

In October 1967 Soeharto denounced religious violence and set in motion a governmental effort to stop it. The government convened an inter-religious dialogue in Jakarta in November, where Christian and Islamic leaders came to the conclusion that there was no basis for compromise. Since both Islam and Christianity are missionary religions, anxious to bring their universal message to all people, to expect either to restrain its mission work is to ask it to be untrue to itself. But Christian and Muslim leaders did at least recognise in each other a genuine devotion to God. Younger Christian and Islamic leaders were more inclined to mutual respect than their elders, perhaps because many had worked together in the political tumult of 1965–6 and because younger Muslim leaders lacked their elders' personal experience of a lifetime of frequent frustration. Furthermore, both sides had acquired a more sober view of the dangers of religious violence, although they did not always seem able or willing to reduce bitterness between their followers. Yet religious violence did decline after 1967, not least because the military made it clear that it was prepared to use force to stop it.

Political party conflicts of the Sukarno era still had resonances in the late 1960s, but the political framework was changing rapidly. In April-May 1967 an attempt was made by Modernist Islamic politicians to revive Masyumi under a different name. Soeharto refused to approve this, for to him the urban Modernist politicians were tainted with the marks of both rebellion and fanaticism. In May 1967 the Dewan Da'wah Islamiyah Indonesia (Indonesian Islamic Mission Council) was founded to promote the further Islamisation of Indonesian society, with Natsir as its chairman. The new order military elite saw this as a proper role for Natsir and for religion; politics was regarded as proper for neither. Leading Muslims suspected the government of a secret anti-Islamic bias. They noted that some senior military men were Christians and that the personal religion of others seemed to be close to Kěbatinan.

PNI and NU came under further pressure from the government in 1967, as did parts of the military. Many military men wanted to be rid of everything connected with the old order, and therefore still hoped to destroy PNI. But Soeharto preferred to preserve it in a weakened, controlled form. Sitor Situmorang, PNI's leading intellectual and former ally of Lekra, was imprisoned in 1967 and held without trial until 1975. Regional commanders in Sumatra, East Java and South Sulawesi subjected PNI to temporary bans and purge orders, but the party survived because Soeharto wished it to. The NU leadership was also subject to adverse criticism, but had less need of Soeharto's protection, for it had a stronger social base in the countryside. Many of the new order elite believed in any case that NU was unlikely to cause trouble so long as its religious interests were not threatened. An attachment to Sukarno remained in parts of the police, navy, air force and army, especially in the Brawijaya Division. In the course of 1967, further purges removed many of these Sukarnoist elements without significant resistance, except for some shooting in June between army and marine units in East Java.

In August 1967 Soeharto abolished the four separate armed forces ministries and placed all services directly under his authority. The Sukarno style of encouraging inter-service rivalry was thus replaced by Soeharto's policy of centralisation. This more centralised military was also taking over regional government. By 1968, 17 out of 25 provinces were governed by military officers and by 1969 over half of all Bupatis and mayors were military men. Centralisation of power within a tight circle of military men around Soeharto was now well advanced.

In March 1968 the Provisional People's Consultative Assembly (MPRS) convened again and elected Soeharto to the Presidency for a five-year term, confirming the success and durability of his control. He installed a new cabinet in June in which civilian technocrats received more places and the military fewer. Sumitro Djojohadikusumo was made Minister of Trade, over the objections of those who disapproved of him for having joined PRRI. The technocrats' influence over policy was considerable, for Indonesia still desperately needed the economic support of noncommunist donors, whose language and policies the technocrats shared. In a later cabinet of 1971 there were ten university professors, the most prominent being the economist Widjojo Nitisastro (b. 1927). But strategy decisions remained firmly in the hands of the inner military circle.

Security problems still arose for the new regime but they were few and quickly dealt with. In 1967 South Blora (north-central Java) witnessed a revival of the Saminist movement led in the early years of the twentieth century by Surantiko Samin. A local holy man named Mbah (grandfather) Suro (1921–67) attracted a large peasant following. The government regarded this as a revival of Communism and sent in troops who killed Mbah Suro and an unknown number of his followers. A more unequivocally Communist underground organisation was discovered in South Blitar (southern East Java) in mid-1968. Surviving PKI leaders had gone into hiding there to prepare for guerilla resistance. They lost control of their *abangan* peasant supporters, who began revenge killings of NU leaders. This revealed the existence of this PKI remnant. In July and August the organisation was wiped out, most of its leaders and 800 followers being taken prisoner. Interrogation of these people led to further purges of several hundred military men with clandestine PKI connections. In West Kalimantan Indonesian and Chinese Communists continued to exist in jungle hideouts but were of little consequence. Joint Malaysian-Indonesian security operations were later mounted against them along the Sarawak border. By the end of 1968 there was no longer a credible PKI threat. Nonetheless the regime's principal security organisation Kopkamtib continued its surveillance of the citizenry, hampered only by the general inefficiency of the nation's administrative apparatus.

In February 1968 a Modernist Islamic political party called Parmusi (Partai Muslimin Indonesia, Indonesian Muslims' Party) was established. Along with NU, in the MPRS session of 1968 Parmusi urged that the Jakarta Charter should be recognised as having legal force, thereby giving constitutional authority to the implementation of Islamic law among Muslims; this proposal was defeated. Then in November Parmusi elected a new leadership which included former Masyumi figures, although not Natsir or Sjafruddin. The government refused to approve this new leadership and thus left Parmusi in something like suspended animation for two years. The government did, however, permit the revival of some formerly banned anticommunist newspapers in 1968, including Mochtar Lubis' *Indonesia Raya* ('Greater Indonesia'), the former Masyumi and now Parmusi paper *Abadi* ('Eternal') and the former PSI paper *Pedoman* ('Guide').

Just as internal politics was now well under control, so foreign policy directions were fixed, with a new Association of South East Asian Nations (ASEAN) as the regional cornerstone. ASEAN was formed in August 1967 by Indonesia, Malaysia, Singapore, Thailand and the Philippines to promote economic and cultural co-operation among the anticommunist states of the region. Down to the mid-1970s, however, ASEAN could find little to do. Its main function was symbolic: it did not exist to promote various projects, rather its meetings and projects existed to justify ASEAN, the central purpose of which was to symbolise regional cooperation and in particular the rehabilitation of Indonesia as a constructive regional actor, free of the Sukarno era's flamboyant and aggressive stances. Adam Malik and the new order elite also hoped that regional cooperation might act as a counterbalance to the otherwise overwhelming influence of Japan and the United States over Indonesia.

Economic structures were also well established by 1968. Oil was the central focus of government economic policy, although other capital-intensive and high-technology extractive industries in minerals and timber were also expanding rapidly. Off-shore drilling began in 1966 and was intense by 1968. In August 1968 the army's role was strengthened by the merger of its oil companies Pĕrtamin (est. 1961) and Pĕrmina into Pĕrtamina (Pĕrusahaan Pĕrtambangan Minyak dan Gas Bumi Nĕgara, State Oil and Natural Gas Mining Enterprise). This was run as a personal empire by Ibnu Sutowo, who soon gained an international reputation for aggressive and visionary management, a reputation which was to be shattered in 1975. Pĕrtamina did little drilling itself; instead it (not the government) had production-sharing agreements with the foreign companies. Oil production grew at about 15 per cent per annum in 1968–9 and nearly 20 per cent in 1970. Meanwhile the technocrats' battle against inflation continued to make progress. Inflation was reduced to about 85 per cent in 1968, but there were pointed questions being asked about when the population at large would see the prosperity which the new order promised.

The year 1969 can be said to mark the end of the transition from the old to the new order. The battle against inflation was at last won, price rises being held to about 10 per cent for the year. On 1 April the government symbolised the turning of its primary attention from economic stabilisation to development with the inauguration of its first Five-Year Development Plan (Rĕpĕlita I: Rĕncana Pĕmbangunan Lima Tahun) for 1969–74. This gave priority to the areas where government investment was expected to produce the highest returns: agriculture, economic infrastructure, expansion of exports and import-substitution industries. Three-quarters of the expenditure under Rĕpĕlita I was to be financed by foreign loans, which grew to US$877 million for its last year. By 1972 the new foreign debts acquired since 1966 would already exceed those inherited from Sukarno's years. In 1969 Indonesia's rehabilitation within the anticommunist world was symbolised by visits from several heads of state, including the American President Richard Nixon. Following Nixon's visit, US military aid to Jakarta increased dramatically, reaching US$40 million in 1976.

Indonesia also settled an old issue in 1969 by the incorporation of Irian as its twenty-sixth province. This followed an 'act of free choice' as called for in the UN-sponsored transfer arrangements, the outcome of which was never in doubt. All of the 1022 Irianese leaders consulted voted for incorporation. With Irian, Jakarta acquired considerable cultural and administrative challenges, as well as a nagging security problem in the form of a resistance movement called Organisasi Papua Mĕrdeka (Free Papua Organisation).

The government was now preparing a final solution to one of its lingering administrative and security headaches, the problem of political prisoners. Throughout the archipelago, jails were bursting with people held without trial since 1965. The numbers of such prisoners is not known with confidence. As late as 1977, Amnesty International estimated that between 55000 and 100000 Indonesians were political prisoners. These people were divided into three categories reflecting alleged proximity to the coup attempt of 1965. Category A was for those directly involved, category B for those indirectly involved (i.e. members of PKI or its mass organisations or sympathisers), category C for those whose connection was more remote than category B (the distinction was often arbitrary). In July 1969 the government announced that it had opened a penal colony for the large number of category B prisoners on Buru island in South Maluku. A release program was announced for category C prisoners, but Islamic and other anti-PKI groups made it clear that they were not prepared to accept these prisoners back into society. It seems, however, that category C prisoners were released quietly over subsequent years. For category B the future was to be permanent imprisonment, either on Buru or in prisons elsewhere. By 1977 there were about 14000 prisoners on Buru. Among them was Pramudya Ananta Tur, who wrote there his tetralogy of historical novels *Bumi manusia, Anak semua bangsa, Jejak langkah* and *Rumah kaca* ('This earth of mankind', 'Child of all nations', 'Footsteps' and 'Glass house') which would win him renewed international recognition in the 1980s. Category A prisoners alone were brought to trial, very slowly, always ending in conviction and almost always in a death sentence.

The final stages in Soeharto's reorganisation of the military also took place in 1969–70. The commanders of the four services were replaced by chiefs of staff and the authority of the Department of Defence and Security (Hankam: Departĕmen

Pĕrtahanan – Kĕamanan) over regional commanders and all the armed forces was increased. Soeharto loyalists dominated the army while the new navy chief of staff was Soeharto's old colleague Rear Admiral Sudomo (b. 1926). A final purge of the navy followed. Some army officers were also arrested in 1970 for alleged links with PKI, a few among them being quite senior. In October 1970 Soeharto lowered the retirement age for officers to 48 and announced that eighty-six generals would be retired over the next two years. From this time on, the military was so effectively centralised that factional disputes were virtually invisible to outside observers.

The government was ready for the postponed elections. In November 1969 parliament (DPR-GR) passed an election law which fixed the membership of a new parliament (DPR) at 360 elected plus 100 appointed members. The whole of this parliament would be incorporated within a 920-seat People's Consultative Assembly (MPR) along with 207 military and functional group members appointed by the President, 131 members elected by provincial parliaments, 112 selected according to party strengths in the election, and 10 appointed from the less successful parties. Thus, the government would directly appoint 22 per cent of the parliament and 33 per cent of the Assembly, sufficient to block constitutional amendment. In February 1970 the government announced that all government employees must observe 'monoloyalty' towards the government. They were not allowed to join any political party and were pressured to join Golkar (Sekber Golkar, Joint Secretariat of Functional Groups), the body established by the army in 1964 to coordinate army-civilian cooperative bodies. At a stroke the government thus undercut whatever remained of PNI's traditional constituency within the bureaucracy. The new order was about to turn Golkar into its vehicle for establishing a military-bureaucratic condominium over the nation.

The government was not certain that it had sufficiently weakened the political parties. So Ali Murtopo interfered in PNI leadership issues and Soeharto imposed a politically reliable chairman upon Parmusi in the person of H. Mohamed Safaat Mintaredja (b. 1921). NU alone among the 'big four' parties of the last national election, that of 1955, still existed in its original state.

There were some doubts about the likely outcome of the election, for public criticism of the regime and particularly of the President's family was increasing. Although many people found Soeharto himself admirable, his wife Siti Hartinah Soeharto (b. 1923), better known as Ibu (mother) Tien, was widely believed to benefit financially from her husband's position. She chaired several foundations with extensive business investments. The President's brother Probosutedjo (b. 1930) and foster-brother Sudwikatmono (b. 1934) were also pursuing business careers the profitability of which was widely thought to owe less to their entrepreneurial talents than to Presidential influence. Student demonstrations against price rises and corruption now led the students into direct opposition to the regime. In June 1970 an anti-corruption team under former Prime Minister Wilopo, with Hatta as a member, reported that there was corruption everywhere. The team then dissolved and nothing of significance was done.

Ali Murtopo, Amir Mahmud (Minister of Home Affairs and hence in charge of the bureaucracy) and Kopkamtib were given the task of ensuring the victory of Golkar in the elections. Kopkamtib screened candidates for all parties and disqualified about 20 per cent for political unreliability. Military officers and officials down to village level were given quotas of votes to deliver. Intimidation was widespread, but it should not be thought that this alone explained the election outcome. Electors who saw the contest as one between Islamic power and the 'secular' (or anti-Islamic), developmental outlook of the government and who distrusted Islam would have supported Golkar willingly; it thereby, ironically, captured much of the former PKI and PNI electoral base.

The scale of Golkar's victory in the July 1971 elections surprised even the government. It captured 62.8 per cent of the votes, winning 236 (65.6 per cent) of the 360 contested seats. PNI won only 6.9 per cent of the votes, its best result being 19.5 per cent in Central Java. NU did the best of the non-governmental parties with 18.7 per cent overall and 35.2 per cent in its heartland of East Java (but even there Golkar beat it with 54.9 per cent). Golkar won absolute majorities in every province except Aceh, Jakarta and Maluku, where it won pluralities. When the appointed seats were added to the elected seats, the government controlled 73 per cent of parliament, the Islamic parties 20.4 per cent and the non-Islamic parties 6.5 per cent. The Assembly would have a government majority of about 82 per cent.

The government did not see this election victory as a sign that political controls could be relaxed, but rather as a justification for completing the destruction of the old political parties. The government pressured them to fuse into two groups. In January 1973 PPP (Partai Pěrsatuan Pěmbangunan, United Development Party) was created out of the Islamic parties, of which NU and Parmusi were the most important. From the non-Islamic parties (Murba, PNI, Catholic, Christian and the minor IPKI) was created PDI (Partai Demokrasi Indonesia, Indonesian Democracy Party). Except at election time, these parties were not to have organisations below Kabupaten level, a restriction which did not apply to Golkar since it was permanently represented by the bureaucracy and, in any case, pretended not to be a political party. From this point onwards the political parties were rarely more than a minor nuisance to the government.

In March 1973 the newly formed People's Consultative Assembly (MPR) met and re-elected Soeharto to a second five-year term. The office of Vice-President which exists under the 1945 constitution was now filled (1973–8) for the first time since Hatta's Vice-Presidency by Sultan Hamengkubuwana IX. He was a man much admired by Soeharto and the Indonesian public. Many hoped that he might restrain some of the less acceptable features of the regime. But in the end, his presence seems to have brought few changes. The only serious trouble in the 1973 Assembly concerned Kěbatinan. Since 1957 Kěbatinan groups had sought recognition as the equal of other religions, which would give them access to Ministry of Religion funds and shield them from persecution. Islamic groups feared that the Soeharto government would finally approve this. But in the end the government recognised Kěbatinan only as 'belief' (kěpěrcayaan), which the 1945 constitution appears to recognise alongside religion (agama), officially regarding it as, in effect, a cultural phenomenon but not a religion, without a section in the Ministry of Religion.

Yet the governing elite was not as firmly in power as it and its external supporters believed and hoped. By the early 1970s the extravagant wealth of some of the elite and of their Chinese cukong allies produced responses ranging from widespread grumbling and black political humour at one extreme to student demonstrations and anti-Chinese violence at the other. Heightened Islamic moral sensibilities and the anger of *pribumi* entrepreneurs from devout Islamic circles coalesced to make religious questions a potential flashpoint. Ali Murtopo was regarded as one of the regime's main anti-Islamic figures. When he supported the idea of a new marriage law which would allow Muslim women to marry non-Muslims and would recognise civil marriages, devout Muslims were furious. In September 1973 Islamic students invaded a sitting of parliament and obliged the government to withdraw the proposal. A revised marriage law was subsequently passed in December, Ali Murtopo and the government having accepted that compromise was unavoidable. The overthrow of the Thai government of Thanom Kittikachorn by student demonstrations in October 1973 both emboldened critics of the Soeharto government and inclined its supporters to contemplate moderation and compromise.

Factional competition within the regime became entangled in public issues, especially regarding the role of Japan. Japan took 53 per cent of Indonesia's exports by 1973 (71 per cent of its oil) and supplied 29 per cent of its imports. Moreover the Japanese were more evident because of their increasing investment in manufacturing industries in Java itself, which put still greater pressure on indigenous entrepreneurs. The Japanese were widely perceived as unprincipled exploiters of the Indonesian economy, aided by people close to the Presidential palace. There was criticism particularly of Ali Murtopo and of another of Soeharto's closest colleagues, Maj. Gen. Sudjono Humardani (1919–86), who was reputed to be the President's mystical guide as well as a broker for foreign (especially Japanese) investors seeking governmental favour. They found themselves facing the head of Kopkamtib Gen. Soemitro (b. 1927), who presented himself as a man open to dialogue with the regime's critics.

A visit by the Japanese Prime Minister Tanaka Kakuei to Jakarta in January 1974 precipitated the capital's worst riots since the fall of Sukarno, an episode known as Malari (from Malapětaka Januari, January Disaster). Students and poor urban youths burned about 800 cars and 100 buildings, and looted many shops selling Japanese goods. At one point an estimated crowd of 20000 surrounded Tanaka's guest house while 5000 surrounded the Presidential palace. Not until the second day of this episode did Kopkamtib step in, a delay which increased suspicions that Soemitro favoured the demonstrators or sought to use the crisis to his political advantage.

The regime clamped down harshly. By 17 January the rioting was suppressed. For the first time, instead of saying that Communists were responsible for the trouble, the government blamed former Masyumi and PSI activists. Kopkamtib arrested 770 people, almost all of whom were released by May 1976. Three student leaders were, however, sentenced to prison terms upon doubtful evidence. Among those arrested was Mochtar Lubis. His newspaper *Indonesia Raya* was closed down, as were *Pedoman, Abadi* and eight other publications. Soemitro was removed from Kopkamtib, which Soeharto again took charge of, with Admiral Sudomo as its chief of staff.

The regime was now operating within a rapidly changing world economic environment, which would make it less dependent upon outside funds and advice. The Arab-Israeli war of October 1973 produced a revolution in oil prices. Indonesia's export price for crude oil rose from US$2.96 per barrel in April 1973 to $12.60 in July 1974. In 1966 oil represented 30 per cent of the value of Indonesia's exports but in 1974 it represented 74 per cent. Under the second Five-Year Development

Plan (Rěpělita II, 1974–9), 72 per cent of expenditure could be financed out of domestic rather than foreign sources. This vast rise in oil prices did not make Indonesia a rich nation. It was by far the most populous and poorest member of the Organisation of Petroleum Exporting Countries (OPEC), with a per capita GNP less than half that of the next poorest member, Nigeria. But economic policy could now swing towards an economic nationalism which was never far below the surface of the regime. The influence of IMF and IGGI policies, and of the Indonesian technocrats who supported them, was thus somewhat weakened for a time.

The government's economic plans depended upon having control of oil revenues, which meant gaining control of Pěrtamina. Under Ibnu Sutowo's directorship, Pěrtamina had grown to be one of the largest corporations in the world. It directly produced 28.2 per cent of the nation's oil at the end of 1973 and had production-sharing agreements with Caltex (producing 67.8 per cent of the oil) and Stanvac (producing 3.6 per cent). It owned Indonesia's seven oil refineries, oil terminals, 116 tankers, 102 other vessels and an airline, was investing in cement, fertiliser, liquid natural gas, steel, hospitals, real estate, a rice estate and telecommunications, and built the Presidential executive office building (Bina Graha) in Jakarta. It was almost entirely free of government control and stood shakily on a foundation of excessive debt, chaotic management and corruption.

In 1973, the government tightened up the conditions under which Ibnu Sutowo could borrow money overseas. In February 1975 Pěrtamina found itself unable to repay loans from American and Canadian banks. The ensuing revelations did much to discredit elite circles in the eyes of both Indonesians and foreigners. The government took over the running of Pěrtamina and undertook to meet its debts, which were subsequently said to exceed US$10 billion. Pěrtamina was under government control, but at a heavy price.

Just as the world economic climate was rapidly changing, so was the international political stage. Nixon's trip to China in 1972 signalled the beginnings of Chinese-American détente, while Soviet-American détente had been a topic of discussion for some time. The 1973 Paris Accord began the American withdrawal from Vietnam, following which US military aid to Indonesia increased. In 1975 the warfare in Indochina ended in Communist victories. The Indonesian military elite was now somewhat uncertain of the external political context and concerned about potential transformations closer to home.

The military's worst fears were confirmed when the sleepy colonial backwater of Portuguese (East) Timor produced a major crisis. The 1974 revolution in Portugal signalled the end of Portugal's decrepit colonial empire. Three political parties sprang up in East Timor. Fretilin (Frente Revolucionária Timor Leste Independente, Revolutionary Front of Independent East Timor) was radical and sought immediate independence. UDT (União Democrática Timorense, Timorese Democratic Union) desired gradual independence. Apodeti (Associação Popular Democrática Timorense, Timorese Popular Democratic Association), the smallest of the three, favoured incorporation within Indonesia. By mid-1975 Fretilin appeared to be gaining the upper hand. Then in August 1975 civil war broke out, as UDT attempted a coup which Fretilin resisted with the support of the local Portuguese military.

Jakarta had no intention of tolerating an independent, and certainly not a leftist, state within its own archipelago, but how far it was prepared to go to prevent this was not clear until Indonesia invaded East Timor on 7 December 1975. Its troops had so little training or experience in anything but internal security operations against civilians that they appear to have performed badly. The government denied reports of torture, rape and looting by its soldiers, who were said to have made Chinese a particular target. Five Australian journalists were killed during the invasion, but Jakarta denied responsibility for their deaths. Some estimates put civilian casualties at 60000, which would be 10 per cent of the population. By April 1976 some 30000–35000 Indonesian troops were there, and about 500 had died in the fighting. Fretilin was driven into the hills, whence it maintained desultory resistance. In July 1976 East Timor was incorporated as Indonesia's twenty-seventh province. Indonesia's Western supporters and neighbours gave greater priority to their relations with Jakarta than to the rights of East Timorese, and accepted the *de facto* conquest of East Timor. In particular, the United States had no intention of challenging Indonesian control of the territory, thereby rendering meaningless the United Nations' continuing recognition of Portugal as the legitimate administering power there. In 1976 IGGI increased its aid, pledging US$990 million in project aid and over $1 billion in supplementary credits. Major investments were promised by Japan, the Soviet Union and Shell.

The conquest of East Timor rounded off Indonesia's territorial boundaries but also gave Jakarta on-going and serious problems. Integrating the East Timorese, with their very different historical experience, into the Indonesian nation presented major cultural problems, developing their territory presented economic and administrative difficulties and their continuing distaste for Indonesian rule presented political and security challenges. Fretilin resistance meant low-level but nonetheless persistent problems for the military. From the initial conquest on, Amnesty International and other human rights organisations condemned the brutalities which accompanied Jakarta's rule over East Timor, but Indonesia refused to bend to such international humanitarian criticisms and did its best to prevent outside scrutiny.

By the beginning of 1976 the new order had achieved a stable, definable form. Here was a regime resting upon the tight centralisation of power in the hands of President Soeharto and a circle of loyal followers. Political expression was repressed by physical violence, arrests and the banning of publications, or by subtle threats of such action. Parties were rendered impotent to change the political order but played their part in the carefully controlled election process which lent the government legitimacy. The military took the main decisions, but shared economic decision-making with technocrats and the administration of the country with the bureaucracy. Golkar was the organisational vehicle for this military-bureaucratic dominion. Economic policy was fixed in favour of capitalist-style development and produced impressive results. The regime's promise to employ development to promote the health and welfare of its citizenry was, however, still little more than a promise. On the other hand, the evidence of the governing elite employing economic development to enrich itself and its business partners was clear. Oil was the crucial element in all economic calculations; the revolution in oil prices after 1973 would make significant new developments possible, as will be seen in the following chapter. Foreign political and economic policy rested on cooperation with Western powers but Indonesia refused, as it had since independence, to join formal military pacts. ASEAN was the regional cornerstone of foreign policy. The nation's boundaries were fixed by the inclusion of Irian and East Timor, both of which regions brought major problems for the regime. Society was changing; it was becoming more multireligious yet *aliran* seemed to be of decreasing significance because of the demise of the political parties which had previously hardened *aliran* boundaries. Major transformation had taken place since the mid-1960s. It is worth noting that this had occurred without any serious challenge to the unity of the nation, but also that it had occurred at unprecedented cost: not since the Dutch colonial conquest had so many Indonesians died or lost their freedom in the name of creating a new political order.

21   The New Order since 1975

Many of the patterns established in the first ten years of the new order government of President Soeharto, as described in the previous chapter, persisted from 1975 to the early 1990s. Certainly there were changes, some of which may ultimately prove to have been significant, but at the time of writing this chapter these developments were too close to judge confidently their longer-term significance. This final chapter therefore merely surveys briefly some of the developments since 1975 which may prove to have been important.

There is no doubt that the revolution in oil prices which followed the Arab-Israeli war in 1973 transformed Indonesia's economic circumstances for about a decade. As was pointed out in the previous chapter, from 1973 to 1974 the price for Indonesia's crude oil more than quadrupled to US$12.60 per barrel, by which time oil represented 74 per cent of the value of the nation's exports. By 1983, the price set by OPEC was $34.50 per barrel. This meant that the majority of expenditures under the second and third five-year development plans (Rĕpĕlita II, 1974–9; III 1979–84) could be financed from domestic sources.

Until international oil prices collapsed again in the 1980s, the new order had resources with which to do two things. Firstly, it could respond to domestic dissatisfaction about the cost of its previous open-door economic policies, especially to indigenous (*pribumi*) entrepreneurs, for it could afford greater economic nationalism. The government began to restrict opportunities for foreign investors and to encourage the development of a domestic industrial base. Particularly the steel, natural gas, oil refining and aluminium industries were developed. The state also encouraged smaller-scale *pribumi* enterprise. Thus it responded to some of the protest described in the preceding chapter, which had emanated from important elements of that coalition which had brought the new order to power in 1965–6: students, indigenous businessmen, urban consumers and devout Muslims.

Secondly, the government could fulfil its promise to improve the welfare of the Indonesian masses, a promise upon which much of its claims to legitimacy rested. Its achievements in agriculture, education and other welfare areas were impressive, especially when compared to the record of the Dutch colonial regime. Indeed, the average welfare of Indonesians may well have reached the most promising levels since the eighteenth century during this period, although it would be difficult to muster hard evidence to prove that this was so. Investment in irrigation, new seed strains, fertilisers and pesticides produced dramatic increases in the production of rice and other foodstuffs. In the 1960s average rice availability was calculated to be less than 100 kg per capita but by 1983 the figure was 146 kg. Rice imports were reduced to virtually nil and Jakarta announced that it had achieved self-sufficiency in rice. Pessimistic predictions that Indonesia must face a food catastrophe now gave way to cautious optimism. This remarkable achievement was a result of technological advances, government policies and the initiative and hard work of ordinary Indonesian farmers.

In education there were rapid advances. Over 100 000 new schools were built, especially in rural areas, and over 500 000 new teachers employed. By 1984 it was reported that 97 per cent of seven- to twelve-year-olds were attending school, as opposed to 57 per cent in 1973. Literacy rates continued to grow. The 1980 census reported 80.4 per cent of males and 63.6 per cent of females to be literate. The benefits of public education in Bahasa Indonesia were seen not only in these literacy figures, but also in the growth of the proportion of the population able to use the national language, from 40.8 per cent in 1971 to 61.4 per cent in 1980. This reflected also, of course, the impact of newspapers and magazines and, perhaps even more, of radio and television.

Other welfare measures also indicated great strides forward, but when results were compared with those in other Asian nations, Indonesia's relative poverty remained clear. The 1971 census had reported one doctor for every 20.9 thousand inhabitants throughout the archipelago. The 1980 census showed a population of 147.3 million, with 12 931 doctors available: one for every 11.4 thousand. The improvement was thus dramatic, but the distribution of medical services remained uneven and the absolute levels far from satisfactory. According to United Nations statistics, among other Asian nations only Afghanistan, Democratic Kampuchea, Laos, the Maldives and Nepal had a lower provision of physicians per capita. At about this time, peninsular Malaysia had one doctor for every 4.2 thousand inhabitants, Thailand one for every 6.9 thousand and the Philippines one for every 6.7 thousand. Similarly, the provision of hospital beds in Indonesia (1:1787 inhabitants in 1979) was one of the worst in Asia, slightly worse than Pakistan (1:1737 in 1982) and only better than Afghanistan, Bangladesh, the Maldives and Nepal.

An increase in annual per capita income to nearly US$600 led the World Bank to reclassify Indonesia as a middle-income country in 1982, but this and the improvement in various welfare measures did not, of course, mean that the awesome race with population and poverty was won in Indonesia. The family planning program had an impressive record of success there, but at the time of writing this chapter scholars nevertheless estimated that the nation's population would grow from the 147.3 million recorded in 1980 to something like 220 million in the year 2000. And very many Indonesians still lived in poverty, with little hope that the lives of their children would be better. Some indicators suggested that the proportion of the population living in poverty in rural Java, for example, was growing in the 1980s.

Political patterns remained generally what they had become by 1975, with President Soeharto skilfully directing a highly centralised power structure. Popular support for the regime was sought, but not popular political mobilisation or involvement. Golkar remained the principal political expression of the structure of the state. It won massive victories in the general elections of May 1977 (62.1 per cent), May 1982 (64 per cent), April 1987 (73 per cent) and June 1992 (68 per cent), which reflected a significant degree of acceptance of the government and its policies, or at least a lack of faith in any alternatives. After the 1987 election the new parliament (DPR) consisted of 500 seats (400 elected and 100 appointed); this was incorporated in an Assembly (MPR) of 1000 seats, the other 500 members of which were appointed partly on the basis of general election results. In the wake of these elections, the MPR reelected Soeharto to the Presidency unopposed every five years. By 1990 he had been President of Indonesia longer than Sukarno.

Soeharto's government continued to give emphasis to security issues and ideological orthodoxy. The Communist victories in Indochina in 1975 led to increased concerns about regional security and greater emphasis on ASEAN as a means of coordinating the foreign policies of its members. In 1976 for the first time the ASEAN heads of state met in Bali and agreed to establish a permanent secretariat in Jakarta. Bilateral military cooperation between ASEAN members also developed further.

Domestically the government sought to forestall ideological threats which it feared both from the left (i.e. Communism) and the right (i.e. militant Islam). It did this partly through compulsory indoctrination in the state philosophy of Pancasila for all citizens. The central figure in arranging this was Roeslan Abdulgani, formerly an active promoter of Sukarno's guided democracy ideology. Beginning in 1978, courses called P4 (Pědoman Pěnghayatan dan Pěngalaman Pancasila; Guidelines for the implementation and experiencing of Pancasila) were introduced into government departments, workplaces, schools and so on. By 1983–5, all political parties and all other organisations were required by law to accept Pancasila as their sole ideological foundation. This clearly caused some difficulty for Islamic bodies, but in 1984 NU adopted a view which allowed it to accept Pancasila as its sole ideology yet to regard itself still as an Islamic body. It then withdrew from formal politics altogether, returning to its 1926 principles as a social and educational organisation. This enabled it to forge closer links with the regime rather than being seen as an opposition political force.

P4 attracted criticism and ridicule from intellectuals. Some critics detected a tendency on the part of President Soeharto to regard himself as the embodiment of Pancasila and to see all criticism of himself as criticism of the very philosophy of the state. The May 1980 'Petition of fifty', signed by fifty prominent citizens, including retired military figures such as Nasution and the former reforming governor of Jakarta Ali Sadikin (b. 1927), reflected such concerns. Repeated episodes of student protest also showed that, for the politically sophisticated and courageous, P4 courses did little to inspire greater affection for the regime. In fact, evidence of the government elite enriching itself from the development process was probably a more powerful factor in shaping popular views of the government.

The regime was also subject to external pressure on human rights grounds. When Jimmy Carter won the American Presidency in the election of November 1976 after a campaign which emphasised human rights issues, Jakarta decided it must do something about the political prisoners still held because of the events of 1965. It first attempted sham release programs, which entailed 'transmigrating' prisoners to what were, in effect, permanent detention and labour camps in the outer islands. By December 1977 the government decided that it must genuinely release those it could not bring to trial. By the end of 1980 all category B and C prisoners appear to have been released. These people often faced severe difficulties in re-entering society. This was not, however, the end of political imprisonment. During 1978 something over 100 people who were suspected of involvement in the events of 1965 but had successfully hidden in the outer islands returned to Java on the presumption that it was now safe to do so, and were promptly arrested. Students and other critics of government were regularly arrested, usually for relatively short periods. Unknown numbers of Islamic activists (certainly several hundred) were arrested and held for longer periods.

In 1984–6 the government faced serious challenges, the surmounting of which demonstrated its durability. In September 1984 serious riots broke out in Jakarta's old port area Tanjung Priok. The riots took an Islamic form but arose fundamentally out of the poverty suffered by people in areas like Tanjung Priok. Up to 28 people were killed. There followed a series of bombings in Jakarta, the first target being the Bank Central Asia owned by Liem Sioe Liong, the principal *cukong* of the new order. More Islamic protests occurred in 1984, including a bombing of the ancient Buddhist temple of Barabudhur (Borobudur) in Central Java. The government also faced a sudden reversal of economic fortunes. Oil prices fell in 1983, requiring a devaluation of the Rupiah by 28 per cent and austerity budgets for the next five-year development plan (Rĕpĕlita IV, 1984–9). The government cracked down. In 1984 three publications were banned for publishing articles about *cukong* connections with the government and the gap between rich and poor. Trials of those involved in the Tanjung Priok riots and the subsequent bombings included some major national figures. Most notably, Lt. Gen. (ret.) Hartono Dharsono, a signatory to the 'Petition of fifty' and former Secretary-General of ASEAN, was sentenced to ten years imprisonment, later reduced to seven years. His trial became a public spectacle in which the regime and its justice apparatus were held up for ridicule and condemnation.

By 1986 the OPEC price of oil had dropped from its 1983 high of $34.50 per barrel to below $10, recovering to $12 in August 1986. Since 60 per cent of government revenue derived from oil, this represented an ongoing regime crisis. The government reacted decisively. The Rupiah was again devalued, this time by 31 per cent, in September 1986. The technocrats resumed much of that influence over government economic policy which had diminished when oil prices were high and again pushed for more open-door policies. Domestic criticism was repressed. In October, one of the nation's most respected newspapers, the Protestant *Sinar Harapan* ('Ray of hope'), was shut down by the government after 23 years of publication. Several PKI prisoners held since 1965–6 were executed, to no other purpose as far as anyone could see than to remind critics of the power of the state. Two thousand oil industry workers were fired for alleged PKI involvement in the 1960s. Pramudya Ananta Tur's new books were banned. When the Australian journalist David Jenkins published an article on the business dealings of the Soeharto circle, Jakarta was outraged and Indonesian-Australian relations were significantly damaged.

The regime thus surmounted the challenges by a combination of repression and careful economic management. By 1988, although oil prices remained around $15 per barrel, modest economic growth was being maintained. This was partly because of a growth in non-oil exports stimulated by the devaluations of the Rupiah. At $11 billion, non-oil exports were over 30 per cent higher than oil exports ($8.3 billion) in 1988. These exports included primary products but also manufactured goods such as plywood, textiles and clothing. Indonesia also acquired very major external debt from the new order's policies. By 1988 the figure stood at $42 billion, the largest in Asia and vastly greater than the debts of the Sukarno era which had once seemed so significant. Servicing this debt required 35.8 per cent of gross export earnings.

The durability of the new order regime was demonstrated also by the succession of a new generation of military men at its top levels. The 'generation of 45', the men whose military careers began in the Revolution, were fast being replaced by men trained in post-revolutionary Indonesia such as L. B. (Benny) Murdani (b. 1932) and Try Sutrisno (b. 1935). Murdani became armed forces commander in 1983 and Minister of Defence in 1988, when Try Sutrisno replaced him as armed forces commander. Yet Soeharto himself remained firmly in control of the regime despite occasional hints of anti-Soeharto factions within the military.

Important social changes accompanied these political, economic and welfare developments, but it is difficult to judge these matters without greater historical hindsight. Two interrelated social transformations nevertheless seem likely to prove significant. In previous chapters there has been discussion of *aliran*, the vertical communal structuring of Indonesian, especially Javanese, society which shaped and was reinforced by the party politicking of the 1950s and 1960s. The Soeharto government itself rode to power on a wave of violence in part determined by *aliran* and was well aware of the potential for conflict which was inherent in such a social structure. In an effort to restrain religious violence generally, to prevent Islamic extremism more particularly and to destroy the influence of the old political parties, the new order followed a policy of undermining *aliran* structures. The destruction of PKI and undermining of PNI quickly left two important *abangan aliran* depoliticised. The fusion of political parties in 1973, government restrictions on their activities between elections and their crushing election defeats at the hands of Golkar effectively destroyed all the political structures which had hardened *aliran* boundaries. While one still heard such terms as *abangan* and *santri* they began to seem like anachronisms in a society which was both less clearly divided on such lines and, at the same time, moving generally towards a deeper understanding of and commitment to Islam, towards a more generally *santri* style.

The decreasing salience of *aliran* might have meant a concomitant rise in class identities, but opinions were divided as to whether this was occurring. Some scholars perceived the emergence of an identifiable and politically significant middle class. This was seen as a group between the ruling elite and the poor, a group of educated and relatively well-to-do urbanites with a more cosmopolitan life style. Certainly such people existed but whether they constituted a self-conscious social class and whether, as some commentators hoped, they would generate demands for a more democratic order, was not yet clear at the time of this writing. Some definitions of who was in this middle class seemed so broad – from senior military men and bureaucrats through *pribumi* entrepreneurs to small traders – that one wondered whether the concept was not too loose to be of value, and the supposed class too amorphous to be significant.

Religious change continued without accompanying social violence of the kind seen in the late 1960s. The 1980 census showed that the proportion of Christians was still growing (to 8.8 per cent), confirming that this was not a short-term phenomenon created by the political crisis of the 1960s. Conversions were still particularly notable in the cities of Central Java, where in Yogyakarta 17.9 per cent of the populace was now Christian, while in Surakarta and Magĕlang the figure reached 18.8 per cent and 17.6 per cent respectively in 1980. Meanwhile a deeper Islamisation of society was also underway among the vast majority (87.1 per cent in 1980) of Indonesians who were Muslim. Islamic *dakwah* activities were visibly successful throughout the nation, confirming the wisdom of those Islamic leaders who had concluded that Islam's political weakness meant that mission work was now the way forward. The new order government did not restrict such activities and, indeed, in many respects supported them.

There were thus several potential sources of change and challenge to the new order's economic, political and social structures, many of them generated by the new order's own past successes. This was true on the boundaries of the state as much as at its centre. Jakarta's integration of Irian Jaya into the nation's provincial structure meant continuing small-scale resistance from OPM guerillas and both local and international protest at the impact of economic development and trans-migration by other Indonesians into that territory. Similarly, in East Timor Frctilin resistance continued and the dominance of non-Timorese Indonesian immigrants fuelled local dissatisfaction. International criticism of Indonesia's conquest of Timor continued – without, however, the support of any foreign government with significant influence over Jakarta – and was given renewed vigour by a massacre of civilians in Dili by Indonesian troops in November 1991. The Indonesian army claimed that nineteen died and a government enquiry put the figure at fifty, but others claimed that it was around 100 or even higher. The regime's educational, welfare and economic successes had perhaps created a middle class which might demand more democratic involvement in the affairs of state, an end to corruption and a more just society. Yet the strongest impression made by the new order of President Soeharto as the 1990s opened was of its durability. There were grounds for thinking that its political, economic and social structures were so deeply rooted that they could survive even the retirement or death of the President.

Notes and References

Chapter 1: The Coming of Islam

On the role of Muslims in Southeast Asia early in the Islamic era, see Nakahara, 'Muslim merchants in Nan-Hai'. The contemporaneous evidence for Islamisation is described in Damais, 'L'épigraphie musulmane dans le Sud-Est Asiatique', with references to previous literature; see also Damais, 'Études javanaises, I: Les tombes musulmanes datées de Trålåjå'; Chen, 'Une pierre tombale retrouvée à Brunei'; and de Casparis, 'Ahmat Majanu's tombstone'. Chinese records are translated in Rockhill, 'Notes on the relations and trade of China with the the eastern archipelago'; Groenveldt, *Notes on the Malay Archipelago and Malacca*; and Ma Huan, *Ying-yai sheng-lan*. On Marco Polo's account see Jack-Hinton, 'Marco Polo in South-East Asia'. Cortesão, *Suma Oriental*, contains the crucial text of Tomé Pires in Portuguese and English translation.

The Indonesian chronicles described above are found in the following: Hill, 'Hikayat Raja-raja pasai'; Brown, *Sějarah Mělayu*; Olthof, *Babad Tanah Djawi*; Djajadiningrat, *Sadjarah Bantěn*. Other legends are described in R. Jones, 'Ten conversion myths'. The two sixteenth-century Javanese Islamic books have both been edited and translated by Drewes: *Javaanse primbon* and *Admonitions of Seh Bari*. See also Drewes, *Early Javanese code*. On the pre-1620 Malay text, see Johns, 'Quranic exegesis'; Riddell, 'Earliest Quranic exegetical activity'.

A survey of some of the controversies surrounding Islamisation, with special attention to the sources of Indonesian Islam, is in Drewes, 'New Light'. Van Bruinessen, 'Bukankah orang Kurdi yang mengislamkan Indonesia?' argues interestingly for indirect Kurdish influence. On the Sufi argument see Johns, 'Sufism as a category'. See also Ricklefs, 'Six centuries of Islamisation'; and Reid, 'Islamization of Southeast Asia'.

Some materials on Islam in the areas outside of Indonesia which are mentioned in this chapter can be found in Hardy, 'Modern European and Muslim explanations of conversion to Islam in South Asia'; and in Majul, *Muslims in the Philippines*.

Chapter 2: General Aspects of Pre-Colonial States and Major Empires, c. 1300–1500

The general principles which underlay Indonesian states have been investigated in Moertono, *State and statecraft in old Java*; Schrieke, *Indonesian sociological studies* (see especially vol. II, p. 102 ff.); and Reid and Castles, *Pre-colonial state systems*;

see also Gullick, *Indigenous political systems of western Malaya*. Fisher, *South-East Asia*; and Pelzer, 'Physical and human resource patterns', describe the geography of the archipelago. Particularly valuable studies of economic (and other) affairs are to be found in Reid, 'Pre-colonial economy of Indonesia' and *Southeast Asia in the age of commerce*.

The standard historical description of Majapahit, now rather out of date, is Krom, *Hindoe-Javaansche geschiedenis*. This is the main source for the discussion in Coedès, *Les états hindouisés*, which has been translated into English as *Indianised states of Southeast Asia*. Slametmuljana, *Story of Majapahit*, contains much useful material, but some of the suggestions seem inadequately documented. For the fifteenth century, all of these works have been superseded by Noorduyn, 'Majapahit in the fifteenth century'. A text and English translation of the *Nāgarakĕrtāgama*, and much other useful information, is given in Pigeaud, *Java in the 14th century*. The *Pararaton* is in Brandes, *Pararaton (Ken Arok)*; there is an Indonesian translation in Padmapuspita, *Pararaton*.

C. C. Berg has published his arguments in several books and articles; see especially his *Rijk van de vijfvoudige Buddha*.

On Malacca, see Wang, 'First three rulers of Malacca'; Wake, 'Malacca's early kings and the reception of Islam'; and the early chapters of Meilink-Roelofsz, *Asian trade and European influence*. An attempt to reconstruct Malacca's origins is Wolters, *Fall of Śrīvijaya*. The major source for its trade is Cortesão, *Suma Oriental*.

Chapter 3: The Arrival of the Europeans in Indonesia, *c.* 1509–1620

The background and development of Portuguese overseas expansion are described in Boxer, *Portuguese seaborne empire*; and in Diffie and Winius, *Foundations of the Portuguese empire* (this, however, has some errors of detail concerning the Malay-Indonesian area). An excellent analysis of Dutch overseas activities is in Boxer, *Dutch seaborne empire*. See also Parry, *Europe and a wider world*, reprinted as *Establishment of the European hegemony*; and Masselman, *Cradle of colonialism*.

An examination of Portuguese and early English and Dutch activities in Indonesia is to be found in Meilink-Roelofsz, *Asian trade and European influence*. Much material is also included in Tiele, 'Europeërs in den Maleischen archipel'. A Malay chronicler's view of the conquest of Malacca is given in Brown, *Sĕjarah Mĕlayu*.

Portuguese and Dutch activities in Maluku are analysed in de Graaf, *Ambon en de Zuid-Molukken*. On sixteenth-century Maluku see also Abdurachman, 'Moluccan responses to the first intrusions of the West'. Abdurachman *et al.*, *Bunga rampai sejarah Maluku (I)*, covers the sixteenth and seventeenth centuries. There is also interesting material collected in da França, *Portuguese influence in Indonesia*. On Solor, see Abdurachman, 'Atakiwan, casados and tupassi' and Barnes, 'Avarice and iniquity at the Solor fort'; on Banda, see Villiers, 'Trade and society in the Banda islands'.

Documents concerning Coen's period are in Colenbrander and Coolhaas, *Jan Pietersz. Coen*. The events surrounding the conquest of Batavia are described in Ricklefs, 'Bantĕn and the Dutch in 1619'; and Abeyasekere, *Jakarta*. An authoritative analysis of VOC financial records is to be found in de Korte, *Financiële verantwoording*. For the social history of Batavia under the VOC, see Blussé, *Strange company*; and Jean Taylor, *Social world*.

Chapter 4: The Rise of New States, c. 1500–1650

There is much miscellaneous material on the states discussed above in Meilink-Roelofsz, *Asian trade and European influence*. Important and stimulating analysis of the economic setting of these new states is contained in Reid's articles 'Age of commerce' and 'Seventeenth-century crisis'.

On Aceh and the states of the western archipelago, see Djajadiningrat, 'Geschiedenis van het Soeltanaat van Atjeh'; and Lombard, *Iskandar Muda*; see also the earlier parts of Andaya, *Kingdom of Johor*.

On Java, see de Graaf and Pigeaud, *Eerste Moslimse vorstendommen op Java*; de Graaf, *Sénapati Ingalaga*; and de Graaf, *Sultan Agung*. The first of these books lacks an index, which is to be found along with English summaries of the other books listed here and other of de Graaf's writings in Pigeaud and de Graaf, *Islamic states*. On the later years of Majapahit see Noorduyn, 'Majahapit in the fifteenth century'. The establishment of Islamic rule in West Java and the role of the Portuguese are discussed in Guillot, 'L'accord luso-soundanais de 1522'.

The earliest Javanese chronicle so far discovered is published in Ricklefs, *Modern Javanese historical tradition*. Some Javanese chronicle views on the fall of Majapahit are also published in Ricklefs, 'Consideration of three versions of the *Babad Tanah Djawi*'. The Cirĕbon manuscript is published and translated into Indonesian in Atja, *Carita Purwaka Caruban Nagari*; its authenticity is doubtful: its paleography and use of Western rather than Javanese dates suggest in fact a twentieth-century origin for the text. See also the Indonesian translation in Sulendraningrat, *Purwaka Tjaruban Nagari*.

For sixteenth-century Java, of course Cortesão, *Suma Oriental*, is a major source. From the seventeenth century onwards, important VOC documents are published in de Jonge and van Deventer, *Opkomst van het Nederlandsch gezag*; and Coolhaas and van Goor, *Generale missiven*. Van Goens's reports are in de Graaf, *Vijf gezantschapsreizen van Rijklof van Goens*.

C. C. Berg's arguments concerning Senapati are found in several of his publications, of which the most important for this purpose is 'Twee nieuwe publicaties betreffende de geschiedenis en de geschiedschrijving van Mataram'. A reply is found in de Graaf, 'Historische betrouwbaarheid der Javaanse over-levering'.

On Makasar see Pelras, 'Religion, tradition and the dynamics of Islamization' and 'Les premières données occidentales concernant Célèbes-Sud'; Noorduyn, 'Islamisering van Makasar'; Reid, 'Rise of Makasar'; Noorduyn, *Kroniek van Wadjo*; and Stapel, *Bonggaais verdrag*. On the Makasarese and Balinese in the Lombok-Sumbawa area see de Graaf, 'Lombok in de 17e eeuw'. Bali in the golden age of Gelgel is discussed in Vickers, *Bali*; and Creese, 'Balinese *babad* '.

Chapter 5: Literary, Religious and Cultural Legacies

There is a vast literature on the subjects covered in this chapter. Excellent, but already rather out of date, introductions to the scholarship on Malay and Javanese are in Teeuw and Emanuels, *Studies on Malay and Bahasa Indonesia*; and Uhlenbeck, *Studies on the languages of Java and Madura*. Religious matters are discussed in Stöhr and Zoetmulder, *Religionen Indonesiens* (also available in a French edition).

The best introduction to classical Malay literature is Winstedt, *History of classical Malay literature*. On the seventeenth-century Acehnese mystics and their doctrines much has been written; see Lombard, *Iskandar Muda*; Johns, 'Malay Sufism', 'Islam in Southeast Asia' and 'Quranic exegesis'; Riddell, 'Earliest Quranic exegetical activity'; van Nieuwenhuijze, *Šamsu 'l-Dīn van Pasai*; al-Attas, *Mysticism of Hamzah Fansuri* and *Rānīrī and the Wujūdiyyah of 17th century Aceh*; Drewes, 'Nūr al-Dīn al-Rānīrī's charge of heresy'; Drewes and Brakel, *Poems of Hamzah Fansuri*; and Ito, 'Why did Nuruddin ar-Raniri leave Aceh?'. An important study of *syair* in general and of a major ninteenth-century centre for *syair* writing is Matheson, 'Questions arising from a nineteenth century Riau syair'. Malay literature available in translation is listed in Chambert-Loir, 'Bibliographie de la littérature malaise en traduction'.

The most comprehensive survey of Javanese literature is in vol. I of Pigeaud, *Literature of Java*. Zoetmulder, *Pantheisme en monisme*, is still the best analysis of mystical Javanese Islam and is now available also in Indonesian under the title *Manunggaling kawula gusti*. Much useful information on Javanese Islam and on Yasadipura I, as well as a valuable text, is contained in Soebardi, *Book of Cabolèk*. Ekadjati, *Ceritera Dipati Ukur*, is an important study of one *babad* tradition, as is Djajadiningrat, *Sadjarah Bantěn*. On the survival of Old Javanese literature in Islamised Java, see McDonald, *Old Javanese literature*; and Ricklefs, 'Unity and disunity'. English versions of three Javanese shadow plays can be found in Brandon, *On thrones of gold*.

On Old and Middle Javanese literature, see Zoetmulder, *Kalangwan*. On Middle Javanese see also Robson, *Wangbang Wideya*. Balinese *babads* are analysed in Worsley, *Babad Buleleng*; Hinzler, 'Balinese babad'; Creese, 'Balinese *babad*'; and Schulte Nordholt, *Een Balische dynastie*.

On Bugis and Makasarese, see especially Noorduyn, *Kroniek van Wadjo*'; Noorduyn, 'Origins of South Celebes historical writing'; and Cense, 'Old Buginese and Macassarese diaries'.

An introduction to Indonesian art is in Holt, *Art in Indonesia*. A good introduction to Indonesian music is found in Hood and Maceda, *Music*; more extensive discussions are contained in Sadie, *New Grove dictionary*. Kunst, *Music in Java*; and Kartomi, 'Music in nineteenth century Java', are important studies. On dance drama, see Soedarsono, *Wayang wong*.

Chapter 6: Eastern Indonesia, c. 1630–1800

Events in South Maluku are described in detail in de Graaf, *Ambon en de Zuid-Molukken*. Knaap, *Kruidnagelen en Christenen*, is an authoritative study of Ambon in the later seventeenth century. On the events in South Sulawesi see Andaya, *Arung Palakka* and 'Kingship in Bone'; Noorduyn, *Kroniek van Wadjo*'; Skinner, *Sja'ir perang Mengkasar*; Stapel, *Bonggaais verdrag*; and Noorduyn, 'Arung Singkang'. See also Wigboldus, 'Minahasa c. 1615–1680'. There is much information on the Makasarese and Bugis and their activities in the western archipelago in Andaya, *Kingdom of Johor*.

The Nusa Těnggara area is subject to penetrating historical and anthropological analysis in Fox, *Harvest of the palm*. Other useful materials are to be found in Noorduyn, *Bima en Sumbawa*. Concerning Bali, see Worsley, *Babad Buleleng*; Vickers, *Bali*;

and particularly the important historical study of Mĕngwi contained in Schulte Nordholt, *Een Balische dynastie*. On the economic history of the VOC see Glamann, *Dutch-Asiatic trade*.

Chapter 7: Java, c. 1640–82

An authoritative discussion of the reign of Amangkurat I is in de Graaf, *Mangku-Rat I*; this work is summarised in English in Pigeaud and de Graaf, *Islamic states*. There is also considerable material in Schrieke, *Indonesian sociological studies*. A major primary source is in de Graaf, *Vijf gezantschapsreizen van Rijklof van Goens*. A critical Javanese view which may be contemporaneous is in Ricklefs, *Modern Javanese historical tradition*.

On the period of the Trunajaya rebellion, see also de Graaf, 'Gevangenneming en dood van Raden Truna-Djaja'; and de Graaf, *Expeditie van Anthonio Hurdt*. Both of these are also summarised in Pigeaud and de Graaf, *Islamic states*. On Bantĕn and West Java generally, see Djajadiningrat, *Sadjarah Bantĕn*; de Jonge and van Deventer, *Opkomst van het Nederlandsch gezag*; and de Haan, *Priangan*.

Chapter 8: Java, Madura and the VOC, c. 1680–1745

There is still much work to be done on the period covered in this chapter. Valuable VOC primary sources are available in de Jonge and van Deventer, *Opkomst van het Nederlandsch gezag*; and Coolhaas and van Goor, *Generale missiven*. One Javanese source is in Ricklefs, *Modern Javanese historical tradition*.

Certain periods and aspects have, however, been covered. Nagtegaal, *Rijden op een Hollandse tijger*, is useful for European and Chinese activities on Java's north coast. The period 1677–1726 is studied in Ricklefs, *War, culture and economy*. A survey of VOC records and a summary of one Javanese chronicle for the period 1726–43 are to be found in Remmelink, *Emperor Pakubuwana II*. Some issues concerning the history of ideas are addressed in Ricklefs, 'Unity and disunity', while certain social, economic and demographic topics are discussed in Ricklefs, 'Statistical evidence'. For a biography of Speelman, see Stapel, *Cornelis Janszoon Speelman*. The Surapati episode is the subject of de Graaf, *Moord op Kapitein François Tack* (this is summarised in Pigeaud and de Graaf, *Islamic states*); and Kumar, *Surapati*. Concerning Raja Sakti, see Kathirithamby-Wells, 'Ahmad Shah ibn Iskandar'.

On social life and health conditions in Batavia, see Jean Taylor, *Social world*; and Schoute, *Geneeskunde*. Vermuelen, *Chineezen te Batavia*, concerns the Chinese massacre and the associated conflict between Valckenier and van Imhoff . A Javanese account of Pakubuwana II's decision to support the Chinese is contained in Ricklefs, 'Crisis of 1740–1'. His adventures after the fall of Kartasura are described in Gijsberti Hodenpijl, 'Zwerftocht van Sultan [sic] Pakoeboewana II'. Hoadley, 'Javanese, *peranakan* and Chinese elites in Cirebon' is important on the late seventeenth and early eighteenth centuries.

Chapter 9: Java and the VOC, c. 1745–92

On Central and East Java in this period see Ricklefs, *Jogjakarta under Sultan Mangkubumi*. The period is also discussed more briefly in Soekanto, *Sekitar*

Jogjakarta. See also Louw, *Derde Javaansche successie-oorlog.* A very important analysis of rural social and economic conditions is found in Carey, 'Waiting for the "just king"'. New light is shed upon Seh Ibrahim in van der Meiden, 'A Turkish mediator'. On Bantĕn see de Jonge and van Deventer, *Opkomst van het Nederlandsch gezag.* On VOC finances in this period, see de Korte, *Financiële verantwoording.*

Chapter 10: Java, 1792–1830

The most important work on this period is Carey's unpublished D.Phil thesis, 'Pangeran Dipanagara'. Other important works by Carey are 'Origins of the Java War', 'Satria and santri', 'Waiting for the "just king"' and 'Changing Javanese perceptions of the Chinese'. See also Ricklefs, 'Dipanagara's early inspirational experience'. On Javanese perceptions of relations with Batavia see Ricklefs, *Jogjakarta under Sultan Mangkubumi;* and on the Sepoy mutiny see Carey, 'Sepoy conspiracy of 1815 in Java'. The standard history of the Java War itself is Louw and de Klerck, *Java-oorlog;* see also Sagimun, *Pahlawan Dipanagara berdjuang.* There is a briefer description in Soekanto, *Sekitar Jogkakarta.* On Sĕntot in Sumatra see Dobbin, *Islamic revivalism.* Concerning the Mangkunĕgaran see Pringgodigdo, *Ondernemingen van het Mangkoenagorosche rijk.* There is also much valuable information contained in Rouffaer, 'Vorstenlanden'.

On colonial issues see Bastin, *Native policies of Sir Stamford Raffles* and 'Raffles' ideas on the land rent system in Java'; Day, *Dutch in Java;* Wright, *East-Indian economic problems;* and Levyssohn Norman, *Britsche heerschappij over Java en onderhoorigheden.* A general analysis of the social and economic circumstances of nineteenth-century Java is Boomgaard, *Children of the colonial state,* but Boomgaard's conclusions sometimes rest upon rather shaky evidence.

Chapter 11: Java, 1830–1900

The most important studies of the *cultuurstelsel* period are Fasseur, *Kultuurselsel en koloniale baten* (also available in English translation as *Politics of colonial exploitation*); and Boomgaard, *Children of the colonial state.* The latter also covers the later nineteenth century, as does Elson, *Javanese peasants and the colonial sugar industry.* Other major works on the nineteenth century are Booth, *Agricultural development* and 'Living standards and distribution of income'; Djoko Suryo, 'Economic crisis' and *Sejarah sosial;* Elson, 'Famine in Demak and Grobogan' and 'Impact of government sugar cultivation'; Fasseur, 'Organisatie en sociaal-economische betekenis', 'Cultivation system and its impact' and 'Purse or principle'; Houben, *Kraton en kumpeni;* Hugenholz, 'Famine and food supply'; Knight, 'People's own cultivations'; Rush, *Opium to Java;* and Van Niel, 'Function of landrent under the Cultivation System in Java' and 'Measurement of change under the Cultivation System in Java, 1837–1851'. Important papers reflecting the current state of knowledge and argument on nineteenth century Java economic history (as well as contributions on other subjects) are found in Booth *et al., Indonesian economic history.* Older but still useful works are Day, *Dutch in Java;* Burger, *Sociologisch-economische geschiedenis;* and especially Furnivall, *Netherlands India.*

A valuable political survey of the years 1839–48 is contained in Arsip Nasional, *Ikhtisar keadaan politik Hindia-Belanda, tahun 1839–1848,* with the original Dutch text and summaries in English and Indonesian. A description of Java in the 1870s is found in Veth, *Java*. On Suryengalaga and other late-nineteenth conspiracies see Kumar, 'Suryengalagan affair'. See also Ruiter, 'Tegal revolt in 1864'. Van Deventer, *Overzicht van den economischen toestand der inlandsche bevolking van Java en Madoera*, is an offical report to the Minister of Colonies and a devastating revelation of the impact of the 'liberal' period upon indigenous society. On Javanese cultural activities see Pigeaud, *Literature of Java*; Soebardi, 'Santri-religious elements as reflected in the Book of Tjěntini'; Kartomi, 'Music in nineteenth century Java'; and Dewantara, *Beoefening van letteren en kunst in het Pakoe-Alamsche geslacht*. An English translation of the *Wedhatama* is in Robson, *Wedhatama*. On nineteenth-century artists see Holt, *Art in Indonesia*; Maronier, *Pictures of the tropics*; Carey, 'Raden Saleh'; and Bachtiar, 'Raden Saleh'. On Raden Saleh's family background see de Graaf, 'Semarangse geslacht Bustam'. The economic activities of the Mangkunĕgaran are analysed in Pringgodigdo, *Ondernemingen van het Mangkoenagorosche rijk*.

On Javanese *bupatis* in this period see Soeria Nata Atmadja, *Regenten-positie*; and Sutherland, 'Notes on Java's regent families'. Drewes, 'Struggle between Javanism and Islam', concerns late-nineteenth-century anti-Islamic writings. On the education of new *Priyayi* see Brugmans, *Geschiedenis van het onderwijs in Nederlandsch-Indië*.Peasant protest is discussed in two works by Kartodirdjo: *The peasants' revolt of Banten in 1888* and *Protest movements in rural Java*; the first of these contains much information on Islam in this period; the second proposes a classification of movements which has, however, been criticised. See also Drewes, *Drie Javaansche goeroe's*; and Wiselius, 'Djǎjǎ Bǎjǎ'.

Important work relevant to nineteenth-century Javanese Islam is found in van Bruinessen, 'Origins and development of the Naqshbandi order'; Johns, 'Quranic exegesis'; Snouck Hurgronje, *Mekka*; and Steenbrink, *Beberapa aspek tentang Islam*. See also Dhofier, *Tradisi pesantren*. Although Christianisation was not a large-scale phenomenon in this period, it is of considerable historical interest; see Guillot, *L'affaire Sadrach*.

Chapter 12: The Outer Islands, *c.* 1800-1910

There has been no full study of the outer islands in this period which analyses Dutch expansion throughout the area, and few local studies which reveal the Indonesian side of events. A survey of Dutch imperial aspects is, however, to be found in Fasseur, 'Een koloniale paradox', which covers 1830–70. A number of important essays is contained in Lapian and Day, *Papers of the Dutch-Indonesian historical conference 1976*. Much information is given in the regional articles in Paulus, *et al.*, *Encyclopaedie van Nederlandsch-Indië*; and in a more abbreviated fashion in Bezemer, *Beknopte encyclopaedie*. Valuable colonial surveys of the whole Indonesian area are contained in Arsip Nasional, *Laporan politik tahun 1837*; and Arsip Nasional, *Ikhtisar keadaan politik Hindia-Belanda, tahun 1839–1848*; both volumes have the original Dutch texts and summaries in English and Indonesian. On Dutch missionary activity in the nineteenth century see vol. I of Swellengrebel, *In Leijdeckers voetspoor*; and Coolsma, *Zendingseeuw*.

On Madura see also Sutherland, 'Notes on Java's regent families'; H. de Jonge, 'State formation by contract', is also useful on the nineteenth century. On Bali and Lombok see Utrecht, *Sedjarah hukum internasional di Bali dan Lombok*. A particularly valuable work on Bali is Schulte Nordholt, *Een Balische dynastie*. Anak Agung Gde Agung, *Bali pada abad XIX*, is a valuable survey of materials from a nationalist perspective. See also Vickers, *Bali*. Van der Kràan, *Lombok*, is important but argues for economic causation in a less than convincing fashion. On Mads Lange's extraordinary role, see Schulte Nordholt, 'Mads Lange connection'. Events in Ambon are described authoritatively in Chauvel, *Nationalists, soldiers and separatists*; see also de Graaf, *Ambon en de Zuid-Molukken*. Fox, *Harvest of the palm*, concerns Nusa Těnggara.

Imperial rivalry in Kalimantan is described in Irwin, *Nineteenth-century Borneo*. See also Soeri Soeroto, 'Beratib Beamaal movement in the Banjar War'. On economic developments in the later nineteenth century in Southeast Kalimantan, see Lindblad, *Between Dayak and Dutch*. Brooke rule in Sarawak is analysed in Runciman, *White rajahs*; and Pringle, *Rajahs and rebels*.

Concerning Palembang, see Woelders, *Sultanaat Palembang, 1811–1825*. The progress of Dutch imperialism in Sumatra is described in Schadee, *Geschiedenis van Sumatra's oostkust*.

Three important articles by Dobbin greatly illuminated the Padri movement: 'Economic change in Minangkabau as a factor in the rise of the Padri movement', 'Islamic revivalism in Minangkabau', and 'Tuanku Imam Bondjol'. Her work has been further developed and extended in Dobbin, *Islamic revivalism*. See also Abdullah, 'Adat and Islam: An examination of conflict in Minangkabau'; and Mansoer *et al.*, *Sedjarah Minangkabau*. For information on the Wahhabis in Arabia, see Hourani, *Arabic thought in the liberal age*.

On Islamic issues generally, see van Bruinessen, 'Origins and development of the Naqshbandi order'; and Steenbrink, *Beberapa aspek tentang Islam*.

Reid, *Contest for North Sumatra*, is an analysis of the origins and progress of the Aceh War, with special attention to diplomatic aspects. On the balance between imperial and economic motivations in the war, see Bakker, 'Economische belang van Noord-Sumatra'. For a description of the war itself see van't Veer, *Atjeh-oorlog*; and Alfian, *Perang di jalan Allah*. See also Alfian, 'Acheh Sultanate under Sultan Mohammad Daudsyah'. Snouck Hurgronje's major study of Aceh is his *Atjèhers*, available in English as *Achehnese*. A convenient analysis of Snouck Hurgronje's ideas is given in Benda, *Crescent and the rising sun*. Concerning the Batak region see Castles, 'Statelessness and stateforming tendencies among the Bataks'.

Chapter 13: A New Colonial Age

Van Deventer's article of 1899 is reprinted (along with much other valuable material) in Fasseur, *Geld en geweten*. Furnivall's *Netherlands India* is an unsurpassed source for subjects covered in this chapter, and for many other aspects of twentieth-century Dutch colonialism which are not discussed above; his *Colonial policy and practice* is also very valuable. On economic aspects see also Allen and Donnithorne, *Western enterprise in Indonesia and Malaya*; Booth, *Agricultural development*; and Elson, *Javanese peasants and the colonial sugar industry*. Breman, *Control of land and labour*, describes agrarian reform experiments in Cirěbon and gives a detailed picture of village life in this period. American economic interests are analysed in Gould, *Americans in Sumatra*. On East Sumatra see Pelzer, *Planter and peasant*. Burger, *Sociologisch-economische geschiedenis*, also contains a stimulating analysis of this period. The beginnings of the oil industry are described in Schadee, *Geschiedenis van Sumatra's Oostkust*; see also Paulus *et al.*, *Encyclopaedie van Nederlandsch-Indië* (or Bezemer, *Beknopte encyclopaedie*); and Bakker, 'Economische belang van Noord-Sumatra'. For a much more detailed account see Gerretson, *Geschiedenis der 'Koninklijke'*, translated into English as *History of the Royal Dutch*.

A general survey is found in Van Niel, *Emergence of the modern Indonesian elite*. The most comprehensive statistical picture of the period is contained in Departement van Economische Zaken, *Volkstelling 1930/Census 1930*. On educational reforms see Brugmans, *Geschiedenis van het onderwijs in Nederlandsch-Indië*; and on population matters see Widjojo, *Population trends in Indonesia*. Boomgaard, 'Welfare services', is valuable. The development of the Indonesian administrative corps in this new age is analysed in Sutherland, *Making of a bureaucratic elite*.

The works cited in Chapters 14 and 15 which concentrate on indigenous Indonesian affairs also contain much material on colonial policy and practice.

Chapter 14: The First Steps towards National Revival, c. 1900–27

The events of this period have attracted much scholarly attention. Van Niel, *Emergence of the modern Indonesian elite*, is still a valuable survey; as is Pringgodigdo, *Sedjarah pergerakan rakjat Indonesia*.

Concerning Abdul Rivai and *Bintang Hindia*, see Poeze, 'Early Indonesian emancipation'. On Budi Utomo see Nagazumi, *Dawn of Indonesian nationalism*. Saminism is discussed in Benda and Castles, 'Samin movement'; Bijleveld, 'Saminbeweging'; and Shiraishi, 'Dangir's testimony'.

McVey, *Rise of Indonesian Communism*, is the most authoritative study of PKI down to 1926–7, and contains much material on the other political movements of the period, particularly SI. Shiraishi, *Age in motion*, analyses radicalism in Java between 1912 and 1926. On ISDV see the introduction in Tichelman, *Socialisme in Indonesië*. On SI see further Korver, *Sarekat Islam*; Kartodirdjo, *Protest movements in rural Java*; Oates, 'Afdeeling B'; Ensering, 'Afdeeling B'; Kuntowijoyo, 'Islam and politics'; and Williams, *Sickle and crescent*. Trade union history is analysed in Ingleson, *In search of justice*. The best analysis of Communism in Minangkabau is in Schrieke, *Indonesian sociological studies*, vol. I. A biography of Tan Malaka down to 1945 is found in Poeze, *Tan Malaka*. Fox, *Harvest of the palm*, decribes developments in Timor; Chauvel, *Nationalists, soldiers and separatists*, analyses Ambon.

On the Javanese principalities in this period, see Larson, *Prelude to revolution*; and van den Haspel, *Overwicht in overleg*.

Noer, *Modernist Muslim movement in Indonesia, 1900–1942*, is a survey of Islamic reform. On the movement in Minangkabau see Abdullah, *Schools and politics*. The role of Singapore in this is described in Roff, *Origins of Malay nationalism*. On the major Islamic reform movements in Java, see also Federspiel's publications 'Muhammadijah' and *Persatuan Islam*. Other important analyses of Islamic issues are found in van Bruinessen, 'Origins and development of the Naqshbandi order'; Steenbrink, *Beberapa aspek tentang Islam*, which contains *inter alia* material on Ahmad Khatib of Minangkabau; Johns, 'Quranic exegesis'; and Baroroh Baried, 'Islam and the modernization of Indonesian women'. Islamic educational developments are analysed in Steenbrink, *Pesantren, madrasah, sekolah*. Valuable essays on the reform movement in Java and on the government-recognised Islamic hierarchies are contained in Pijper, *Studiën over de geschiedenis van de Islam in Indonesia, 1900–1950.* Hourani, *Arabic thought in the liberal age,* describes the Middle Eastern background of Islamic reform.

Surjomihardjo, 'National education', describes Indonesian educational efforts, including women's movements. The origins of Taman Siswa are described in Surjomihardjo, *Ki Hadjar Dewantara;* and McVey, 'Taman Siswa and the Indonesian national awakening'. See also Surjomihardjo, 'Suwardi Surjaningrat's ideals and national-revolutionary actions'. On the Javanese *priyayi* elite in this period see Sutherland, *Making of a bureaucratic elite.* Suryadinata, *Peranakan Chinese politics,* covers Chinese aspects of the period.

Chapter 15: Repression and Economic Crisis, 1927–42

A general survey of the events of this period is in Pluvier, *Overzicht van de ontwikkeling der nationalistische beweging in Indonesië in de jaren 1930 tot 1942.* Pringgodigdo, *Sedjarah pergerakan rakjat Indonesia,* also covers this period. For a detailed analysis concentrating on the urban 'secular' movements of 1927–34 see Ingleson, *Road to exile.* For the period 1936–42 see Abeyasekere's publications 'Partai Indonesia Raja', 'Soetardjo petition', and *One hand clapping.* See also O'Malley, 'Pakempalan Kawulo Ngajogjakarta'.

There have been several studies of Sukarno; the best is Legge, *Sukarno: A political biography.* There is also much valuable material on Sukarno's thinking in Dahm, *Sukarnos Kampf um Indonesiens Unabhängigkeit* (in English under the title *Sukarno and the struggle for Indonesian independence*), but Dahm's interpretations of this material and his attempt to link it closely to traditional Javanese cultural phenomena have been criticised. Sukarno's four letters of 1933, first analysed in Ingleson, *Road to exile,* are discussed further in Kwantes, 'Soekarno's vier brieven'; and Hering, 'Nogmaals de vier brieven'. Noer, *Mohammad Hatta;* and Rose, *Indonesia free,* offer political biographies of Hatta. On the PNI-Baru, see Legge, *'Daulat Ra'jat'.*

On Islamic matters see Noer, *Modernist Muslim movement in Indonesia, 1900–1942.* Events in Minangkabau are treated in detail in Abdullah, *Schools and politics;* see also A. Kahin, 'Repression and regroupment'. Federspiel, *Persatuan Islam,* should also be consulted.

Probably the best general survey of the impact of the Depression in Indonesia is in O'Malley's unpublished doctoral dissertation 'Indonesia in the Great Depression'. Furnivall, *Netherlands India;* and van Gelderen, *Economic foreign policy,* are still valuable although both were published in 1939. More recent contributions which should be consulted are Booth's 'Living standards and distribution of income' and *Economic development.* A useful general account which includes a comparison with India is Goswami, 'Depression'. For more detailed local analyses, see Ingleson, 'Urban Java during the Depression'; and Elson, *Javanese peasants and the colonial sugar industry.* A major survey of the economy in the later years of Dutch rule is found in vol. I of Sutter, *Indonesianisasi.*

The Javanese bureaucratic class is treated in Sutherland, *Making of a bureaucratic elite.* The background to World War II in Indonesia is covered in Aziz, *Japan's colonialism and Indonesia.*

On the development of modern Indonesian literature, see Teeuw, *Modern Indonesian literature,* which analyses major works briefly and includes extensive bibliographies. See also Teeuw, 'Impact of Balai Pustaka on modern Indonesian literature'; Sutherland, 'Pudjangga Baru'; Foulcher, '*Pujangga Baru*'; Jassin, *Pudjangga Baru*; and Jassin, *Amir Hamzah*. On pre-war literature and Islam, see Kratz, 'Islamic attitudes'.

European issues are explored in Fasseur, 'Nederland en het Indonesische nationalism'; and Drooglever, *Vaderlandse Club*. On connections between events in the Philippines and Indonesia, see Bootsma, *Buren in de koloniale tijd*.

Chapter 16: World War II and the Japanese Occupation, 1942–5

No entirely satisfactory work covering the whole of Indonesia during World War II has been published. The best available survey is Aziz, *Japan's colonialism and Indonesia*. A comprehensive, but rather undigested, collection of material is in Waseda University, *Japanese military administration in Indonesia*. A briefer survey is to be found in Reid, 'Indonesia: From briefcase to samurai sword'. Benda, *Crescent and the rising sun*, is a valuable work, but its isolation of Islam as the primary topic tends to obscure other aspects. A substantial analysis emphasising economic matters is in vol. I of Sutter, *Indonesianisasi*.

Husken, 'Islam and collective action', analyses the violence at the beginning of the occupation. B. Anderson has greatly illuminated the later stages of occupation in Java; see his 'Japan: "The light of Asia"', *Some aspects of Indonesian politics under the Japanese occupation*, and *Java in a time of revolution*. Legge, *Sukarno: A political biography*; Noer, *Mohammad Hatta*; and Rose, *Indonesia free* (on Hatta) are valuable. Legge, *Intellectuals and nationalism*, is a study of Sjahrir's circle. Some important interpretative issues concerning Java under the Japanese are considered in Sluimers, '"Nieuwe orde" op Java'. See also Kurasawa, 'Propaganda media on Java'.

There has so far been little serious study of areas occupied by the navy, except for Chauvel, *Nationalists, soldiers and separatists*, on Ambon. On Sumatra see Piekaar, *Atjèh en de oorlog met Japan*; Reid, 'Japanese occupation and rival Indonesian elites'; Reid, *Blood of the people*; and van Langenberg, 'North Sumatra 1942–1945'. Friend, *Blue-eyed enemy*, is a comparative analysis of Java and Luzon under the Japanese.

A good survey of the Japanese background to events can be found in Beasley, *Modern history of Japan*. See also F. Jones, *Japan's new order in East Asia*; and Elsbree, *Japan's role in Southeast Asian nationalist movements*. Shimer and Hobbs, *Kenpeitai in Java and Sumatra*, presents the Kenpeitai's own view of its role.

Chapter 17: The Revolution, 1945–50

The Revolution has produced much scholarly writing of high quality. Reid, *Indonesian national revolution*, is the best guide to the Revolution throughout Indonesia. An earlier and more detailed study which concentrates on Java, and which ranks as one of the classic works of Indonesian history, is G. Kahin, *Nationialism and revolution*. Legge, *Sukarno: A political biography*, is also valuable. For an extensive study by a major participant, see Nasution, *Sekitar perang kemerdekaan Indonesia*. Vol. II of Sutter, *Indonesianisasi*, covers the Revolution with an emphasis on economic aspects.

The years 1945–6 in Java are analysed in B. Anderson, *Java in a time of revolution*. On West Java in the same period see Smail, *Bandung in the early revolution.* Lucas, 'Social revolution in Pemalang', and *One soul, one struggle* (in Indonesian as *Peristiwa tiga daerah*), cover the three regions affair. Events in Surakarta are described in Soejatno (Sujatno), 'Revolution and social tensions in Surakarta' and 'Perubahan-perubahan sosial politik di Surakarta'. On Yogyakarta see Selosoemardjan, *Social changes in Jogjakarta.* The Revolution in Surabaya is analysed in Frederick, *Visions and heat.* Cribb, *Gangsters and revolutionaries*, sheds interesting light on the Revolution in Jakarta. The Madiun rebellion is discussed in Swift, *Road to Madiun*; and in D. Anderson, 'Military aspects of the Madiun affair'. For studies of major military figures, see Nugroho, 'Soedirman: Panglima yang menepati janjinya'; and Penders and Sundhaussen, *Nasution.* See also Sundhaussen, *Road to power.* Noer, *Mohammad Hatta*, and Rose, *Indonesia free*, analyse the role of Hatta.

The Revolution outside of Java has so far received rather less attention. For essays on Aceh, East Sumatra, West Sumatra, South Sulawesi and Ambon, as well as parts of Java, see A. Kahin, *Regional dynamics.* On Bali, see Robinson, 'State, society and political conflict in Bali'; and Vickers, *Bali.* On the early stages in South Sulawesi, see Reid, 'Australia's hundred days'. Chauvel, *Nationalists, soldiers and separatists*, provides an authoritative account of Ambon. Reid, *Blood of the people* (available in Indonesian as *Perjuangan rakyat*), covers the early years of the Revolution in Aceh and East Sumatra. On the initial stages in Aceh, see also Piekaar, *Atjèh en de oorlog met Japan.* See also Reid, 'Birth of the Republic in Sumatra'.

The final stages of the Revolution are covered in Feith, *Decline of constitutional democracy.* On international diplomatic aspects see A. Taylor, *Indonesian independence and the United Nations*; and McMahon, *Colonialism and cold war*; the more general diplomatic context is described in Colbert, *Southeast Asia in international politics.*

Islamic aspects are covered in Boland, *Struggle of Islam.* See van Dijk, *Rebellion under the banner of Islam*; Soebardi, 'Kartosuwiryo'; and Horikoshi, 'Dar ul-Islam movement', on Kartosuwirjo and Darul Islam. On literature see Teeuw, *Modern Indonesian literature*; on art see Holt, *Art in Indonesia.* The role of van Mook is described in Yong, *van Mook.*

Chapter 18: The Democratic Experiment, 1950–7

Feith, *Decline of constitutional democracy*, is an exhaustive study of this period. Studies of various constituents of the political scene may be found in Hindley, *Communist party of Indonesia*; Mortimer, *Indonesian Communism under Sukarno*; McVey, 'Post-revolutionary transformation of the Indonesian army'; Legge, *Sukarno: A political biography*; Boland, *Struggle of Islam*; Noer, *Mohammad Hatta*; Rose, *Indonesia free* (on Hatta); and Penders and Sundhaussen, *Nasution.* On Lekra, see Foulcher, *Social commitment.*

Booth, *Agricultural development*, is an important work for this period. For East Sumatran agrarian issues, see Pelzer, *Planters against peasants.* On population growth see Widjojo, *Population trends in Indonesia.* A brief collection of useful statistics is given in Brand, 'Some statistical data'. Economic affairs down to 1955 are analysed in vols. III and IV of Sutter, *Indonesianisasi.*

Local studies of Javanese society are found in Selosoemardjan, *Social changes in Jogjakarta*; Castles, *Religion, politics and economic behaviour in Java*; Jay, *Religion and politics in rural Central Java*; and Kuntowidjojo, 'Sikap ekonomi dan keagamaan pengusaha didesa industri' (available in English as 'Economic and religious attitudes of entrepreneurs in a village industry'). Geertz, *Religion of Java*, contains much information, but has been criticised for appearing to equate communal identities (*santri* and *abangan*) with a social class category (*priyayi*).

An analysis of the 1955 (and 1971) elections is in van Marle, 'Indonesian electoral geography'. On foreign policy see Fifield, *Diplomacy of Southeast Asia*; Bone, *Dynamics of the Western New Guinea (Irian Barat) problem*; and Mozingo, *Chinese policy toward Indonesia*.

Indonesia's regional crises have been analysed in several important works. See Sjamsuddin, *Republican revolt*, on Aceh. On Sulawesi see Harvey's works *Pemberontakan Kahar Muzakkar* and *Permesta*. Van Dijk, *Rebellion under the banner of Islam*, describes Darul Islam in Java, Sulawesi, Kalimantan and Aceh. A case study of Darul Islam life is in K. Robinson, 'Living in the hutan'. Leirissa, *PRRI Permesta*, employs much oral evidence from participants. See also Smail, 'Military politics of North Sumatra'.

Chapter 19: Guided Democracy, 1957–65

No general study of the guided democracy period has yet been published. The years 1957–9 are covered in detail in Lev, *Transition to guided democracy*. Analyses extending to 1962 are found in Feith's 'Dynamics of guided democracy' and 'Indonesia'. Hindley, *Communist Party of Indonesia*, extends to 1963. See also Reeve, 'Sukarnoism and Indonesia's "functional group" state'.

Leirissa, *PRRI Permesta*, is an important study of that rebellion, using both documentary sources and oral evidence of participants; Mossman, *Rebels in paradise*, is an older journalistic account. On the Sulawesi rebellion see also Harvey, *Permesta*.

Studies covering the whole period with emphasis on particular aspects are found in Crouch, *Army and politics*; Mortimer, *Indonesian Communism under Sukarno*; Legge, *Sukarno: A political biography*; Boland, *Struggle of Islam*; and McVey, 'Postrevolutionary transformation of the Indonesian army'; all but the last of these include analyses of the 1965 coup attempt and its various interpretations. The economic troubles of the period are described in Mackie, *Problems of the Indonesian inflation*. On military aspects, see further Sundhaussen, *Road to power*; and Penders and Sundhaussen, *Nasution*. Coppel, *Indonesian Chinese*, covers the period. Other valuable studies are found in Foulcher, 'Survey of events surrounding "Manikebu"'; Lee, 'Taman Siswa in postwar Indonesia'; and Rocamora, 'Partai Nasional Indonesia, 1963–1965'. Teeuw, *Modern Indonesian literature*, includes the writers of this period. Literary issues are also covered in Foulcher, *Social commitment*; and Kratz, 'Islamic attitudes'. Concerning the murders of the generals in 1965, see B. Anderson, 'How did the Generals die?'

Feith and Castles, *Indonesian political thinking*, contains valuable primary sources for this period (and before). Sukarno's own *Autobiography as told to Cindy Adams* gives much insight into his mind in this period. The general inclination of scholars to see Sukarno as a social conservative despite his revolutionary rhetoric is challenged in Hauswedell, 'Sukarno: Radical or conservative?'

The foreign policy of this period has received considerable attention. See Bunnell, 'Guided democracy foreign policy'; and Mackie, *Konfrontasi: The Indonesia-Malaysia dispute*. Weinstein, *Indonesian foreign policy*, concentrates on the post-Sukarno years but includes material on this period. On China's role see Mozingo, *Chinese policy toward Indonesia*; and Jay Taylor, *China and Southeast Asia*; both of these include analyses of the 1965 coup attempt. American involvement is discussed in Bunnell, 'Central Intelligence Agency – Deputy Directorate for Plans 1961 secret memorandum'; and Fifield, *Southeast Asia in United States policy*, which extends to c. 1962. Regarding the Gilchrist document, see the first chapter of Mody, *Indonesia under Suharto*.

Chapter 20: Creating the New Order, 1965–75

A description of the Soeharto era down to 1985 is found in Mody, *Indonesia under Suharto*. Polomka, *Indonesia since Sukarno*, is a valuable analysis down to c. 1970; H. McDonald, *Suharto's Indonesia*, is a wide-ranging account covering events to c. 1979. Crouch, *Army and politics*, is an important analysis to c. 1976 concentrating on military aspects. See also Sundhaussen, *Road to power*. Roeder, *Smiling general*, is an authorised biography of Soeharto extending to 1968. For Soeharto's own reflections, see his autobiography *Pikiran, ucapan dan tindakan saya*. Oey, *Indonesia after the 1971 elections*, contains several useful articles. The period of transition from old to new order is described in the above works. For more specific analyses, see Paget, 'Military in Indonesian politics'; Hindley, 'Alirans and the fall of the old order'; Cribb, *Indonesian killings of 1965–1966*; Webb, 'Sickle and the cross'; and Samson, 'Islam in Indonesian politics'. Studies of various aspects of domestic politics are found in McVey, 'Post-revolutionary transformation of the Indonesian army', which extends to 1969; McIntyre, 'Divisions and power in the Indonesian National Party, 1965–1966'; Nishihara, *Golkar and the Indonesian elections of 1971*; and Ward, *Foundation of the Partai Muslimin Indonesia*. Boland, *Struggle of Islam*, extends to 1969. On the 1971 elections see Ward, *1971 election*; and van Marle, 'Indonesian electoral geography'. Jassin, *Angkatan '66*, contains early literary works of the 'generation of '66'. On Chinese aspects, see Coppel, *Indonesian Chinese*.

Political imprisonment down to mid-1977 is analysed in *Indonesia: An Amnesty International report*; the Indonesian edition of this (*Indonesia: Sebuah laporan Amnesti International*) has an introduction covering mid-1977 to October 1978. Several studies have been published concerning East Timor; the best are Jolliffe, *East Timor*; and Dunn, *Timor: A people betrayed*. Osborne, *Indonesia's secret war*, is a serious journalistic account of Irian Jayan resistance.

Religious issues have received considerable scholarly attention, and are discussed in several of the works referred to above. Regarding Islam, other important works are McVey, 'Faith as the outsider'; Nakamura, *Crescent arises over the banyan tree*, covering the period to 1970; and Hefner, 'Islamizing Java?'. See also Dhakidae, 'Manusia dan agama'. For basic statistics resting upon the censuses of 1971 and 1980 see Biro Pusat Statistik, *Beberapa ciri pemeluk agama*. G. Jones, 'Religion and education', analyses Christianisation. Hadiwijono, *Man in the present Javanese mysticism*, contains an important study of Kĕbatinan. See also Mulder, *Mysticism and everyday life*; Stange, '"Legitimate" mysticism'; and Subagya, *Kepercayaan*, which is written from a critical Christian viewpoint. Islamic educational work and related matters are discussed in Steenbrink, *Pesantren, madrasah, sekolah* (of which there are both Dutch and Indonesian editions); and Sudjoko Prasodjo *et.al.*, *Profil pesantren*.

On the ending of confrontation see Weinstein, *Indonesia abandons confrontation*; and Mackie, *Konfrontasi: the Indonesia-Malaysia dispute*. For foreign relations in general see Weinstein, *Indonesian foreign policy*, which extends to *c.* 1974; and Heinzlmeir, *Indonesiens Aussenpolitik nach Sukarno, 1965–1970*. On ASEAN see Jorgensen-Dahl, *Regional organisation and order in South-East Asia*. Mozingo, *Chinese policy towards Indonesia*, extends to 1967; Jay Taylor, *China and Southeast Asia*, extends to 1972.

Economic affairs are analysied in Booth and McCawley, *Indonesian economy during the Soeharto era*; and in Booth, *Agricultural development*. An important analysis of the connections between politics and economic policy is Liddle, 'Relative autonomy'. An analysis from a more critical standpoint is in Palmer, *Indonesian economy since 1965*. Radical criticism is also found in Payer, 'International Monetary Fund and Indonesian debt slavery'. Rĕpĕlita I is analysed in Rudner, 'Indonesian military and economic policy'. Robison, *Indonesia: Rise of capital*, analyses the business affairs of the new order elite within the general context of new order society and economics down to the mid-1980s. On oil, see especially Carlson, *Indonesia's oil*, which was written before the consequences of the Pĕrtamina crisis of 1975 had become clear. Drake, *National integration*, is a valuable statistically based study focussing on the new order period into the 1980s. Indonesia's economy and society are seen within a wider ASEAN context in Kühne, *Bevölkerungs und Beschäftigungsentwicklung*, which extends to *c.* 1971; and Wong, *ASEAN economies in perspective*, which extends to *c.* 1976.

Social statistics are available in Biro Pusat Statistik, *Sensus penduduk 1971/1971 population census*; a useful guide to this census data is P. McDonald, *Pedoman*. Soetjipto Wirosardjono *et al.*, *Gita Jaya*, is an official analysis of Jakarta's development during 1966–77; on this see also Abeyasekere, *Jakarta*.

Chapter 21: The New Order since 1975

Several of the works cited for Chapter 20 extend to the period since 1975. In particular Mody, *Indonesia under Suharto*; and Robison, *Indonesia: Rise of capital*, extend to the mid-1980s. Booth and McCawley, *Indonesian economy during the Soeharto era*, covers down to about 1980; while Booth, *Agricultural development*, discusses affairs to *c.* 1985. Liddle, 'Relative autonomy', extends to the late 1980s. Hefner, 'Islamizing Java?' is particularly important on religious issues.

There are many sources available for events since 1975 which have not already been cited for Chapter 20; not a few of these are of a polemical nature. Scholarly annual surveys of events in Indonesia during the preceding year may be found in the monthly journal *Asian Survey*, normally in the second (February) issue of each year. A major study of political history from 1975 to 1983 is Jenkins, *Suharto and his generals*. On Pancasila and P4, see Morfit, 'Pancasila'. One significant aspect of Indonesian foreign relations to 1990 is covered in Suryadinata, 'Indonesia-China relations'.

Economic aspects are analysed in Booth, 'State and economic development'; and Hadi Soesastro, 'Political economy of deregulation', which is set in the context of the 1980s generally. A rather pessimistic view of the future is in Young, 'Transformation or temporary respite?'. Arndt, 'Transmigration' is an important general analysis of the role and achievements of transmigration. Analyses of the life of people seeking survival in the urban informal sector are to be found in Jellinek, *Wheel of fortune*, and Bijlmer, *Ambulante straatberoepen*.

Van Bruinessen, 'Indonesia's ulama and politics'; and Aswab Mahasin, 'Islam in Indonesia', are important sources on religious aspects of this period.

For sources on such matters as population, welfare and religious affiliation the publications of Biro Pusat Statistik are valuable. Its *Statistik Indonesia 1986* has been particularly helpful for the topics in this chapter. Comparative information is available in United Nations *Statistical yearbooks*; that for *1983/84* has been useful here. For discussions of emerging social class issues, see Tanter and Young, *Middle class Indonesia*.

Bibliography

Abbreviations of journals

AS	*Asian Survey*
BEFEO	*Bulletin de l'École Française d'Extrême-Orient*
BIES	*Bulletin of Indonesian Economic Studies*
BKI	*Bijdragen tot de Taal-, Land- en Volkenkunde*
BSOAS	*Bulletin of the School of Oriental and African Studies*
JAS	*Journal of Asian Studies*
JMBRAS	*Journal of the Malaysian Branch, Royal Asiatic Society*
JSEAH	*Journal of Southeast Asian History*
JSEAS	*Journal of Southeast Asian Studies*
MAS	*Modern Asian Studies*
MIISI	*Majalah Ilmu-Ilmu Sastra Indonesia /Indonesian Journal of Cultural Studies*
RIMA	*Review of Indonesian and Malayan Affairs*
TBG	*Tijdschrift voor Indische Taal-, Land- en Volkenkunde uitgegeven door het (Koninklijk) Bataviaasch Genootschap van Kunsten en Wetenschappen*
VBG	*Verhandelingen van het (Koninklijk) Bataviaasch Genootschap van Kunsten en Wetenschappen*
VKI	*Verhandelingen van het Koninklijk Instituut voor Taal-, Land- en Volkenkunde*

Abdullah, Taufik. 'Adat and Islam: An examination of conflict in Minangkabau'. *Indonesia*, no. 2 (Oct. 1966), pp. 1–24.

―――― *Schools and politics: The Kaum Muda movement in West Sumatra (1927–1933)*. Ithaca: Cornell Modern Indonesia Project Monograph Series, 1971.

―――― and Sharon Siddique (eds). *Islam and society in Southeast Asia*. Singapore: Institute of Southeast Asian Studies, 1986.

Abdurachman, Paramita R. 'Atakiwan, casados and tupassi: Portuguese settlements and Christian communities in Solor and Flores (1536–1630)'. *Masyarakat Indonesia*, vol. 10, no. 1 (1983), pp. 83–117.

―――― 'Moluccan responses to the first intrusions of the West'. Pp. 161–88 in Soebadio and Sarvaas, *Dynamics of Indonesian history* (see below).

―――― *et al.* (eds). *Bunga rampai sejarah Maluku (I)*. Jakarta: Lembaga Penelitian Sejarah Maluku, 1973.

Abeyasekere, Susan. *Jakarta: A history.* Singapore, etc.: Oxford University Press, 1987.

_____ *One hand clapping: Indonesian nationalists and the Dutch, 1939–1942.* [Clayton, Victoria:] Monash Papers on Southeast Asia no. 5, 1976.

_____ 'Partai Indonesia Raja, 1936–42: A study in cooperative nationalism'. *JSEAS*, vol. 3, no. 2 (Sept. 1972), pp. 262–76.

_____ 'The Soetardjo petition'. *Indonesia*, no. 15 (Apr. 1973), pp. 81–107.

Alfian, Teuku Ibrahim. 'Acheh Sultanate under Sultan Mohammad Daudsyah and the Dutch war'. Pp. 147–66 in Kartodirdjo, *Profiles* (see below).

_____ *Perang di jalan Allah: Perang Aceh 1873–1912.* Jakarta: Pustaka Sinar Harapan, 1987.

Allen, G. C. , and Audrey G. Donnithorne. *Western enterprise in Indonesia and Malaya: A study in economic development.* London: George Allen & Unwin, 1957.

Anak Agung Gde Agung, Ide. *Bali pada abad XIX: Perjuangan rakyat dan raja-raja menentang kolonialisme Belanda 1808–1908.* Yogyakarta: Gadjah Mada University Press, 1989.

Andaya, Leonard Y. *The heritage of Arung Palakka: A history of South Sulawesi (Celebes) in the seventeenth century.* VKI vol. 91. The Hague: Martinus Nijhoff, 1981.

_____ *The kingdom of Johor, 1641-1728.* Kuala Lumpur: Oxford University Press, 1975.

_____ 'The nature of kingship in Bone'. Pp. 115-25 in Reid and Castles, *Pre-colonial state systems* (see below).

Anderson, B. R. O'G. 'How did the Generals die?' *Indonesia* no. 43 (Apr. 1987), pp. 109-134.

_____ 'Japan: "The light of Asia"'. Pp. 13-50 in Josef Silverstein (ed.), *Southeast Asia in World War 11: Four essays.* [New Haven:] Yale University Southeast Asian Studies Monograph Series no. 7, 1966.

_____ *Java in a time of revolution: Occupation and resistance, 1944-1946.* Ithaca: Cornell University Press, 1972.

_____ *Some aspects of Indonesian politics under the Japanese occupation, 1944-1945.* Ithaca: Cornell Modern Indonesia Project Interim Reports Series, 1961.

Anderson, David Charles. 'The military aspects of the Madiun affair'. *Indonesia* no. 21 (Apr. 1976), pp. 1-63.

Arndt, H. W. 'Transmigration: Achievements, problems, prospects'. *BIES* vol. 19, no. 3 (Dec. 1983), pp. 50-73.

Arsip Nasional Republic Indonesia. *Ikhtisar keadaan politik Hindia-Belanda, tahun 1839-1848.* Jakarta: Arsip Nasional R. I. , 1973.

_____ *Laporan politik tahun 1837 (Staatkundig overzicht van Nederlandsch Indië, 1837).* Djakarta: Arsip Nasional R. I. , 1971.

Aswab Mahasin (ed.). 'Islam in Indonesia: In search of a new image'. *Prisma: The Indonesian Indicator* no. 35 (Mar. 1985).

Atja (ed. & transl.). *Carita Purwaka Caruban Nagari: Karya sastra sebagai sumber pengetahuan sejarah.* 2nd revised edn [Bandung:] Proyek Pengembangan Permuseuman Jawa Barat, 1986.

Attas, Muhammad Naguib al-. *The mysticism of Hamzah Fansuri.* Kuala Lumpur: University of Malaya Press, 1970.

_____ *Rānīrī and the Wujūdiyyah of 17th century Acheh.* Singapore: Monographs of the Malaysian Branch of the Royal Asiatic Society no. 3, 1966.

Aziz, M. A. *Japan's colonialism and Indonesia.* The Hague: Martinus Nijhoff, 1955.

Bachtiar, Harsja W. 'Raden Saleh: Aristocrat, painter, and scientist'. *MIISI* vol. 6, no. 3 (Aug. 1976), pp. 31-79.

Bakker, H. 'Het economisch belang van Nord-Sumatra tijdens de Atjehoorlog, 1873-1910'. Pp. 41-65 in A. H. P. Clemens and J. Th. Lindblad (eds), *Het belang van de buitengewesten: Economische expansie en koloniale staatsvorming in de buitengewesten van Nederlands-Indië, 1870-1942.* Amsterdam: NEHA, 1989.

Barnes, R. H. 'Avarice and iniquity at the Solor Fort'. *BKI* vol. 143, nos 2-3 (1987), pp. 208-36.

Baroroh Baried. 'Islam and the modernization of Indonesian women'. Pp. 139-54 in Abdullah and Siddique, *Islam and society in Southeast Asia* (see above).

Bastin, John. *The native policies of Sir Stamford Raffles in Java and Sumatra: An economic interpretation.* Oxford: Clarendon Press, 1957.

_____ *Raffles' ideas on the land rent system in Java and the Mackenzie land tenure commission. VKI* vol. 14. 's-Gravenhage: Martinus Nijhoff, 1954.

Bayly, C. A. , and D. H. A. Kolff (eds). *Two colonial empires: Comparative essays on the history of India and Indonesia in the nineteenth century.* Dordrecht & Boston: M. Nijhoff Publishers, 1986.

Beasley, W. G. *The modern history of Japan.* 3rd edn London: Weidenfeld & Nicolson, 1981.

Benda, Harry J. *The crescent and the rising sun: Indonesian Islam under the Japanese occupation, 1942–1945.* The Hague & Bandung: W. van Hoeve, 1958.

_____ and Lance Castles. 'The Samin movement'. *BKI,* vol. 125, no. 2 (1969), pp. 207–40.

Berg, C. C. *Het rijk van de vijfvoudige Buddha.* (Verhandelingen der Koninklijke Nederlandse Akademie van Wetenschappen, Afd. Letterkunde, vol. 69, no. 1.) Amsterdam: N.V. Noord-Hollandsche Uitgevers Maatschappij, 1962.

_____ 'Twee nieuwe publicaties betreffende de geschiedenis en de geschiedschrijving van Mataram'. *Indonesië,* vol. 8 (1955), pp. 97–128.

Bezemer, T. J. (ed.) *Beknopte encyclopaedie van Nederlandsch-Indië, naar den tweeden druk der encyclopaedie van Nederlandsch-Indië.* 's-Gravenhage & Leiden: Martinus Nijhoff & E. J. Brill, 1921.

Bijleveld, J. 'De Saminbeweging'. *Koloniaal Tijdschrift,* vol. 12 (1923), pp. 10–24.

Bijlmer, Joseph Johannes Maria. *Ambulante straatberoepen in Surabaya: Een studie naar kleinschalige economische activiteiten.* Doctoral thesis, Vrije Universiteit te Amsterdam. Amsterdam: VU Uitgeverij, 1987.

Biro Pusat Statistik. *Beberapa ciri pemeluk agama di Indonesia 1980.* Jakarta: Biro Pusat Statistik, Bagian Statistik Kesejahteraan Rakyat, [1984].

_____ *Sensus Penduduk 1971 / 1971 population census.* 33 vols. Jakarta: Biro Pusat Statistik, 1971–75.

_____ *Statistik Indonesia 1986.* Jakarta, 1987.

Blussé, Leonard. *Strange company: Chinese settlers, mestizo women and the Dutch in VOC Batavia. VKI,* vol. 122. Dordrecht & Riverton: Foris Publications, 1986.

Boland, B. J. *The struggle of Islam in modern Indonesia. VKI,* vol. 59. The Hague: Martinus Nijhoff, 1971.

Bone, Robert C. , Jr. *The dynamics of the Western New Guinea (Irian Barat) problem.* Ithaca: Cornell Modern Indonesia Project Interim Reports Series, 1958.

Boomgaard, Peter. *Children of the colonial state: Population growth and economic development in Java, 1795–1880.* Amsterdam: Free University Press, 1989.

―――― 'The welfare services in Indonesia, 1900–1942'. *Itinerario,* vol. 10, no. 1 (1986), pp. 57–81.

Booth, Anne. *Agricultural development in Indonesia.* Sydney, etc.: Allen and Unwin, 1988.

―――― *The economic development of Southeast Asia, 1870–1985.* Clayton: Monash University Centre of Southeast Asian Studies Working Paper 63, 1990.

―――― 'Living standards and the distribution of income in colonial Indonesia: A review of the evidence'. *JSEAS,* vol. 19, no. 2 (Sept. 1988), pp. 310–34.

―――― 'The state and economic development in Indonesia: The ethical and new order eras compared'. Pp. 111–26 in R. J. May and William J. O'Malley (eds), *Observing change in Asia: Essays in honour of J. A. C. Mackie.* Bathurst: Crawford House Press, 1989.

―――― and Peter McCawley (eds). *The Indonesian economy during the Soeharto era.* Kuala Lumpur, etc.: Oxford University Press, 1981.

―――― *et al.* (eds) *Indonesian economic history in the Dutch colonial era.* New Haven: Yale University South-East Asia Studies Monograph Series, 35, 1990.

Bootsma, N. A. *Buren in de koloniale tijd: De Philippijnen order Amerikaans bewind en de Nederlandse, Indische en Indonesische reacties daarop, 1898–1942. VKI,* vol. 119. Dordrecht & Riverton: Foris Publications, 1986.

Boxer, C. R. *The Dutch seaborne empire, 1600–1800.* London: Hutchinson & Co., 1965; Harmondsworth: Penguin, 1973.

―――― *The Portuguese seaborne empire, 1415–1825.* New York: Alfred A. Knopf, 1969.

Brand, W. 'Some statistical data on Indonesia'. *BKI,* vol. 125, no. 3 (1969), pp. 305–27.

Brandes, J. L. A. (ed. & transl.).*Pararaton (Ken Arok) of het boek der koningen van Tumapěl en van Majapahit.* 2nd edn, ed. N. J. Krom. *VBG,* vol. 62 (1920).

Brandon, James R. (ed.). *On thrones of gold: Three Javanese shadow plays.* Cambridge, Mass.: Harvard University Press, 1970.

Breman, Jan. *Control of land and labour in colonial Java: A case study of agrarian crisis and reform in the region of Cirebon during the first decades of the 20th century. VKI,* vol. 101. Dordrecht & Cinnaminson, N.J. : Foris Publications, 1983.

Brown, C. C. (transl.). *Sějarah Mělayu, or Malay annals.* Kuala Lumpur: Oxford University Press, 1970. Originally published in *JMBRAS,* vol. 25, pts. 2–3 (Oct. 1952).

Brugmans, I. J. *Geschiedenis van het onderwijs in Nederlandsch-Indië.* Groningen & Batavia: J. B. Wolters' Uitgevers-Maatschappij N. V. , 1938.

Bruinessen, Martin van. 'Bukankah orang Kurdi yang mengislamkan Indonesia?' *Pesantren,* vol. 4, no. 4 (1987), pp. 43–53.

―――― 'Indonesia's ulama and politics: Caught between legitimising the status quo and searching for alternatives'. *Prisma,* no. 49 (June 1990), pp. 52–69.

―――― 'The origins and development of the Naqshbandi order in Indonesia'. *Der Islam,* vol. 67, pt. 1 (1990), pp. 150–79.

Bunnell, Frederick P. 'The Central Intelligence Agency-Deputy Directorate for

Plans 1961 secret memorandum on Indonesia: A study in the politics of policy formulation in the Kennedy administration'. *Indonesia*, no. 22 (Oct. 1976), pp. 131–69.

——— 'Guided democracy foreign policy: 1960–1965'. *Indonesia*, no. 2 (Oct. 1966), pp. 37–76.

Burger, D. H. *Sociologisch-economische geschiedenis van Indonesia.* Intro. by J. S. Wigboldus. 2 vols. Amsterdam: Koninklijk Instituut voor de Tropen; Wageningen: Landbouwhogeschool; Leiden: Koninklijk Instituut voor Taal-, Land- en Volkunkunde, 1975.

Carey, P. B. R. 'Changing Javanese perceptions of the Chinese communities in Central Java, 1755–1825'. *Indonesia*, no. 37 (Apr. 1984), pp. 1–47.

——— 'The origins of the Java War (1825–30)'. *The English Historical Review,* vol. 91, no. 358 (Jan. 1976), pp. 52–78.

——— 'Pangeran Dipanagara and the making of the Java War'. Unpublished D. Phil. thesis, Oxford University, 1975.

——— 'Raden Saleh, Dipanagara and the painting of the capture of Dipanagara at Magelang'. *JMBRAS*, vol. 55, pt. 1 (1982), pp. 1–25.

——— 'Satria and santri: Some notes on the relationship between Dipanagara's kraton and religious supporters during the Java War (1825–30)'. Pp. 271–318 in Ibrahim Alfian *et al.* (eds), *Dari babad dan hikayat sampai sejarah kritis: Kumpulan karangan dipersembahkan kepada Prof. Dr. Sartono Kartodirdjo.* Yogyakarta: Gadjah Mada University Press, 1987.

——— 'The Sepoy conspiracy of 1815 in Java'. *BKI*, vol. 133, nos. 2–3 (1977), pp. 294–322.

——— 'Waiting for the "just king": The agrarian world of South-Central Java from Giyanti (1755) to the Java War (1825–30)'. *MAS*, vol. 20, pt. 1 (Feb. 1986), pp. 59–137.

Carlson, Sevinc. *Indonesia's oil.* Washington, D. C. : Center for Strategic and International Studies, Georgetown University, 1976. Reprinted Boulder, Colo.: Westview Press, 1977.

Casparis, J. G. de. 'Ahmat Majanu's tombstone at Pengkalan Kempas and its Kawi inscription'. *JMBRAS*, vol. 53, pt. 1 (1980), pp. 1–22.

Castles, Lance. *Religion, politics and economic behavior in Java: The Kudus cigarette industry.* New Haven: Yale University Southeast Asia Studies Cultural Report Series no. 15, 1967.

——— 'Statelessness and stateforming tendencies among the Bataks before colonial rule'. Pp. 67–76 in Reid and Castles, *Pre-colonial state systems* (see below).

Cense, A. A. 'Old Buginese and Macassarese diaries'. *BKI*, vol. 122, no. 4 (1966), pp. 416–28.

Chambert-Loir, Henri. 'Bibliographie de la littérature malaise en traduction'. *BEFEO*, vol. 62 (1975), pp. 395–439.

Chauvel, Richard. *Nationalists, soldiers and separatists: The Ambonese islands from colonialism to revolt, 1880–1950.* VKI, vol. 143. Leiden: KITLV Press, 1990.

Chen Dasheng. 'Une pierre tombale du début du XIVe siècle retrouvée à Brunei'. *Archipel,* no. 42 (1991), pp. 47–52.

Coedès, George. *Les états hindouisés d'Indochine et d'Indonésie.* New edn. Paris: Editions E. de Boccard, 1964.

_____ The Indianized states of Southeast Asia. Transl. Susan Brown Cowing. Ed. Walter F. Vella. Honolulu: East-West Center Press, 1968.

Colbert, Evelyn. Southeast Asia in international politics, 1941–1956. Ithaca & London: Cornell University Press, 1977.

Colenbrander, H. T. , and W. Ph. Coolhaas (eds). Jan Pietersz. Coen: Bescheiden omtrent zijn bedrijf in Indië. 7 vols. 's-Gravenhage: Martinus Nijhoff, 1919–53.

Coolhaas, W. Ph., and J. van Goor (eds). Generale missiven van Gouverneurs-Generaal en Raden aan Heren XVII der Verenigde Oostindische Compagnie, vols I–. 's-Gravenhage: Martinus Nijhoff, 1960–.

Coolsma, S. De zendingseeuw voor Nederlandsch Oost-Indië. Utrecht: G. H. E.Breijer, 1901.

Coppel, Charles A. Indonesian Chinese in crisis. Kuala Lumpur, etc.: Oxford University Press, 1983.

Cortesão, Armando (ed. & transl.). The Suma Oriental of Tomé Pires and the book of Francisco Rodrigues. 2 vols. London: The Hakluyt Society, 1944.

Creese, Helen. 'Balinese babad as historical sources: A reinterpretation of the fall of Gèlgèl'. BKI, vol. 147 (1991), nos 2–3, pp. 236–60.

Cribb, Robert. Gangsters and revolutionaries: The Jakarta people's militia and the Indonesian Revolution, 1945–1949. North Sydney: Asian Studies Association of Australia in association with Allen and Unwin, 1991.

_____ (ed.). The Indonesian killings of 1965–1966: Studies from Java and Bali. Monash Papers on Southeast Asia no. 21. Clayton: Monash University Centre of Southeast Asian Studies, 1990.

Crouch, Harold. The army and politics in Indonesia. Ithaca & London: Cornell University Press, 1978.

Dahm, Bernard. Sukarno and the struggle for Indonesian independence. Transl. Mary F. Somers Heidhues. Ithaca & London: Cornell University Press, 1969.

_____ Sukarnos Kampf um Indonesiens Unabhängigkeit: Werdegang und Ideen eines asiatischen Nationalisten. Berlin & Frankfurt am Main: Alfred Metzner Verlag, 1966.

Damais, Louis-Charles. 'L'épigraphie musulmane dans le Sud-Est Asiatique'. BEFEO, vol. 54 (1968), pp. 567–604.

_____ 'Études javanaises, I: Les tombes musulmanes datées de Trålåjå'. BEFEO, vol. 48, pt. 2 (1957), pp. 353–415.

Day, Clive. The policy and administration of the Dutch in Java. New York: The Macmillan Company, 1904. Reprinted Kuala Lumpur, etc.: Oxford University Press, 1966.

Departement van Economische Zaken. Volkstelling 1930 / Census of 1930 in the Netherlands Indies. 8 vols. Batavia: Landsdrukkerij, 1933–6.

Deventer, C. Th.van. Overzicht van den economischen toestand der inlandsche bevolking van Java en Madoera. 's-Gravenhage: Martinus Nijhoff, 1904.

Dewantara, Ki Hadjar. Beoefening van letteren en kunst in het Pakoe-Alamsche geslacht. Djokjakarta: H.Buning, 1931.

Dhakidae, Daniel (ed.). 'Manusia dan agama: mencari ufuk baru'. Prisma, vol. 7, no. 5 (June 1978).

Dhofier, Zamakhsyari. Tradisi pesantren: Studi tentang pandangan hidup kyai. Jakarta: LP3ES, 1982.

Diffie, Bailey W. , and George D.Winius. Foundations of tbe Portuguese empire,

1415–1580. Minneapolis: University of Minnesota Press & Oxford University Press, 1977.

Dijk, C. van. *Rebellion under the banner of Islam: The Darul Islam in Indonesia. VKI,* vol. 94. The Hague: Martinus Nijhoff, 1981.

Djajadiningrat, Hoesein. *Critische beschouwing van de Sadjarah Bantĕn: Bijdrage ter kenschetsing van de Javaansche geschiedschrijving.* Haarlem; Joh. Enschedé en Zonen, 1913.

_____ 'Critisch overzicht van de in Maleische werken vervatte gegevens over de geschiedenis van het Soeltanaat van Atjeh'. *BKI,* vol. 65 (1911), pp. 135–265.

Djoko Suryo. 'Economic crisis and its impact on rural Java: A case study of the Semarang residency in the latter half of the 19th century'. Pp. 115–30 in Taufik Abdullah and Sartono Kartodirdjo (eds), *Papers of the fourth Indonesian-Dutch history conference, 24–29 July 1983.* 2 vols. Yogyakarta: Gadjah Mada University Press, 1986.

_____ *Sejarah sosial pedesaan Karesidenan Semarang 1830–1900.* Yogyakarta: Pusat Antar Universitas Studi Sosial, Universitas Gadjah Mada, 1989.

Dobbin, Christine. 'Economic change in Minangkabau as a factor in the rise of the Padri movement, 1784–1830'. *Indonesia,* no. 23 (Apr. 1977), pp. 1–38.

_____ *Islamic revivalism in a changing peasant economy: Central Sumatra, 1784–1847.* London & Malmö: Curzon Press, 1983.

_____ 'Islamic revivalism in Minangkabau at the turn of the nineteenth century'. *MAS,* vol. 8, no. 3 (1974), pp. 319–45.

_____ 'Tuanku Imam Bondjol (1772–1864)'. *Indonesia,* no. 13 (Apr. 1972), pp. 5–35.

Drake, Christine. *National integration in Indonesia: Patterns and policies.* Honolulu: University of Hawaii Press, 1989.

Drewes, G. W. J. (ed. & transl.). *The admonitions of Seh Bari.* The Hague: Martinus Nijhoff, 1969.

_____ (ed. and transl.). *An early Javanese code of Muslim ethics.* The Hague: Martinus Nijhoff, 1978.

_____ *Drie Javaansche goeroe's: Hun leven, onderricht en messiasprediking.* Leiden: Drukkerij A. Vros, 1925.

_____ (ed. & transl.). *Een Javaanse primbon uit de zestiende eeuw.* Leiden: E. J. Brill, 1954.

_____ 'New light on the coming of Islam to Indonesia?' *BKI,* vol. 124, no. 4 (1968), pp. 433–59.

_____ 'Nūr al-Dīn al-Rānīrī's charge of heresy against Hamzah and Shamsuddin from an international point of view'. Pp. 54–9 in Grijns and Robson, *Cultural contact* (see below).

_____ 'The struggle between Javanism and Islam as illustrated by the Sĕrat Dĕrmagandul'. *BKI,* vol. 122, no. 3 (1966), pp. 309–65.

_____ and L. F. Brakel (eds and transls). *The poems of Hamzah Fansuri.* Dordrecht and Cinnaminson: Foris Publications, 1986.

Drooglever, P. J. *De Vaderlandse Club 1929–1942: Totoks en de Indische politiek.* Franeker: Uitgeveriji T. Wever B. V. , 1980.

Dunn, James. *Timor: A people betrayed.* Milton, Qld.: The Jacaranda Press, 1983.

Ekadjati, E. Suhardi. *Ceritera Dipati Ukur: Karya sastra sejarah sunda.* Jakarta: Pustaka Jaya, 1982.

Elsbree, Willard H. *Japan's role in Southeast Asian nationalist movements, 1940 to 1945*. Cambridge, Mass.: Harvard University Press, 1953.

Elson, Robert. 'The famine in Demak and Grobogan in 1849–50: Its causes and circumstances'. *RIMA*, vol. 19, no. 1 (Winter 1985), pp. 39–85.

—— 'The impact of government sugar cultivation in the Pasuruan area, East Java, during the cultivation system period'. *RIMA*, vol. 12, no. 1 (June 1978), pp. 26–55.

—— *Javanese peasants and the colonial sugar industry: Impact and change in an East Java Residency, 1830–1940*. Singapore, etc.: Oxford University Press, 1984.

Ensering, Else. 'Afdeeling B of Sarekat Islam: A rebellious Islamic movement'. Pp. 99–122 in Kooiman, *Conversion, competition and conflict* (see below).

Fasseur, C. 'The cultivation system and its impact on the Dutch colonial economy and the indigenous society in nineteenth-century Java'. Pp. 137–54 in Bayly and Kolff, *Two colonial empires* (see above).

—— 'Een koloniale paradox: De Nederlandse expansie in de Indonesische archipel in het midden van de negentiende eeuw (1830–1870)'. *Tijdschrift voor Geschiedenis*, vol. 92 (1979), pp. 162–86.

—— (ed.). *Geld en geweten: Een bundel opstellen over anderhalve eeuw Nederlands bestuur in de Indonesische archipel.* 2 vols. Den Haag: Martinus Nijhoff, 1980.

—— *Kultuurstelsel en koloniale baten: De Nederlandse exploitatie van Java 1840–1860*. Leiden: Universitaire Pers, 1975.

—— 'Nederland en het Indonesische nationalisme: De balans nog eens opgemaakt'. *Bijdragen en mededelingen betreffende de geschiedenis der Nederlanden*, vol. 99, no. 1 (1984), pp. 21–44.

—— 'Organisatie en sociaal-economische betekenis van de gouvernements-suikerkultuur in enkele residenties op Java omstreeks 1850'. *BKI*, vol. 133, nos. 2–3 (1977), pp. 261–93.

—— *The politics of colonial exploitation: Java, the Dutch and the cultivation system.* Trans. R. E. Elson and Ary Kraal. Ithaca: Cornell University South-East Asia Program, 1992.

—— 'Purse or principle: Dutch colonial policy in the 1860s and the decline of the cultivation system'. *MAS*, vol. 25, no. 1 (1991), pp. 33–52.

Federspiel, Howard M. 'The Muhammadijah: A study of an orthodox Islamic movement in Indonesia'. *Indonesia*, no. 10 (Oct. 1970), pp. 57–79.

—— *Persatuan Islam: Islamic reform in twentieth century Indonesia*. Ithaca: Cornell Modern Indonesia Project Monograph Series, 1970.

Feith, Herbert. *The decline of constitutional democracy in Indonesia*. Ithaca: Cornell University Press, 1962.

—— 'Dynamics of guided democracy'. Pp. 309–409 in McVey, *Indonesia* (see below).

—— 'Indonesia'. Pp. 183–278 in George McTurnan Kahin (ed.), *Governments and politics of Southeast Asia*. 2nd edn. Ithaca: Cornell University Press, 1964.

—— and Lance Castles (eds). *Indonesian political thinking, 1945–1965*. Ithaca & London: Cornell University Press, 1970.

Fifield, Russell H. *The diplomacy of Southeast Asia, 1945–1958*. New York: Harper & Row, 1958. Reprinted [Hamden, Conn.:] Archon Books, 1968.

—— *Southeast Asia in United States policy*. New York: Frederick A. Praeger, 1963.

Fisher, Charles A. *South-East Asia: A social, economic and political geography.* London: Methuen & Co.; New York: E. P. Dutton & Co., 1964.

Foulcher, Keith R. *'Pujangga Baru': Literature and nationalism in Indonesia 1933–1942* [Adelaide:] Flinders University Asian Studies Monograph no. 2, 1980.

———— *Social commitment in literature and the arts: The Indonesian 'Institute of People's Culture' 1950–1965.* Clayton: Centre of Southeast Asian Studies, Monash University, 1986.

———— 'A survey of events surrounding "Manikebu": The struggle for cultural and intellectual freedom in Indonesian literature'. *BKI*, vol. 125, no. 4 (1969), pp. 429–65.

Fox, James J. *Harvest of the palm: Ecological change in eastern Indonesia.* Cambridge, Mass. & London: Harvard University Press, 1977.

França, Antonio Pinto da. *Portuguese influence in Indonesia.* Djakarta: Gunung Agung, 1970.

Frederick, William H. *Visions and heat: The making of the Indonesian Revolution.* Athens: Ohio University Press, 1989.

Friend, Theodore. *The blue-eyed enemy: Japan against the West in Java and Luzon, 1942–1945.* Princeton: Princeton University Press, 1988.

Furnivall, J. S. *Colonial policy and practice: A comparative study of Burma and Netherlands India.* Cambridge: University Press, 1948.

———— *Netherlands India: A study of plural economy.* Intro. by A. C. D. de Graeff. Cambridge University Press, 1939. Reprinted 1967.

Geertz, Clifford. *The religion of Java.* Glencoe: The Free Press, 1960.

Gelderen, J. van. *The recent development of economic foreign policy in the Netherlands East Indies.* London, etc.: Longmans, Green & Co., 1939.

Gerretson, [F.]C. *Geschiedenis der 'Koninklijke'.* 3 vols. in 4. Haarlem: J. Enschedé, 1932–41.

———— *History of the Royal Dutch.* 4 vols. Leiden: E. J. Brill, 1958.

Gijsberti Hodenpijl, A. K. A. 'De zwerftocht van Sultan Pakoeboewana II na diens vlucht uit den kraton te Kartasoera op 30 Juni 1742'. *BKI*, vol. 74 (1918), pp. 562–614.

Glamann, Kristof. *Dutch-Asiatic trade 1620–1740.* Copenhagen: Danish Science Press; The Hague: Martinus Nijhoff, 1958.

Goswami, O. 'The Depression, 1930–1935: Its effects on India and Indonesia'. *Itinerario*, vol. 10, no. 1 (1986), pp. 163–76.

Gould, James W. *Americans in Sumatra.* The Hague: Martinus Nijhoff, 1961.

Graaf, H. J. de (ed.). *De expeditie van Anthonio Hurdt, Raad van Indië, als Admiraal en Superintendent naar de binnenlanden van Java, Sept.–Dec. 1678, volgens het journaal van Johan Jurgen Briel, Secretaris.* 's-Gravenhage: Martinus Nijhoff, 1971.

———— *De geschiedenis van Ambon en de Zuid-Molukken.* Franeker: T. Wever B. V. , 1977.

———— 'Gevangenneming en dood van Raden Truna-Djaja, 26 Dec. 1679–2 Jan. 1680'. *TBG*, vol. 85, pt. 2 (1952), pp. 273–309.

———— 'De historische betrouwbaarheid der Javaanse overlevering'. *BKI*, vol. 112, no. 1 (1956), pp. 55–73.

———— 'Lombok in de 17e eeuw'. *Djåwå,* vol. 21, no. 6 (Nov. 1941), pp. 355–73.

_____ De moord op Kapitein François Tack, 8 Febr. 1686. Amsterdam: H. J. Paris, 1935.

_____ De regering van Panembahan Sénapati Ingalaga. VKI, vol. 13. 's-Gravenhage: Martinus Nijhoff, 1954.

_____ De regering van Sultan Agung, vorst van Mataram 1613–1645, en die van zijn voorganger Panembahan Séda-ing-Krapjak 1601–1613. VKI, vol. 23. 's-Gravenhage: Martinus Nijhoff, 1958.

_____ De regering van Sunan Mangku-Rat I Tegal-Wangi, vorst van Mataram 1646–1677. 2 vols. VKI, vols. 33, 39. 's-Gravenhage: Martinus Nijhoff, 1961, 1962.

_____ 'Het Semarangse geslacht Bustam in de 18e en 19e eeuw: Afkomst en jeugd van Radèn Salèh'. BKI, vol. 135, nos 2–3 (1979), pp. 252–81.

_____ (ed.). De vijf gezantschapsreizen van Rijklof van Goens naar het hof van Mataram, 1648–1654. 's-Gravenhage: Martinus Nijhoff, 1956.

_____ and Th. G. Th. Pigeaud. De eerste Moslimse vorstendommen op Java: Studiën over de staatkundige geschiedenis van de 15de en 16de eeuw. VKI, vol. 69. 's-Gravenhage: Martinus Nijhoff, 1974.

Grijns, C. D., and S. O. Robson (eds). Cultural contact and textual interpretation: Papers from the fourth European colloquium on Malay and Indonesian studies, held in Leiden in 1983. VKI, vol. 115. Dordrecht & Cinnaminson: Foris Publications, 1986.

Groeneveldt, W. P. Notes on the Malay Archipelago and Malacca compiled from Chinese sources. VBG, vol. 39, pt. 1 (1877).

Guillot, C. 'L'affaire Sadrach: Un essai de christianisation à Java au XIXe siècle. Paris: Editions de la Maison des Sciences de l'Homme, 1981.

_____ 'La nécessaire relecture de l'accord luso-soundanais de 1522'. Archipel, no. 42 (1991), pp. 53–76.

Gullick, J. M. Indigenous political systems of western Malaya. London: The Athlone Press, 1958.

Haan, F. de. Priangan: De Preanger-Regentschappen onder het Nederlansch bestuur tot 1811. 4 vols. [Batavia:] Bataviaasch Genootschap van Kunsten en Wetenschappen, 1910–1912.

Hadi Soesastro, M. 'The political economy of deregulation in Indonesia'. AS, vol. 29, no. 9 (Sept. 1989), pp. 853–69.

Hadiwijono, Harun. Man in the present Javanese mysticism. Baarn: Bosch & Keuning, 1967.

Hardy, P. 'Modern European and Muslim explanations of conversion to Islam in South Asia: A preliminary survey of the literature'. Journal of the Royal Asiatic Society 1977, no. 2, pp. 177–206. Reprinted pp. 68–99 in Levtzion, Conversion to Islam (see below).

Harvey, Barbara S. Pemberontakan Kahar Muzakkar: Dari tradisi ke DI/TII. Jakarta: Pustaka Utama Grafiti, 1989.

_____ Permesta: Half a rebellion. Ithaca: Cornell Modern Indonesia Project Monograph Series, 1977.

Haspel, C. Ch. van den. Overwicht in overleg: Hervormingen van justitie, grondgebruik en bestuur in de vorstenlanden op Java, 1880–1930. VKI, vol. 111. Dordrecht & Cinnaminson: Foris Publications, 1985.

Hauswedell, Peter Christian, 'Sukarno: Radical or conservative? Indonesian politics 1964–5'. *Indonesia*, no. 15 (Apr. 1973), pp. 109–43.

Hefner, Robert W. 'Islamizing Java? Religion and politics in rural east Java'. *JAS*, vol. 46, no. 3 (Aug. 1987), pp. 533–54.

Heinzlmeir, Helmut. *Indonesiens Aussenpolitik nach Sukarno, 1965–1970: Möglichkeiten und Grenzen eines bündnisfreien Entwicklungslandes.* Hamburg: Mitteilungen des Instituts für Asienkunde, 1976.

Hering, B. B. 'Nogmaals de vier brieven van Ir. Soekarno'. *BKI*, vol. 145, nos 2–3 (1989) pp. 281–94.

Hill, A. H. (ed. & transl.). 'Hikayat Raja-raja Pasai: A revised romanised version of Raffles MS 67, together with an English translation'. *JMBRAS*, vol. 33, no. 2 (1960), pp. 1–215.

Hindley, Donald. 'Alirans and the fall of the old order'. *Indonesia*, no. 9 (Apr. 1970), pp. 23–66.

——— *The Communist Party of Indonesia, 1951–1963.* Berkeley & Los Angeles. University of California Press, 1966.

Hinzler, H. I. R. 'The Balinese babad'. Pp. 39–52 in Kartodirdjo, *Profiles* (see below).

Hoadley, Mason C. 'Javanese, *peranakan* and Chinese elites in Cirebon: Changing ethnic boundaries'. *JAS*, vol. 47, no. 3 (Aug. 1988), pp. 503–17.

Holt, Claire. *Art in Indonesia: Continuities and change.* Ithaca: Cornell University Press, 1967.

Hood, Mantle, and José Maceda. *Music.* Handbuch der Orientalistik, dritte Abteilung: Indonesien, Malaysia und die Philippinen unter Einschluss der Kap-Malaien in Südafrika, sechster Band. Leiden & Köln: E. J. Brill, 1972.

Horikoshi, Hiroko. 'The Dar ul-Islam movement in West Java (1948-62): An experience in the historical process'. *Indonesia* no. 20 (Oct. 1975), pp. 59-86.

Houben, Vincentius Johannes Hubertus. *Kraton en Kumpeni: Surakarta en Yogyakarta, 1830-1870.* Doctoral thesis, Leiden University, 1987.

Hourani, Albert. *Arabic thought in the liberal age, 1798-1939.* London: Oxford University Press, 1970.

Hugenholtz, W. R. 'Famine and food supply in Java, 1830-1914'. Pp. 155–88 in Bayly and Kolff, *Two colonial empires* (see above).

Hüsken, Frans. 'Islam and collective action: Rural violence in North Central Java in 1942.' Pp. 123-54 in Kooiman, *Conversion, competition and conflict* (see below).

Indonesia: An Amnesty International Report. London: Amnesty International Publications, 1977.

Indonesia: Sebuah laporan Amnesti Internasional. London: Amnesti Internationa Publications, 1979.

Ingleson, John. *In search of justice: Workers and unions in colonial Java, 1908-1926.* Singapore, etc.: Oxford University Press, 1986.

——— *Road to exile: The Indonesian nationalist movement 1927-1934.* Singapore, etc.: Heinemann Educational Books (Asia), 1979.

——— 'Urban Java during the Depression'. *JSEAS* vol 19, no. 2 (Sept. 1988), pp. 292-309.

Irwin, Graham. *Nineteenth-century Borneo: A study in diplomatic rivalry.* Singapore: Donald Moore Books, 1967. Originally published as *VKI* vol. 15 (1955).

Ito, Takeshi. 'Why did Nuruddin ar-Raniri leave Aceh in 1054 A. H?' *BKI* vol. 134, no. 4 (1978), pp. 489-91.

Jack-Hinton, Colin. 'Marco Polo in South-East Asia'. *JSEAH* vol. 5, no. 2 (Sept. 1964), pp. 43-103.

Jassin, H. B. (ed.). *Amir Hamzah: Radja penjair Pudjangga Baru.* Djakarta: Gunung Agung, 1962.

―――― (ed.). *Angkatan '66. Prosa dan puisi.* Djakarta: Gunung Agung, 1968.

―――― (ed.). *Pudjangga Baru: Prosa dan puisi.* Djakarta: Gunung Agung, 1963.

Jay, Robert R. *Religion and politics in rural Central Java.* New Haven: Yale University Southeast Asia Studies Cultural Report Series no. 12, 1963.

Jellinek, Lea. *The wheel of fortune: The history of a poor community in Jakarta.* Sydney, etc.: Asian Studies Association of Australia in association with Allen and Unwin, 1991.

Jenkins, David. *Suharto and his generals: Indonesian military politics, 1975-1983.* Ithaca: Cornell Modern Indonesian Project Monograph Series, publication no. 64, 1984.

Johns, A. H. 'Islam in Southeast Asia: Reflections and new directions'. *Indonesia* no. 19 (Apr. 1975), pp. 33-55.

―――― 'Malay Sufism, as illustrated in an anonymous collection of 17th century tracts'. *JMBRAS* vol. 30, pt. 2 (no. 178) (Aug. 1957).

―――― 'Quranic exegesis in the Malay world: In search of a profile'. Pp. 257-87 in A. Rippin (ed.), *Approaches to the history of the interpretation of the Qur'an.* Oxford: Oxford University Press, 1988.

―――― 'Sufism as a category in Indonesian literature and history'. *JSEAH* vol. 2, no. 2 (July 1961), pp. 10-23.

Jolliffe, Jill. *East Timor: Nationalism and Colonialism.* St. Lucia: University of Queensland Press, 1978.

Jones, F. C. *Japan's new order in East Asia: Its rise and fall, 1937-45.* London: Oxford University Press, 1954.

Jones, Gavin W. 'Religion and education in Indonesia'. *Indonesia* no. 22 (Oct. 1976), pp. 19-56.

Jones, Russell. 'Ten conversion myths from Indonesia'. Pp. 129-58 in Levtzion, *Conversion to Islam* (see below).

Jonge, Huub de. 'State formation by contract: The Madurese regency of Sumenep, the VOC and the Netherlands East Indies, 1680-1883'. *RIMA* vol. 16, no. 2 (1982), pp. 37-58.

Jonge, J. K. J. de, and M. L. van Deventer (eds). *De opkomst van het Nederlandsch gezag in Oost-Indië: Verzameling van onuitgegeven stukken uit het oud-koloniaal archief.* 16 vols. 's-Gravenhage: Martinus Nijhoff, 1862-1909.

Jorgensen-Dahl, Arnfinn. *Regional organization and order in South-East Asia.* London & Basingstoke: The Macmillan Press Ltd., 1982.

Kahin, Audrey R. (ed.). *Regional dynamics of the Indonesian Revolution: Unity from diversity.* Honolulu: University of Hawaii Press, 1985.

―――― 'Repression and regroupment: Religious and nationalist organizations in West Sumatra in the 1930s'. *Indonesia* no. 38 (Oct. 1984), pp. 39-54.

Kahin, George McTurnan. *Nationalism and revolution in Indonesia.* Ithaca: Cornell University Press, 1952.

Kartodirdjo, Sartono. *The peasants' revolt of Banten in 1888, its conditions, course and sequel: A case study of social movements in Indonesia. VKI* vol. 50. 's-Gravenhage: Martinus Nijhoff, 1966.

―――― (ed.) *Profiles of Malay culture: Historiography, religion and politics.* [Jakarta:] Directorate General of Culture, Ministry of Education and Culture, 1976.

―――― *Protest movements in rural Java: A study of agrarian unrest in the nineteenth and early twentieth centuries.* Singapore, etc.: Oxford University Press, 1973.

Kartomi, Margaret J. 'Music in nineteenth century Java: A precursor to the twentieth century'. *JSEAS* vol. 21, no. 1 (Mar. 1990), pp. 1-34.

Kathirithamby-Wells, J. 'Ahmad Shah ibn Iskandar and the late 17th century "holy war" in Indonesia'. *JMBRAS* vol. 43, pt. 1 (1970), pp. 48-63.

Knaap, G. J. *Kruidnagelen en Christenen: De Verenigde Oost-Indische Compagnie en de bevolking van Ambon 1656-1696. VKI* vol. 125. Dordrecht & Providence: Foris Publications, 1987.

Knight, G. R. '"The people's own cultivation"': Rice and second crops in Pekalongan residency, north Java, in the mid-nineteenth century'. *RIMA* vol. 19, no. 1 (Winter 1985), pp. 1-38.

Kooiman, Dick, Otto van den Muijzenberg and Peter van der Veer (eds). *Conversion, competition and conflict: Essays on the role of religion in Asia.* Amsterdam: Free University Press, 1984.

Korte, J. P. de. *De jaarlijkse financiële verantwoording in de Verenigde Oostindische Compagnie.* Leiden: Martinus Nijhoff, 1984.

Korver, A. P. E. *Sarekat Islam 1912-1916: Opkomst, bloei en structuur van Indonesië's eerste massabeweging.* Amsterdam: Historisch Seminarium van de Universiteit van Amsterdam, 1982.

Kraan, Alfons van der. *Lombok: Conquest, colonization and underdevelopment, 1870-1940.* Singapore, etc.: Heinemann Educational Books (Asia) Ltd., 1980.

Kratz, E. U. 'Islamic attitudes toward modern Indonesian literature'. Pp. 60-93 in Grijns and Robson, *Cultural contact* (see above).

Krom, N. J. *Gouverneur Generaal Gustaaf Willem van Imhoff.* Amsterdam: P. N. van Kampen & Zoon, 1941.

―――― *Hindoe-Javaansche geschiedenis.* 2nd. ed. 's-Gravenhage: Martinus Nijhoff, 1931.

Kühne, Dietrich. *Bevölkerungs- und Beschäftigungsentwicklung in den ASEAN-Ländern seit 1960.* Hamburg: Mitteilungen des Instituts für Asienkunde, 1975.

Kumar, Ann (ed. & transl.). *Surapati, man and legend: A study of three babad traditions.* Leiden: E. J. Brill, 1976.

―――― 'The "Suryengalagan affair" of 1883 and its successors: Born leaders in changed times'. *BKI* vol. 138, nos 2-3 (1982), pp. 251-84.

Kunst, J. *Music in Java: Its history, its theory and its technique.* 3rd enlarged ed., ed. E. L. Heins. 2 vols. The Hague: Martinus Nijhoff, 1973.

Kuntowijoyo (Kuntowidjojo). 'Economic and religious attitudes of entrepreneurs in a village industry: Notes on the community of Batur'. Transl. Mitsuo Nakamura. *Indonesia* no. 12 (Oct. 1971), pp. 47-55.

―――― 'Islam and politics: The local Sarekat Islam movements in Madura, 1913-20'. Pp. 108-38 in Abdullah and Siddique, *Islam and society in Southeast Asia* (see above).

―――― 'Sikap ekonomi dan keagamaan pengusaha didesa industri: Komentar tentang masjarakat Batur'. *Buletin Fakultas Sastra dan Kebudajaan* no. 4

(1971), pp. 163-72.

Kurasawa, Aiko. 'Propaganda media on Java under the Japanese 1942-1945'. *Indonesia* no. 44 (Oct. 1987), pp. 59-116.

Kwantes, R. C. 'Ir. Soekarno's vier brieven'. *BKI* vol. 143, nos 2-3 (1987), pp. 293-311.

Langenberg, Michael van. 'North Sumatra 1942-1945: The onset of a national revolution'. Pp. 33-64 in McCoy, *Southeast Asia under Japanese occupation* (see below).

Lapian, A. B. , and Anthony Day (eds). *Papers of the Dutch-Indonesian historical conference held at Noordwijkerhout, the Netherlands, 19 to 22 May 1976.* Leiden & Jakarta: Bureau of Indonesian Studies, 1978.

Larson, George D. *Prelude to revolution: Palaces and politics in Surakarta, 1912-1942.* *VKI* vol. 124. Dordrecht & Providence: Foris Publications, 1987.

Lee Kam Hing. 'The Taman Siswa in postwar Indonesia'. *Indonesia* no. 25 (Apr. 1978), pp. 41-59.

Legge, John D. '*Daulat Ra'jat* and the ideas of Pendidikan Nasional Indonesia'. *Indonesia* no. 32 (Oct. 1981), pp. 151-68.

_____ *Intellectuals and nationalism in Indonesia: A study of the following recruited by Sutan Sjahrir in occupation Jakarta.* [Ithaca:] Cornell Modern Indonesia Project Monograph Series, 1988.

_____ *Sukarno: A political biography.* 2nd ed. Sydney, etc.: Allen & Unwin, 1985.

Leirissa, R. Z. *PRRI Permesta: Strategi membangun Indonesia tanpa komunis.* Jakarta: Pustaka Utama Grafiti, 1991.

Lev, Daniel S. *The transition to guided democracy: Indonesian politics 1957-1959.* Ithaca: Cornell Modern Indonesia Project Monograph Series, 1966.

Levtzion, Nehemia (ed.). *Conversion to Islam.* New York & London: Holmes & Meier Publishers, 1979.

Levyssohn Norman, H. D. *De Britsche heerschappij over Java en onderhoorigheden (1811 -1816).* 's-Gravenhage: Gebroeders Belinfante, 1857.

Liddle, R. William. 'The relative autonomy of the third world politician: Soeharto and Indonesian economic development in comparative perspective'. *International Studies Quarterly* vol. 35 (1991), pp. 403-27.

Lindblad, J. Thomas. *Between Dayak and Dutch: The economic history of Southeast Kalimantan, 1880-1942.* *VKI* vol. 134. Dordrecht & Providence: Foris Publications, 1988.

Lombard, Denys. *Le carrefour javanais: Essai d'histoire globale.* 3 vols. Paris: Éditions de l'École des Hautes Études en Sciences Sociales, 1990.

_____ *Le Sultanat d'Atjéh au temps d'Iskandar Muda, 1607–1636.* Paris: École Française d'Extrême-Orient, 1967.

Louw, P. J. F. *De derde Javaansche successie-oorlog (1746–1755).* Batavia: Albrecht & Rusche; 's Hage: M. Nijhoff, 1889.

_____ and E. S. de Klerck. *De Java-oorlog van 1825–30.* 6 vols. 's Hage: M. Nijhoff; Batavia: Landsdrukkerij, 1894–1909.

Lucas, Anton. *One soul, one struggle: Region and revolution in Indonesia.* Sydney: Asian Studies Association of Australia in association with Allen and Unwin, 1991.

_____ *Peristiwa tiga daerah: Revolusi dalam revolusi.* Intro. by Sartono Kartodirdjo. Jakarta: Pustaka Utama Grafiti, 1989.

———— 'Social revolution in Pemalang, Central Java, 1945'. *Indonesia,* no. 24 (Oct. 1977), pp. 87–122.

Ma Huan. *Ying-yai Sheng-lan: 'The overall survey of the ocean's shores' (1433).* Ed. and transl. J. V. G. Mills. Cambridge: University Press, 1970.

McIntyre, Angus. 'Divisions and power in the Indonesian National Party, 1965–1966'. *Indonesia,* no. 13 (Apr. 1972), pp. 183–210.

McCoy, Alfred W. (ed.). *Southeast Asia under Japanese occupation.* [New Haven:] Yale University Southeast Asia Studies Monograph Series no. 22, 1980.

McDonald, Barbara. *Old Javanese literature in eighteenth-century Java: A consideration of the processes of transmission.* Clayton: Monash University Centre of Southeast Asian Studies Working Paper no. 41, [1986].

McDonald, Hamish. *Suharto's Indonesia.* Sydney: Fontana/Collins, 1980.

McDonald, Peter F. (ed.). *Pedoman analisa data sensus Indonesia 1971–1980* [Yogyakarta:] Australian Vice-Chancellor's Committee, Australian Universities International Development Program, 1983.

Mackie, J. A. C. *Konfrontasi: The Indonesia-Malaysia dispute, 1963–1966.* Kuala Lumpur, etc.: Oxford University Press, 1974.

McMahon, Robert J. *Colonialism and cold war: The United States and the struggle for Indonesian independence, 1945–1949.* Ithaca: Cornell University Press, 1981.

McVey, Ruth T. 'Faith as the outsider: Islam in Indonesian politics'. Pp. 199–225 in James P. Piscatori (ed.), *Islam in the political process.* Cambridge, etc.: Cambridge University Press in association with The Royal Institute of International Affairs, 1983.

———— (ed.). *Indonesia.* New Haven: HRAF Press, 1963.

———— 'The post-revolutionary transformation of the Indonesian army'. *Indonesia,* no. 11 (Apr. 1971), pp. 131–76; no. 13 (Apr. 1972), pp. 147–81.

———— *The rise of Indonesian Communism.* Ithaca: Cornell University Press, 1965.

———— 'Taman Siswa and the Indonesian national awakening'. *Indonesia,* no. 4 (Oct. 1967), pp. 128–49.

———— *Problems of the Indonesian inflation.* Ithaca: Cornell Modern Indonesia Project Monograph Series, 1967.

Majul, Cesar Adib. *Muslims in the Philippines.* 2nd edn. Quezon City: University of the Philippines Press, 1973.

Mansoer, M. D. , *et al. Sedjarah Minangkabau.* Djakarta: Bhratara, 1970.

Marle, A. van. 'Indonesian electoral geography under Orla and Orba'. Pp. 37–59 in Oey, *Indonesia after the 1971 elections* (see below).

Maronier, J. H. *Pictures of the tropics: A catalogue of drawings, water-colours, paintings and sculptures in the collection of the Royal Institute of Linguistics and Anthropology in Leiden.* 's-Gravenhage: Martinus Nijhoff, 1967.

Masselman, George. *The cradle of colonialism.* New Haven & London: Yale University Press, 1963.

Matheson, Virginia. 'Questions arising from a nineteenth century Riau syair'. *RIMA,* vol. 17 (1983), pp. 1–61.

Meiden, G. W. van der. 'A Turkish mediator between Mangkubumi and the Dutch East India Company (1753–1754)'. *RIMA,* vol. 15, no. 2 (1981), pp. 92–107.

Meilink-Roelofsz, M. A. P. *Asian trade and European influence in the Indonesian Archipelago between 1500 and about 1630.* The Hague: Martinus Nijhoff, 1962.

Mody, Nawaz B. *Indonesia under Suharto.* New York: Apt Books, Inc., 1987.

Moertono, Soemarsaid. *State and statecraft in old Java; A study of the later Mataram period, 16th to 19th century.* Revised edn. Ithaca: Cornell Modern Indonesia Project Monograph Series, 1981.

Morfit, Michael. 'Pancasila: The Indonesian state ideology according to the new order government'. *AS,* vol. 21, no. 8 (Aug. 1981), pp. 838–51.

Mortimer, Rex. *Indonesian Communism under Sukarno: Ideology and politics, 1959–1965.* Ithaca & London: Cornell University Press, 1974.

Mossman, James. *Rebels in paradise: Indonesia's civil war.* London: Jonathan Cape, 1961.

Mozingo, D. *Chinese policy toward Indonesia, 1949–1967.* Ithaca & London: Cornell University Press, 1976.

Mulder, Niels. *Mysticism and everyday life in contemporary Java: Cultural persistence and change.* Singapore: Singapore University Press, 1978.

Naerssen, F. H. van, and R. C. de Iongh. *The economic and administrative history of early Indonesia.* Handbuch der Orientalistik, dritte Abteilung; Indonesien, Malaysia und die Philippinen unter Einschluss der Kap-Malaien in Südafrika, siebenter Band. Leiden & Köln: E. J. Brill, 1977.

Nagazumi Akira. *The dawn of Indonesian nationalism: The early years of the Budi Utomo, 1908–1918.* Tokyo: Institute of Developing Economies, 1972.

Nagtegaal, Lucas Wilhelmus. *Rijden op een Hollandse tijger: De noordkust van Java en de V. O. C. 1680–1743.* Doctoral thesis, Rijksuniversiteit te Utrecht, 1988.

Nakahara, M. 'Muslim merchants in Nan-Hai'. Pp. 1–10 in Raphael Israeli and Anthony H. Johns (eds), *Islam in Asia,* vol. II: *Southeast and East Asia.* Jerusalem: The Magnes Press, The Hebrew University, 1984.

Nakamura, Mitsuo. *The crescent arises over the banyan tree: A study of the Muhammadiyah movement in a central Javanese town.* Yogyakarta: Gadjah Mada University Press, 1983.

Nasution, A. H. *Sekitar perang kemerdekaan Indonesia.* 11 vols. Bandung: Penerbit Angkasa, 1977–9.

Nieuwenhuijze, C. A. O. van. *Šamsu'l-Dīn van Pasai: Bijdrage tot de kennis der Sumatraansche mystiek.* Leiden: E. J. Brill, 1945.

Nishihara, Masashi. *Golkar and the Indonesian elections of 1971.* Ithaca: Cornell Modern Indonesia Project Monograph Series, 1972.

Noer, Deliar. *The Modernist Muslim movement in Indonesia, 1900–1942.* Singapore, etc.: Oxford University Press, 1973.

_____ *Mohammad Hatta: biographie politik.* Jakarta: LP3ES, 1990.

Noorduyn, J. (ed.). *Bima en Sumbawa: Bijdragen tot de geschiedenis van de Sultanaten Bima en Sumbawa door A. Ligtvoet en G. P. Rouffaer.* VKI, vol. 129. Dordrecht & Providence: Foris Publications, 1987.

_____ *Een achttiende-eeuwse kroniek van Wadjo': Buginese historiografie.* 's-Gravenhage: H. L. Smits, 1955.

_____ 'Arung Singkang (1700–1765): How the victory of Wadjo' began'. *Indonesia,* no. 13 (Apr. 1972), pp. 61–8.

_____ 'De Islamisering van Makasar'. *BKI,* vol. 112, no. 3 (1956), pp. 247–66.

_____ 'Majapahit in the fifteenth century'. *BKI,* vol. 134, nos. 2–3 (1978), pp. 207–74.

_____ 'Origins of South Celebes historical writing'. Pp. 137–55 in Soedjatmoko *et al.* (eds). *An introduction to Indonesian historiography.* Ithaca: Cornell University Press, 1965.

Nugroho Notosusanto. 'Soedirman: Panglima yang menepati janjinya'. Pp. 47–62 in Taufik Abdullah *et al.*(eds), *Manusia dalam kemelut sejarah.* Jakarta: Lembaga Penelitian, Pendidikan dan Penerangan Ekonomi dan Sosial, 1978.

Oates, William A. 'The afdeeling B: An Indonesian case study'. *JSEAH,* vol. 9, no. 1 (Mar. 1968), pp. 107–16.

Oey Hong Lee (ed.). *Indonesia after the 1971 elections.* London & Kuala Lumpur: Oxford University Press, 1974.

Olthof, W. L. (ed. & transl.). *Babad Tanah Djawi in proza: Javaansche geschiedenis.* 2 vols. 's-Gravenhage: M. Nijhoff, 1941.

O'Malley, William J. 'Indonesia in the Great Depression: A study of East Sumatra and Jogjakarta in the 1930's'. Ph.D. thesis, Cornell University. Ann Arbor: University Microfilms, 1977

_____ 'The Pakempalan Kawulo Ngajogjakarta: An official report on the Jogjakarta People's Party of the 1930s'. *Indonesia,* no. 26 (Oct. 1978), pp. 111–58.

Osborne, Robin. *Indonesia's secret war: The guerilla struggle in Irian Jaya.* Sydney, etc.: Allen and Unwin, 1985.

Padmapuspita, J. (ed. & transl.). *Pararaton.* Jogjakarta: Taman Siswa, 1966.

Paget, Roger K. 'The military in Indonesian politics: The burden of power'. *Pacific Affairs,* vol. 40, nos. 3–4 (Fall and Winter 1968), pp. 294–314.

Palmer, Ingrid. *The Indonesian economy since 1965: A case study of political economy.* London: Frank Cass, 1978.

Parry, J. H. *Europe and a wider world.* London: Hutchinson & Co., 1949. Reprinted as *The establishment of the European hegemony, 1415–1715.* New York & Evanston: Harper & Row, 1961.

Paulus, J. , *et al.* (eds). *Encyclopaedie van Nederlandsch-Indië.* 8 vols.'s-Gravenhage: Martinus Nijhoff; Leiden: E. J. Brill, 1917–40.

Payer, Cheryl. 'The International Monetary Fund and Indonesian debt slavery'. Pp. 50–70 in Mark Selden (ed.), *Remaking Asia: Essays on the American uses of power.* New York: Pantheon Books, 1974.

Pelras, Christian. 'Les premières données occidentales concernant Célèbes-Sud'. *BKI,* vol. 133, nos. 2–3 (1977), pp. 227–60.

_____ 'Religion, tradition and the dynamics of Islamization in South Sulawesi'. *Archipel,* no. 29 (1985), pp. 107–35.

Pelzer, Karl J. 'Physical and human resource patterns'. Pp. 1–23 in McVey, *Indonesia* (see above).

_____ *Planter against peasants: The agrarian struggle in East Sumatra 1947–1958. VKI,* vol. 97. 's-Gravenhage: Martinus Nijhoff, 1982.

_____ *Planter and peasant: Colonial policy and the agrarian struggle in East Sumatra, 1863–1947. VKI,* vol. 84. 's-Gravenhage: Martinus Nijhoff, 1978.

Penders, C. L. M. , and Ulf Sundhaussen. *Abdul Haris Nasution: A political biography.* St. Lucia, etc.: University of Queensland Press, 1985.

Piekaar, A. J. *Atjèh en de oorlog met Japan.* 's-Gravenhage & Bandung: Hoeve, 1949.

Pigeaud, Theodore G. Th. *Java in the 14th century: A study in cultural history.* 5 vols. The Hague: Martinus Nijhoff, 1960–3.

_____ *Literature of Java: Catalogue raisonné of Javanese manuscripts in the library of the University of Leiden and other public collections in the Netherlands.* 4 vols. The Hague: Martinus Nyhoff; Leiden: Bibliotheca Universitatis Lugduni Batavorum; Leiden University Press, 1967–80.

_____ and H. J. de Graaf. *Islamic states in Java, 1500–1700: Eight Dutch books and articles by Dr H. J. de Graaf, as summarised by Theodore G. Th. Pigeaud, with a comprehensive list of sources and a general index of names composed by H. J. de Graaf.* VKI, vol. 70. The Hague: Martinus Nijhoff, 1976.

Pijper, G. F. *Studiën over de geschiedenis van de Islam in Indonesia, 1900–1950.* Leiden: E. J. Brill, 1977.

Pluvier, J. M. *Overzicht van de ontwikkeling der nationalistische beweging in Indonesia in de jaren 1930 tot 1942.* 's-Gravenhage & Bandung: W. van Hoeve, 1953.

Poeze, Harry A. 'Early Indonesian emancipation: Abdul Rivai, van Heutz and the *Bintang Hindia*'. *BKI*, vol. 145, no. 1 (1989), pp. 87–106.

_____ *Tan Malaka: Strijder voor Indonesië's vrijheid; Levensloop van 1897 tot 1945.* VKI, vol. 78. 's-Gravenhage: Martinus Nijhoff, 1976.

Polomka, Peter. *Indonesia since Sukarno.* Harmondsworth: Penguin Books, 1971.

Pringgodigdo, A. K. *Geschiedenis der ondernemingen van het Mangkoenagorosche rijk.* 's-Gravenhage: Martinus Nijhoff, 1950.

_____ *Sedjarah pergerakan rakjat Indonesia.* Djakarta: Pustaka Rakjat, 1949.

Pringle, Robert. *Rajahs and rebels: The Ibans of Sarawak under Brooke rule, 1841–1941.* Ithaca: Cornell University Press, 1970.

Reeve, David. 'Sukarnoism and Indonesia's "functional group" state'. Part one: 'Developing "Indonesian democracy"', *RIMA*, vol. 12, no. 2 (1978), pp. 43–94. Part two: 'Implementing "Indonesian democracy"', *RIMA*, vol. 13, no. 1 (1979), pp. 53–115.

Reid, Anthony. 'An "age of commerce" in Southeast Asian history'. *MAS*, vol. 24, no. 1 (1990), pp. 1–30.

_____ 'Australia's hundred days in South Sulawesi'. Pp. 201–24 in David P. Chandler and M. C. Ricklefs (eds), *Nineteenth and twentieth century Indonesia: Essays in honour of Professor J. D. Legge.* Clayton: Centre of Southeast Asian Studies, Monash University, 1986.

_____ 'The birth of the Republic in Sumatra'. *Indonesia*, no. 12 (Oct. 1971), pp. 21–46.

_____ *The blood of the people: Revolution and the end of traditional rule in northern Sumatra.* Kuala Lumpur, etc.: Oxford University Press, 1979.

_____ *The contest for North Sumatra: Atjeh, the Netherlands and Britain, 1858–1898.* London, etc.: Oxford University Press, 1969.

_____ 'Indonesia: From briefcase to samurai sword'. Pp. 16–32 in McCoy, *Southeast Asia under Japanese occupation* (see above).

_____ *The Indonesian national revolution, 1945–1950.* Hawthorn, Vic.: Longman, 1974.

_____ 'The Islamization of Southeast Asia'. Pp. 13–33 in Muhammad Abu Bakar et al. (eds), *Historia: Essays in commemoration of the 25th anniversary of the Department of History, University of Malaya.* Kuala Lumpur: The Malaysian Historical Society, 1984.

_____ 'The Japanese occupation and rival Indonesian elites: Northern Sumatra in 1942'. *JAS*, vol. 35, no. 1 (Nov. 1975), pp. 49–61.

_____ *Perjuangan rakyat: Revolusi dan hancurnya kerajaan di Sumatra.* Jakarta: Pustaka Sinar Harapan, 1987.

_____ 'The pre-colonial economy of Indonesia'. *BIES*, vol. 20, no. 2 (Aug. 1984), pp. 151–67.

_____ 'The rise of Makassar'. *RIMA*, vol. 17 (Winter/Summer 1983), pp. 117–60.

_____ 'The seventeenth-century crisis in Southeast Asia'. *MAS*, vol. 24, no. 4 (1990), pp. 639–59.

_____ *Southeast Asia in the age of commerce 1450–1680.* 2 vols. New Haven & London: Yale University Press, 1988– .

_____ and Lance Castles (eds). *Pre-colonial state systems in Southeast Asia: The Malay Peninsula, Sumatra, Bali-Lombok, South Celebes.* Kuala Lumpur: Monographs of the Malaysian Branch of the Royal Asiatic Society no. 6, 1975.

Remmelink, Willem Gerrit Jan. *Emperor Pakubuwana II, priyayi & Company and the Chinese War.* Doctoral thesis, Leiden University, 1990.

Ricklefs, M. C. 'Bantĕn and the Dutch in 1619: Six early "*pasar* Malay" letters'. *BSOAS*, vol. 39, pt. 1 (1976), pp. 128–36.

_____ 'A consideration of three versions of the *Babad Tanah Djawi,* with excerpts on the fall of Madjapahit'. *BSOAS*, vol. 35, pt. 2 (1972), pp. 285–315.

_____ 'The crisis of 1740–1 in Java: The Javanese, Chinese, Madurese and Dutch, and the fall of the court of Kartasura'. *BKI*, vol. 139, nos 2–3 (1983), pp. 268–90.

_____ 'Dipanagara's early inspirational experience'. *BKI*, vol. 130, nos 2–3 (1974), pp. 227–58.

_____ *Jogjakarta under Sultan Mangkubumi, 1749–1792: A history of the division of Java.* London, etc.: Oxford University Press, 1974.

_____ *Modern Javanese historical tradition: A study of an original Kartasura chronicle and related materials.* London: School of Oriental and African Studies, 1978.

_____ 'Six centuries of Islamization in Java'. Pp. 100–28 in Levtzion, *Conversion to Islam* (see above).

_____ 'Some statistical evidence on Javanese social, economic and demographic history in the later seventeenth and eighteenth centuries'. *MAS*, vol. 20, no. 1 (1986), pp. 1–32.

_____ 'Unity and disunity in Javanese political and religious thought of the eighteenth century'. *MAS*, forthcoming.

_____ *War, culture and economy in Java, 1677–1726: Asian and European imperialism in the early Kartasura period.* Sydney: Asian Studies Association of Australia in association with Allen & Unwin, 1993.

Riddell, Peter. 'Earliest Quranic exegetical activity in the Malay-speaking states'. *Archipel*, no. 38 (1989), pp. 107–24.

Robinson, Geoffrey. 'State, society and political conflict in Bali, 1945–46'. *Indonesia*, no. 45 (Apr. 1988), pp. 1–48.

Robinson, Kathy. 'Living in the hutan: Jungle village life under the Darul Islam'. *RIMA*, vol. 17 (Winter/Summer 1983), pp. 208–29.

Robison, Richard. *Indonesia: The rise of capital.* North Sydney: Allen & Unwin, 1986.

Robson, S. O. (ed. & transl.). *Wangbang Wideya: A Javanese Pañji romance.* The Hague: Martinus Nijhoff, 1971.

_____ (ed. and transl.). *The Wedhatama: An English translation.* KITLV working paper 4. Leiden: KITLV Press, 1990.

Rocamora, J. Eliseo. 'The Partai Nasional Indonesia, 1963–1965'. *Indonesia*, no. 10 (Oct. 1970), pp. 143–81.

Rockhill, W. W. 'Notes on the relations and trade of China with the eastern archipelago and the coast of the Indian Ocean during the fourteenth century'. *T'oung Pao*, vol. 14 (1913), pp. 473–6; vol. 15 (1914), pp. 419–47; vol. 16 (1915), pp. 61–159, 236–71, 374–92, 435–67, 604–26.

Roeder, O. G. *The smiling general: President Soeharto of Indonesia*. Djakarta: Gunung Agung, 1969.

Roff, William R. *The origins of Malay nationalism*. London & New Haven: Yale University Press, 1967.

Rouffaer, G. P. 'Vorstenlanden'. *Adatrechtbundels*, vol. 34, pp. 233–378.

Rose, Mavis. *Indonesia Free: A political biography of Mohammad Hatta*. Ithaca: Cornell Modern Indonesia Project Monograph Series no. 67, 1987.

Rudner, Martin. 'The Indonesian military and economic policy: The goals and performance of the first Five-Year Development Plan, 1969–74'. *MAS*, vol. 10, no. 2 (1976), pp. 249–84.

Ruiter, Tine. 'The Tegal revolt in 1864'. Pp. 81–98 in Kooiman, *Conversion, competition and conflict* (see above).

Runciman, Steven. *The white rajahs: A history of Sarawak from 1841 to 1946*. Cambridge: Cambridge University Press, 1960.

Rush, James R. *Opium to Java: Revenue farming and Chinese enterprise in colonial Indonesia, 1860–1910*. Ithaca & London: Cornell University Press, 1990.

Sadie, Stanley (ed.). *The new Grove dictionary of music and musicians*. 20 vols. London: Macmillan, 1980.

Sagimum. *Pahlawan Dipanagara berdjuang (Bara api kemerdekaan nan tak kundjung padam)*. Djakarta: Gunung Agung, 1965.

Samson, Allan A. 'Islam in Indonesian politics'. *AS*, vol. 8, no. 12 (Dec. 1968), pp. 1001–17.

Schadee, W. H. M. *Geschiedenis van Sumatra's Oostkust*. 2 vols. Amsterdam: Oostkust van Sumatra-Instituut, 1918–19.

Schoute, D. *De geneeskunde in den dienst der Oost-Indische Compagnie in Nederlandsch-Indië*. Amsterdam: J. H. de Bussy, 1929.

Schrieke, Bertram. *Indonesian sociological studies: Selected writings of B. Schrieke*. 2 vols. The Hague & Bandung: W. van Hoeve, 1955–7.

Schulte Nordholt, Hendrik Gerard Christiaan. *Een Balische dynastie: Hierarchie en conflict in de negara Mengwi 1700–1940*. Doctoral thesis, Vrije Universiteit te Amsterdam, 1988.

—— 'The Mads Lange connection: A Danish trader on Bali in the middle of the nineteenth century: Broker and buffer'. *Indonesia*, no. 32 (Oct. 1981), pp. 16–47.

Selosoemardjan. *Social changes in Jogjakarta*. Ithaca: Cornell University Press, 1962.

Shimer, Barbara Gifford, and Guy Hobbs (transls). *The Kenpeitai in Java and Sumatra (Selections from Nihon Kenpei Seishi)*. Intro. by Theodore Friend. Ithaca: Cornell Modern Indonesia Project translation series publication no. 65, 1986.

Shiraishi, Takashi. *An age in motion: Popular radicalism in Java, 1912–1926*. Ithaca & London: Cornell University Press, 1990.

—— 'Dangir's testimony: Saminism reconsidered'. *Indonesia*, no. 50 (Oct. 1990), pp. 95–120.

Sjamsuddin, Nazaruddin. *The republican revolt: A study of the Acehnese rebellion* [Singapore:] Institute of Southeast Asian Studies, 1985.

Skinner, C. (ed. & transl.). *Sja'ir perang Mengkasar (The rhymed chronicle of the Macassar war) by Entji' Amin. VKI*, vol. 40. 's-Gravenhage: Martinus Nijhoff, 1963.

Slametmuljana. *A story of Majapahit.* Singapore: Singapore University Press, 1976.

Sluimers, L. '"Nieuwe orde" op Java: De Japanse bezettingspolitiek en de Indonesische elites, 1942–1943'. *BKI*, vol. 124, no. 3 (1968), pp. 336–67.

Smail, John R. W. *Bandung in the early revolution, 1945–1946: A study in the social history of the Indonesian revolution.* Ithaca: Cornell Modern Indonesia Project Monograph Series, 1964.

_____ 'The military politics of North Sumatra: December 1956–October 1957'. *Indonesia*, no. 6 (Oct. 1968), pp. 128–87.

Snouck Hurgronje, C. *The Achehnese.* Transl. A. W. S. O'Sullivan. 2 vols. Leyden: E. J. Brill, 1906.

_____ *De Atjèhers.* 2 vols. Batavia: Landsdrukkerij; Leiden: E. J. Brill, 1893–4.

_____ *Mekka in the latter part of the nineteenth century: Daily life, customs and learning; the Moslims of the East-Indian-Archipelago.* Transl. J. H. Monahan. Leyden: E. J. Brill; London: Luzac & Co., 1931.

Soebadio, Haryati, and Carine A. du Marchie Sarvaas (eds). *Dynamics of Indonesian history.* Amsterdam, etc.: North-Holland Publishing Company, 1978.

Soebardi, S. (ed. & transl.). *The book of Cabolèk: A critical edition with introduction, translation and notes, a contribution to the study of the Javanese mystical tradition.* The Hague: Martinus Nijhoff, 1975.

_____ 'Kartosuwiryo and the Darul Islam rebellion in Indonesia'. *JSEAS*, vol. 14, no. 1 (March 1983), pp. 109–33.

_____ 'Santri-religious elements as reflected in the book of Tjĕnṭini'. *BKI*, vol. 127, no. 3 (1971), pp. 331–49.

Soedarsono. *Wayang wong: The state ritual dance drama in the court of Yogyakarta.* Yogyakarta: Gadjah Mada University Press, 1984.

Soejatno. 'Perubahan-perubahan sosial politik di Surakarta sesudah 1945'. *Buletin Fakultas Sastra dan Kebudajaan*, no. 4 (1971), pp. 186–94.

_____ 'Revolution and social tensions in Surakarta, 1945–1950'. Transl. Benedict Anderson. *Indonesia*, no. 17 (Apr. 1974), pp. 99–111.

Soeharto. *Pikiran, ucapan dan tindakan saya: Otobiografi.* As explained to G. Dwipayana and Ramadhan K. H. [Jakarta:] Pt. Citra Lamtoro Gung Persada, 1989.

Soekanto. *Sekitar Jogjakarta, 1755–1825 (Perdjandjian Gianti-perang Dipanagara)* Djakarta & Amsterdam: Mahabarata [1952].

Soeria Nata Atmadja. *De regenten-positie.* Bandoeng: A. C. Nix & Co., [1940].

Soeri Soeroto. 'The Beratib Beamaal movement in the Banjar War'. Pp. 167–77 in Kartodirdjo, *Profiles* (see above).

Soetjipto Wirosardjono *et al.* (eds). *Gita Jaya: Catatan H. Ali Sadikin, Gubernur Kepala Daerah Khusus Ibukota Jakarta 1966–1977.* Jakarta: Pemerintah Daerah Khusus Ibukota, [1977].

Stange, Paul. '"Legitimate" mysticism in Indonesia'. *RIMA*, vol. 20 (Summer 1986), pp. 76–117.

Stapel, F. W. *Het Bonggaais verdrag.* ['s-Gravenhage: no publ.,] 1922.

_____ *Cornelis Janszoon Speelman.* 's-Gravenhage: Martinus Nijhoff, 1936. Originally published in *BKI*, vol. 94 (1936), pp. 1–222.

Steenbrink, Karel A. *Beberapa aspek tentang Islam di Indonesia abad ke-19.* Jakarta: Bulan Bintang, 1984.

_____ *Pesantran, madrasah sekolah: Pendidikan Islam dalam kurun moderen.* Jakarta: LP3ES, 1986.

_____ *Pesantren, madrasah, sekolah: Recente ontwikkelingen in Indonesisch Islamonderricht.* Meppel: Krips Repro, 1974.

Stöhr, Waldemar, and Piet Zoetmulder. *Die Religionen Indonesiens.* Stuttgart, etc.: W. Kohlhammer Verlag, 1965.

_____ and _____ *Les religions d'Indonésie.* Transl. L. Jospin. Paris: Payot, 1968.

Subagya, Rahmat. *Kepercayaan, kebatinan kerohanian, kejiwaan dan agama.* [Yogyakarta:] Kanisius, [1976].

Sudjoko Prasodjo *et al. Profil pesantren: Laporan hasil penelitian Pesantren al-Falak dan delapan pesantren lain di Bogor.* [Jakarta:] Lembaga Penelitian, Pendidikan dan Penerangan Ekonomi dan Sosial [1975].

Sukarno. *Sukarno: An autobiography as told to Cindy Adams.* Hong Kong: Gunung Agung, 1966.

[Sulendraningrat, P. S.] *Purwaka Tjaruban Nagari.* Djakarta: Bhratara, 1972.

Sundhaussen, Ulf. *The road to power: Indonesian military politics 1945–1967.* Kuala Lumpur: Oxford University Press, 1982.

Surjomihardjo, Abdurrachman. 'An analysis of Suwardi Surjaningrat's ideals and national-revolutionary actions (1913–1922)'. *MIISI*, vol. 2, no. 3 (1964), pp. 371–406.

_____ *Ki Hadjar Dewantara dan Taman Siswa dalam sejarah Indonesia modern.* Jakarta: Penerbit Sinar Harapan, 1986.

_____ 'National education in a colonial society'. Pp. 277–306 in Soebadio and Sarvaas, *Dynamics of Indonesian history* (see above).

Suryadinata, Leo. 'Indonesia-China relations: A recent breakthrough'. *AS*, vol. 30, no. 7 (July 1990), pp. 682–96.

_____ *Peranakan Chinese politics in Java, 1917–1942.* Revised edn. Singapore: Singapore University Press, 1981.

Sutherland, Heather. *The making of a bureaucratic elite: The colonial transformation of the Javanese priyayi.* Singapore, etc.: Heinemann Educational Books (Asia), 1979.

_____ 'Notes on Java's regent families'. *Indonesia*, no. 16 (Oct. 1973), pp. 113–47; no. 17 (Apr. 1974), pp. 1–42.

_____ 'Pudjangga Baru: Aspects of Indonesian intellectual life in the 1930s'. *Indonesia*, no. 6 (Oct. 1968), pp. 106–27.

Sutter, John O. *Indonesianisasi: Politics in a changing economy, 1940–1955.* 4 vols. Ithaca: Cornell Southeast Asia Program Data Paper no. 36, 1959.

Swellengrebel, J. L. *In Leijdeckers voetspoor: Anderhalve eeuw Bijbelvertaling en taalkunde in de Indonesische talen.* 2 vols. *VKI*, vols. 68, 82. 's-Gravenhage: Martinus Nijhoff, 1974, 1978.

Swift, Ann. *The road to Madiun: The Indonesian Communist uprising of 1948.* Ithaca: Cornell Modern Indonesia Project Monograph Series, 1989.

Tanter, Richard, and Kenneth Young (eds). *The politics of middle class Indonesia.*

Monash Papers on Southeast Asia no. 19. Clayton: Centre of Southeast Asian Studies, Monash University, 1990.

Taylor, Alastair M. *Indonesian independence and the United Nations*. Ithaca: Cornell University Press, 1960.

Taylor, Jay. *China and Southeast Asia: Peking's relations with revolutionary movements*. Revised edn. New York: Praeger Publishers, 1976.

Taylor, Jean Gelman. *The social world of Batavia: European and Eurasian in Dutch Asia*. Madison: University of Wisconsin Press, 1983.

Teeuw, A. 'The impact of Balai Pustaka on modern Indonesian literature'. *BSOAS*, vol. 35, pt. 1 (1972), pp. 111–27.

_____ *Modern Indonesian literature*. 2nd edn. 2 vols. The Hague: Martinus Nijhoff, 1979.

_____ with the assistance of H. W. Emanuels. *A critical survey of studies on Malay and Bahasa Indonesia*. 's-Gravenhage: Martinus Nijhoff, 1961.

Tichelman, F. (ed.). *Socialisme in Indonesië: De Indische Sociaal-Democratische Vereeniging, 1897–1917*. Vol. I. Dordrecht & Cinnaminson: Foris Publications, 1985.

Tiele, P. A. 'De Europeërs in den Maleischen archipel'. *BKI*, vol. 25 (1877), pp. 321–420; vol. 27 (1879), pp. 1–69; vol. 28 (1880), pp. 260–340, 395–482; vol. 29 (1881), pp. 153–214, 332; vol. 30 (1882), pp. 141–242; vol. 32 (1884), pp. 49–118; vol. 35 (1886), pp. 257–355; vol. 36 (1887), pp. 199–307.

Uhlenbeck, E. M. *A critical survey of studies on the languages of Java and Madura*. 's-Gravenhage: Martinus Nijhoff, 1964.

United Nations. *Statistical yearbook / annuaire statistique*, vol. 34: *1983/84*. New York, 1986.

Utrecht, E. *Sedjarah hukum internasional di Bali dan Lombok (Pertjobaan sebuah studi hukum internasional regional di Indonesia)*. [Bandung:] Sumur Bandung,1962.

Van Niel, Robert. *The emergence of the modern Indonesian elite*. The Hague & Bandung: W. van Hoeve, 1960.

_____ 'The function of landrent under the cultivation system in Java'. *JAS*, vol. 23, no. 3 (May 1964), pp. 357–75.

_____ 'Measurement of change under the cultivation system in Java, 1837–1851'. *Indonesia*, no. 14 (Oct. 1972), pp. 89–109.

Veer, Paul van't. *De Atjeh-oorlog*. Amsterdam: Uitgeverij de Arbeiderspers, 1969.

Vermeulen, J. Th. *De Chineezen te Batavia en de troebelen van 1740*. Leiden: N. V. Boek- en Steendrukkerij Eduard Ijdo, 1938.

Veth, P. J. *Java: Geographisch, ethnologisch, historisch*. 3 vols. Haarlem: Erven F. Bohn, 1875–82.

Vickers, Adrian. *Bali: A paradise created*. Ringwood, Vic. etc.: Penguin Books, 1989.

Villiers, John. 'Trade and society in the Banda islands in the sixteenth century'. *MAS*, vol. 15, no. 4 (1981), pp. 723–50.

Wake, Christopher. 'Malacca's early kings and the reception of Islam'. *JSEAH*, vol. 5, no. 2 (Sept. 1964), pp. 104–28.

Wang Gungwu. 'The first three rulers of Malacca'. Pp. 97–107 in Wang Gungwu, *Community and nation: Essays on Southeast Asia and the Chinese*. Singapore & North Sydney: Heinemann Educational Books (Asia) Ltd. & George Allen & Unwin Australia, 1981. Originally published in *JMBRAS*, vol. 41, pt. 1

(1968), pp. 11–22.

Ward, K. E. *The foundation of the Partai Muslimin Indonesia.* Ithaca: Cornell Modern Indonesia Project Interim Report Series, 1970.

_____ *The 1971 election in Indonesia: An East Java case study.* [Clayton, Vic:] Monash University Centre of Southeast Asian Studies Papers on Southeast Asia no. 2, 1974.

Waseda University, Okuma Memorial Social Sciences Research Institute. *Japanese military administration in Indonesia.* Washington, D.C. : US Department of Commerce, Office of Technical Services, Joint Publications Research Service, 1963. Transl. of *Indonesia ni Okeru Nihon Gunsei no Kenkyu.* Tokyo: Kinokuniya Shoten, 1959.

Webb, R. A. F. Paul. 'The sickle and the cross: Christians and Communists in Bali, Flores, Sumba and Timor, 1965–67'. *JSEAS*, vol. 17, no. 1 (Mar. 1986), pp. 94–112.

Weinstein, Franklin B. *Indonesia abandons confrontation: An inquiry into the functions of Indonesian foreign policy.* Ithaca: Cornell Modern Indonesia Project Interim Reports Series, 1969.

_____ *Indonesian foreign policy and the dilemma of dependence: From Sukarno to Soeharto.* Ithaca & London: Cornell University Press, 1976.

Widjojo Nitisastro. *Population trends in Indonesia.* Ithaca & London: Cornell University Press, 1970.

Wigboldus, Jouke S. 'A history of the Minahasa *c.* 1615–1680'. *Archipel*, no. 34 (1987), pp. 63–101.

Williams, Michael C. *Sickle and crescent: The Communist revolt of 1926 in Banten.* Ithaca: Cornell Modern Indonesia Project Monograph Series no. 61, 1982.

Winstedt, Richard. *A history of classical Malay literature.* Kuala Lumpur, etc.: Oxford University Press, 1969. A reprinting of the revised edition originally published in *JMBRAS*, vol. 31, pt. 3 (1958; but published in 1961).

Wiselius, J. A. B. 'Djåjå Båjå, zijn leven en profetieën'. *BKI*, vol. 19 (1872), pp. 172–217.

Woelders, M. O. *Het Sultanaat Palembang, 1811–1825. VKI*, vol. 72. 's-Gravenhage: Martinus Nijhoff, 1975.

Wolters, O. W. *Early Indonesian commerce: A study of the origins of Śrīvijaya.* Ithaca: Cornell University Press, 1967.

_____ *The fall of Śrīvijaya in Malay history.* Ithaca: Cornell University Press, 1970.

Wong, John. *ASEAN economies in perspective: A comparative study of Indonesia, Malaya, the Philippines, Singapore, and Thailand.* London & Basingstoke: The Macmillan Press, 1979.

Worsley, Peter John (ed. & transl.).*Babad Buleleng: A Balinese dynastic genealogy.* 's-Gravenhage: H. L. Smits; The Hague: Martinus Nijhoff, 1972.

Wright, H. R. C. *East-Indian economic problems of the age of Cornwallis & Raffles.* London: Luzac & Company, 1961.

Yong Mun Cheong. *H. J. Van Mook and Indonesian independence: A study of his role in Dutch-Indonesian Relations, 1945–48.* The Hague: Martinus Nijhoff Publishers, 1982.

Young, Kenneth R. 'Transformation or temporary respite? Agricultural growth, industrialisation and the modernisation of Java'. *RIMA*, vol. 22, no. 2 (Summer, 1988), pp. 114–32.

Zoetmulder, P. *J. Kalangwan: A survey of Old Javanese literature.* The Hague: Martinus Nijhoff, 1974.

_____ *Manunggaling kawula gusti: Pantheïsme dan monisme dalam sastra suluk Jawa: suatu studi filsafat.* Transl. Dick Hartoko. Jakarta: Perwakilan Koninklijk Instituut voor Taal-, Land- en Volkenkunde, Lembaga Ilmu Pengetahuan Indonesia, Penerbit PT Gramedia, 1990.

_____ *Pantheisme en monisme in de Javaansche soeloek-litteratuur.* Nijmegen: J. J. Berkhout, 1935.

Maps

Note: these maps necessarily contain place-names which are not contemporaneous with one another.

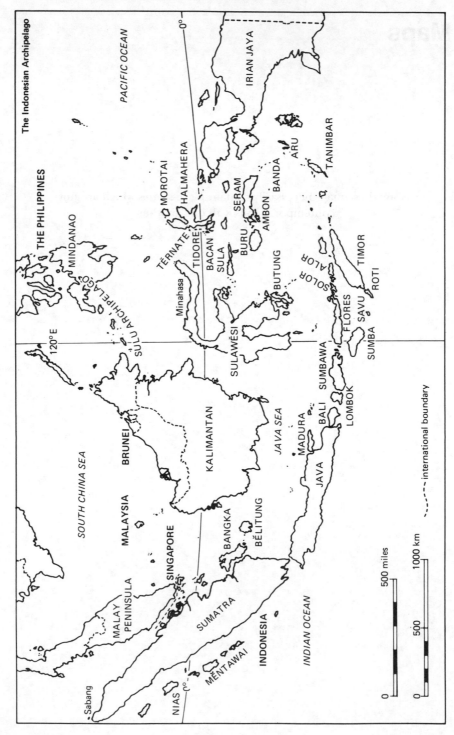

The Indonesian Archipelago

Sumatra and the Malay Peninsula

100° E

PENANG

Kĕdah

Trĕngganu

Sabang
Banda Aceh (Kutaraja)
Pĕdir
Aceh
Daya   Samudra/
Pasai
Minye Tujoh
Pĕrlak

Perak

Pahang

Aru
Alas   Langkat
Medan
Dĕli   Sĕrdang
Pĕmatangsiantar

SIMEULUĔ

Kuala Lumpur

Pĕngkalan
Kĕmpas

Singkil   LAKE
TOBA
Barus   Bangkara

Malacca

RUPAT
BĔNGKALIS

Johor

SINGAPORE

STRAITS OF MALACCA

Sibolga

Tapanuli

Gunungsitoli

NIAS

Daludalu

BINTAN
RIAU
ARCHIPELAGO

Siak

Pakanbaru   Kampar

0°   0°

Indĕragiri

LINGGA
ARCHIPELAGO

Minangkabau

Padang

MĔNTAWAI ARCHIPELAGO

Muarakumpe

Jambi

BANGKA

Palembang

Bĕngkulu

Lampung

Tulangbawang

Tĕlukbĕtung

Bonjol
Limapuluh
Agam   Kota   Lintau
Tiku
LAKE MANINJAU   Bukittingi
Padangpanjang   Tanah Datar
LAKE SINGKARAK
Pariaman

Padang

0   100   200 miles

0   100   200   400 km

0   25   50 miles

0   50   100 km

international boundary

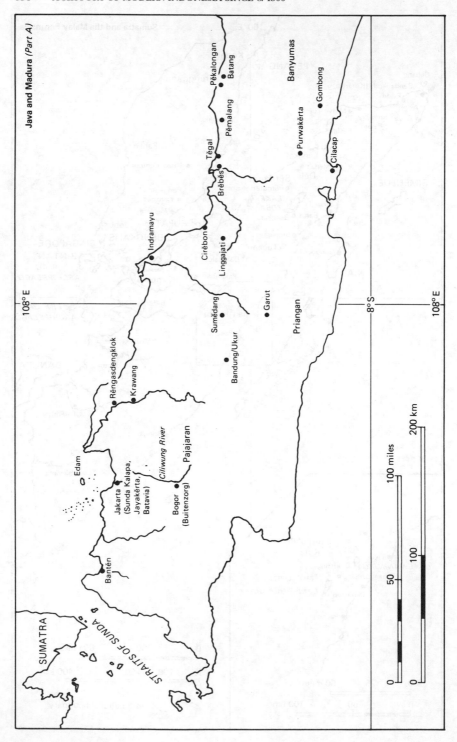

Java and Madura (Part A)

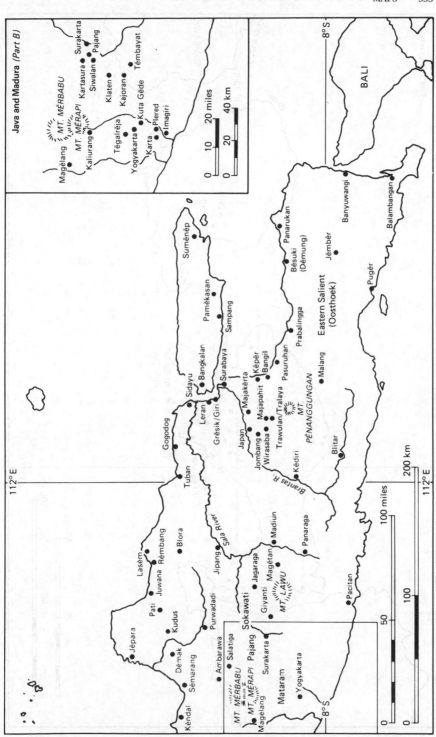

Java and Madura *(Part B)*

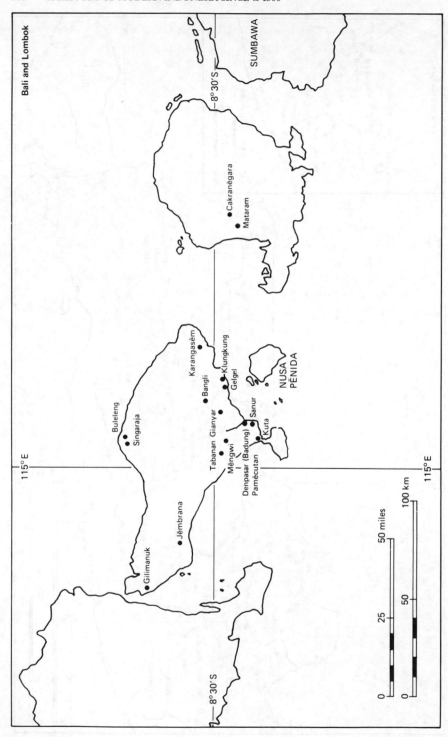

Bali and Lombok

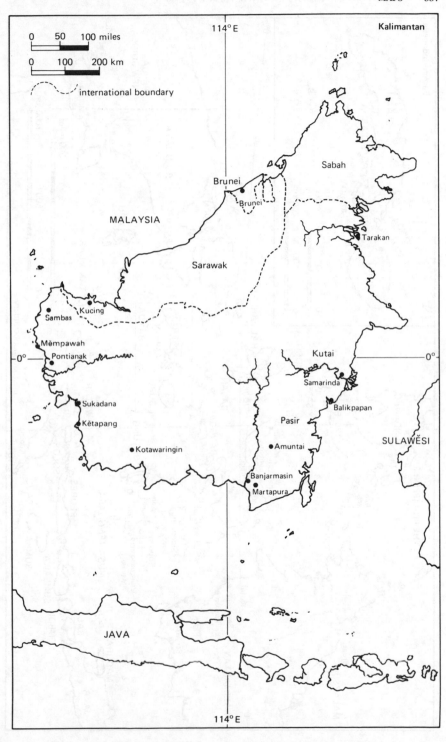

Kalimantan

114° E

0   50   100 miles

0   100   200 km

- - - - international boundary

Sabah

Brunei

Brunei

MALAYSIA

Tarakan

Sarawak

Kucing

Sambas

Mĕmpawah

0°   Pontianak

Kutai

0°

Samarinda

Sukadana

Balikpapan

Kĕtapang

Pasir

SULAWĚSI

Kotawaringin

Amuntai

Banjarmasin

Martapura

JAVA

114° E

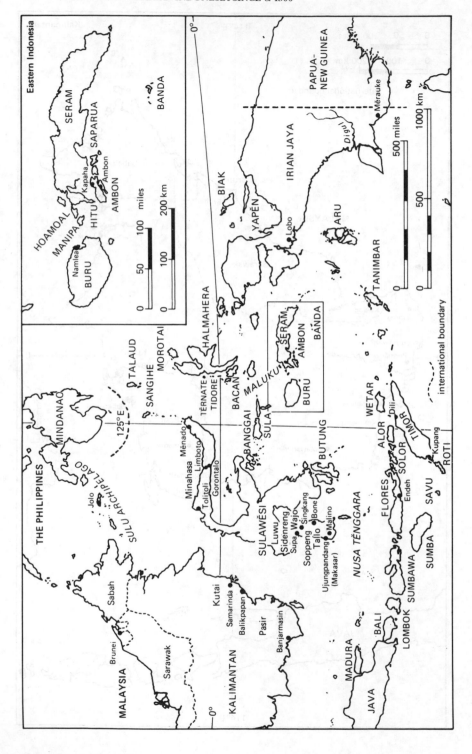

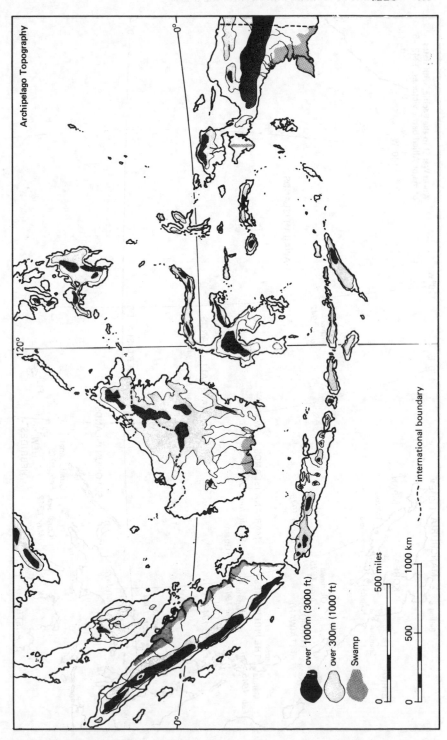

Archipelago Topography

over 1000m (3000 ft)

over 300m (1000 ft)

Swamp

international boundary

500 miles

1000 km

0   500

0   500   1000 km

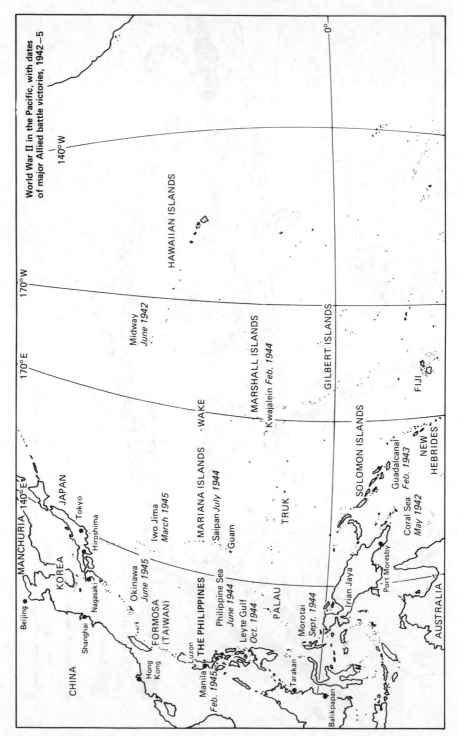

World War II in the Pacific, with dates of major Allied battle victories, 1942–5

Index

Note: Readers who fail to locate a twentieth-century Indonesian personal name or publication title under the expected spelling should check possible alternate spellings (see p. xiv above)

Abadi, 296, 300
abangan (Javanese nominal Muslims), 163–4, 174, 181, 182, 219, 221, 227, 229, 240, 244, 249, 274, 288, 293, 295, 308
'Abduh, Muhammad, 168, 170
Abdul Aziz, Sayyid, 9
Abdul Hamid II, Sultan of Pontianak, 225, 233
Abdul Kadir, 98
Abdul Karim Amrullah, Haji, *see* Rasul, Haji
Abdul Rahman, Tungku, 273, 275
Abdul Rakhman (of Banjarmasin), 138–9
Abdul Razak, Tun, 290
Abdullah Muhammad Maulana Matarani, Sultan, 47
Abdurrauf of Singkil, 51, 130
Abendanon J. H., 156–7
Abikoesno Tjokrosoejoso, 202, 209
Abulmafakhir Mahmud Abdulkadir, Sultan of Bantĕn, 47
Aceh, 7, 16, 17, 24, 29, 32, 33, 34, 35, 36, 48, 50–2, 54, 142–6, 147, 152, 163, 200, 203, 220, 230, 247, 251, 254, 262, 265, 266, 269, 294, 299; foundation of, 6; Islamisation of, 6, 7; becomes Special District, 265; Aceh War, 111, 144–6, 152, 220
'act of free choice' in Irian Jaya, 271, 297
Adabiyah school, 170
Adam, Sultan (of Banjarmasin), 138–9
adat (customary law), 115, 141, 142, 146, 168, 170, 176, 265
Adat, Raja, 140
Adi Santika, Pangeran Arya, 104, 105
Adityavarman, 141
'Afdeeling B', *see* Section B
Affandi, 215
Afghani, Jamal ad-Din al-, 168
Afghanistan, 305
Africa, 19, 20, 22, 26, 28, 144, 248
Agam, 141
Agĕng, Ratu, 115
Agĕng, Sultan of Bantĕn, 78–9, 82
Agrarian Law, 124
Agung, Sultan of Mataram, 34, 40, 41, 43–7, 54, 69, 70, 71, 73, 74, 96, 104, 126, 257
Agung, Cokorda Gusti, 68
Ahmad, Sultan of Malacca, 23
Ahmad Hanapi, 53
Ahmad Khatib (of Sambas), 130, 168
Ahmad Khatib, Shaikh (of Minangkabu),

170, 171
Ahmad Syah, Sultan of Pahang, 34, 35
Ahmad Syah ibn Iskandar, 83
Ahmat Majana/Majanu, 6
Aidit D. N., 228, 229, 241, 243, 249, 252, 255, 259, 268, 269, 271, 274, 278, 279, 281, 282, 288; father of, 243
Aisyiyah, 171
Akbarnama, 52
Alam, Raja, 140
Alas, 144
Alauddin Riayat Syah I, Sultan of Johor, 32, 33
Alauddin Riayat Syah II, Sultan of Johor, 34
Alauddin Riayat Syah al-Kahar, Sultan of Aceh, 33
Alauddin Riayat Syah al-Mukamil, Sultan of Aceh, 33
Alauddin Tumenanga ri Gaukanna, Sultan of Gowa, 48
Albuquerque, Afonso de, 23
Alĕngkajĕng, Gusti Agung Made, 68
Alexander the Great, 52
Algemeene Studieclub, 183
Ali, Mohammad, 248
Ali Alauddin Mansur Syah, Sultan of Aceh (Tuanku Ibrahim), 143
'Ali-Baba' firms, 247
Ali Mughayat Syah, Sultan of Aceh, 6, 32–3
Ali Murtopo, 276, 290, 298, 300
Ali Sadikin, 306
Ali Sastroamidjojo, 184, 246–8, 249, 251, 253, 254, 255, 264, 279, 281, 290
Alimin Prawirodirdjo, 178, 182, 252
aliran, 241, 285, 288, 303, 308
Alit, Pangeran, 69–70
All-Aceh Union of Ulamas, *see* PUSA
All-Indonesia Congress of Islamic Scholars (1957), 261
Alor, 136
aluminium, 304
Amangkurat, Ratu (mother of Pakubuwana II), 88, 89, 91
Amangkurat I, Susuhunan of Mataram, 41, 47, 69–75, 77
Amangkurat II, Susuhunan of Mataram and Kartasura: as crown prince, 72–5; as king 76–7, 79, 80, 81–5
Amangkurat III, Susuhunan of Kartasura, 84–6, 92, 98
Amangkurat IV, Susuhunan of Kartasura, 87

Ambarawa, 216
Ambon, Ambonese, 24, 25, 26, 28, 29, 39, 61, 62, 63, 64, 69, 84, 85, 86, 104, 105, 112, 116, 117, 137, 142, 147, 160, 168, 216, 233, 242, 263
'Amboyna Massacre', 29
America, United States of, Americans, 120, 141, 143, 144–5, 146, 152, 160, 182, 186, 192, 194, 195, 201, 207, 208, 209, 213, 215, 225, 226, 228, 230, 231, 239, 244, 254, 262, 263, 269, 271–2, 273, 274, 275, 276, 277, 278, 280, 281, 289, 291, 296, 297, 301, 302, 306
Amir Hamzah (poet), 192, 220
Amir Hamzah (uncle of the Prophet), 52, 53, 55
Amir Machmud, 298
Amir Sjarifuddin, 192, 203, 217, 218, 221–30
Amnesty International, 297, 302
Amongraga, Seh, 54, 126
AMS (General Middle School), 158, 159, 189
Amuntai, 203
Anak semua bangsa, 297
Anbiya, 55
Anggĕr-Agĕng, 99
Anggĕr-Arubiru, 99
angkatan 45, 215, 308
angkatan 66, 284
Anno Javanico, adoption of, 46
Anom, Gusti Agung, 67–8
Anrangkusuma, patih of Kartasura, 82, 83
Ansor, 259, 274
Antasari, Pangeran, 139
Antwerp, 29
Apodeti, 301
Aqsa, al-, 38
Arabia, Arabs, 3, 6, 7, 9, 12, 20, 22, 24, 36, 104, 122, 125, 127, 141, 169, 170, 171, 184, 192, 267, 300, 304. See also Mecca
Arabic language and literature, 4, 5, 6, 8, 9, 10, 11, 38, 47, 51, 52, 53, 54, 56, 13 167, 170, 193, 205
areca, 20
Arjuna Sasrabau, 53, 54
Arjunawijaya, 53
Arjunawiwāha, 53
Armed Forces Day, 280, 287
army, (Indonesian): in Revolution, 221–2, 223–5, 227–32; since independence, 239 ff. passim; size of, 228, 239, 269; preponderance of Javanese in, 264. See also Bantĕng Division, Brawijaya Division, Diponĕgoro Division, Kostrad, paracommandos, Siliwangi Division
Aru, 33, 34, 137
arumpone (king of Bone), 64, 214, 222
ASEAN (Association of South East Asian Nations), 296, 303, 306, 307
Ashanti War, 144
Asian-African Conference (Bandung), 247, 248
Asrama Indonesia Mĕrdeka, 207
Asrar al-'arifin, 51
Assembly for Federal Consultation, 226
atomic bomb, 209, 210, 277, 280
attoriolong, 56

Australia, Australians, 195, 201, 216, 222, 225, 226, 302, 307
Austria, 193
Azahari, Shaikh A. M., 272

Baab Ullah, Sultan of Tĕrnate, 25
babad, see chronicles and historical traditions and individual titles
Babad Giyanti, 55
Babad Kartasura, 54
Babad Kraton, 100
Babad Tanah Jawi, 9–10, 41, 54
Bacan, 8
Badaruddin, Mahmud, Sultan of Palembang, 139–40
Badruddin of Dĕmak, 36
Badung, 132, 133, 134, 135
Bagĕlen, 121
Baghdad, 12
Bagus Buang, Ratu, 105
Bahrum Rangkuti, 215
Bajra, Carik, 54
Balai Pustaka, 185–6, 192
Balambangan, 10, 39, 42, 44, 46, 47, 67, 68, 90, 99
Bali, Balinese, 8, 13, 18, 20, 39, 46, 47, 48, 50, 55, 56, 57, 67–8, 69, 70, 81, 82, 83, 84, 85, 87, 89, 90, 92, 93, 98, 99, 105, 132–6, 143, 160, 163, 181, 207, 214, 216, 224, 241, 250, 255, 274, 276, 287, 288, 306; literature of, 55; music of, 57; Dutch conquest of, 135, 136; cattle, 136
Balikpapan, 215
Banda, Bandanese, 8, 25, 29, 30, 62, 85, 86, 137, 140, 185, 191
Banda Aceh (Kutaraja), 144, 145, 146, 220
Bandung, 105, 156, 158, 165, 177, 182, 183, 185, 189, 207, 215, 216, 220, 222, 225, 232, 238, 247, 248, 265. See also Asian-African Conference
Bangil, 85
Bangka, 131, 139, 222
Bangkalan, 132
Bangkara, 142
Bangli, 134, 135
Banjarmasin, 45, 47, 66, 93, 138–9, 207; Banjarmasin War, 139
Bank Central Asia, 307
Bank of China, 277
Bantĕn, 10, 17, 27, 28, 29, 30, 31, 35, 36, 37, 38, 42, 44, 45, 46, 47, 69, 70, 71, 73, 74, 75, 78, 79, 82, 83, 84, 86, 89, 90, 104–5, 121, 125, 130, 158, 178, 179, 200, 225, 229; foundation of, 38
Banteng, Barisan, 223
Banteng Division, 254
Barabudhur, 40, 307
Bari, Seh, text ascribed to, 11
Barisan Tani Indonesia, see Peasant Front, Indonesian.
Baron Sakendher, 110
Barus, 142
Bastin, John, 114
Bataks, 33, 141, 142, 157, 185, 186, 192, 200, 220–1, 222, 252, 254

Batavia, *passim*; foundation of, 30–1; Javanese
    attacks on, 45; epidemics in, 89; massacre
    of Chinese in, 90, 93; renamed Jakarta, 202
batik (dyed fabric), 56, 57, 127, 166, 167
Batuah, Haji Datuk, 176
Baturenggong, Dalĕm, 48
bauxite, 194
Bayat, Sunan, 10, 46, 73
Bĕbĕluk, Ki, 54
Beijing (Peking), 259, 277, 278, 280, 290
Belenggoe, 192
Belgium, 26, 119, 226
Bĕlitung, 139, 222
Bĕndara, Ratu, 98
Bengal, Bangladesh, 12, 305
Bĕngkulu (Bencoolen), 79, 117, 140, 143, 191
benteng-stelsel, 117
benzoin, 20
Berg, C. C., 18, 40, 41
Bergson, H., 165
'Berkeley mafia', 291
Berlin blockade, 230
bestuurshervormingwet (1922), 160
Bĕsuki, 73
betel, 10, 129, 141
Bhāratayuddha, 52, 53, 55
bhinneka tunggal ika, 256
bid'a, 169, 170
Bijeenkomst voor Federale Overleg, 226
Bina Graha, 301
Bintan, 34
Bintang Hindia, 164, 165
Bintang, Zacharias, 84
birds of paradise, 137
'black Portuguese', 66
Blitar, 46, 208, 289, 295
Blitar, Pangeran (brother of Amangkurat
    IV), 87
Blora, 167, 295
Bodi Caniago, 141
Body for the Supporters (or Spreaders) of
    Sukarnoism, 276
Bogor (Buitenzorg), 105, 139, 166, 243, 268,
    282, 289, 293
bonang, 57
Bonang, Sunan, 10
Bone, 48, 63–4, 66, 67, 76, 136, 137, 214, 222
Bonjol, 141, 142
Boomgaard, P., 121
Borneo, 8, 138, 209, 210, 272. *See also*
    Kalimantan
Borneo Oil Company, 152
Bosch, Johannes van den, 119–20, 131
Both, Pieter, 43
Boven Digul, 179, 191
Brantas river, 15, 42, 43, 83
Bratayuda, 53, 54
Brawijaya Division, 263, 264, 277, 280, 281,
    292, 295
Brazil, 26
Brĕbĕs, 219
Britain, British, English, 28–9, 30, 45, 48,
    78, 79, 83, 84, 90, 93, 105, 110, 111, 112,
    113–14, 120, 124, 126, 132, 133, 136, 137,
    138, 139–40, 141, 142–5, 152, 153, 169,
    186, 195, 209, 210, 213, 215, 216, 217, 218,

222, 224, 225, 239, 272, 273, 275, 279,
    291. *See also* East India Company
Brooke, James, 138
Brunei, 4, 6, 8, 20, 138, 272, 273; early
    gravestones at, 4
bubonic plague, 155
Buddhism, *see* Hindu-Buddhism
budi and *buda*, 129
Budi Utomo, 164–6, 168, 171, 172, 173, 183,
    190, 191
Bugis, 8, 16, 20, 36, 48, 49, 56, 63, 64, 65, 66,
    76, 85, 103, 137, 147, 214, 224; literature,
    48, 56. *See also* Bone
Buitenzorg, *see* Bogor
Bukittingi, 207, 262, 263
Buleleng, 67, 68, 132, 133, 134
Bulog, 292
Bumi manusia, 297
bupati (Javanese lords, senior courtiers),
    110, 111, 116; (Javanese officials of Dutch
    colonial regime), 120, 128, 129; (during
    Revolution), 219; in nineteenth-century
    Minangkabau), 142
Bupatis' Union, 165, 172
bureaucracy, size of, 239
Burhanuddin Harahap, 249, 251, 262,
    263, 270
Burma, 19, 205, 206, 208, 209, 230, 247,
    265; (Pegu), 21
Buru, 297
'business cabinet', 258, 262
Bustan as-Salatin, 51
Butung, 64

Cabolek, Ki (*Sĕrat Cabolek*), 54, 55
Cairo, 168, 170, 177, 190
Cakrajaya, *patih* of Kartasura, 88
Cakranĕgara, 135
Cakraningrat II, Panĕmbahan of Madura, 85
Cakraningrat III, Pangeran of Madura,
    85, 86, 87
Cakraningrat IV, Pangeran of Madura, 87–9,
    91, 92, 93
Cakraningrat line of Madura, 44, 132
Caliph, Caliphate, 9, 177, 190
Calon Arang, 55, 56
Caltex, 152, 239, 262, 263, 278, 292, 301
Calvinism, *see* Protestantism
Cambodia, 19, 280, 305
camphor, 16, 20
Canada, 301
cannibalism, 142, 146
Canton, 3, 39
Cape of Good Hope, 23, 79, 88, 93, 112
Capellen, G. A. G. Ph van der, 116, 136, 137
Carter, J., 306
cassava, 124, 153
Catholic Party, *see* Partai Katholik
Catholicism, Catholics, 25, 26, 28, 62, 168,
    172, 240, 242, 255, 259, 287, 299
cattle, 67, 136
Cek Ko-po, 36
cĕlĕmpung, 57
cement, 301
Cĕnthini, 126

Centraal Sarekat Islam, see CSI
Central Advisory Board (Chuo Sangi-in):
in Java, 205, 208; in Sumatra, 207
Central Intelligence Agency (American),
276, 281
Central Intelligence Board (Indonesian), 272
centuries, cycle of, in Java, 73, 100
Ceylon, 84, 85, 86, 87, 88, 105, 247
Chaerul Saleh, 258, 266, 275, 276, 278, 281,
289, 292
Chairil Anwar, 215
Champa, 19
Chen Dasheng, 4
Chen Yi, 277
China, Chinese, 3, 4, 5, 7, 12, 16, 18, 19, 20,
21, 25, 28, 31, 36, 37, 38, 39, 78, 90–3, 98,
114, 115, 116, 121, 122, 123, 124, 125, 129,
138, 139, 143, 152, 155, 158, 159, 160, 161,
166, 167, 169, 172, 173, 184, 187, 192, 200,
203, 216, 225, 229, 230, 238, 239, 247,
248, 249, 252, 253, 259, 264, 267, 268,
269, 272, 273, 274, 276, 279, 280, 290,
292, 293, 294, 296, 299, 301, 302; role in
Islamisation, 6. See also China, People's
Republic of
China, Peoples Republic of, relations with
Indonesia, 248, 267, 273, 274, 277–8, 290
cholera, 115, 117, 121, 133, 145
Christian Party, see Parkindo
Christianity, Christians, 22, 24, 25, 26, 28,
33, 34, 48, 61, 62, 63, 66, 74, 75, 79, 84,
136, 137, 142, 157, 160, 171, 183, 184,
186, 192, 200, 213, 214, 221, 222, 224,
233, 240, 241, 242, 250, 252, 259, 265,
266, 285, 293, 294, 295, 299, 308, 309;
Christian population, 25, 294, 308–9. See
also Catholicism, Protestantism
Christison, Sir Philip, 216
chronicles and historical traditions: Balinese,
55; Bugis and Makasarese, 56; Javanese, 10,
18, 37, 39-41, 42, 43, 46, 54, 55, 56, 75, 100,
115; Malay, 52, 56. See also individual titles
Chuo Sangi-in, 205
Cianjur, 139
Cik di Tiro, Teungku, 145
Cikini, attempt to assassinate Sukarno at,
261, 262
Ciliwung river, 45
cinnamon, 124
Cirĕbon, 38, 42, 44, 45, 70, 74, 79, 80, 83,
85, 86, 90, 112, 123, 125, 200, 210, 224;
foundation of, 37
Cloon, Dirk van, 89
clove, 16, 20, 22, 29, 39, 61, 62, 63, 105,
124, 137
coal, 138, 139, 225
cockfighting, 141
coconut, 153
Coen, Jan Pieterszoon, 29–30, 45, 82
coffee, 65, 86, 90, 105, 112, 115, 119, 120, 121,
123, 124, 125, 127, 133, 141, 152, 153, 186
Colijn, Hendrikus, 188
Colombo powers, 248
Comintern, 172, 178
Comité voor het Javaansch Nationalisme, 176
'Communism, national', 221, 229, 240

Communist Party of Indonesia, see PKI
'confrontation', 272–5, 280, 290
Constantinople, 22
Constituent Assembly, 246, 251, 261, 264–6
Constitution, Indonesian: of 1945, 209, 213,
218, 264–5, 266, 290; of 1950, 233. See
also Constituent Assembly
Constitutional Regulation of 1854, 121
copper, 133
copra, 152, 153
Coral Sea, battle of, 201
Coromandel, 12
corruption: before 19th century, 23, 62, 81,
82, 90, 97, 105; in 19th century, 111, 115,
120; in 20th century, 156, 201, 219, 237,
239, 247, 250, 253–5, 260, 261, 265, 274,
276, 283, 284, 287, 290, 291, 293, 298,
301, 306, 309
cotton, 20, 67
Council of the Indies (Raad van Indië),
creation of, 28; reduction of powers of, 161
councils, 160–1. See also Volksraad
coup attempt of 1965, 280–2, 289, 291,
292, 297; killings which followed, 287–8;
imprisonment which followed, 288, 290,
295, 297, 306
Crawfurd, John, 113
CSI (Sarekat Islam Central headquarters),
167, 173, 174, 175, 176
cukong, 292, 293, 299, 307
Cultural Manifesto, 275
cultuurstelsel (cultivation system, 'culture
system'), 119–24, 126, 128
Czechoslovakia, 193, 230

Daendels, Herman Willem, 111-12, 113, 114,
118, 132, 138
Daha (Kĕdiri), 7
Dahlan, Kyai Haji Ahmad, 171
dakwah, 285, 309
Dalat, 210
Dale, Thomas, 30
Daludalu, 142
Damais, Louis-Charles, 5
Damar Wulan (Damar Bulan) stories, 52, 53
dance, 56, 57
Danes, 48, 78, 134
Danurĕja, patih of Kartasura, 88
Danurĕja I, patih of Yogyakarta, 110
Danurĕja II, patih of Yogyakarta, 110, 112, 113
Danurĕja IV, patih of Yogyakarta, 116
Darsono, 174, 176, 178
Darul Islam, 227–8, 240, 244, 246, 247, 256,
262, 265, 269, 270
Daud Beureu'eh, Mohammed, 200, 230,
247, 254, 265–6
Daud Syah, Tuanku Muhammad (Sultan
Ibrahim Mansur Syah) of Aceh, 145, 146
Daya, 32
Dayaks, 139, 203
'debt of honour', 151, 154
debt, external, 291, 297, 307-8
decentralisation, 160
Delacroix, F., 127
Dĕlanggu, 227

Dĕli, 33, 34, 143, 200
Dĕmak, 8, 16, 18, 36, 37, 38, 40, 41, 42, 54,
    84, 85, 91, 100
Democratic League, 268
Dĕmung, 73
Den Pasar, 135, 224
Depression of 1930s, 153, 155, 159, 161, 181,
    186–8, 194, 201
desascholen, 159
Deventer, C. Th van, 125, 151
Dewa Agung: of Gelgel, 46, 67; of Klungkung,
    67, 68, 134, 135–6
Dewa Anom of Sukawati, 68
Dewa Ruci, 55
Dewan Da'wah Islamiyah Indonesia, 294
Dewantara, Ki Hadjar (Suwardi
    Surjaningrat), 171, 176, 182, 190, 204,
    209, 251
Dharmaśûnya kakawin, 53
Dharsono, Hartono, 307
diamonds, 20
Dias, Bartolomeu, 23
Diem, Ngo Dinh, 275
Diemen, Antonio van, 61–2
Dili massacre, 309
Diniyah School, 170
Dipanagara, Pangeran (son of Hamĕng-
    kubuwana III), 115–17, 174
Dipanagara, Pangeran (son of Pakubuwana
    I), 87
Diponĕgoro Division, 263, 264, 277,
    280–2, 290
Djajaadiningrat, Raden Adipati Arya, 157
Djajadiningrat, Hoesein, 158
Djambek, Shaikh Muhammad Djamil, 170
Djawi Hisworo, 176
Djuanda Kartawidjaja, 258–9, 260, 261, 263,
    264, 266, 275
doctors, numbers of: in 1930, 155–6; in
    1974, 286; in 1980, 305
Doktĕr-Jawa school, 129, 157, 164, 165
Dominican order, 25
Door duisternis tot licht, 157
Douwes Dekker, E. F. E., 171, 174, 182, 195
Douwes Dekker, Eduard, 124, 171
DPR (Peoples' Representative Council):
    established, 242; in 1945 constitution, 264;
    dissolved, 268; re-established, 298, 306
DPR-GR (Mutual Cooperation Peoples'
    Representative Council), appointment
    of, 268, 292
Drake, Sir Francis, 28
Drewes, G. W. J., 11
Du Bus, Fort, 137
Dulles, J. F., 263
Dutch, passim; arrival in Indonesia of, 27
Dwiwarna (red and white Indonesian flag)
    see Sang Merah-Putih
dysentery, 117, 133

East India Company, English, 29, 45, 83. See
    also British
East India Company, Dutch, see VOC
East Indonesia state (NIT), 224, 233
East Java state, 226

East Sumatra state, 226, 233
Eastern Salient (Oosthoek) of Java, 10, 38,
    39, 43, 47, 48, 67, 68, 69, 70, 83, 87,
    89, 92, 98–9, 225. See also Balambangan,
    Pasuruan
eclipses, 73
Edam island, 104
education: Rotinese, 66, 136; in 19th-century
    Java, 128; Ethical period reforms of, 156–9;
    Western, Indonesian desire for, 164, 165;
    Islamic, 160, 170, 177–8, 200, 205; during
    World War II, 201, 202, 204, 205, 227; in
    1950s, 238, 267; after 1965, 286, 304, 305.
    See also Taman Siswa, pesantren
'eereschuld, Een', 151
Egypt, 12, 170, 177, 184, 190, 245, 249
elections: Volksraad, 161, 172, 173; of 1955,
    246, 248, 250–1, 252, 256; of 1957, 252,
    260, 262; of 1971, 298–9, 305; of 1977
    and after, 305
elephants, 34
Elizabeth I, queen of England, 29
elmu nabi Adam, 167
emigration (from Java to outer islands),
    152, 155
English, see British
English War, Fourth, 109
Erbervelt, Pieter, 90
Eru Cakra, 167
Ethical policy, 135, 151–62, 165, 186, 192, 284

Fadhillah Khan, 38
Fakhruddin, Muhammad, Sultan of Jambi,
    140
'Falatehan', 38
Fasseur, C., 121
Fatahillah, 38
fertiliser, 301, 304
Ficus elastica, 152
'fifth force', 278, 279, 280
First Class schools, 158, 159
Flores, 8, 66, 136, 191
Fock, Dirk, 157, 161
Formosa, see Taiwan
Fox, James J., 136
France, French, 29, 48, 89, 105, 110, 111,
    112, 143, 144–5, 194
Frederikse, Jochum, 87
Freitas, Jordão de, 25
Fretilin, 301–2, 309
Front Demokrasi Rakyat, see People's
    Democratic Front
functional groups, 255, 259, 264, 265, 268,
    276, 298

Gajah Mada University, 220
Gama, Vasco da, 23
gambier, 141
Gambir, 129
gambling, 10, 141
gamĕlan (orchestra), 57, 164
ganyang Malaysia, 273
GAPI, 193–4
Garĕndi, Raden Mas, 92, 98

Garibaldi, G., 183
Garut, 174, 227
Gelgel, 46, 48, 67, 68
Generation of 45, 215, 308
Generation of 66, 284
Gĕrakan Hidup Baru, 260
Gĕrakan Rakyat Baru, 209, 260
Gĕrinda (local Yogyakarta party), 189
Gĕrindo (Indonesian People's Movement), 192, 200
Germany, Germans, 173, 193, 194, 200, 209, 278, 287
Gĕrwani (Indonesian Women's Movement), 271, 281, 282
Gĕstapu, 287, 288. See also September 30 Movement
Gianyar, 68, 134, 135
Gibraltar, Straits of, 29
Gids, de, 151
Gilchrist letter, 279
Giri, 10, 39, 46
Giri, Panĕmbahan, 74, 76
Giri, Sunan, 10, 39, 40, 41, 46, 61
Girīndrawardhana Raṇawijaya, king of Majapahit, 36
Gīriśawardhana, king of Majapahit, 18
Giyugun, 206, 214
Goa (India), 23, 24, 271
Goddess of the Southern Ocean, 41, 44, 47, 100, 101, 115, 117
Goens, Rijklof van, 40, 61, 70, 76
goeroe ordonnantie (teacher ordinance): of 1905, 178; of 1925, 178, 205
Gogodog, 74
gold, 16, 19, 20, 22, 33, 138, 141, 144, 245
Gold Coast, 144
gold standard, 187
Golkar (Sekber Golkar, Joint Secretariat of Functional Groups), 276, 298, 299, 302, 305, 308
Gombong, 195
gong, 57
Good Offices Committee, 226, 230
Gorontalo, 64, 263
gotong royong, 255, 268
Governor-General of VOC, creation of position of, 28
Gowa, 17, 48–9, 61–5, 70, 72, 73, 137
Graaff, Simon de, 161
Graeff, Andries C. D. de, 185, 189
Greater East Asia Co-Prosperity Sphere, 199, 201
Greeve, Jan, 103
Grĕsik, 10, 12, 38–9, 42, 43; early gravestone at, 5
Guadalcanal, 201
Guiana, Dutch, see Surinam
guided democracy: origins of, 251, 254, 255; general nature of, 257–8
guitar, 26
Gujerat, Gujeratis, 12, 20, 21, 45, 51
Gunseikan (Military Governor), 202, 204, 206, 210
Guntur, Raden Mas, 86, 98
Gunungjati, Sunan, 10, 37–8
Gunungsitoli, 143

Guomindang, 264

Hadhramis, 169
Hadikusumo, Ki Bagus, 205, 209
Hadisubeno Sosrowerdojo, 279, 290
Hadith, 169
Hairun, Sultan, 25
Haji, Sultan of Bantĕn, 78–9, 83
hajis (pilgrims who have been to Mecca): as money lenders and landowners, 125, 130; 19th-century numbers of, 130; as religious and popular leaders, 130, 141, 174, 207; travel via Singapore, 169
Halim Pĕrdanakusumah air base, 279, 280–2, 287
Halmahera, 207
Hamĕngkubuwana I, Sultan of Yogyakarta (Pangeran/Sultan Mangkubumi), 92, 94–104, 109, 110
Hamĕngkubuwana II, Sultan of Yogyakarta: as crown prince, 100; as Sultan, 100, 101, 104, 109–13, 115, 116
Hamĕngkubuwana III, Sultan of Yogyakarta, 110, 112, 113, 115
Hamĕngkubuwana IV, Sultan of Yogyakarta, 115
Hamĕngkubuwana V, Sultan of Yogyakarta, 116, 126
Hamĕngkubuwana VIII, Sultan of Yogyakarta, 219
Hamĕngkubuwana IX, Sultan of Yogyakarta, 219, 231, 232, 243, 245, 246, 262, 263, 287, 289, 290, 299
Hamzah Pansuri, 51, 52
Hanafi school of law, 4
Hanbali school of law, 177
Hankam, 297–8
Hardi, 259, 264, 279, 290
Harian Rakjat, 248, 269, 282
Harṣawijaya, 55
Hartingh, Nicolaas, 96
Hartsinck, Andries, 102–3
Hasanuddin, king of Bantĕn, 38
Hasanuddin, Sultan of Gowa, 64, 70
Hasjim Asjari, Kyai Haji, 177, 206, 207
Hassan, A., 177, 190
Hatta, Mohammad, 184–5, 188, 189, 191, 203–13, 217, 218, 223, 225–33, 244, 253, 254, 255, 258, 260, 261, 262, 263, 264, 268, 298, 299
Hayam Wuruk, king of Majapahit, 18
HBS (Higher middle-class school), 158, 181–2
head-hunting, 137, 146
Heeren XVII (Directors of the VOC): role, 27, 30; dismissal of, 110
Hegel, G. W. F., 165
Heiho (Auxiliary Forces), 204, 206, 210, 214, 215, 221
Henry 'the Navigator', prince, 22
Heroes Day (Hari Pahlawan), 217
Heutsz, Joannes Benedictus van, 145–6, 156, 157, 159, 165
Hevea brasiliensis, 153
Hidayatullah, 139
hijrah (non-cooperative movement), 176,

177, 192
Hikayat Aceh, 52
Hikayat Amir Hamzah, 52, 55
Hikayat Iskandar Dhulkarnain, 52
Hikayat Pandawa Jaya, 52
Hikayat Raja-raja Pasai, 8, 9, 13
Hikayat Sĕri Rama, 52
Hindu-Buddhism, Hinduism, Buddhism,
    3, 4, 5, 7, 8, 11, 12, 13, 17, 18, 19, 20, 36,
    37, 38, 39, 40, 46, 52, 53, 54, 55, 56, 99,
    134, 142, 164, 167, 182, 241, 307; revival
    of, 293
Hiroshima, 209
HIS (Dutch-Native school), 158, 159
Hitler, A., 193, 194
'Hitoe, Kapitein', 61, 62
Hitu, 24, 28, 39, 61, 62
Hizbullah, Barisan (God's Forces), 208, 215,
    227, 240
Hoamoal, 61–3, 65
Hohendorff, Johan Andries Baron von, 92, 95
Hollandsch-Chineesche schools, 158
honey, 20
Hong Kong, 195
hongi, 63
hoofdenscholen (chiefs' school), 128, 156
Hoorn, Joan van, 84
Horie Choso, 204
hormat circulaire (etiquette circular), 128, 129
horses, 20, 34, 72, 84, 136
Houtman, Cornelis de, 27
Hurdt, Anthonio, 76
'hydraulic society', 16

Ibadat, Raja, 140
Ibn Battuta, 4
Ibn Sa'ud, 177
Ibnu Sutowo, 262, 296, 301
Ibrahim, Seh, 96
Ibrahim, Tuanku (Sultan Ali Alauddin
    Mansur Syah) of Aceh, 143, 145
Ibrahim Mansur Syah, Sultan of Aceh, 145
Idenburg, Alexander W. F., 151, 156, 167
Idham Chalid, Kyai Haji, 259, 265, 266, 289
IGGI, 291, 301, 302
ijma', 169
ijtihad, bab al- ijtihad, 169
Iljas Jacub, 190, 191
Imagiri, 47
imam (religious leader) in Aceh, 36
Imam al-, 169
Imam Bonjol, Tuanku, 141, 142
Imam Sjafei, 289
Imhoff, Gustaaf Willem Baron van, 93, 94–5
Indĕragiri, 34, 142
India, Indians, 3, 4, 6, 7, 8, 9, 11, 12, 13, 16,
    20, 21, 23, 29, 45, 46, 51, 52, 53, 55, 56,
    76, 78, 111, 113, 114, 126, 127, 138, 143,
    144, 152, 169, 174, 177, 185, 216, 217, 225,
    247, 267, 271
Indië weerbaar (defence of the Indies)
    movement, 161, 172, 173
indigo, 86, 115, 120, 122, 123, 124, 133
Indische Partij, 165, 171, 172, 176, 182
Indische Vereeniging, 184

Indochina, French, 194. *See also* Vietnam,
    Cambodia, 19
Indo-Europeans, 165, 171, 172, 182, 187,
    192, 216
Indonesia, University of, 275, 289
'Indonesia Raya' (anthem), 205, 211, 224
Indonesia Raya (newspaper), 296, 300
Indonesia tumpah darahku, 186
Indonesian language (*Bahasa Indonesia*):
    origins, 185; during World War II, 202;
    used in educational system, 238
Indonesian literature, modern, 185, 186,
    192, 215
Indonesian Nationalist Party, *see* PNI
inflation, 175, 201, 220, 227, 239, 247, 267,
    271, 275, 280, 289, 291, 293, 296, 297
Ingalaga, Susuhunan, *see* Pakubuwana I
Inggit Garnasih, 182
inlander, 194
Insulinde, 172, 173, 174
International Monetary Fund, 272, 280,
    290, 291, 301
Interpol, 280
Investigating Committee for Preparatory
    Work for Indonesian Independence,
    208, 209
Iqbal, Muhammad, 215
Iraq, 184, 265
Irian Jaya, 137, 179, 215, 232, 242–3, 248,
    251, 252, 256, 261, 262, 269, 270–1, 297,
    303, 309
iron, 20
irrigation: expansion of, under Ethical policy,
    129, 152, 154; under new order, 304
Irshad, al-, 170, 193
ISDV (Indies Social-Democratic Association),
    172, 173, 174, 178
Iskandar Muda, Sultan of Aceh, 33, 34,
    35, 51, 52
Iskandar Syah, Sultan of Malacca, 19, 20
Iskandar Thani Alauddin Mughayat Syah,
    Sultan of Aceh, 35
Islam, *passim*; coming of, 3–14, 19–20, 38,
    39, 48, 99. *See also* Modernism, Orthodox
    Islam, Shafi'i school of law, Sufis, *and*
    individual names and terms
Islam dan kĕbangsaan, 190
Islamic Communism, 174, 175, 176, 179
Islamic Community, Preparatory Union
    of, 202
Ismail, Shaikh, 9
Israel, 248, 300, 304
Italy, 194
Itinerario naer Oost ofte Portugaels Indien, 26
Iwojima, 209

Jagaraga, 41, 87
Jaka Tingkir, 40, 41
Jakarta, 30, 37, 202 ff. *passim*; becomes capital
    of Indonesia, 233; population, 238. *See*
    also Jayakĕrta
Jakarta Charter, 209, 213, 264, 265, 266, 296
Jakarta-Pnom Penh-Hanoi-Beijing-
    Pyongyang axis, 280
Jambi, 29, 34, 70, 140, 143

Jam'iyyat Khair, 170
Jangrana II, 86
Jangrana III, 87
Janssens, Jan Willem, 112-13
Japan, Japanese, 21, 25, 28, 29, 78, 86, 127,
    129, 146, 152, 161, 186, 187, 189, 191, 192,
    193–5, 199–222 passim, 227, 237, 239, 240,
    244, 258, 259, 278, 286, 290, 291, 296,
    300, 302
Japan (place in Java), 42
Jassin, H. B., 275
Java Sea, battle of, 195
Java War, 111, 112, 116-17, 119, 137, 142, 174,
    193, 217
Javanese literature, 9–11, 51, 52–5, 56, 115,
    126. See also chronicles and historical
    traditions and individual titles
Javanese Wars of Succession: First, 85;
    Second, 87; Third, 95–7, 104, 105
Jawa Hokokai, 206, 207, 208, 209, 213
Jayakěrta, 29, 30, 37
Jayalěngkara, king of Surabaya, 44
Jayanagara, king of Majapahit, 18
Jayapuspita, 87
Jazirat al-Muluk, 24
Jehovah's Witnesses, 293
Jejak langkah, 297
Jělantik, Gusti Gěde, 135
Jěmbrana, 134
Jenkins, D., 307
Jěpara, 29, 32, 36, 38, 43, 45, 71, 73, 76, 81,
    83, 84, 87, 92, 94, 157
Jerusalem, 38
Jesuit order, 25
Jipang, 40, 41
Johns, A. H., 12, 130
Johor, 16, 24, 32, 33, 34, 35, 36, 38, 75, 83
Jolo, 6. See also Sulu archipelago
Jombang, 177, 206
Jong Java, 168, 182
Jong Minahasa, 168
Jonge, Bonifacius C. de, 188, 191
Jonker, Captain, 84
Jortan, 43
'July 3rd Affair', 223–4
Juwana, 74, 85, 91

Kabinet Karya, 258
Kabinet Kěrja, 266
kafir, 177, 205
Kahar Muzakkar, 244, 269
Kajoran, Raden, 73, 76
Kakiali, 39, 61–2
Kalijaga, Sunan, 10, 40, 41
Kalimantan, xi, 8, 16, 18, 20, 29, 39, 42, 65,
    66, 70, 86, 93, 105, 130, 138, 143, 152,
    168, 178, 199, 201, 203, 209, 215, 224, 232,
    233, 255, 262, 269, 272, 275, 276, 296;
    Dutch conquest of, 138–9, 143. See also
    individual place-names
Kalinyamat, Ratu, queen of Jěpara, 38
Kaliurang, 230
Kamaruddin of Děmak, 36
KAMI, 287, 289
Kampar, 34

Kant, I, 165
Kapaha, 62
kapok, 153
KAPPI, 287
Karangasěm (Bali), 67, 68, 132, 133, 134, 135
Karta, 44, 70
Kartasura, 53, 54, 77, 82–94 passim, 100,
    101; foundation of, 77, 100; conquests of,
    92; abandonment of, 94
Kartini, Raden Ajěng, 157
Kartini Fonds, 'Kartini schools', 157
Kartosuwirjo, S. M., 227, 228, 242, 244,
    247, 270
KASI, 287
kaum (in Aceh), 33
Kaum Bětawi, 168, 188
kauman (in Java), 166
kawin gantung, 182
Kěbatinan, 293, 295, 299
Kědah, 34
Kědiri, 7, 36, 37, 41, 42, 75, 76, 79
Kědu, 121
Keibodan, 204
Kennedy, J. F., 269, 271
Kennedy, R. F., 271, 275
Kenpeitai (Japanese Military Police), 202,
    203, 216
Kěpěr, 76
kěroncong, 26
Kěrtarājasa Jayawardhana, king of Majapahit,
    18
'Kew letters', 112
Khrushchev, N., 269, 277
Kidul, Kangjěng Ratu or Nyai Lara see
    Goddess of the Southern Ocean
kidung, 55
Klungkung, 67, 68, 133, 134, 135
KNIP (Central Indonesian National Com-
    mittee), 213, 214, 218, 225, 226; Badan
    Pěkěrja KNIP, 218
Koga (Vigilance Command), 275–6
Koiso Kuniaki, 207, 209
kongsi, 138
Koninklijke Nederlandsche Maatschappij
    tot Exploitatie van Petroleum-bronnen in
    Nederlandsch-Indië, 'de Koninklijke', 152
Kopkamtib, 287, 296, 298, 300
Korea, 248, 263, 280
Korean War, 242, 245
Kostrad (Army Strategic Reserve), 274, 276,
    281, 282
Kota Piliang, 141
Kotawaringin, 138
KPM line, 239, 261
Krakatau, 133
kretek, 293
kris (dagger), 56, 57, 86, 135
Kuala Lumpur, 273, 290
Kucing, 138
Kudus, 38, 42
Kudus, Sunan, 10, 38, 40
Kuning, Sunan (in Java), 92
Kupang, 66
Kuta Gěde, 42, 44
Kutai, xi, 39, 66, 152
Kutaraja see Banda Aceh

Kwajalein, 207
kweekscholen, see teacher-training schools
kyai (religious teacher), 104, 105, 116, 117,
    130, 166, 171, 174, 177, 178, 204, 205, 206,
    207, 215, 217, 227, 240, 259, 286

La Galigo, 56
La Ma'dukĕllĕng, 66
La Mappanjuki, 214
La Tenritatta to Unru', see Arung Palakka
Lajar terkembang, 192
Lampung, 35, 38, 86, 104, 155
Lancaster, Sir James, 29
'land rent' (land tax), 114, 119–20, 125
Lange, Mads, 134
Langkat, 144, 152
Laos, 305
Lasĕm, 43
lasykar rakyat, 220
Law College (Rechtshoogeschool), 158
League of Supporters of Indonesian
    Independence (IPKI), 265, 299
Lee Kuan Yew, 280
Left Wing (Sayap Kiri), 225, 226, 227
Leiden University, 145, 158, 219
Leimena, Johannes, 259, 266, 275, 277,
    281, 289
Lekra (People's Cultural Institute), 259,
    271, 275, 295
Lenin, V., 174, 175
Lcran gravcstonc, 3
Lesser Sunda Islands, see Nusa Tĕnggara
Leyte Gulf, 208
'liberal' period, 124–5, 128, 151
Liem Sioe Liong, 307
Limapuluh Kota, 141
Limboto, 64
Limburg Stirum, J. P. Count van, 173–4
Lincoln, A., 183
Linggajati agreement, 224–5
Linschoten, Jan Huygen van, 26
Lintau, 142
Lipura, 41
Lisbon, 7, 27, 29
literacy: in 1930, 160; in 1961, 238; in 1971,
    286; in 1980, 305
LKN (National Cultural Institute), 271, 275
Lobo, 137
Lokapala, 53, 55
Lombard, Denys, xiii, 33, 35
Lombok, 8, 20, 39, 47, 48, 55, 65, 67, 86,
    133, 134–5, 136, 160, 216; Dutch conquest
    of, 135
Loyola, St. Ignatius, 25
Lubis, Zulkifli, 253, 260, 261, 262, 269
Lukman, M. H., 228, 229, 241, 243, 268,
    281, 288
Luwu, 222
Luzon, 208

Macao, 25
Macapagal, Diosdado, 272, 275
macapat, 53, 55
mace, 16, 20, 22, 61

Madiun, 37, 41, 84, 87, 228, 229, 240, 241,
    282; PKI rebellion at, 229, 264
Madiun river, 41
Madura, Madurese, 8, 27, 39, 43–4, 47, 57,
    73, 77, 81, 85, 86, 87, 92, 93, 103, 109, 116,
    132, 147, 154, 155, 160, 164–5, 172, 199,
    223, 224, 225, 226; literature of, 56; music
    of, 57; state of, 226. See also Cakraningrat
Maeda Tadashi, 207, 210
Maetsuycker, Joan, 61, 64, 76
Magĕlang, 117, 156, 216, 218, 294, 309
Magĕtan, 87
Mahabhārata, 52
Mahkota Sĕgala Raja-raja, 51
Mahmillub (Extraordinary Military Courts),
    289, 292
Mahmud Syah, Sultan of Aceh, 144–5
Mahmud Syah, Sultan of Malacca, 23, 32
Ma Huan, 5
Maimun, daughter of, 3
maize, 124
Maja, Kyai, 116, 117, 174
Maja Agung, 43
Majakĕrta, 129, 181
Majapahit, 4, 5, 8, 10, 13, 15, 16, 17–19, 36–7,
    38, 39, 40, 41, 43, 47, 55, 68, 74, 100, 140,
    174; golden crown, 76, 83
Makasar, Makasarese, 8, 20, 29, 39, 47, 48–9,
    61, 62, 63, 64, 66, 67, 75, 86, 105, 117,
    207, 233, 255, 294; literature, 48, 56, 65,
    66, 72, 73, 74, 75, 76, 77, 78, 81, 84, 85,
    137, 138, 214. See also Gowa
Malabar, 12
Malacca, 5, 6, 8, 9, 10, 15, 16, 17, 18, 19–21,
    23–4, 25, 26, 28, 32, 33, 34, 35, 36, 38, 42,
    46, 50, 61, 63, 75; as centre of Islamisation,
    5–6; Islamisation legend concerning, 9;
    Portuguese conquest of, 7, 24, 32; Dutch
    conquest of, 62; British occupation of,
    112, 143
Malang, 37, 43, 85, 97, 98, 99, 215, 222
Malari riots, 300
malaria, 117, 137, 155
Malay literature, 50–2, 56. See also chronicles
    and historical traditions and indvidual titles
Malaya: British, 153, 169, 195, 209, 210, 230,
    272; Federation of, 263, 272–3. See also
    Malaysia
Malaysia, Federation of, 272–3, 274, 275,
    278, 290, 296, 305. See also Malaya
Maldives, 305
Malik, Adam, 222, 223, 276, 278, 289, 290,
    291, 296
Malik as-Salih, Sultan of Samudra, 4, 9, 12
Malik az-Zahir, Sultan, 4
Malik Ibrahim, 5, 12
Maliki school of law, 4
Malino conference, 224
Mallaby, A. W. S., 217
Maluku (Moluccas, 'Spice Islands'), 8, 16,
    19, 20, 24, 25, 26, 27, 28, 29, 30, 39, 42,
    43, 48, 49, 61, 62, 63, 65, 69, 94, 160, 233,
    255, 297, 299. See also Ambon, Banda,
    Hitu, South Malaku, Tĕrnate, Tidore
Manar, al-, 38
mancanĕgara (outer districts of Javanese

kingdom), 110, 112, 117
Manchuria, 193, 210
Mandala Command, 270
Mandarsyah, king of Tĕrnate, 63
Mangkubumi, Pangeran (brother of
    Pakubuwana II), see Hamĕngkubuwana I
Mangkubumi, Pangeran (uncle of
    Dipanagara), 117
Mangkunĕgara, Pangeran Arya (brother of
    Pakubuwana II), 88
Mangkunĕgara I, Pangeran Adipati (Raden
    Mas Said), 88, 92, 94–103
Mangkunĕgara II, Pangeran Adipati Arya,
    110, 111, 114, 118
Mangkunĕgara IV, Pangeran Adipati,
    126, 127
Mangkunĕgara VIII, Pangeran Adipati
    Arya, 223
Mangkunĕgaran: status under Dutch rule,
    126; success in adjusting to colonial
    rule, 127
Mangkunĕgaran Legion, 111, 113, 114,
    116, 127
Manikĕbu, 275
Manila, 207, 208
Manipol (—USDEK), 267, 271, 275
Mansur, al-, king of Tidore, 8
Mansur, Kyai Haji Mas, 204, 206, 209
Mansur Syah, Sultan of Malacca, 6, 143, 145
mantri-guru, 129
Manuel, Dom, of Tĕrnate, 24
Maphilindo, 273
Marah Rœsli, 185
Mardijkers, 85
Maring, G., 172
marriage law (1973), 300
martabat, 51
Ma'ruf Syah, Sultan of Pĕdir, 6
Marxism, 174, 180, 182, 183, 184, 189, 222,
    241, 249, 268, 290. See also PKI
Masjid al-Haram, 170
Masyumi, 206, 208, 209, 215, 217, 221, 226,
    227, 228, 229, 240–55, 259–68, 270, 276,
    287, 294, 296, 300; banned, 265, 268
Mataram (in Java), 31, 36, 39–115 passim;
    foundation of, 40–2; fall of, 41, 73, 75
Mataram (in Lombok), 133, 135
Mataram, Pangeran Arya (uncle of
    Amangkurat IV), 87
Matulesia, Thomas, 137
Mauritius, 105, 112
Max Havelaar, 124, 151
Mecca, 9, 37, 38, 47, 71, 125, 130, 141, 169,
    170, 171, 176, 177, 190, 205, 249, 265
Medan, 216, 220, 225, 238, 243, 246, 254,
    263, 278
Medan Mĕrdeka, 215, 281
Medical College (Geneeskundige
    Hoogeschool), 158
Mediterranean, 19, 20, 22
Mĕgat Iskandar Syah, Sultan of Malacca, 20
Mĕlaka, see Malacca
Mĕmpawah, 138
Mĕnado, 64, 117, 126, 140, 142, 214, 263
Menak Amir Hamsa, 53
Menak stories, 53, 55

Mĕngwi, 67–8, 134
Mĕntawai, 146
Merah Silau/Silu, 9
Mĕrapi, Mt., 73, 116, 282
Mĕrbabu, Mt., 282
MIAI (Supreme Islamic Council of Indo-
    nesia), 193, 194, 203, 205, 206
Middle Javanese literature, 18, 55
Middleton, Sir Henry, 29
Midway, 201
Minahasa, 64, 157, 168, 252
Minangkabau, Minangkabaus, 7, 56, 83,
    84, 117, 133, 140–2, 146, 163, 164, 169,
    170, 171, 173, 174, 175, 176, 178, 179, 184,
    185, 186, 189, 190, 191, 192, 193, 195,
    200; Islamisation of, 7, 140; language and
    literature, 56
Mindanao, 6
Mintaraga, 53, 54
Mintaredja, H. Mohamed Safaat, 298
Minye Tujoh gravestones, 4, 6
Misbach, Haji, 174
Mochtar Lubis, 215, 253, 296, 300
Modernism, Islamic, 168 ff. passim; origins
    and nature of, 168–71
Molana Usalam, 10
Molana Yusup, king of Bantĕn, 38
Moluccas, see Maluku
Mongolia, Outer, 248
Mongols, 12
'monoloyalty', 298
Mook, Hubertus J. van, 216, 217, 218, 223,
    225, 226; van Mook line, 226, 229, 230
Moro, Morotai, 25, 207, 215
Moses, story of, 10
Mountbatten, Lord Louis, 216
MPR (People's Consultative Assembly): in
    1945 constitution, 264; established, 298,
    299, 306
MPRS (Provisional People's Consultative
    Assembly), appointment of, 268, 290–1,
    292, 295, 296
Muarakumpe, 140
Muchtar Lutfi, 190, 191
Muhammad, the Prophet, 9, 51, 52, 53, 169,
    171, 176
Muhammad Sĕman, Sultan, 139
Muhammad Syah, Sultan of Aceh, 143
Muhammad Syah, Sultan of Malacca, 9, 20
Muhammad Syah, Sultan of Pahang, 6
Muhammadiyah, 171, 175, 176, 177, 187, 189,
    193, 204, 205, 206, 208, 221, 286, 288
Muis, Abdul, 173, 174, 175, 192
mukim (in Aceh), 35
MULO (More Extended Lower Education
    school), 158, 159, 177, 286
Multatuli, 124, 171
Munggu, Gusti Agung Made, 68
Munir, al-, 170
Murba Partai (Proletarian Party), 229, 240,
    250, 254, 255, 276, 299; banned, 278
Murdani, L.B., 308
Murya, Sunan, 10
music, 57, 126, 164
Muslimin, wong, 166
Musso, 178, 179, 182, 228–9, 274

Musyawarah Nasional, Musyawarah Nasional Pěmbangunan (1957), 260
Muwardi, 223
Muzaffar Syah, Sultan of Malacca, 20
Muzaffar Syah, Sultan of Pědir, 6
mysticism, Islamic, see Sufis

Nāgarakěrtāgama, 18, 19
Nagasaki, 210
Nahdlatul Ulama, see NU
Najamuddin, Ahmad, Sultan of Palembang, 140
Napoleon, Louis, 111
Napoleon Bonaparte, 111; Napoleonic Wars, 112, 114, 119
Napoleon III, 144
Naqshabandiyya order, 130, 135, 142, 168, 170
Nasakom, 268, 275, 278, 279
Nasiruddin, Abdul Rahman, Sultan of Jambi, 140
Nasser, G. A., 248
Nasution, A. H., 222, 227–9, 231, 240, 245–6, 249, 251, 252–3, 255, 259–82 passim, 287, 288–9, 306
Natadiningrat, Pangeran, 112
Natakusuma, Pangeran (brother of Haměngkubuwana II), see Pakualam I
Natakusuma, patih of Kartasura, 89, 91–2
National Conference, National Development Conference (1957), 260
National Council, 255, 259, 260, 266
National Front (of guided democracy period), 269, 275
National Front for the Liberation of West Irian, 262, 269
National Front government (Madiun rebellion), 229
National Party (Nationale Fractie), 188
National Planning Council, 266
'national united front' strategy: adopted by PKI, 243; endangered by PKI, 274
nationalism, 'secular': beginnings of, 179, 181, 182–4; Islamic opposition to, 177, 183, 184, 189–90
Natsir, Mohammad, 189–90, 221, 240, 242–4, 254, 262, 263, 264, 265, 269–70, 291, 294, 296
natural gas, 301, 304
Nawawi, Syaikh Muhammad al-, 130
Neck, Jacob van, 27
Nederlandsch Indische Vrijzinnige Bond, 173
něgara ikut tuan, 224
Negara Islam Indonesia, 227
Něgěri Sěmbilan, 6
Nehru, J., 248, 271
Neighborhood Associations, 206
Nepal, 305
Netherlands Trading Company (NHM: Nederlandsche Handelmaatschappij), 120, 123
New Life Movement, 260
'new order': origin of term, 284; compared with Dutch rule, 284–5, 286, 304
New People's Movement, 209, 260

newspapers: numbers of, 185, 267; circulation of, 238, 248–9, 267
Ngampel-Děnta Sunan, 10, 44, 46
Nias, 34, 143
Nigeria, 301
Nirartha, 48
Nītiśāstra kakawin, 55
Nixon, R., 297, 301
Njono Prawiro, 289
Njoto, 228, 241, 243, 269, 271, 281, 288
'November promises', 174
NU (Nahdlatul Ulama, the Rise of the Religious Scholars), 177, 184, 193, 204, 206, 207, 217, 221, 241, 244–55 passim, 259–68 passim, 274, 276, 278, 282, 287, 295, 296, 298, 299, 306
Nu, U, 248
Nur ad-daqa'iq, 51
Nusa Těnggara, 66, 136, 143, 255. See also individual place-names
nutmeg, 16, 20, 22, 25, 61, 124

'October 17 affair', 245–6, 249, 251, 253
Oetoesan Hindia, 182
Office for Religious Affairs, 202, 204, 207
oil, 146, 152, 153, 186, 194, 225, 239, 254, 262, 263, 273, 292, 296, 300–1, 302, 304, 307
Okinawa, 209
Old Javanese literature, 18, 52, 53, 54, 55
Old Malay, 4
Omar Dhani, 270, 275, 276, 279, 280, 281, 282, 289, 292
Oosthoek, see Eastern Salient
OPEC, 301, 304, 307
opium, 76, 79, 81, 82, 86, 115, 122, 125, 133, 135, 141, 168, 176
Opsus, 276, 290
orang kaya, 25, 35
orang laut, 19
Organisasi Papua Měrdeka, 297, 309
Ormuz, 23
Orthodox Islam, 4, 11, 168, 171, 177, 184, 190, 193, 219, 240, 244, 259, 261, 266, 268, 285, 286. See also Shafi'i school of law, NU
OSVIA (Training School for Native Officials), 156–7, 158, 164, 166
Outhoorn, Willem van, 84

P4, 306
Padang, 105, 112, 141, 143, 170, 216, 225, 262, 263
Padangpanjang, 170
Padris, Padri War, 117, 141, 142, 163
Pahang, 6, 34, 35
painting, 127, 215
Pajajaran, 7, 37, 38, 41, 110
Pajang, 39–41, 43, 54, 76, 77, 100
Pakěmpalan Kawula Ngayogyakarta, 189
Pakěmpalan Politik Katolik Jawi, 168
Pakistan, 215, 247, 265, 305
Pakualam I, Pangeran Adipati (Pangeran Natakusuma), 110, 112, 113–14
Pakualam II, Pangeran Adipati, 126
Pakualam III, Pangeran Adipati, 126

Pakualam VIII, Pangeran Adipati, 219
Pakualaman: status under Dutch rule,
    126; members play roles in early anti-
    colonialism, 164, 176
Pakualaman Corps, 114
Pakubuwana I, Susuhunan of Kartasura
    (Pangeran Pugĕr, Susuhunan Ingalaga),
    73, 75, 76–7, 83, 84–7, 88, 98
Pakubuwana II, Susuhunan of Kartasura
    and Surakarta, 88–9, 91, 92, 93, 94–5
Pakubuwana III, Susuhunan of Surakarta,
    95, 96, 97, 98, 99, 101, 102
Pakubuwana IV, Susuhunan of Surakarta,
    98, 102–3, 109–14
Pakubuwana V, Susuhunan of Surakarta, 126
Pakubuwana VI, Susuhunan of Surakarta, 117
Pakubuwana XII, Susuhunan of Surakarta,
    223
Palakka, Arung, 63–5, 73, 76
Palembang, 7, 19, 34, 38, 47, 70, 71, 72, 83,
    105, 139–40, 143, 152, 167, 183, 216, 225,
    238, 261
Palm, W. A., 102
Pamanahan, Kyai Gĕdhe, 40
Pamĕcutan, 135
Pamĕkasan, 73, 132
Panaraga, 41, 42, 87
Panarukan, 37, 46
Pan-Asianism, 175
Pancasila (five principles), 246, 247, 261,
    264, 275, 292, 306; origin of, 209
Pane, Armijn, 192, 202
Pane, Sanusi, 185, 192, 202
panĕmbahan, 40, 42, 43, 73, 74, 76, 85
Panggung, Sunan, 54
Pan-Islam, 173, 175, 179, 190
Panitisastra, 55
Panji Sakti, Ki Gusti Ngrurah, 67
Panji stories, 52, 53, 54, 55, 56
pantun (Malay verse form), 52, 185
paracommandos (RPKAD), 287, 289
Paramayoga, 126
Parameswara, 19
Parameswara Dewa Syah, king of Malacca, 20
Pararaton, 18, 55
Pariaman, 29
Parindra (Greater Indonesia Party), 191,
    192, 193
Parkindo (Indonesian Christian Party), 240,
    242, 250, 259, 265, 266, 299
Parman, S., 277, 281
Parmusi, 296, 298, 299
Partai Islam Indonesia, 193
Partai Katholik (Catholic Party), 240, 242,
    250, 255, 299
Partai Sarekat Islam, 176, 183, 184
Partai Sarekat Islam Indonesia, *see* PSII
Partai Sosialis (Socialist Party), 221
Partai Sosialis Indonesia, *see* PSI
Partindo (Indonesian Party), 188, 189, 190,
    191, 192, 221
Pasai, 4, 7, 8, 9, 12, 13, 15, 33, 37, 51
Pasir, 39, 66
Pasundan: (organisation), 168; state, 226,
    231, 232
Pasuruan, 37, 39, 42, 43, 83, 85, 93, 122

Patah, Raden, of Dĕmak, 37
Pati, 42, 45, 85
patih (administrative grade under Dutch
    rule), 128
patih (chief official of Javanese kingdom),
    73, 82, 88, 89, 91, 92, 94, 96, 99, 101,
    110, 112, 113, 116; abolition of position in
    Yogyakarta, 219
Patras, Abraham, 89
Pattimura, 137
patturioloang, 56
pawnshops, 125, 129, 168, 175, 187
PDI (Indonesian Democratic Party), 299
Peace Corps, 278
Pearl Harbor, 195
pearl, mother-of-pearl, 137
Peasant Front (Indonesian) (BTI), 248,
    271, 278
Pĕdir, 6, 33, 141
Pedoman, 296, 300
Pegu, 21
Pĕkalongan, 121, 123, 216, 219
Pĕkik, Pangeran, 44, 46, 70, 72
pelog, 57
Pĕlopor, Barisan, 208
Pĕmalang, 219
Pĕmuda Rakyat (People's Youth), 248, 259,
    271, 280, 281, 282
Penang, 29, 113, 141, 143
Pĕnanggungan, Mt., 37
Pĕnangsang, Arya, 40
Pĕndidikan Nasional Indonesia, *see* PNI-Baru
Pĕngging, 40
pĕnghulu (Minangkabau clan head), 141,
    142, 146, 200
Pĕngkalan Kĕmpas stone, 6
Pĕnyadar PSII, Barisan, 192
People's Congress, Indonesian, 194
People's Council, *see* Volksraad
People's Democratic Front, 227, 228, 229
People's Party, Brunei, 272
People's Security Army, 217
pepper, 16, 19, 20, 22, 27, 29, 33, 35, 38, 65,
    69, 71, 78, 79, 82, 104, 115, 124, 139, 143,
    144, 152, 153
'pepper *rajas*', 133, 143
Perak, 33
Perdjuangan kita, 218
Pĕrhimpunan Indonesia, 184, 244
pĕrintah halus, 159
pĕrjuangan, 212; *badan pĕrjuangan*, 215
Pĕrlak, 4
Pĕrmesta rebellion, 255, 260, 262, 269, 291
Pĕrmi (Indonesian Muslims' Union), 190, 191
Pĕrmina, 262, 292, 296
Pĕrmufakatan Islam, 177
Pĕrsatuan Bangsa Indonesia (Indonesian
    People's Union), 188, 191
Pĕrsatuan Islam (Islamic Union), 177, 182,
    189, 190, 193
Pĕrsatuan Pĕrjuangan, 222
Pĕrsĕrikatan Kommunist di India, 174
Pĕrsĕrikatan Nasional Indonesia, 183
Persia, Persian, 12, 20, 34, 51, 52, 72, 78,
    86, 184
'Pĕrsis', 177

Pěrsyarikatan Ulama, 171
Pěrtamina (State Oil and Natural Gas Mining Enterprise), 296, 301
pěsantren (Islamic religious schools in Java), 115, 166, 171, 177, 178, 204, 205, 206, 217
Pěsindo (Indonesian Socialist Youth), 221, 222, 248
Peta (Protectors of the Fatherland), 206, 208, 210, 214, 215, 221
'Petition of fifty', 306, 307
Pham Van Dong, 248
Philippine Sea, battle of, 207
Philippines, Filipino, 6, 22, 28, 78, 127, 160, 192, 195, 205, 207, 208, 230, 263, 272, 273, 275, 296, 305. *See also* Mindanao, Sulu
Piagam Jakarta, *see* Jakarta Charter
Pidari, orang, 141
pigs, 67, 133
Pinang, Pulau, *see* Penang
Pires, Tomé, 7-8, 12, 13, 20, 30, 33, 36, 39
pitch, 20
PKI (Indonesian Communist Party): 1920-7 period, 161, 174, 175, 176, 178–9, 181, 182, 183, 184; underground 1935–45 period, 219, 228; in Revolution, 219, 221, 228–30; after independence, 241–55, 259–82, 284–90, 293, 295–6, 297, 299, 307; outlawed, 289–90, 308; membership, 174, 243, 248, 271, 279
PKN, 189
Plered, 70, 72, 73, 75, 77, 100
plywood, 308
PNI (Indonesian Nationalist Party): before World War II, 183, 185, 188: in Revolution, 213, 221, 226, 229, 244; after independence, 240–55, 259–66, 268, 271, 274, 275, 278, 279, 288, 290, 295, 298, 299, 308
PNI-Baru, 188, 189, 190, 191, 193, 203
Poedjangga Baroe, 192–3
poison, 72, 87, 115, 140
Poland, 194
Polem Muhammad Daud, Panglima, 146
'police actions': first, 225, 226; second, 230–1
political prisoners, since 1965, 297, 306–7
Polo, Marco, 4
Pontianak, 138, 225, 233
population: before *c.* 1800, 15, 16, 17, 99, 109; in Java in 19th-century, 121; in Indonesia in 1905, 147; growth of 1905–30, 155; in Indonesia in 1939, 161; during World War II, 201; growth of 1950–61, 237–8; urban, 238, 286, 294; in 1971 and after, 286, 294, 305; movements of, 86, 89, 122, 123, 127, 132, 136; of Europeans in Indonesia, 31; of Chinese in Indonesia, 90
Portugal, Portuguese, 7, 21, 22–6, 27, 28, 29, 32–3, 34, 35, 36, 37, 38, 46, 48, 61, 63, 64, 66, 84, 136, 271, 301, 302; language, 50, 85
Potsdam, 209
poultry, 67, 72
PPP (United Development Party), 299
PPPKI, 184
Prabalingga, 156
Prambanan, 40
Pramudya Ananta Tur, 215, 259, 271, 287, 297, 307

Prangwadana, Pangeran (Mangkuněgara II), 110
Prawata, Sultan of Děmak, 38
Preparatory Committee for Indonesian Independence, 209–10, 213
Priangan, 76, 79, 86, 104, 105, 119, 120, 124, 142, 178, 179, 207
pribumi, 293, 300, 304, 308
primbon, 16th-century Javanese, 11
Pringgalaya, *patih* of Kartasura and Surakarta, 94
priyayi (member of the official class), 129, 164, 165, 166, 167, 174, 178, 182, 189, 200, 206, 214; 'new' or 'lesser' *priyayi,* 129, 163–6, 183, 242
Probosutedjo, 298
Protestantism, Protestants, 26, 28, 34, 62, 137, 240, 307. *See also* Christianity, Parkindo
PRRI (Revolutionary Government of the Indonesian Republic), 262–4, 265, 268, 269–70, 272, 291, 295
PSI (Indonesian Socialist Party), 226, 240–55 *passim,* 259, 260, 262, 263, 264, 266, 267, 268, 270, 276, 287, 296, 300; banned, 265, 268
PSII (Indonesian Islamic Union Party), 184, 190, 191, 192, 193, 202, 203, 208, 227, 250
Pugěr, Pangeran (half-brother to Krapyak), 42
Pugěr, Pangeran (son of Amangkurat I), *see* Pakubuwana I
puputan, 135–6
Purbaya, Pangeran (brother of Amangkurat IV), 87
Purbaya, Pangeran (brother of Sultan Agung), 70, 74
Purbaya, Pangeran Arya, *patih* of Kartasura, 89
Purwaka Caruban Nagari, 38
PUSA (All-Aceh Union of Ulamas), 200, 247
pusaka (holy regalia in Java), 41, 75, 85–6, 101, 287
Pustakaraja Purwa, 126
Putěra, 204, 206
putihan, 166
Putri Cina, 37

Qadiriyya order, 130, 142, 168
Qadiriyya wa Naqshabandiyya, 130, 168
Quanzhou, 4
Quds, al-, 38
Qur'an, 5, 9, 10, 12, 52, 130, 160, 169, 286

Raad van Indiě, *see* Council of the Indies
Radjiman Wediodiningrat, 165, 172, 208, 210
Raffles, Thomas Stamford, 113–5, 118, 132, 140, 143
railways and tramways, construction of, 154
'raja mogok', 175
Rájasanagara (Hayam Wuruk), king of Majapahit, 18
Rájasawardhana, king of Majapahit, 18
Rama, 52, 53, 54
Rama, Panembahan, *see* Kajoran

Rāmāyana, 52, 53, 55
Rangga, Raden, 112
Rangga Lawe, 55
Rangoon, 209
Raniri, Nuruddin, ar-, 51, 56
Rasul, Haji (Haji Abdul Karim Amrullah), 170, 171, 176, 195, 205
rattan, 20
Ratu, Pangeran, king of Bantĕn, 47
Ratu Adil, 167, 174, 189
Ratulangie, G. S. S. J., 214, 222
Raymond, George, 29
rĕbab, 57
Red Sea, 130
Reede tot de Parkeler, J. Fr. Baron van, 110
regent, 120, 142
Regentenbond, see Bupatis' Union
Reid, A., 15, 16
Rĕmbang, 84, 91, 92, 93, 94, 152, 157
Rĕngasdengklok, 210
Renville, USS, agreement aboard, 226, 227
Rĕpĕlita, 297, 301, 304, 307
Retnadhoemilah, 164
Riau, 222
Rida, Muhammad Rashid, 168, 170
Rivai, Abdul, 164, 173
'Rodim', 36
Roeslan Abdulgani, 253, 259, 289, 306
romusha, 206
Ronggawarsita, Raden Ngabei, 126
Rooseboom, W., 135
rosewater, 20
Roti, Rotinese, 66, 136, 168
'Rotterdam', 64
Round Table Conference, 231, 232, 248, 251, 252
Royal Mail Steam Packet Company (KPM), 239, 261
RPKAD (paracommandos), 282, 287, 289
rubber, 152–3, 186, 187, 194, 201, 225, 239, 245, 252
Rukun Tĕtangga, 206
Rumah kaca, 297
Russia, Russians, see Soviet Union

Sabah, 272, 273
Sabang, 220
Sabilillah, Barisan (Forces in the Path of God), 215, 240
Said, Raden Mas, see Mangkunegara I
Said, Sultan of Tĕrnate, 25
Saigon, 210
Saint-Martin, Isaac de, 79
Saipan, 207
Śaka era, 4–6; abandonment of, in Java, 46
Sakirman, 277
Sakti, Raja, 83, 84
Sala (Solo), see Surakarta
Salah asuhan, 192
salah Idenburg, 277
Salahuddin, Sultan of Aceh, 33
Sala river, 15, 41, 85, 94, 154
Salatiga, 97, 113
Saleh, Raden, 127
Salim, Haji Agus, 173, 175, 176, 178, 182,

183, 190, 192, 208, 209, 230
salt, 22, 132, 141
Samanhudi, Haji, 166
Sambas, 130, 138, 168
Samin, Surantika, 167, 295
Sampang, 44
Samudra, 3, 4, 6, 8, 9
sandalwood, 8, 16, 20, 66
Sang Merah-Putih (red and white Indonesian flag), 205, 207, 211
Sangihe, 64
Sanskrit, 4, 37, 52
santri (Javanese strict Muslim), 42, 166, 219, 227, 228, 229, 249, 259, 274, 288, 308
sanyo (advisers), 205, 208, 213; Dewan Sanyo, 208
Saparua, 137
Sarawak, 138, 272, 273, 296
Sarekat Adat Alam Minangkabau, 176
Sarekat Ambon, 168
Sarekat Dagang Islamiyah, 166
sarekat hijau, 178
Sarekat Islam, see SI
'Sarekat Islam B', see Section B
Sarekat Kaum Buruh Indonesia, 185
Sarekat Rakyat (People's Union), 176, 178
Sarekat Sumatra, 168
sarengat, 54
Sarifa, Ratu, 104
Sasaks, 134, 135
Sasraningrat, Raden Mas Adipati Arya, 157
Savu, Savunese, 66, 136, 168
Schakelschool, 159
schools, see education
scripts: Arabic, 4, 6, 11, 52, 53, 178; Indian, 11; Javanese, 11, 52, 53, 56; paleo-Sumatran, 4, 6
Second Class schools, 158–9
Section B (of SI), 173, 174, 178, 182
Seda ing Krapyak, Panĕmbahan, 42
Seinendan, 204
Sĕjarah Bantĕn, 10, 158
Sĕjarah Mĕlayu, 9, 50
Sekber Golkar, see Golkar
Sela Gilang, 41, 75
Sĕmarang, 76, 81, 83, 84, 85, 86, 91, 92, 94, 98, 113, 125, 127, 152, 157, 173, 216, 225, 238
Semaun, 173, 174, 175, 176, 178, 182, 184
Senapati Ingalaga, Panĕmbahan, 40–2, 44, 75
Sĕntot, 112, 117, 174
Sepoys, 113, 114
September 30 Movement, 281–2, 287
Sequeira, Diogo Lopes de, 23
Seram, 61, 62. See also Hoamoal
Sĕrdang, 143
Serrão, Francisco, 24
Seventh-Day Adventists, 293
Shafi'i school of law, 4, 51, 168, 170, 177, 193. See also Orthodox Islam
Shanghai, 277
Sharab al- 'ashiqin, 51
Shari'ah, 54, 169
Shattariyya order, 141, 142, 168
Shell, Royal Dutch, 152, 153, 188, 239, 261, 262, 278, 292, 302

Shell Transport and Trading Company, 152
Shi'ah, 168
Shibata Yaichiro, 217
Short Declaration, 146
Shu Sangi-kai, 205
SI (Islamic Union), 166, 167, 172, 173, 174, 175, 176, 177, 178, 181, 182, 183. *See also* Partai Sarekat Islam, PSII
Siak, 34, 142, 143, 144
Siam, 19, 20, 21, 65, 78, 83, 206. *See also* Thailand
Sidayu, 27, 42
Sidenreng, 67
Sihanouk, N., 248
Siliwangi Division, 222, 226, 227–8, 229, 230, 253, 263, 264, 281
silk, 20
Simatupang, T. B., 222, 240, 245, 246
Simbolon, Maludin, 252, 253, 254, 260, 262, 269–70, 291
Sinar Harapan, 307
Singapore, 115, 133, 138, 143, 144, 146, 169, 177, 178, 179, 195, 199, 204, 209, 263, 272, 273, 280, 296
Singasari, Pangeran (brother of Pakubuwana II), 92, 94, 98
Singasari, Pangeran (son of Amangkurat I), 74
Singhawikramawardhana, king of Majapahit, 18
Singkang, Arung, 66–7
Singkil, 142
Si Singamangaraja, 142
Siti Inggil, 89
Sitijĕnar, Sunan, 10, 54
Sitor Situmorang, 271, 295
Sitti Noerbaja, 185
Siwa (Śiva), 19
Siwalan, 43
Sjafruddin Prawiranegara, 242, 262, 263, 269–70, 291, 296
Sjahrir, Sutan, 184, 188, 191, 203, 207, 210, 213, 218, 221, 222–6, 230, 240, 244, 245, 270
Sjam (Kamarusaman bin Ahmad Mubaidah), 259, 276, 277, 281, 292
slavery, slaves, 20, 26, 30, 35, 48, 63, 66, 67, 79, 81, 82, 90, 120, 123, 132, 133, 135, 136, 143, 146
slendro, 57
Sloot, Jan Albert, 76
smallpox, 121, 133, 136, 139
Sneevliet, H. J. F. M., 172, 173, 174, 182
Snouck Hurgronje, Christiaan, 145–6, 156, 157, 169, 284
SOBSI (All-Indonesia Workers' Organization Centre), 241, 244, 247, 260, 261, 271, 289
Sociaal Democratische Arbeiderspartij, 173
'social revolutions', 218–21
Socialist Party of Indonesia, *see* PSI, Partai Sosialis
Socotra, 23
Soedirman, 206, 222, 223, 224, 228, 229, 231, 264
Soeharto, 195, 231, 270, 274, 276, 277, 280 ff. *passim*
Soeharto, Siti Hartinah, 298

Soemitro, 300
Soenting Melajoe, 170
Soetardjo Kartohadikoesoemo, 191–2, 194, 209
Soetomo ('Bung Tomo'), 217. *See also* Dr Sutomo
Sokawati, 94
Solor, 8, 25, 136
Soppeng, 64
Sorāndaka, 55
Sosrokardono, 173, 174, 178
Soumokil, 233
South Africa, 248
South Maluku, Republic of, 233
South Sumatra state, 226
Southeast Asia Command, 216, 222
Soviet Union, Russia, Russians, 172, 174, 175, 178, 210, 225, 228, 230, 252, 253, 259, 269, 271, 273, 274, 276, 277, 278, 280, 291, 301, 302
Spain, Spanish, 26, 28, 29, 48, 61, 62, 63, 64
Spanish Civil War, 193
Special Bureau (Biro Khusus), 277, 281
Special Operations (Opsus), 276
Speelman, Cornelis Janszoon, 61, 64–5, 75, 76, 81–2
Spice Islands, *see* Maluku
Sri Lanka, *see* Ceylon
Sri Tanjung, 55
Śrīvijaya, 3
staatsinrichting of 1925, 161
Stalinism, 221, 228, 229
Standaardscholen, 159
Stanvac, 152, 239, 262, 278, 292, 301
Starkenborgh Stachouwer, W. L. Tjarda van, 188, 194, 195
States-General (of the Netherlands), 27, 28, 123, 151, 161, 172
steam navigation, impact of, 124
steel, 301, 304
Stevenson Rubber Restriction Scheme, 153
STOVIA (School for Training Native Doctors), 157, 158, 164
Struggle Union, 222
study clubs, 183, 188
Subandrio, 258, 266, 268, 272, 273, 274, 275, 276, 278, 281, 288, 289, 292
Sudamala, 55
Sudan, 170, 265
Sudisman, 228, 241, 292
Sudjojono, 215
Sudjono Humardani, 300
Sudomo, 298, 300
Sudwikatmono, 298
Suez Canal, 124, 130
Suffah Institute, 227
Sufis, Sufism (Islamic mystics, mysticism): in Islamisation, 5, 11, 12–13; in pre-colonial Aceh and Java, 51, 54; in 19th century, 130, 141, 142; in 20th century, 168, 170, 175, 176
sugar, 26, 76, 81, 90, 115, 120, 122, 123, 124, 125, 127, 152, 153, 155, 168, 186, 187, 201, 225
sugar beet, 125, 127, 186
Sugar Law, 124

Suhitā, queen of Majapahit, 18
Sukadana, 29, 42, 43, 47
Sukamiskin prison, 185
Sukarno, 181–5, 188, 189, 191, 203–93
    passim, 306
Sukarno, Barisan, 288
Sukawati, 68
sukeë, 33
Sukiman Wirjosandjojo, 183, 184, 193, 221,
    240, 243, 244, 263
Sulaiman, Sultan of Aceh, 143
Sulawesi, see individual ethnic and place names
suling, 57
sulphur, 20
Sulu archipelago, 6, 8, 272
Suma Oriental, 7, 8, 36, 39
Sumatra Chuo Sangi-in, 207
Sumatra Thawalib, 176
Sumatranen Bond, 168
Sumba, 8, 20, 66, 136
Sumbawa, 8, 20, 47, 48, 64, 65, 67, 132, 136
Sumĕdang, 46
Sumĕnĕp, 132
Sumitro Djojohadikusumo, 260, 262,
    269, 295
Sumual, H. N. V., 255, 260, 269, 291
sunan, 10
Sunda, Straits of, 28, 105
Sunda, Sundanese, 7, 20, 37, 38, 55, 56, 57,
    121, 123, 124, 147, 154, 165, 168, 228, 252
Sunda Kalapa, 37
Sunnah, 169
Sunni, 168. See also Orthodox Islam
Supa, 224
Supardjo, 281, 292
Supĕrsĕmar, 289, 290
Supreme Advisory Council, 266, 269
Supreme Operations Command (KOTI),
    270, 273–4
Surabaya, 7, 8, 36, 37, 39, 42–4, 45, 46, 70,
    74, 75, 84, 85, 86–7, 92, 93, 94, 98, 132,
    152, 157, 166, 171, 172, 173, 174, 182, 183,
    188, 215, 216, 217, 218, 225, 238, 277;
    battle of, 217
Surachman, 289
Surakarta (Javanese court city), 39, 54, 94
    ff. passim; foundation of, 94; status under
    Dutch rule, 126
Surakarta (name for Jayakĕrta), 37
Surapati (of Banjarmasin), 139
Surapati (of Java), 67, 82–4, 85, 87;
    descendants of, 87, 88, 93, 97, 98
Surat, 86
Surengrana, 87
Surinam (Dutch Guiana), 123, 144
Surjadarma, Surjadi, 268, 270
Surjodiningrat, Pangeran, 189
Surjopranoto, 175, 176, 178, 193
Surkati, Shaikh Ahmad, 170
Suro, Mbah, 295
Surya Raja, 100
Suryengalaga, Pangeran, 126
Susuruh, Raden, 41
Sutan Maharadja, Datuk, 170, 176
Sutomo Dr, 183, 188, 191. See also Soetomo
    ('Bung Tomo')

Suwardi Surjaningrat, see Dewantara, Ki
    Hadjar
Suzuki Kantaro, 209
Switzerland, 270
syahbandar (port master), 95
syair (Malay verse form), 52, 185
Syamsuddin of Pasai, 51
syari'at, 54
Syria, 20, 29

Tabanan, 68, 134, 135
Tabariji/Tabarija, king of Tĕrnate, 24
Tack, François, 76, 79, 83
'Tagaril', 38
Taha Saifuddin, Ratu, of Jambi, 140
Tahir Jalaluddin, Shaikh (Muhammad Tahir
    bin Jalaluddin al-Azhari), 169–70
Taiwan (Formosa), 201, 263, 264, 273
Taj as-Salatin, Tajusalatin, 51, 55
Taj ul-Alam, queen of Aceh, 35, 51
Takdir Alisjahbana, 192
Talaud, 64
Taman Siswa, 177, 182, 188, 190, 204, 251, 259
tamarind, 20
Tambora, Mt., 132–3
Tamjidillah, Sultan of Banjarmasin, 138–9
Tan Malaka, 175, 178, 184, 221, 222, 224,
    228, 229, 231, 240, 254, 258
Tanah Datar, 141
Tanaka Kakuei, 300
Tanimbar, 137
Tanjung Priok riots, 307
Tapa, Kyai, 104–5
Tapanuli, 142, 221, 227, 254
Tapel Adam, 55
Tarakan, 215
tarekat (Islamic mystical brotherhood), see
    Sufis, Sufism
tea, 65, 105, 124, 152, 153, 201
Teacher Ordinance, see goeru ordonnantie
teacher-training schools, 158, 164, 177
Technical College (Technische
    Hoogeschool), 158, 182, 183
Tĕgal, 45, 75, 76, 84, 219
Tĕgalrĕja, 115, 116
Tĕgal-Wangi, 75
Telukabesi, 62
Tĕmbayat, 46, 73
Tĕntara Kĕamanan Rakyat, 217
Tĕntara Nabi Muhammad, 176
Terauchi Hisaichi, 210
Tĕrnate, 8, 24, 25, 28, 29, 39, 62, 63, 64, 65,
    86, 140
textiles, 16, 20, 21, 65, 76, 79, 81, 82, 86,
    141, 293, 308. See also batik
Thailand, 245, 265, 273, 296, 300, 305. See
    also Siam
Thamrin, Muhammad H., 188, 191, 194, 195
Thanom, Kittikachorn, 300
Thawalib school, 170
Thedens, Johannes, 93
Theosophy, 129, 165, 181
'three regions affair', 219
Tidore, 8, 24, 25, 28, 29, 63, 65
Tien, Ibu, 298

timber, 31, 43, 69, 71, 81, 83, 86, 296
Timor, 8, 20, 66, 84, 105, 136, 147, 168,
    301–2, 303, 309
Timorsch Verbond, 168
tin, 19, 131, 136, 139, 152, 153, 194
Tirtawiguna, 54
Tirtayasa, Sultan of Bantĕn (Sultan Agĕng),
    78
Tirtoadisurjo, 166
Tjipto Mangunkusumo, 165, 171, 172, 173,
    174, 182, 185
Tjokroaminoto, H. O. S., 166–7, 173, 174,
    175, 177, 178, 182, 190, 191, 202, 227
tobacco, 124, 141, 152, 153, 186, 201
To-Indo, 207
Tojo Hideki, 205, 207
Tokyo, 187, 204, 205, 275, 290
Tolitoli, 174
'Topasses', 66
Toraja, 137
Tralaya gravestones, 4, 5, 7
'transmigration', 155, 286, 309
Trawulan gravestone, 4, 5, 7
Treaties, contracts and agreements: of
    Bungaya, 64, 136–7; Dutch–Bantĕn,
    78, 82; Dutch–Javanese, 71, 72, 75,
    76, 81, 86, 88, 92, 94–5, 96, 103,
    110, 111, 112; Dutch–Palembang, 71; of
    Giyanti, 96, 97; Dutch–Balinese, 133–4;
    Dutch–Lombok, 134; Dutch–Portuguese,
    136; Dutch–Kalimantan, 138;
    Dutch–Jambi, 140; Dutch–Minangkabau,
    142; Dutch–Indĕragiri, 142; Dutch–Siak,
    142, 143, 144; Anglo–Dutch, 144; of
    London, 143, 144; of Sumatra, 144; of
    Revolutionary period, 223, 224, 225,
    226, 231, 232; Indonesia–USA, 244;
    Indonesia–China, 248; ASEAN, 296
Trĕnggana, king of Dĕmak, 36, 37, 38, 40
Trĕngganu stone, 4
Tribhuwană Wijayottunga Dewī, queen of
    Majapahit, 18
Tripartite Pact, 194
Triple A. Movement, 202, 204
Trunajaya, Raden, 65, 73–6, 79, 81, 84, 85, 92
Try Sutrisno, 308
tuanku, 141
Tuban, 7, 37, 42, 43, 74
Tulang Bawang, 104
Turkey, Turks, 22, 96, 144–5, 177, 184
typhoid, 121, 123

UDT, 301
Ujungpandang, 64, 233, 255, 294. See also
    Gowa, Makasar
Ukur, 46
ulama (Islamic scholars) in Aceh, 200, 203,
    220, 247, 254
uleëbalang (hulubalang) (war leaders,
    Acehnese aristocrats), 35, 36, 145–6,
    200, 220
umbul, 72
'unilateral action' campaign, 274, 276, 278
Union, Netherlands-Indonesian, 248, 251,
    252

unions, 168, 173, 175, 176, 177, 178, 185,
    187, 241, 247, 261, 278. See also SOBSI
United Nations (UN), 222, 225–6, 230–1,
    242, 248, 261, 271, 278, 290, 297, 302, 305
United States of Indonesia, 224, 226, 232, 233
Untung, 280, 281, 289
USSR, see Soviet Union
'Uthman, 3

Valckenier, Adriaan, 90, 93
Valentyn, Fr., 42
Van Niel, Robert, 121
Velsen, Johannes van, 91
Vereenigde Oost-Indische Compagnie, see VOC
Vervolgscholen, Inlandsche, 159
Vichy, 194
Victoria, fort, 28
Vienna, Congress of, 119
Vietnam, Vietnamese, 19, 78, 127, 229, 273,
    275, 277, 278, 280, 301
Village Regulation of 1906, 156
village schools, 159
Vlaming van Outshoorn, Arnold de, 62–3
VOC (Dutch East India Company), 27–110
    passim; foundation and organisation of, 27,
    28; military role in Java, 77–8; dissolved, 110
Volksraad, 160–1, 172, 173, 174, 176, 188,
    190, 191, 192, 194, 195, 208
volksscholen, 159
vorstenlanden (Central Javanese
    principalities), 126, 214. See also individual
    principalities and rulers
vrije woord, het, 175
VSTP (Railway and Tram Workers' Union),
    168, 173, 176

Wachid Hasjim, Kyai Haji, 206, 207, 209,
    244, 245
Wahhabi, 141, 177
Wahidin Soedirohoesodo, 164, 165
Wajo, 66–7
Walilanang, Sunan, 10
walis (apostles of Islam in Java), 5, 9,
    10, 37, 38, 39, 43, 46, 53, 54. See also
    individual names
Washington, G., 183
wax, 20
wayang (shadow play), 52, 53, 55–6, 57, 126,
    127, 164, 202, 258, 289
wĕdana, 128
Wedhatama, 126
Weltevreden, 129, 157, 164
West Indies, 29, 120
West Kalimantan state, 224, 233
West New Guinea, see Irian Jaya
Westerling, Raymond 'Turk', 224, 232, 233
Widjojo Nitisastro, 295
widow-burning, 8, 135, 146
Wijayakrama, Pangeran, 30
Wijayaparākramawardhana, king of
    Majapahit, 18
Wikramawardhana, king of Majapahit, 18
Wilatikta, Tumĕnggung, 10
'wild schools ordinance', 190

wilde vaart, 27
Wilhelmina, queen of the Netherlands, 151, 172
William V of the Netherlands, 112
Wilopo, 243, 244, 245, 246, 298
Wiraguna, Tuměnggung, 69
Wirasaba, 42, 43
Wisnu (Viṣṇu), 19
Wiwoho Poerbohadidjojo, 193, 194
'working cabinet', 266
World Bank, 280, 291, 305
World War I, 172, 173
World War II: approach of, 193–5; in Indonesia, 199–210

Xavier St. Francis, 25
Xinhua news agency, 290

Yamin, Muhammad, 185, 186, 192, 202, 209, 222, 223, 224, 243, 246, 258, 266
Yani, Achmad, 263, 270, 271–2, 273–4, 275,

276, 277, 279, 280, 281
Yasadipura, 54–5
Yogyakarta (Yogya), 39, 95, 97 ff. *passim*; foundation of court, 97; conquest of in 1812, 113–14; status under Dutch rule, 126; capital of Republic, 220, 223
Youth Congress, Youth Pledge, of 1928, 186
Yudanagara Wulang, 54
Yunus, king of Děmak and Jěpara, 36, 38
Yusup, 53
Yusup, Shaikh, 78, 79

Zainal Abidin, king of Těrnate, 39
Zainuddin, Ahmad, Sultan of Jambi, 140
Zainul Arifin, Sultan of Bantěn, 104–5
Zainul Asyikin, Sultan of Bantěn, 105
Zeeland, 26
Zeven Provinciën, 191
Zheng He (Cheng Ho), 19
Zhou Enlai (Chou En-lai), 248, 277, 278, 279
Zijlker, A. J., 152
zuama, 247, 254